THE

The Opinionated Spectator:

Born to be Muslim

Pat Wary

PAT WARY

Copyright © 2022 by Pat Wary

Cover design and photography by Pat Wary

Cover copyright © 2022 by Pat Wary

All rights reserved. The scanning, uploading, and distribution of this book without permission is a theft of the author's intellectual property.

Independently published by Kindle Direct Publishing: August 2022

Printed in the United States of America.

Library of Congress Cataloging-in-Publication Data
Wary, Pat
The Opinionated Spectator: Born to be Muslim
Includes text, photograph(s), artwork.
ISBN-13: 979-8847734646 (paperback)

Contents

Introductory comments	5
Anticlimactic Prologue	8
A Slice of Heaven	13
The Original Sin	29
The Apple of Adam's Grandchildren	40
Starving Humanity	
I: Poverty of Avarice	50
II: Hunger for Gluttony	62
The Darwinian Dilemma	67
The Inconvenient Truth	
I: The Other Idea	80
II: Solutions From False Premises	93
III: The Muslims are Here	104
Road to Decivilization	
I: An Idea is Like a Virus	110
II: Development of the Idea	119
III: Manifest Idea	130
IV: Family Legacy	137
Rebels With A Cause	148
Trouble in Paradise	
I: Cain's Boundaries	167
II: Who Owns Democracy?	174
III: The Empire Strikes	180
Center Align	
I: What Now?	200
II: Sirat al-Mustaqim	210

Glass Castles   218

A Fateful Interlude   232

The Untraceables   236

The World Outside the Cone   250

The Blind Scholar   265

How to Unlearn   283

Holy Time   300

The Quarks That Make Us   316

Blinding Light   325

To Dust We Return   339

Notes   351

INTRODUCTORY COMMENTS

"Actions are judged by their intentions, so each man will have what he has intended," said the Messenger of God (peace and blessings be upon him). (Sahih al-Bukhari 1)

History is politically incorrect, written by opinionated spectators. The winners in this global chess game are busy moving pieces and plotting while the defeated become victims of their misery. Most of us are mere commentators. We allow oppression while seeking peace and feigning neutrality, thus tolerating the intolerant through our inertia. We reason with our intellect and speculate through frustration. Sometimes we cheer, and other times we hold moments of silence, sending our thoughts and prayers. We debate, write, and discuss trenchantly but ultimately remain bystanders.

This book attempts to provide a balanced Western perspective and counteract extreme viewpoints without relying on personal authority. The goal is to dissect and understand the world we occupy to redirect our focus and efforts to the lagom. Perhaps all the information packed within this book defies wisdom. Though it may sometimes take an academic tone, it is meant for a general audience who must forgive such impressions as necessary for the cynics. Today's breadth of available knowledge makes its mastery impossible, leaving any audacious attempt destined to fall short. Its enormity hinders our understanding and renders it incomprehensible, which was remarkably noted by Ibn Khaldun even during his time.[1] Experts in the fields discussed would undoubtedly find many gaps in understanding and lapses in judgment. Consequently, they are shared with much trepidation and perseverance, given the dangers of cognitive bias and limited knowledge.

Although a "lack of expertise" is frequently charged to dismiss an otherwise intellectual perspective, knowledge itself is not equivalent to understanding or its prerequisite. Therefore, historian Abul-Feda (1273-1331 CE) considered knowledge of a part *better than ignorance of the whole*. The following discussions are done with scholarly intent without pontification, even if they appear to extend beyond aptitude. Nowadays, similar academic jargon frequents the mainstream narrative, and we must explore their true meanings and motivations before acceptance. If you are reading this book, chances are you have already been exhausted by such attacks. Unfortunately, contemplative reading has diminished significantly in our internet era, further propagating most contemporary pathologies.

The Islamic *way of life* is not confined to religious practices but knitted into all academic disciplines. The discussions to follow may superficially appear scattered from our compartmentally trained minds but deeply coherent in a nonlinear form. As the goal is to introduce various concepts and plant seeds of curiosity, detailed explanations of fairly well-known topics will be deferred to the reader's research to avoid lengthy tangents. To properly explain it all would take volumes which I neither have the time to write nor do you have to read. If you can persevere through the thickets of this book, the world will make a little more sense when you turn over the last page. The contents are ultimately nothing new in our worldly version of Jorge Borges's *Library of Babel*. The difference lies in their presentation through the lens of a Muslim without diluting the narrative down in attempts to make it "palatable." To reiterate Ibn Taymiyya (1263-1328 CE), all of it may be Western solutions to Western problems, which are still urgent in today's global Western village.

The references from the Qur'an (literally, *the Recital*) and *ahadeeth* (plural for *hadith*) are intended to provoke thought, not provide exegesis. *God* is used in this book in His singular meaning and is interchangeable with the Arabic *Allah*. A prayer always follows all mentions of Prophet Muhammad in Islamic traditions as a sign of respect and divine command: peace and blessings of God be upon him (Arabic: *sallallahu 'alayhi wa sallam*, or the symbol ﷺ). Similarly, the names of other prophets and pious predecessors are followed with *'alay-hi 's-salām* (Arabic: عليه السلام). Both are mentioned here and recommended for readers but excluded in the text hereafter for ease of reading.

The content of this moral exhortation resulted from years of research and contemplation for personal edification. The main intention is to bring the focus back to Revelation and share certain *truths* that may continue to benefit others. Perhaps it is an attempt to communicate with the future, which may nevertheless be impossible by nature. Winston wrote, "Either the future would resemble the present, in which case it would not listen to him, or it would be different from it, and his predicament would be meaningless."[2] The author invites readers on a journey to appreciate the complexity and beauty of our existence, concluding that ultimately, God knows best (Arabic: الله أعلم). Any misinterpretations or assumptions are solely the opinions of the spectator at hand, for which I seek God's refuge and forgiveness.

Learn wisdom from the pupil of the eye, which sees everything but is blind to itself. (Persian proverb)

ANTICLIMACTIC PROLOGUE

Say [Prophet], "If the whole ocean were ink for writing the words of my Lord, it would run dry before those words were exhausted"—even if We were to add another ocean to it. (al-Kahf 18:109)

Imagine sitting across a friend on a calm, cloudy day. As you sip on a cup of warmth, you ask, "How are you?" Not as a formality, but with true care and curiosity to understand the deep hiatus. An inquiry of kindness with attention and active listening that may produce a solemn sigh. "Well, there are some things on my mind if you wish to know...

Our pursuit of knowledge is driven by a desire to comprehend ourselves and our surroundings, revealing a vast and interconnected network extending beyond our intellect. This complexity challenges our inclination to categorize things into separate compartments such as religion, philosophy, politics, and science. Over time, we forget that these boundaries are artificial constructs that ultimately fail to capture the intricate web of existence. Then, where do we even begin to understand it all?

Dissecting complex phenomena into smaller, more manageable parts is an effective solution. In medicine, for example, this involves studying various subjects, such as anatomy, biochemistry, genetics, and neuroscience, until it all comes together into a macroscopic understanding of the body and its healing process. Mathematics similarly tackles complex problems through the Infinity principle, breaking them down into simpler parts that are analyzed and combined to explain the original. This logical breakdown became *derivative* and *integral* calculus, which are the foundations of our technological achievements today. Mathematics, being the most *rational* of all sciences, can perhaps help us find a starting point. Let us then begin breaking the complexity of our shared existence into simpler parts.

Knowing oneself is key to understanding, as noted by philosophers like Socrates (470-399 BC) and Ibn 'Arabi (1165-1240 CE). Its significance unites us beyond our perceived differences, but we must go back even further to understand how we got here. "Go back to where you started," demanded James Baldwin, "examine all of it, travel your road again, and tell the truth about it." While he provided an activist's perspective on the importance of studying our history, even biological and physical reasons exist for undertaking such endeavors. For us to be here today, trillions of atoms had to come together in an incredibly unique, organized manner to define our individual identities in the universe's timeline. Physicists describe our entire existence as a *sum-over history* of ourselves, which is one of the key factors defining our identity.[3] While our personal memories define us individually, our collective memory tethers us to this relatively *grainy* spacetime we occupy.

The stories of Adam and Eve's children resonate with us, but the way they are told and remembered is subjective. Thus, history is more related to the art of the humanities than science, as the past can never be directly proven but must be reconstructed indirectly through contemporary records. Even these records are only retrospective recollections of events from memory, which is notoriously uncertain. We all remember the past differently as we change and evolve. It is embedded within the word *his*-story. Much of it also depends on who is included when we are considering *us*. Recognizing this, both Giambattista Vico (1668-1744 CE) and Karl Marx (1818-83 CE) observed that, ultimately, men make their own history within which they also reside.

In shuffling through the endless variations of the past, it becomes crucial to recognize the credibility and caliber of the narrators to stitch together the most transparent picture with the least amount of cognitive bias. While few historians can resist naturally falling into the pitfalls of subjectivity, studying it allows us to understand its complexity, where things are not always clearly demarcated. The more we broaden our viewing window, the smaller each individual existence becomes. The breadth of it all humbles us —or, at least, it should. History books are colored with civilizations similar to ours, whose rise and fall are tales as old as the hour. The problem is that not everyone finds these stories entertaining, which can often seem prosaic, repeating like a broken record even when no one is listening. This cyclical pattern was apparent to many (like Ibn Khaldun, P. R. Sarkar, Polybius, and Sima Qian, to name a few), leading to various proposed models to explain its inner workings. However, the overall theme remains the same, like the background noise of the universe.

The rise of civilization often stems from chaos with a desire for unity and order. Psychologically, as "people move out of Apathy and Grief to overcome Fear as a way of life, they begin to want; Desire leads to frustration, which in turn leads to Anger," explained Dr. Hawkins, a renowned psychologist.[4] This anger then catapults an oppressed generation to fight for its freedom. The birth of a nation then reflects these values painstakingly upheld by its founders and those who remember the original struggle. To what extent they succeed is a different discussion, but when they do, it leads to a general sense of security, providing fertile ground for new ideas and innovations. The succeeding posterity near its peak is removed from the original struggle far enough to become complacent. Feeling comfortable with the perceived stability, they neglect the entropy lurking around the corner. The higher purpose that initially held that community together gradually deteriorates towards personal gains at the cost of others. Society begins to rust and lean more towards individualism and avarice. This loss of morality eventually brings us back to the original chaos that shakes the foundation again.

In this diseased state, Friedrich Nietzsche (1844-1900 CE) assigned civilization's healing to its sages and philosophers. Here, nihilism reemerges in a society, which Nietzsche described as a revaluation of values rather than its pop-cultural posturing—drowning in despair without tackling the responsibility of necessary change. Historically, this is when prophetic figures were sent with revolutionary ideologies for realignment from the *status quo* rather than the destruction of authority. Humanity evolves technologically, with surviving advancements serving as a starting point for the next civilization. Hence, through the rise and fall of individual empires, we evolved from the Stone Age to the Bronze to the Iron, and so on. This progression, however, is not to be confused with a gradual betterment of humankind or increasing civility, as we will soon discover.

Morality (or ethics), on the other hand, is timeless, contrary to the cynical assertions of postmodernists like Walter T Anderson. The ethical principles prevalent today were established at the birth of humanity beyond our subjective interpretations. How a society values or implements them at any given moment varies along its trajectory. Over the last few centuries, there has been a gradual trend away from the divine moral standard toward a secular tradition, which defines *ethics* as "the free consensus of the citizens of a democratic society."[5] This secular view may sound intelligent on paper, but it becomes a moving base that creates room for anything from the Holocaust to nuclear oblivion.

The modern understanding of secularism against a theocracy is incompatible with Islamic philosophy, where such distinctions between sacred and profane realms do not exist.[6] These terms are derived from a line of logic that cannot be applied to Islam without the confusion and deviation that resulted in their pursuit and application in the West. In the following chapters, we will explore this further to separate political secularism from philosophical and present the Islamic prescription of a balanced middle. Moral values or rules, therefore, follow an identical overlapping cyclical pattern as civilization. The rise of civilization follows these values; the loss of them, in turn, is followed by their collapse. Thus, the Prophet exclaimed: "How can God sanctify a nation if their strong do not support their weak?" (*Sunan Ibn Mājah* 4010). Furthermore, God confirms: "Can you see any trace of them now?" (*al-Haqqah* 69:8).

Historian Arnold Toynbee observed that promiscuity and moral degradation are hallmarks of declining civilizations.[7] Even psychologically, all humans demonstrate a hierarchy of values constantly manifested through actions. Religion attempts to unify diverse values through absolute authority, preventing conflicts that can result from individual whims and idols. Of course, this oversimplification does not apply to all civilizations. Sometimes, the original chaos creates a power vacuum, aspirating in a profligate despot, which does not necessarily mean an end to suffering for the people; rather, an ephemeral chapter adding to the chaos until the next upturn of events. For example, the complacency and corruption that started to rot the Islamic Empires and Central Asia in the 13th century opened the doors to Mongol invasions. Their devastating ruthlessness served as a forceful cleansing process that brought people back to the necessary struggle to strive for a better cause.

Ultimately, it is the balance of justice, not religion, that determines success in earthly power (*Sahih al-Bukhari* Book 65, Hadith 206). Initially, Genghis Khan did not appear to have any plans to invade Muslims. He first attempted to establish trade with the Khwarezmid Empire bordering his Mongol Khanate. Unfortunately, his 500-man trade caravan was raided by Inalchuq, the governor of the Khwarezmian city of Otrar. His request to Shah Ala ad-Din Muhammad for repudiation was answered with the beheading of the Mongol ambassadors, along with the execution of the entire caravan. It was that tipping point of injustice that caused Genghis to gather his people in 1219 and start an invasion that changed the known world.

"If God did not drive some back utilizing others, the earth would be completely corrupt, but God is bountiful to all" (*al-Baqarah* 2:251). After turning the largest mosque of Bukhara into a stable in 1220, Genghis took the pulpit and told everyone that he was the punishment from God. That hometown of none other than al-Bukhari was called the "cupola of Islam" before the Mongol plague. Soon, monstrous pyramids were built with the severed heads of men, women, and children, causing many to mistake them for Gog and Magog. They were not that far off, as some estimate the Mongols to have slaughtered 90% of the densely populated central Asia in their rage.[8]

Others in the West celebrated Genghis as Prester John—a rumored Christian King sent to exterminate Islam—which only lasted until they faced the same plague.[9] In Balkh and Nishapur, after slaughtering everyone in sight, a point was made by even killing every chicken, cat, and dog.[10] One day, sybaritic Caliph al-Musta'sim indulged in his treasure trove, and the next day, he was trampled within it.[11] Even those apathetic to the annals and current events were not spared, ultimately becoming forgotten footnotes in history. The unimaginable massacre awakened a generation to fight for a better society, uprooting greed and comfort in the ruling class that inhibited social reform.

The Mongols were finally beaten back in 1260 at 'Ain Jalut, modern day Galilee, at the same springs where David once brought down Goliath. They were defeated again at Marj al-Saffar in 1303, with Ibn Taymiyya fighting within the ranks of the Mamluk army. This likely saved Europe from total Mongol domination, perhaps allowing it to become a continent.[12] Nevertheless, the subsequent Mongol plague of Europe and Asia in the form of the Black Death was only reenacted by the European invasion of the Americas. Then the Ottomans saw their virtuous rise and inevitable fall through their climactic corruption and transgression, all within this epic game of empires.

It almost seems a utopian society would be sustained if we could only hold on to the golden period of a civilization marked by tolerance, justice, and morality. What is it then that makes us deviate from the clear solution? Why would anyone choose chaos? This age-old question was asked first by the angels upon God's introduction of Adam. However, God did not deny their knowledge of the unseen but only reminded them: "Certainly, I know what you know not" (*al-Baqarah* 2:30).

The Prophet said: "Be mindful of God, and He will protect you. Be mindful of God, and you will find Him before you. When you ask, ask God, and when you seek aid, seek God's aid. Know that if the entire creation gathered together to do something to benefit you—you would never get any benefit except that God had written for you. And if they gathered to do something to harm you— you would never be harmed except that God had written for you. The pens are lifted, and the pages are dried." (Jami at-Tirmidhi Book 37, Hadith 2706)

A SLICE OF HEAVEN

To understand why anyone would choose chaos, we need to meander a little and explore the motivations behind all human actions. John Locke (1632-1704 CE) observed that all of our desires are moved by seeking happiness, whose necessary counterpart and companion is misery.[13] Indeed, a misguided pursuit of happiness is the common denominator in history. Aristotle spent a significant portion of his *Nicomachean Ethics* defining happiness for similar reasons, which need not be repeated here. Although his view conforms with the religious, most secular understanding and pursuits of happiness today lack that spiritual remedy, which aims not only for temporal pleasures but for a supreme ideal that gives a purpose to our existence through meaningful struggles.

Recently, there has been a renewed interest in happiness as a subject of scientific research, with a formal branch of psychology established by Dr. Martin Seligman in 1998. While the outcome of this *happiness revolution* was a mountain of studies proving the obvious, the focus only reflects the global pandemic of depression. Instead of addressing its roots, we are looking for a scientific solution in the form of a miracle pill to make us happy. Since our existence, we have been on a utilitarian quest for happiness, spending every moment on reaching that goal. True happiness, however, has always been understood as more than the pursuit of desires and is inextricably tied to meaningful efforts toward kindness and compassion.

Initially, everything we needed for survival was provided free by nature with little effort. We gradually made it difficult for ourselves by chasing our unlimited desires. We were all rich until our greed introduced poverty through competing luxuries, making it justifiable for some to hoard while preventing others from having their bare necessities. One of the first human experiences was likely hunger. Although any sustenance would have sufficed, only some released the endorphins that made us epicurious. Then we sought it in every meal, even when it got our parents expelled from paradise. I am just as guilty, expecting the next meal to be more than its true purpose of providing enough energy to stand straight in prayer (*Sunan Ibn Majah* 3349). Similarly, the warmth of the fire eventually caged us into the ease and comfort of a home with a controlled temperature. Essentially, we are not too different from the rats in Edward Thorndike's experiments, always looking for more efficient ways of getting to the cheese.

Consequently, the more physical comfort we achieved, the less prepared we became to deal with emotional strife. With each new addition of comfort came the added economic strife. "Competing for more distracts you until you go into your graves," reminds God (*at-Takathur* 102:1-2). We are still unsatisfied and constantly trying to invent ways to decrease the effort required, with the ultimate goal of perhaps being happy all the time. Some find it through various intoxicants and hallucinogens, replacing religion with narcotics as the opium of the people, resulting from the global secularizing process. Whether it is pharmacologic or organic, the aftereffects of heightened stimulation of our brain's pleasure center are the same: immediate torpidity and habituation requiring *more* for the next episode.[14] After all, it was a paradise where we had originated and now wish to return. Is it so bad that we cut to the chase and try to create our slice of heaven here on earth?

For al-Kindi, it is foolish to seek pleasure through sensible things that are transitory by nature. Thus, it would be unnatural to expect something from nature that does not exist.[15] Our first experience with pleasure is usually incidental but, once felt, becomes addictive. The catch-22 is that when we make happiness our goal, we initiate our paths of misery, as noted in various psychological studies.[16] Happiness has been observed to be an independent risk factor for depression, as it focuses our current state in a negative light.[17] It is not to denounce all such pursuits but to reframe our understanding in a more balanced approach, which is otherwise unattainable without a belief in God and an afterlife. At any given moment, we are surrounded by countless blessings that require some attention to appreciate. Recognizing them in real-time leads to a lasting joy that remains stable through our necessary trials to find meaning. Happiness can be either the byproduct of a noble cause or the temporary pleasure from a sordid act. While the former is sustainable, the latter is momentary and comes at a high cost.

It is ultimately *an ideal* that every person craves—*the cause* of Dostoevsky that drives every physical body to action. God provides us with the most worthy and balanced ideal of peace and submission. Without that belief in an afterlife, we become slaves of instant gratification. Even our ever-faster microchips cannot keep up with our competing need for speed, while we feel entitled to demand instant delivery of everyday purchases from our beds. Such fetishism of commodities culminates in our dehumanization of those who are abused for our demands by an animated smile on a box awaiting our doors from an insatiable click. "If the Son of Adam had a valley of gold, then he would still like to have a second," warned the Prophet. "And nothing fills his mouth but dust, God turns to whoever repents" (*Jami` at-Tirmidhi* 2337).

Humanity's Achilles' heel is this incessant pursuit of pleasures and simultaneous gravitation towards comfort. Yet, like all human states, happiness can only be realized through its opposite. Just as one becomes patient by demonstrating it with others during agitation, he achieves lasting happiness not through pleasures but by reducing the pain of others. Thus, the Prophet's advice for sadness and a hardened heart was to bring an orphan close, pat his head, and treat him to one's food (*Makārim al-Akhlāq lil-Kharā'iṭī* 661). Unfortunately, the only way these evident principles can be presented to today's distracted audience is through a secular context via scientific investigations into the most commonsensical concepts. But that process itself is a fatal blow to the principles at hand due to their severance from their *telos*, which is evident from everything that prevailed since the Enlightenment.

The prophets and sages have exemplified this balance by reaching a state of peaceful equilibrium with their *presence*, which reveals the temporal nature of this world. When offered even the most mundane earthly comfort, the Prophet responded: "What do I have to do with the world! I am not in the world, but as a rider seeking shade under a tree, then he catches his breath and leaves it" (*Jami` at-Tirmidhi* 2377). Dismissing their divinely guided wisdom for our devilish desires misses the mark of internal peace that only manifests as external chaos. Hence, *missing the mark* is the linguistic root of *sinning*.

Among the things that genuinely make us happy is being satisfied with our lot in life. Timeless Prophetic traditions advise us to look at those less fortunate to be content with what we have and fully appreciate God's favors (*Sahih Muslim* 2963c). Recent research has also chimed in, demonstrating happiness to be a function of one's outlook in life, which is influenced by a tendency to compare.[18] In fact, we *are* happy for most of our lives (89% based on a recent study), which should reflect our state of gratitude.[19] This recognition also leads to joy, thus completing the loop by psychologically amplifying the good in our lives.[20] If we bridge the gap by striving to reach a constant state of thankfulness, we have the benefit of living happier and 14% longer than the rest.[21] Thus, in the Qur'an, God considers gratitude as the opposite of disbelief, which is at the core of today's global emotional crisis.

We have briefly discussed how the initial struggle that builds a civilization stems from an individual and general chagrin. It is not simply a fleeting feeling but an unshakeable void that breaks our inertia. As long as we feel safe in our homes, even if outside events upset us, most would not take the extra step to jeopardize our comfort and demand change. Some remain sycophantic or even go so far as to promote chaos for immediate gains at others' expense. When it finally invades our homes and destroys our perceived safety bubble, enough momentum is gained for the masses to rise and come out onto the streets. Though most of us empathize with injustice, we fail to take action until it directly affects us, like the apocryphal frog that remains stolid in slowly boiled water until it is too late. Unfortunately, the time it takes for things to reach that level can vary from decades to centuries, and the irreversible damage done during that incubation period is painted all over history.

Ironically, when achieved, the same pursuit of happiness that fuels the birth of civilization creates stagnation, resulting in its downfall. That push is initially for a communal wellbeing, which later shifts to the individual. We always hear our elders speak of the "better days," but some historical trends have remained relatively unchanged. It is uncanny to read Imam al-Nawawi's (1233-77 CE) writings about his generation's neglect of *enjoining good and forbidding evil*, which sounds more applicable to our current times.[22] The entire matter of Islam nonetheless stands upon that principle, for its failure results in our collective punishment (*Musnad Ahmad*, Book 1 Hadith 16). Such broad generalizations often hide motivated individuals who are always struggling for a just cause in its backdrop, resembling a swing between them and those who are stagnant. One end of the pendulum is the birth of a nation, where there is a brawl for betterment. Over time, it sways to the opposite end, where a few are struggling with little effect, while the majority are complacent.

Since complacency marks the beginning of a civilization's decline, the solution must lie in the *labor* into which we were born. Perhaps it is deep within our DNA to live a life of conflict, not simply in terms of our sufferings and trials, but a continuous effort to make ourselves and our world better as part of the evolving process of God's creations. "Verily We have created man into toil and struggle," confirms God (*al-Balad* 90:4). It is manifested at the very moment of our birth trauma when the lungs are expunged of the amniotic fluid, allowing for the first breath to jump-start our lives. When the pursuit of happiness derails us from that personal battle, we lose sight of our true purpose and suffocate, allowing for the deterioration of society around us.

Some spend their entire lives trying to escape their trials when the only escape is death. It is the most widely accepted and ignored reality, which makes us postpone conscious living for a self-delusional future until it comes knocking on our doors when least expected. "Death will overtake you no matter where you may be, even inside high towers," reminds God (*an-Nisa* 4:78). The attempted escape is itself a quixotic quest perpetuating more despair. Ignorance only creates personal dissatisfaction with an outward mask of the vanity of pleasures. "The trance of death will bring the Truth with it: 'This is what you tried to escape'"(*Qaf* 50:19).

While conflicts are woven deeply within our fabric, we must distinguish between that which leads to happiness versus despair. Misunderstood pain and suffering can often be paralyzing, as demonstrated in catatonics. For the rest of us, a negative outlook on affliction results in a sense of failure that often leads to anxiety and intolerance when faced with difficulties.[23] Pain also has the power to move our desires as pleasure, where the same objects and ideas often produce both. Locke noted: "This their near conjunction, which makes us often feel pain in the sensations where we expected pleasure, gives us a new occasion of admiring the wisdom and goodness of our maker, who designing the preservation of our being, has annexed pain to the application of many things to our bodies, to warn us of the harm that they will do; and as advices to withdraw from them."[24]

In Islam, all physical and mental struggles are seen as tests that help us improve and get closer to God, who promises to reward us accordingly. Contrarily, a secular understanding forces us down a path of false associations and presumed causalities, which lead to ever-changing solutions that only result in more harm. "No fatigue, nor disease, nor sorrow, nor sadness, nor hurt, nor distress befalls a Muslim, even if it were the prick he receives from a thorn, but that God expiates some of his sins for that," explained the Prophet (*Sahih al-Bukhari* 5641, 5642). They all have meanings, serving a higher purpose, which helps frame our point of reference during hardship. At the same time, God reassures us repeatedly that He only wants ease for us (*al-A'la* 87:8). Even the most defining pillar of Islam—the five daily prayers—is shortened by His mercy when we are on a journey. Accordingly, in all our endeavors, we are divinely guided toward a balanced middle path toward His blessing.

For those still averse to this process of purification, God reminds: "Did you think you would enter the Garden without God first proving which of you would struggle for His cause and remain steadfast?" (*al-'Imran* 3:142). Psychologists Greg Lukianoff and Jonathan Haidt address this recent antipathy to toil in their book, *The Coddling of the American Mind*. They describe several "Great Untruths" that plague us today, including beliefs like: "Anything that doesn't kill you makes you weaker" and "Always trust your feelings." Unfortunately, these have gradually become mantras that drive postmodernist actions, which explain much of our current bewilderment, acting as a global "reverse cognitive behavioral therapy."[25]

Just like happiness, pain also has distinct psychological and physical aspects regarding its source, manifestation, and aftereffects. During infancy, we develop various neurological pathways for the reflexive muscle memory to painful stimuli, like withdrawing immediately after accidentally touching a hot stove. Before this, we are unable to demonstrate a psychological manifestation of physical pain, as experimentally demonstrated by Ronald Melzak in puppies. Losing this pathway later in life can lead to disfigurations seen in leprosy and various Charcot arthropathies. Pain is crucial in our physical and spiritual well-being, which strengthens us and helps us appreciate its opposite. It not only makes us aware of the different parts of our body but also unites the entire humanity through its universality, allowing us to empathize with even those far removed.

Such understanding of our purpose requires a *presence* only achieved through *taqwa* or God-consciousness. God commands us to be conscious of our actions and emotions as a divine remedy, which is also described as the most effective way to reduce worry in psychotherapy. Ancient philosophers like Epictetus called this *prosoche* or mindfulness, which allows us to bring our attention back from future concerns to living in the present.[26] Thus, the people of *taqwa* are relieved from any future worries or past griefs through God's promise (*al-Baqarah* 2:112). In contrast, most of us today live in a trance-like sleepwalking state with our minds somewhere in the distance. The secular promotion of mindfulness also fails to define what the mind should be full of instead. It is another principal artifice of the devil to influence us into rushing through our lives—distracting us from the endless blessings at hand—and failing to act like human *be*-ings with that literal emphasis.

Aristotle distinguished between wish and choice as one relating to the end, and the other to the means.[27] Since happiness itself is not a choice within our power *per se*, we can only *wish* to be happy by *choosing* to be present. "Life is very brief and anxious for those who forget the past, neglect the present, and fear the future," wrote Seneca. "When they reach life's end, the poor wretches realize, too late, that they've been busy for a long time doing nothing."[28] There is a direct correlation between living such a rushed and inattentive life with the high prevalence of behavioral disorders today, where 20% of the people in this country suffer from anxiety disorders. Seneca's remedy for freeing up time was to seek voluntary poverty and appreciation for simple things, for even half of the millionaires are sick of worrying about wealth.[29]

Most days, we cannot even recall how we get to work, as it all becomes mundane somnambulism, leaving us looking desperately for meaning elsewhere. So we try to document and share every experience to create a facade of happiness, which prevents us from enjoying the very thing we are documenting. Ironically, angels are constantly recording our actions to be played back on the Day regardless of our embarrassments. In contrast, the Prophet's emphatic *presence* was evident from the numerous supplications he left for nearly every activity of daily life. Such a remarkable level of conscious spirituality sounds mythical or even abnormal to those of us not even aware of our breaths. Mufti Hussain Kamani shares an incredible story of his *hadith* teacher rushing to clean his utensils after every meal as a sign of gratitude and respect for even those inanimate objects that sacrificed their cleanliness for our comfort. The opposite is reflected in our routine use of dishwashers and single-use utensils, and the environmental consequences resulting from that mindset with a global impact.

Dr. Hawkins attributed the source of one's pain and suffering to the ego from a misunderstanding of God's providence. He reported some remarkable cases where he used the power of *presence* to cure catatonics. While the cynic in us questions the method, his assessments have valuable insights. His work in kinesiology found negative stimuli affecting all research subjects, except for students of spiritual disciplines, who saw themselves at the mercy of God rather than their tribulations. He concluded: "The great tragedy of human life had always been that the psyche is so easily deceived; discord and strife have been the inevitable consequence of mankind's inability to distinguish the false from the true."[30] This was remarkably written before the advent of the internet and the global social media pandemic, making the Prophet's prayer even more prevalent for our era: "God, show me the truth as truth and guide me to follow it. Show me the false as false and guide me to avoid it" (*Sharḥ al-Muntahá al-Irādāt* 3/497).

Our current age of filtered reality created by social media goes hand-in-hand with the high rate of depression, dependence on antidepressants, substance abuse, and self-destructive behavior.[31] It serves as the culmination of all the major sins that have individually been perfected through various aspects of our global culture.[32] This emotivist display of all emotions openly and indiscriminately starves our intimate relationships, leaving no private feelings to be shared with our special ones. "All those famous men you see strutting about grandly possess gold-leaf happiness," wrote Seneca two millennia ago. "Look inside, and you'll see how much corruption lies beneath that flimsy veneer of status."[33]

Seneca certainly was in a place to make that observation as the second most powerful man in Rome and the teacher of emperor Nero. Unfortunately, those plagued by it are worse equipped to realize the problem, as studies have found those with lower emotional intelligence to be unaware of their shortcomings, dismissive of any feedback, and reluctant to seek help for improvement.[34] To make matters worse, from birth, we are constantly told that our happiness is tied to "more," to the point that we cannot think or question otherwise. The result is endless consumerism of all things superficial without an honest distinction between one's *needs* versus *wants*. The Prophet warned of such hedonic adaptation and described those partaking as the worst of his *ummah* (*al-Mu'jam al-Kabīr* 7512).

As Seneca noted, the timeless condition of human suffering can often be unbearable, making it rather courageous to live joyfully.[35] For Aristotle, that courage is only praiseworthy for the associated pain and struggle.[36] Mitch Alborn's memoir of his final lessons with Professor Morrie Schwartz reveals insights into the human condition commonly associated with a deep understanding of death. Like the classic epistemological premise, life also can only be appreciated through its opposite. Such a level of compassion and clarity provided by death would be more beneficial if obtained through conscious internal spiritual discussions earlier in life. The Prophet frequently visited the graveyard and advised us to do the same (*Riyad as-Salihin* 580). However, some are aghast by even the thought of spending time alone and would rather be distracted by the lives of others. We are so engulfed by entertainment and an altered virtual reality that the everyday world appears too prosaic. The little breaks of reflection we used to get throughout the day—whether waiting in line at the store or at a traffic stop—are now replaced by reflexive browsing on our smartphones and social media, whose sole focus is competition for our attention.

Not only is unlimited entertainment made acceptable today, but it is an encouraged vice promoting a thriving global industry. Its ties with greed make it another limitless goal fused with habituation and boredom, necessitating an ever-increasing need for *more*. Indeed, boredom—a term nonexistent in premodern language—is only a symptom of unhappiness stemming from a lack of purpose. Pascal identified that as the source of our misery, leading to all the violence we create in vanity to fill a fenestrated heart.[37] Hasan al-Basri (641-728 CE) warned that when God removes his providential care from a people, they are preoccupied with things that do not involve them. It was based on Prophetic traditions like: "Part of the excellence of a man's Islam is that he leaves what does not concern him" (*Muwatta Malik* Book 47, Hadith 3). The point here is not to impart knowledge but, through it, initiate inner changes that would create a better community without playing into today's "woke culture."

In *The Republic,* Plato stressed the importance of stories in shaping a child's soul and signifying the cultural values of a society. Such stories today take the form of the entertainment industry, and the "reality" portrayed by the reality shows paints our current pathetic intemperate state. Prophets were sent to people in the past who excelled in a particular sin, while the promotion of all sins today is writing the final chapter of humanity following the seal of prophethood. What concerns the average person today, and what value does it add to his existence? Our consumerist material worldview is formed even before we learn to speak, causing us never truly to understand our pure identity. Consequently, our attention is more in tune with the dramatized gossip than real-world events, which we deem demoralizing. Nevertheless, should we ignore history because learning about the past makes us sad? What satisfaction can such a life provide to an individual? What society would such individuals create?

Only when we embrace reality and strive towards meaningful struggles can we serve our purpose and find our slice of heaven on earth.[38] *Meaningful* here is defined as that which not only benefits self but the global humanity. It broadens our minds in seeing our petty problems in a realistic light. Our self-worth and happiness are tied to our compassion and generosity, resulting in lasting satisfaction. The prophets exemplified that lifestyle, personified by the righteous *ulama* thereafter. "If the kings knew the pleasure we are in, they would send their armies with swords to take it away from us," said Imam Abu Hanifa (699-767 CE). Even a brief look into his life makes it apparent that it was not the material pleasure he was describing, for the trials of his journey were immense. He died from injuries following his imprisonment and torture by Caliph al-Mansur, ultimately embodying the eudaemonia of the Stoics.

The Prophet reached this spiritual apotheosis at its highest level, describing the world as a prison for the believer but paradise for the disbeliever dogging all its pleasures (*Jami` at-Tirmidhi* 2324). A study of his life (Arabic, *seerah*) reveals perfection in character and action achieved through immense trials. All the discussions on the definition of justice in Plato's *Republic* only serves as a footnote to the *ahadeeth* and *seerah*. The Prophet taught that true success in life depends on submission to God and being fully content with His decree (*Sahih Muslim* 1054). Only an exceptional few who see beyond an anthropomorphic conception of God accomplish this cosmic level of consciousness. Albert Einstein saw it as an individual realizing the futility of human desires in comparison, for "individual existence impresses him as a sort of prison, and he wants to experience the universe as a single significant whole."[39]

A timeless wisdom spans all cultures for those who embark on this journey. True happiness is necessarily linked with our knowledge of God, which only frees our spirit from material deceptions. Imam al-Ghazali explained that each of our faculties delights in what it was created for—lust is pleased with desire, anger in vengeance, sight in beauty, ear in harmony, etc. Accordingly, the highest function of our soul is the perception of truth, which delights it the most. "Thus he who has raised himself above the alms-basket, and not content to live lazily on scraps of begged opinions, sets his own thoughts on work, to find and follow truth, will (whatever he lights on) not miss the hunter's satisfaction; every moment of his pursuit, will reward his pains with some delight; and he will have reason to think his time not ill spent, even when he cannot much boast of any great acquisition," wrote Locke.[40] Perhaps his reference to the hunt here is an homage to Aristotle's archer in *Nicomachean Ethics*.

When we are dissatisfied with common pleasures, many specialists provide various diagnoses and nostrums. "'Thus far their wisdom reaches,' says the Qur'an. It does not occur to them that...the Almighty has a concern for the welfare of that man, and has therefore commanded His servants, the planets or elements, to produce such a condition in him that he may turn away from the world to his Maker," explained al-Ghazali.[41] This understanding of self is derived from a belief in a most loving, most merciful God, who is the most accessible and most near to even the lowest of His creations (*al-Baqarah* 2:186). When we deviate from that relationship with God, we only end up devaluing ourselves in a "meaningless" world. "So remember Me, and I shall remember you; give thanks to Me and do not be ungrateful to Me for My favors" (*al-Baqarah* 2:152).

Many degrees of pleasure and pain are embedded in all that concerns us, blending to redirect us back to God. We find Him through virtuous acts that habituate our desires to seek purity, and experience beauty and perfection in all creation as an expression of God's love and mercy. When we reach a peaceful state, our will merges with divine Will—God's commands embodying our actions, thoughts, and desires—in a joyous *presence* symbolizing Rumi's poem: *What you seek is seeking you.* Our effort on that journey is what proves to be ultimately satisfying, not necessarily winning every battle, for many in history have never lived to see the tremendous impact their struggles had in shaping the world after them. "Those only are happy, who have their minds fixed on some object other than their own happiness; on the happiness of others, on the improvement of mankind, even on some art or pursuit, followed not as means, but as itself an ideal end," observed JS Mill (1806-73 CE). "Aiming thus at something else, they find happiness by the way."[42] This path of selfless actions along with spiritual devotion has been provided as a time-tested solution by nearly all major philosophies and religions, as epically conveyed through the Bhagavad Gita.

There is an element of stoicism in finding contentment in one's lot in life, but without turning into a passive quietist. Passivity is a symptom of apathy, while acceptance is realizing that nothing "out there" can make one happy. The possibility of living a happy life is fully available in the present, and we only have to actively seek it by living in the moment. Realizing that even a pinprick is a decree and test from God that serves to erase our sins through *taqwa*, gratitude turns that physical pain into spiritual joy and enlightenment (*Sahih Muslim* 2572g). Such belief would provide the foundational balance to one's "ABC Theory of Emotion," where an activating event in that light would always lead to a positive emotional response or consequence.

Stoics divide all occurrences into those in our control and those that are not. The latter group belongs to routine natural events that are not inherently good or bad but only from our mental point of reference, which psychologists call the *cognitive theory of emotion*. Essentially, it all gets reduced to our point of view, which we can certainly control to overcome all negative emotions, worry, and anxiety. The Prophet also advised against placing negative connotations on things as "bad omens" but encouraged a positive evaluation to find goodness in everything (*Al-Adab Al-Mufrad* 913). Otherwise, the mind's house of mirrors can turn into a feedback loop of happiness or meta-anxiety, where "each person is as miserable as he imagines himself to be."[43]

The virtues of wisdom, justice, courage, and moderation with excellence have been recognized by all humans since birth, which is another sign of our *fitra* (i.e. natural disposition) and common origin. Tolstoy masterfully painted this in his portrayal of *Hadji Murat*. A similar path brought El-Hajj Malik El-Shabazz (1925-65 CE) the realization that he, too, would die by violence. His infamous rise to fame came under the flagship of the Nation of Islam as Malcolm X, which is far from mainstream Islam. It was during his pilgrimage to Mecca that he was introduced to the core of Islam, which significantly changed his worldview and political strategy thereafter. Unfortunately, he never had a chance to execute his new plans as he was gunned down in broad daylight at forty. Only after the death of Elijah Muhammad in 1975 was his successor WD Mohammed allowed to gradually transform the Nation back to true Islamic principles, himself becoming the first Muslim to perform the morning prayers in the US Senate in 1992.

We have commanded people to honor their parents...In time, when the child

reaches their prime at the age of forty, they pray, "My Lord! Inspire me to be thankful for Your favors which You blessed my parents and me with, and to do good deeds that please You. And instill righteousness in my offspring. I truly repent to You, and I truly submit." (al-Ahqaf 46:15)

Perhaps, this search for meaning at the turn of a man's fourth decade of life leads to the so-called midlife crisis at the peak of his self-awareness. It was the same age when prophet Muhammad started to spend more time in solitude in the cave of Hira. Not surprisingly, this also appears to be the age divinely selected for prophethood (except for Yahya and Jesus). Approaching this age, Imam al-Ghazali left his astounding academic position at the Niẓāmiyyah college at Nishapur to seek seclusion in Damascus. There he achieved his mountain of knowledge through his battle with radical skepticism that has continued to supply fertile minds for generations.

This concept of struggles leading to happiness resembles *nirvana* in Buddhist philosophy. The Buddha (563-480 BC) is said to have realized the truth of suffering. His solution was to leave its causes, which to him were all human desires and pleasures—both related to greed and essentially insatiable. This almost has a tone of Plotinus's Neoplatonic view of the mystic. The Buddhist path to nirvana thus leads away from all personal desires, but without leaving social responsibilities (as opposed to Jainism). Based on that philosophy, the Dalai Lama summarizes the purpose of existence as the pursuit of happiness, which also echoes *Nicomachean Ethics*. In Islamic traditions, the ultimate objective of our lives is instead to serve God, which in turn results in our happiness. God, in His perfect wisdom, shifts our focus from *happiness* itself being the ultimate goal to the higher objective of His servitude (adh-Dhariyat 51:56). One of the reasons is to solve the dilemma of continued servitude on the righteous path while facing adversity, which otherwise gainsays temporal happiness.

Interestingly, Boethius (480-524 CE) makes a similar case in *The Consolation* of true contentment existing in all things good, whose perfection exists only in God. Essentially, *ideals* are the sole driver of human desires, and God consciousness (*taqwa*) is their purest form. "It is that all-powerful urge of the human mind which Freud misinterprets as an urge for sex, Adler misunderstands as an urge for power, McDougall mistakes as a mysterious outcome of the combination of all the animal instincts of man, and Karl Marx misrepresents as an unconscious distortion of the economic urge in the human being," explained Dr. Rafi-ud-din.[44] The higher desires of man supersede their animalistic counterparts by resulting in pleasures of a far superior quality and intensity. Thus, a pure ideal can dominate all desires at both psychological and biological levels through its overarching effects.

Today's promotion of pursuing the lower desires is a rather sharp departure from all classical understanding of its ramifications. The conditioning starts as soon as an infant can look at a screen and use opposable thumbs to navigate the ways to instant gratification on a tablet of modern life. From then on, the same algorithm is only repeated in schools, workplaces, personal relationships, entertainment, and all other things that have an app. The resulting diseased state then produces addicted bots unable to function without constant stimulation in all aspects of life. Reframing this entire concept is necessary to de-emphasize happiness as a *right*, which attempts to justify any means required to reach that goal. Only then would we refrain from transgressing on others' basic human rights to achieve temporal pleasures on earth.

Secular practice reduces the self to following lusts like the lower class of animals, which moves us away from God-consciousness. Anthropologist Joseph Unwin demonstrated how abandonment of chastity rapidly leads to societal demise in *Sex and Culture*, along with a reduction of creativity and arts. Instead, what truly brings happiness is a habitual denial of carnal pleasures. "The mind cannot become stable unless it stops wandering," wrote Seneca.[45] In pursuing desires, not only the mind wanders but individuals also try to run away from their problems and even themselves for the lack of a set goal. God provides us with a fixed destination in the hereafter that serves to focus our thoughts, actions, and purpose. So Islam becomes a *way of life* on a balanced *path* to a permanent destination, not just an exciting philosophy.

Still, the wisdom and lessons taught by the Dalai Lama are timeless, as is the humility of his likeness in admitting not having the answers to all human inquiries. He admits that practices such as *Tong-Len* were never expected to apply to everyone. Similarly, the Buddha never claimed divinity or any inspiration from any god. On the other hand, the Prophetic traditions differ in their divine guidance in having the perennial answer to every human condition in their all-encompassing applicability. While many other spiritual practices and philosophies correlate with Islamic principles, the latter supersedes via its source code. For instance, the Stoics employed *delay* to overcome anger, which modern psychologists like Victor Frankl also stressed as the decisive moment between stimulus and response. The Prophet took it even further by advising one to leave the state of anger by changing posture or washing oneself in preparation for prayer, all of which provide sufficient *delay* (or cognitive distancing) and turn a vice or passion into a virtue (e.g., *Sunan Abī Dāwūd* 4782-4).

The Buddhists emphasize compassion as an aspect of the meaningful struggle that makes our human experience worthwhile. Islam internalizes such commitment through its bigger picture: "God commands justice, doing good, and generosity towards relatives, and forbids what is shameful, blameworthy, and oppressive. He teaches you, so that you may take heed" (*al-Nahl* 16:90). Hence, all different philosophical understandings of virtue were imparted upon humanity through God's initial teaching of Adam with their revival through the fraternity of prophets and messengers thereafter. The entire life of the Prophet was an unwavering practical demonstration of compassion as guided by the divine light, not only in a theoretical plane but in its actual application in all the diversely complex human interactions. The rest of us deviating from it do it through our shortcomings. Our imagination also limits us in walking in others' shoes, as studies have consistently shown the inefficacy of such roleplay.[46] A better method is to seek such perspectives from direct interactions with individuals of opposing views while keeping our emotional biases in check.

Interestingly, the early Vedic texts described an afterlife consisting of heaven and hell based on one's actions in life.[47] Historian al-Biruni noted how the educated Hindus of his time believed in monotheism in a striking resemblance to Muslims.[48] Later Vedic thinkers introduced *samsara* in their attempts to reconcile the inequality of morality in life, resulting in an endless cycle of rebirth commonly associated with Hinduism and Buddhism today.[49] While our souls are unique, a form of "rebirth" can still be appreciated through our earthly bodies, which are made of an arrangement of atoms that countless others have shared throughout the universe's history. Perhaps a spiritual rebirth in the form of resurrection with eternal life in heaven is a better consolation for our earthly sufferings than *samsara*, which frankly sounds more like a hellish punishment through repeated terrestrial toil. In fact, that **is** the concept of hell on earth in Sikhism. Accordingly, the caste system and even the serfdom of old Tibet appear to rival the latter. On a side note, the propagandized Chinese takeover of Tibbet usually neglects that it abolished serfdom and slavery, which oppressed the main populace for centuries. Thus, ordinary Tibetans largely opposed the CIA-trained elite uprising, which caused its failure.[50]

Nirvana is similar to *moksha* as they both offer an escape from *samsara*. Still, death appears to be the only way to escape life's pains. But there has to be a middle path without a cromulent life of misery to attain permanent happiness. While the Buddha's solution is understandable in light of his early life of vanity and crapulence, it nevertheless is just as myopic. Either of these extremes—a life full of pleasure or utterly devoid of it—would only force out extreme human characteristics. The celibacy adopted by the Catholic Church created a legacy of paraphilia that they have continuously struggled to contain.[51] Ironically, if we were to leave *all* desires, the human race would cease to exist. Civilization would collapse if we all became vagrant cynics (or ascetics) like Diogenes of Sinope (400-325 BC).

Even notable stoics like Seneca (4 BC-65 CE) and Marcus Aurelius (121-180 CE) died as wealthy men. Passions and pleasures are like all other faculties given in divine wisdom for us to master and control. They, too, have important functions, which in their own right are essential to our well-being. Thus, God tells us that He has made all good and pure things lawful for us along with our desires for them (*al-Ma'idah* 5:5). We should strive to control them with our reason and intellect to express them as divinely instructed, for that is the true purpose of this world, serving as a training ground for us to grow spiritually. According to Orientalist Thackston Jr, this latter view elaborated by many Sufi thinkers resulted in the greater social context of Sufism compared to their counterparts in the Christian West.[52]

What you have been given is only the fleeting enjoyment of this world. Far better and more lasting is what God will give to those who believe and trust in their Lord (Ash-Shuraa 42:36)

What the later Vedic thinkers did with the original concept of an afterlife has interesting similarities to Rabbinic Jewish traditions. Both of them, representing two of the world's oldest religions, have gradually moved away from an afterlife consisting of well-defined heaven and hell; some sects today do not even believe in a God. The result is confusion among followers regarding the proper role of morality in one's life. This uncertainty is even more prevalent in the nonreligious denominations of the world, who still refuse to accept a connection.

Today, some champion their irrational acts with the dictum, "You only live once," or "YOLO." God addresses this timeless pathology and says: "And they argue, 'There is nothing beyond our worldly life. We die; others are born. And nothing destroys us but [the passage of] time.' Yet they have no knowledge [in support] of this [claim]. They only speculate" (*al-Jathiya* 45:24). A genuine belief in an afterlife allows us to live the best version of our lives both for the rewards and the fear of eternal consequences. That is the divine solution with positive and negative reinforcements for our behavior. When our actions are not clearly related to consequences, the reasons for abiding by those rules become vague. As a result, people start to focus more on rituals, overlooking their practicality. Critical thinking, therefore, is discouraged, often firmly put down by threats of exclusion.

Poet al-Mutanabbi (915-65 CE) once said: "Nothing will be considered correct by the mind if you even have to prove the sun is shining during daytime." What is even the point of scientifically demonstrating compassion's physiological and psychological benefits to those unwilling to accept it at its inherent wellness? If a study someday shows no benefit or even some negative effect of benevolence, would that cause us to abandon our humanity? It is, therefore, worth reflecting on God's clear promise: "As for those who reject Our signs, We will lead them gradually (towards their punishment) in a way that they do not know" (*al-'A'raf* 7:182).

THE ORIGINAL SIN

Have you not considered how God has made everything on the earth of service to you? That ships sail the sea at His command? That He keeps the heavens from falling down on the earth without His permission? God is most compassionate and most merciful to mankind. (al-Hajj 22:65)

Following our brief investigation into our motivations, next, we must inquire about the source of our infatuation with our intellect. It distinguishes us from the rest of creation and aids our incessant attempts to separate from the divine solution for success. Essentially, all movements toward secularism originate from our pride in attempting to mask the limitations of our intellect. To visualize it through a Freudian scope, it is our totalitarian *ego* seeking a potential solution to the *id's* struggle to submit. The goal becomes to redefine and confine religion to prevent its application in a broader, conflicted world that we cannot understand sensibly.

Freud's *id*, *ego*, and *superego* are curiously similar to the Islamic forces of *shaytan*, *nafs*, and *angelic*.[53] We take pride as intelligent beings having dominion over our world. It is inconceivable for such a dominating creation to accept defeat by not mastering it all. Furthermore, submitting to a singular all-knowing Master requires a level of humility that is unimaginable for some. "From pride, from pride, our very reas'ning springs," wrote Alexander Pope. "Account for moral as for nat'ral things: Why charge we Heav'n in those, in these acquit? In both, to reason right is to submit."[54]

The first command of the Qur'anic revelation was to "Read" (*al-'Alaq* 96:1) in search of wisdom from the Creator's generous bestowment of knowledge unto humanity (*al-'Alaq* 96:2-5). It is telling that the subsequent *ayats* describe us as: "Most certainly, one exceeds all bounds once they think they are self-sufficient," and the most fitting reminder, "[But] surely to your Lord is the return [of all]" (*al-'Alaq* 96:6-8). Today we are as "self-sufficient" as we have ever been, becoming used to the inevitability of our emergence as Earth's dominant species to the point of preaching our freedom from God. While we have not managed to cure ourselves of death, we have only succeeded in ignoring our mortality and purpose.

Man's titanic arrogance is quick to claim invincibility, especially when drowning in an ocean of blessings. Perhaps our pride comes from a misinterpretation of the source material: "We create man in the finest state" (*al-Tin* 95:4). Setting aside the evident mastery of our planet, throughout history, we have gradually dominated every obstacle and bent the will of every-*thing* to suit our needs. Occasionally, we succumb to the tiniest of God's creations, but eventually, we win over them as well by the Prophetic promise (*Sahih al-Bukhari* 5678). However, taking pride as the best of creation is ostentatiously ignorant because we had no role in our formation. We have the potential to be great at birth, only judged at death based on the legacy we leave behind. But to be proud of our existence is plagiarism at a divine level. Our capacity for eternal progress should not delude us from our fragility in this temporal sphere, where we are constantly troubled by hunger, thirst, heat, cold, pain, and waste.

Humility and submission are the defining features of Islam, while arrogance is the antithesis. The latter is arguably the original sin in the scriptures, even though later Biblical interpretations related it to something more convoluted. Of note, St. Augustine believed that redemption was only possible through God's mercy despite his Paulian belief that all men are born in sin. He held that repentance alone does not guarantee one's entry into heaven, which is similar to the Islamic view. The Catholic Church eventually traded his philosophy for Boethius (480-524 CE), who believed in a more Aristotelian non-omnipotent, minimally-invasive God. Aristotle nevertheless asked, "How can gods who need food be eternal?"[55] Thus, God also reminds us through His final Prophet: "And even before your time, all the messengers We sent were only men We inspired—if you [disbelievers] do not know, ask people who know the Scripture—We did not give them bodies that ate no food, nor were they immortal" (*al-Anbiya* 21:7-8).

The Arabic word commonly translated as sin is *dhulm* (ظلم), which more accurately means to be unjust, oppressive, or deprive oneself of what is rightfully his.[56] It better portrays the self-destructive nature of the act of sinning, essentially depriving us of our spiritual enlightenment. "The sinner sins against himself," wrote Marcus Aurelius. "The unjust man does injustice to himself by making himself bad."[57] While the Bible speaks of other celestial creations like demons and Seraphim (*Isaiah* 6:2), the Qur'an clarifies that God created two entities with free will who are held accountable for their actions: humans and *jinns*. The latter were created before us from smokeless fire and are the likely suspects for many paranormal activities worldwide. One of their notable leaders was Iblis (Azazil), whose devotion over the years had raised him to a station amongst the angels in heaven. All the while, his achievements took root as pride and arrogance with a sense of entitlement. Although he continued to maintain his outward piety, God being all-knowing was aware of what he buried deep inside (i.e., the literal translation of *kufr* or disbelief in Arabic). With that mise-en-scène, God in the heavenly arena debuted the creation of humankind, which simultaneously brought Iblis's faith to the test. It allowed him a shot at redemption or outright disobedience, for the middle ground is plain hypocrisy.

Frankly, *faith* does not apply here as it implies believing in the *unseen*. When standing in front of God, having total belief in Him is not faith but a simple reality. Like the Taoist assertions in *The Book of Balance and Harmony*: "to sense and comprehend after action is not worthy of being called comprehension…To know after seeing is not worthy of being called knowing."[58] This answers common questions like: *Why doesn't God make Himself visible to everyone? Why does He only communicate through select messengers? (al-Baqarah* 2:118). Such arguments come from a place of arrogance that originated with Iblis, who served as a case in point that even when God is visible, that pathology of one's heart and thought can still prevent him from full submission. Ordinary beings demanding such miracles from God fail to realize His magnificence and would not demand the same from far lesser human kings or rulers. It is exponentially more illogical than to ask for the president to come and explain the laws personally to earn one's trust—except it is we who depend on God for everything while He does not need anything from us.

Humbling ourselves to our relative existence amidst God's magnanimous creations reveals the infinite miracles surrounding us as proof of His presence. If He had sent an angel with the message, it would have been unrelatable for us, just as if the messenger was a human from a different nation. Thus, God selects messengers from amongst the people who have proven to be the most virtuous throughout their lives *before* receiving revelation (*ali-'Imran* 3:164). Pre-prophethood, Muhammad lived forty years among his people with a legacy that earned him the nickname of "the trustworthy." During his early adulthood, he was even noted to work the shift of a sick person to earn his livelihood for him. Those demanding a direct message from God to believe usually do not achieve such qualifications, while placing conceited stipulations on God without putting in the work.

On the Day of Judgment, when all things become apparent, we would have no choice but to believe unconditionally, forcing some to beg for a second chance—just like the pharaoh when he tasted the saltwater of the Red

Sea. God describes the scene in the Qur'an: "There [in hell] they will be [fervently] screaming, 'Our Lord! Take us out [and send us back]. We will do good, unlike what we used to do.' [They will be told,] 'Did We not give you lives long enough so that whoever wanted to be mindful could have done so? And the warner came to you. So taste [the punishment], for the wrongdoers have no helper'" (*Fatir* 35:37). For every day when we wake up from our temporary deaths in sleep serves as yet another of the thousands of chances we are given to repent and submit.

Nonetheless, when God commanded all in heaven to bow down before Adam, Iblis's pride got the best as he refused to obey a direct command. "He said, 'Never would I prostrate to a human whom You created out of clay from an altered black mud.' [God] said, 'Then get out of it, for indeed, you are expelled'" (*al-Hijr* 15:32-34). That was the single most important event summarizing the entire human experience, which is the focus of our current discussion. Right before the command of prostration, God reminded how He knows "what you reveal and what you conceal" (*al-Baqarah* 2:33). That was an indirect warning towards Iblis in attendance, as well as for the rest of us. The angels, in their innocence, also wondered about Adam's creation (*al-Baqarah* 2:32). In sharp contrast to Iblis, when the angels witnessed Adam's intellect, they glorified the source of all knowledge and fell into prostration. Even with their immense grasp of the unseen, they demonstrated humility, for our understanding is ultimately just a drop of God's perfection in wisdom. It revealed the two paths for humanity and our free will: those who question with humility versus those who transgress out of arrogance. Perhaps that is why Frost wrote: "Two roads diverged in a wood, and I—"

Iblis's refusal to submit was, therefore, the *original sin*. He showed how knowledge itself is never enough to attain wisdom as we continue to question our way to defiance. When God asked about his truculence, he claimed superiority not because of his rank and devotion but for his creation from fire—something he had no control over. It further illustrates the inanity of arrogance displayed around us even today. History is full of people claiming superiority through birth, skin color, and place of origin, none of which they achieved or influenced. As a result, the actions motivated by that unfounded foolish hubris only take one down the same path of Iblis's original racism—being cast out of heaven forever. Iblis also cunningly left out the fact that Adam's uniqueness hinged on his fashioning with intellect and a soul (*al-Hijr* 15:29). It helped him demote humankind down to the level of dirt, which has been since used as a strategy by his army. When we secularly downgrade ourselves as nothing more than the downstream silt of evolution from amoebas and monkeys, we devalue ourselves from that superior status. Such degradation of the soul results in a lack of self-worth where we are in constant need of external social affirmation to survive.

It is only fair then that one's willful refusal to obey simultaneously forfeits His divine guidance (*al-Nahl* 16:106-8). Each haughty sin earns him another that follows, for existence is nothing but successive choices. The *choice* of sin only confirms one's *wish* for eternal damnation. Iblis's monumental arrogance in the presence of clear truth resulted in his heart being sealed. The sin that followed was his asking for God's respite till the final Day to lead humanity astray. "Iblis said, 'I swear by Your might! I will tempt all but Your true servants'" (*Sad* 38:82-3). Even in disobedience, he swore by God's glory and asked permission to be nefarious while praising His might. As absurd as it may seem, it also exemplifies God's infinite mercy when He granted him that respite.

It is also infamy of all those who follow in Iblis's path that they mistake God's respite as His favor, which further makes them ruin their afterlife. "God is mocking them, and allowing them more slack to wander blindly in their insolence" (*al-Baqarah* 2:15). Iblis technically never lost his faith nor denied God's existence. In his arrogance, he consciously traded his afterlife to prove a point—that humankind is not deserving of his submission and can easily be led to deny its creator. At the same time, even the devil is aware of God's might and does occasionally regret his actions while continuing on the same spiteful path (*Mishkat al-Masabih*, Book 4, Hadith 319). Thus, evil was born by God's leave through the means of free will and *Satan*: the sobriquet Iblis earned on that momentous day. The word *devil* also shares its linguistic roots with Iblis through its Greek *diabolos*. It is all in there if you look closely.

The immediate reward for a good deed is also another opportunity to repeat that action. All that is good originates with the Creator, and no evil can be attributed to God, where even the word itself is His linguistic extension. Hence, Rumi considered it a logical absurdity to think that God would create His opposite. What appears to us as ugly or evil is only with the good and beauty within our universe to allow us to differentiate.[59] Satan has no true power except for what is permitted by God and manifested through our free will, which is the fallacy of Satanism. The apparent power of evil only highlights God's majesty as His creations include entities that are even more sublime. Therefore, Dr. Yasir Qadhi suggests that if Kierkegaard had read the Qur'anic narrative and Ibn Taymiyya's writings on Abraham's sacrifice, perhaps he would not have spiraled down his path of *Fear and Trembling*.

The Prophet said: "No one will enter Paradise in whose heart is an atom's weight of arrogance, and no one will enter Hell in whose heart is an atom's weight of faith." A man said: What if I like my clothes to look nice and my

shoes to look nice? He said: "Verily God loves beauty; rather arrogance means rejecting the truth and looking down on people." (At-Tirmidhi 1999)

Since God frees Himself from evil, it cannot exist within His pure domain. Thus, Iblis's arrogance effectively exiled him from heaven along with all that was *evil*, for that is one of the descriptions of eternal paradise. What remained were the angels, incapable of free will and the embodiment of good. Contrary to another misconception, God states at the beginning of this story that He created humankind to inhabit the earth. We were neither sent here as a punishment nor born in sin. We are only responsible for our own actions (*al-Ma'idah* 5:105) and are born in the perfect spirit in our *fitra*, whose later corruption calls for a devolution back to its original state of purity.

Every time God mentions this story in the Qur'an, He says explicitly that both *Adam and Eve* ate from the tree. It abrogates Eve and all women from the blame placed upon them in the Testaments and Judeo-Christian scholarship (e.g., *Ecclesiastes* 7:26-8, *Ecclesiastes* 25, *Genesis* 3, *Timothy* 2). The blame was elaborated in the writings of notable theologians like Rabbi Yitzhak b. Avdimi (*Eruvin* 100b:20), St. Paul, St. Tertullian, St. Augustine, St. Thomas Aquinas, and others. In one particular instance in the Qur'an, God even singles out Adam saying: "So, both Ādam and Eve ate from it, and their parts of shame were exposed to them, and they started stitching on themselves some of the leaves of Paradise. And '**Ādam disobeyed his Lord, and erred**" (*Taha* 20:121).

Our first orientation to Satan's animosity was this persuasion of our parents into following in his footsteps by disobeying a command of God. It demonstrated his divide-and-conquer policy that will become a recurrent theme in our earthly interactions. Focusing on the tree here makes us miss the hypothetical forest, which was only Adam's temporary educational stop. Earth had already been created for his children to prove their magnificence by separating from all evil spells. Here on earth, we are to be enemies while being deceived by its beauty like a counterfeit gilded coin. The scorching trials of our lives act as a sieve to purify us and help us become worthy of our original home in heaven.

God gives us the clear answer: "[He is the One] Who created death and life to test which of you is best in deeds" (*al-Mulk* 67:2). Is it then surprising that the devil drives many to question God's presence? While proving our worth, many of us encounter immense trials and tribulations; some pay the ultimate price of death. Others would argue that a higher price is paid by living a torturous life. The injustice and chaos around us can be overwhelming and illogical at times, which made Auden violently protest his pre-WW-II poem's ending: "We must love one another or die." Witnessing the extent of human cruelty, he later only allowed reprints with the ending: "We must love one another and die."[60] Even then, we should not succumb to despair, as the better Prophetic advice was to place our faith in God's judgment for whichever is better for us (*Sahih al-Bukhari* 5671). Indeed, "God alone is sufficient for us and He is the best Protector" (*ali-'Imran* 3:173).

Some are left wondering why would so much chaos be allowed if God is perfect. God answers: "And if God were to take mankind to task for what they did, He would not have left a living creature on its back, but He delays them up to an appointed time. So when their time comes, then God is the One who will see His slaves" (*Fatir* 35:45). God's *slaves* here may refer only to those who obeyed Him during their earthy lives, indicating an ominous disregard for those who disobeyed. While we all demand justice, it is God's mercy that we should seek instead, as He chooses *ar-Rahman* and *ar-Raheem* from all His names to introduce Himself to us (*al-Fatihah* 1:1). Otherwise, even the noblest of us would have to expiate the insects and plants we unknowingly crush on our daily strides. Therefore, it is not simply *justice* that Islam aspires to, but all-encompassing *excellence* (Arabic: *ihsan* إحسان) in its perfection. That comes with the appropriate reward because: "Is there any reward for excellence except excellence?" (*ar-Rahman* 55:60).

A denial of God also accompanies a dismissal of the devil's plots, which is perhaps his greatest gambit. Instead of training and building a fortress around our souls to protect us from his whispers, some contest his mere existence. Consequently, they are prayed upon unnoticed. Why would evil not encircle us from all directions if this is its main domain? We were meant to return to heaven leaving it behind to rot here on earth, followed by eternal damnation. If we succumb to evil powers, we do so through that *original sin* of arrogance, which we share with the roots of all that is vile. If we truly want good, we must seek it through its source beyond this world—from the heavens and the sole Creator.

The Prophet described our actions as deposits made in the banks of goodness and evil, with our intentions serving as the keys (weak chain, *Sunan Ibn Majah* 237 & 238). Forever digging deeper into worldly matters, we must remind ourselves of its temporal nature and detach from it all to experience every moment fully. Eventually, the most oppressed and the worst oppressors share the same fate. "Every soul will taste death. And We test you with evil and with good as a trial, and to Us, you will be returned," reminds God (*al-Anbya* 21:35). Imagine all the people we interact with during our short lives: how many of them will stand between us and our Paradise on the Day when God promises to account for *every* injustice? The point is not to delude ourselves into creating our temporary paradise on earth but to invest in the eternal domain of the hereafter that is to follow. We can still enjoy our stay here, just as long as we do not transgress the rights of others and God's commands. For God swears by His Grandeur that He would never allow us to be fearful twice—if we fear Him in this life, He promises us safety in the hereafter. However, if we feel safe from His punishment here, the resulting actions would cause us much to fear in the afterlife (*Sahih Ibn Hibban*; *al-Ihsan* 640).

Human beings are born in hardship in a world created to exile evil. Many have died unjustly throughout history, proving the injustice of humanity. At the same time, much of the injury is done by those seeking justice, both genuinely and spuriously. Then how can we expect to find fairness here? "Do you suppose that you will enter the Garden [of Paradise] without first having suffered like those before you?" asks God and reassures: "They were afflicted by misfortune and hardship, and they were so shaken that even [their] messenger and the believers with him cried, 'When will God's help arrive?' Truly, God's help is near" (*al-Baqarah* 2:214). Some of the most deserving people face the toughest trials, while the depraved live the lavish lives of the elite. The inequity of arrogance is not new to world history, which we are finally ready to dissect after meandering considerably to set the foundations for our discussion.

As an American, perhaps it is most fitting to start at home. For instance, the European colonization of the Americas caused 8-138 million Native American casualties over 200 years. This wide range further highlights the (lack of) value of minority life in historical accounts. It is no small feat to convince a whole nation that the resistance of the natives against foreign invaders is "savagery" justifying their extermination. The first governor of California, Peter Burnett (1807-95 CE), took office promising "a war of extermination until the Indian race becomes extinct," and "Let the first man who says treaty or peace be regarded as a traitor."[61] Pompous "experts" like Lewis Cass (1782-1866 CE)—Secretary of War and governor of the Michigan territory—made academic arguments for the removal of the natives, resulting in an honorary doctorate from Harvard in 1836. Similar establishment apologists continue to climb the ranks in prestigious institutions across the country even today.

A witnessing federal agent once wondered the obvious moral question of "Which of these people are the savages?"[62] Rare defenders like Senator Theodore Frelinghuysen (1787-1862 CE) of New Jersey cried: "We have crowded the tribes upon a few miserable acres…Do the obligations of justice change with the color of the skin?"[63] Nevertheless, they have been gradually reduced to their current sad state where the invaders dare to yell, "Go back to your country," confusing them for immigrants at local Walmarts. After his contribution to the genocide, President John Quincy Adams (1833-94 CE) pitied "that helpless race of native Americans, which we are exterminating with such merciless and perfidious cruelty among the heinous sins of this nation, for which I believe God will one day bring [it] to judgment."[64] Indeed, God warns: "And [remember] when We took your covenant that you would neither shed each other's blood nor expel each other from their homes…But here you are, killing each other and expelling some of your people from their homes, aiding one another in sin and aggression…Do you believe in some of the Scripture and reject the rest? Is there any reward for those who do so among you other than disgrace in this worldly life and being subjected to the harshest punishment on the Day of Judgment? For God is never unaware of what you do" (al-Baqarah 2:84-5).

Dr. Martin Luther King Jr. gave our nation too much credit for being the "only one" that exterminated its indigenous people as a national policy.[65] In reality, the Australians have done it to the Aboriginals; the Europeans did it in their colonized lands everywhere; the Mongols did it all over Eurasia; the Ottomans did it to the Armenians; the Russians did it during the Circassian genocide and later again in Bosnia; the Maori did it to the Moriori; the Germans to the Jews, who are now doing it to the Palestinians; the Japanese to the Chinese, who are now doing it to the Uyghurs, demonstrating techniques they mastered in Tibet; the Christian Serbs did it to the Muslims in Chechnya and Kosovo; the Burmese are doing it to the Rohingya as the Indians are to Muslims; the list goes on. It may even go as far back as 40,000 years ago, with the Cro-Magnons annihilating the Neanderthals from the planet.

It is easy to get bogged down with such historical accounts of godless men competing in arrogance. While they champion the devils in their war against God, the resulting injustices seem inscrutable if we consider our earthly life as our only existence. Thus, the Prophet warned that the first matter concerning which judgment will be passed on the Day of Resurrection is bloodshed (Sunan Ibn Majah 2615). That belief is the only fair outcome of history, providing strength and meaning through life's difficulties. Neurologist Victor Frankl concluded the same through his research and personal experience as a Holocaust survivor. Yet the same injustice and chaos meant to remind us of our purpose cause many to turn away from God. That denouncement does not bring justice but only leads to an existential crisis. *Why would God even give us such qualities to transgress and allow so much suffering?* It is not that we do not know the answer but it is difficult for us to accept due to our arrogance.

Our passions indeed serve a purpose and God only asks us to restrain them. It allows us to earn His mercy and forgiveness for our minor sins through our avoidance of the greater. Whenever we are blessed with abundance and good times, we seem to forget our dependence on God and, as a result, start our transgressions against Him through His creations. In divine wisdom, He then tests us with afflictions to help us return to Him. "Indeed, We have sent messengers before you [O Prophet] to other people who We put through suffering and adversity [for their denial], so perhaps they would be humbled" (*al-An'am* 6:42). It is a sign of His infinite mercy and love that He does not immediately condemn us for our defiance. Instead, He promises to test us only with what we can bear to atone for our conceit with chances of redemption. "As for those who repent, believe, and do good deeds, they are the ones whose evil deeds God will change into good deeds. For God is All-Forgiving, Most Merciful" (*al-Furqan* 25:70).

This concept of trial and error, leading to our gradual improvement, is deeply woven into our DNA. Its importance to our spiritual development is also reflected through the Prophetic tradition that if humanity ceased sinning, God would replace it with another that would continue to sin and repent to earn His forgiveness (*Muslim*). The entire process requires a leap of faith and *submission*, which for many is unacceptable, just as it was for Iblis. Our free will and intellect make us the most powerful creatures on earth, which creates a sense of pride that rises to the level of questioning God. Still, we cannot even grasp the galaxy's vastness nor the smallness of the protons that make us—which are made of even smaller quarks. We make clamorous demands to understand it all just like Iblis, as he stood in front of God and refused to submit. Therefore, some follow his path and separate from all that is good while fueling the fire of injustice.

Corruption has flourished on land and sea due to people's actions, and He will make them taste the consequences of some of their actions so that they may turn back. (ar-Rum 30:41)

Heaven is a choice. Hell is a choice. Meanwhile, we are stuck here with free will, like *The Stranger* on a sunny beach in Albert Camus's existence. We are ultimately free to do as we please as long as we accept the consequences. The absurdity of absurdism is blatantly denying the meaning of it all through our frustration with the world. Often debating endless tangential philosophies like existentialism that only attempt to furiously hang onto one aspect of the elephant in the room while vehemently ignoring the rest. "I am as My servant thinks of me," reminds God (*Sahih al-Bukhari* 7405). So we must positively reacquaint ourselves with God in the way He presents Himself in the Qur'an and not aid Satan in fulfilling his arrogant promise.

The world we live in is anything but just. Still, we fight evil to prove our worth in hopes of returning to our original home. Albeit most struggling on that path do not live to see the fruits of their labor, they still find happiness through their journey. We must strive to bring positive changes around us in hopes of collectively making the world a better place. The goal is to eventually earn our place back in heaven, away from all that pushes us towards hell during our temporal commune here on earth. "Looking back on one's lifetime, you say...have I done enough for the world to justify being here?" asked vaccinologist Maurice Hillerman. "There is a great joy in being useful, and that is the satisfaction you get from it."

God does not change the condition of a people unless they change what is in themselves, but if He wills harm on a people, no one can ward it off—apart from Him, they have no protector. (al-Ra'd 13:11)

THE APPLE OF ADAM'S GRANDCHILDREN

> Look next on Greatness say where Greatness lies?
> "Where, but among the Heroes and the Wise?"
> Heroes are much the same, the point's agreed,
> From Macedonia's madman to the Swede;
> The whole strange purpose of their lives, to find
> Or make, an enemy of all mankind!
> Not one looks backward, onward still he goes,
> Yet ne'er looks forward farther than his nose.
>
> [ALEXANDER POPE, AN ESSAY ON MAN IV:216-24]

The eschatological duel between good and evil is constantly on display. Still, Heraclitus and Lao Tzu saw harmony in our variance with our surroundings, like the bow and the lyre. We are to balance ourselves in that tug-of-war with repeated chances for redemption. When we become obdurate in selfishness and greed, the only remaining option becomes our replacement with people of better ethics.

Greed lies at the heart of our infamies that James Ogilvy describes as the fulcrum turning love into lust, leisure into sloth, hunger into gluttony, honor into pride, righteous indignation into anger, and admiration into envy.[66] Nevertheless, all the "greats" in history repeatedly fell into its trap. Cyrus's great ambition, for instance, resulted in a consolidated Persia around 550 BC. By the time of his twelfth successor Darius III (381-330 BC), the empire became consumed with corruption, allowing the unprotested conquest by Alexander *the Great* in 330 BC. Within days his army razed Persepolis to the ground, essentially replacing Darius's lust for pleasure with his greed for conquest.

"Two hungry wolves sent amid a flock of sheep are no more destructive to them than a man's greed for wealth and fame is to his *deen*," warned the Prophet (*At- Tirmidhi; Riyad as-Salihin* 484). There is also no end to coveting, which renders even the most affluent person poor. Perhaps the lack of further characterization of *the Greats* includes their great brutality and ego, as both Cyrus and Alexander left a trail of burnt cities, tortured prisoners, and pillages to satisfy their grand ambitions. Unlike Ashoka (304-232 BC) in Kalinga, these men were not moved by their victims' mourning and continued their great aggression till death. One wonders how satisfied they were when they met their eventual ends.

A poet once sang: "I obeyed the things I coveted, and they enslaved me; If only I had been satisfied, I would have been free."[67] History books are plagued with such "great" men, but should a man's legacy be judged by his most significant accomplishment or worst atrocity? For God warns: "We shall certainly give the disbelievers a taste of severe punishment. We shall repay them according to their worst deeds" (*Fussilat* 41:27). Still, men are not binary but full of complex nuances, like Cyrus's spectacular garden that he tended to daily. It was his pride and joy with a massive underground irrigation system imitating the cascading rivers beneath the gardens of Paradise. It is only fitting that he called his garden *pairidaeza*, where we derived the word *paradise* from the Greek *paradeisos*. Interestingly, the same *al-Firdous* is also the Arabic term for a garden in the Qur'an.

The lessons from the Achaemenid destruction by Alexander parallel the Abbasids' by the Mongols in 1258 CE. Corruption within the ruling class had seeped so deep that rebuilding from the ashes was the only remaining redemption. Consequently, Persepolis and Baghdad suffered similar fates fifteen centuries apart. "That was a nation which has passed; they will have what they earned, and you will have what you earned, and you will not be questioned concerning what they used to do," reminds God (*al-Baqarah* 2:134). Indeed, anyone with any knowledge of history would have seen this coming, but that would require some introspection and a receptive heart. "Is it not clear to those who inherit the land from former generations that We can punish them too for their sins if We will? And seal up their hearts so that they cannot hear?" asks God (*al-A'raf* 7:100).

What is even the point if we cannot learn from past mistakes? Einstein defined *insanity* as doing the same thing repeatedly but expecting different results, which makes our entire existence appear unhinged. Perhaps we do not study history to prevent the future but to understand and find meaning in the present. Another benefit is to familiarize ourselves with prior failed attempts for the next wily usurper's promise to *make us great again*. Yet, every generation thinks they have discovered a new technique to go down the same time-tested path to destruction without meeting the same end. We repeatedly double down on past mistakes in a pattern known in psychology as the *escalation of commitment*, where we validate erroneous decisions in search of self-justification.[68] That egotistical rationalization ignores the inevitability: "Before you people, We destroyed whole generations when they did evil—their messengers brought them clear signs, but they refused to believe. This is how We repay the guilty. Later We made you their successors in the land, to see how you would behave" (*Yunus* 10:13-14).

Repetition is the only guarantee in history, where Roman brutalities rolled over to the Byzantine Empire, ultimately sealing their fates. Although the pennant of justice was again raised by the Qur'an, the Islamic Caliphate also became corrupt through political greed. God alludes to this and says: "Then We made to inherit the Book those whom We have chosen from among Our slaves. But among them are some who wrong themselves, some follow a middle course, and some are foremost in good deeds with God's permission" (*Fatir* 35:32). "That is the great bounty," for it shows the elegant diversity of faith and the heterogeneity of creation that demonstrates God's grandeur, mentioned in the preceding *ayats* of the same *surah*.

Opinions on early Muslims' political and geographical success are as ubiquitous as minds willing to cogitate. Nevertheless, the contrasting lessons from the Battles of Badr and Uhud are self-explanatory. Even though the Prophet spent his entire life fighting sacrosanct tribalism, political power remained within the tribe of Quraysh for hundreds of years after his death. The fates of his family and companions following his passing are utterly heartbreaking. Re-emergence of the fissiparous infighting between the Qurayshi tribes (similar to the times of *jahiliyyah*) eventually weakened the bond that had allowed them to come out of a barren desert and rule the known world in the first place.

The successors of the Prophet and scholars who shaped early Islam were persecuted not by outsiders but by Muslim rulers from within the Caliphate. Muslims were the ones who laid siege to the sacred cities and massacred the Prophet's family and companions. The Kufan's innovative lamentation of that guilt for abandoning the Prophet's grandson at Karbala gradually transformed a political schism into a new religious sect. Jerusalem was also lost to the Crusaders during its rule under the Caliphate. Islamic morale was so low during that period that some leaders of the *ummah* even aided the Crusaders in massacring their Muslim neighbors, while others simply looked away. Therefore, the subsequent revival of Islamic teachings had to come from the outside under the Ottoman banner.

Many today, reminiscing about the golden years, overlook these hard historical facts and fail to learn from their lessons.

These examples follow the same pattern at both ends, marked by a power grab by local factions because it is much harder to reconstruct than to demolish. For the ancient Greeks, there were the smaller city-states claimed by Alexander's generals. For the Romans were the Germanic tribes and the Burgundians. For the Ottomans was the mutilation through the Sykes-Picot agreement, which "transformed what had been relatively quiet provinces of the Ottoman Empire into some of the least stable and most internationally explosive states in the world."[69] These only represent a buffer till the next empire—all revolving around the inevitable cycle of civilization.

We shall certainly make them taste a nearer torment [in this life] prior to the greater torment, so that perhaps they may return [to the right path]. (as-Sajdah 32:21)

Naturally, we must be wondering where in the cycle of civilization are we today?

Over the last several centuries, humanity has gone through exponential technological and unparalleled scientific advancements. In contrast, the Stone Age lasted about 2.5 million years, with successive periods gradually becoming shorter. Perhaps the lack of written records makes us ignorant, as our knowledge of even those living a thousand years ago falls sharply. Contrasting that to the commonly estimated 100-200 thousand years of humanity's existence puts us in the dark regarding 99% of human history. Hence, our many theories significantly underestimate their accomplishments to the point that other hominids and Neanderthals before them do not even stand a chance. Although Hippocratic medicine was practiced for a millennium, it makes today's physicians sneer and assume all that preceded to be more hysterical than his "wandering womb." Then we are humbled by discoveries like the Neanderthals' use of salicylates and penicillins for toothaches some 40,000 years ago.[70]

The classification of historical periods based on weaponry is skewed by a European perspective, which has been endemic to carnage since its conception. That struggle fueled their leaps of advancements in warfare compared to the rest. As a result, casualties of armed conflicts rose from hundreds to millions, making persecution on a massive scale possible. The worst wars and genocide in history "had their origins and execution in Europe; these were the latest chapters in a long-running story of brutality and violence," writes historian Frankopan. "Thus, while focus normally falls on the investment in art and the impact of new wealth on culture in the sixteenth and seventeenth centuries, it is perhaps more instructive to look to the parallel advances in weapon-making in this period."[71]

To keep up with gunpowder, horses suddenly needed to become bulletproof. That need partly drove the Industrial Revolution and marked the beginning of our current era. It became a race between offense and defense between powers, the likes of which the world had never seen before. Richard Gatling hoped his invention of the first machine gun in 1862 would reduce the American Civil War deaths by showing the futility of combat. Instead, it ended up being quite effective in exterminating Native Americans in the war's aftermath.[72] The members of the Manhattan Project were also rather pollyannish about their atom bomb and giving birth to the nuclear age. In similar irony, the German-Jewish chemist Fritz Haber, whose synthetic ammonia allowed the world unlimited population growth, was the father of mass chemical warfare later used against his own extended family.

The incredible rate of our recent technological advancements is partly fueled by a population growth whose collective genius and sheer brainpower may surpass the totality of our existence. One of the defining moments was the second agricultural revolution of the 17th and early-18th centuries when the global population exponentially rose from half a billion to today's eight billion. At this point in the race, we are virtually rising faster than our synaptic recovery to fully grasp the consequence of being too close to the sun. Yet, we all know what happens next.

Imagine the thousands of years the world enjoyed the wheel compared to the new iPhone released every year—each a monumental achievement in its own right. We relish these technologies making our lives seem *heavenly* to anyone from a few generations ago. Despite the physical pleasures, we are still drowning in anti-depressants, for our spiritual starvation is inevitable from the reduced struggle. Our generation may be the last to recall the joy and personal connection penned within a handwritten letter, otherwise lost in the pixelated virtual world. In a single lifetime, we have seen the incredulous efficiency of the global postal service to letters becoming a thing of the past. We have even escaped our atmosphere into outer space to create a Space Force and ensure our continued warring behavior above and beyond. At this visible peak of our achievement, we feel invincible and immortal in our controlled paradise, demanding the bite from the next *Apple*.

Each technological achievement, in turn, made our world relatively smaller. As if it is humanity's own Napoleon complex to make up for the gradual shorter stature since Adam by virtually shrinking the planet. These are unprecedented times and hardly resemble anything that came before, making it difficult for us to relate to our history. The result is a societal Heisenberg uncertainty that, positioned at this moment in time, we cannot determine our current trajectory. However, not much has changed in our *nature* since Adam. Technology aside, the same human characteristics continue to plague our societies with a higher prevalence. Instead of being humble and grateful for all the blessings, we voluntarily dive into disbelief. We live in a global village where the entire world is at our fingertips. Even with all this access, *truth* is constantly slipping through the massive amount of disinformation shoved at our faces. "It is from the conditions of the Last Hour that knowledge would be taken away and ignorance would prevail, the liquor would be drunk, and adultery would become rampant," foretold the Prophet, which sends shivers down our spines when transposed over our current reality (*Sahih Muslim* 2671).

Constantly looking at our screens at arm's length, we have gradually become nearsighted in a physical sense and shortsighted in a metaphoric. We no longer look beyond the horizon but only down at our smartphones and tablets rivaling the one Preserved (Arabic, *al-Lawhu 'l-Mahfuz*). Within an ever-increasing population, we are rather individually isolated. We are content not knowing our neighbors or those we share our walls with. Arguably, do we even exist if we do not ration it with others in a positive manner? Sure, a falling tree might scream in an empty forest, but is it relevant? (Not to Locke as sound isn't one of his *primary qualities*; nor to George Berkeley as *to be is to be perceived*).

A recent Harvard study concluded that *the absence of conflict is not harmony, it is apathy.*[73] Not all strifes are harmful, as some are deeply ingrained into our well-being. The Population Reference Bureau, through complex mathematical algorithms, estimated that about 108 billion humans had been born since humanity's "Great Leap Forward" some 50,000 years ago. It calculates to an astounding 7-8% of the entire human existence currently alive today. Disputes have always risen where people flourished. The difference is that historically we thrived periodically at a handful of epicenters worldwide, limited by our geographical isolation and shorter lifespan. In contrast, our recent global spread resulted in the rise and fall of contemporary *empires*, the likes of which were separated by centuries before. Thus, the previous power struggles between the few and far between now become internecine World Wars, the devastation of which is sickening. Today's nuclear capability yet again risks our complete extinction after the next global discord.

The global childhood mortality rate for the first five years of life was as high as 40% until the turn of the last century. The average life expectancy was also around forty years until then. With most of our prior limitations solved, we can now live twice as long and die less. Hence, death is perceived to be so far from us that it almost seems foreign, as most of us are afforded the luxury of living without paying much attention to it. Until recently, our loved ones died at home with us exposed to the entire process. Nowadays, the ill get shipped off to a hospital or a nursing facility until their relatives are notified of their demise and then visited one last time at their funerals prepared by strangers.

Technology undoubtedly improves our general quality of life but at the cost of a critical shift in perception. Without the clarity provided by death, the true purpose of life becomes blurry and the entire process is seen as an anomaly, or a failure "of some system, as an infringement on our guaranteed right to happiness!" observed Russell.[74] If we truly believed in our mortality, perhaps we would act differently. To contemplate one's death and loved ones is not to be morbid but to appreciate the gift of life in the present. This *memento mori* for Muslims is divinely prescribed through the five daily prayers, which act to refocus our perspective throughout the day.

Elizabeth Kubler-Ross's ground-breaking research helped us appreciate the many stages of death and grief. Some of her interviews of dying patients were particularly revealing in their dire loneliness, highlighting the Prophetic command to visit the sick as a form of worship (*Sahih al-Bukhari* 3046). That interaction has profound mutual benefits for the visitor and the visited endangered by our current practice. Even though we now live longer, our final years are plagued by calamities of a different kind. Some suffer from conditions that make us forget our identities, reducing us to mere shells like mannequins. Then again, God did tell us: "If We extend anyone's life, We reverse his development. Do they not use their reason?" (*Ya-Sin* 36:68).

This longevity becomes so burdensome that even our offspring cannot care for us. We wither away in loneliness, waiting for a death that is constantly pushed away from us unnaturally.[75] Unsurprisingly, in a secular world, this leads to the legalization of euthanasia worldwide as we continue to find absurd bandaids for our unethical progress. Russell summed it up as a form of "chemical imperialism," where we try to transform as much of the planet's resources into *human bodies* as possible. "Domestication of animals, agriculture, commerce, industrialism has been stages in this process." While much of our efforts have been directed towards this, perhaps it would be more intelligent to pursue "worthier ends, concerned with the quality rather than the quantity of human life."[76]

If one squints through the fog, he can almost make out the outlines of the cyclical pattern of civilization at national levels. We see internal struggles within every country with the rise and fall of governments that fit the aforementioned cycle or empires. However, it all comes at a high cost to the planet. An unsustainable need for raw materials fueled our industrial revolution. The more power we sought, the more technologically advanced we had to become, which required more control of global resources. It was the overwhelming theme of world history until the Second World War.

As the major world powers rushed to control these resources—petroleum, metal ores, rubber, coal, indigo, bauxite, cotton, silk, etc.—to guarantee their war effort, a simultaneous chemical revolution waged on to make us free from such limitations.

We came out of the War into the synthetic age, where we can "synthesize absolutely anything," bragged Richard Feynman.[77] Losing access to the Panama Canal at the start of the War made the US build 134 bases in Panama. Our independence from natural resources then made us abandon them all at the War's end, along with our prior need to annex new territories. It entered the developed countries into a new age of global politics, which is not simply resource-dependent. It became a complex game where developed economies could have anything they *decided* to have limited only by their foreign policies, noted the UN secretary general of the '60s, U Thant.[78] Therefore, our empire-building shifted from territorial possessions to control through foreign bases and corporations.

The synthetic age reduced the need for a slew of raw materials with one major exception: oil. Empires of the past and new made many chemistry-for-colonies exchanges where petroleum substituted for other materials to make synthetic rubber and plastic. The US had an early advantage holding 59% of the world's oil reserves within its borders in 1945. Oil export was only second to cotton in America in the late-19th century, with Rockefeller's Standard Oil accounting for 90%. That soon changed with the discovery of foreign reserves, which single-handedly pushed politicians back to "the old logic of empire," writes historian Immerwahr. "When faced with an Arab oil embargo, Henry Kissinger suggested that the United States 'may have to take some oil fields.' 'I'm not saying we have to take over Saudi Arabia,' the secretary of state continued. 'How about Abu Dhabi or Libya?'"[79]

Such moves are only natural outcomes of Darwinian economics, which unconditionally promotes neo-imperialism. The armed forces then became critical in maintaining "national interests," which are mainly capitalistic. After studying all of the important US leaders, historian Richard Hofstadter (1916-70 CE) came to that conclusion in *The American Political Tradition*. He wrote: "The range of vision embraced by the primary contestants in the major parties has always been bounded by the horizons of property and enterprise...They have accepted the economic virtues of capitalist culture as necessary qualities of man...That culture has been intensely nationalistic..."

Switching to oil from coal at the turn of the 20th century was a milestone moment. As the British Empire became increasingly insecure about the rising Russian influence, the imperials played a complex game of musical chairs of alliances. It was a game of greed where even the tiny monarchy of Belgium had colonies abroad. Britain allied with Russia to avoid direct conflict, but realized that by the end of WWI, they needed to secure their oil supply to maintain dominance.[80] Its Foreign Secretary stated: "I do not care under what system we keep the oil, whether it is by perpetual lease or whatever it may be, but I am quite clear it is all-important for us that this oil should be available."[81] The same need for oil during WWII caused both Britain and Russia to simultaneously invade Iran with the backing of the US, without any regard for their sovereignty. When the Shah resisted, he was promptly replaced with his Westernized brother.[82] What started as William Knox D'Arcy's Anglo-Persian Oil then turned into British Petroleum, initiating the subsequent struggle over Middle Eastern Oil that is all too familiar.

The overall effect of human ambition on the planet has been a tragedy that would even humble Shakespeare. Furthermore, the outcry of the scientific community regarding global warming has been largely ignored.[83] Unfortunately, the most recent UN scientific report of 2022 called it too late, predicting grimmer consequences than the Ukrainian conflict, yet without similar media outrage.[84] Corporate and political leaders at the forefront of the counter-propaganda campaigns are fully aware of the threat but are overpowered by their greed to maximize profit and market share.

The sad reality is that if they do not, someone else will. "The fate of our grandchildren counts as nothing when compared with the imperative of higher profits tomorrow," observes Chomsky.[85] An overwhelming majority of global greenhouse gasses result from the production of electricity compared with 5% from the cars we drive. Yet, the most significant push for change has been toward the conversion to electric cars. Today as the world burns, these propagandas are becoming a tough sell against the smoking ashes. Natural historian David Attenborough's 2020 witness statement on our dying planet is one of the worst atrocities of our generation. Within one lifetime, we destroyed the wildlife he once explored at the beginning of his career.

On our current course, we are looking at another mass global extinction event within the next generation. Still, seeing the disappearing glaciers, we ran straight to bottling them directly for consumption and profit. Our governments boast about the responsible disposal of radioactive waste while inconspicuously throwing it overboard for decades onto the Farallon Islands. When the cartoonish drums failed to sink, the Navy gunners reflexively sunk them with bullets, not caring for the leaked radioactive waste. This practice reportedly stopped in the 1990s, but by then *millions* of drums were dumped by nearly all European nations (plus Russia, China, Japan, and New Zealand).[86] Thus, in 2015 the *Bulletin of the Atomic Scientists* advanced the Doomsday Clock to 3 minutes before midnight, condemning the world leaders for failing to act in a manner to prevent a potential catastrophe.[87] The clock then advanced to two-and-a-half minutes as soon as President Trump took office.[88]

Only recently have we started to appreciate the complexity of the world we have inhabited for eons. It resembles a living organism similar to our bodies—with the flowing rivers as its bloodstream and the mycorrhizae as its nervous system. Trees have evolved to communicate with one another and allocate resources to allow every species a chance to fruit.[89] Some trees even participate in mast fruiting globally in unison to maximize their use of resources and survival.[90] In contrast, humans have gradually devolved from a parasitic relationship with nature to a deadly secular virus plaguing its limbs from all directions. We have failed to see nature's communication to ensure communal well-being over the individual. So we project our selfishness and greed onto it to promote an *unnatural* selection.

Neuroscientist Robert Sapolsky's studies with wild baboons found the alpha males who were friendlier during their rule to be much better off after their downfall.[91] Yet our current path of social Darwinism demands the struggle for ever-increasing greed or death, with no apparent middle ground. The survivors are driven by the efficiency of their consumption as cutting back risks being overrun in the global power struggle, premised on Hobbes's pursuit of "power after power that ceaseth only in death." Hence, the central theme of the US foreign policy became the right to dominate hidden under the stated right to defend. As the world population continues to increase, the need for *all* resources is constantly rising. "There is obvious (or, perhaps, willful) blindness to the fact that it is impossible to attain infinite growth on a finite planet," noted Dr. Hathout.[92] Ironically, the success of this process also leads to our demise—therefore, the *death* of the fittest, regardless.

This desperation then trickles down to every aspect of our lives. The privation of depleting resources forces us to think more from an individual perspective where my clamorous individuality demands that I have the right to speak and be heard; I have the right to own and hoard; I have the right to exist at any cost; I even have the right to consume and cause my destruction. These "rights" championing an emotivist individualism represent a relatively recent innovation with little to no rational foundation when uprooted from their religious roots.[93] As Attenborough realized after his lifelong experience, while it was our intelligence that brought us here, it is our wisdom that will ultimately secure our survival.

It is God who produces both trellised and untrellised gardens, date palms, crops of diverse flavors, the olive, the pomegranate, alike yet different. So when they bear fruit, eat some of it, paying what is due on the day of harvest, but do not be wasteful: God does not like wasteful people. (al-An'am 6:141)

STARVING HUMANITY

Man never tires of asking for good, but if evil touches him, he loses all hope and becomes despondent. Whenever We let him taste some of Our mercy after he has been afflicted, he is sure to say, "This is all my own doing: I do not think the Hour will ever come, but even if I were to be taken back to my Lord, the best reward would await me with Him." We shall most certainly inform the disbelievers of what they have done and give them a taste of severe torment. Whenever We are gracious to man, he goes away haughtily, but as soon as evil touches him, he turns to prolonged prayer. (Fussilat 41:49-51)

I: Poverty of Avarice

Capitalism grew from a reinvigorated individualism sprouting from the ashes of the French Revolution. Even today's concept of the left and the right came from the respective revolutionary and royalist sides of the French National Assembly. Ideally, the result of that Revolution—opposing both Church and monarchy—should have been a philosophy of social reform for the collective betterment. Instead, it was the "cult of the individual" that prevailed, as noted by philosophers like Emile Durkheim (1858-1917 CE). As a result, they ended up throwing out the proverbial baby with the bathwater.

Although our drive to own and profit in this depleting world is framed through a "basic survival instinct," the true motivations are nothing short of selfish greed and arrogance. What guidance or motivation could override that instinct other than a strong belief in God and an afterlife? We are all essentially miniature imperialists trying to transform as much of our environment into ourselves and our offspring as possible.[94] Paul Valéry's (1871-1945 CE) *une machine puissante* reflected that dominant

Occidental attitude of the era.[95] But in the aftermath of all revolutions, the impoverished masses are always betrayed by the imperialism of the intellectuals and elites. "Progressivism aims above all at the liberation of an elite whose ascent requires the disassembling of norms, intermediating institutions, and thick forms of community, a demolition that comes at the expense of these communities' settled forms of life," explains Professor Deneen.[96] Once the dust from all the sociopolitical theories settles, we are left with the central issue of faith: what do we believe to be the source of our provisions? Who ultimately is responsible for providing our next meal?

God answers by informing us that there is no moving creature on earth, but its sustenance depends on Him (*Hud* 11:6). At the same time, we must work for those provisions and not take a lazy, passive approach. Even when Mary was alone in isolation during labor, God asked her to shake the tree before its fruits were made available (*Maryam* 19:24-5). It was not the force of her hands that caused them to fall but the step she took toward God's mercy that resulted in its fruition. Moses was also asked to strike with his staff for the Red Sea to part. Similarly, we are to work towards our livelihood but realize that the next meal (or *rizq*) will ultimately come from God. This balance allows us to share without diving into a selfish hoarding mentality, frowned upon by most faiths.

Jesus compared one's love for this world to drinking seawater, which only increases thirst. His brother in mission, prophet Muhammad, warned about the difficulty of abstaining from materialism by comparing it to swimming without getting wet. Both of them warned us against the antichrist, who will be the ultimate materialist. Thus, both of them also demonstrated their firmness in faith and spirituality by being *as generous as the wind*—not hesitating to share even the last date or bowl of milk for their household. We can emulate such unwavering faith in God's promise as exposure therapy by living, eating, and dealing like the prophets to bring more fulfillment to our lives. Without that firmness of faith, we are constantly threatened with poverty and hunger, which in a secular culture promotes trust in money and an overflowing fridge over God.

Such replacement and abandonment of spirituality leave us with only our generosity when it comes to the welfare of society without a failsafe to protect the weak. While that may be enough for some philanthropists, it does not allow guidance for the profligate. Even the strongest proponents of individualism would beg for help if they were destitute, perhaps driven by that same selfishness. Unfortunately, that same mentality would preclude anyone from coming to their aid in an individualistic society, which is not far from today's lived reality. Hunger is a powerful motivator that cannot be empathized with by those with a full stomach. According to the UN, we lose about 25,000 people daily to global hunger.[97] It amounts to about 9 million hunger and malnutrition-related deaths annually worldwide. It is far greater than the deaths from COVID-19 but without comparable global efforts towards eradication because poverty does not affect the elite and the powerful indiscriminately like a virus.

"In the long run, a hierarchical society is only possible on the basis of poverty and ignorance," observed Orwell.[98] Thus, we live in a failed system, desperately looking for patchwork on a sinking ship. This practice of fixing *effects* instead of their *causes* is similar to only treating a symptom of an infection—like fever or pain—without appropriate antibiotics or intervention. It is the main factor in the delayed progression of humanity from an ethical sense that resembles stagnation if not regression. It is noteworthy that today's global food production is enough to sustain a 3000-calorie diet for every individual. With thousands of years of existence, even after revolutionizing food production, we have failed to solve fundamental problems like hunger and shelter. We may deem ourselves too sophisticated and evolved to need primitive religions, but that secularization only ruins everything we touch, including ourselves.

With polluted minds, we search for answers overlooking the apparent, further complicating the picture. "Liberalism has failed because liberalism has succeeded," stresses Professor Deneen. "As it becomes fully itself, it generates endemic pathologies more rapidly and pervasively than it is able to produce Band-aids and veils to cover them."[99] However, this is not a support for contemporary conservatism, which essentially is only the other side of the same coin.[100] Greed and arrogance are at the heart of it, defying the nature of everything else in the universe. "Again I tell you, it is easier for a camel to go through the eye of a needle than for someone who is rich to enter the kingdom of God," reminded Jesus (*Matthew* 19:24). That camel reemerges in the Qur'an as God warns those who arrogantly deny such revelations, for "the gates of heaven will not be opened for them, nor will they enter Paradise until a camel passes through the eye of a needle. This is how We reward the wicked" (*al-A'raf* 7:40).

Why must we help the poor? Why should I give away my hard-earned money to those who are lazy? Many such arguments are convenient myths based on a few case reports supporting one's selfishness.[101] Societal choices typically reflect decisions made on sentiment, political and media pressure, prejudice, and false statistics that guarantee failure. In Islam, the entire mindset is reversed through God's promise: "Indeed, those men and women who give in charity and lend to God a good loan will have it multiplied for them, and they will have an honorable reward" (*al-Hadid* 57:18).

God's blessings given to some are not theirs to hoard, but a test and part of the divine plan to help others through them. Hence, His Messenger sought out the weak and the needy and taught us that it is through them the rest of us receive our sustenance (*Jami`at-Tirmidhi* 1702; Book 23, Hadith 33).

The power given to the sun is shared to bring life and warmth to an entire solar system, just like the universal economy that generously provides us with every breath. "Satan threatens you with the prospect of poverty and commands you to do foul deeds; God promises you His forgiveness and His abundance: God is limitless and all-knowing, and He gives wisdom to whomever He will. Whoever is given wisdom has truly been given much good, but only those with insight bear this in mind" (*al-Baqarah* 2:268-9).

While God is perfectly capable of directly providing for everyone, involving others makes it a shared experience for humans who need such meaning. It is only fair that whoever lessens the burden of a destitute person will have God reduce his on the Day of Judgment (*Sunan Ibn Majah* 225). Come to think, we do not own any of it as we all have an equal birthright to this planet's limited resources. If we hoard an unequal piece of the pie for ourselves, we wrongfully prevent others from their fair share. What some earn is not simply for their efforts since two people can exert equally and not be similarly fortunate. Some even inherit a fortune by being born into the right family, which makes it even more appalling when they refuse to share.

Believers, many rabbis, and monks wrongfully consume people's possessions and turn people away from God's path. [Prophet], tell those who hoard gold and silver instead of giving in God's cause that they will have a grievous punishment: on the Day it is heated up in Hell's Fire and used to brand their foreheads, sides, and backs, they will be told, "This is what you hoarded up for yourselves! Now feel the pain of what you hoarded!" (at-Tawbah 9:34-5)

Ignoring the socioeconomic factors that lead to wealth disparity does not free us from our responsibility and guilt. It only propagates a chain of events that affects all of us globally.[102] All the data is out there and a simple Google search away. It would cost us much less to solve global poverty than what we pay for the criminal justice system that results from it.[103] However, those benefiting from the *status quo*—like the private prisons, the entire industry supplying law enforcement, wealthy elites, and politicians —would have us focus on the myths to shift attention away from their daylight robbery.

From 1977 to 1999, the top 1% of household income in the US grew by 85%, the top 10% grew by 45%, and the bottom 20% fell by 13%.[104] As this trend continues worldwide, we only see empty political rhetoric without any substance to alleviate inequality. According to *Forbes*, in 1982, the 400 wealthiest families owned $92 billion. The same magazine reported Elon Musk's net worth alone to be $219 billion in 2022. "He is not a believer whose stomach is filled while his neighbor goes hungry," warned the Prophet (*Al-Adab Al-Mufrad* 112). We are all neighbors in an earthly sense, especially in today's global village. Mortality from hunger anywhere is an entirely unacceptable humanitarian failure. To accept the obvious would be an existential threat for many, but not seeing it as such is a complete failure of any society.

While divine laws in Islam mandate social services like a flat 2.5% tax on individual annual *surplus* (i.e., *zakat* or alms distributed to the needy), a secular system fights to free us of such governmental oversight. God-forbid one even mentions anything remotely similar to *shari'ah law!* And the critics would defenestrate screaming fearful propaganda. Behind their thick wall of excuses lies the simple fact of their predatory greed. Compare that to the ~37% income tax that enables our government to fund global terrorism over which we have no influence. Much of that tax revenue ends up in the pockets of the elites, who prevent any expenditure towards social services while paying the least/no federal income tax themselves.

A side note here about the fashionable contempt towards divine laws or *shari'ah*, while lawyers generally have always been among the most prestigious in all societies. A reverence for law and order in all civilizations is demonstrated for pronounced reasons, as they are the foundations upon which a society is built. Men are often not good when left alone and unguided, which is why we have a law enforcement system. While man-made laws are strictly enforced to modulate our behavior from speeding to even how we interact with others, our disdain for the laws of the Creator of the *entire universe* is quite baffling. God reminds: "I bring My punishment on whomever I will, but My mercy encompasses all things. I shall ordain My mercy for those who are conscious of God and pay the prescribed alms; who believe in Our Revelations" (*al-A'raf* 7:156).

A selfish, individualistic point of view is not just a "difference of opinion" when it leads to the demise of other members of society. Precisely why *zakat* (literally, *purification*) is a central pillar of Islam right next to the obligatory daily prayers, and deemed significant enough for the first Caliph Abu Bakr (573-634 CE) to go to war over. "Righteousness is not in turning your faces towards the east or the west," reminds God. "Rather, the righteous are those who believe in God, the Last Day, the angels, the Books, and the prophets; who give charity out of their cherished wealth to relatives, orphans, the poor, travelers, beggars, and for freeing captives; who establish prayer, pay zakat/alms-tax, and keep the pledges they make; and who are patient in times of suffering, adversity, and in battle. It is they who are true [in faith], and it is they who are mindful [of God]" (*al-Baqarah* 2:177).

Imagine one of your children with a bellyful of candy sitting with a bag of extra 100 pieces of M&Ms. For him not to be willing to share just a few pieces with his brother who has none is **not** a difference of opinion but a punishable crime. No species can thrive with such predatory behavior nor prosper. These principles are timeless, as even reflected in Seneca's letters stating: "society can only remain healthy through the mutual protection and love of its parts," the opposite of which today signs our ailment.[105] Pew research in 2014 found 99% of a decade's growth going into the pockets of the top 1%, with inequality approaching that of the Great Depression.[106] Even through the COVID-19 pandemic, Wall Street gained 56 new billionaires totaling $4 trillion at the expense of starving families.[107] It is certainly no small feat for these greedy "too big to fail" corporations to repeatedly convince hardworking people to bail them out of their mismanagement, often giving their "starving" CEOs millions in bonuses. At the same time, they manipulate the same taxpayers to vomit even at the notion of universal healthcare, which would only harm the private insurance companies.

Interestingly, economist Dean Baker demonstrated how the entire deficit could be solved by just replacing our dysfunctional privatized healthcare with far better options adopted from other industrial societies. A Harris/Harvard Public Health Poll in 1989 showed that 61% of Americans favor a single-payer system like the Canadian. However, such solutions are frowned upon by our financial institutions and the pharmaceutical industry, who are quick to point out potential problems with any alternatives while maintaining the *status quo*.[108] In 2013, Bloomberg News reported that the taxpayers gave the big banks about $83 billion a year, which was nearly their entire "profit."[109] As domestic unemployment in 2010 neared depression levels following the financial crisis, one of its principal architects, Goldman Sachs, announced $17.5 billion in compensation and gave its CEO Lloyd Blankfein a $12.6 million bonus, while his base salary more than tripled.[110] It is *them* always counting on a handout, not the hardworking destitute victims of their greed. But the kicker is when all of it escapes media and public attention, and the blame is placed on the public sector workers.

We saw it again during the 2020 pandemic like clockwork, based on Reaganite imagery of black mothers driving in their limousines to pick up welfare checks. The next useful target is teachers, which has the added benefit of destroying public education to maintain a subaltern, leading us to the best time-tested target: immigrants. An ironic example was the Antiterrorism and Effective Death Penalty Act of 1996 following the Oklahoma City bombing. Although its perpetrator, Timothy McVeigh, was American by birth, the law allowed the deportation of any immigrant with any criminal history, even if they were lawful residents. Then to win his reelection, President Clinton covered all the bases by cutting back on healthcare and welfare assistance to the poor.

Darwin once wrote: "If the misery of the poor be caused not by the laws of nature, but by our institutions, great is our sin." Nevertheless, Darwinian economics gradually evolved to today's extreme capitalism and global hegemony. In 2019, the US spent more on defense—a staggering $732 billion—than the following ten countries combined.[111] Stephen Semler points out that this number, in reality, adds up to over a trillion when considering additional military-related expenditures, nearly half of which are towards the private sector. This enormous drain of taxpayer money since the infancy of this nation has resulted in a tremendous stagnation of social and public services necessary to maintain a healthy civilization.

The critics of the 2020 CARES Act bickered over the $300 billion taxpayer money going back to the taxpayers. However, they ignored the $500 billion towards large corporations—which again pay little to no federal income tax—and the rest to other businesses and state and local governments.[112] For some perspective, the $1.5 billion spent on the *Trident* submarine turned out to be completely useless, which would have otherwise funded a five-year global immunization program preventing some five million deaths worldwide (Ruth Sivard, *World Military and Social Expenditures*). Now compare that to the Lockheed Martin F-35 failure that cost a staggering $1.5 Trillion. Does anyone even remember President Reagan's Star Wars program? Yet, how dare we give some of the tax revenue back to those who actually pay taxes?

The Prophet said: "The signs of a hypocrite are: whenever he speaks he lies, whenever he makes a promise he does not fulfill it, and whenever he is entrusted he betrays." (Jami` at-Tirmidhi 2631)

Amazon CEO Jeff Bezos made $48 billion during the pandemic bringing his net worth as of June 2020 to over $160 billion. Even if we subtract a generous billion for his annual expenses, we are left with a 2.5% tax on his surplus of $4 billion. Something like that would be obligatory upon him in a system where wealth is fairly distributed. With that in mind, the $100 million he donated to the food bank during the pandemic is a shameful chump change. It is a disgrace considering what would be required of him in a just system where the top is not squeezing those underneath for profit. That is without even mentioning the abuse of workers within the Amazon warehouses.

Capitalism is designed for private gain via maximizing profits from the labor of others, which is in direct conflict with social services. However, capital by itself cannot create anything—including jobs—without labor, which makes its neglect of the latter unsustainable.[113] If all the billionaires gave just that bare minimum to support the poor, the current wealth disparities of the world would vanish. Karl Marx criticized this predatory nature of the political economy in *Das Kapital*. Usually, one's enemies are his truest critics, and such practices are not limited only to foreign lands. Communist obloquy aside, he shed light on how capitalists maximize the production process by suppressing wages in the Third World.[114] It is done by presenting arguments like: *those in a developing country do not have a Western standard of living to require the same wage for similar work.* This projection only hides underlying racist propaganda, perpetuating continued oppression and subjugation of the Third World, while simultaneously preventing them from economic prosperity. Much of the developed countries' wealth is made through similarly absurd arguments and practices easily debunked with the abundant available evidence.

A point of consideration here is that much of the Third World is resource-rich—yet, its people are poor from overexploitation. From 1970 to 1980, the US invested about $8 billion in the Third World while taking $63.7 billion, which is medically comparable to a massive hemorrhage that always leads to death. The money invested into those places only benefits their elites through practices promoting capitalism. Therefore, countries in Asia and Africa simultaneously become significant exporters of food while their poor starve. Choice land is taken by agribusinesses for export cash crops and livestock, turning land previously used for local consumption into profitable gains for the rich. Thus, in Mexico, exported livestock consumes more grains than the country's entire rural population.[115] Another real-time example of this is demonstrated through the European colonization project in Palestine, where the natives are forcefully expelled from their ancestral lands by a murderous army recruited from the global pool of bloodthirsty psychopaths.

We could spend volumes listing the absurdities of our current global economy that are all out in the open. Those who are blind or neglectful are unlikely to benefit from such catalogs. The solution requires a supreme ideal to curb our appetites. Notably, there was a time during the early Islamic Caliphate when fair—as opposed to *faire*—economics made it challenging to find people to receive charities. "Surely man is ungrateful to his Lord—and He is witness to this—he is truly excessive in his love of wealth" (al-'Adiyat 100:6-8). In a way, the rapid expansion of the Umayyad dynasty mimicked capitalistic principles, which directly resulted in their downfall, similar to nearly all empires in history. Hence, there is a close relationship between all exploitative empires, capitalism, and corruption—sharing a common goal to expropriate others' land and labor.

Today there is a prevalent doctrinal misconception that a transfer of power from the public sector to the market economy promotes individual freedom. The entire process is a gamble of sorts where no one is safe. This top-down propaganda is debunked by the current state of affairs and simple common sense. Only a few benefiting from such practices enjoy that economic freedom, while the rest carry invisible chains to work their *fields*. In reality, the poor are deluded by the *idea* of wealth, used like a carrot on a stick to lure them into opposing social services that would benefit them.[116] This *idea* is further propagated by an education system and various institutional "experts" funded by the elite to condition the masses away from the apparent.

Studies in psychology have repeatedly shown that even when we "fake it," like a smile, it can eventually lead to a meaningful positive change within us, like authentic happiness.[117] Similarly, prescribed religious acts like prayer, fasting, and almsgiving modify our behavior by training the animal in us to become human. Thus, the Prophet advised us to practice regular good deeds as they are the most beloved to God, even if small (*Sunan Ibn Mājah* 4240). At the same time, we cannot just donate to charities and wash our hands clean while being part of the problem. Farid Esack points out that any religiosity failing to see the connections between poverty and the socio-political structures that breed and sustain it is unjust and complicit in the original crime.[118] In our haste to serve the victims, we ignore the underlying issues and only become an extension of those structures. Islam's inherent egalitarianism makes it imperative for Muslims to be aware of these factors and strive to improve unjust social structures.

But would We treat those who believe and do good deeds and those who spread corruption on earth as equal? Would We treat those aware of God and those who recklessly break all bounds in the same way? (Sad 38:28)

Another sensitive example is the Saudi Royal family's net worth, which is estimated at $1.4 trillion. The *zakat* on that would be more than enough to solve the Middle Eastern humanitarian crisis. Arguably, the profit from all natural resources can be claimed by any earthling from the same birthright to the land. While everyone has the right to enjoy their wealth to a reasonable limit, bereft of social responsibilities, we see disgraceful vanities like the golden toilets of the Royal family and their unfathomable prodigal expenditures. There is a story of a Roman elite named Apicius whose sybaritic ambitions once led him to spend a hundred million sesterces on fine dining. When he realized he *only* had ten million left, he committed suicide fearing poverty.[119]

All the while, pilgrims in Mecca have to navigate through countless panhandlers and refugee children to get to the holiest of places. In one of the first revelations, God said, "Have you considered the person who denies the Judgment? It is he who pushes aside the orphan and does not urge others to feed the needy. So woe to those who pray but are heedless of their prayer; those who are all show and forbid common kindnesses" (*al-Ma'un* 107:1-7). Some caretakers of the *haram* today remain in power while committing atrocities. Nevertheless, God warns sternly: "Do you consider giving water to pilgrims and tending the Sacred Mosque to be equal to the deeds of those who believe in God and the Last Day and who strive in God's path? They are not equal in God's eyes. God does not guide such benighted people" (*al-Tawbah* 9:19).

Such deviation is also reflected in their implementation of Islam, which often reduces *shari'ah* to a few selected items without regard for the full context. "Meting out harsh punishment for petty crimes without any attempt at addressing the massive corruption in the ruling circles and their greedy exploitation of the nation's resources in total absence of accountability can never pass as Islamic," rebuked Dr. Hathout.[120] The wealth of these billionaires did not just grow out of thin air but was made on the backs of the poor, often wrongfully. Still, their greed further pushes them to point iron at their brothers next door and slaughter them with bombs and famine to gain control over their resources, taking a page from their Western ally's playbook.

"Verily, there is a trial for every nation, and the trial for my nation (or *ummah*) is wealth," foretold the Prophet (*at-Tirmidhi, Riyad as-Salihin* 480). Our current state is similar to Pax Romana at the time of Jesus, which he aggressively condemned (*Matthew* 21:12-13). Roman and Temple's prosperity was built on brutal oppression and taxation of their subjects that the elites proudly enjoyed as *the new world order*. The Prophet, however, warned that none of us truly believe until we love for others what we love for ourselves (*Sunan an-Nasa'i* 5039). Accordingly, one of the first policies he implemented in Medina was the elimination of usury as commanded by God. Although that caused friction between him and the Jewish elites who profited from money lending, it was an effective measure to alleviate the ridiculous wealth disparity. It contrasts sharply with the capitalist's push to eliminate government oversight for maximal private interest.

Often we become so used to certain practices that their absurdity goes unrecognized, not too different from past practices of infanticide or mortuary cannibalism. Usury is a similar concept at the core of the current global economy, which is why it is forbidden in all Abrahamic traditions. If we only dissect it without preconceived notions—the fact that those with money only allow those without to have some by asking more in return—its farcical nature becomes apparent. By design, it perpetuates a lower class by guaranteeing their exploitation, who are also tasked to bail out the same financial system when they go bankrupt through greedy mismanagement. Thus, Aristotle considered it the most hated and unnatural mode of gaining wealth.[121] "But those who take usury will rise on the Day of Resurrection like someone tormented by Satan's touch," warns God (*al-Baqarah* 2:275).

Islamic economics is a much larger topic, the scope of which is beyond this book. Some interesting work in this arena has been done by Ayatollah Mahmud Taliqani, Mustafa Mahmud, M. Umar Chapra, Timur Kuran, and many others. It is sufficient to say that the main goal is to prevent economic injustice while promoting the fairest market, which cannot be compartmentalized into capitalism, socialism, or communism. Imam al-Shāṭibī (1320-88 CE) emphasized that human welfare is the basis for the *shari'ah*.[122] Resistance to such social justice perspectives and ideologies only reflects a position of asymmetrical privilege. The other economic principles take a narrower approach to some aspects of a fair system, drastically deviating from the middle by losing sight of the ultimate goal: to not hoard wealth but to create a just society. All of it ignores God's command: "Do not consume one another's wealth unjustly, nor deliberately bribe authorities in order to devour a portion of others' property, knowing that it is a sin" (*al-Baqarah* 2:188).

Those benefiting from injustice will always defuse any threat to their established system by marginalization. In the case of Islam, its economic guidelines for a just society are then disregarded as "religion" to maintain secular rapacity. All people of faith should instead unite to lift humanity from economic disparity. How can we expect the despots and the politicians to favor fair economics when they get there through avarice? Clair Patterson (1922-95 CE) experienced it firsthand, fighting the oil industry to remove tetraethyl lead from gasoline, resulting in even "neutral" government institutions like the US Public Health Service canceling his research funding.[123] Ethyl Corporation continues to exist today, without acknowledging its contribution to global lead poisoning, ozone depletion, or association with Thomas Midgley's chlorofluorocarbons.

Over the recent decades, the cost of US elections has skyrocketed, causing politicians to reach even deeper into the pockets of the highest corporate bidders. Both political parties then compete in auctioning off Congressional leadership positions that compel the winners to become servants of private capital instead of the people.[124] The 2010 Supreme Court decision on *Citizens United v Federal Election Commission* further opened the doors to such capitalistic corruption. Hence, Orwell saw power not as a means but as an end, as no one ever seizes it intending to relinquish it.[125] Psychologically, the weak are attracted to leaders who empower them with the glamor of force.[126] At the same time, no progressive or beneficial change is ever made by any ruling body without forceful measures by the masses. Therefore, Georg Hegel's interpretation of virtue as total obedience to the State serves only to benefit the tyrants but would fail in a true democracy.

"Governments which rule with a view to the private interest, whether of the one, or of the few, or of the many, are perversions," was Aristotle's assessment.[127] Interestingly, he considered democracy to be a similar perversion placing the interest of the needy over the common good, which nevertheless often hides an underlying oligarchy. Plato considered democracy the worst form of government when all the other types are virtuous.[128] Many political scientists of recent times—such as John Dewey, Walter J Shepard, Jason Brennan, Bryan Caplan, and Jeffrey Friedman—have also come to the same conclusion based on the results of our democratic experiment.[129] Many governmental policies of one political party in our current system either come to a halt or are completely reversed as soon as the opposition takes power. Over time, it only achieves stagnation at the cost of tax revenue that would have better served various social services. It also fails to protect basic human rights by allowing fascism to thrive under its Darwinian delusions.

That is not to mistake Islam for a reactionary or a violent ideology, as conflicts are antithetical to its values.[130] Ironically, confrontations and conflicts are Hegelian concepts that originated in Europe with the belief that to construct something new, it was necessary to destroy the old. That is also similar to the Marxist worldview, who himself never worked a day in his life. Regardless of their religion or beliefs, many at the top are guilty of the same crime. It is a fraternity that unites them through their shared interests and goals across all perceived differences. They are the slaves of their desires and serve that master to the fullest. They only help each other in their evil as long as it benefits them. For that, they will be ridiculed by God on Judgment Day: "What is the matter with you that you can no longer help each other?" (*as-Saffat* 37:25). Although they are smaller in number, it is astonishing how they manipulate the other 99% proles to fight for their interest using fear and scare tactics. The rest are the mice tearing each other apart for the benefit of the vultures, who are always profiting from them, dead or alive.

We never seem to truly internalize that we can take none of our wealth with us to the next life. "No one hoards but the sinner," warned the Prophet (*Sahih Muslim* 1605). Many Pharaohs have tried to take their riches to their graves, only to have them looted by others with similarly diseased hearts. That wealth helped transport their preserved mummified bodies to their next worldly lives as museum displays. Yet, how magnificently lavish rituals those funeral processions entailed. "Woe to every backbiter, slanderer, who amasses riches, counting them over, thinking that their wealth will make them immortal!" curses God (*al-Humazah* 104:1-3). Perhaps the only things worth *hoarding* are knowledge and good deeds, as they are among the things that carry over to the afterlife.

Know that this worldly life is no more than play, amusement, luxury, mutual boasting, and competition for wealth and children. It is like rain that causes plants to grow, to the delight of the planters. But later, the plants dry up, and you see them wither, then they are reduced to chaff. And in the Hereafter, there will be either severe punishment or forgiveness and pleasure of God, whereas the life of this world is no more than the delusion of enjoyment. (al-Hadid

57:20)

II: Hunger for Gluttony

While poverty and famine in certain parts of the world are shocking, a significantly higher number of people die daily from overconsumption. Today, the leading causes of mortality worldwide include heart disease, strokes, and other vascular diseases resulting from our eating habits, along with metabolic syndrome and the diabetes epidemic. In speaking of the end of times, the Prophet warned of such disabling diseases, obesity, unstabling senility, and sudden death, which we now see with increasing frequency (*Tirmidhi, Riyad as-Salihin* 577; *Riyad as-Salihin* 508). The rise of all types of cancers can also be traced back to the carcinogens we consume. Common diseases like diverticulosis propagated by industrialization were unheard of before the advent of processed food. Yet, postmodern theories today turn towards obscurity, deflecting all scientific data to the apparent.[131] Worldwide obesity is now the new norm to the point that even mentioning it is socially unacceptable. The resultant rise of mood disorders further pushes us into a vicious cycle that is only cured by death.

Even in the 14th century, Ibn Khaldun recognized food as the origin of all illnesses.[132] We are what we eat and what we have been eating is processed garbage. We have been manipulated into trusting a system that is poisoning us to benefit big businesses, as detailed by Rachel Carson in *Silent Spring*. Sadly, certain real-life facts today sound like conspiracy theories because of their blatant and greedy disregard for societal well-being. Large corporations bribe lawmakers to produce chemical and bioengineered foods without demonstrating safety, while the Environmental Protection Agency (EPA) is simultaneously crippled from policing with cutbacks.[133] Even the "organic" food that most people pay extra for is not truly organic.[134]

A National Research Council study in 1984 found no safety data on 78% of the commercially used chemicals, with another update decades later showing no significant change in that number.[135] On average, the government's National Toxicology Program tests ten to twenty chemicals a year—even those tested only for carcinogens—while five hundred to a thousand new chemicals are introduced to the market annually.[136] As a result, nearly all safety research is left to the industry, which also decides when to release them to the EPA. Needless to say, the industry has a long track record of lying—take 3M and per- and polyfluoroalkyl substances (PFAS), for example. Furthermore, those chemicals banned domestically are sold to foreign countries without any disclosure.

A landmark Australian study in 1984 showed significant improvement in obesity, diabetes, hypertension, and metabolic syndrome among its urbanized Aboriginal participants within weeks of returning to the wilderness and a traditional hunter-gatherer lifestyle.[137] Accordingly, there was a sharp decline in heart disease during WWII from reduced consumption of pretty much everything and increased activity from the rationing of gasoline.[138] Today, there is a large discrepancy between the US's healthcare expenditure and life expectancy. Among various factors, the daily stressors of urban life have also been shown to have detrimental effects on our health through repeated studies since the 1930s.[139]

Besides the nutritional benefits, what we consume also has long-term psychological and spiritual effects. We have just recently started to uncover the surface of this profound interaction that highlights God's mandate for us to only consume lawful and wholesome food (*al-Baqarah* 2:168). Several recent studies have found our normal gut bacteria to have a significant role in maintaining our immune system and reducing anxiety conveyed by the vagus nerve.[140] The overuse of antibiotics—both medically and through the agricultural industries—disrupts this complex homeostasis with our gut flora.[141] The result is an increase in overall mood disorders, autoimmune diseases, and a wide spectrum of cancers.[142] If this makes you anxious, it likely has much to do with what you had for your last meal.

Despite our profound understanding of physiology, we fail to act accordingly. When we eat, the expanding stomach and its stretched wall allow our brain to gauge satiety. Consequently, the more we eat, the more our stomachs stretch, making it harder for us to feel full after each subsequent meal. With that knowledge, the next outcome, of course, was for us to invent procedures to cut off or exclude part of the stomach to allow us to feel stuffed again. Changing the crapulent behavior that leads to that state is unrealistic, as we cannot even conceive of curbing our consumption. In fact, psychological studies done by Stanley Schachter in the 1960s and thereafter documented our incapability of internally controlling our appetite.[143] Hence, we continue our oral fixation just like our material greed without ever feeling satisfied.

"The human does not fill any container worse than his stomach," said the Prophet. "It is sufficient for the son of Adam to eat what will support his back for worship," was his lesser-known context for the oft-quoted advice: "If this is not possible, then a third for food, a third for drink, and third for his breath" (*Jami` at-Tirmidhi* 2380). Gluttony has both physical and psychological effects on one's self. Physically, we experience blood rushing to our guts resulting in the well-known *food coma*. We feel its immediate effect of torpidity that also perpetuates a sedentary lifestyle, further propagated by the difficulty of being active while obese.

It, in turn, manifests through various psychological effects like depression and addiction, for overconsumption itself is the result of both. While it supports a thriving pharmaceutical industry, recent studies found exercise to be just as effective in treating depression.[144]

"The existence of pious men and ascetics is, therefore, restricted to the desert, whose inhabitants eat frugally," observed Ibn Khaldun.[145] The Prophet also warned that those who eat their fill in this world will be the most hungry on the Day of Resurrection (*Sunan Ibn Majah* 3351). Through such habituation, we lose sight of spirituality and any meaningful purpose other than consuming. Mentally we become stagnant as we despair in our repugnant condition, only contemplating the next meal. With the current fad of intermittent fasting, it is remarkable that Muslims are obligated to fast an entire month of Ramadan every year as a divine prescription of behavioral therapy. The Prophet fasted often throughout the year and recommended that we fast at least three days a month even outside of Ramadan (*Sunan an-Nasa'i* 2414).

Imam al-Ghazzali saw all of our illnesses from overconsumption as God's way of clarifying the truth.[146] We can get closer to God through them as He even tested His beloved prophets like Ayyub (Job) through illness and poverty. All the adverse effects of gluttony redirect us towards the lagom, while ignoring the clear signs only digests us into a miserable existence. With the discovery of kinases like mTOR, we are starting to see how even our cells understand the dangers of abundance and the importance of struggle. When we ignore the subtle grades of depression that manifest as-and-from gluttony, we fail to see it as the most significant cause of mortality in our world today. No antidepressant can alleviate such a spiritually based disease that originated not in the organic cerebral dysfunction but from our deviation from the middle balance.

While times of prosperity provide us an opportunity to share the wealth, times of desperation serve to define our true beliefs. It may seem like a philosophical discussion, but it became a lived reality during the COVID-19 pandemic. The abruptness of it revealed the ugliness of individualism and our over-consumptive behavior as we saw toilet paper—of all things —disappear from store shelves. Just the thought of an uncertain future instantly drove people to hoard without a care for their neighbors. The rights of one's neighbors are so sacred in the sight of God that Archangel Gabriel continually advised the Prophet to the point that he started to think the neighbors would also be included as one's heirs (*Jami` at-Tirmidhi* 1943).

Arguably, that panic to secure toilet paper was simply the byproduct of our voracious behavior. The ensuing chaos tore our presumed safety bubbles from living in a developed country. We watched our supply chains crumble under their unsustainable foundations, and the resultant crop waste happening simultaneously as scarcity at the local groceries. Capitalistic bureaucracy prevented plain solutions from implementation, while we suffered from failed dissolute leadership. We heard the rise of disinformation and preference for dramatized propaganda over apparent veracity. We even saw people protest for their right to infect others by refusing to wear masks—not too different from the lynching threats towards Dr. Charles Stiles in the early 1900s, when he tried to deworm the "lazy white Southerner" population.[147]

Similarly, there was renewed rhetoric against Dr. Anthony Fauci even from some healthcare professionals. We became closely acquainted with "anti-vaxxers," some of whom deferred to treating themselves with animal dewormers and bleach rather than a simple shot. When such bizarre opinions and misinformation cause harm, perhaps they should serve as grounds for dismissal to hold people responsible for jeopardizing public health. Nevertheless, we continue to live through strange times with our forced isolation in a poignantly sordid state. Interestingly, Dr. Larry Scherwitz found individualism—as manifested by the frequent uses of "I," "me," and "my"—linked to a higher risk of coronary artery disease.[148] This individual "I" in Sikhism is called the *haumai*, which refers to the human ego. Guru Nanak attributed all evil to *haumai* and compelled his followers to abandon it. It is a teaching shared by nearly all religions and philosophers across the board.

The life of this world is alluring to those who reject faith, and they scoff at those who believe. But the righteous will be above them on the Day of Resurrection, for God bestows His abundance without measure on whom He will. (al-Baqarah 2:212)

Our planet does not have the resources to support a large carnivorous species like the current human population. When we see our craving for meat and its horrendous carbon footprint, we start to appreciate the wisdom behind the Prophetic advice towards limiting its consumption (*Muatta Malik* Book 49, Hadith 36). Today trawlers as big as cruise ships scrape the ocean clean with nets big enough to hold a dozen jumbo jets to feed our demand.[149] By that method, about a quarter of the "catch" is then dumped back into the seas as unwanted corpses. The result is a tremendous loss of biodiversity caused directly by the commercial fishing industry that nearly all global watchdogs ignore due to conflicts of interest. We currently constitute 36% of all mammalian biomass on earth. An additional 60% are those we raise for our consumption. It leaves only 4% representing all of the remaining mammalian wildlife on our planet, from the tiniest shrew to the elephants and whales.[150]

Our overconsumption is replacing the world's biodiversity like an unsustainable plague on track to make even our own species extinct within the next hundred years. According to paleontologist David Raup, the background rate of extinction for our planet has been, on average, one species every four years throughout its biological history. Recent findings suggest our current human-caused extinction rate be 120,000 times that level.[151] Long before this, Tolstoy mourned: "What a destructive, cruel being man is, how many different living creatures and plants he has annihilated to sustain his own life!"[152] As it would appear, that annihilation also includes ourselves and the planet we call home.

God presents the example of a town that was secure and at ease, with provisions coming to it abundantly from all places. Then it became ungrateful for God's blessings, so God afflicted it with the garment of famine and fear for what its people had done. (al-Nahl 16:112)

THE DARWINIAN DILEMMA

The Prophet said: "None of you [truly] believe until your desires are subservient to that which I have brought." (Hadith 41, 40 Hadith an-Nawawi)

In a self-centered world, all outsiders become potential *enemies*. Secular ethics leads to a sense of insouciant entitlement where **my** right to live **my** life the way **I** want supersedes my responsibilities towards my family. Similarly, my family's need to live comfortably triumphs over anyone else's; therefore, it is okay if someone's rights are trampled for me to live to my fullest. It is justifiable for my city to prosper at the expense of its neighbor. Of course, it is only patriotic for my country to dominate the world at the expense of another.

Dr. Hawkins defined this ubiquitous human ego as merely an "it" rather than an "I," which reveals an endless cosmic illusion serving as the wellspring of all suffering. Our exhaustive efforts to explain the inexplicable are only the vanity of our ego's failure to comprehend reality.[153] Unfortunately, this trend has become pervasive in our diseased state, where individuals no longer associate their actions with the group. This peculiar mindset has been an *unnatural* selection of extreme liberalism that dismantles timeless norms of humanity and starts to resemble anarchy. The resulting chaos manifests as psychosocial stressors leading to higher criminal behavior because *hurt people hurt people*.[154] Naturally, it leads to a society's degradation, as classically explained by Aristotle.[155] Today's observable disintegration of established familial, societal, and economic norms is another sign of the end of times in the Qur'an.[156] Yet, how much have we truly evolved?

Liberalism's design was to free individuals from natural and religious constraints toward unlimited freedom, which has also opened doors to many innovations that are best left closed. Focusing on our individual needs makes us more willing to sacrifice others. Ultimately, it becomes justifiable for many to die for one in a Darwinian society. This line of thinking encourages similar philosophies where one's survival may even be beneficial, as it would testify to their fitness for passing on their genes for the greater good of the species. We can see the dangers of such a mindset, which enlightened Europeans unsurprisingly used to justify colonialism and eugenics.[157] Liberal imperialism is one of its inevitable outcomes, where even forceful enslavement of "uncivilized" people was seen as necessary to help them transition into more productive economic lives.[158]

As we make such sacrifices on this lonesome path, we leave behind a trail of destruction that lacks humanity. Instead of facing this horror, it is easier to rewrite history and paint it with a more suitable color. Orwell explained this type of political writing as "the defense of the indefensible," where language is used as a political weapon to defend injustice.[159] This path of destruction is suicidal by design and has far-reaching consequences. Just as an eye for an eye leaves the world blind, individualism leads straight to our extinction. Since it contradicts all religious values, God was abandoned on this journey along with morality which no longer fueled our ambition for a greater good. Instead, our actions were motivated by coveting, leading us to capitalism—an unsustainable system solely driven by profit.

Have you seen the one who has taken their own desires as their god? Will you then be a keeper over them? Or do you think that most of them listen or understand? They are only like cattle—no, more than that, they are astray from the [Right] Way! (al-Furqan 25:43-4)

To serve this new master, we had to free ourselves from religious limitations. Sociopolitically, we sought secularism and screamed for a redefined "freedom," which was classically understood as liberating the self from one's desires and reactions through the cultivation of virtues. It was noted in the very first line of Seneca's *Letters* in its original Latin. Epictetus ("owned" in Greek) was himself an emancipated slave and equated the Stoic training of the mind to manumission.[160] But in our material world, freedom has been weaponized to enslave us to our desires, which are subtly manipulated by every click and swipe. Then to justify the whims, it becomes imperative to rationalize them exhaustively.

An awkward emphasis on reason was evident in post-Newtonian deism's ordering of "the Laws of Nature and of Nature's God." This audacious step separated God from "Natural Laws," thus promoting all human intellectual contrivances over divine oversight. Economically we sought capitalism, which is only economic Darwinism, where the elite will naturally devour the weak. Here again, divine faith tries to free us from the shackles of ignorance and subjective intellectual bias. With all of their exhaustive efforts, every philosopher and thinker since the Enlightenment has failed to provide a satisfactory rationale for their claimed natural rights and utility, ultimately leading them to give up and simply call them "self-evident." Each piling upon the predecessors' delusions built on false premises that have gradually deteriorated the foundations of morality and ethics.[161] We cannot avoid going right back into the dark embrace of our evil earthly companions. Their calls are mellifluous for us as we drift like moths to a flame entranced; or like the freed followers of Moses reminiscing about the food under Pharaoh's oppressive rule while enjoying freedom on the other side of the Red Sea. "And it is God's Will to lighten your burdens, for humankind was created weak" (*an-Nisa* 4:28).

Hitherto we have briefly discussed various extra-biological manifestations of the theory of evolution that is popularly attributed to Charles Darwin (1809-88 CE). Now we will focus on the actual theory, which continues to be a controversial affair. Interestingly, there was little surprise or discussion upon its presentation at the Linnaean Society meeting in July 1858. Professor Haughton of Dublin even snickered: "All that was new in them was false, and what was true was old."[162] This is precisely the Islamic view of the entire contention. It may surprise some readers that evolution had been a known phenomenon for centuries before Darwin. It was widely accepted and taught throughout the Muslim world during the Golden Age due to its revelation in the Qur'an in many *ayats*, such as: "And God has created from water every living creature. Some crawl on their bellies, some walk on two legs, and some walk on four. God creates whatever He wills. Surely God is Most Capable of everything" (*al-Nur* 24:45).

While the Catholic Church was preaching fossils as Satan's deceptions buried in place to lead humanity astray, Muslim scholars across the sea were writing books on evolution. Nearly 400 years before Darwin, Ibn Khaldun described the evolutionary process from minerals to men.[163] For similar insights, historian Arnold Toynbee considered the *Muqaddimah* to be "undoubtedly the greatest work of its kind that has ever yet been created by any mind in any time or place."[164] Other polymaths like Abu Bakr Ibn Tufail (1110-85 CE) made evolution the theme of his novel, *The Story of Hayy Ibn Yaqzan*, which became an instant bestseller. Its English translation by Simon Ockley in 1708 became widely popular in Europe, further inspiring Daniel Defoe's *Robinson Crusoe* just eleven years later. The list of imitators includes Rudyard Kipling's Mowgli and Edgar Burroughs's Tarzan, which even borrows from the name Yaqzan.[165]

There is little doubt about Darwin's familiarity with such works found in the personal libraries of most European scholars of his time. His grandfather even wrote a rendition of Ibn Tufail's classic in *The Temple of Nature*. The similarities between Darwin's ideas and existing Muslim scholarship did not go unrecognized by his contemporaries. In writing, John William Draper criticized him: "Sometimes...we meet with ideas with which we flatter ourselves with having originated in our own times. Thus, our modern doctrine of evolution and development was taught in [Muslim] schools. In fact, they carried them much further than we are disposed to do, extending them to inorganic or mineral things...[Christian] theologian authorities were therefore constrained to look with disfavor on any attempt to carry back the origin of the earth to an epoch indefinitely remote, and on the Muhammadan theory of evolution which declared that human beings developed over a long period of time from lower forms of life to their present condition."[166]

As a graduate of the Cambridge divinity school, Darwin's inexperience as a naturalist was demonstrated through his failure to catalog the origins of the specimen he had gathered from the Galapagos Islands. Hence, the story of him noting the beaks of finches is apocryphal and was actually discovered by his ornithologist friend John Gould. Darwin never really used phrases like "survival of the fittest" or "evolution" in his original print of *On the Origin of Species*—they were coined by his contemporaries thereafter. During the time he shelved his theory, another book was published anonymously in 1844 by Robert Chambers called *Vestiges of the Natural History of Creation* that suggested human evolution from primates.[167] A Scottish gardener, Patrick Matthew, published a similar theory of natural selection in *Naval Timber and Arboriculture* the same year Darwin set sail on the *Beagle*; Alfred Wallace published a similar paper titled "On the Tendency of Varieties to Depart Indefinitely from the Original Type." To top it all, the one thing Darwin failed to explain in his magnum opus was how species originated.

It is not a testament against Darwin's character but to familiarize ourselves with the reality of the *evolution* of his theory. His legacy served as an instrument of European intellectual hegemony that aggressively erased contributions of the Islamic world to the point that much of what is discussed in this chapter would be news to even educated Muslims. The motivations behind it are quite complex, and it is not simply an all-encompassing conspiracy but an evolving—partly intentional and partly subconscious—phenomenon of identity. Even when Bryson mentions the concept of evolution as "already decades old by the 1830s"[168] and Erasmus Darwin's book, he fails to connect the links back to Ibn Tufail. While the scholars of Orientalism erased the Islamic theory of evolution, the secular forces within the Occident pushed that theory further and further away from where Muslim polymaths had left off.

Stephen Hawking stated that the eventual goal of science is to provide a single theory that describes the whole universe. He admitted the difficulty of devising such a theory given the complexity of our universe, which leaves us with only partial theories to get us by. While they do the trick, for the most part, Hawking realized how contradictory these theories are, citing the example of the general theory of relativity and quantum mechanics. Nevertheless, he unsuccessfully pursued a single unified theory throughout his life's work, just like Einstein before him. While he pointed out the problems with the Biblical narratives, he overlooked the answers provided by the Qur'an, perhaps out of simple ignorance and unfamiliarity. The latter is evident through his grouping of all three Abrahamic faiths together in their "belief in a relatively young universe."

Although the Judeo-Christian traditions dated the birth of the universe around 6,000 years ago, Islam shares no such estimation. Among the treasures lost with the destruction of the great Alexandrian Library was a three-volume history of the world by Berossus that reportedly detailed 432,000 years before the Flood in its first volume.[169] Nevertheless, the calculation of Archbishop James Ussher of the Church of Ireland in 1650 ushered in the creation myth of earth at midday on October 23, 4004 BC. Al-Biruni, for one, criticized this idea in *Tahdid nihāyāt al-amākin li-tashīh masāfāt al-masākin* and put his mathematical deduction to be around "billions of years."[170] It was also the common belief of most respectable geologists of Darwin's time, including Reverend Buckland (1784-1856 CE) and his student Charles Lyell (1797-1875 CE). Therefore, Darwin's estimate of 306,662,400 years in the first edition of his book was nothing more than a gross miscalculation.

Alternatively, the ontologically unified God in Islam, or *tawhid*, is the unifying force that connects our universe. It is reminiscent of William of Occam's (1285-1347 CE) principle of not multiplying entities unnecessarily —Occam's razor. The unity of God pervades every human experience and should be taken into account in all intellectual pursuits. A purely secular worldview, on the other hand, distorts reality, revealing our inherent biases and weaknesses. Hawking acknowledged the fundamental paradox of his search having the equipotential outcome of arriving at both the right and the wrong conclusions. It sadly echoes the philosophy of Immanuel Kant, where he discussed the contradictions of having equally compelling arguments for believing the thesis and the antithesis (similar to the Skeptics like Pyrrho and Sextus Empiricus). This is where divine guidance through revelation becomes critical. Its absence is evident among all who observe with a cloudy vision. Kant himself contradicted much of his own edifice in a later work called the *Critique of Practical Reason*, demonstrating the sheer madness of relying solely on reason without common sense.[171] It overlooks the wisdom of others, like Imam al-Ghazali, marveling at the complexity of the human hand and its five unequal fingers, each with a unique function that could not be improved by human intervention.[172]

Ultimately, based on Darwinism, Hawking proposed that we may have an evolutionary advantage for arriving at the correct conclusions about the universe. Then he quickly realized that these same advantages had led us to the brink of destruction with our nuclear weapons. Perhaps, annihilation is the curse of the atheist thinker. Feynman candidly admitted that our scientific theories are incomplete and flawed, leaving us with only imperfect theories to rely on.[173] Despite such limitations of science, many still prefer to bet against God. But as Blaise Pascal (1623-62 CE) demonstrated mathematically, that is an unwise gamble, as God holds the advantage of knowing the future.[174]

Meanwhile, our evolutionary drive towards secularism has not necessarily led to global peace and justice. Instead, the disruptions caused by Western civilization's imposition of its artificial ways of living have created many of the problems faced by Third World countries today. "The messengers of progress and civilization destroyed what they had not built and ridiculed what they did not understand," noted Feyerabend. "It would be shortsighted to assume that they alone now possess the keys to survival.[175] Darwin's observations only captured one aspect of our universe and failed to constitute the unified theory that many assume it to be. Its overemphasis conceals the observer bias that underlies it and its damaging effect in various fields. The "survival of the fittest" has been distorted and applied *unnaturally* to justify humanity's aggressive practices, disregarding the delicate balance between predators and prey in our environment. Darwin may not have intended his ideas to be interpreted in this way, and he might have even disapproved of how his theory was used to justify eugenics, slavery, and extreme poverty through capitalism.

Recognizing this bias challenges the foundations of evolutionism, making it less rigid and dogmatic. It is difficult to see what survival benefit my seasonal allergy may possess when a simple walk to my car evokes a deathly spell of sneezes and ocular pruritus. These same traits without the synthetic antihistamines would have been fatal to many Cro-Magnons. Even Alfred Wallace (1823-1913 CE), a co-creator of the modern theory of evolution, expressed doubts about the theory's ability to explain certain human characteristics that remain unsolved.[176] Biologist Motoo Kimura argues that most genetic changes are selectively neutral, challenging the theory's core assumptions. This myth of the scientific age may be a result of our sense organs' misinterpretation of environmental data, as proposed by anthropologist Claude Levi-Strauss (1908-2009 CE). Nevertheless, scientists have rather adamantly been diverting more energy towards finding evidence to support it instead of using the evidence at hand to revise a better one.

Jean-Baptiste Lamarck (1744-1829 CE) proposed a theory before Darwin suggesting that acquired traits could be inherited, which bet on nurture's effect at a genetic level. Lamarckism was initially discredited by most geneticists, who preferred Darwin's slow evolution over a much longer time. However, Lamarckism resurfaced through the work of evolutionary biologist Paul Kammerer (1880–1926), who observed that environmental factors during early development could lead to measurable genetic manifestations within a generation.[177] Although his observations with midwife toads were contested and largely dismissed, recent studies with rats suggest similar epigenetic effects through the biochemistry of methyl groups.[178]

Even more fascinating is the evidence from genealogical records in Överkalix, Sweden, suggesting that exposure to starvation just before puberty can confer unique survival benefits to the progeny. This observation was confirmed in the Uppsala Multigeneration Study, where the paternal grandfather's food access in pre-puberty predicted his male grandchildren's all-cause mortality.[179] During these prepubescent years, more energy is diverted away from physical growth and towards sperm development, which can incorporate some environmental factors to be passed on to the next generation. Thus, it is not simply a matter of genetics or evolution but a complex interplay of both.

Our library of fossils reveals a lack of enough intermediate species to support the neo-Darwinian evolutionary synthesis. Paleontologist Steven Stanley points out that there is no record of phyletic evolution to validate gradualism as proposed by this theory. David M Raup also maintains that "instead of gradual unfolding of life, what geologists of the present day actually find is a highly uneven or jerky record."[180] This is where Nils Eldredge and Stephen Gould's punctuated equilibria come in to explain the void. However, the process of fossilization leaves us with a very skewed history of the past, with only a pixel of the entire image from which all deductions are made. Most of the fossils on display at museums around the world are, in fact, artificial casts, including the impressive features at the entrances of the Natural History Museums in London and New York.[181] The theoretical aspect of the entire thing can easily be lost within the heated discussions surrounding events like the Cambrian explosion. Paleoanthropologist Ian Tattersall describes the sparse fossilized records as only providing fragmentary pieces that are more different than similar.[182] Psychologically, it does not take long for one to say something repeatedly before he and others start to see it as an undeniable fact. Hence, Bryson reminds us, "These are all just informed guesses," which leaves us with "tons of conjectures and very little evidence."[183]

What is the matter with you? Why will you not fear God's majesty when He has created you stage by stage? (Nuh 71:13-4)

The Qur'an supports evolution as a modus operandi of creation through the various names of God—including *ar-Rabb, al-Khaliq, al-Baari,* and *al-Musawwir*—within the scope of their classical Arabic definitions. God gives examples of His creations reaching their predestined perfection through gradually evolving stages, including the universe, the skies, the heavens, and even humankind. Though the exact process is not disclosed, God alludes to a period when man was nothing, emphasizing the irrelevance of such knowledge (*al-Insan* 76:1). It may be the time Adam was left in his clay form (*Sahih Muslim* 2611), the time we spent as an embryo, or the time we took evolving. Classical discussions suggest that Adam was gradually formed through different stages of clay followed by a period of rest before the infusion of his soul (i.e., مَا مَسْنُون, *al-Hijr* 15:28). Additionally, the Qur'an implies a sequence of events through *ayats* such as "Who created you, fashioned you, and perfected your design, molding you in whatever form He willed" (*al-Infitar* 82:7-8) and "You will progress from stage to stage" (*al-Inshiqaq* 84:16-9).

Prophetic traditions parallel the creation of humans at the very end of the evolutionary spectrum of our 14-billion-year-old universe (e.g., *Sahih Muslim* 2789). An interesting hadith suggests that the initial gathering of clay on earth was followed by the shaping of Adam into his perfect form in a timeless paradise, where the soul was blown into him after a prolonged period (*Sahih Muslim* 2611). Many classical scholars, including Ibn Abbas (619-87 CE), shared this view.[184] Another narration reports: "Indeed God Most High created Adam from a handful that He took from all of the earth. So the children of Adam come in accordance with the earth, some of them come red and white and black, and between that, and the thin, the thick, the filthy, and the clean" (*Jami` at-Tirmidhi* 2955). Adam's name suggests an African origin with its possible Arabic roots *adim* and *udama* meaning "a dark/brown-skinned person who lives on the surface of the earth."[185] Those rejecting it based on the timeline and linguistic origin of the Arabic language should consider that the name was given by God, who is the ultimate creator of all languages. Furthermore, the naming event took place in a spacetime unlike ours, where time may be completely absent or differ from what we are familiar with (more on this concept in a later chapter).

As I type these words, I am reminded of the millions of evolutionary processes that have led to my existence. We must acknowledge the environmental stressors that have shaped our evolution and accept the challenges that come with our soul's journey toward the next stage. Our virtues must similarly evolve to adapt to the heavenly environment of Paradise or devolve to be more fit for the conditions of Hell. Sufi scholars viewed man's organic and inorganic characteristics as the microcosm of the universe, evolving from the nadir of pure matter to the highest of the angels.[186] God creates everything perfectly and guides it with divine precision (*al-A'la* 87:1-3). This makes scientists see the process as an inevitability, like "an obligatory manifestation of matter, bound to arise wherever conditions are appropriate," according to Nobel laureate Christian de Duve.[187] It is this *guidance* that composes in concert numerous variables in the evolutionary process that we do not even recognize. God points out: "If there had been any gods but Him, both heavens and earth would be in ruins: God, Lord of the Throne, is far above the things they say: He cannot be called to account for anything He does, whereas they will be called to account" (*al-Anbiya'* 21:22-3).

The problem lies in our textbooks, where secular ideologies are preached as facts instead of theories. Scientific history is summed up as a neatly aligned pursuit along an imaginary trajectory to the truth devoid of their actual diversities and dilemmas. Most elementary textbooks, for instance, provide Robert Boyle's definitions of an element, overlooking the fact that it was a paraphrase of a traditional concept he used to argue against its existence.[188] Nonetheless, students accept these theories based on the authority of their teachers and text, rather than on evidence.

Most of us presume them to be hard facts and approach Revelation from that secular paradigm which is inherently flawed, resulting in conflicts. "The philosopher must drag such beliefs into the light of day and see whether they still survive," demanded Russell, "Often it will be found that they die on exposure."[189] In the Qur'an, God repeatedly questions our closed-mindedness and compels us to use our intellect. It is a sign of our intellectual evolution to be able to shift through the deceiving sense-data in our progress beyond the rational into the spiritual realm. Unfortunately, most of us fall shy and remain deluded in Rumi's *primitive stage* of serving *other than God* and held in bondage to money, power, and vain intellect.

Although all evidence points towards divine guidance, some call it "natural." However, what is nature without God?[190] Researchers agree that even the dehydration linkage necessary for life—turning monomers into polymers—would not have been favored in Darwin's primordial soup because of the mass action law. It is analogous to putting sugar in water and expecting it to spontaneously become a cube. While everyone agrees that the ancient Archaean world was not suitable for life, some panspermians would rather believe the help came from other extraterrestrial sources like a meteorite or an alien species. These fringe theories were even believed by the co-discoverer of DNA, Francis Crick (1916-2004 CE), a Nobel laureate.[191] In his excuse, he was only following Fred Hoyle's lead, whose nucleosynthesis study nevertheless made him blurt: "The universe looks like a put-up job."[192] God rebukes such hubris and reminds us that those *confidently* arguing against Revelation simply *were not there* to have an opinion on such matters (e.g., *al-Qasas* 28:44).

There have been many discussions regarding the locations of Eden—in heaven, outskirts of heaven, a different realm altogether, within our universe, versus on earth—all of which are speculative and frankly irrelevant (الله أعلم). According to the Qur'an, the earth was already in existence before Adam, divinely planned for his eventual destination after his brief educational stay in Eden. Meanwhile, the evolutionary preparation of the earth had already been underway for billions of years to accommodate its prized guests with an environment more suitable for humans. When the evolutionary spectrum finally arrived at the early hominids, it perhaps marked the readiness of the planet and God's infusion of the first man's soul into his human shell made from clay.

Maybe it was at this time when God offered humankind the Covenant (*al-Ahzab* 33:72), making us the only creation tested and *Trusted* to balance their natural tendencies. (To answer Kierkegaard's question, *the self* was indeed asked if it wanted to accept the Covenant and be born.[193]) Although that natural state causes us to sin, we are commanded to repent and refrain, to prove our status over the rest of creation, who follow their natural laws in complete obedience. This is just another theory like Darwin's without going against the revealed *truth* from the Creator, and its evidence will be presented shortly.

He is the One Who has placed you as successors on earth and elevated some of you in rank over others, so He may test you with what He has given you. Surely your Lord is swift in punishment, but He is certainly All-Forgiving, Most Merciful. (al-An'am 6:165)

It is interesting to note the parallels between the scientific theories and the Qur'anic concept of our creation and succession on Earth. While the prevailing theory suggests that humanoids existed for 4 million years, the sudden emergence of *Homo sapiens* and their subsequent migration out of Sub-Saharan Africa 200 thousand years ago raises questions about the nature of human progress and development. The Qur'anic report of the perfect man, Adam, created de-novo ex-nihilo in heaven and sent down to earth, implies a divine intervention in human history. All debates regarding Adam's timeline are ignorant of the nature of *time* from theoretical physics, where the "single quantity 'time' melts into a spiderweb of times," explains physicist Rovelli. "We do not describe how the world evolves in time: we describe how things evolve in local time, and how local times evolve *relative to each other."*[194]

This *local time* on earth would be different from the time of the heavenly arena where Adam was created. It will make more sense in a later chapter, but for now, it is fair to state that our attempts to relate things based on our observations are dubious from the start due to *false premises*. We have many proposed theories for these sudden changes circumnavigating the enormity of humanity's inertia for the remaining 3,800,000 years. Then we are told of another enormous leap toward the domestication of plants around 8500 BC. The likelihood of us being grossly wrong in these assumptions is statistically and significantly higher than the available evidence. The only saving grace for such sudden milestone events would be outside intervention to the otherwise *status quo* stagnation in the form of divine guidance or a heavenly descent.

The Qur'anic term *khalifah* (2:30, 6:165, 27:62; Arabic: خليفة), which refers to humankind as successors on earth, is understood by many scholars (such as al-Farāhīdī, Muqātil ibn Sulaymān, and al-Samarqandi) as a group replacing an existing group, paralleling the anthropological concept of Homo sapiens replacing pre-existing humanoids. There is a fascinating scholarly tradition (not rooted in revelation) of pre-human creatures (*al-hinn, al-binn*) who were replaced because they spilled blood on earth (mentioned by Ibn 'Umar and Qatada Ibn Di'ama). Ibn Hajar al-Asqalani described these creatures as distinct tribes that existed before humankind, which sounds remarkably similar to the conflict between the Cro-Magnons and the Neanderthals, with the former completely wiping the latter off the planet 40,000 years ago. These add another dimension to the angels' curiosity at the creation of Adam, as if comparing our potential corruption with those already inhabiting the planet with similar features and characteristics (*al-Baqarah* 2:30).

Still, Gould asked: "Why did the Lord see fit to make so many kinds of hominids, and why some of his later productions, Homo-erectus in particular, look so much more human than the earlier models?"[195] Ibn 'Arabi's concept of the perfect man excelling above the animal man to receive God's blessing of the knowledge of all things provided a framework for understanding this dilemma.[196] This reconciliation of different hominid species, far removed from the perfected humans, offers a unique perspective on human evolution and its place in the divine scheme of things. Therefore, Adam, the first *perfect man*, became God's vicegerent on earth to be inherited by his offspring. "Surely in this are signs for those who contemplate" (*al-Hijr* 15:75).

Some experts speculate that Ibn 'Arabi learned about evolution from al-Ikhwan al-Safa's *Rasa'il*, a collection of essays by an 8th-century secret society. It features Jalaluddin Rumi's *Masnavi*, whose father was a student of Ibn 'Arabi.[197] Al-Biruni identified hominids of varying statures through the bones he found in the caves of the Median mountains.[198] In fact, evolution has a long and rich history that extends to different parts of the world and time periods. Even the Popol Vuh of the Quiche Maya likened monkeys to ancient human-like beings who had not yet achieved perfection. Darwin, of course, is the most well-known figure associated with the theory of evolution. He famously stated that if any complex organ existed that could not have formed through gradual modifications, his theory would fail.[199] However, the absence of a direct skeletal link between apes and humans is enough evidence to challenge Darwin's theory.

Such is He who knows all that is unseen and what is seen, the Almighty, the Merciful, who gave everything its perfect form. He first created man from clay, then made his descendants from an extract of underrated fluid. Then He molded him; He breathed from His Spirit into him; He gave you hearing, sight, and mind. How seldom you are grateful! (as-Sajdah 32:6-9)

Scholars such as Ibn-Miskawayah, Ibn al-Haitham (965-1040 CE), al-Masudi (896-956 CE), and al-Jahiz (776-868 CE), among others, wrote about the evolution of animals and their transition from animality to humanity. Allamah Iqbal (1877-1938 CE) summarized Ibn-Miskawayah's (930-1030 CE) views as humanity passing from barbarism to civilization as animals evolve psychologically and spiritually.[200] From Khurasan to Sham, to Ifriqiya, to Andalucia, throughout Islamic lands, the theory of evolution was widely accepted and taught, much of which was later translated and studied by the next generation of European thinkers. As such, Darwin's ideas resemble al-Biruni's in *Fi Tahqiq Ma Li'l Hind* without acknowledgment. (Allowing for the difference in translation, reference passages from *The Origin of Species*[201] read nearly verbatim to al-Biruni's[202].)

The similarities between Darwin's theories and those of his predecessors do not necessarily imply plagiarism. Nor can we establish his intent retrospectively in what is called an intentional fallacy, but the only crime is what is attributed to him thereafter by others with ignorant ploys. Al-Biruni observed: "You find the functions of nature which it is her office to fulfill, some fault, but this only serves to show that the Creator who had designed something deviating from the general tenor of things is indefinitely sublime, beyond everything which we poor sinners may conceive and predicate Him."[203] Independent observers are undoubtedly capable of formulating common theories following similar rational paths. Perhaps the only "missing link" in Darwinian evolutionism is the presence of God whose *guidance* allows the "imperfect" nature to follow its divine course. While the Occidental scientists were undoubtedly inspired by

Islamic scholarship, unfortunately, some subsequent Muslims took after the misguidance of the Judeo-Christian delusion of creationism, losing ties to their Golden roots.

Even if someday all the skeletal records are laid out in front of us, the sequence of events would still be our most educated guess. As of now, there is little evidence to support Darwin's theory, which nevertheless "serves as the creation myth of our time, assigning properties to nature previously assigned to God," writes Berlinski.[204] It is futile to debate over such issues that will forever be from the unknown with little benefit to our faith. Regardless of whom we consider our ancestors, there remains a colossal difference between humans and all the other animals regarding intelligence and capabilities. While some wish to reduce themselves to apes, the apparent leap of perfection still differentiates us from the rest.

There are [countless] signs on earth for those with sure faith, as there are within yourselves. Can you not see? (adh-Dhariyat 51:20-21)

THE INCONVENIENT TRUTH

The Prophet said about the signs of the Hour: "...when you see barefooted, naked, deaf and ignorant as the rulers of the earth—and destitute shepherds competing in making tall buildings." (Sahih Muslim 10; Sunan an-Nasa'i 4990)

I: The Other Idea

The world today celebrates the West as the pinnacle of civilization, with a narrative that highlights the Greco-Roman legacy as crucial to the Caucasian identity. This revisionist view of history enables the West's "othering" of the East, a phenomenon that Edward Said called Orientalism. It parallels the postcolonial theory, where the West defines itself through opposition. The use of the prefix "post" in these modern movements may suggest going beyond old practices but only serves to perpetuate them through the same Darwinian dominance.[205]

The amount of scholarship that went into the development of Europe's Oriental framework is noteworthy, with an estimated 60,000 books written about the Near Orient between 1800 and 1950. Amazingly, as historian R. W. Southern noted, all of it only refined and propagated Western ignorance over time.[206] Till today, books taught in our schools contain gross misinformation about Islam and racist rhetoric toward Muslims.[207] William Muir's works on Islam are still revered in the West, stating: "The sword of Muhammad, and the Koran, are the most stubborn enemies of Civilization, Liberty, and the Truth, which the world has yet known."[208] The entire field revolves around similar judgments against Islam substantiated by a chain of "experts" who continue to give significance to former bigotry legitimizing their personal biases. The entire "expert" culture of our modern-era bureaucracy was masterfully debunked by MacIntyre in *After Virtue*, alongside many similar myths surrounding social sciences. Psychologically, this forms organizational disidentification, where one's identity is defined by their adversaries, fueling stereotypes and animosity.[209] It also makes reconciliation difficult, as even giving an ear to the other side threatens one's ego.

The concepts of the "Orient" and the "East" are not actual geographic places but imaginary fields demarcated by Western minds, often grouping people with few commonalities. Various stories, ideas, and characters are then created to enrich these fields. They are then studied and academically intellectualized into a "knowledge base" and projected onto *others* as needed. One such example is d'Herbelot's *Bibliotheque orientale*, which categorized every known misconception and bigotry of the era from A to Z. Postcolonial Orientalism had existed since the construction of Europe, dating back to antiquity, as Edward Said demonstrated in *Orientalism*. As a nascent Europe grew in the shadows of Al-Andalus and Islam, it formed a peculiar inferiority complex giving rise to its military, theological, and intellectual aggression against Islam and the entire world.

The problem with questions based on false premises is that they lead to erroneous answers and solutions. The birth of Europe and its association with the Western Church was not driven by an unselfish ideology but rather by a power struggle for both to survive each other's long history of brutality. Merging the warring Franks, Visigoths, Lombards, and other Germanic tribes with the Western Church created "the question of Islam," providing historians with ample material for failed solutions. Ironically, the same barbarians that had clashed with civilized Rome and faced defeat demonstrated their military prowess against the Islamic civilization under a theology entirely antithetical to the message of Jesus.

With that false premise, even when Europe gained the upper hand of power, it demonstrated unbalanced aggression and greed. Its intellect and achievements only brought arrogance and enhanced destruction to anything it touched. It saw the rest of the world with a view from power, making any outside attempts of correction an attack on Western intellect and reason. Islam became whatever the European minds saw fit from their baseline assumption of the superiority of their beliefs, whether it be Christianity, science, or hedonism. Thus, all semites were primitive, Islam "organized hypocrisy," and Muhammad a "ruthless crypto-Jesuit."[210] This view eventually became a matter of fact that was backed by all enlightened sciences, and any opinion to the contrary was blasphemous. Newton's successor William Whiston was even expelled from Cambridge in 1709 for his honest enthusiasm toward Islam. This kind of worldview, by definition, makes its holder racist, ethnocentric, and imperialist. Edward Said highlights the presence of a "field" such as Orientalism as proof itself, along with the absence of a corresponding equivalent field of Occidentalism.

R. N. Cust noted at the Orientalist meetings that even after centuries of scholarly work on Orientalism, there is a profound stagnation in their understanding of Islam.[211] Accordingly, we do not see any significant study of Islam until 1966 with Maxime Rodinson's *Islam and Capitalism*. The romanticized Western view of the East took precedence over truth, often extending to nonscientific literature such as Mark Twain's *The Innocents Abroad*. The power of *discourse*, as explained by Michel Foucault, is demonstrated in the negative connotation of terms like "revisionist history," which is often inaccurately applied to cases where history was written with significant subjective liberty in its first draft. In such cases, revision is not only a good thing but imperative at the risk of nit-picking like a postmodernist.

This discourse of Orientalism is so ingrained into the Western rhetoric that notable revolutionaries like Karl Marx could not break free from its prejudices.[212] Outbursts of undiagnosed bigotry reek even from open-minded scholars like Feyerabend, reducing the complex, multifaceted early Islamic history down to "Moslem conquests," similar to the "crusaders" and "discoverers of new continents."[213] Among the many ignored nuances is the lack of historical evidence for forced conversions or pillaging following the early Muslim expansions, which otherwise dominated the history of the others. In addition, while all the different ethnicities of "Moslems" are grouped under their religious belief, the Crusaders escaped their Christianity even when their savageries were unleashed by direct papal blessing.

Gross misinterpretations of Islam are readily evident from its most learned to the least in a remarkable consistency maintained even today through the rhetoric of various "experts" on TV. As Said wrote half a century ago, "Whereas it is no longer possible to write learned (or even popular) disquisitions on either 'the Negro mind' or 'the Jewish personality,' it is perfectly possible to engage in such research as 'the Islamic mind,' or 'the Arab character.'"[214] Orientalism's political incorrectness today only makes it subversive in all of its neo-imperial motifs but with consistent Occidental representation.

The French contribution to Orientalism's philological roots and quasi-material knowledge was implemented politically by British colonial ambitions. After the Second World War, the US inherited this Anglo-French imperial tradition, redefining it in politics and policymaking. Orientalism's philological roots were traded for social sciences, where even the mastery of the Oriental language was abandoned. That came with a reduced emphasis on literature in the area studies which, along with their group portrayal in popular culture and media, led to further dehumanization.

Throughout history, the Orient has been consistently disregarded and misrepresented by the West. Despite being capable of representing themselves, the West has repeatedly chosen to speak on their behalf, perpetuating the mutilation of their culture and values. For instance, the *Report on Current Research* by the Middle East Institute in 1958 included a contribution titled "Present State of Arabic Studies in the United States" by a Hebrew Professor. In the *New York Times Magazine* coverage of the Arab-Israeli war in 1973, the Israeli side was presented by an Israeli lawyer, while the Arab side was presented by a former American ambassador who lacked any former training.[215] This adulteration has been only superseded by a deep hatred for all things Islamic in America's popular culture and its schools—from Hollywood to elementary textbooks to the rhetoric within institutions of higher learning (Gustave von Grunebaum, Bernard Lewis, and Thomas Sowell, among others).

Such academic and intellectual vitriol perhaps arises from the fact that the West has never been able to conquer Islam politically despite its relentless efforts. Thus, it became endless quasi-scientific propaganda at an academic level, giving importance to egos that personify the original comment of Benjamin Disraeli: *The East is a Career* (Tancred, II, xiv). In the neo-imperial era, it manifested in discourse, where the resistance of an occupied *other* became a *lack of understanding of democracy and self-governance as we do*. The occupied *other's* class, political, and economic nuances are irrelevant as they are all *terrorists at the bottom*. This notion is epitomized by Bernard Lewis, who believes that if Arab Palestinians oppose Israeli-European settlement and occupation of their lands, then that is merely "the return of Islam." Lewis defines Islamic opposition to non-Islamic peoples as a principle of Islam enshrined in the 7th century, completely disregarding the history, politics, and economics that underpin the conflict. This kind of reductive thinking allows the West to view the Orient as a monolithic entity that can be easily conquered and controlled, without taking into account the complexities of their culture and society.[216]

When the Orient was given a place in history in the 20th century, it was through the vision of the Orientalist as enacted by its imperial agents like T. E. Lawrence, Roosevelts, and Bushes. Accordingly, an Iraqi fighting an American invasion becomes a terrorist, while a Ukrainian opposing the Russians is a freedom fighter. Of course, a Palestinian trampled under occupied forces inside a holy mosque is a *status quo* not worth reporting. "Modern European racism and biblical constructs and prejudices towards the Philistines have survived in the derogatory and offensive connotation of the modern Western term: 'a *philistine* is a person ignorant of, or smugly hostile to, culture,'" explains Professor Masalha.[217] Occidental humanitarians vituperating about Qatar's hosting the FIFA World Cup in 2022 somehow lost their voices in 2018 when Russia was actively involved in massacring an estimated 23,000 civilians in Syria.[218] Nor did they demand banning Russia or Israel from the games, as they will again forgo when the US becomes the host.

Anthropologist Eric Wolf (1923-99 CE) summarized the sentiment: "Ancient Greece begat Rome, Rome begat Christian Europe, Christian Europe begat the Renaissance, the Renaissance the Enlightenment, the Enlightenment political democracy and the industrial revolution. Industry crossed with democracy, in turn, yielded the United States, embodying the rights to life, liberty and the pursuit of happiness."[219] Some historians would instead call it *neo*-naissance to highlight the myth of Europe's *re*-birth, as it lacked any prior history of enlightenment. The more linguistically accurate renaissance of that period took place in the East during the rise of the Ottoman and Mughal Empires. The Orientalists of Europe, however, were unaware of this history—whether deliberately or as a consequence of their Orientalism. Instead, they revised a history where Europeans were the epitome of all things civilized as if humanity only existed through them.

Chateaubriand completely denied the aggression of the Crusades and considered them to be "more about knowing which would win on the earth, a cult that was civilization's enemy, systematically favorable to ignorance [this was Islam, of course], to despotism, to slavery, or a cult that had caused to reawaken in modern people the genius of a sage antiquity, and had abolished base servitude?"[220] In such a "civilized" take on the history of the *others*, it would appear they were quite uneducated of their own history. This theme of the West teaching *others* the meaning of liberty and democracy continues in today's mainstream narrative. Chateaubriandesque smugness is timeless in spewing bigotry like: "Of Liberty, they know nothing; of propriety, they have none: force is their God."[221] His take on the Qur'an makes one wonder if he even bothered to read it, saying: "This book preaches neither hatred of tyranny nor love of liberty."[222] Therefore, it again becomes the West's Christian (now secular) mission to conquer others, which somehow is their "liberation" as it continues to be the case in the Middle East and Afghanistan.

The roots of white supremacy lie in the papal law of *limpieza de sangre* (cleanliness of blood) which emerged in the aftermath of the Crusades.[223] The legal precedence was borrowed from Roman *terra nullius*, where any land not occupied by Europeans was up for grabs through either occupation or settler colonization. The Age of Enlightenment was even more farcical as the "great" European minds of that era somehow made leaps in every field with complete disregard for basic human rights. While they embraced reason and shifted from religion to secularism, "giving science the ultimate authority over truth and knowledge," they also developed the "modern scientific concept of race as a natural category."[224] Their accomplishments were nonetheless financed by the prosperous slave trade, which they also justified with more "enlightened" ideas about race, natural selection, and eugenics. As MacIntyre pointed out, for the typical Enlightenment writers like Montesquieu, Voltaire, and Helvetius, the notable "rights" were only meant for the lords and the intellectuals like themselves. Everyone else was grouped in Voltaire's "rabble" with the expected *status quo* order of obedience.[225]

Carl Linnaeus (1707-78 CE) cataloged all living things in *Systema Naturae* and separated *Homo sapiens* into four races, linking stereotypes with anthropology as the scientific basis for white supremacy.[226] The Europeans were at the top with positive traits, including flowing blond hair and inventiveness, while Africans were placed at the bottom with negative features like sluggishness and craftiness.[227] Such narcissism manifested in the placement of Europe at the top of the world map, opposing most classical Islamic maps with the entire global south rising above the European dark ages. Although prejudice has existed throughout history, the concept of race and racism as we know it today is a social construct created by the leading figures of the European Enlightenment to justify their global exploits.[228] Even peeling away from the Church, they clung to the belief that *God had created only the European race in His image*.[229] Such enlightened minds secularized their racism by inventing a scientific basis for subjugating the world. "For every idea about 'our' art spoken for by Arnold, Ruskin, Mill, Newman, Carlyle, Renan, Gobineau, or Comte, another link in the chain binding 'us' together was formed while another outsider was banished," wrote Said.[230] Today we study Locke, Hume, and other empiricists without contextualizing how their philosophies influenced the racial theory of Europe, justifying centuries of slavery and colonialism. Locke even enriched himself from his investments in the silk and slave trades.

The disconnect between the West's philosophical ideals and its practices persists today. However, the ideological nature of liberalism makes it difficult to perceive this disconnection, as the failure to achieve these ideals is now endemic to liberalism itself.[231] Celebrated Western apologists, such as Thomas Sowell, have attempted to whitewash the horrors of racial slavery by equating it with the chattel slavery that has plagued humanity since ancient times. In his book *Black Rednecks and White Liberals*, Sowell boldly claims that Western empires were responsible for abolition against Oriental resistance. In reality, the Occident became "appalled" by their racial slavery only *after* they had exploited it for centuries and risen to world dominance. John Newton, a former slave trader who became an anti-slavery leader, once wrote of Sierra Leone: "The state of slavery, among these wild barbarous people, as we esteem them, is much milder than in our colonies...no call for that excessive, unintermitted labour, which exhausts our slaves: so, on the other hand, no man is permitted to draw blood even from a slave."[232] Their subsequent abolishment was politically motivated and designed to cripple their competition. One can draw an analogy with a hypothetical abolishment of drug trafficking by the world's largest global cartels after they have made their fortunes and spent centuries building a complex supply chain economy.

It is baffling to see such circular arguments from Ivy League scholars that only reveal the means behind their success. Sowell further attempts to refute the idea that the Western Industrial Revolution was financed by slavery by arguing that the regions where slavery was allowed in both the US and Brazil were poorer than others. But within a page, he admits to the frugal lifestyles of slave owners while ignoring the fact that cotton, made possible by slave labor, was the largest American export on the eve of the Civil War. The success of the colonies relied on the strength of its African resources, which they increasingly capitalized on through the booming transatlantic slave trade. Sowell admits that in the non-Western world, slaves were often sources of domestic amenities and displays of wealth rather than sources of wealth themselves. Yet, he fails to see the irony.[233] Meanwhile, Napoleon Bonaparte was astonished in Egypt when he witnessed: "The slave inherits his master`s property and marries his daughter...They began their lives by performing the most menial services in the houses of their masters and were subsequently raised in status for their merit or by favour. In the West, on the contrary, the slave has always been below the position of the domestic servants; he occupies the lowest rug."[234]

In the classic Orientalist tradition, Sowell repeatedly puts *Western* civilization against *Islam*, as if the latter represents a geographical locality of uniform geopolitics. He follows the general blueprint of a few acceptable ideas and facts leading to overreaching assumptions, which are only applauded and celebrated by a target audience of similar ignorance. The results are outlandish claims, such as "On the issue of slavery, it was essentially Western civilization against the world...Some Moslems regarded attempts to abolish slavery as impious, since the Koran itself accepted slavery as an institution, while trying to ameliorate the lot of the slave."[235] These only prove his knowledge of Islam at an abecedarian level, as his saying "Moslems" in the 21st century is a telltale sign of his camp. More honest historians note that the Islamic precedents set by the Qur'an and *sunnah* only lead to a natural ebbing of slavery when put into practice with sincerity.[236] "Islam in its original form is a theology for liberation," writes Michael Mumisa.[237] Freeing one from slavery, as well as any other form of bondage, is one of the conditions of faith and ways to enter Paradise (*al-Balad* 90:11-18). Essentially, the *shari'ah* abolished all forms of slavery except war, which itself was closer to indentured servitude or today's mortgage system, as quipped by Shaikh Hamza Yusuf.[238] The objective of the Qur'anic instructions regarding slavery was to gradually prepare Muslims for a free world, similar to the rulings against alcohol.

Another neglected fact in the narrative is the origin of the core group of American frontier settlers from the Ulster Scots, who were originally Scottish Protestants recruited by Britain to drive out indigenous Irish farmers of Ulster in Northern Ireland.[239] This took place in the early 17th century, coinciding with the North American settlements, where the same settler colonial tactics were employed. The Protestant Scots brought with them the covenant ideology of Calvinism developed by John Knox, which was later secularized into a "contract" by Locke, who was also of Scottish descent. "Before ever meeting Indigenous Americans, the Ulster settlers had perfected scalping for bounty, using indigenous Irish as their victims," writes historian Dunbar-Ortiz. "As Calvinists (mostly Presbyterian), they added to and transformed the Calvinism of the earlier Puritan settlers into the unique ideology of the US settler class."[240] They formed the backbone of the US's revolutionary war and continued to see themselves as the true patriots—God's chosen people to transform the land into the new Israel.[241]

It becomes an essential clue once we realize that seventeen US presidents have been of Ulster-Scot lineage—including Andrew Jackson, Ronal Reagan, Theodore Roosevelt, the Bushes, Bill Clinton, and Obama on his mother's side. Ironically, because of their deep antisemitism, they dumped the "new-Israel" project on Palestine. Rabbi Yaakov Shapiro's book, *The Empty Wagon*, on this issue is noteworthy. Even "humanists" like Walt Whitman, when not writing songs about the glorified Anglo-American super-race, were predating eugenics by prescribing: "The nigger, like the Injun, will be eliminated; it is the law of the races, history…A superior grade of rats come and then all the minor rats are cleared out."[242] As the Bob Marley song noted, the Buffalo Soldier regiments directed against the Native Americans served to remedy these problems by winning "the war for America." Similar celebrated writers served as contemporary propaganda machines to rev up the war machine at the backbone of the US Empire's economy since its conception.

Nearly all of the empire's leading minds were keenly aware of race and imperialism, as even J.S. Mill made it clear that Indians were an inferior race in *On Liberty* and *Representative Government*.[243] Their successors continued to benefit from the racist *status quo* while hiding under their feigned academic "neutrality," which is nothing short of biased rationalization of the bigotry hidden in the rhetoric of many like Bernard Lewis, Jordan Peterson, and Sam Harris. The consistency in their message over time only portrays the personality of the West more than their object of study. Said was a pioneer in confronting such academic dishonesty, which gradually made "Orientalism" politically incorrect, only to be expressed under other monikers. It is not a unified Western conspiracy against the Orient but a deliberate cultural ignorance of such bigotry at every level that perpetuates a general theme, over time becoming a phenomenon. The only unifying element here is the unrecognized ploys of the devils in dividing humanity for an easy conquest.

In attempts to create this illusion of the West's apocryphal separate identity, the Renaissance of the Islamic Golden Age was forcefully omitted. It did not go unnoticed by many like the French surgeon turned social anthropologist Robert Briffault (1876-1948 CE). John William Draper also recognized it centuries ago and wrote: "I have to deplore the systematic manner in which the literature of Europe has contrived to put out of sight our scientific obligations to the Muhammadans. Surely they cannot be much longer hidden. Injustice founded on religious rancor and national conceit cannot be perpetuated forever."[244] The only reason the Greco-Roman heritage even survived the European Dark Ages was their preservation and translation by Islamic scholars, contrasting the suppression of free thought by the contemporary Church. It was a Christian mob that torched the treasures held within the famous library of Alexandria in 391 CE; Byzantine Emperor Zeno closed Edessa's school of Hippocratic medicine in 489 CE; Christian King Justinian closed Plato's academy in 529 CE exiling all its scholars and students to Persian lands. Along with them went the ancient knowledge, later nurtured by state-commissioned scholars under Caliph al-Ma'mun (786-833 CE) and translated into Arabic. The Caliph then appointed a Nestorian Christian, Hunayn Ibn Ishaq, as the head of the intellectual center *Bait al-Hikma*, and paid him its weight in gold for every classic manuscript he translated.

At the height of the Islamic enlightenment, more books were published yearly than in modern New York.[245] Further expansion in those fields—by the likes of Ibn Musa al-Khwarizmi (aka Algoritmi, 780-850 CE), Abbas Ibn Firnas (aka Armen Firman, 810-87 CE), al-Razi (aka Rhazes 854-925 CE), al-Zahrawi (aka Abulcasis, 936-1013 CE), al-Haytham (aka Alhazen, 965-1040 CE), al-Biruni (973-1050 CE), Ibn Sina (aka Avicenna, 980-1037 CE), Ibn Tufail (aka Abubacer, 1110-85 CE) and his student Ibn Rushd (aka Averroes, 1126-98 CE), Ibn al-Nafis (1213-88 CE), and Ibn Khaldun (1332-1406 CE)—laid the foundations of the European Renaissance as well as most modern sciences.

The Islamic Renaissance not only produced scientific advancements but also gave birth to the scientific method. Al-Ghazali preceded Bacon in asserting that true knowledge is inductive, not deductive, as previously claimed by Aristotle. This progress was made possible by the emphasis on the pursuit of knowledge demanded by God in the Qur'an. The first university in the world, al-Azhar, was established in Cairo in 970 CE and still stands today, while the first hospital, or *bimaristan*, was built in Baghdad in 805 CE by Caliph Harun al-Rashid. The Islamic educational system was unrivaled in history and had a profound influence on the formation of the Christian and Western systems of education, as Professor George Makdisi explains in his work, *The Rise of Colleges*.

The recent deterioration of Islamic values and the rise of extremism worldwide can be attributed in part to attacks on this robust Islamic educational system, intentional or otherwise, and centuries of destruction at centers of Islamic scholarship. (Gaza serves as a quintessential example where the entire education system was just recently bombed into oblivion along with its students who were previously known for their high level of literacy.) Nascent Europe was aware of these achievements and sent their brightest minds, such as Adelard of Bath, to explore the libraries of Antioch and Damascus. He returned with algorithmic tables that served as the foundation of mathematics in the Christian world, while Leonardo Fibonacci learned the Arabic-Hindu arithmetic in Muslim lands before bringing it to Europe.[246] Al-Haytham's ingenuity spanned numerous fields, including calculating volumes of solids that Archimedes never considered.[247] Even Descartes' rediscovery of Snell's sine law, published in 1637 in *Dioptrics*, was formulated by al-A'la Ibn Sahl in 984.[248] Algebra derives its name from *al-jabr*, meaning "reunion of broken parts." Thales learned "Greek" geometry in ancient Egypt, while the Pythagorean theorem originated in Babylon; Pythagoras himself was from a western island of modern Turkey, once known as Samos. Nearly all notable scholars and predecessors of the prestigious European academia traveled through Muslim lands before their revolutionary ideas.

The Qur'an's emphasis on every Muslim's reading and understanding of Revelation starkly contrasted with the exclusivity of the Latin priests. During the same period when Pope Alexander III (1100-81 CE) banned the study of medicine, citing a belief that illnesses were the result of demonic possessions that required exorcism, Muslim scholars made unparalleled advancements in the field.[249] Abu Zayd al-Balkhi's description of Obsessive-Compulsive Disorder (OCD) from a thousand years ago is strikingly similar to the current DSM-5.[250] The *Cannon* and the *Continens*, written by Ibn Sina and al-Razi, were the standard medical texts in the West for nearly a millennium. People from all over the world traveled to Toledo to learn Arabic and study medicine. Soon, even non-Muslims preferred Arabic, which made the archbishop of Cordoba lament that his fellow Christians "know only the language and the literature of the Arabs."[251] That is how a Christian physician named Robertus Ketenensis came to translate the first Latin Qur'an in 1143 at the request of Peter the Venerable, abbot of

Cluny, though the title, *Lex Mahomet pseudoprophete* ("The Law of the false prophet Muhammad"), revealed his ignoble intent. That was the standard Qur'an for Europeans until the 18th century and influenced Riccoldo da Monte di Croce's *Confutatio Alkorani* ("Confutation of the Qur'an"), printed in 1500.[252] Interestingly, Martin Luther studied both extensively leading up to his 95 revolutionary opinions that gave birth to the Protestant Reformation, many of which conformed to Islamic doctrine.

"From the beginning, then, Islam was a religion of the book and of learning, a society that esteemed knowledge and education above almost every other human activity," notes Professor Berkley.[253] The Arab invention of a fretboard allowed musical tuning to the Pythagorean scale. The roots of today's soul music can be traced back to the melancholic Qur'anic recitations and *adhan* of enslaved African Muslims, and a combination of the two led to the creation of blues, rock-and-roll, and other popular genres.[254] Muslims invented the alphabetic musical notation used today and the popular canon style, while the guitar evolved from the *kaitara*.[255] The Arabic origin of many English words serves as evidence of that neglected history. (For example: admiral, alchemy, algorithm, alkali, almanac, atlas, chemistry, chess, cipher, coffee, drug, earth, elixir, fret, guitar, julep, magazine, marzipan, mattress, rocket, sofa, syrup, tambourine, zenith, zero, etc.)

Non-muslims living in the Islamic lands also participated in the flow of ideas. It allowed for Maimonides's (1138-1204 CE) complete revival of Jewish theology, bringing it out of a long decline. Until recently, most Jewish scholars had to learn Arabic to study their religious texts preserved in Muslim lands. He was a student of Ibn Rushd and served as the personal physician of Sultan Salah ad-Din (1138-93 CE), who liberated Palestine from the brutal occupation of Christian Crusaders. While the Crusaders under the leadership of Richard the Lionheart (1157-99 CE) preferred slaughtering everyone in sight, Salah ad-Din's treatment of the Crusaders, on the other hand, was directly responsible for even saving Richard's life.

Such was the tolerance under Islamic Rule as demonstrated in the rulings of prominent jurists like Imam al-Juwaynī (1028-85 CE).[256] It is evident from the centuries it took for Muslims to be a majority in many conquered lands, like Andalucia, Egypt, and Syria. Only 56 people became Muslim on the day of the Prophet's near-bloodless conquest of Mecca surrounded by about 60,000 of his companions. Places like India enjoyed a Hindu majority even during and after over one thousand years of Muslim rule. This unique history of Islam is denied by the Occidental crude reductionist narrative, which predominantly draws from exceptional cases, often taken out of context and even exaggerated. Still, those exceptions found contemporary Muslim scholars risking their lives to defend minorities in Muslim lands. Examples include Imam al-Awzā'ī protecting the Christians of Lebanon in the 2nd century A.H.; Imam Zarrūq and his teacher, Shaykh al-Qūrī's protection of the Jewish minority communities in Morocco; and Imam al-'Izz bin 'Abd al-Salām's protection of Egyptian Copts during the Crusades.[257]

According to the Israeli scholar and erstwhile foreign secretary Abba Eban (1915-2002 CE), Muslim Spain was one of the only two times in history where Jews were treated justly. Hasdai Ibn Shaprut, a Jewish vizier of Caliph Abd al-Rahman III, was one of the most powerful men in Muslim Spain. Jewish documents written during this period referred to Islam as "an act of God's mercy," which was in sharp contrast to the legacy of Jewish persecution by Kings Reccared, Sisibut, Egica, and Witiza, promoted by the bishops of the concurrent Catholic Church of Hispaniola.[258] Jews of the Iberian Peninsula sought aid from Muslims of North Africa and Mesopotamia for deliverance from escalating antisemitism, which was reflected in the charges against them in the 17th Toledo Council of 694.[259] Such injustices served as the premise for Muslim campaigns across the strait that still bears the name of Tariq Ibn Ziyad (670-720 CE).

Sylvester II, the first "Scientist Pope," received much of his training and knowledge in al-Hakam II al-Mustansir's (915-76 CE) Cordoba. He revolutionized the Christian world with Arab-Hindu mathematics, which raised suspicions of demonic powers from his colleagues.[260] Letters from both Timothys—head of the Eastern Church in Baghdad in the late 8th and 9th centuries—report the senior Christian clerics enjoying personal relations with the Caliph and sending evangelical missions from there to India, China, Tibet, and North Africa.[261] This is the history of the long coexistence of all three Abrahamic religions in Muslim lands before the corruption and revision of our recent era.[262]

Our history books omit the pre-Columbian trade and commerce between Muslim West Africa and the Americas, despite their mention by nearly all European explorers, including Columbus and Balboa. While European sailors limited themselves to coastal explorations of their flat-earth, Muslim scientists under Caliph al-Ma'mun (786-833 CE) calculated the earth's circumference with remarkable precision in the 9th century. With al-Battani's (858-929 CE) compass, al-Biruni's (973-1048 BC) latitude and longitude, and al-Zarqali's (1029-87 CE) astrolabe, Muslim sailors were at the forefront of transoceanic exploration. Al-Idrisi (1100-65 CE) created the most studied world map under the commission of King Roger II of Sicily. Their accuracy and acumen allowed them to sail to the Americas centuries before Columbus without ever confusing Central America for India (e.g. Khashkhash Ibn Saeed in 889 CE and Ibn Farrukh in 999 CE).[263]

Sadly, even contemporary writers like Jared Diamond fail to acknowledge these accomplishments and continue to write: "Pizarro came to Cajamarca by means of European maritime technology..."[264] Sir Francis Drake (1540-96 CE) offloaded 200 Arab and Turkish Muslims on Roanoke Island in 1586, who then assimilated into North Carolina's native Cherokee tribes. Turkish influence in Native American languages of Cherokee, Seminole, Algonquin, Powhatan, and Chippewa demonstrates blatant ignorance of etymology. Places like Kentucky and Chicago share their Indian names with similar Turkish words like *kan-tok* and *chee-kahkah*.[265] Interestingly, California was so named by the Spanish explorers as "the city of the Caliph."[266]

A Moravian missionary named JC Pyrlaeus compiled a Nanticoke Indian vocabulary on the shores of Maryland in 1750, documenting them speaking the same Muslim Mandinka language of West Africa. The traditional garments of the Cherokee before 1832 included a turban for men and a head covering for women, which is strikingly Islamic and different from other natives. Cherokee and Creek Indians wore turbans in a Turkish *fez* style with a single feather, like those worn in the 16th-century Ottoman Empire. The similarities continue to the names of Cherokee chief Stand Watie's sons, Saladin and Solon.

Columbus learned about Muslim trade with the Americas while traveling along the West African trade routes. He even had a copy of al-Idrisi's book with him in *Santa Maria*, indicating his knowledge of prior Muslim transatlantic expeditions. Perhaps the difference is that Muslims explored for trade, not exploitation of natives and claiming an already inhabited land for themselves. It explains the friendliness of the Aztecs and the Incas towards the invading Europeans, given their familiarity with centuries of preceding commerce with Muslims. The common misconception of them confusing the Conquistadors for gods is yet another ignorant Occidental shameless projection, demonstrating the remarkable narcissism that plagues their academics. Just as they fantasize about a conservative Arab world's harem life by projecting their hypersexual misogyny onto them.[267] That self-discovering theme is recurrent in nearly all major Orientalist works, from Flaubert to Gide.[268]

In today's world, the presence of a double standard and blatant hypocrisy necessitates the clarification of some common-sensical matters. Noam Chomsky aptly argues against even the phrase "double standard" as there is only a single standard where all Occidental aggression is noble, and all Oriental resistance or reaction is considered criminal.[269] Although Islam represents a divine ideal, humans will always fall short in practice. *Insaan* (Arabic, humans), with their insanities, will often confuse the actions of a suboptimal Muslim for the message of Islam. If all Muslims were perfect, there would be no need for a Day of Judgment. Islam provides the divine solution to all human problems, which many Muslims fail to implement and convey. However, the failure of the people is independent of the ideals, and an honest study of them reveals their perfection.

Despite our imperfect application of those ideals, the only time in history we ever came close to a utopian society was through Islamic values. This undeniable fact can only be argued and misconstrued by those with polluted minds and nefarious agendas. Raphael recognized such contributions by including Ibn Rushd in his fresco alongside Aristotle and Plato. Similarly, Thomas Aquinas quoted Ibn Rushd and Ibn Sina extensively in his scholasticism, which became the official doctrine of the Catholic Church. Aquinas's theory of knowledge and religious realism were heavily influenced by the writings of al-Farabi (870-950 CE).[270] With such a legacy, it is astonishing to see the forceful exclusion of Muslims from Western discourse and texts like Philip Stokes's *100 Essential Thinkers*, which includes obscurists like Parmenides of Elea with minimal documented work. All of it is skipped over as the scientific heritage is connected from the classical period to Western Europe by even best-selling Cambridge scholars like Stephen Meyer. His emphasis on the Judeo-Christian heritage in *The Return of the God Hypothesis* only emphasized the active exclusion of Islamic contributions at the highest levels of Western academics.

In contrast, Peter Adams of King's College London argues that Ibn Sina is the single most influential philosopher in European history. It is not to be pejorative of Western scholars, who are brilliant in their own right, but to undo current misconceptions and give credit where it is due. By encouraging the truth in our popular culture and correcting the disinformation in our education system, we can nurture a better understanding of Muslims that will promote recognition and respect from the West to reciprocate the same from *others*.

The Jews say, "The Christians have nothing to stand on," and the Christians say, "The Jews have nothing to stand on," although both recite the Scriptures. And those [pagans] who have no knowledge say the same [about people of faith]. Surely God will judge between them on the Day of Judgment regarding their dispute. (al-Baqarah 2:113)

II: Solutions From False Premises

The responsibilities of intellectuals have always belonged in two competing categories: the moral obligation to use their privilege and status to further the causes of freedom, justice, mercy, and peace, versus the expectation that they will play their roles as "technocratic and policy-oriented intellectuals" to serve the leadership and established institutions. As Chomsky notes, those who fall into the latter category are often seen as "responsible intellectuals," while those in the former are dismissed or denigrated, at least within their own societies.[271] By examining the treatment of intellectuals by ruling powers and their rhetoric, we can classify them into these two groups, which helps to clarify the often complex global picture.

Despite being domestically criticized for speaking out against their governments and foreign policies, some intellectuals in countries such as Iran are considered courageous and honored dissidents in the West. As Sa'id ibn al-Musayyib (637-715 CE) warned, any scholar who becomes too close to rulers risks losing their integrity and becoming a "thief" (al-Ādāb al-Shar'īyah 477). Even the famous Muslim scholars of the eponymous schools were subjected to torture and imprisonment by contemporary authorities. Similarly, all of the prophets and messengers of God can be seen as dissidents who spoke out against the corruption within their rulers and elites. However, their moral nonconformity should not be confused with political movements against authority; they were all attempting to right the wrongs within their established communities without bringing down the entire structure.

It is worth noting that Nelson Mandela was only removed from the official State Department terrorist list in 2008. Until then, he was listed as the leader of the world's "most notorious terrorist group" in a Pentagon report, which justified American support for the South African apartheid regime that resulted in 1.5 million deaths.[272] The US was the largest trading partner of that apartheid regime, providing up to a third of its international credit.[273] Similarly, today we label Hamas as a terrorist organization while continuing to support an exponentially worse apartheid, genocidal regime that is causing mounting Palestinian casualties even at this very moment.

Although Jews and Muslims were initially grouped as Semites, in the latter 20th century, Jews received much more favorable treatment. Perhaps owing to their Jewish State, which, naturally from their European origin, adopted the same Orientalist viewpoint in dealing with their Semitic coinhabitants. A consistent demonstration of their colonial mindset is evident in all Zionist rhetoric dating back to its founder, Theodor Herzl (1860-1904 CE).[274] For instance, in 1982, General Sharon invaded Lebanon with 17,000 civilian casualties. When pressed by American Ambassador Morris Draper, Sharon bluntly said, "So we'll kill them. They will not be left there. You are not going to save them."[275] His "mop up" massacres in Sabra and Shatila refugee camps stand as the general theme of the entire occupation. Still, he was named a partner in "peace" with George W. Bush without much dissent from the intellectual community.[276] Evidence of such atrocities is abundant, as even Dov Weisglass, a confidant of Sharon, forthrightly explained. Learning from the Nazi tactics, Israeli experts calculated precisely how many calories Gazans needed per day for bare survival and then placed them on that diet—just enough to make them not die of hunger while depriving them of a decent life and medicine.[277] Untill their outright genocide and ethnic cleansing, of course, where they did not even shy away from using starvation as a tactic.

All peace attempts are met with demands of strict preconditions intentionally designed to sabotage negotiations. Although Hamas won a democratic election deemed "free and fair" by international monitors in January 2006, all of Palestine was immediately punished collectively for voting the wrong way. "The pretense of opposition reached the level of farce in February 2011, when Obama vetoed a UN Security Council resolution calling for the implementation of official US policy (and also adding the uncontroversial observation that the settlements themselves are illegal)," adds Chomsky.[278] In fact, Hamas accepts the two-state settlement per the international consensus and always observes the ceasefire agreements. Israel then disregards whatever agreement is in place with increasingly violent tactics leading to a Hamas response, which is then reflexively followed by even fiercer Israeli brutality.[279] It is reminiscent of the numerous treaties forced upon the Native Americans, nearly all of which were eventually broken by the settlers as they were gradually pushed out of their native lands and exterminated.

In 2021 we witnessed it all over again with the continued forceful eviction of native Palestinians from their ancestral homes in Sheikh Jarrah by naturalized Jewish immigrants from as far as Brooklyn. They apparently have more rights to those homes according to the asinine judicial system of the apartheid regime.[280] Perhaps it is only natural for the US to sympathize with those illegal settlements as this country was founded on the same maneuvers. Our Supreme Court was not different in the *Dred Scott v Stanford* and *Williams v Lee* rulings, with the former yet to be reversed. Only when enough desired territory is annexed a "peace" deal is made, offering the natives whatever is left of the undesired wasteland. *Déjà vu*: when Cherokee landowners could do nothing but watch Georgians distribute Cherokee land to whites by lottery in the early 19th century. Even their Westernized Christian Chief, John Ross, was not spared when one day he found a white squatter in his home, forcing him to move out of his large estate to a one-room log cabin.

Jefferson dreamt of continental-scale apartheid in America for its natives.[281] By 1879, nearly all the natives were forced into Oklahoma, only to have illegal white settlers follow in defiance, claiming: "We are here with our axes and our plows...Hundreds and thousands of our friends are on their way to join us from all States of the West. We are here to stay. We deny the right of any man, or mob of men, whether in uniform or plain clothes, to molest us."[282] Thus, in 1893, white settlers on horses sprinted to claim the last remaining native territory for themselves at the shot of a government official's gun. It instantly resonates with the current tactics in Palestine, where similar settler-government relations are reenacted under state protection.

When the expected protests arose in Jerusalem in 2021, the brutes-in-boots in sheer chutzpah stormed into a religious sanctuary during the holiest time to bring down their wrath on unsuspecting worshippers. They only mimicked their mentor's long history of doing the same, as demonstrated in the Ponce massacre on Palm Sunday of 1937. The resulting outrage served as a pretext for yet another bombing of Gaza, demolishing what remained of vital infrastructures with an unfathomable civilian casualty. A ceasefire was reached, only for it to be broken again by Israel within weeks. It was met with little to no outcry from international leaders or media, while similar Russian tactics against Ukraine found a remarkably different global reaction. Like clockwork, repeated assaults on Gaza and al-Aqsa during every Ramadan also met paralyzed media attention. Yet, these are all war crimes under the current international law.

The plan has always been clear and simple: a colonial Zionist state of Israel composed exclusively of Jews by birth, which necessarily requires an extermination campaign of the indigenous population. Moshe Dayan stated Hobson's choice clearly, suggesting his party tell the Palestinians: "We have no solution, you shall continue to live like dogs, and whoever wishes may leave, and we will see where this process leads."[283] Excusing such state-sponsored terrorism allows similar injustices to be allowed elsewhere. Instead of noting the manifest distinction between right and wrong, we see blatant hypocrisy with convoluted arguments justifying absurdity. The simplest method to check one's bias is to reverse the script of any argument to see if the opposite would also be true. When one argues Israel's right to self-defense, would he also afford the Palestinians an equal right? If that causes one to stutter or search for excuses to deny the other side the same rights, that is a telltale sign of prejudice. Then it comes as no surprise to see the US and Israel's full support for India's military occupation of Kashmir with arms and professional training to run another apartheid open-air prison.[284]

The term "prison" also wrongfully implies its victims have committed some crime other than being born within a fascist movement and a depraved global leadership. What right does an occupier have to defend anyway? Indeed, it is only the right to resist an occupation under international law that is constantly being violated with an egregious cover-up by the Western powers. Today it is *de rigueur* to desecrate the holiest sites of Islam like Masjid al-Aqsa annually, often during the last ten days of Ramadan, which are of the utmost importance to Muslims. It is commonplace to witness the occupying terrorist army storming the premises, fully armed, just like the Neo-Babylonian and Roman soldiers of the past. Their actions violate the rights of peaceful worshippers and often incite violence. Nevertheless, when the oppressed stand their ground with bare hands and stones, all the world leaders express their solidarity for the right of the tyrants to "defend" in unison with hatred and bigotry, for they are all guilty of the same crime. David's slingshot today is hopelessly comical against Goliath's advanced war machines. But God clarifies: "They do not fight you, even assembled, but in fortified towns, or from behind the walls. Their battle between themselves is severe. You think that they are united while their hearts are divided. That is because they are a people who have no sense" (*al-Hashr* 59:14).

At home, we have casually moved from one president's reign of torture of captives, who are *guilty until proven guilty*, to the next's team of special forces and drone assassination of anyone deemed *dead until proven guilty*. "And we should remember that this is an international terrorist campaign," reminds Chomsky. "If you're living in a village in Yemen or North Waziristan and you don't know whether in five minutes a sudden explosion across the street will blow away a bunch of people who are standing there, and maybe hit you as well, you're terrorized."[285]

It is difficult to find words for policies like President Obama's counting all males over 16 years in a strike zone as non-civilian combatants until posthumously proven innocent.[286] Perhaps that is relatively merciful, considering civilian casualties in the two decades of Afghan slaughter were not even counted. Consequently, children in those regions have learned not to play outside on a clear day and to run for cover whenever they hear a *humming* above. In effect, Obama's actions in office were the completion of Donald Rumsfeld's plans for an *unmanned army*, given America's low threshold for its own casualties.[287] That solves the age-old problem of all imperialist regimes: accountability. With few boots on the ground, there is less public knowledge of foreign involvements and, as a result, less public outcry. Accordingly, there were significantly fewer protests against the Afghanistan War than in Vietnam, although the former cost a lot more time and money.[288]

Leaving these countries defeated, how much does the US owe those people in blood money, pain and suffering, and damage to infrastructures? At the very least, the "victors" are owed an admission of wrongdoing and a fair trial. Let us now reflect upon Article 3 of the Geneva Conventions barring "the carrying out of executions without previous judgment pronounced by a regularly constituted court, affording all the judicial guarantees which are recognized as indispensable by civilized peoples." Not to mention the divine sanctity of life stressed in all religions and the simple common-sensical notion of ethics. Even some of the worst war criminals were given a trial at the end of WWII at Nuremberg, which is denied to many innocent civilians today.

As noted by military historian John Grenier, such unlimited warfare has been deeply ingrained within the US's DNA since its early settlement days. It effectively destroys the enemy's resistance by attacking civilians and destroying infrastructures, the same way the colonial militias employed it against indigenous communities. That extravagant violence gradually developed into racial hatred, which continues to play a role in this nation's identity, forming an ironic full circle from the Crusades to today's anti-Muslim aggression. Notable leaders of the colonial armies—including John Smith of Virginia, Myles Standish of Plymouth, John Mason of Connecticut, and John Underhill of Massachusetts—had a history of fighting bloody religious wars in Europe.[289] They blurred the lines between combatants and civilians by scalping Native Americans, which was a precursor to today's indiscriminate aerial warfare. The similarities continue to an enemy territory still designated "Indian Country" by the US military.[290] The irony was not lost during the Gulf War when a proud retired commander boasted about the famed scouting Second Armored Cavalry Regiment's origin in the 1830s to fight the Seminoles.[291]

Today, war has become a remote bureaucratic play of numbers against a dehumanized enemy. There are no veterans of the US's war with Yemen to speak of the horrors on the ground, while nearly the entire mainland remains unaware.[292] Groups are added and removed from the Foreign Terrorist Organizations (FTOs) list to suit temporal whims when other methods such as removing aid, bombing, blockading, and sanctions fail. In the '80s, Iraq was swiftly removed from the list and replaced by Iran to sell weapons to Saddam because Secretary of State George Shultz considered it strategically important.[293] The same administration later sold weapons to Iran through Israel while pressuring others not to do so.[294]

The CIA even factored in the Contras in Nicaragua in their illegal "generosity" during that decade. When the word got out, everyone scrambled to shred all documents while the president feigned dementia during the Congressional mock trial.[295] The climactic scene was the chalking-up of the who's-who list of scapegoats, most of whom were promptly dropped and the rest forgiven by the next president, who also happened to be Reagan's VP involved in the same affair.[296] Bill Breeden, a Unitarian minister from Odon, Indiana, was the only person jailed from the entire Iran-Contra affair. It was Reagan's National Security Adviser Admiral

Poindexter's hometown where Bill, out of principle, stole a street sign named "John Poindexter Street."

Then it was only natural to reimpose sanctions on Iraq just a few years after for crimes done under our government's watch. What we Americans fail to realize or care for is that these actions have real-life consequences. "It is easy to forget that, in a developing world, cents can make a difference between life and death; the enforcement of embargoes can mean silent suffocation for those whose voices cannot be heard—mothers in the slums of Mumbai, basket weavers in the suburbs of Mombasa or women trying to oppose illegal mining activities in South America," writes Frankopan. "And all so that Iran is forced to disavow a nuclear programme built on US technology sold to a despotic, intolerant and corrupt regime in the 1970s."[297]

When one president added the Houthis—the de-facto government of Yemen—to the FTO list on his way out of office, it became illegal for even charity organizations to continue their aid in that devastated war-torn country and left millions of children to continue to starve to death. What is more striking is the fact that the Houthis were actively fighting al-Qaeda until the US recruited the latter to help defeat Yemen's de facto government.[298] The perpetual drone attacks to "neutralize" potential suspects have killed as many as 50 civilians in a single raid in Syria, likely even more undisclosed. Drones take a Machiavellian approach to Sun Tzu's strategy of *winning without a fight*. They blur the lines of war as most of their uses have been in "friendly" nations, killing more than two thousand people in Pakistan by CIA's own estimates.[299]

Given the current state of affairs, sometimes philosophical discussions take a psychopathic turn as one finds himself comparing human atrocities. For example, the 1370 massacre of 300 civilians in Limoges by the Black Prince showcased England's brutality. However, when considering the 56.4 million deaths during WWII, the Limoges massacre pales in comparison. ISIS's beheadings are deplorable, but the civilians' blown-to-pieces after drone strikes overshadow them. After each drone attack, the locals have to gather those pieces in hopes of identifying and burying their loved ones properly.

In 1998, President Clinton authorized the bombing of a Sudanese pharmaceutical plant that made half the country's medicine, including antimalarials. At the same time, sanctions against them prevented medicine imports, resulting in tens of thousands of deaths in one of the world's poorest countries.[300] These sanctions are nothing short of medieval sieges with expectant civilian casualties, which should reflexively raise the question: how is sanctioning not a form of active warfare? They are indeed the lowest forms of warfare, as noted by Master Sun in *The*

Art of War. The intentions behind such acts are made explicit by our government's offer to remove Sudan from the terrorist list if they paid $335 million and supported US and Israel's Middle East aggressions.[301] That sort of extortion of one of the poorest nations following years of siege tactics at drone diplomacy by the largest global power is wrong on many levels. Interestingly, the Prophet foretold of the Antichrist being followed by *drones* (Arabic: غاسيب) in his destructive path around the world (*Jami` at-Tirmidhi* 2240).

It is not surprising then to see many of the patriotic young souls operating these drones questioning the true motives behind their indiscriminate murders. Our imperial army has a legacy of dissent from soldiers trained through a moral plight only to be sent to slaughter civilians, as detailed in Chris Lombardi's *I Ain't Marching Anymore*. Thus, we have conscientious whistleblowers like Brandon Bryant, Daniel Hale, Chelsea Manning, and Edward Snowden, whose bravery is punished with incarceration. At the same time, the masterminds of the entire thing are praised and awarded.

How America celebrates its warring concepts by projecting hyperbolized values onto its forced immoral actions also has schizophrenic traits.[302] When Air Force pilot Charles Clement became disillusioned with US activities abroad and refused to fly any missions, he was committed to a psychiatric hospital and then dishonorably discharged. Afterward, he completed medical school and volunteered as a physician helping the guerrillas in El Salvador. While civilians bully soldiers into submission by saluting their patriotism, any time actual soldiers question the immorality of war, they are met with harsh punishments. Hence, the system breeds immorality and only allows the corrupt to climb to the top, punishing out all with a conscience. Even Jack Ryan, a twenty-one-year veteran FBI agent, was fired for refusing to investigate nonviolent activists in 1987, eventually rendering him destitute and homeless.

Veterans are tossed away like used napkins upon their return, as the society no longer has any need for their post-war-torn selves or opinions. Those surviving combat suffer withdrawal symptoms from intoxicating violence, often leading to other forms of addiction and suicide. Within the causal debates surrounding catastrophes like the World Wars, centuries of greedy imperial ambitions leading up to them are overlooked. When imperial bluffs culminate in stand-offs, ignorant civilians are sent to fight for the elites' egos. Thus, we had an imperialist Churchill writing from the safety of his mansion about the martyrdom of soldiers "inspired not only by love of country but a widespread conviction that human freedom was challenged by military and Imperial tyranny [not Brittain's, of course]. If two lives or ten lives were required by their commanders to kill one German, no word of complaint ever rose from the fighting troops [dead soldiers seldom complain]...No slaughter however desolation prevented them from returning to the charge."[303] This convenient revision hides over 300,000 British military court offenses of dissent during the war and the senseless suffering on fields like Somme.[304]

Lines of justice are redrawn, erasing the Allies' military and imperial tyranny that jeopardized the freedom of the defeated. Dehumanization of the enemy further attempts to justify the silence of the fallen, as if the ones on the other side were not victims of the same "nightmarish game of chess where all possible moves are bad."[305] Churchill's attitude towards the Germans only surfaced his racism towards the entire Orient, where even Gandhi was not spared.[306] His imperialist and racist views were transparent in his 1896 article in *The Saturday Review*, where he shrieked at the potential success of the Cuban revolution: "after years of fighting, another black republic."[307] The US swiftly answered his prayers. After getting the green light from the bankers, brokers, and businessmen, public opinion was manufactured to "free Cuba," which was then invaded and won from Spain in 1898 with immediate foreign economic ventures. The Cubans were not allowed to come to the negotiations, nor was their fighting force allowed to enter Santiago.

Almost poetically, the Old World's Imperial struggles resulted in their bankruptcy and destruction, which financed and propelled the New World's Imperialism.[308] A desperate British Empire then frantically retreated from its Oriental colonies, leaving a trail of lesser-known war casualties.[309] Their retreat from the Indian subcontinent and Palestine resembled evasion of crime scenes with devastating consequences. Perhaps things would have been different if they had even a little skin in the game rather than all-out profit from their market shares.

Meanwhile, opportunists exploit soldiers' honest patriotism with impunity. Retired army officer Daniel Sjursen's work, including *Patriotic Dissent*, in this regard is noteworthy. Perhaps, the best way to support our troops would be to avoid sending them to die in unjust for-profit wars. This simple concept is obscured by the alternative reality argued by the media, politicians, and high-ranking military officials. They all are united in their economic incentives, which becomes more apparent during times of stress.[310] At the turn of the 20th century, all the famous industrialists were amassing their fortunes at the cost of wretched working conditions that led to many violent protests and labor riots. In 1914, the National Guards violently subdued a similar protest at Ludlow, Colorado. *The New York Times* describes the desperate workers as "savage-minded men" who must be "quelled by force." Woodrow Wilson complied by sending federal troops leading to another massacre of sixty-six men, women, and children without addressing the conditions that led to their suicidal path.[311]

All of our (social)media does a remarkable job of keeping the masses misinformed, for the majority are too apathetic. Although almost the entire British army was wiped out within the first three months of World War I, none of it was reported domestically. Instead, the media blatantly lied about the cargo of *Lusitania* that led to its sinking, which manufactured consent for the US to join the war. Of the few reports that remained true from that period were the writings of Du Bois in the *Atlantic Monthly*. While historical revisions portray national support for the war, the actual public opinion was best demonstrated through the many protests leading to President Wilson's passing of the Espionage Act of 1917.

Most of them gain directly from their investments in the military-industrial complex. Even "non-profit" organizations like NPR depend on contributions from these same industries, which is reflected in the tone of their reporting—perhaps even more by the things they choose not to report. Air Force veteran Christian Sorensen details much of this in his book *Understanding the War Industry*. Massive rewriting of the Vietnam War continues in both academic reporting and mainstream entertainment.[312] This allowed for another eighteen years of economic war behind our backs in that same country following the US's withdrawal. (Similarly, the economic war in Afghanistan continues today even after the US's official departure.[313]) Unsurprisingly, historian Bruce Franklin's book detailing such crimes only received nominal media coverage. Another by Michael Lind justifying the war was paraded across the mainstream media, including Op-Eds in the *New York Times* and the *Washington Post*.[314]

Many government officials come directly from these war industries. A notable example is the Council of Foreign Relations (CFR), which has consistently supplied top members to the presidential cabinets since 1921. There are additional profiteers that we may not readily recognize, like Wall Street.[315] The loop is then closed by many high-ranking military officials retiring to top positions in these industries, as well as lobbying to continue their financial gains from their knowledge while receiving six-figure pensions. These revolving doors between the regulators and regulated are not limited to the arms industry but a wide array of companies, including the media giants and special interest groups. The fools are the ones regurgitating propaganda, who believe that there is no conflict of interest nor incentive in allowing the foxes to manage the slaughterhouse. Sociologist Arlie Hochschild once lived among the right-wing base studying the great political paradox of why people vote for politicians who only harm them and wrote a book about it.[316] In summary, the recipe calls for desperation, bad education, and propaganda simmered with a dash of truth.

Blind faith in our politicians and leaders is certainly not well-founded. The declassified Kennedy tapes and documents detailing the October 1962 events provide chilling details of how close we came to obliteration without any consideration for morality. Their lack of communication and arrogance only reveal a divine miracle that allowed us to persist despite the failure of global leadership. Yet, little seems to change through the revolving cabinets and foreign policies. Even with the world watching, as the US left war-torn Afghanistan in August 2021, one of its last acts of blatant terrorism was to bomb a car, killing seven children of the same family. The media immediately called it a "righteous act" with no supporting evidence or repercussions.[317] Similarly, no evidence was demanded from the ever-lying Zionist regime's October 7th claims before the entire Western civilization gave it a carte blanche for a genocide in Gaza.

One may wonder what gives the government the right to commit such crimes. Turns out, it is each and every one of us in our times of despair, anger, and hatred, passing resolutions like the Authorization for the Use of Military Force (AUMF). It gave the President unrestrained authority "to use all necessary and appropriate force..." This single sentence served as the legal pretext for all the tortures, unlawful detentions, collective punishments, and air and ground terrors that lasted over two decades. We should have known better, as a similar resolution was also given to President Lyndon Johnson in 1964 for his manufactured Gulf of Tonkin attack, authorizing him to "take all necessary measures to repel any armed attack against the forces of the United States and to prevent further aggression."

It is darkly comical that our aggressive war machine is called the Department of Defense, as we ever had the need. Our leaders act with impunity and slaughter millions with the stroke of a pen, then profit further by admitting it in their memoirs. Historically, most acts of gross human rights violations were done under this same "defense" claim. Hitler's invasion of Poland comes to mind, which he ironically modeled after the US's legacy of deceiving the public through staged border incidents and attacks, leading to invasions under the pretense of seeking peace. Or as Israel calls it, "de-escalation through escalation." Who can hold *US* accountable, when we even refuse to be a part of the International Criminal Court (ICC)?

At this point, it is hard to trust our government, the CIA, and the media given their history of deceit. For instance, Nayirah's Congressional testimony about Saddam's troops leaving babies to die in incubators turned out to be a fabrication.[318] Nor was there any evidence of Gadhafi's soldiers using Viagra for rape in the aftermath of their government's overturn.[319] Nevertheless, every US intervention in foreign lands was done through a humanitarian plight that caused awful atrocities, leaving the regions in a far worse condition. While President Obama rushed in to save the Libyans from a ruler who had provided them with free healthcare, he soon left them *free* to starve and be slaughtered by the extremists. It was only a completion of the prior attacks on Tripoli in 1986, also under false pretenses, which were deservingly described as acts of terrorism by Professor Stephen Shalom.[320]

These are not isolated incidents but a pattern of behavior that has been going on for centuries. Those in power masterfully exploit the goodwill of the majority through these staged premises. It is all a twisted version of the "Noble Lie" of Plato in the *Republic*. We still see shameless public pleas for such foreign intervention like the essay by Paul Johnson in the April 18, 1993 issue of *The New York Times Magazine* titled "Colonialism's Back-And Not a Moment Too Soon." In reality, our government could care less about anything other than its financial interests. Thus, our full support for similar terrorist regimes worldwide as they follow in America's footsteps in raining down airstrikes on civilians without due process. Often, such discussions with unlearned hatemongers are extremely disheartening and unproductive. Their counterarguments serve to obfuscate the truth and distract from the real motives of arrogance and avarice.

III: The Muslims are Here

The Prophet said: "Let him who believes in God and the Last Day speak good, or keep silent; let him who believes in God and the Last Day be generous to his neighbor; let him who believes in God and the Last Day be generous to his guest. (Sahih al-Bukhari 6136)

In the past, Orientalists erroneously called it Muhammadanism, but Islam derives its name from the concepts of submission (*taslim*) and peace (*salam*). Specifically, it is submission to the oneness of God with an emphasis on establishing peace on earth, as exemplified by the final messenger (*Sunan Ibn Majah* 3694). This reflexive definition needs to be internalized for anyone who can attest to it is Muslim, as God declares: "Abraham was neither a Jew nor a Christian; he was a Muslim [submitted in all uprightness] and was not a polytheist" (a*l-'Imran* 3:67).

Classifying Islam as a *religion* can also be misleading. Some scholars of comparative religion, like Wilfred Cantwell Smith, have even proposed abandoning the term "religion" for its distorted view. The Arabic word *deen*, commonly translated as "religion" in the Qur'an, actually represents only one-half of the Islamic way of life, with *dunya* being the other half. Denying either half would make the other unrealizable. "The 'political' nature of Islam must not be understood as an attempt to increase the political power of an institutionalized Islam, as neo-orientalist commentators like Daniel Pipes wrongly contend in portraying Islam as a threat to the West," explains Shedinger. "The creation of such a power imbalance would be un-

Islamic. Rather, the 'political' aspect of Islam serves the interests of the 'spiritual' aspect, which itself drives the realization of the political ideal of justice and egalitarianism."[321]

Secularism, as it is understood in the West, is inherently contradictory to Islam. Any attempt at secularization also corrupts Islam's fundamental values. Nearly all such terms have developed from a misunderstanding of religion in the West, which cannot be applied to Islamic theology due to their different source codes. However, from a proper perspective, all of the secularization's integral components—the disenchantment of nature, the desacralization of politics, and the deconsecration of values—are already inherent in the core Islamic values.[322] They enabled Islam to timelessly merge with different cultures in forming "innumerable, alternative social and cultural blueprints for the conduct of human life on earth," explains Professor Karamustafa.[323]

The Qur'an is the verbatim words of God, sent down via Archangel Gabriel through His final messenger, making it inimitable. It rejects *any* religion's claim to sole ownership of God and the afterlife. "Say, [O Prophet,] 'He is God —One [and Indivisible]; God—the Sustainer [needed by all]. He has never had offspring, nor was He born. And there is none comparable to Him'" (*al-Ikhlas* 112:1-4). The Hebrew word translated in English as "God" in the Old Testament is *Elohim* or *El-Elohim*, the same as the ones in its sister language, Arabic *Allah* or *Al-Ilah*. Therefore, even linguistically, all three Abrahamic faiths pray to the same God.

Islamic doctrine and laws are above all failures of human misinterpretations. Shaikh Bayyah stresses the seriousness of engaging with these texts through reception, comprehension, and application, and not subjecting them to the whims of individuals, groups, or misconceived interests.[324] It is uncouth to attack Islam by citing examples of failed corrupt leaders claiming the banner of Islam. Anyone making such claims should first measure the representative group's adherence to the core Islamic values and their application. Western discourse's tendency to demonize the politicization of Islam serves to maintain the rhetorical structure that constructs the West as the seat of civilization and progress while portraying the Muslim world as backward and primitive.[325]

For the West, Islam had long been contained within the Muslim world, out of sight...or so it is made to appear. In reality, Muslims have always been in Europe, and even here in America, dating back to the 9th century, long before Protestantism existed.[326] The entire Christian Reformation movement was likely inspired by those European Muslims and the Qur'an. Early non-native explorers of the Americas included notable Muslims, who assimilated into native tribes and left many visible traces. So many Turkish Muslims lived in Jamestown in the 1600s that a law was passed prohibiting any further addition of such "infidels" into the colony.[327] The Wahab brothers established the Wahab Village in North Carolina in the 1700s, and Yusef bin 'Ali, also known as Joseph Benhaley, fought as a scout under General Sumter in the American Revolutionary War.

Jefferson not only owned a copy of the Qur'an but also explicitly included Muslims in his republic's vision.[328] The recognition of the Prophet as one of eighteen great law-givers in history reflected the founders' reverence for Islamic ideals. (Such reverence is accompanied by a suboptimal understanding of the faith as demonstrated through the injudicious frieze of the Prophet between Charlemagne and Justinian on the north wall of the US Supreme Court.) Muslims have also served in the US Army, with Hajji 'Ali's epitaph now erected in Quartzsite, Arizona. American sympathy towards Algerian revolutionary Emir Abdelkader (1808-83 CE) led to the naming of Elkader, Iowa in 1845. Mecca, Indiana, was founded in 1873 by Muslim Arab immigrants. Albanian Muslims established a mosque in Michigan as early as 1912, where thousands of Arab immigrants were welcomed by Henry Ford to power his industry for their strong work ethics and prohibition of intoxicants.

Many Americans also discovered Islam through their personal pursuits, such as Mohammed Alexander Russel Webb (1846-1916 CE), publisher of the *Missouri Republican* and *St Joseph Gazette*. After spreading the message of Islam worldwide, he established the first Muslim American periodical in 1893 called the *Muslim World*. From the West Coast was the famed political cartoonist Homer Davenport (1867-1912 CE), who acquired the largest export of pure Arabian horses due to his surreptitious conversion to Islam in 1906. Wali Akram (1904-94 CE), formerly Walter Gregg, founded the United Islamic Society of America and started the first halal grocery in St Louis and Cleveland in the 1920s. And who can forget the widely broadcasted Islam of the youngest heavyweight champion of the world, Muhammad Ali, in 1964?

With the fall of the last Ottoman Caliphate at the end of World War I, suddenly, there came a moment when no single Muslim country remained in the entire world. The continuous Caliphate that led the *ummah* since the Messenger was dismantled (although the *leading* by then was mostly symbolic). Then the exponential rise of global migration through shifting political and socio-economical climates and the ease of travel opened the entire world to the message of Islam.

The Prophet said: "Imminently, there will come a time when the nations gather against you, just as people gather around a feast...you will be numerous in those times, but you will be as useless as the foam of the sea, and God will remove the fear that your enemies used to posses from you from their chests, and He will place al-Wahn (love of life, and hatred of death) in your hearts." (Sunan Abu Dawud 2/210)

Once unleashed, it only became a matter of time before the West started to see the appeal of Islam's message, which posed a threat to the elite's capitalistic *religion*. Therefore, the top-down propaganda machine revved up the fear and hate within the common people, and the media gave preferential attention to prominent American Christians like Pat Robertson and Jerry Vines who labeled Islam as "evil" and its prophet a "terrorist."[329] It is the same Prophet regarding whom the Creator said: "And Verily, you [O Muhammad] are on an exalted [standard of] character" (*al-Qalam* 68:4). To defame a messenger of God whom God Himself venerated only illustrates the unsavory character of the accuser. Historian Thomas Carlyle once said, "The lies which well-meaning zeal has heaped round this man [Muhammad] are disgraceful to ourselves only." Muslims have been even labeled as "Satan worshippers" but God's promise is clear: "Those who insult God and His Messenger will be rejected by God in this world and the next—He has prepared a humiliating torment for them—and those who undeservedly insult believing men and women will bear the guilt of slander and flagrant sin" (*al-Ahzab* 33:57-8).

Today, Islamophobia is constantly being normalized, with the media selectively focusing on the acts of deranged extremists who claim to be Muslims without giving actual Muslims equal time to respond to the malicious distortions of their faith. The world's leaders drop everything to join in solidarity against Islam in classic Orwellian *doublethink*, while the media looks the other way when barbarous atrocities are directed against Muslims in places like Palestine, Bosnia, Srebrenica, India, and Xinxiang. Professor Deepa Kumar explores much of this in *Islamophobia and the Politics of Empire*. Except, the more hatred they spewed, the more they helped spread the message of Islam to those who would have otherwise lived their entire lives unassumed. "They try to extinguish God's light with their mouths, but God insists on bringing His light to its fullness, even if the disbelievers hate it," says God (*at-Tawbah* 9:32). At the end of the day, religion is interpretation, which displays all of our shortcomings. Ibn Qayyim al-Jawziyyah discussed this classic problem in *I'lam al-muwaqqi'in* back in the 8th century in a chapter entitled, "On the inappropriateness of calling a fatwa the 'ruling of God.'"[330] Hence, any interpretation of Islam that misses its goals of promoting peace and the well-being of humanity cannot be Islamic.

They plotted and planned, but We too planned, even while they perceived it not. See how their scheming ended: We destroyed them utterly, along with all their people. As a result of their evil deeds, their homes are desolate ruins—there truly is a sign in this for those who know. (an-Naml 27:50-2)

It is unacceptable for any non-practicing pedant to define Islam as akin to a non-practicing medical specialist commenting on the standard of care. Even in our flawed judicial system, we recognize the importance of being judged by one's peers—in this case, practicing Muslims with knowledge and values consistent with the core of Islam. While outside criticism can sometimes be valuable, they often have underlying prejudice or misunderstanding from the lack of personal experience, for Islam is a lived reality. Anyone allowing such rhetoric from hatemongers disguised as panjandrums is also culpable, regardless of their excuses. Dr. Yasir Qadhi accurately labels them as ultracrepidarian pseudo-intellectuals.

This book may not be a Pulitzer candidate, but many "winning" discussions by non-Muslims are plagued with errors that even novice students of knowledge can identify. Their contemned disdain beats like the telltale heart of their narrative, just like the "knowledgeable" discourse of the Orientalists of the past like Arthur Balfour and Lord Cromer.[331] It was simply "knowledge" that, after decades of governing in the Orient, Cromer deduced: "Accuracy is abhorrent to the Oriental mind...The European is a close reasoner; his statements of fact are devoid of any ambiguity; he is a natural logician, albeit he may not have studied logic; he is by nature sceptical and requires proof before he can accept the truth of any proposition; his trained intelligence works like a piece of mechanism."[332] Perhaps making such bold claims without proof argues otherwise.

Imam al-Shāṭibī explained this classic pathology of "the ignorant arguing their positions using erroneous proofs or using sound proofs while neglecting other proofs or failing to take into account others."[333] Malcolm X was victimized by the contemporary media and warned of their deceiving the masses into hating the oppressed and loving the oppressors. Our privatized media plays an incriminating role in manufacturing consent for their corporate motives disguised as a top-down objective facade. When some of it leaks into the back page of some media outlet, it does not serve as a *non sequitur* "proof" against the overall theme. Janine Jackson's work on *Fair* is just the tip of the iceberg, attempting to highlight much of this debauchery.

Abu al-Qasim al-Samarqandi (874-956 CE) once attributed all of the world's tribulations to news transmitters, consumers, and seekers.[334] They do not care to be openly hateful, yet we are too worried about political correctness to call them racist bigots. Kierkegaard, centuries before the advent of television and social media, warned of *the daily press* as *the evil principle* of the modern world, whose capacity for *degeneration is sophistically without limit*. He warned against its ability to manipulate the masses beyond reason or control. His prediction of a convenient "talking tube" that could be heard worldwide was remarkable in its farsight, as was his fear of its rendering the realization of any religious values impossible.[335] The Prophet also warned of the end of times when falsehood would rise to the clouds and instantly reach the horizons.

Muslims have been—and continue to be—heavily persecuted and brutally murdered around the world by terrorists belonging to all faiths, far more than their publicized counterparts. "As for the disbelievers, they are guardians of one another. And unless you [believers] act likewise, there will be great oppression and corruption in the land," warns God (*al-Anfal* 8:73). The conditions of Muslims in many places are already at advanced stages of genocide based on Dr. Gregory Stanton's classification.[336] Perhaps this, in time, will unite the divided ummah, just like the Mongol brutality once united all the different Christian churches. Most reasonable people can see the atrocities in plain sight. Those who continue to deny and argue otherwise are extremists with blood on their hands. Just as in their own judicial system, denying an evident crime is meaningless to the jury; the evidence stacked against such rabid terrorists makes their arguments and denials moot.

"There is no doubt that a central aim of the Qur'an is to establish a viable social order on earth that will be just and ethically based," wrote Fazlur Rahman.[337] It brought Arabia and the known world out of *jahiliyyah* within a few generations of Islam's renewal. Living on the same planet and coming from the same parents, when did humanity become so mindless and cruel as not to offer others the same treatment we demand for ourselves? While wishing better for our fellow humans would be ideal, we cannot even meet the bare minimum. Was there ever a time in human history when we transcended such animalistic behavior that lowered us from all that is supposed to make us the more advanced species?

Do not argue with the People of the Book unless gracefully, except with those who act wrongfully. And say, "We believe in what has been revealed to us and what was revealed to you. Our God and your God is One. And to Him we [fully] submit." (al-'Ankabut 29:46)

ROAD TO DECIVILIZATION

Say, "Would you dispute with us about God, while He is our Lord and your Lord? We are accountable for our deeds and you for yours. And we are devoted to Him [alone]. Do you claim that Abraham, Ishmael, Isaac, Jacob, and his descendants were all Jews or Christians?" Say, "Who is more knowledgeable: you or God?" Who does more wrong than those who hide the testimony they received from God? And God is never unaware of what you do. (al-Baqarah 2:139-40)

I: An Idea is Like a Virus

> The conquest of the earth, which mostly means the taking it away from those who have a different complexion or slightly flatter noses than ourselves, is not a pretty thing when you look into it too much. What redeems it is the idea only. An idea at the back of it; not a sentimental pretense but an idea; and an unselfish belief in the idea—something you can set up, and bow down before, and offer a sacrifice to...[Joseph Conrad, *Heart of Darkness*]

The true weight of civilization is demonstrated through how those in power treat the ones they have authority over. This chapter aims to explore how we measure up thus far and whether we have maintained civility. Let us travel all the way back to the beginning.

Although Adam and Eve's *submission* made them the first *Muslims* on earth, it did not take long for the first murder in our history (i.e., Cain and Abel). This schism within their family continued to engulf their descendants until the time of Noah, whose 950 years of preaching resulted in only a handful of followers. (Perhaps it is somewhat encouraging given the significantly larger number of believers spread all across the earth today.) With the few remaining *Muslims* aboard the Ark, humanity got a reboot while the wrongdoers drowned in their arrogance.

However, this kerfuffle of yore did not take long to resurface. Among Noah's lineage was a remarkable *Muslim*, Abraham, whom God calls an *ummah* of his own for his *submission* to the oneness of God (i.e., *tawhid*) and fathering the three major monotheistic religions of today. "We sent Noah and Abraham, and gave prophethood and scripture to their offspring: among them, there were some who were rightly guided, but many were lawbreakers," informs God (*al-Hadid* 57:26). Abraham's sons—Ishmael and Ishaq—followed in his legacy and were devout Muslims themselves. Ishaq/Isaac was the father of Yaqub/Israel, whose son Yusuf/Joseph played a pivotal role in the rise of Egypt's Middle/New Kingdom. Yaqub's twelve sons gave rise to the twelve tribes of Israel, whose lineage includes Moses and Jesus. On the other side of Abraham's family was Ishmael, whose lineage came down to Prophet Muhammad. In poetic symmetry, Ishmael also had twelve sons forming the twelve Arabized tribes of Mecca.

This distinction going back to the sons of Abraham has resulted in an asymmetric *otherization* of Muslims vs. Judeo-Christians, overlooking their similarities and fueling an updated form of Denys Hay's "idea of Europe."[338] Islam's recognition of Judaism and Christianity makes it nearer to both than they are to each other. "In this respect it would seem that the term 'Judeo-Christian' is a misnomer...coined, politically, for the sole purpose of excluding Muslims," wrote Dr. Hathout. "A more appropriate description of our current civilization would be Judeo-Christian-Islamic,"[339] highlighting the collaboration between the faiths that ultimately led to our civilization.

The fact that Islam is a continuation of the *same* message from the *same* God is often lost in discourse. According to God, all righteous people of *tawhid* before the Qur'an's revelations were also *Muslims*. "The Jews and Christians each say, 'Follow our faith to be [rightly] guided.' Say, [O Prophet,] 'No! We follow the faith of Abraham, the upright—who was not a polytheist'" (*al-Baqarah* 2:135). This shared lineage unites all Judeo-Christian-Muslims as *Semites*, referring to the lineage of Shem, son of Noah. Thus, the history of Muslims naturally takes us back to Adam through all three Abrahamic faiths, which deserves a review to understand our current world.

The Semitic people had lived around Palestine dating as far back as the

3rd millennia BC and were often referred to as the Caananites of many separate tribes. However, the origin of the term "Hebrew" is as uncertain as their migration into Canaan, which is estimated to be around 1400 BC.[340] Some believe that the term originated as an outsider's description of the Israelites, as *ibrim/ivri* appears in the Hebrew Bible as another name for Abraham.[341] After moving from Ur to Haran to Egypt, Abraham settled in Hebron, while the Hebrews slowly migrated into the region. Their territorial possession remained transient and nominal until the establishment of the Kingdom of David in the 1st millennium BC.[342]

Then the Bible mentions the Kingdom of Solomon splitting into the Kingdom of Israel (Samaria) to the north and the Kingdom of Judea in the south, with Solomon's descendants ruling the latter. The historic veracity of this Biblical narrative, however, is highly contested. Nevertheless, the Neo-Assyrian Empire conquered Samaria in 722 BC, and the Neo-Babylonian Empire conquered Judea in 538 BC. Many of the previously exiled Jews then returned to Jerusalem to build the Second Temple. After Alexander's conquest of the Achaemenid Empire in 332 BC, Judea fell under Greek rule and split into traditional and Hellenized influences. Then the Maccabean Revolt in 164 BC saw Jerusalem freed from the Seleucid Empire, with the cleansing of the Temple marking the subsequent Hanukkah celebration.

Judea was conquered again and turned into a Roman province in 64 BC. During the Jewish-Roman Wars of 66-136 CE, many Jews were expelled from the region, with some remaining in Galilee, which gradually became Christian after the 3rd century. In 70 CE, Emperor Titus destroyed the Second Temple along with nearly all of Jerusalem's inhabitants, fulfilling God's warning to the disciples (*al-Ma'idah* 5:115). The Jews were not allowed to occupy the city until the Sasanian conquest in 614, at which point only 10-15% of the population of Palestine was Jewish. After withstanding three centuries of Christian persecution, the Byzantine Jews again related their deliverance by the Persians to that of Cyrus over a thousand years ago. Vengeance was immediate with the massacre of thousands of Christians across Mesopotamia, including Patriarch Anastasius.

The "deliverance'" was short-lived when Khosrow II ordered Jews to leave Jerusalem to accommodate the Gentiles' rebuilding of the city.[343] In 630, Heraclius rode victoriously through Jerusalem's Gate of Repentance and returned the True Cross to the apse of the Church of the Resurrection, as miraculously foretold in the Qur'an (*ar-Rum* 30:2-4). It was the same year as the Prophet's triumphant return to Mecca, but in stark contrast to his remarkable amnesty, Heraclius immediately authorized the massacre of Jews throughout the empire.[344] The fall of Jerusalem resulted in another round of rape and pillage, with some accounts reporting thirty thousand civilian casualties. Even patriarchs like Sophronius and his predecessor contributed to the persecution of Jews and Monophysite Christians, which only opened the doors for the next succession.

By the time Muslims entered Jerusalem, the Temple Mount had been turned into a sewage dump. In 638 CE, the city became part of the Caliphate, ushering in a period of stability that lasted for centuries. In 1099 CE, the Crusaders launched a brutal invasion, killing almost all of the city's 70,000 inhabitants. After a century's occupation, Jerusalem was liberated by Salah al-Din in 1187, on the very slopes where Jesus once delivered his sermon following the evening of *qadr*. European ambitions for reconquest thereafter were thwarted by their newfound interest in the Far East and the New World, which presented higher monetary gains. It allowed another stretch of relatively peaceful Ottoman rule from 1517 to World War I.

Meanwhile, in Christian Europe, Jewish persecution increased dramatically after the mid-14th century, with vicious pogroms and expulsions from various cities.[345] They were vituperated even for the Bubonic Plague. Martin Luther, a revered leader of the Protestant Reformation, advocated for the complete segregation of Jews from Christians, forced labor, and the destruction of Jewish homes and synagogues in his 1524 publication, ominously entitled *On the Jews and Their Lies*.[346] It would appear that Adolf Hitler got his hands on a copy of that book and took a page from it.

Islamic societies, on the other hand, were known for their tolerance and justice towards Jewish refugees from all persecuted lands.[347] Such egalitarian values were founded on the Qur'an and the teachings of the Prophet, as exemplified by Caliph 'Umar's demolition of a mosque constructed illegally on Jewish property in Damascus. In doing so, he was merely following the Prophet's warning that those who wrong a Jew or a Christian will have him as his accuser on the Day of Judgment.[348]

Although the initial relationship between the Ottomans and the British was "friendly," the latter's ambition soon brewed animosity with active schemes of conquest. A rising Western elitist zeal for Zionism at the turn of the 19th century further aided it along with the discovery of Mid-East oil. European Zionism eventually culminated in the Balfour Declaration of 1917, which with remarkable vagueness, allowed the creation of an illegal Jewish nation on Muslim land. In desperation to win WWI and secure oil interests, the Brits promised this same land simultaneously to local Arabs, Armenians, Palestinians, Husayn Sharif of Mecca, and Zionists, while secretly claiming it for themselves through the Sykes-Picot agreement. It was also motivated by deep British antisemitism towards its own "great and abiding Jewish problem."[349]

Thus, Lord Balfour wrote in secrecy to one of the most prominent Zionists of the time, Lord Rothschild: "His Majesty's Government [viewing] with favour the establishment in Palestine of a national home for the Jewish people."[350] Rothschild, along with Baron Maurice de Hirsch's Jewish Colonization Association, later financed much of the extensive early Zionist land grabs and subsidies.[351] Hitler initially spoke in support of deporting German Jews in the spring of 1938, except no European nation was willing to take them in (something Netanyahu would later reenact with the Gazans).[352] Additionally, a Zionist Israel offered a solution to Britain's "Jewish problem" and provided access to Persian pipelines and potential Palestinian reserves.[353] Balfour clearly stated the game plan for the subsequent century: "The four Great Powers are committed to Zionism. And Zionism, be it right or wrong, good or bad, is rooted in age-long traditions, in present needs, in future hopes, of far greater import than the desires and prejudices of the 700,000 [Palestine] Arabs who now inhabit that ancient land."[354]

The outcome was clear as President Wilson's foreign policy adviser, Edward House, observed the French and the British to be "making [the Middle East] a breeding place for future war."[355] The settler colonizers were first armed by Britain and Communist Czechoslovakia, setting off the dramatically imbalanced perennial David vs. Goliath cliche, culminating in a drawn-out Palestinian genocide. Ethnic cleansing of the native communities was immediately apparent at the onset. A refusal to even recognize the 91% Arab population of the land by calling them "non-Jewish" from the start was a Zionist political strategy that has been continually employed.[356] Additionally, the narrative that Israel was created in an empty desert after the Holocaust is patently false, as the region is one of the longest continually inhabited lands on earth. A malicious slogan popularized by Israel Zangwill—A land without a people for a people without a land—hid the typical racist European supremacy. Concern for the natives who did not "deserve" the land from that mindset was expressed by the first president of Israel, Chaim Weizmann, saying: "The British told us that there are some hundred thousand niggers and for those there is no value."[357]

It highlights the racist mindset of the Zionists, only reflecting the European colonial *status quo* deployed globally. This politicide of Palestinians is at the core of Zionism and was in full display even in the British Mandate of 1922.[358] The Crane-King Commission of 1919, the Haycraft Commission of 1921, the Shaw Commission of 1930, the Hope-Simpson Commission of 1930, and the French Commission of 1931 and 1932 have all documented the grave injustices committed against the Arab Palestinians. They recommended that Jewish immigration should be suspended indefinitely and that a government representing the population should be installed.[359] Instead, the partition of 1947—initially proposed by the Peel Commission in 1937—granted the Jews, who accounted for only 32.5% of the population occupying 5.77% of the land, an astounding 56% of the total land.

Even that was not enough for the illegal apartheid regime. It immediately launched a barbaric offensive on the eve of its birth by forcefully occupying over 80% of the land. The result was the savage expulsion of Arabs from their ancestral homes (i.e., the first *Nakba* or Catastrophe, النكبة) with the final goal per Joseph Weitz (the administrator of Jewish colonization) stated: "Between ourselves it must be clear that there is no room for both people together in this country...the only solution is a Palestine without Arabs...not one village, not one tribe, should be left."[360] Their tactics were harsher than the Nazis, massacring unarmed men, women, and children in places like Deyr Yasin, Ein al-Zeitun, Lydda, Safsaf, Saliha, and Duwaima. An Israeli soldier at Duwaima recounted: "They killed some eighty to one hundred Arabs, women and children. Their children were killed by smashing their skulls with clubs."[361] Such events were simultaneously broadcast on the radio to frighten other Palestinians to also run for their lives.

Even when the massacres were state-sponsored, blame was quickly diverted to the flanks, which continues to mask the mainstream moral depravity of the occupation. For instance, both the Stern gang and Lehi were officially declared terrorist groups after the assassination of Count Folke Bernadotte in 1948. The few members of those terrorist groups that were arrested in the initial public display were soon pardoned and released in 1949. The rest of those terrorists were then integrated into the Israeli army that continues to use the same unlimited violent tactics under a defensive disguise. Folke's assassination was one of the first of many to follow of anyone who dared to express any concerns about the apparent ethnic cleansing that continues to this day. The general pathology of the occupation is thus evident through the election of officially recognized terrorists like Yitzhak Shamir, the Lehi leader who ordered the assassination of Folke, as their leader for two terms. Similarly, Avraham Stern became a national hero celebrated through an annual memorial day and an official postage stamp. Even the street where Stern was assassinated was later named after him, and the building turned into a museum called Beit Yair under the patronage of the defense ministry.

Entire cities were violently depopulated and rebuilt with Hebrewised names to erase them from collective memory. Popular beach resorts and theme parks were developed over mass graves. Elsewhere, the Jewish

National Fund initiated the "Plant A Tree" campaign over hundreds of destroyed villages to bury indigenous culture and rewrite history. Today, many non-native pine trees hide their crimes in plain sight, aiding Israel's origin myth of a "land without people," yet highlighting their true origin by resembling European forests.[362] Defense Minister Moshe Dayan boasted in 1969: "Jewish villages were built in the place of Arab villages. You do not even know the names of these villages, and I do not blame you because geography books no longer exist...Nahlal arose in the place of Mahlul... There is not a single place in this country that didn't have a former Arab population."[363] This method has only been perfected by the Zionist slaughterhouse as they continue to effortlessly drop "dumb bombs" to flatten entire crowded city blocks of Gazans while auctioning off the land to their global financiers.

When Christian extremism under Nazi Rule displaced more European Jews, they were again welcomed into Palestine with remarkable Arab hospitality. Some of these same refugees then went on to expel native Palestinians of all three faiths from their homes. As archeologist William Baker clarified, the present-day Jews now occupying Palestine are not traceable to the former Hebrews or Habiru who once conquered the land of Canaan. In contrast, those Palestinian Arabs still living in Palestine are the true descendants of the original Semitic inhabitants who have always known Palestine as their homeland.[364] The name of the neo-colonial project of Israel is not to be confused with the Biblical Israel referring to the original tribes Jacob, a majority of whom have since become Muslims as demonstrated through simple DNA tests. Some Zionists in Palestine even went back to fight for their fatherland, Germany, during WWI.[365] In the same vein, today, Zionist psychopaths from all over the world flock in to massacre the indigenous population on behalf of the terrorist army. The ethnic cleansing of the Palestinians is clear to even Israeli historians like Ilan Pappe, whose exposition of the truth resulted in his expulsion.

The Prophet advised: "When two disputants sit before you, do not judge between them until you listen to the second one as you listened to the first. If you do that, the verdict will become clear to you." (Musnad Ahmad 882)

Aside from political and economic motives, Western support for the apartheid regime also derives from cultural factors. It is worth noting that Zionism was founded by Christians, while Rabbinic Judaism historically opposed it. Europeans have always been the original antisemites in its broadest form in their hatred towards Jews and Muslims. In fact, Christian Zionism and the colonization of Palestine played a significant role in the US's involvement in WWI, which is apparent from its discussions with Britain.[366] Thus, General Edmund Allenby's entrance into Jerusalem was celebrated in the American media as "Richard the Lion-Hearted, who had at last won the Crusades and driven the pagans out of the Holy Land. The next step was for the Chosen People to return to the land promised to them by the Lord."[367] This way, the media laid the groundwork for the next set of events to follow. A significant number of Baptists still believe that the messiah's return will only occur when Jerusalem is under Jewish control, leading to their blind support for the massacre of Palestinians. Their apocalyptic zeal culminates in a hell on earth for the locals with raining bombs and annihilation of entire bloodlines. Today, the Christians United For Israel (CUFI) lobby is even bigger than AIPAC with massive funding for the expansion of illegal settlements in the West Bank.

Former Prime Minister Shamir described Palestinians as "grasshoppers compared to us [whose heads should be] smashed against the boulders and walls."[368] These were far from empty threats, as repeatedly demonstrated by the settler-military terror exemplified in Halhul in December 1982. No mercy was shown when a tank rolled over a white flag-waving cripple Kemal Zughayer, splitting his face in half; or Jamal Rashid, found crushed in his wheelchair along with his entire family in his home in Jenin by the US-supplied Israeli bulldozer in 2002. The desperate screaming eyes of a 12-year-old Mohammad al-Durrah, forever captured in photographs till his demise by Israeli snipers, are not easily forgotten, nor is the hopelessness of his father's attempt to shield his son from bullets with his bare hands. He survived to bury more family members two decades later when Israeli bombardments flattened entire Gazan neighborhoods.

Regrettably, these are far from sentinel events, but the norm that continues today with full Western support. We would not even dare to treat animals that way. Even when we agreed to support the UN Security Council resolution for the investigation of war crimes in Syria in May 2014, it was with the condition that the US and Israeli involvement in the region must be excluded.[369] If condemning such a terrorist regime brings an accusation of antisemitism, then perhaps the accusers are the real antisemites for equating Judaism with oppression and injustice. Yet, such excoriations are not spared even for the children of Holocaust survivors like political scientist Norman Finkelstein.

God does not forbid you from dealing kindly and fairly with those who have neither fought nor driven you out of your homes. Surely God loves those who are fair. (al-Mumtahinah 60:8)

It is a shameful reality that our government consistently vetoes internationally proposed two-state and ceasefire solutions while aiding Israel with money, weapons, and mainstream propaganda. This ongoing cycle opposes diplomacy and perpetuates aggressive terrorism, all the while feeding the people an opposite narrative. Moreover, it works, as obviated by the normalized anti-Islamic theme of today. The master plan also includes the suppression of education among occupied Palestinians, thereby ensuring a future of enslavement through economic despair. After all, that is a page right from Uncle Sam's playbook, which many domestic bigots still use to criticize an entire race struggling to emerge from 400 years of slavery at home.

The same tactics are currently being used to falsely claim that Palestine was an empty desert prior to Jewish settlements. If this continues, future historians and experts will discuss *various environmental factors that led to the decline of Palestinian natives in the 20th century*, similar to the "attrition by disease" of the millions of Native Americans whose massacre remains hidden. To report just one of the countless routinely ignored instances: a Palestinian girl named Intissar al-Atar was shot and killed by a Jewish settler in a schoolyard in Gaza just before the Infifada in 1987, which the Israeli court deemed not even severe enough for detention. Just as the murderer was being released, another Israeli army patrol fired into a West Bank refugee camp schoolyard, wounding five children, also without any repercussions. The Israeli press called it an "illiteracy as punishment" program, using gas bombs and rifle butts to beat students for intimidation while barring them from medical aid.[370] It stands along similar grotesque official policies such as Yitzhak Rabin's "break-their-bones" and the "disproportionate force" of the Dahiya Doctrine.

Meanwhile, Israel continues to forcefully expel native Palestinians from their ancestral homes, burying them within if they refuse, and building lavish illegal settlements around starving locals—all with full US support, as even Israeli scholars have detailed.[371] The atrocities are remarkably blatant and numerous, yet completely ignored. They echo the aftermath of the 1785 Treaty of Hopewell, where illegal settlements into the Cherokee territory eventually culminated in their near-complete extermination.[372] Despite multiple UN and International Council resolutions deeming these settlements illegal, they continue to expand, further demonstrating the castrated existence of the international community. Even when the ICC declares Israeli leaders as war criminals and issues an arrest warrant, the US responds by inviting the same criminals to the White House With a standing ovation from the entire Congress.

For the victims, however, the cumulative effect of this oppression is like magma under a volcano until their anger finally erupts. Then the oppressors immediately point fingers, confirming how "animalistically violent" these Arab ants are, thus justifying the Western boot. After a time, even death seems preferable to the continued daily oppression under such a barbarous regime denying basic human dignity. As for the Oslo scams, described by historian Hilde Waage, "could serve as the perfect case study for flaws...conducted on Israel's premises, with Norway acting as Israel's helpful errand boy."[373]

Many books have been written about nearly every line of this chapter to explain the nuances and complexities lost in such generalizations. Nonetheless, what penetrates through an honest reflection is the untenable Jewish historical claim to Palestine. As Lang puts it, "The possession by force of scattered parts of a territory for a few centuries more than two thousand years ago no more entitles today's Jews to that land than it would entitle today's Arabs to Spain, which they possessed for several centuries."[374] Novelist Haruki Murakami said it best during his acceptance of the Jerusalem Prize in 2009: "If there is a hard, high wall and an egg that breaks against it, no matter how right the wall or how wrong the egg, I will stand on the side of the egg."

Regarding the Abrahamic or Semitic origins, all three faiths have equal claim to that region, which ultimately is only symbolic when compared with the rights of the natives of the land. Dehumanization is done with malicious intent by excluding some from the consideration of "human." Similarly, redefining "semitism" with the exclusion of Arabs, yet including non-semitic Europeans only highlights the underlying racism of neocolonialism. The assertion itself is antisemitic in its deepest form and furthers the association of such evil with Abrahamic traditions. The apartheid occupation has persisted for so long that demanding a complete reversal would be unrealistic. Instead, this review aims to raise awareness in hopes of halting the continued aggression and oppression, which is the first step towards reconciliation. Denial and ignorance of these atrocities should be made just as criminal as the denial of the Holocaust, if not more, due to their continued prevalence. Understanding conflicts helps us not only resolve them but also avoid them altogether.

God only forbids you from befriending those who have fought you for [your] faith, driven you out of your homes, or supported [others] in doing so. And whoever takes them as friends, then it is they who are the [true] wrongdoers. (al-Mumtahinah 60:9)

II: Development of the Idea

The Prophet said: "When the sword is imposed on my ummah, it shall not be removed from it until the Day of Resurrection." (Jami` at-Tirmidhi 2202)

At the height of the Islamic conquests, it appeared as if all of Europe was about to come under its control. Then Charles Martel halted the Umayyad's advance into France by defeating Abdul Rahman al-Ghafiqi in the Battle of Tours/Poitiers in October 732. Although that battle has since been inflated to represent Christian Europe's existential resistance, it is nothing short of an anachronism as the term *European* nor their unified identity had yet been created.

The neologism "Europenses," coined by Isidore Pacensis in the 16th century to describe the battle, introduced a holistic concept that replaced the lost *civitas romanum* with a meta-category that transcended savage particularisms. As Catholicism and Europe became synonymous, the Austrasian Franks and their Nestorian cousins were credited with "saving" Christian civilization and creating a new people in history.[375] However, the Battle of Toulouse between Duke Odo and Amir al-Samh eleven years earlier was arguably more significant, even though neither battle was fought for anything more than personal honor and regional power.[376]

The defeat of Duke Odo by Charles Martel in 731 corroborated the aphorism where the winners erased his legacy from history, raising the latter on a pedestal of hindsight (through the *Continuations of Fredegar* and the *History of the Lombards*). In reality, Charles robbed the Church, just as his father Pippin did, to finance his expeditions, which gradually deprived the once flourishing Benedictine prosperity.[377] This extortion cornered the Church into modeling itself on a similar imperial papacy for survival, as demonstrated by Pope Stephen's presentation of a forged *Donation of Constantine* to Pepin III in 754.[378] It granted him papal sanction to save the Western Church from Lombard obliteration and officially break away from the Eastern Church by refusing to return Ravenna to the Byzantine Empire.

To sanctify Pipin's lineage, the early years of his famed son Carolus (Charlemagne, 747-814 CE) were officially erased by even the earliest biographers like Einhard—to remove charges of incest and polygamy that were otherwise common at that time and locale.[379] It is only befitting that the son later updated the forged document as the *Donation of Charlemagne* to restore the *quid pro quo* between the nascent religious-secular relationship.[380] One of his immediate acts as *patricius Romanorum* was the remorseless ethnic cleansing of the neighboring Saxons in 775, who conveniently became "heathens."[381] Then in 778, he led an army from virtually every corner of the realm across the Pyrenees in a humiliating pre-crusade against Muslims that succeeded in sacking the only Christian city on the way (Pamplona). These historical developments are critical in understanding the evolution of Christianity as a European phenomenon, where even Jesus became caucasian in his later depictions.

The petering Muslim advance beyond the Pyrenees was not because of Christian military success but from internal stresses within the Muslim

World (*Dar-ul-Islam*).[382] According to French historians Jean-Henri Roy and Jean Deviosse had the Muslim *regnum* succeeded, Europe might have been spared three centuries of religious wars.[383] Nonetheless, Muslims were just the remedy the warring European powers later needed to unite against a common foe. That *defining enemy* helped Europe gradually develop its White-Christian-European identity and come out of the dark ages. Islam as a culturally and militarily formidable competitor to Christianity was reflected in the works of all of its earliest scholars, which have persisted to the present day portraying Islam as "belonging to a part of the world—the Orient—counterposed imaginatively, geographically, and historically *against* Europe and the West."[384]

This antagonistic view of Islam manifests as systematic Islamophobia at the heart of all nations sprouting from that ideology. It is present in works such as *La Chanson de Geste,* Voltaire's *Mahomet le Prophète ou le Fanatisme*, Dante's distasteful depiction of the Prophet in *La Divina Commedia*, and Chaucer's Man of Law—all taught to generations of high-schoolers. "In that perspective, the Battle of Poitiers and the *Song of Roland* are pivotal moments in the creation of an economically retarded, balkanized, and fratricidal Europe that, by defining itself in opposition to Islam, made virtues out of hereditary aristocracy, persecutory religious intolerance, cultural particularism, and perpetual war," writes Professor Lewis.[385]

France had been at the forefront of this ideology, which gradually became a literary battle to compensate for their dwindling imperial prowess. While Meursault's killing of an Arab in French Algiers in *The Stranger* was an "existential crisis," the reverse would have probably been an "act of terrorism." The French have also shown their *absurdity* on many occasions outside of literature. They showed their antisemitism and radicalization at the turn of the 20th century through the Dreyfus affair. Not only in Algeria for over a century, but also in 1961 in Paris, and on numerous other occasions since then under the guise of *laïcité*.[386]

Such atrocities go back to their extermination of the entire Lucera Muslim population in 1301 CE, calling them a "disease and infection." Their continued misogyny and religious intolerance are demonstrated by their more recent ban on the hijab and halal meat. Today, Muslims make up half the prisoners in France despite being only 8-10% of the population.[387] Of course, none of these would fit their version of "historic Truth" and would be punishable under the Gayssot Law, highlighting their ingenuine respect for freedom of expression and speech, perhaps not different from how their brain-bashing founding father Chlodowech (Clovis) would have dealt with similar matters.[388]

Ironically, much of the literary talent of Europe trickled down from the

Islamic Golden Age. After battles like Barbastro in 1064 CE, thousands of captives were taken to southern France, including many *qiyans* who ended up in the victors' courts.[389] The resulting spread of poetry influenced troubadours like William of Aquitaine, the father of Provencal poetry.[390] Similarly, *The Divine Comedy* appears to have been plagiarized from Ibn al-'Arabi's *Al-Futuhat al-Makkiyah*, written 25 years before Dante was born, as exhaustively proven in Miguel Palacios's book *Islam and the Divine Comedy*. Both works were, in turn, inspired by the Prophet's original Night Journey.

Ibn Tufail's *Hayy Ibn Yaqzan* set the scene for all spiritual journeys out of Europe, from Dante's *Divine Comedy* to Bunyan's *Pilgrim's Progress*.[391] It predated *Don Quixote* by four centuries, despite the latter winning the title of the first modern novel. Although Dante metaphorically demonstrated his prejudice towards Muslims in his book for "splitting" the Christian world, his mentor Pietro d'Abano was a staunch Averroist, which explains Dante's generosity in placing Ibn Sina and Ibn Rushd in Limbo rather than Hell. That anti-Islamic sentiment is so contagious that it even spread to the neighboring regions, where Spain continues to struggle with an identity crisis. It was Islam that ultimately brought Spain out of the darkness and instability left by the Romans, the Visigoths, and the Vandals, contrary to the fabrications of medievalist Henri Pirenne's *Mohammed and Charlemagne*.[392] Their barbaric legacies are forever imprinted on the origins of the words goth and vandalism.

More honest historians acknowledge that forced conversion was alien to Islam everywhere in the *ummah*, including Al-Andalus. Muslims made it a pinnacle of civilization described by a Christian nun from Europe, Hroswitha of Gandersheim, as "the brilliant ornament of the World."[393] Even with occasional tensions, the respect for human dignity in Muslim lands was a significant advancement compared to the treatment of non-Christians in Europe, where heretics were routinely tortured and executed.[394] The brutality of Christian Europe only heightened in 1478 when King Ferdinand and Queen Isabella were given a papal bull by Pope Sixtus IV authorizing the Inquisition. With this history, today's *us versus them* mentality comes to light, as the roots of global politics and Islamophobia stretch back to the Battle of Tours and the conception of Europe.

The Reconquista movement united warring Christian kingdoms of Spain to expel Muslims from the peninsula, despite Muslim acceptance of Christians and Jews. They did not reciprocate similar hospitality and instead offered a legal pronouncement of forced conversion or death, known as *requerimiento*, which was later also brought to the New World. The Catholics were even less tolerant than they were towards Arianism following the Seventh Toledo Council.[395] When Barbastro was besieged under the pope's banner in 1064, more than six thousand Muslims were slaughtered in a celebration of violence.[396] This persecution of Muslims persisted in Spain until the early 18th century, even during the concurrent Age of Enlightenment. After savagely expelling all non-Christians out of the peninsula, Spain now boasts its Catholic-Caucasian heritage while much of its history is Islamic. Its legacy of Muslim persecution developed into traditions like the hanging hams in its restaurants and bars still seen today. It is deeply ingrained in their language, culture, architecture, music, food, agriculture, and more.

An overlooked fact is the importance of warfare in its mastery and evolution of weaponry. Ceaseless conflicts and savagery in Europe over time gave them an aggressive advantage over Muslims, who predominantly enjoyed the luxury of peace. It debunks the common Occidental claim of a civilized West and its allegation of the "spread of Islam by the sword." Reputable historians have already exposed this myth, as there is little evidence of violent conquest in the archeological records across Syria and Palestine.[397]

In contrast, the entire feral heathenism of the European landmass was gradually consolidated and forcefully converted to Christianity as a counterforce against the Islamic civilization in principle and practice. There was endless savagery within Christendom, exemplified by the Thirty Years' War (1618-48 CE), which established the first nation-states. Nearly all Western advancements result from weapons research even today, where the US military is decades ahead in technology made available to the general masses. In a letter to Gandhi, Tolstoy once complained that even though in "Christianity the law of love had been more clearly and definitely given than in any other religion, and that its adherents solemnly recognized it…they deemed the use of force to be permissible, and based their lives on violence—so that the life of the Christian nations presents a greater contradiction between what they believe and the principle on which their lives are built."[398]

The idea that an Islamic state with a population of only 2.5 million in the 7th century could conquer a land of 35.6 million using only swords and spears is a preposterous notion. Such a scenario may only seem believable in light of modern Western drone warfare, where a few individuals can dominate millions worldwide. Belgian historian Henri Pirenne (1862-1935 CE) even blamed Islam as the cause of the European Dark Ages, which has since been disproven.[399] In reality, it was the trade with the Umayyads that supported the Carolingian economy and helped bring it out of the darkness.[400] Trading with Muslim Andalus financed the Danish and Norwegian Viking's transformation into French-speaking Normans. Just as the trade with the Muslim Levant financed the Swedish Viking's (aka Rūs) transformation into Slavic-speaking Russians in and around Kyiv.[401]

Contemporary historians have provided ample evidence of local populations inviting and aiding Muslims against their oppressors. In North Africa, Arian Christians quickly embraced Islam due to the similarities in their beliefs with Islam, contrasting Byzantine Christianity. Similarly, Jewish tribes learned about the Charter of Medina and allied with Muslims during their conquest. When the news reached the persecuted Jews of Iberia, they also looked to Muslims for deliverance.[402] As city after city fell in Iberia, their liberated inhabitants welcomed a new era of tolerance that is arguably unmatched in non-Muslim Europe. The level of intolerance that dominates wherever Islamic values fade is a testament to this.

Roman historian Ammianus Marcellinus (330-95 CE) documented that "no wild beasts are so hostile to men as Christian sects in general are to one another."[403] Brutal Byzantine persecution of Jews and dissident Christians, such as the Nestorians and Jacobites, similarly resulted in their allegiance to Muslims. The wholesale massacre of Jews and Christians in Roman and Persian lands was the only unfortunate constant in their ever-revolving imperial successions. Some saw the dismemberment of Phocas in 610 as an exquisite comeuppance for his rampage against the Gentiles. There was also a monetary incentive, as the *jizyah* collected under Muslim rule was much less than the taxes collected by the Christian governments. The poll tax or *jizyah* for non-Muslims was comparable to the *zakat* Muslims were obligated to pay, both serving as a civic responsibility to help the poor. It also exempted non-Muslims from military service during conflicts, while those ineligible for the army (eg. women, children, and the elderly) were absolved from it all.

Caliph 'Umar personally guaranteed the life and property of all Christians living in Jerusalem, Lod, and Bethlehem and prohibited the desecration of any church or monastery. Such practices were corroborated through the writings of contemporary Christians like Yohannan bar Penkaye.[404] This protection was enjoyed by the Nestorian patriarch, Yeshuyab III (650-660 CE), who later wrote to the bishop of Persia that Muslims "have not attacked the Christian religion, but rather they have commended our faith, honored our priests...and conferred benefits on churches and monasteries."[405] Historians have noted that one of the main goals of early Muslim conquests was to establish religious freedom rather than forceful conversion, which is strictly prohibited in the Qur'an (*al-Baqarah* 2:256).[406] The Prophet demonstrated this principle through numerous expeditions during his lifetime, further exemplified by his miraculous conquest of Mecca in January of 630 CE.

Al-Kala'i and al-Balādhurī reported Abū 'Ubaydah (583-639 AD), the commander of the Muslim army in Greater Syria, returning the collected *jizyah* in Homs upon his early departure from the region. The Christians of

Homs replied: "May God bring you back to us and grant you victory over [the Byzantines]. If it were they who ruled over us, they would have never returned anything to us; they would have taken everything. Your rule and justice are more desirable to us than our previous state of oppression and tyranny."[407] Abū 'Ubaydah did the same with the people of Damascus when preparing for the Battle of Yarmuk, following the teachings of the Prophet. Orientalist Thomas Arnold (1864-1930 CE) confirmed this in his book *The Preaching of Islam*, further crediting Muslims for saving all religious denominations from Roman brutalities.

The stereotype of Islam as a "warrior religion" goes back to the Crusades when papal propaganda described Muslims as "the soldiers of the Antichrist in blasphemous occupation of the Holy Lands (and, far more importantly, of the silk route to China)," explains Aslan.[408] The discourse of Orientalism then engraved this European projection into a "fact," which is even believed by some Muslims today. However, the actual history of the world tells a different story.

During the Inquisition, Muslims and Jews were subjected to a variety of inventive tortures as penance, with some infamous torture devices on display at the Museo de la Tortura in Toledo. Roughly 13,000 Jews were killed, and an estimated 200,000 were expelled in 1492, leading Sultan Bayezid II (1447-1512 CE) of the Ottoman Empire to send a fleet to rescue them from Spain. "You call Ferdinand a wise ruler? He impoverishes his own country to enrich mine," he famously remarked.[409] It was not just political lip service; Jewish refugees were truly welcomed with protection, respect, and even financial assistance to start anew. "Tolerance was a staple feature of a society that was self-assured and confident of its own identity —which was more than could be said for the Christian world where bigotry and religious fundamentalism were rapidly becoming defining features," writes Frankopan.[410] Most Jews of modern-day Turkey are descendants of those rescued from Christian persecution.[411]

The Andalucian expulsion of Muslims was enacted in 1607, leading many to relocate as Moriscos (forcefully converted Muslims) and later as Huguenos (a newly formed Protestant denomination) in southern France, and then to migrate to America as some of the first European settlers of South Carolina.[412] The Portuguese Inquisition was even more severe than its Spanish counterpart, resulting in a mass migration of Muslims from there as well. The King of Portugal explicitly stated in a letter to the Pope that his reason for the transatlantic expedition was to reach "the Indians who, it is said, worship the name of Christ, so that we can...persuade them to come to the aid of the Christians against the Saracens."[413] Ironically, even those Christians of India directly resulted from the evangelical missions sent from the diaspora in the tolerant Muslim lands.

It is as if they all compete in their animosity and savagery against Muslims. We know about Vasco da Gama's celebrated expedition around Africa to India, where he was welcomed into the ports of Calicut by Muslim merchants. Few hear about his capture of a ship filled with hundreds of Muslims returning from their pilgrimage to Mecca. He not only burned it down with all the screaming men, women, and children but watched them die gleefully as drowning women held up their infants in vain till their last breath.[414] They did not just travel around the African coast but attacked and sacked many ports along the way. Even Jeddah, Muscat, and Qalhat were not spared with their mosques burnt to the ground.[415]

The same year Muhammad XII surrendered the Emirate of Granada to Queen Isabella I of Castile, Columbus arrived at her court asking for financial support for his expedition to the New World. Had the support come from the Nasrid Emirate, imagine how different the world would look today. While even the most austere historian can hardly avoid hypothetical fantasies, there is enough archaeological evidence available for the Mandinka (a Muslim West African ethnic group) expedition to the Americas—to Brazil, then through the Amazon, and up to the Cave Dwellers of Four Corners, Arizona.[416] Thus, historian U. B. Phillips (1877-1934 CE) complained over a century ago about the historical errors woven into the records by the Puritan institutions of Boston and New Haven.[417] We can even hear it from the coveter's mouth, as Columbus wrote in his journals about Muslim West African trading ships sailing for the Americas during his voyages. He also made a semi-circle by bringing traded gold made by Muslim metallurgists of Guinea from America to Europe.[418]

His son Ferdinand wrote in *The Life of the Admiral Christopher Columbus* how his father met Africans in Honduras, just as Gomara wrote about similar encounters by Vasco Nunez de Balboa in Panama in 1513. Several Native American tribes also have Arabic names, such as the Garifuna of Carib, the Almamys and the Jaras of Honduras, and the Mandingas of Central America. Martin and Vincente Pinzon, captains and part owners of the *Pinta* and the *Nina*, were descendants of the Marinid sultan of Morocco, Muhammad Ibn Yaqub. Francisco was the third brother on that 1492 voyage, along with another African Morisco named Pedro. Rodrigo de Triana was the first to sight land, who converted to Islam upon his return to Spain in 1493, even with the hostile anti-Islamic environment. One of the four survivors of the ill-fated 600-men Narvaez expedition was Estevanico Mustafa Azemmouri, an enslaved Moroccan Muslim who was the first to explore the southern United States and Mexico in the early 1500s and led an expedition for the fabled Seven Cities of Gold (Cibola).

Columbus is known for his transatlantic voyage, but few know about his earlier travels and his animosity towards Muslims. Growing up during the Ottoman conquest of Constantinople, he harbored a deep resentment towards the Islamic Empire. He worked as a sailor's apprentice during his teenage years in the Mediterranean, where he encountered Muslim explorers from North Africa. Later, he explored Muslim West Africa and participated in the fight to expel Muslims from the Iberian Peninsula before embarking on his journey across the Atlantic.

Motivated by his crusader mentality, Columbus sought to find a trade route to the East that would avoid Muslim lands, even while living in a converted mosque. Hence, his surprise to see some Native American women wearing scarves, which made him confuse them for Moors. Similar associations were also made by Hernán Cortés of the Aztecs, referring to Montezuma as a *sultan*. Cortés curiously reported finding more than 400 mosques during his travels through Texas and Mexico.[419] In fact, all European voyages of that period were a transoceanic extension of their overland Crusades. Professor Alan Mikhail argues that this anti-Islamic worldview of such conquerors later influenced their treatment of the indigenous people, who were butchered like animals as woefully described by contemporary accounts.[420]

Following the expulsion of Muslims, the Christian kingdoms of the Iberian peninsula fell back into internal quarrels. The Catholic Church struggled to find its foothold in the north, where *the Song of Roland* became a defining factor in the European sense of self and otherness.[421] Given France's origin story of fighting Muslims, it then comes as no surprise that the reunification attempt also came from there—under Pope Urban II's declaration of a genocidal holy war (*sacrum bellum*) against Muslims at the Council of Clermont on November 25, 1095. The Crusades that followed from 1095 to 1492 ultimately distracted their people from raging havoc in their own lands and brought their raping and pillaging to the unsuspecting East for four centuries, leaving behind a trail of indelible savagery that remains largely overlooked.

"Crusading was thus a murderous device to resolve a contradiction by bringing baron and commoner together in the cauldron of religious war," summarizes Linebaugh.[422] This concept of *holy war* was very familiar to the Catholic Church, dating back to St. Augustine in the 4th century. Even during World War II, the Church did not denounce the religious motivations behind the Nazi Christian holy war, while vehemently opposing communism.[423] The Qur'anic concept of a just war differs from Augustine and Ambrose in that it does not legislate fighting nonaggressive pagans or violently extinguishing others' religions. Rather, the Qur'an resembles Lockean philosophy on warfare, which would take another thousand years to develop in Europe and fail forever to manifest.[424]

The campaigns of the Prophet and the Caliph's armies adhered to a strict code of conduct, which the West never really adopted, even after the Geneva Conventions. Caliph Abu Bakr's instructions for the Muslim army, for instance, included ten rules for the battlefield, which charged them to adhere to the right path and avoid treachery. They were not to mutilate dead bodies or harm children, women, or aged men. The army was to bring no harm to the trees, especially those that were fruitful. They were only allowed to slay the enemy's flock for their food, and they were to leave alone those who devoted their lives to monastic services.[425]

The Catholic Church, on the other hand, promised complete forgiveness (i.e., plenary indulgence) to those on its mission to massacre civilians and ravage foreign lands. The Miriam-Webster definition of the Crusades refers to them as "expeditions," a term that downplays the egregious terrorism they represented. The alternate definition, which describes the Crusades as a "remedial enterprise undertaken with zeal and enthusiasm," is equally insulting. In a strange turn of revisionist history, the Crusades, an actual Christian holy war, get turned into a beautiful *expedition*. Yet, the term *holy war* gets attached to Muslim *jihad*, which is another gross misinterpretation.

Jihad is a secular Arabic word that would be interchangeable with "struggle" throughout this book and remain closer to its meaning. The term *infidel* is also of European origin dating back to the Crusades, referring to the Saracens they were slaughtering with much "zeal and enthusiasm." Today *infidel* is something a typical-Akhmed would scream at the civilized Henry Walton on screen. In all the political rhetoric about how Muslims live for martyrdom, the balanced teachings of the Prophet get ignored. The Prophet emphasized a life of worship over a martyr's death in terms of a person's rank among the righteous (*Musnad Ahmad* 1403). Martyrdom alone does not grant one forgiveness for his aggression against humanity (*Riyad as-Salihin* Book 11, Hadith 28). In contrast, the Bible, in many instances, even condones genocide—for example, *Leviticus* 26:7-9, *Numbers* 33:52-53, 55, I *Samuel* 15:18, and almost the whole book of *Joshua*.

By the time the crusaders were done, an estimated two to five million unsuspecting civilians were massacred. The piety of the Crusaders is questionable, as most tagged along to escape from their squalid feudal life in search of easy riches to be gained in foreign lands. The final siege of Jerusalem in July 1099 epitomized their brutality, not even sparing Arab Christians. Between 40,000 to 70,000 civilians were murdered, and Jews barricading themselves in synagogues were incinerated. A crusader's report of that day stated: "With drawn swords our people ran through the city; nor did they spare anyone, not even those pleading for mercy. If you had been there, your feet would have been stained up to the ankles with blood. What more shall I tell? Not one of them was allowed to live. They did not spare the women or children, the horses waded in blood up to their knees, nay, up to the bridle. It was a just and wonderful judgment of God."[426]

In fact, the wrongdoers merely follow their desires with no knowledge. Who then can guide those God has left to stray? They will have no helpers. (al-Rum 30:29)

Another Crusader, Raymond of Aguiles, wrote of Jerusalem: "Wonderful sights were to be seen. Some of our men cut off the heads of their enemies; others shot them with arrows, so that they fell from towers; others tortured them longer by casting them into the flames. Piles of heads, hands and feet were to be seen in the streets of the city. It was necessary to pick one's way over the bodies of men and horses. But these were small matters compared to what happened at the Temple of Solomon, a place where religious services are normally chanted...in the Temple and porch of Solomon, men rode in blood up to their knees and bridle reins."[427]

The Jews encountered on the way to the Holy Land served as a prelude to the Crusaders' main objective.[428] One Crusader wrote, "We have set out to march a long way to fight the enemies of God in the East, and behold before our very eyes are his worst foes, the Jews. They must be dealt with first."[429] And they did deal with them in thousands, all under the support of the Catholic Church.

In December 1098, after invading Ma'arra, the Crusaders again spent three days slaughtering the entire city and engaging in mass cannibalism. Radulph of Caen wrote: "In Ma'arra our troops boiled pagan adults in cooking pots; they impaled children on spits and devoured them grilled." "Not only did our troops not shrink from eating dead Turks and Saracens; they also ate dogs!" reported Albert of Aix.[430] In Acre, the Crusaders enslaved the Persian poet Saadi Shirazi (1210-91 CE) for seven years digging trenches. His words, which reflect a famous Prophetic narration, are now immortalized at the entrance of the UN headquarters: "All of the sons of Adam are part of one single body, they are of the same essence. When time afflicts us with pain in one part of that body, all the other parts feel it too. If you fail to feel the pain of others, you do not deserve the name of man."

After the Crusaders sacked Bilgays in 1168, they ruthlessly massacred the city's entire population, sparing none in their indiscriminate slaughter. Then they turned against their hosts, laying siege to Constantinople and declaring the Byzantines as "the enemies of God."[431] When they unleashed the usual savagery against fellow Christians, some declared them to be "the forerunners of the Antichrist." By capturing the most significant city in Christendom, the Crusaders proved that they would go to any lengths to acquire power and wealth. Sadly, the same theme continues today as bloodthirsty psychopaths pour in from all over the world to massacre native Palestinians in their homes with advanced Western weaponry and cheering global leadership.

On the other hand, Odo de Diogilo (1110-62 CE), the private chaplain to King Louis VII, wrote about Muslim's compassion and mercy towards the destitute Crusaders. The Muslims helped them with food, money, and medical treatment. It contrasted with the Crusaders' treatment at the hands of their co-religionists, resulting in the conversion of thousands of surviving Crusaders to Islam and joining the Muslim army.[432]

As historian Steven Runciman (1903-2000 CE) once quipped, "The Crusades were launched to save Eastern Christendom from the Moslems. When it ended the whole of Eastern Christendom was under Moslem rule." The subsequent accounts demonstrate the art of history, where a couple of keystrokes turn barbarian zealots into cowboys in chainmail, fighting for civilization in a barren desert of turbaned Indians. Historians have often propagated the myth that the Crusades brought Greek wisdom back to Europe, which serves as a convenient consolation prize. In reality, "only by asserting its power over the weak and the helpless in America, Africa, and Asia could Christendom salvage its pride and prestige," concludes historian Graham.[433]

The Prophet said: "A nation will not be sanctified if the weak cannot take their rights without surmounting obstacles." (Sunan Ibn Mājah 2426)

III: Manifest Idea

While some may feel these to be jejune historical events, the West still retains the same subversive attitude, consistently blending its avaricious politics with religious motives. Whether it is the rationalization of Machiavellian agendas by kings and politicians under the guise of religious values or the Church's use of religious doctrines to mask its political ambitions, these two forces have constantly vied for easier sources of money and resources since their inception. (Now it is the religion of capitalism preached by its priests in academic circles and politics.) As such, both Catholics and Protestants have demonstrated a similar passion for progressive activism, leading to the spread of industrial capitalism wherever their missionaries go.[434]

It is therefore unsurprising that the end of the Crusades in 1492 coincided with Columbus's voyage to the New World. His intentions were transparent and accurately reflected the contemporary European mindset. He described the Arawaks as a peaceful, healthy people without advanced weaponry, who offered to share all of their possessions. Sadly, his immediate conclusion foreshadowed subsequent world history: "They would make fine servants... With fifty men we could subjugate them all and make them do whatever we want." The entire thing was done with remarkable religious zeal and papal blessing, reflected by Columbus's writing: "Thus the eternal God, our Lord, gives victory to those who follow His way over apparent impossibilities... Let us in the name of the Holy Trinity go on sending all the slaves that can be sold."[435]

To clarify, the eternal God certainly does not condone such behavior. Instead, that worship's "holy trinity" is greed, gall, and gluttony. Genuine people of faith, like the young priest Bartolome de las Casas, were horrified by the invaders' cruelty. His *History of the Indies* details events such as: "Two of these so-called Christians met two Indian boys one day, each carrying a parrot; they took the parrots and for fun beheaded the boys."[436] Without their surviving documentation, we would not have learned about the extermination of over three million natives of Hispaniola (modern Haiti and Dominican Republic) alone between 1494 to 1508. In the absence of any remaining accounts of the rest, some estimates suggest that over one hundred million deaths resulted from Columbus's journey. It easily ranks as the worst historical catastrophe, overshadowing even the World Wars combined.

Portugal is credited with starting the European Age of Discovery with the conquest of Ceuta, Morocco, in 1415. It even received a papal blessing in 1455 to seize West Africa. One cannot help but admire the euphemism with the renaming of the colonial age of global exploitation as the "Age of Discovery." It is worth noting that the original Visigoth economy of the Iberian Peninsula was built on slavery, which Spain and Portugal were about to revive with renewed fervor.[437] The apogee of Slavic enslavement throughout Europe (and Arab lands) is also where the origin of the word *slave* lies.

Unfortunately, this new form of oppression never ceased. It has only been refined through the Darwinian process into much more efficient forms of Western hegemony, changing its name from New Imperialism and postcolonialism to today's neo-colonialism. The original Doctrine of Discovery continued to play a role in the papal-initiated Treaty of Tordesillas and in all of the European settler colonial projects of the 19th and 20th centuries. Jefferson claimed it to be a form of international law applicable to the US government in 1792, which was again reaffirmed by a Supreme Court decision in *Johnson v. McIntosh* in 1823.[438]

The colonizer scribes of this segment of history have conveniently erased and tucked away most of their heinous acts. Still, the little surviving evidence paints a horrific picture. It is estimated that Belgian King

Leopold II's occupation of Congo alone killed 8 million people between 1885-1908, all in the name of rubber.[439] That entire continent of Africa represents a legacy of brutal subjugation and exploitation by one colonizer after another. Even the Western depiction of Africa on most maps is a gross misrepresentation of its vastly larger size. Up until that Age of the European Discovery of Africa's rich resources, there was much cultural and industrial progress in Africa, which was ultimately no match for the European "civilized" war machines.[440] (The Battle of Omdurman in 1898 serves as a case in point with over 12,000 Sudanese mowed down by Maxim guns and less than 50 British casualties. Interestingly, a 23-year-old Winston Churchill was among the British lines.) Replacing their technologies with imperial trade of only raw materials—including humans—set the entire continent back to the Stone Age, which was then ironically used against them to justify their continual exploitation.

Then entered Great Britain as the next global power. Not only did it absorb Spanish and Portuguese racial caste systems but also implemented its Protestantism starting with Ireland. Sir Humphrey Gilbert, the official in charge of the 16th-century Irish province of Munster, had mastered his terror campaign there before settling the first English colonies in Newfoundland in 1583. His tactics were brutally implemented on the North American natives with renewed vigor.[441] Essentially, wherever the Europeans went they asserted their hegemony by forcefully subjugating the natives. It was often done through Christian missionaries to "civilize" the world as it best profited them. It became "The White Man's Burden" to convert the entire world to Christianity at gunpoint with the ultimate goal of capitalism, as the Church itself was a capitalist imperial power. The choice was to either do as the *white master* said or die similar to the *requerimiento* of the Conquistadors. This differentiation and persecution of natives have been a standard field-tested method for maintaining control over territories throughout colonialism and neo-colonization, which is evident from abundant research. It only appears conspiratorial due to the colonial scholars' willful ignorance of facts. The available documents from monasteries like the Franciscan in California were overlooked by most historians up until the civil rights era, which detailed heinous atrocities within the missions by even the beatified Junipero Serra (1713-84 CE).[442]

During the entire process, Satan's classic divide-and-conquer policy was in full effect. To this end, well-thought-out strategies were implemented by the French in Algeria, the Belgians in Rwanda, and the British in the Middle East.[443] The repercussions of those divisions continued long after the expulsion of the colonists, which left them in deep political and economic turmoil. They were unable to unite and rebuild their national identity due to manufactured differences, leaving them forever dependent on their former masters. Similarly, the recent US withdrawal from Afghanistan was summarized by a trail of desperate Afghans clinging to the wings and landing gears of the last army planes leaving the runway, ultimately falling to their demise on the rooftops of Kabul.

It is fascinating to picture men of power sitting around a table, marking up territories on maps with little regard for those occupying them. Portugal and Spain did it during their Papal arbitration with the treaties of Tordesillas in 1494, just as the Allies did at the end of WWI through the Sykes-Picot Agreement. The US finally realized the value of the Middle East during WWII from the geologic survey of Everette DeGolyer.[444] This time, the US and Britain were sitting around the table: the "oil in Persia was [British]...we both had a share in Iraq and Kuwait and...Bahrain and Saudi Arabia were American."[445] Initially, Africa was thrown to the European allies to exploit per George Kennan (1904-2005 CE).[446] Then the US changed its mind and joined China in further destruction of the continent. Today, much of the US and its allies' involvement in sub-Saharan Africa flies under the radar, as Nick Turse details in *Tomorrow's Battlefield*.

The answers to many of our current global problems become apparent when we delve just a little under the surface. Malcolm X, through his prison library, astutely analyzed Western animosity towards China, tracing it back to centuries of exploitation. European empires and Christian traders exported millions of pounds of opium into China for financial and psychosocial hegemony, resulting in addiction and associated socio-criminal issues. When a desperate Chinese government cracked down and destroyed twenty thousand chests of opium in 1839, the British Empire launched the first Opium War, using its own gunpowder to destroy the soul of China. The Treaty of Nanking forced China to pay for the destroyed opium, open its remaining ports to British trade, abandon Hong Kong, and fix a lopsided import tariff, crippling its industrial development. After the Second Opium War, the Tientsin Treaties again legalized the opium trade and a British-French-American control of China's customs.[447]

The Europeans flooded the coasts of India to plunder its riches, touting their higher moral values and enlightened civilization. As Lord Curzon (1859-1925 CE) said: "To feel that somewhere among these millions you have left a little justice or happiness or prosperity, a sense of manliness or moral dignity, a spring of patriotism, a dawn of intellectual enlightenment, or a stirring of duty, where it did not before exist—that is enough, that is the Englishman's justification in India."[448] In that pursuit, they instilled evangelical Christian missionaries at every high post and pushed to convert the entire subcontinent, unmasking their brutality through the wholesale massacre during the Sepoy rebellion of 1857. It raises questions about the real motives behind such Christian values, which deviate drastically from divine laws and ethics. It is not an opprobrium of Christianity as theology, but rather the corruption within its institutions that has led it astray from its noble roots. Nevertheless, let us reserve further discussion of this topic for the next chapter.

Britain's primary objective during the colonial era was to secure complete control of the opium trade, making it one of the largest narco-traffickers in history, a practice similar to recent US involvement in Afghanistan. In essence, it was a refinement of the drug trade that fueled European colonization of the New World, consisting of tobacco, sugar, and alcohol.[449] Cecil Rhodes (1853-1902 CE), the founder of De Beers diamond company, expressed his sentiment: "We Britons are the first race in the world, and the more of the world we habit, the better it is for the human race."[450] The Governor of Madras, Sir Charles Trevelyan (1807-86 CE), stated their actual goal as "nothing short of the conversion of the natives to Christianity," which was rightfully seen by the natives as a threat to their identity and existence. "Excepting the African slave trade, nowhere has history recorded any more unnecessary bestial and ruthless human carnage than the British suppression of the non-white Indian people," commented Malcolm X.[451] These atrocities inspired JS Mill to write an essay on humanitarian intervention, urging Britain to complete the liberation of India (from Indians). Even when some of them recognized their brutalities, they still could not stop their Occidental outlook and aggression.

Political scientist R.J. Rummel (1932-2014 CE) estimates the death toll from 20th-century colonialism alone at about 50 million. These are not just numbers on paper, but they represent individuals with families and loved ones. By reducing people to numbers for gains, humanity is lost, and the transatlantic slave traders stand as an example. The colonialists understood their liberal ideas as they applied to themselves only, while pillaging the colonies for all they had. It caused Muhammad Abduh (1849-1905 CE) to fume: "We Egyptians believed once in English liberalism and English sympathy; but we believe no longer, for facts are stronger than words. Your liberalness we see plainly is only for yourselves, and your sympathy with us is that of the wolf for the lamb which he designs to eat."[452]

Such tyranny over destitute natives engendered opposition from others like Jamal ad-Din al-Afghani (1838-97 CE), who was pursuing higher education in India during the Sepoy Rebellion. Sir Sayyid Ahmed Khan (1817-98 CE) tried to bridge the gap in his book *The Causes of the Indian Revolt*. His solution was to modernize Islamic education by founding the Aligarh School. It was countered by Mawlana Maududi's (1903-79 CE) *Jama'at-i Islami* movement resisting modernization, but both played into revitalizing Ibn Khaldun's *group morale* and eventually expelling the British from India.

The colonial education system remains one of the most potent and unrecognized weapons that continues to exert its effects. Professor Ogunnaike explains that "the conquest is complete when you teach the conquered that their conquest was actually a liberation as has happened worldwide."[453] Shaykh al-Hind Mahmud Hasan Deobandi (1851-1920 CE) recognized this threat and urged his people to develop their own education system to free themselves from colonial oppression. He was promptly imprisoned by the British in Malta and unsuccessfully tortured to give a *fatwa* against rebellion.

The powerful elites have always been a small minority, which repeatedly presented them with the problem of controlling a large group of colonized people. Consequently, they implemented reeducation programs to eliminate cultural identities. It was often done by physically removing native children and placing them in boarding schools for Westoxification. Just like the Romans two millennia prior, the US did it in the Philippines under *Benevolent Assimilation,* overlooking the lessons taught by Arminius in the Teutoburg forest.[454] The Trump administration used a similar tactic of separating children from their parents as a deterrent to address the ever-growing unauthorized border crossings. Ironically, its neo-imperial stepchild employs the same in Palestine by terrorizing the entire indigenous population with perennial "mowing the lawn" and kidnapping of children to keep, use, and abuse as hostages. To make matters worse, Israel has also been a safe haven for pedophiles from all over the world, with documented abuse of these kidnapped children within its torture centers.[455]

The resultant breakdown of families in native communities due to sexual, physical, and emotional abuse in boarding schools persists as social and familial dysfunctions.[456] Even after the expulsion of colonizers, these education systems continued because of the lack of the forgotten alternative. It is debatable how much of this is intentional versus a result of colonialism, but it ultimately led to the most recent triumph of Orientalism. Most of the places of higher education in these regions follow inherited systems from their former colonial powers, with overcrowded facilities and undervalued faculty who are often political appointments. The most promising students often immigrate to developed countries to continue their education, adopting a Western view of their identity. When they return from the brain drain, they propagate Western dogmas based on their foreign education. Meanwhile, the uneducated mimic the elite and their Hollywood-inspired reality, unaware of their rich heritage. It influences subsequent generations to feel subservient and always looking towards the West for all things "better," like flightless baby birds in a nest awaiting the return of their parents with vomit. That brings about the final triumph of Orientalism: *consumerism in the Orient.*[457]

Ibn Khaldun's observation that "those who are conquered always want to imitate the victor in his distinctive mark(s), his dress, his occupation, and all his other conditions and customs" is demonstrated today as indigenous communities trade their colorful heritage for all things Western.[458] At the same time, the West gradually devolves to a state of nakedness, parallelling the ancestral story of Adam and Eve in Eden. The only difference is the voluntary disrobing of the Occident, demonstrating the true conqueror to be the devil himself. This dark history of colonialism and exploitation makes any shifting of blame to the Third World absurd. Convenient labeling of these destitute conflict zones as warring nations also overlooks their imperial puppeteer's strings.

Many fail to connect the dots between the economic hardship faced by India after two centuries of British humiliation, followed by the theft of $45 trillion of its resources and wealth.[459] In 1773, a House of Commons Select Committee calculated that just the conquest of Bengal resulted in the removal of over £2 million (tens of billions today) from the Bengalis, which directly led to a devastating famine with a death toll in the millions.[460] The resulting loss of workforce in Bengal pushed the East India Company to near bankruptcy, which was only prevented by the Tea Act in 1773, initiating a series of events that led to the American Revolution.[461] This is how the dying Bengalis helped the American independence, connected by one Lord Clive.

Thievery of this magnitude is still perpetuated by developed countries through loansharking tactics of institutions like the World Bank and the International Monetary Fund. It is a calculated method to keep their control over the colonized land while preventing them from achieving full sovereignty. As President John Adams preached, "There are two ways to conquer and enslave a nation. One is by the sword. The other is by debt." Paraguay serves as a case in point, where 80% of its export earnings went towards paying interest on its $2 billion foreign debt by 1986.[462] Accordingly, there was no outcry when the entire country of Zambia defaulted during a pandemic due to the developed world's exploitation of their copper mines.[463] Or the Gazan genocide for the mining of natural gas along its shores.

Despite the recent media focus on the loss of Afghan liberties due to the Taliban takeover, we must not forget the unlawful foreign occupation and exploitation of Afghanistan that occurred for two decades prior. Such media bias was analyzed by Professor Deepa Kumar, concluding that humanitarian concerns are only highlighted when they serve the war effort.[464] A similar tactic was used to justify the US's entry into WWII, even though the plight of the Jews and fascism were not the Allies' main concerns.[465] In fact, both antisemitism and fascism are just as prevalent among the Allies as anywhere else even today. As mainstream narratives fumed over the few opposing the withdrawal from Afghanistan for personal gains, they ignored the US's refusal to count civilian casualties during their oppressive invasion. Recent reports with careful cross-checking revealed that on average, each Afghan family lost ten to twelve civilians in what the locals call the "American War."[466] That wholesale massacre was justified in the name of democracy and expiation for the 2,977 lives lost at home. Some lives are obviously worth a lot more than others, which are not even worth counting. If we consider this scenario fairly, we must ask: if the heinous murder of nearly three thousand civilians justifies a decades-long brutal global war, what does the murder of millions of civilians by the US justify from the other side?

These policies reflect George Kennan's (former chair of the US State Department's policy planning) recommendation of maintaining a "position of disparity" to separate America's enormous wealth from the poverty of others. He argued that we should not talk about "vague and...unreal objectives such as human rights, the raising of the living standards, and democratization" but instead "deal in straight power concepts" and not be "hampered by idealistic slogans" about "altruism and world-benefaction."[467] President Lyndon Johnson went so far as instructing the Junior Chamber of Commerce not to help the rest of the world to the same blessings as us because he did not want to exchange places.[468] This mentality can be traced back to Richard Greenville's first landing in Virginia in 1585 when he burned an entire Powhatan village over a stolen silver cup.

IV: Family Legacy

The Prophet said: "Whoever sets free his share of a slave, and he has sufficient wealth to set him free completely by paying the price of the slave, then he should set him free with his own wealth." (Sunan an-Nasa'i 4699)

Even though European colonialism brought slavery to the Americas, it did not leave with their expulsion. The dark history of racial slavery was just too profitable and convenient to be abandoned. Kidnapping free people from one continent—kings and queens, scholars (like Bilali Mohamed, Kunta Kinte, and Omar Ibn Said) and priests, rich and poor the same—and forcing them to live as subhumans for generations lasting 400 years, is an egregious crime. People of color during this period had a life expectancy of only six to fifteen years. Approximately three to six million African Muslims were also enslaved in the Americas, with their legacies often lost due to their Biblical renaming, as explained by Toni Morrison in *Song of Solomon*, which was originally the song of Ayuba Suleyman Diallo.[469] Hence, many Muslims played critical roles in organizing and leading slave revolts, including the *Amistad*, Haitian, and Bahia revolts.

Arguably, slavery never ended, as it still exists in different forms within this country's social and legal systems. It was only a matter of time before the enslaved masses traded their rich heritage for the *jahili* practices of their southern masters.[470] Today, those same customs are used against black Americans as "proof" of their ignorance. How are the people—now supposedly free—to feel about the *great* founding fathers who conveniently left them out of the equation? Sure, Jefferson's child slave was human enough to bear his offspring, but not deemed economical or practical to be freed and given the same God-given rights. "Human" may not have been a factor as the 1662 Virginia law decreeing children of black women as slaves gave him monetary incentive. This incentive is perhaps reflected by Carolina's Black population of 39,100, exceeding its 20,000 whites by 1740.[471]

Protection of slavery was such a motivator for the American Revolution that it made Samuel Johnson (1709-84 CE) famously quip: "We hear the *loudest yelps* for liberty among the drivers of negroes."[472] While Jefferson wrote, *We hold these truths to be self-evident*, our sciences have since revealed that "things that seemed self-evident to us were really no more than prejudices."[473] If we judge not by propaganda but by facts, then the true motives are made clear by the stark increase in violence against natives and blacks following America's independence from Britain.

How are the oppressed supposed to feel about the government that has consistently failed to enforce its laws and constitutional values of freedom and equality since its conception? While historians write about the great Fourteenth and Fifteenth Amendments, all the presidents that followed failed to execute them, along with the laws passed in the 1860s. Instead, those in power looked the other way, sometimes even ordering the execution of those they were supposed to protect. Some technocratic scholars today attempt to credit those same politicians with all social justice gains while willfully ignoring the activism that forced their necks to turn.

During the Civil Rights movement, with tensions mounting, the federal and local authorities refused to protect those fighting for their rights— the Freedom Riders, black voters, and activists like James Chaney, Fred Hampton, and Mark Clark, among others—which only makes them all complicit. What was once considered *just another conspiracy theory* soon became apparent as evidence of the FBI's counterintelligence program (COINTELPRO) became public, with 295 documented covert actions against black organizations. Only after all their violent tactics failed to control the rage of the oppressed did they finally pass the Civil Rights laws, which were still only reluctantly enforced with constant gnawing back since. Every step forward is met with endless "random" acts of periodic racist violence against minorities from the nation's DNA.

Jefferson scientifically explored his racism in the *Notes on the State of Virginia* treatise in 1781. He justified the exclusion of African Americans, concluding: "This unfortunate difference in colour, and perhaps in faculty, is a powerful obstacle to the emancipation of these people."[474] Such prejudices cannot be excused by citing their environment and time, for fundamental values of morality and justice are timeless. It is demonstrated by better contemporary minds, such as Quaker preacher John Woolman (1720-72 CE). Deviation from basic morality is only possible in a society where true religious guidance is abandoned. Good-ol' Ben (Franklin) argued in *Observations Concerning the Increase of Mankind* against African imports to stop "darkening" the New World to save white purity. Perhaps that should be a summation of his legacy rather than the apocryphal kite.

Referring to Jamestown as the birthplace of American democracy and freedom is not only a blatant lie but also reveals the intended recipients of those principles. The persistent injustice and inequality in our nation are not happenstance but masterfully planned and executed by the powerful.[475] Unsurprisingly, a report in 2018 found no improvement in African American homeownership, unemployment, and incarceration since the Civil Rights Movement.[476] Those who deny it are either oblivious of their surroundings or privileged beneficiaries of injustice. If we are to be accurate in our designation, then we must call this entire thing "American white supremacy" until the day it aspires to true democracy.

We still live among a generation that faced brutal opposition to desegregation and their simple right to be treated as human beings. While Abraham Lincoln opposed the institution of slavery, even he did not recognize blacks as his equals, nor was he an abolitionist.[477] Therefore, the reconstruction following the Civil War was not radical but a safer and more profitable approach. The audacious attempts by some "experts" to contextualize this dark past within the framework of slavery are outright shameful. Perhaps those downplaying it should be chained by their necks and feet in the suffocating below-deck of a slave ship for a more expert opinion. Criticism of them and subsequent government policies is not an attack on America, but the most American thing to do, as it is the principal civic duty that defines the US.

It is telling that the most revered philosopher of Western civilization, Aristotle, also failed to consider a world without slavery in *Politics*. He and Plato were both agreeable to slavery and even justified oppression while serving tyrants.[478] The Roman Republic, which Western civilizations modeled themselves after, relied heavily on slavery. Any Roman with less than four slaves was living below the poverty line, while the wealthy elites owned up to fifty thousand slaves.[479] Today, our consumerism results in a similar dependance on slave labor worldwide. During the time of Jesus, over 25% of the Roman empire consisted of slaves, whose misery served as a fertile ground for Pauline theology. This is not to boorishly disregard any good such men do, as we all have our faults and make regrettable mistakes. The Founding Fathers' efforts to maintain religious freedom in the original Constitution are commendable, despite their degradation over the last few centuries. It nevertheless hides the persecution of all religions by Puritans and evangelical Protestants in this country.[480] At the same time, it is another extreme to excuse all of their crimes as a fallacy of anachronism.

In America, the battle over memory has always been about what we choose to remember. Events like the Stone *Rebellion* or the 1811 Slave *Revolt* are painted in a tone to revise an enslaved and dehumanized people's revolutionary plight for freedom. It is inaccurate to describe the treatment of slaves as animalistic based on the humane treatment of animals. Imagine what it would take for someone to claim complete ownership over you and force you to do anything they wished. Subjugating humans with their sense of free will, pride, and rebellious nature requires overpowering, fear-inducing violence, which dehumanizes the slavers as monstrous brutes. A similar appeal in 1829 by a freeborn David Walker resulted in a $10,000 bounty on his head by the state of Georgia. He challenged: "Show me a page of history, either sacred or profane, on which a verse can be found, which maintains, that the Egyptians heaped the insupportable insult upon the children of Israel, by telling them that they were not of the human family."[481]

The power of language used as a weapon is demonstrated in naming events like the Boston *Massacre* with a death toll of five; yet when hundreds of Seminole and Lakota were slaughtered by the army at Sand Creek and Wounded Knee, it is somehow a *Battle*. Such tactics are only refined today when disenfranchised protesters are portrayed by the media and politicians alike as *rioters*. *What could these people possibly be so angry about if it was not simply in their nature?* Frederick Douglass once exploded, asking: "What have I, or those I represent, to do with your national independence? Are the great principles of political freedom and of natural justice, embodied in that Declaration of Independence, extended to us?"[482]

It is not to excuse all reactionary violence but to understand the factors leading to such aggressive displays of emotions. Similar inequity caused Reverend Earl Little (1890-1931) to believe that "freedom, independence and self-respect could never be achieved by the Negro in America."[483] He came to it through his experience as a black man in the American

South after seeing his brothers lynched and murdered. Later his son would describe his earliest vivid memory as barely escaping death along with his family at the hands of white supremacists. Rev. Little then suffered the same fate as his brothers, as did his son decades later. His wife succumbed to psychosis from a life of repeated trauma and repression. Such is the setup for millions (if not billions) worldwide, while some on the other side completely deny its effects. Not long ago, a black person was being lynched every four days in America.[484] In some places, it became a popular pastime, as some fifteen thousand spectators participated in the lynching of a teenage Jesse Washington in Waco, Texas. One of the last publicized lynchings in America was as recent as 1981 in Alabama of Michael Donald.

"The degree of civilization in a society can be judged by entering its prisons," observed Dostoevsky. Today, nearly a quarter of the entire world's prisoners are in the US, and a third of them are black. Adding Hispanics into the equation makes it over 70% of the prisoners while representing only a fifth of the population. Ibn Khaldun considered forced labor as one of the greatest forms of injustice, as it destroys a people's incentive to work, their cultural enterprise, and group morale.[485] Yet nearly four centuries after the Royal African Company received its charter, prison labor continues to exploit minorities for capitalism and corporate America.

Indeed, the prisons in this country only represent extreme manifestations of the nation's deep class disparities, racism, and lack of freedom. The single thing the system fails to represent is justice, serving long sentences to the poor and minorities for petty crimes while the wealthy are afforded clemency for daylight robberies. George Jackon served as a case in point— serving over a decade for a $70 robbery in a California prison. When his revolutionary book *Soledad Brother* became widely popular, he was shot in the back by guards at San Quentin prison in 1971. The underlying philosophy of the penitentiary was summed up by a warden: "To reform a criminal you must first break his spirit." Such methods are more likely to create sociopaths. In contrast, the Prophetic teachings advocate for appealing to one's humanity through love and care, God-consciousness, and helping them overcome their struggles to improve their lives in this world and the next.

The history of the US prison system is closely tied to slavery and racism. Michigan, for example, built a large state prison in Jackson within a year of formally abolishing slavery, while Pennsylvania built the nation's first penitentiary soon after passing its earliest abolition acts.[486] Although slavery has always been around, American slavery was worse in many ways, including its abolishment of manumission, which naturally evolved into the penitentiary system. Instead of recognizing the apparent disparity, those who use today's prison statistics as evidence to discriminate are the actual criminals not worthy of roaming freely.

The use of tear gas and chemicals in warfare was banned after World War I due to their inhumane psychological effects, yet these tactics have been used often against black demonstrators in the US.[487] As recently as 2020, we saw black men chased down and murdered in Georgia in broad daylight; and in Kenosha by a teenage vigilante from out of state with an illegal assault rifle, only to be given immediate police protection. He was soon bailed out by the generous fundraising of his fellow Christians.[488] If "faith" compels one to be blind, unjust, and hateful, then there should be no confusion as to the source of that satanic motivation. A jury of his peers later acquitted him after a trial paid for by the generous support of politicians and police. Yet the same police force did not think twice before shooting down a black child with a toy gun on a playground.

Malcolm X once wondered, "In the racial climate of this country today, it is anybody's guess which of the 'extremes' in approach to the black man's problems might *personally* meet a fatal catastrophe first—'non-violent' Dr. King, or so-called 'violent' me."[489] It turned out to be both, as the powers that benefit from such a *status quo* will not allow any success whatsoever to that end. The massive inertia of injustice appears too much for a few to shift. Commemorating a day in their name does not erase the dark history of our government's efforts to discredit them in life and its probable role in their assassinations. The extent of pathology is exemplified by practices like the segregation of black and white blood by the Red Cross until the mid-20th century, despite a black surgeon named Charles Drew developing the entire process. He was fired from being in charge of the blood bank for even attempting to end racial segregation.

Children continue to be taught similar lies in schools about the foundation of this country on freedom. In reality, this empire was built on the same settler-colonial framework as its parent and consciously conceived enslavement of an entire race.[490] George Washington described the US as a "rising empire" as early as 1783.[491] It is a truism that people of the past also have the same consciousness as us and the same sense of morality, which is evident from works like the *Nicomachean Ethics*. Western apologists often highlight internal conflicts among the founding fathers, emphasizing their chained hands by contemporary culture and laws. The argument boils down to excusing the subjugation of an entire race due to the *potential* inconvenience of the politicians. "The slave codes of 1705 are among American history's most striking evidence that our nation's greatest sins were achieved with clear forethought and determined maintenance," refutes Wright.[492]

So if they fail to respond to you, then know they only follow their desires. And who could be more astray than those who follow their desires with no guidance from God? Surely God does not guide the wrongdoing people. (al-Qasas 28:50)

All the while, there was little redirection of these policies from the contemporary Catholic Church, which has always played a central role in Western politics. Holy Roman Emperors like Frederick (1194-1250 CE) not only led the Crusades but also ethnically cleansed Muslim Sicily in 1224 CE. Yet, he kept Arabic manuscripts in his University of Naples and Muslim women in his harem, which earned him a place in Dante's *Inferno*. Papal intolerance of other faiths was demonstrated by many, like Pope Gregory (540-604 CE). During European colonialism, the Bible was used to even support white supremacy and justify the subjugation of Africans as descendants of Ham (*Genesis* 9:18-27).

European slavers initially enslaved "African heathens" by proclaiming a natural right to freedom reserved for Christians. It became problematic when some slaves began to convert, causing the Dutch Reformed Church to protect their business by ending the baptism of blacks in 1656.[493] This profit-based religion was at the heart of Europe's conquest culture, and the resulting nations continue to demonstrate their forged origin stories justifying an exceptionalist ideology of the Old Testament covenant. Examples include the US and the apartheid states of South Africa and Israel, which also explain the cultish zeal of their nationalists towards their constitutions as well as their support for each other.[494]

While many Christians believe that the creation of a just world is inherent in Christian identity, their history shows that the Church often prioritizes its well-being over that of society.[495] Professor David Chidester has shown that the development of comparative religion was indeed a strategy of 19th-century European scholars that helped advance the cause of colonialism and the "domestication" of the African people. A visiting Father Patrick Smyth from Ireland documented how the Catholic Church's expansion following the American Revolution directly partook in slavery.[496] His contemporary Brissot de Warville exposed the systemic rape of slaves on church plantations, where priests were "keeping harems of Negro women, from whom was born a mixed race."[497] In 1610, a conflicted Catholic priest wrote to his superiors about the legality of slavery. Brother Luis Brandaon responded: "I think your Reverence should have no scruples on this point because this is a matter which has been questioned by the Board of Conscience in Lisbon...Nor did the bishops who were in Sao Thome, Cape Verde, and here in Loando—all learned and virtuous men—find fault with it...Therefore we and the Fathers of Brazil buy these slaves for our service without any scruples."[498] There were exceptions, such as missionaries Samuel Worcester and Elizur Butler, who sympathized with native Cherokees and were arrested, tortured, and imprisoned in 1831 by Church authorities.

Meanwhile, Ibn Khaldun had already explained in the 1300s that skin color was merely a result of one's environment.[499] Alas! Common sense existed even in 14th-century North Africa but was thrown overboard centuries later during the middle passage. Historian Tisby highlights the hypocrisy of white Christians who claimed their religion condemned darker-skinned people to slavery, yet worshiped a brown-skinned Jewish man who was put to death by an imperial power.[500] Shedinger describes this *discourse of domestication* as a Western strategy to protect imperialist interests by removing the revolutionary impulse of oppressed people to resist their oppression.[501]

Slavery existed in many forms throughout human history. Perhaps it was a necessary institution for the most humane treatment of prisoners of war, as argued by Mohammad Qutb (1919-2014 CE). Nonetheless, with the rise of Islam and the teachings of the Prophet, the notion of racial and tribal superiority was ripped out of people's hearts. Islam's egalitarianism allowed Bilal, a freed slave of African origin, to be the first person to climb on top of the Ka'ba and call for prayer. Throughout Islamic history, leaders of various ethnicities rose to power, including many *mamluk* (slave) dynasties. Unfortunately, we also saw a reemergence of slavery from a substitution of Islamic values for material gains.

Therefore, it is possible to achieve equality as exemplified by the Prophet, without the need for apologist rationalization centuries later. Even with the blatant racism of today, it is like pulling teeth to get some to admit to the systemic problem. Feeling superior to another human being is the original sin of Satan and all actions deriving from that mindset are truly satanic. Thus, the Prophet emphasized in his final sermon: "O people! Your God is one and your forefather is one. An Arab is not better than a non-Arab, and a non-Arab is not better than an Arab, and a red person is not better than a black person, and a black person is not better than a red person, except in piety" (*Musnad Ahmad* #22978).

Myths of Anglo-Saxon purity have been common among US presidents and leading figures, and even recent presidents have won elections with openly racist rhetoric. It breaks the illusion of progress that we have been led to believe, as nearly half the country is willing to overlook a candidate's crimes just to unite in their hatred towards Muslims and all foreigners. We fail to realize the effect of racism on the psyche of the racist. While we have learned about the effect of slavery on the minds of black people through the experiments of Drs. Kenneth and Mamie Clark, where are the studies demonstrating its counter effects on the minds of the white people in America? Or, for that matter, the effect of centuries of colonialism on the minds of all Europeans? Is it then surprising to see persistent negative feelings towards non-European *foreigners* all over the world?

We watched silently as the leader of the free world openly supported far-right terrorists and refused to denounce white supremacists, while career politicians debated whether he was a racist ad nauseam. Unsurprisingly, a recent study found a direct correlation between a history of Klan activity and Republican votes in America.[502] The "proud boys" flying nazi-confederate-Trump flags being told to "stand by" by their Führer in 6MWE shirts ("six million wasn't enough") still somehow deserve our benefit of the doubt regarding their true motives. While some politicians' unorthodox showmanship invokes our reaction, the more professional politicking of others with the same global outcome goes unnoticed.

How can we rid ourselves of this illness that has taken hold since the birth of this country? President Woodrow Wilson was sympathetic to the Klan and staged a special screening of *The Birth of a Nation* in the White House. Five months later, he reenacted the plot in the black republic of Haiti by sending the Marines in an occupation lasting until 1934. His father was a Southern pastor who defended slavery in a pamphlet titled *Mutual Relation of Masters and Slaves as Taught in the Bible*.[503] Accordingly, he went into WWI with his glamorous talks of liberation and came out redistributing defeated colonies among the victors as "mandates" and vetoing all talks of racial equality in the League of Nations. "Clearly, Wilson had no intention of applying the principle to most of those who took them as inspiration for their hopes of national liberation," notes historian Khalidi. "Indeed, he confessed that he was bewildered by the plethora of peoples, most of whom he had never heard of, who responded to his call for self-determination."[504]

Those who did not live through a president's daily outlandish social-media rhetoric will never understand the insanity hidden in the short excerpts in history books written in its aftermath. History similarly hides many sociopaths like Andrew Jackson, as we continue to make excuses for such behavior and ignore the common trend. "If you look through high school textbooks and elementary school textbooks in American history you will find Jackson the frontiersman, soldier, democrat, man of the people—not Jackson the slaveholder, land speculator, executioner of dissident soldiers, exterminator of Indians," observed historian Zinn.[505] The Confederates and the Nazis were open enemies of America that many Americans sacrificed their lives to defeat. To think that flying those flags within this country would be anything but treason is just another example of white privilege. Instead, journalists who dare to expose our government's malicious actions face such charges and are reprimanded. The anathema towards all foreigners among the evangelical base is such that they would lock up and deport the dark-skinned Palestinian Jesus if he were to return today. Our government would accuse him of "corrupting souls, and in due course, society as a whole" for his critical geopolitical analysis and condemnation of the elite.[506]

The right-wing extremism of this country stretched beyond its birth to the first settlements when laws like the 1667 Virginia Assembly set the foundations of white Christian supremacy. Hitler admired America's genocidal treatment of its indigenous people, and in *Mein Kampf* called it "the 'one state' making progress toward the creation of the kind of order he wanted for Germany."[507] He dreamt the Volga would become Germany's Mississippi, while modeling his invasion of Russia after the British.[508] Millions of North American natives were massacred by the US Army and settlers alike for centuries down to the creation of America's coast-to-coast barren land myth. In that process, even millions of buffalos spanning the entire continent were not spared.[509]

Hate and fear often stem from a lack of understanding, but history has proven that hate only begets more hate. *Yet love is the only rational act.* Malcolm X's original views on race were shaped by his environment but changed within days of his exposure to the true message of Islam during his pilgrimage to Mecca. Muslim brotherly kinship demonstrated across all races and ethnicities showed him the true potential of its values. He concluded: "If white Americans could accept the Oneness of God, then perhaps, too, they could accept *in reality* the Oneness of Man—and cease to measure, and hinder, and harm others in terms of their 'differences' in color. With racism plaguing America like an incurable cancer, the so-called 'Christian' white American heart should be more receptive to a proven solution to such a destructive problem."[510]

Over time, the discourse of *otherization* creates stereotypes and prejudices that justify harming one's rivals for selfish benefits. Psychologist Adam Grant illustrates similar practices in sports, where a team celebrates the injury of a key player on the opposite team and provides his professional opinion: "With all due respect, if you care more about whether your team wins a game than whether a human being is hurt in real life, you might be a sociopath."[511] We must always be on guard to recognize when such tactics are being employed to manipulate our emotions and actions, lest we become devils ourselves. Hindsight criticism matters little if present actions lack fortitude, while the departure of commonsense in civil discourse marks the end of justice for all. God reminds us: "And the [faithful] slaves of God Most Gracious are those who walk on the earth in humility and sedateness, and when the foolish address them [with ignorance] they reply back with mild words of gentleness" (*al-Furqan* 25:63).

To contain Islam, it is also being *religionized* within the Western concept. That allows Muslims to continue their religious practices without interfering with politics or similar entities. "If defining Islam as religion plays into social discourses designed to maintain the privilege of the powerful at the expense of the powerless, then challenging the idea of Islam-as-religion itself becomes an act of resistance against hegemonic powers," explains Shedinger. Western civilizations have done the same with Judaism and Christianity, which made them compatible with global injustice.[512] Therefore, Islam, as the last remaining threat, is also being gradually forced to undergo the same *discourse of domestication* to allow neo-imperialism to persist.

And whoever is mindful of God, He will make a way out for them and provide for them from sources they could never imagine. And whoever trusts God, then He [alone] is sufficient for them. Certainly, God achieves His Will. God has already set a destiny for everything. (at-Talaq 65:2-3)

REBELS WITH A CAUSE

"Every Prophet before me was under obligation to guide his followers to the good and to warn against the evil. As for my ummah, it will have a sound state in its early stage; but the last phase of its existence will be faced with tremendous trials, one after the other, and to each the believer will say, 'That is it...This is going to bring about my destruction.' When it passes, another calamity will approach and he will say: 'This surely is going to be my end.' Whoever wishes to be removed from the Fire (Hell) and admitted to Paradise should die with faith in God and the Last Day; and he should treat others as he wishes to be treated." (Riyad as-Salihin Hadith 667)

Global oppression against Muslims today is the unfortunate *status quo*. This manufactured alienation disappears if we look into the Qur'an, which closely maintains Judeo-Christian traditions. Islam is often mistaken for "the next" or "the newest" religion, which could not be furthest from the truth. The entire Muslim perspective derives from the belief that it is the oldest *and* the original religion for humanity, taught to the first human by the Creator. All the other religions are understood as human corruptions thereafter, which necessitated God's messengers to come and restore.

God commands: "Say, [O Prophet], 'We believe in God and what has been revealed to us and what was revealed to Abraham, Ishmael, Isaac, Jacob, and his descendants; and what was given to Moses, Jesus, and other prophets from their Lord—we make no distinction between any of them, and to Him we (fully) submit'" (al-'Imran 3:84). Along the way, Judaism was codified by Ezra and the Men of the Great Assembly in the 4th century BC. Then Christianity was codified through Paul's teachings during the Councils of Nicea and Chalcedon thereafter. The Jewish Bible confirmed: "Hear O Israel, the Lord our God, the Lord is One" (*Deuteronomy* 6:4). And the Christian Bible reinforced: "'Which commandment is the first of all?' Jesus answered, 'The first is, 'Hear, O Israel: the Lord our God, the Lord is one" (*Mark*

12:28-9). Prophet Muhammad accordingly described himself as bearing the closest kinship to Jesus as there was no other messenger between them (*Sahih Muslim* 2365).

Moses is mentioned the most by name in the Qur'an, while the reverence for Jesus is reflected by an entire chapter named after his mother, which is longer than that of the Bible. She is mentioned over thirty times by name and described as one of the noblest women of Paradise (*al-'Imran* 3:42). Muslims believe in Jesus's return before the end of times to lead all those who *submit* to God, deemed the remaining *Muslims* on earth (*al-'Imran* 3:55). After completing his final years, he would then die and be buried next to the graves of the Prophet, Abu Bakr, and 'Umar in Medina.

Every prophet was met with resistance, leading to subsequent factions and deviations into various faiths with a spectrum of shared beliefs. Nevertheless, the core of Islam remains a straight arrow shot from Adam to Muhammad. Only the *shari'ah* or laws of the Islamic way of life changed to fit human evolution through different times and places. Those rebelling against this divine change gradually split into various divisions, which is reflected even within the names of nearly all world religions, typically denoting a person, object, or philosophy of worship. In contrast, the oldest world religion of *Islam*, chosen by God for us, fittingly translates to a lifestyle of peace and submission to Him alone.

Linguistically, Muslims are those who *submit* their entire existence to serve God's commands with sincerity (Arabic, *naseehah*; *Sunan an-Nasa'i* 4199). "In fact, any who direct themselves wholly to God and do good will have their reward with their Lord: no fear for them, nor will they grieve," confirms God (*al-Baqarah* 2:112). In essence, there have always been two groups of people since Adam: those who *submit* to God and those who do not. In Arabic, it translates to those who are *Muslims* and those who are not, which is even echoed in the Bible: "*Submit* yourselves therefore to God" (*James* 4:7)—where the term in Arabic would again translate back to *Islam*. Therefore, to not be a Muslim only linguistically states one's rebellion against God. Then those continuously at war against God and Muslims, whose path are they truly on?

God has called you Muslims—both in the past and in this [message]—so that the Messenger can bear witness about you and that you can bear witness about other people. So keep up the prayer, give the prescribed alms, and seek refuge in God: He is your protector—an excellent protector and an excellent helper. (al-Hajj 22:78)

From this perspective, we can trace the various deviations back to their primary source and identify their evolution. It would be impossible for any world religion to develop without borrowing from "meta"-Islam, which is evident in the way certain words and concepts have been translated and adapted over time. For example, the word *messiah* was translated from Hebrew (מָשִׁיחַ, Mašíaḥ) into Greek as chrīstós (χριστός, "anointed one"), which is where we get *Christ* with the same meaning. It phonetically resembles *Krishna*, whose origin story in *Mahabharata* parallels that of Moses and Jesus. While the events in the epic anecdotally took place between the 9th and 8th centuries BC, its textual compilation did not occur until the 4th century CE. By this time, Alexander's invasion of India had brought many cultures together, and his men had assimilated into the subcontinent, bringing with them the stories of all cultures along the way.

Accordingly, Dio Chrysostom (40-120 CE) and Plutarch (46-119 CE) reported that Homer's *Iliad* was sung all the way to India. The *Ramayana* borrows heavily from the *Iliad* and the *Odyssey*, with Ravana's abduction of Sita echoing that of Helen of Troy.[513] This intermixing of cultures explains the merging of Moses and Jesus into Krishna, paralleling the Hebrew *messiah*. Such blending of concepts was not limited to Hinduism; the idolization of the Buddha began in western India only after the arrival of the cult of Apollo, just as the appearance of Christ on Roman coins countered the *shahada* on Islamic coins.[514]

It is interesting to note that the letter "J" was not in use during the time of Jesus, and the original pronunciation of his name would have been closer to the Arabic 'Isa. Additionally, being a Palestinian, Jesus would have had a darker complexion, as noted in Islamic traditions. Jews and Christians have long debated over Jesus's messianic status with the gradual reversal of his revolutionary zeal and message. However, the setting of his birth reveals a different reality. At that time, the Kingdom of Judea had become a Roman vassal-state, which represented a continuation of a long history of Jewish persecution since the destruction of Solomon's Temple in 586 BC by Nebuchadnezzar. Herod's (72-4 BC) brutal rule only exacerbated this resentment among his subjects, who were anxiously waiting for the *messiah's* arrival. This is a recurrent concept in Judaism, and one of the 13 principles of faith in orthodoxy, where someone rises to save them from suffering and reestablishes the Temple. Many contenders around that time were raised to messianic status, such as Cyrus (590-529 BC) for rescuing the Jews from Babylon. The Bible is quite graphic in its resentment: "O daughter of Babylon, doomed to be destroyed, blessed shall he be who repays you with what you have done to us! Blessed shall he be who takes your little ones and dashes them against the rock!" (*Psalm* 137). Ezra and Nehemiah were then sent to Jerusalem to establish a Persian-governing system with a priestly elite controlling the population, similar to what the Romans did a few centuries later.

In the Qur'an, God reminds us: "And We certainly delivered the Children of Israel from the humiliating torment" (*al-Dukhan* 44:30). They had been God's chosen people since Jacob/Israel, with the blessing of a continuous chain of prophets that led to their expectation of the next divine deliverance. Judas Maccabeus was another such messiah who led a successful revolt against the Seleucid Empire in 167-160 BC, commemorating the subsequent Hanukkah celebration. Simon of Perea was disputed as a messiah and executed by the Romans close to the birth of Jesus. The group of eighteen psalms written in the 1st century BC reflected this theme and the rising tensions. There also was a shepherd named Arthrongaeus, whose terrorist activities led to the Romans crushing his followers and sending a message by burning an entire town, killing tens of thousands of Galileans.

That was the standard treatment for anyone claiming to be a messiah, representing an act of sedition. Similar movements by Hezekiah and Judas the Galilean were also brutally crushed, just like those of their progeny, leading to a growing anti-Roman sentiment within the Jewish Kingdom. Thus, many recent scholars of religion—such as Warren Carter, Richard Horsley, William Herzog, and John Dominic Crossan—rejected the traditional Christian apolitical view of Jesus contradicting his message within the Bible itself. Some Christian scholars have even gone so far as to suggest that Jesus is more consistent with the Islamic interpretation as a prophet of the Islamic message of justice than with the Christian understanding of him. They argue that Christianity has lost the spirit of Jesus by allowing itself to become "religionized."[515]

In that tumultuous political environment, Mary gave birth to Jesus through an immaculate conception, which God describes as a "Word" from Him— a simple divine command coming into existence. While the first miracle of Jesus in the Bible is his turning water into wine, in the Qur'an, it is him speaking as a newborn—which is also found in the non-canonical *The First Gospel of the Infancy of Jesus Christ* 1:2. A newborn Jesus declared, "I am truly a servant of God. He has destined me to be given the Scripture and to be a prophet. He has made me a blessing wherever I go, and bid me to establish prayer and give alms-tax as long as I live, and to be kind to my mother" (*Maryam* 19:29-32). From the start, God upholds Mary's integrity and establishes Jesus's messianic prophethood. The fact that none of those present at his birth and early life contributed significantly to the canonized Bible explains the omission of major theological concepts that gave rise to later disagreements. Unfortunately, it is impossible to say anything about Jesus's early life with certainty due to the lack of records. "That is because before Jesus was declared messiah, it did not matter what kind of childhood a Jewish peasant from an insignificant hamlet in Galilee may or may not have had," explains Aslan. "After Jesus was declared messiah, the only aspects of his infancy and childhood that did matter were those that could be creatively imagined to buttress whatever theological claim one was trying to make about Jesus's identity as Christ."[516]

Except for the gospel of Luke, none of the gospels were penned by their eponyms and were retrospective narratives written decades to centuries after Jesus's time. They promote the writer's motives without consensus (Arabic: تواتر, *tawatur*), resulting in an image of God with anthropomorphic attributes and ultimately taking human form on earth. This practice of weaving myth and reality to achieve a spiritual message was common at the time, where facts took a back seat to the overall theme.[517] Therefore, it is essential to study the character and motives of the narrators to consider the accuracy of their reporting. Stories such as Herod's dream, the Massacre of the Innocents, and coming out of Egypt are all uncorroborated with contradictory contemporary assertions. Nevertheless, if we were to pause and reflect on events like the Massacre of the Innocents, we would see a single mother from today's West Bank area fleeing south through Gaza to save her son from the slaughter of the leader of Judea. As a result, much has been said about Jesus, turning him into one of the most controversial and disputed figures in history. Perhaps that is why God takes it upon Himself to rectify the allegations against one of his famed prophets: "Indeed, this Quran clarifies for the Children of Israel most of what they differ over" (*al-Naml* 27:76).

From the scant available clues, it can be gathered that Jesus was born in the small, impoverished, off-the-map village of Nazareth, which adhered more to the traditional teachings of the Torah than Jerusalem. "We made the son of Mary and his mother a sign; We gave them shelter on a peaceful hillside with flowing water" (*al-Mu'minun* 23:50). He grew up following the Laws of Moses with the guidance of his pious mother, who was a scholar of Torah herself. Jesus being circumcised speaks to that devotion and continuation of the Old Testament, which he also confirms in the New Testament: "Do not think that I have come to abolish the Law of Moses or the teaching of the prophets. I have not come to abolish but to fulfill what they said" (*Matthew* 5:17). His twelve apostles symbolized a reconfiguration and revival of the twelve tribes of Israel who had lost their ways. Until the end, all of them, including Jesus, claimed their original submission (i.e. Islam) to the *shari'ah* of Moses. Moreover, none of them ever identified as Jews or Christians.[518]

During his early life, Jesus followed the contemporary prophet Yahya/ John the Baptist and was baptized by him. The gospel writers gradually downplayed this implication of his subservience to another prophet in their chronological order to a complete reversal, as it conflicted with his deification. After Herod Antipas executed Yahya, Jesus received the scepter of prophethood at the age of thirty with an addendum to the Torah, easing some of the prohibitions the children of Israel brought upon themselves over the years. Jesus's prayer in the Bible is described as bowing, kneeling, and falling on his face, which resembles Muslim prayer the most (*Matthew* 26:39). Centuries later, at the Council of Nicea, kneeling and prostration were forbidden, which some of the Eastern Churches refused to accept. They continued to pray like Jesus, as corroborated by Salman al-Farsi (568-652 CE) through his journey to Islam from Christianity. Interestingly, if someone saw Jesus praying and preaching today, they might even confuse him for a Palestinian Muslim. "This is the prophet Jesus from Nazareth in Galilee" (*Matthew* 21:11).

As the last of a continuous lineage of prophets to the children of Israel, Jesus presented a totality of the miracles given to them to bring them back to *tawhid* (oneness of God) and the *shari'ah* of Moses. "But they have split their community into sects, each rejoicing in their own," says God (*al-Mu'minun* 23:53). Josephus (37-100 CE) mentioned over twenty-four sects of Judaism around Jerusalem at that time, including the Pharisees, the Sadducees, the Essenes, and the Zealots. Jesus rebuked their corruption, which was quite the opposite of their expectations of a messiah. Instead of simply reestablishing the Temple, he was asking for the people within to correct their ways and return to the straight path. Following Palm Sunday, he walked into the temple complex, overturned the tables of the money changers, and let loose the sacrificial animals, calling them hypocrites and snakes. He accused them of shedding the blood of previous prophets and warned them of the consequences of being condemned to hell (*Matthew* 23:29-34).

Remarkably, these are the same accusations God puts forth against the children of Israel in the Qur'an (*al-Nisa'* 4:155). The similarities only indicate a common source and the prophethood of Jesus and Muhammad belonging to the same fraternity since Adam. To diverge from this is illogical, as repeatedly stressed by God: "The Messiah, son of Mary, was no more than a messenger. [Many] messengers had [come and] gone before him. His mother was a woman of truth. They both ate food. See how We make the signs clear to them, yet see how they are deluded [from the truth]!" (*al-Ma'idah* 5:75). While God's reasoning is simple, deviations from it require a more convoluted line of rationales. A distinction is made here between the established *revealed* religions versus Christianity, which is more of a historical and cultural development. Jesus was not given a new Covenant nor any new set of Laws, which makes Christianity more of a sect of Judaism as Shi'ism is to Islam. Additionally, the gospels in today's Bible are not equivalent to those given to Jesus, as reaffirmed in the Qur'an.

If Yahya's fate, along with the prophets before him, were of any indication, it comes as no surprise that there was almost immediate persecution of

Jesus and his coterie of followers by Rome and the Jewish elite alike. Muslims believe that God saved Jesus at this point, and one of his disciples with his resemblance voluntarily took his place out of devotion (similar to 'Ali taking the Prophet's place during the night of his migration to Medina). This was also the belief of the Gnostic Christians, who were heavily persecuted. This extraordinary ascension of a man may have confused many naive eyes witnessing the event, for the death of the man with Jesus's resemblance on the cross is clear as day. But God strongly condemns them "for their denial and outrageous accusation against Mary, and for boasting, 'We killed the Messiah, Jesus, son of Mary, the messenger of God.' But they neither killed nor crucified him—it was only made to appear so. Even those who argue for this [crucifixion] are in doubt. They have no knowledge whatsoever—only making assumptions. They certainly did not kill him. Rather, God raised him up to Himself. And God is Almighty, All-Wise. Every one of the People of the Book will definitely believe in him before his death. And on the Day of Judgment Jesus will be a witness against them" (*al-Nisa'* 4:156-9).

Some might have even confused his prophecy of returning towards the end of time as the resurrection of the man they watched die on the cross. That was one way to have him retain his messianic status, for his unvictorious "death" would otherwise disprove such claims. Others adjusted the traditional expectation of the messiah to fit Jesus's story, as seen in the apocalyptic imagery of *1 Enoch* and *4 Ezra*. The early Church used both to invent "a new, post-Jewish Revolt paradigm of the messiah as a preexisting, predetermined, heavenly, and divine Son of Man, one whose 'kingdom' was not of this world...But Jesus's kingdom—the Kingdom of God—was very much of this world," argues Aslan.[519]

Following the crucifixion, local unrest was exacerbated exponentially. Facing active persecution from Romans and Jewish elite alike, the original disciples were forced to practice in secrecy, without any formal orthodoxy to preserve Jesus' message. The disciple's lack of authority also resulted in the spread of Jesus's message without any central guidance to preserve its authenticity. "And that is the value of Abu Bakr to Muhammad," explains Shaikh Omar Suleiman. "When a prophet leaves this earth, there is an attempt to switch him to all different directions. Ibn Qayyim said, had Abu Bakr not shut down Musaylimah and all the attempts to change the message of the Prophet, it would have been unrecognizable to us."

Suddenly, a dominating voice emerged from the outside. Paul, an erstwhile Jewish Pharisee, who opposed Jesus while alive, resembles Musaylimah to Prophet Muhammad. Despite never having met Jesus, he suddenly appeared with a new "prophecy" rejected by the original disciples. "When [Paul] had come to Jerusalem [after three years of preaching the son of god], he attempted to join the disciples; and they were all afraid of him, for they did not believe that he was a disciple" (*Acts* 9:26). The story of his "vision" was never told by Paul, but created by his sycophant Luke in his attempted eulogy in *Acts*. His claim that "Christ is the end of the Torah" (*Romans* 10:4) would have been blasphemous to Jesus, who had clearly said to have come to only fulfill it. "In fact, Paul shows no interest at all in the historical Jesus," writes Aslan. "There is almost no trace of Jesus of Nazareth in any of his letters…[nor does he] narrate a single event from Jesus's life," sometimes even directly contradicting Jesus.[520]

Jesus's brother, James the Just, led the apostles and criticized Paul as those who "look at themselves in the mirror…and upon walking away, immediately forget what they looked like" (*James* 1:23). With James as the undisputed leader of the movement after Jesus, the Bishop of Bishops, it begs the question why we end up with Peter and Paul becoming the major contributors to the religion. It turns out that James's hapless execution by Ananus in 62 CE followed the complete obliteration of Jerusalem and the Hebrew assembly in 70 CE. It sealed the fate of Jerusalem in joining the list of people incurring God's wrath for their disobedience despite receiving direct miracles through a prophet, as Jesus warned (*al Ma'idah* 5:115). In their aftermath, the only things remaining of Christianity were Paul's letters and the diaspora of the Hellenist camp.

Divorced from Judaism, this version gained popularity among the Gentiles who were already familiar with Paul's pagan innovations. The gospel writers showed similar zeal and creativity as the Kharijites, justifying their fabrications by the preservation of faith. Written sixty years after the events, the resurrection stories have little historical basis and preemptively present rebuttals for all of their critics over the years. God rebukes such acts by saying: "So woe to those who write something down with their own hands and then claim, 'This is from God,' in order to make some small gain. Woe to them for what their hands have written! Woe to them for all that they have earned!" (*al-Baqarah* 2:79).

Hence, Paul essentially became a prophet and founder of what gradually evolved into Christianity, resembling a combined influence of Roman lands. The faith branched off the central and original message of Islam, with practically everything written about Jesus being by those who never met him. The task of defining Jesus' message fell to a new crop of educated, urbanized, Greek-speaking Diaspora Jews who became the primary vehicles for the expansion of the new faith.[521] This new faith certainly does not resemble the original message of Jesus even within the framework of the Bible, leading to many contradictions. It would later undergo another iteration in pre-medieval Europe, incorporating its pre-Christian past and social forms, "so that the pagan warrior-king could emerge as the Christian knight, remarkably unchanged," explains MacIntyre.[522]

The actual disciples and early Christians were heavily persecuted for over three hundred years, culminating in the Diocletianic Persecution (303-12) when they refused to go along with the concept of divinity. What survived those trying times was only what Diocletian's successors Constantine and Theodosius allowed and later deemed fit for the struggling Roman Empire to recover.[523] In their conformity with modernity, progressive Christian theologians today often claim roots of secularization within the gospels, which rather traces the footsteps of Paulian theology and its subsequent Hellenization. Christianity provided the much sought-after Greek philosophical materialization of *logos*. Thus, the Christian god became a fusion of the Greek *theos*, Hebrew *Yahweh*, Western *Deus*, and other inherently conflicting concepts that naturally give rise to doubt. Similar attempts of "modernizing" Islam only have an underlying scheme of repeating a similar fate while simultaneously paraded as "revolutionary," "courageous," and "maturity" of an "inevitable evolutionary" process.[524] That is just another scheme of the Devil as he was, in essence, the first *progressive*.

He has revealed to you [O Prophet] the Book in truth, confirming what came before it, as He revealed the Torah and the Gospel. (al-'Imran 3:3)

In his analysis of the origins of the New Testament, Aslan argues that Mark was not writing for a Jewish audience, but for Romans in Rome.[525] As the city had just experienced the destruction of Jerusalem, Mark tailored his writing to appeal to Roman sensibilities and reinforce their rule. Such influences are reflected in the canonized New Testament containing only "one letter from James, the brother, and successor of Jesus, two letters from Peter, the chief apostle and first among the Twelve, three letters from John, the beloved disciple and the pillar of the church, and fourteen letters from Paul, the deviant and outcast who was rejected and scorned by the leaders in Jerusalem."[526] Hence, Jesus turned into a Roman Herculean-like *son* with the same birthday as Mithra/Mithras and the resurrection story of Osiris. That was the most effective Roman socio-political way of dealing with the "Jesus/messianic problem" against the existence of their Empire, which then allowed them to survive and continue to exert their rule as the *Roman* Catholic Church. The Jews who followed Jesus had only one option left to survive in Rome: completely separate themselves from Judaism and turn Jesus into a pacifist who was killed by the Jews, absolving Rome of any blame. That was Mark's mission for mainly evangelical purposes. Over time, this shifting of blame continued to stretch to the point of justifying two thousand years of Christian antisemitism.[527]

The gospels also chronologically ascribed more divinity to Jesus, further solidifying Paul's prophetic status and highlighting the authors' motives. It takes after the rabbinic traditions in the Midrash, where the Jewish sages often took the liberty to veer off from scripture and go so far as to invent new books entirely. In fact, Jesus never calls himself the "son of god" in the early gospels, which nevertheless was a traditional title given to Israel's kings like David in *2 Samuel* 7:14; *Psalms* 2:7, 89:26; *Isaiah* 42:1.[528] Perhaps that consuming term was an ill-suited mistranslation which can make average Jews think of themselves as the only beloved people of God, while average Christians may take it literally.

Jesus identifies himself as the "Son of Man" over eighty times in the New Testament. This term translated from Greek (*ho huios tou anthropou*) would have been *bar enash(a)* in Jesus's native Aramaic and *ben adam* in Hebrew: all translating simply to "man." Same as the Arabic *bani adam* (بني آدم, literally: descendants of Adam), which is how God describes us in the Qur'an. But the miracle of the Qur'an's divine origin lies in its technicalities, where God takes it a step further to acquit Jesus's legacy by referring to him not as "son of man" but "son of Mary" (Arabic, ٱبْنُ مَرْيَمَ). "When the disciples said, 'Jesus, son of Mary, can your Lord send down a feast to us from heaven?' he said, 'Beware of God if you are true believers'" (*al-Ma'idah* 5:112). Jesus also distinguished himself by uniquely referring to his people as "O Children of Israel" instead of "O my people" like the rest of the noble prophets in the Qur'an—because in his tradition people belonged to the tribe of their fathers. God alludes to such perfection in asking: "Will they not think about this Quran? If it had been from anyone other than God, they would have found much inconsistency in it" (*an-Nisa* 4:82).

O children of Israel! Remember My favors upon you. Fulfill your covenant and I will fulfill Mine, and stand in awe of Me [alone]. Believe in My revelations which confirm your Scriptures. Do not be the first to deny them or trade them for a fleeting gain. And be mindful of Me. (al-Baqarah 2:40-1)

The early independent churches of Christianity, such as the Anomoeism, Arianism, Ebionites, Elkesaites, Nestorianism, and others, varied in their recognition of the various gospels, religious doctrines, and dogma, much of which were consistent with Islam. This was particularly true in Palestine and Sinai, where many Christian communities strongly opposed the conclusions reached at the Council of Chalcedon in 451 regarding the precise meaning of the divine nature of Jesus Christ, and suffered formal persecution as a result.[529] It was natural for those closer to the birthplace of Jesus to have the most resistance to any corruption of his message. Thus, the standardization of the New Testament in the 6th century CE necessitated the birth of the next messenger in the same century. Today, those dissenting Christian views are rare, having been persecuted early on and naturally accepting Islam since the 7th century.[530]

The formation of the Roman Catholic Church is also ironic, given Jesus's zeal against the Temple establishment. When Jesus told his disciples to take up the cross (*Mark* 8:34), he meant it in the contemporary punishment of sedition for going against the Temple (thus, Roman) authorities. Accordingly, his miracles, like healing the blind as stated in the *Gospel of John*, directly attacked the Deuteronomic view of suffering, which helped domesticate the Jewish people under Persian and Roman Rules. The Sanhedrin's suppression of the Jewish fighting spirit would later parallel the Church's pacification of Jesus's message, as reenacted during American slavery. This ingenious time-tested method necessitated an institutionalized system of atonement through official mediators, which kept the masses under the control of the Temple priests, who were themselves representatives of Rome. Atoning for sin then essentially enriched the Roman treasury. By Constantine's time, the Roman emperors had nominal control over their denizens, while the underground Christian movement had organized into a church mediating all things at local levels. Hence, it is not surprising to see his incorporation of Christianity into the empire and the Church's attempts at global domination thereafter.

The result was not divinely liberating but humanly corrupt, as evident through the misogyny of *1 Timothy* 2:11-15, stripped of the radical sociopolitical message of Jesus.[531] Within a century, the revolutionary tone of the Gospels changed to a more domesticated one: "For the Lord's sake accept the authority of every human institution, whether of the emperor as supreme, or of governors, as sent by him to punish those who do wrong and to praise those who do right" (*1 Peter* 2:13-4). Also, "Slaves, accept the authority of your masters with all deference, not only those who are kind and gentle but also those who are harsh" (*1 Peter* 2:18). Such verses make more sense as imperial propaganda than scripture. It was a direct result of the Jewish Roman Wars (66-73 CE) with total obliteration of Judea and Jerusalem, as noted earlier. Afterward, the messianic tradition, the Zealots, and the Sicarii were all blamed for ruining the Temple-centric Judaism. This gave rise to a Rabbinic Orthodoxy that rejected overt political ambitions, which also gave into Mark's apolitical reorganization of Christianity, written "not in Hebrew, the language of God, nor in Aramaic, the language of Jesus, but in Greek, the language of the heathens," notes Aslan.[532] The survivors of the Roman purge displayed a similar psychological process in the gospels with Roman swords held at the neck, which nevertheless contradicts the Bible: "Do not think that I have come to bring peace on earth. I have not come to bring peace, but the sword," (*Matthew* 10:34, *Luke* 12:51). Although, some have argued the latter to represent a spiritual war, that may be a selective restrictive interpretation.

The Jews say, "Ezra is the son of God," while the Christians say, "The Messiah is the son of God." Such are their baseless assertions, only parroting the words of earlier disbelievers. May God condemn them! How can they be deluded [from the truth]? (al-Tawbah 9:30)

Jewish authorities also had to denigrate Jesus to reject his inconvenient message. "It has been taught: on the eve of Passover they hanged Yeshu [Jesus]...because he practiced sorcery and enticed and led Israel astray" (Baraitha, *Babylonian Talmud,* Sanhedrin 43a). Gradually, his legacy was reduced to the only nonchalant half-sentence from the 1st-century Jewish historian Josephus. This *ad hominem* political weapon is as old as time and was also used against Prophet Muhammad in Medina. Jesus's virgin birth was corrupted by his mother's character assassination, leading to the ultimate rejection of his prophethood and labeling him as a false messiah. That certainly was not the first occurrence of such heinous allegations against prophets in Jewish tradition. It was done to many previous prophets whose message was too disruptive for the elite. The children of the namesake Israel left Joseph for dead and conspired against their father, both of whom were prophets. Fast-forwarding to Moses, the rescued children of Israel rebelled against him even after witnessing the parting of the Red Sea. His complaints are immortalized in the Qur'an: "'O my people! Why do you hurt me when you already know I am God's messenger to you?' So when they [persistently] deviated, God caused their hearts to deviate. For God does not guide the rebellious people" (*as-Saf* 61:5).

Such aggression against God was demonstrated in the beheading of John the Baptist during Jesus's lifetime. It remains in the Old Testament where unspeakable things are said about Noah, Abraham, Lot, and others. Christianity shares similar allegations against prophets while the pope is infallible.[533] What does it say about a god who would allow the divine message to be conveyed by immoral men? Or are those men later dissipated for the people to justify their own sins? Sins that include the use of historical facts to justify antisemitism by nearly all Church leaders.[534]

In contrast, the Qur'an upholds the messengers as humans of the highest moral caliber, who are within our reach as role models. "They are exonerated of the gross sins attributed to them in the Old Testament, but are not raised to the level of divine perfection as Jesus often is in popular Christianity, despite his very human image in the Gospels," explains Lang. "Both of these tendencies may lead to excessive negativism and pessimism, for in the first, the examples are hardly worth following, and in the second, such an attempt would not be realistic."[535] Some of the gospels paint Jesus' exclusivity only to Jews (*Matthew* 15:24) and prejudice against Gentiles: "Go nowhere near the gentiles and do not enter the city of the Samaritans" (*Matthew* 10:5-6); "Let the children [of Israel] be fed first, for it is not right to take the children's bread and throw it to the dogs [gentiles]" (*Mark* 7:27). When they stress love for the neighbor, they mean it within the children of Israel (*Leviticus* 19:18). The Torah goes further by commanding the Israelites to drive out other nations and make no covenant with them (*Exodus* 23:31-33). Such exclusivity and prejudice do not align with the benevolent prophets of God described in the Qur'an, and may only reflect the motives of the authors.

They have taken their rabbis and monks as well as the Messiah, son of Mary, as lords besides God, even though they were commanded to worship none but One God. There is no god [worthy of worship] except Him. Glorified is He above what they associate [with Him]! (at-Tawbah 9:31)

The first Temple of Solomon established a centralized prophet-king, but after his passing, a power struggle ensued as the religious elite systematically carved up a societal hierarchy based on nepotism and greed. This gradually led to a wealth and class disparity that worsened after external powers took over the Kingdom. Eventually, the Temple structure became too powerful for even a prophet or a messiah to overturn. Despite Mosaic Law forbidding usury, the Royal Portico became the center for money-changing and loan-sharking, which sustained the Temple economy. Religious activities were performed by arbiters who took full advantage, much like their pagan counterparts. Both parties even made the same daily sacrifices to the Roman Emperor at the Temple. When Judas son of Sepphoraeus and Mathias son of Margalus planned to steal the Roman golden eagle from the Temple's main gate, both rabbis and their students were burned alive by the Sanhedrin.

The costly and laborious ritual of cleansing a leper performed only by a Temple priest illustrates systemic corruption. To be considered free of sin, the leper had to procure two clean birds, cedarwood, crimson yarn, hyssop, two male lambs, and one ewe free of blemishes, and participate in an eight-day ritual. Only then would he be allowed to rejoin the community of God (*Leviticus* 14). Allowing direct access to God causes political structures to lose power since they also become subservient to divine laws. It is an existential crisis for all oppressive regimes, which must restructure power in some way to assume control. "[This] is an important degree stabilized by the formation of a special priestly caste which sets itself up as a mediator between the people and the beings they fear, and erects a hegemony on this basis," explained Einstein. "In many cases a leader or ruler or a privileged class whose position rests on other factors combines priestly functions with its secular authority in order to make the latter more secure; or the political rulers and the priestly caste make common cause in their own interests."[536]

That recurred with the construction of the Catholic Church, similar to the destroyed Temple, ultimately deviating from the teachings of both Jesus and Moses. Essentially, one has to confess not to God directly but to another man of the cloth, assuming the power of salvation (i.e., *extra ecclesiam nola salus*). It was not a coincidence that the pope was initially called *pontifex maximus*, a title previously held by Rome's high pagan priest. Such power allowed them to control the masses as they pleased. God, through his messengers, reclaims that power to free humanity from its manufactured shackles. Yet, we cannot help but fall right back into the same patterns by voluntarily forfeiting our freedom.

A similar concept later created a schism in Islam where: "Karbala became Shi'ism's Garden of Eden, with humanity's original sin being not disobedience to God, but unfaithfulness to God's moral principles," writes Aslan. In Christianity, Jesus' crucifixion was reinterpreted as a conscious and eternal decision of self-sacrifice, while in Shi'ism, Husayn's martyrdom was seen as an atonement through sacrifice. "There developed in Shi'ism a distinctly Islamic theology of atonement through sacrifice, something alien to orthodox, or Sunni, Islam. 'A tear shed for Husayn washes away a hundred sins,' the Shi'ah say," notes Aslan.[537] Origen (184-253 CE), a revered Christian theologian of the 3rd century, rejected the concept of salvation through the crucifixion of Jesus, which only resembles the high-priest's annual atonement for his nation on Yom Kippur.[538] In contrast, every Muslim is responsible for his actions and forgiveness through direct private repentance. "Each soul is responsible for its own actions; no soul will bear the burden of another. You will all return to your Lord in the end, and He will tell you the truth about your differences," clarifies God (*al-An'am* 6:164).

Surely those who conceal any part of the Book that God has revealed and take for it a small price, they eat nothing but fire into their bellies, and God will not speak to them on the day of resurrection, nor will He purify them, and they shall have a painful chastisement. (al-Baqarah 2:174)

The Kingdom of God attributed to Jesus in the gospels is a prophecy of overturned Rome *and* Temple, vowing "not one stone would be left upon another; all will be thrown down" (*Mark* 13:2). In the end, Jesus told the high priest Caiaphas: "And you will see the Son of Man sitting at the right hand of the Mighty One and coming on the clouds of heaven" (*Mark* 14:62). This was a direct reference to prophet Daniel's vision in the Old Testament of someone yet to come (*Daniel* 7:13). The Romans ultimately destroyed the Temple in 70 CE, fulfilling half of Jesus's mission, which the Qur'an alludes to: "We sent Our messengers in succession: whenever a messenger came to a community they invariably called him a liar, so We destroyed them one after the other and made them into cautionary tales. Away with the disbelievers!" (*al-Mu'minun* 23:44). Of note, the Arabic term for "disbeliever" here again refers to those who knowingly bury the truth. The subsequent "triumph" of Christianity, however, maintained its *Roman* Catholic name with re-establishment of a similar Temple structure. The new empire was only called the Byzantine by later historians, while its occupants considered themselves "Roman." Then what of Jesus's prophecy and the continued suffering of his true followers after his ascension?

Jesus presented himself as God's messenger to the children of Israel, confirmed the Torah, and gave the good news of the final messenger named Ahmad who would establish a new world order (*al-Saff* 61:6). A text from the 2nd century describes Rabbi Shim'on b Yohai's sorrow after Herclius' destruction of the Second Temple. An angel reportedly came to his consolation and "reassured him, for God is 'bringing about the kingdom of [the Arabs] only for the purpose of delivering you from that wicked [Rome]. In accordance with His will, He shall raise up over them a prophet. And he will conquer the land for them, and they shall come and restore it with grandeur.'"[539] It seems that the *son of man* Jesus prophesied was none other than the final Prophet Muhammad, whom the high priest refused to accept, and the later gospel writers concealed or lost in translation.

The descriptions in *Isaiah* 42:1-25 are more accurate for Prophet Muhammad than for Jesus. In particular, verses 16-17 refer to a prophet sent to idol-worshippers—while Jesus was sent to monotheists—to make "crooked things straight," otherwise the straight path or Arabic ٱلصِّرَٰطَ ٱلْمُسْتَقِيمَ (*al-Fatihah* 1:6). While all Muslim prayers start with asking God's guidance to that straight path, it ends with a prayer asking God's blessings for Abraham at least seventeen times a day. Interestingly, God told Abraham: "And I will bless them that bless thee, and curse him that curseth thee: and in thee shall all families of the earth be blessed" (*Genesis* 12:3). Today, no religion sends blessings upon Abraham daily except Islam, while others go so far as to say horrendous things about his character.

The actual word translated as "advocate" in the Bible (e.g., *John* 16) is from Greek *parakletos*, which is *shafi'* in Arabic (Han's Wehr's dictionary) used to describe Prophet Muhammad. A single switch of a letter in translation would have made it *pariklytos*, which translates to *Ahmad* (i.e., most praised) in Arabic.[540] The name Muhammad itself was uncommon in Arabia at the time of his birth.[541] It is no less than another miracle that it is now the most common name in the world as well as the Prophet indeed the most praised human. Although the *Gospel of Barnabas* provides more blatant proof, its authenticity is contested. Linguist Giorgio Levi Della Vida illustrated the problem of mistranslation even with the first sentence of the Bible, where *Bereshita bara* is ungrammatically translated as "In the beginning God created." The actual Hebrew *Bereshit bro* would more accurately be translated as "At the outset of creation, there was chaos."[542] Similarly, a lot can be lost both intentionally and unintentionally through translation.

Rome was ultimately defeated and Jerusalem was liberated, as predicted, by the first Caliph of Islam, establishing the true all-inclusive Kingdom of God on earth—or *new world order*. Perhaps this gives the followers of the entire prophetic lineage—including Abraham, Moses, David, Jesus, and Muhammad—the right to claim the historical Jesus saved by God. Those attributing divinity to him can claim the non-human Christ who was crucified. "Despite the fact that I myself bring a Christian perspective, I firmly believe that the life and work of Jesus as recorded in the Gospels resonate more with…the Islamic tradition than with common Western articulations," writes Shedinger.[543] After the Jews asked John the Baptist if he was the Christ or Elias, he was asked if he was "that prophet" (*John* 1:19). Indicating the foretelling of a prophet other than the two mentioned, just as confirmed in the Qur'an. Furthermore, if you look up the Mirriam-Webster definition of "the prophet," you will also be directed to Muhammad.

Additional clues foreshadowing the final messenger are present in the gospels even with their alterations. God immortalizes Abraham's prayer in the Qur'an: "Our Lord! I have settled some of my offspring in a barren valley, near **Your Sacred House**, so that they may establish prayer" (*Ibrahim* 14:37). After building the Ka'ba with Ishmael, he prayed: "Our Lord! Raise **from among them a messenger** who will **recite to them Your revelations**, teach them the Book and wisdom, and purify them" (*al-Baqarah* 2:129). It echoes the New Testament: "I will raise them up a Prophet from among their **brethren**, like unto thee, and will put **my words in his mouth**; and he shall **speak unto them** all that I shall command him" (*Deuteronomy* 18:18). The only other *brethren* to declare prophethood among the lineage of Abraham was Muhammad. He was also the only messenger miraculously given **God's words in his mouth** in the form of the Qur'an. His return to Mecca with ten thousand Muslims was from the direction of "Sinai, and rose up from Seir unto them; he shined forth from mount **Paran**, and he came with ten thousands of saints: from his right hand went a fiery law for them" (*Deuteronomy* 33:2).

In the Bible, God reassures Abraham by telling him that Ishmael would be blessed with twelve sons, who would father a great nation (*Genesis* 17:20). After Abraham left his wife and infant son in the middle of a barren desert, the Bible mentions an angel guiding Hagar to a miraculous well of water, "and God was with the lad; and he grew, and became an **archer**. And he dwelt in the wilderness of **Paran**" (*Genesis* 21:17-21). The Prophet reported that Abraham visited his son in Mecca to find him behind the Zamzam well, mending his **arrows** (*Sahih al-Bukhari* 3365). *Habakkuk* 3:3 also says "the Holy One" came "from Mount Paran." *Numbers* 10:12 places the wilderness of Paran from northeastern Arabia down to Mecca, and Mount Paran within the Sirat Mountains surrounding that city.[544] There are few contenders for the water well other than the Zamzam next to the Ka'ba. Geographer Al-Muqaddasi described the Red Sea branching "at the extremity of *al-Hijaz* at a place called Faran,"[545] as the letter P does not exist in Arabic. Pre-Islamic Arabic folklore also corroborates Faran hill on Mecca's outskirts, as mentioned in *Kitab al-Tijan* by Wahb Ibn Munabbih.

In *Genesis* 25:13, Kedar is listed as one of Ishmael's sons who would produce the final prophet in **Paran**. Over time, many Jews migrated along southern Arabia down to Yathrib (later renamed Medina) in anticipation of his arrival in several waves since the Babylonian and Roman exiles.[546] "When you see kingdoms fighting among themselves then look for the footsteps of the Messiah," warned their scholars with a specific date of 4291 of the Hebrew calendar correlating with the 6th century CE—when Muhammad was born.[547] Perhaps this was known to the ancient Greeks, as Euripides referred to Arabia as the land of the blessed (i.e. *Arabia Felix*, Ancient Greek: Εὐδαίμων Ἀραβία, *Eudaemon Arabia*).[548] *Isaiah* 60:7 states, "All the flocks of Kedar shall be gathered together unto thee, the rams of Nebaioth shall minister unto thee: they shall come up with acceptance on mine altar, and I will glorify **the house of my glory**." What could this glorified house of God in the lands of Kedar be other than the Ka'ba built by Abraham and Ishmael, where a *great nation* continues to flock in millions every year as God's answer to their prayers?

As in the Qur'an (*al-Baqarah* 2:132-3), the Bible also reports Jacobs's parting words to his sons, where he passes the scepter of prophethood to Judah. "The scepter will not depart from Judah, nor the ruler's staff from between his feet, **until he to whom it belongs shall come** and the obedience of the nations shall be his" (*Genesis* 49:10). The original Hebrew of the bolded phrase is *ad ki-yavo Shiloh*. According to the Rabbinic scholar Rashi's commentary, *Shiloh* translates to "praise/tribute to him," which again translates to the Arabic *Ahmad*. Additionally, the entire Judeo-Christian prophetic lineage remained within the nation of Judah from Moses down to Jesus until the scepter was passed to the only remaining side of the receiver of the original Covenant, Muhammad through Ishmael, who successfully brought the obedience of all the nations. The Prophet said: "I am the chief of the children of Adam on the Day of Judgment and I am not boasting, and in my hand is the **banner of praise**, and I am not boasting, and there has been no Prophet since Adam or other than him, except that he is under my banner" (*Jami` at-Tirmidhi* 3148). It is the same banner of praise —the scepter, the *Shiloh*, the *Maqam al-Mahmud*—that will be passed from all the previous prophets until the final Messenger accepts to begin his intercession as the "advocate" or *parakletos* on the Day of Judgment.

The vision of a sealed revelation in the Old Testament echoes the first Qur'anic revelation. "The vision of all this has become for you like the words of a sealed document. If it is given to those who can read, with the command, 'Read this,' they say, 'We cannot, for it is sealed.' And if it is given to those who cannot read, saying 'Read this,' they say, 'We cannot read'" (*Isaiah* 29:11-2). It prophesied a future end to idolatry and peace through the defeat of warring kingdoms (*Isaiah* 2:4). It was Islam that finally ended idolatry in the fertile crescent through the defeat of warring Persians and Romans. When Archangel Gabriel came upon the Prophet in the cave of Hira (with the sealed message) and commanded him to "Read," he responded, "I do not know how."[549] The chapter ends in the Greek Old Testament, Septuagint, promising: "They that erred in spirit shall know understanding, and the murmurers shall learn obedience, and the stammering tongues shall learn to speak peace" ((*Isaiah* 29:24). This is finally fulfilled by the Muslim greeting of "Peace be upon you."

Much has been written addressing the topics mentioned above since the time of the Prophet. What is mentioned here is only the tip of the iceberg. The rest is for the reader to investigate and contemplate, for that is a divine command. Or we can let the One who created everything clarify the matter based on His expertise:

We ordained for them in the Torah, "A life for a life, an eye for an eye, a nose for a nose, an ear for an ear, a tooth for a tooth—and for wounds equal retaliation." But whoever waives it charitably, it will be atonement for them. And those who do not judge by what God has revealed are [truly] the wrongdoers. Then in the footsteps of the prophets, We sent Jesus, son of Mary, confirming the Torah revealed before him. And We gave him the Gospel containing guidance and light and confirming what was revealed in the Torah —a guide and a lesson to the God-fearing. So let the people of the Gospel judge by what God has revealed in it. And those who do not judge by what God has revealed are [truly] the rebellious. We have revealed to you [O Prophet] this Book with the truth, as a confirmation of previous Scriptures and a supreme authority on them. So judge between them by what God has revealed, and do not follow their desires over the truth that has come to you. To each of you We have ordained a code of law and a way of life. If God had willed, He would have made you one community, but His Will is to test you with what He has given [each of] you. So compete with one another in doing good. To God you will all return, then He will inform you [of the truth] regarding your differences. (al-Ma'idah 5:45-9)

TROUBLE IN PARADISE

Humanity was once nothing but a single community [of believers], but then they differed. Had it not been for a prior decree from your Lord, their differences would have been settled [at once]. (Yunus 10:19)

I: Cain's Boundaries

Our chances of living peacefully perhaps ended with the devil's original vow of envy. His skills were demonstrated with our parents' slippage while surrounded by heavenly conditions. With the limited resources of our earthly lives, Satan can easily exploit this familiar angle to sow animosity among brothers. His guile sharpened within the first-generation immigrants on earth, who fell into the same trap knowing first-hand about the forbidden fruit. Cain's jealousy bested him as he felt more deserving of his brother's blessings to the point of bludgeoning Abel to death, even when he refused to defend himself.

The Prophet spoke of jealousy and hatred as an inherited disease of previous nations that destroys religious commitment. He emphasized the importance of loving one another and spreading peace as conditions of one's faith (*Musnad Ahmad* 1412). However, many psychologists today do not consider jealousy and envy as pathologies, even when all human sufferings can be traced back to them. Nor would they treat them—instead, in some instances, even promote them under the guise of *healthy competition* and *building confidence*. Imam al-Ghazali recognized such diseases of the heart a millennium ago and prescribed remedies, making our current mainstream psychology appear nascent.

And do not be like those who forgot God, so He made them forget themselves. It is they who are [truly] rebellious. (al-Hashr 59:19)

Cain's legacy then resembled Iblis's with his exile from the family's dwelling. "[Cain] replied. 'Am I my brother's keeper?' The Lord said, 'What have you done? Listen! Your brother's blood cries out to me from the ground" (*Genesis* 4:9-10). He settled down in the valley with his wife and children, laying the foundation of sedentary city life with its first boundaries. Meanwhile, Adam and his family of shepherds continued their nomadic hunter-gatherer life in the mountain wilderness. A divergence emerged between city and rural life, stemming from Cain's individualism and Abel's communalism. This may correlate with the first signs of agriculture arising around 11,000 years ago, as carbon dating places the earliest plant and animal domestication at the fertile crescent at around 8,500 BC. Despite the abundance of human activity in Mesopotamia and Asia Minor since the dawn of civilization, their plains and valleys today remain remarkably empty. It is not for their lack of ingenuity but rather the destructive ambitions of endless demigods and demagogues through the ages, rendering the land desolate. Places like Balkh, for instance, have yet to recover from the utter Mongol destruction.

Individualism is not inherently sinful, but when it is pursued selfishly, it leads down an iniquitous path. As historian Diamond points out, societies of hunter-gatherers never developed institutions like money, rule by kings, stock markets, or income taxes, nor did they produce modern innovations like copper or steel tools, automobiles, or atomic bombs.[550] All such innovations of our current civilization that its proponents' marvel would drown in the murky waters of their ethical essence. Ironically, the narcissistic philosophy that drives individualism is harmful even to the self, as it fools one to forgo his well-being both in this life and hereafter. "Humans are ever inclined to selfishness. But if you are gracious and mindful [of God], surely God is All-Aware of what you do," reminds God (*al-Nisa'* 4:128). We should rather channel that natural inclination of selfishness to benefit our hereafter by being virtuous in this life in an apparent "selfless" way. Thus, the Stoic Emperor asked, "Have I acted unselfishly? Then I have benefited. Hold fast to this thought, and keep up the good work."[551]

To draw broadly from these lessons, when one's libertarianism becomes an existential crisis for others, the result is a divine curse of absurdism and famine. As God told Cain: "Now you are under a curse and driven from the ground, which opened its mouth to receive your brother's blood from your hand. When you work the ground, it will **no longer yield its crops** for you. You will be a restless wanderer on the earth" (*Genesis* 4:11-12). Hence, we find humanity at the height of our sedentary existence again faced with atheism and global warming, giving life to God's warning: "...as for the disbelievers, because of their misdeeds, disaster will not cease to afflict them or fall close to their homes until God's promise is fulfilled: God never fails to keep His promise" (*al-Ra'd* 13:33).

Man is created of haste. I will show you My Ayât [torments, proofs, evidence, lessons, signs, revelations, etc.]. So ask Me not to hasten [them]. (al-Anbiya' 21:37)

Settling down in the valley from the mountain wilderness mirrors Adam's descent from heaven and Satan's expulsion down to earth. Even now, the busiest part of a city is called a "downtown," which is also a satirical epithet of the devil's domain. Following Abel's demise, Adam's legacy continued through the lineage of Seth down to Enoch, Noah, and the rest of us. This thematic *descent* into city life recurs with Enoch in the antediluvian Bible, who eventually deserted Babylon to escape its heedless inhabitants. Meanwhile, some of Seth's children also settled in the city because of its more leisurely lifestyle. That ease, however, comes at the cost of spirituality and plays right into the cyclical pattern of civilization.

Again we find *struggle* right at the center of our well-being. "Indeed, it can be observed that there are few religious people in towns and cities, inasmuch as people there are for the most part obdurate and careless, which is connected with the use of much meat, seasonings, and fine wheat," observed Ibn Khaldun.[552] Just as our physical struggle at the gym builds muscles, our philosophical struggle on earth builds character. Seneca wrote an entire book stressing this point *On Providence*. Without it, we atrophy and become easily preyed upon by Satan's illumination of the dark alleys for instant gratification. God warns: "Do not let Satan deceive you as he tempted your parents out of Paradise and caused their cover to be removed in order to expose their nakedness. Surely he and his soldiers watch you from where you cannot see them. We have made the devils allies of those who disbelieve" (*al-A'raf* 7:27). As a city's inhabitants multiply, they compete for its limited resources, which feeds into greed and envy. Our growth is eventually stunted like a bacteria colony on a petri dish. Perhaps that is why God repeatedly commands us to travel through the land to broaden our outlook and tolerance (*Ghafir* 40:21).

Our ancestral ties to the Garden of Paradise compel us to seek and find it in nature and solitude. The hike up Jabal al-Nour was not easy, yet the Prophet frequented it to escape Meccan city life and ascend to the apotheosis of his pre-prophethood spirituality. Jesus similarly went into the wilderness after his baptism, following in the footsteps of his mentor John. Recent studies found that astronauts became more concerned with universalism upon their return from space, demonstrating the power of perspective gained from removing oneself from material things.[553] "From out there on the moon, international politics looks so petty. You want to grab a politician by the scruff of the neck and drag him a quarter of a million miles out and say, 'Look at that, you son of a...'" said Edgar Mitchell from Apollo 14.[554] This "view from above" is also a classic Stoic practice attributed to Marcus Aurelius.

All things considered, it must have been difficult for Cain to leave his birthplace of memories, just as it was for Enoch to leave Babylon. Still, they were only leaving their people, not necessarily a nation. Today's world of nation-states is a relatively recent innovation whose borders vanish when we look at any aerial map. The first artificially defined border on record was Andorra's 120 km border with France and Spain, fixed in a feudal charter in September 1278. Continents themselves are a much more recent invention. Until then, borders were more loosely defined by geographical landmarks, constantly shifting through raids. Those residing within the fluctuating boundaries were more attached to their local villages, with loyalties belonging to local factions, extended families, or tribes, even within large empires.

The remnants of tribalism still linger in geographically isolated regions today. Loyalty and love for one's land and culture are experiences tied to the people who inhabit it. While these constants remain, the artificial lines drawn on maps and the powers that control them are mere variables. Although these borders may achieve material gains, their mental constraints are overshadowed by the conflicts they often ignite. Europe, for instance, has been plagued by continuous fighting over these lines, which were only stalemated by the destructive capability of the advanced 20th-century weaponry. Today, Europe may be integrated through the Union, but it is in the form of a capitalistic bureaucracy from Brussels thwarting regional democracy. This conflict deepens the schism to the point that people of the same land start to see each other as different. In such cases, a Bengali may consider a Rohingya a foreigner, just as a Han may feel towards the Uyghur. Even if one country pushes the border over, the *occupied* people would resist out of their newfound nationalism. However, this love is no longer for the people or the land, as neither changes, but for the manufactured concept of a nation.

Many of today's conflicts between nations take advantage of hard-lined patriotic values, which are not as well-founded as they appear. For instance, the patriotic emotions displayed in the Indian subcontinent only date back to the British occupation. Throughout history, many empires pursued the subcontinent for its natural resources, which were otherwise enjoyed by the *people of the land* living in jagged harmony. Typical local battles over land and legacy changed little at the village level. Invaders like the Kushans, the Hephthalite Huns, and the Mughals also assimilated within a few generations. The British, however, came only to exploit, displaying exceptional brutality and profound arrogance towards the locals. This marriage under duress was destined for a divorce, which ultimately came in 1947. The independence movement spawned from their love for the land predating today's nationalism. In their last-ditch effort, the shrewd Empire left the subcontinent with artificially drawn lines on a map based on differences invented from their three centuries of divide-and-rule policy.[555]

Unfortunately, people do not live on a map but on land where that line went through villages, families, and even houses, tearing them apart. More than half a million people were butchered in one of the largest relocation catastrophes, all of which were preventable. A border dividing the *same land* inhabited by the *same people* with no such loyalties before that artificial line. Not unsurprisingly, even the term Hinduism was coined by the British to smash together a blend of local religious practices to prop them up against Muslims who have otherwise lived harmoniously for over a thousand years. It further highlights the historically invalid arguments of the current Hindutva movement which has direct ties with the origin of Nazism. Similarly, while the Koreans celebrated their freedom from Japanese occupation at the end of WWII, the Allies carved up the region in a way that continues to keep them divided. All of the conflicts in Africa can also be traced back to the artificial borders created by the imperial powers of England, France, Belgium, and Germany.[556] Then how do we define or justify the love for the countries that came out of those lines? It is nothing but politically manufactured ignorance that overlooks the exploitative nature of such arbitrary borders.

Pride and patriotism are flimsy concepts that often lead to arrogance, division, and denial. Yet their power makes them easily exploitable. They are enough to run the armed forces, providing self-esteem for a soldier's desperate rise out of the ghetto to become a respected marine, serving as a psychological balm for his pain. "Pride generally has a good reputation and is socially encouraged, yet...it's sufficiently negative," explained a renowned psychiatrist. "The problem is...Pride is defensive and...can be knocked off its pedestal back to Shame, which is the threat that fires the fear of loss and pride."[557] Pride prevents us from asking if it is truly patriotic to support unjust wars waged by our leaders. What is the duty of a patriot when his nation commits atrocities? Maybe his loyalty should instead be to an ideal—a constant worth fighting for.[558] Only when a nation upholds those virtues does it deserve our allegiance. When a nation falls short, it no longer deserves such devotion until the expectations are restored.

Believers fight for the cause of God, whereas disbelievers fight for the cause of the Devil. So fight against Satan's [evil] forces. Indeed, Satan's schemes are ever weak. (al-Nisa' 4:76)

A similar pride was prevalent in the pre-Islamic Arab world (of *jahiliyyah*), laden with never-ending conflicts. Each round of fighting only fueled a higher level of hatred, resulting from the bloodshed and injustice from the prior, leading to the next. This created perceived differences that even the most intelligent amongst them could not overlook. It is miraculous how the Prophet brought those same people together within a few decades of preaching his divine message. While he had to demonstrate an unimaginable amount of wisdom, patience, and equanimity, the resulting unity is unmatched in all human history. It serves as a unique exception to the overwhelming natural course of humanity, made possible by the realignment of the people to a new purpose and loyalty towards a divine ideal, superseding their differences. "God brought their hearts together. Had you spent all the riches on the earth, you could not have united their hearts. But God has united them. Indeed, He is Almighty, All-Wise" (*al-Anfal* 8:63).

The prophet's wisdom and examples "are among the treasures of mankind, not merely Muslims," remarked Mahatma Gandhi.[559] That renewed vigor allowed Khalid Ibn al-Walid (592-642 CE) to simultaneously bring down two of the world's greatest empires with his band of bedouins from the desert. His strategies and tactics are strikingly similar to Sun Tzu's aphorisms, which he most likely never studied. Still, we fail to see much in the Western textbooks/scholarship about perhaps the greatest general in human history or the civilization that stretched from the Indian Ocean to the Atlantic. It is particularly amusing to see the endless explanations for the miraculous success of Islam by one Occidental guru after another, all circumnavigating the clearest elephant in the middle.

The first Caliph Abu Bakr's oath of leadership in 632 CE reflected this ideology. He urged his people to obey him only if he adhered to the guidance from the Qur'an and *sunnah*, demonstrating the historical establishment of the separation of religion and state. If he failed, they were no longer obligated to follow his commands. Now that is an aplomb Caliph, whose successors like 'Ali Ibn Abi Talib also demonstrated those values in his dealing with the Kharijites. Unfortunately, they resemble fictional paragons rather than realistic expectations from our current world leaders. Such nobility is dangerous for today's leaders as it risks their control of the masses. Instead, most leaders promote Hegel's definition of virtue as complete obedience to the government with resolute patriotism. Concentrating power under one leader in today's sizable *ummah* poses significant risks than benefits, as colorfully demonstrated in history. On the other hand, all leaders rise from the people who share some of the blame, as we have forgotten the etiquette of a follower. When a man questioned 'Ali about the growing unrest during his caliphate, he replied: "It is because Abu Bakr and 'Umar ruled over people like me, while I rule over people like you."

It is easy to criticize German support for Nazi rule before WWII but overlook our national tendencies towards similar extremism. The utter humiliation of Germans by the Allies following WWI through the Treaty of Versailles only solidified their isolation. It was as counterproductive as the terms against Russia at the end of the Crimean War in 1856.[560] Alienated and ostracized, the Germans were coerced into extreme nationalism while faced with a crippling recession, as predicted by Keynesian economics in *The Economic Consequences of Peace*. Hence, it became criminal not to be patriotic and make the rest of the world pay. That sentiment was brilliantly exploited by the Nazis, leading to their outrageous crimes against humanity. But the aftermath of the Nazi defeat conveniently hides Western Europe's pride and self-exoneration "without paying the price of recognizing its role in its genesis," points out Frankopan.[561]

"Jews had won over half of Germany's Nobel Prizes," noted Malcolm X. "Every culture in Germany was led by the Jew; he published the greatest newspaper. Jews were the greatest artists, the greatest poets, composers, stage directors...And the next thing they knew, there was Hitler, rising to power from the beer halls—with his emotional 'Aryan master race' theory."[562] Even with the Nazi's polarizing ideology, most Germans were trapped by national pride. This blind, obsequious love prevented them from seeing the atrocities until it was too late. Its roots go back to German philosopher Johann Gottfried Herder (1744-1803 CE), credited with the European nationalistic movement. He believed it to be the natural state of humanity, superseding any religious morality. The latter he outright dismissed, pulling the prideful blanket over our history that gradually blurred the line of divine laws of the previous millennia.

Today, similar paradigm blindness makes some like Sam Harris and David Irving suggest that the Jews had somehow brought the Holocaust upon themselves for "their refusal to assimilate."[563] Ironically, Zionists employ the same excuse to justify their continuous onslaught against Palestinians. It is a quintessential case study of how the victims of tremendous atrocities let their trauma transform them into their monstrous oppressors. To prevent similar history from repeating, we must refrain from such blind love and hate. Our loyalty and primary focus must always be on upholding peace and justice. Justice, not only in its restorative sense but also in its primary distribution amongst everyone. All other matters must fall under and be held to that standard.

Those who take protectors other than God can be compared to spiders building themselves houses—the spider's is the frailest of all houses—if only they could understand. (al-'Ankabut 29:41)

II: Who Owns Democracy?

Despite being one of the earliest forms of democracy and the first written constitution, the Prophet and the succeeding Caliphs' rule have been largely neglected in Western dialogues. Although it may not align perfectly with our current democratic definition, that form of popular sovereignty and pluralism was unique, and it took centuries to emerge in Europe. The Orwellian dictum goes, "Who controls the past controls the future: who controls the present controls the past."[564] Democracy, in turn, has become a political weapon with an ever-changing definition to suit the wielder's needs. Similar trigger words, such as freedom, patriotism, terrorism, and treason, are part of the mainstream gaslighting campaign and are often used with unilateral exceptionalism by those who desecrate them.[565]

The Prophet's implementation of the Qur'anic principles led to one of the most robust and fair governments in human history. He reinstated the precedent of consultation (Arabic, *shura*) among the believers to elect a capable leader, which was a significant departure from the nepotism that characterized much of human history (*Ash-Shuraa* 42:38). The consultants were chosen by the people based on their character and qualifications. The constitution of that government was the Qur'an and *sunnah*, superseding the inseparable greedy motives behind all human constructs. This divine filter satisfied Aristotle's primary considerations for all governments, namely whether any particular law is good or bad and its consistency with the idea and character that the lawgiver has set before his citizens.[566] Ultimately, God is the supreme lawgiver who clarifies the good and the bad, even in the face of unrelenting human corruption.

The *shura* also protected that divine constitution from fallible human misinterpretation, thus preventing it from turning into an authoritarian theocracy. It preceded centuries of feudalism in the West, which remained in the dark ages until the philosophies of the Islamic world penetrated the minds of their revolutionaries. We need not look further than our judicial system to see how our interpretations of a non-divine constitution can easily be exploited. Unsurprisingly, similar misguided secularizing outside the Islamic world asymmetrically elevated individualism and socialism. While the former led to our extreme capitalistic society, the latter evolved into communism—both far removed from a fair system. Hence, all democratic processes evolving from those ideals are also far from the middle balance, as they attempt to solve problems originating from a false premise: the elimination of divine boundaries. Both extremes share a passion for secularism, which only fuels hedonism. All of their thinkers tried to redefine *religion*, like Emile Durkheim, Sigmund Freud, Karl Marx, and Clifford Geertz, among others—each only differing from the other in their brilliant ways of opening up all roads to divinely censured vices that only champion devilish ways to civilization's ruin. This dualistic worldview separating the sacred and profane realms is an Occidental construct that only trades one set of problems for another.

In their hearts is a disease [of doubt and hypocrisy] and God has increased their disease. A painful torment is theirs because they used to tell lies. (al-Baqarah 2:10)

This nation was founded on escaping religious persecution by the Catholic Church, which shaped the way it developed its worldview, similar to the Sapir-Whorf hypothesis of linguistic determinism. The resulting theme of the constitution became the "separation of church and state" as enshrined in the First Amendment. However, this concept was not an original achievement, as it had already been implemented by the Prophet in a pluralistic Medina, where the subsequent Caliphs had no religious authority over the community. Moreover, the notion of completely removing religious influences from the government is misguided and unachievable. In fact, religion has been deeply embedded in every aspect of American life since the very beginning.[567] The secularization process only makes it impossible to achieve constitutionally guaranteed religious freedom, as recently exemplified by the Supreme Court's order for a Jewish university to recognize student groups challenging its core values.[568]

This civilization was founded on Judeo-Christian laws that are deeply ingrained into its constitution. Right after its declaration in 1776, the states legislated taxes that mandated supporting Christianity. In 1892, Supreme Court Justice David Brewer even declared the US a Christian nation.[569] It is also difficult for our Judicial branch to coherently define *religion*, as shown by Professor Winnifred Sullivan's works. Nevertheless, most prohibitions within our legal system are based on religious values established within humanity to promote our well-being. Opting between similar divine laws only deceives our "intellect" to promote injustice. God warns, "Satan only makes them [false] promises and deludes them with [empty] hopes. Truly Satan promises them nothing but delusion" (*al-Nisa'* 4:120). Decriminalizing prohibitions like adultery in our attempts to "secularize" only promotes our desires and lust to make what was divinely forbidden to protect the family structure lying at the center of all civic values. Would we then decriminalize murder too since it has its roots in religion to become more secular and leave it up to each individual's judgment? "Whence comes the Innovator's authority to pick and choose?" asked C.S. Lewis.[570] Then who gets to decide where we draw the divine-secular line?

It behooves one to realize that the One who created us in our diversity knows the best laws and standards of living for us. God's commands are not just "interesting" and up for debate but the clear instruction manual from the Maker. It is essential to understand the motives behind any "secular" movement and how that term is used. The goal should not be to divorce ourselves from divine guidance, but only to prevent the interpretation of religion through political motives. Religion as a way of life for the people, however, can never be apolitical as it supersedes all human entities to define the boundaries of our passions. Therefore, any effort to make it apolitical is futile and can only be achieved with a complete abandonment of God. As Aristotle stated, man is "by nature a political animal."[571] In this way, Islam promotes global democracy, where even those living outside the artificial boundaries of a nation are represented by its laws and protected from its aggression.

God's warning is clear: "But whosoever turns away from My Reminder [i.e., neither believes in this Qur'an nor acts on its teachings] verily, for him is a life of hardship, and We shall raise him up blind on the Day of Resurrection" (*Taha* 20:124). Yet, while witnessing the resultant hardship, we are perplexed by its etiology. "In matters of faith, He has laid down for you the same commandment that He gave Noah, which We have revealed to you [Muhammad] and which We enjoined on Abraham and Moses and Jesus: 'Uphold the faith and do not divide into factions within it'—what you [Prophet] call upon the idolaters to do is hard for them; God chooses whoever He pleases for Himself and guides towards Himself those who turn to Him" (*Ash-Shuraa* 42:13).

Throughout history, humans have demonstrated their ability to change their environment to meet their needs. We have done so with our own laws and the divine, sometimes even changing the status of the messenger, as we explored in the previous chapter. Then God sent His final messenger to rectify and correct, solidifying the message to prevent it from further corruption (and obviating the need for any more messengers). The Prophet represents a culmination of the evolution of human consciousness and spirituality, expressed through a perfected ideology.[572] The Qur'an is unique in its divine guarantee of protection, which is also evident in its miraculous transmission history. "Indeed, it is We who sent down the message [the Qur'ān], and indeed, We will be its guardian," assures God (*al-Hijr* 15:9). Deviating from its supreme laws only promotes a perverse individualism veiled under various ideologies to feed a capitalistic appetite that ultimately ruins the individual and the community.

Except for God's messengers, there are absolutely no incorruptible humans in existence. As a result, all attempts to secularize free us from divine laws that are set in place in divine wisdom to prevent us from the traps of oppression and injustice. "Fair retribution saves life for you, people of understanding, so that you may guard yourselves against what is wrong," reminds God (*al-Baqarah* 2:179). Instead, when these secular forces cut their ties with divinity to broker principles of justice and fairness based on their acumen, they inevitably fall short along a broad spectrum without exception.

This was clearly demonstrated at the start of WWI, with all democratic claims culminating in the US's global empire project at its end, where not a single territory was liberated. Indeed, the entire war was fought for the industrialist's control of colonies and spheres of influence at the cost of ten million impoverished soldiers and twenty million civilians. Soon after their return from the slaughter abroad, General MacArthur and Major Eisenhower were tasked with violently evicting twenty thousand hungry and unemployed veterans encamped around the capital with their wives and children. Instead of helping them, they were given the boot, bullets, and tear gas, as the truest sign of their democracy.

Islamic democracy, on the other hand, strives for pluralism rather than secularism, promoting acceptance, peace, tolerance, and justice through the governing bodies instead of unlimited greed and survival of the fittest. It aims to honor equality and sees other people as having the same rights as oneself. While Islam is a divine religion, its history is human, and there have been both exemplary and chaotic periods depending on adherence to its ideals. Muslims enjoyed a thriving and vibrant civilization as long as they maintained those values. Today, those same ideals lie behind the success of the West and the tipping of global power. To reclaim our heritage, Muslims must reject extremism on both sides and recognize the Quran's reverence for a just world that includes all humanity. Movements that deviate from this balance not only deprive non-Muslims of God's mercy but also do not spare Muslims. As Dr. Hathout wrote, "It is doubtful that the politicians and financiers of the world possess the necessary vision, wisdom, and ability to undergo a dramatic self-change. The only hope is a massive campaign to educate the public who, as voters, remain the final arbiters at the end of the day."[573]

The persistence of authoritarian rule in Muslim lands today is supported by Western powers who justify their existence by playing on the fear of an Islamist-state alternative.[574] The US and its allies have been actively preventing authentic democracy globally to maintain their hegemony with an external veneer of support.[575] The Ayatollah's words against the US implanted Manchurian monarch still ring true: rulers should live like ordinary citizens and be open to criticism.[576] However, the overwhelming Muslim support for democratic ideals is not tolerated by those who benefit from the existing inequalities. This reveals the true imperial colors of the US, which is further reflected by the geographic spread of its corporations and armed forces. America's history is inextricably tied to its territorial empire, as highlighted by the origins of WWII and the "war on terror" beginning with a military base. Even everyday items like birth control pills, chemotherapy, plastic, and Godzilla have their roots in the territorial empire.[577]

Low voter turnout in the US and the perception that politicians do not care about improving people's lives have a long history. Over the last century, only about half of the eligible US voters have participated in the elections.[578] This was the original intent of the founders who laid the groundwork for a republic—not a democracy—as stated by Madison in *Federalist 10*.[579] Keep that in mind the next time the media describes an election as a "landslide" or "overwhelming." Elected officials still make consistent efforts to decrease participation further by passing more restrictive voting legislation. Regardless of the terms attached to describe such a system, it is by definition not a majority rule.

Western democracy is plutocracy at its core, evolving within its boundaries over centuries and unlikely to survive if transplanted to a different environment.[580] Societies are no different from the individuals they are composed of, where no single formula applies to all. Nations must develop democratic formulas that best fit their socio-cultural dimensions without outside interference to allow them to be nurtured and mature. Unfortunately, the chances of that happening are slim to none. Former US Marine General David Sharp once stated that if the US would keep its "dirty, bloody, dollar-soaked fingers" out of the business of other nations, they would arrive at their own solutions, even if it necessitated a violent revolution.[581] Nearly all recent cases in the world where non-democratic institutions have failed involve Western manipulation and interference, making objective scientific criticism impossible.

On the other hand, the "success" of our democratic process is due to our global exploitation, putting us on a similar trajectory as many empires of the past. Like all things in our civilization, democracy also comes secondary to the primary *religion* of capitalism, motivating our bureaucratic actions. This is exemplified by the US imposing trade embargoes on a leftist Nicaraguan government in the 1980s to pressure them to become more "democratic," while refusing to do the same to the South African apartheid government, claiming it would thwart democracy. Concentrating economic power among a handful of elites and big businesses dismantles democracy by shifting all true political power to serve their interests, leaving average citizens with little influence. A clear case in point was United Fruit's involvement in the planning and executing of a coup against Guatemala's democratic government in 1953, in response to the expropriation of the company's uncultivated lands.[582]

This nation was modeled after the Roman Republic of landowners and expectedly underwent a *deja-vu* imperial transition. The proof is all around us if one only cares to look. Our government seldom passes any policy without the approval of large international lobbies and powerful interest groups.[583] Thus, every Republican sided with the American Israel Public Affairs Committee (AIPAC) against the Iran nuclear deal in striking solidarity across party lines, which is rare in most other issues. Historian Gareth Porter, among others, has documented speeches made verbatim by members of Congress that were written by such lobbies. Even the Supreme Court is in on it through such actions as overturning the Voting Rights Act.[584] With that set-up, our electoral college, and the two-party system, the whole democratic process, in essence, becomes nothing more than a glass menagerie of sham deception to give the masses the illusion of power.

Basic human survival necessitates one to invest all efforts in the preservation and protection of livelihood. If a salesperson fails to sell his product with a smile, he will be unemployed and fail to provide for his family. If career politicians fail to get reelected, it jeopardizes their source of income, necessitating selling their power to the highest bidder. Accordingly, Peabody Energy, one of the largest private coal producers on the brink of bankruptcy, saw its stock prices soar with the election of Trump.[585] It became even more flagrant during his reelection with donations from global billionaires who promptly received expected returns on their investments. A sincere politician in our current system would never get endorsed nor make it on the ballot. Realizing this truth, a frustrated Carlos Peña Romulo once complained that Washington was "'crowded with little Neros, each fiddling away blithely' while the empire burned."[586]

The Republicans, having abandoned the pretense of a normal parliamentary party, mobilize extremist evangelical Christians, remnants of former slaveholding states, and nativists to attract votes.[587] The Democrats are not far behind in their fervor for corruption and immorality. Those with better policies and qualifications have no real chance against such a massive bureaucracy. While we may deduce why politicians would argue otherwise, those siding with them can only be classified as hypocrites or gullible dullards. We should not jump for the first banana that is presented to us. Instead, we must evolve to ask about the motives behind that particular banana; how it compares to the rest of the bananas in the bunch; who owns the plant and the forest it came from; and how it was produced.

The strength of a foundation is tested only during strong winds or aftershocks. While we do not shy away from flashing our democratic nationalistic badge to the rest of the world, we saw it all shatter with the slightest glimpse of tension in 2021 that we have been dishing out to the rest of the world. Nepotism within the presidential family became apparent as they joined their friends in thievery that affected the entire nation, albeit not for the first time. The "checks and balances" supposedly in place to prevent corruption failed to prevent the lunacy of a government that did not win by popular vote in the first place.

After witnessing such events, only a blind fool would make baseless claims in an attempt to out-bray a donkey. The application of the Bill of Rights has diminished considerably, as has the spirit of our Constitution. Unconstitutional laws are being passed without much protest, while federal and local agencies are routinely resorting to totalitarian tactics. Perhaps we can learn from medicine where disease prevention is the key, and palliative care only leads to an easier death.

III: The Empire Strikes

We shall assign that home of the Hereafter [Paradise] to those who rebel not against the truth with pride and oppression in the land nor make mischief by committing crimes. And the good end is for the Muttaqûn [the righteous]. (al-Qasas 28:83)

Although the ones fighting the empire's wars are invariably from the lowest economic status, the call to arms is made by the powerful, wealthy elite. How else to pocket the enormous $3.5 trillion annual tax collected exclusively from the poor but by manufacturing consent from those same people in exchange for their naive pride? In reality, soldiers do not die for our freedom, but only to secure the insatiable lavish lifestyles of the establishment. General Smedley Butler once confessed: "I spent thirty-three years in the Marines, most of my time being a high-class muscle man for Big Business, for Wall Street and the bankers. In short, I was a racketeer for capitalism."[588]

Our government had little hesitation in testing chemical warfare on over sixty thousand of its own men' during WWII, leading to debilitating aftereffects such as cancer, lung disease, eye problems, scarred genitals, and psychological damage.[589] It tested biological weapons on big cities, including San Francisco, Tampa Bay, St. Louis, and New York, with many fatalities.[590] While fighting the Nazis, America conducted its own racial experiments to test the effect of mustard agents on African Americans, Japanese Americans, and Puerto Ricans. The latter were also sent to San Jose Island near Panama for chemical weapons testing.[591] All of it earned the Army's chief of medical division, Dr. Cornelius Rhoads, a Legion of Merit award. This war hero then took the leftover mustard gas from WWII to continue his research on cancer patients with a sizable grant from his friend Alfred P. Sloan, then president of General Motors.

Today, Rhoads is known as an accomplished director of both Manhattan's Memorial Hospital and the Sloan Kettering Institute. Not for his confession letter from his station in Puerto Rico, describing the locals as "beyond doubt the dirtiest, laziest, most degenerate and thievish race of men ever inhabiting this sphere." He even wished to "exterminate the population" through a natural disaster and furthered "the process of extermination by killing off 8 and transplanting cancer into several more...The matter of consideration for patients' welfare plays no role here—in fact, all physicians take delight in the abuse and torture of the unfortunate subjects," he boasted.[592]

Naturally, he made the *Time* magazine cover in 1949 and was honored by the American Association for Cancer Research's prestigious annual award, commemorating his name. It is just one example of the elites in our system, rotating through various positions of power without the slightest accountability. When we speak of the US and its activities, we refer to the interests of such aristocracy and their financial motives, which are packaged and sold as national interests. Adam Smith criticized these "masters of mankind" of his day, who have only perfected their techniques in the subsequent era.

Developed countries only praise and support democracy as long as it promotes their capitalist interests, veiled with whatever is convenient to make it palatable to the *religious* masses. They have caused the rise and fall of many regimes worldwide and often supported those antithetical to their "core values" for short-term gains. The US confiscated the western half of this continent from Mexico by manipulating them into conflicts to fulfill its *manifest destiny*, only to have them work its fields as "aliens" to their native land. This term served America's aggressive imperialism since conception, which has been the motive behind every one of its wars, just like *la mission civilisatrice* (the civilizing mission) was for the French—both having a much more positive tone than the genocides they symbolize.

The two World Wars essentially destroyed European colonial rule but shifted power to the Soviets, who emerged victorious (not without paying for their role in initiating conflict). Gradually, its imperial power only matched that of the US, which naturally ushered in the Third World War, colloquially known as the Cold War. It would be unnatural to expect Russia not to make attempts for its lost territories after the forced dismantling of the Soviet Union, the same way the US resisted the breaking away of the South. However, Orwell's *Cold War* is incorrectly applied here as it ignores the active warfare between these empires in their proxy lands, who bore the totality of the suffering. The only *cold* thing about it was the lack of morality during the entire catastrophe, as detailed by Vijay Prashad in *Washington Bullets*.

Vietnam narratives often gloss over Ho Chi Minh's efforts to expel the French and Japanese imperial occupation at the end of WWII. A popular democratic republic was then established with a Declaration of Independence inspired by the French and American Revolutions, both of whom soon taught it a crucial lesson. The Republic lasted a solid week in September 1945—the only time in Vietnam's history when it was completely free from foreign domination. The declassified *Pentagon Papers* revealed the motives of the imperial powers, as they immediately went to work to split the region. Initially, China occupied the north while Britain occupied the south. Then the US persuaded both to deliver their halves back to France without consulting the Vietnamese, who had fought hard for their sovereignty. Ho Chi Minh's eight letters to President Truman reminding him of the Atlantic Charter promises went unanswered.[593]

Subsequent resistance to French occupation led to an eight-year war, where 80% of the French war effort was supplied and financed by the US. Secretary of State Dulles even generously offered France nuclear weapons in their final Vietnam days, which France gracefully declined.[594] In 1954, France finally withdrew in defeat, signing an international peace agreement in Geneva that promised the Vietnamese an election to choose their government. Unfortunately, the prior year a US Congressional report declared: "The area of Indochina is immensely wealthy in rice, rubber, coal, and iron ore. Its position makes it a strategic key to the rest of Southeast Asia." Thus, the US jumped in to prevent unification (just as in Korea) by forming a "South Vietnam [which] was essentially the creation of the United States," confessed the *Pentagon Papers*. The CIA trained and placed Ngo Dinh Diem as the prime minister, whose atrocities soon led to a coup assassination in 1963 with US backing, of course. Within a year, the US officially declared war using the fabricated events of the Gulf of Tonkin. The rest is history revolving around the wheel of Catherine costing over two million civilian lives.

The casualties in Vietnam continue to this day from Agent Orange, intentionally used to destroy food crops and poison soil. More than double the number of bombs were dropped in that country than the total of Europe and Asia in WWII, resulting in over twenty million craters. The war cost Vietnam 17% of its population compared to 0.1% for the US.[595] National Security Adviser Henry Kissinger's open orders for genocide were recorded and carried out by sending "anything that flies on anything that moves."[596] The infamous My Lai massacre was initially covered up by Colonel Oran Henderson, who later confessed: "Every unit of brigade size has its My Lai hidden someplace." Even when the pictures and stories leaked into the international press, the domestic media paid no attention. Despite all of President Carter's heartfelt remarks on racial, socioeconomic, and foreign policy issues, his actions in office remained within the traditional framework. He also pardoned Lieutenant William Calley of the My Lai massacre, where he was documented throwing a crawling baby by a leg and shooting the infant point-blank.[597]

What level of savagery is reached by intentionally destroying the food supply by poisoning arable land that affects peasants and children the most? Admiral William Leahy remarked in 1944 that a similar proposal to destroy Japanese rice crops would "violate every Christian ethic I have ever heard of and all known laws of war."[598] Yet, all mentions of the US's chemical warfare in our media only focus on how it affected our soldiers while completely ignoring the large local populations that continue to suffer.

The US bombed Cambodia mercilessly during that period and helped a regime that perpetrated mass genocide. It covered Laos with aerial bombs, 30% of which remain unexploded and continue to maim civilians, adding to the twenty thousand death toll.[599] Deputy Chief of Mission Monteagle Stearns gave the reason: "Well, we had all those planes sitting around and couldn't just let them stay there with nothing to do."[600] Such is the value of minority life reduced to Orwell's *unpeople*: "They arise out of the earth, they sweat and starve for a few years, and then they sink back into the nameless mounds of the graveyard and nobody notices that they are gone. And even the graves themselves soon fade back into the soil."[601] The US backed a military coup in Indonesia in 1965 by General Suharto, who carried out a "staggering mass slaughter" compared by the CIA to those of Hitler, Stalin, and Mao.[602] Many such moves are unknown and undisclosed to the average man, confused about the world's angst against our noble values.

The former "white man's burden" has only changed its name today to a more politically correct theme of Western domination. It is now the

Western "moral supremacy," where America and its allies have a carte blanche to terrorize the world with impunity. "No better instance exists today of what Anwar Abdel Malek calls 'the hegemonism of possessing minorities' and anthropocentrism allied with Europocentrism: a white middle-class Westerner believes it his human prerogative not only to manage the nonwhite world but also to own it, just because by definition 'it' is not quite as human as 'we' are. There is no purer example than this of dehumanized thought," explained Said.[603]

Aggression has always existed in human history, bringing conquests through death and suffering. However, periods of explosive expansion across Asia and North Africa, such as during the spread of Islam and the Mongol conquests, were followed by long periods of stability, peace, and prosperity. In contrast, Europe faced neverending conflicts that seminal works like Thomas Hobbes' *Leviathan* pointed out. "Only a European author could have concluded that the natural state of man was to be in a constant state of violence; and only a European author would have been right," writes historian Frankopan.[604]

Despite such honest narratives, centuries of Orientalist propaganda have created a twisted groupthink projection that perpetuates oft-repeated lies and dogmas that are employed politically toward imperialist ends.[605] As a result, launching terrorist attacks against countries like Cuba is acceptable, while it is unacceptable for them to arm themselves against an imminent US invasion. To the average American, it would seem blasphemous to learn of Kennedy's arrogance that brought the world to the brink of nuclear oblivion, which was eventually prevented by Khrushchev's sanity. It is a divine miracle that we even survived that debacle, as chronicled in Eric Schlosser's *Command and Control*. Yet, JFK remains one of the many untouchable saints of the American *religion* of Panglossian capitalism.

The number of times errors within the system brought the world to the edge of doomsday is absurd. We are lucky to exist due to the miraculous disobeying of orders by unknown heroes like Stanislav Petrov, Vasili Arkhipov, and John Borden, among others. When asked for his reason, Petrov famously replied, "God told me not to." Few know about the forced evacuation of the inhabitants of the Bikini Atoll to use their homeland as a nuclear testing site during the Cold War, as well as the evacuation of the inhabitants of Thule in Greenland. When the natives of Chagos were forcibly expelled to make another base in 1968, they were made to watch their pet dogs rounded up by the soldiers and burned.[606] The concern was expressed by Secretary of State Kissinger when asked about Micronesians: "There are only ninety thousand people out there. Who gives a damn?"[607] Nor are we aware of the many accidental nuclear-bomb-carrying B-52 crashes around the world; one over a populated Spanish village of

Palomares in 1966, carrying a hydrogen bomb seventy-five times more powerful than Hiroshima, landing 80 yards from an elementary school.[608] In 1961, two nuclear bombs 1,800 times more potent accidentally fell over North Carolina and failed to detonate by mere luck.

President Carter's secretary of defense Perry recently warned: "Right now, we are closer to having a nuclear war happen, even by accident, than we were during the Cold War...[and it's] not fearmongering."[609] The *realpolitik* discourse of our politicians is alarmingly ignorant of a nuclear winter that could have extinction-level consequences for the planet. Even the most circulated magazine during the Cold War, *Reader's Digest*, downplayed the deadly effects of atomic tests in synchrony with the Atomic Energy Commission. When Richard Garwin first designed the prototype of a new thermonuclear "Super" bomb in 1952—a thousand times more powerful than the Big Boy dropped on Hiroshima—his mentor Enrico Fermi broke ranks. He declared it "an evil thing...its very existence and the knowledge of its construction a danger to humanity as a whole."[610] When it was test-fired in the Marshall Islands, an entire Elugelab island disappeared into a two-mile-wide crater. Seeing its sheer mass-extermination capability, the US war planners frenzied into stockpiling 31,255 of these Super-bombs by 1967, each of which could level any major city with casualties in the tens of millions. "The Final Solution called for the extermination of all of Europe's millions of Jews and millions more people the Nazis considered subhuman," writes Jacobsen. "The plan for General Nuclear War [the SIOP] ...called for mass extermination of some 600 million...that the U.S. defense scientists calculated would be caught in the crosswinds."[611]

Kissinger expressed his optimism in his 1957 book that "with proper tactics, nuclear power need not be as destructive as it appears," which is disturbing. Various polls during and since the Cold War have demonstrated overwhelming global civilian support for nuclear disarmament, as these weapons do not make us any safer. The pronouns used in such rhetoric are also misleading. We must remind ourselves that "we" are not consenting to build such weapons yet are counted as acceptable collateral to such warfare by "our" leaders. Thus, Sagan pointed out, "military secrecy makes the military the most difficult sector of any society for the citizens to monitor. And with the rewards so substantial, with the hostile military establishments beholden to each other in some ghastly mutual embrace, the world discovers itself drifting towards the ultimate undoing of the human enterprise."[612]

Howard Zinn asked the palpable question ignored by most seasoned historians and analysts: who does all this bloodshed and deceit benefit? Persuasive arguments justifying them are ubiquitous from the likes of Stalin, Churchill, Truman, Obama, and others. In truth, it primarily benefits the upper class, with some trickle-down effects on the middle class, while the lower class, both at home and abroad, pays the price—literally and figuratively. It is always the lower class who are the "necessary sacrifice" for "human progress." Atrocities perpetrated by empires, such as the Spanish and British, brought temporary glory and financed local wars of dominance, but did not make their average citizens any richer nor lead to everlasting empires. Hans Koning pointed out: "They ended up losing those wars anyway, and all that was left was a deadly inflation, a starving population, the rich richer, the poor poorer, and a ruined peasant class."[613] Sadly, this seems to describe our current situation following prolonged Middle East interventions. Then why are the ones benefiting from the enterprise making decisions for the ones being sacrificed?

"Where systems of injustice are enforced by violence, the perpetrators of that violence and those who support them have little moral authority to decry the violence of resistance," writes Shedinger. Meaning, that the violence directed at the West can be deplored as long as those same individuals also show the same level of outrage for the violence done by the Western "military-industrial complex that can rain down terror on an unprecedented scale."[614] The *doublethink* becomes clear when we ask questions like what happened after the Russian threat disappeared in 1989? "The answer: everything continued much as before. The United States immediately invaded Panama, killing possibly thousands of people and installing a client regime...All routine. And all forgotten (which is also routine)," answers Chomsky.[615] Hence, government advisor Samuel Huntington (1927-2008 CE) explained during the Cold War: "You may have to sell [foreign policy] in such a way as to create the misimpression that it is the Soviet Union that you are fighting. That is what the United States has been doing ever since the Truman Doctrine."[616]

Any study into the matter reveals how much of the "arms race" was manufactured by falsely hyperbolizing the Soviet threat, who never really could invade the US as the latter did in 1918. The actual events resemble an arms chase by the Soviets to keep up with the US to prevent another invasion, as the NATO forces continue to surround them from all sides.[617] That is not to downplay the Soviet threat but to understand the multifaceted motives behind power. The CIA even admitted to exaggerating Soviet military expenditure in 1984 to inflate the US military budget.[618] Such noble confessions of that year were paired with their concurrent hidden atrocities in Nicaragua, including blowing up ships in their harbors. Of course, when some of their activities leaked out, the Secretary of Defense Weinberg went on ABC News to faithfully reassure the Americans that "The United States is not mining the harbors of Nicaragua."[619]

Millionaires and billionaires are born through global calamities as noted by Engelbrecht and Hanighen in *Merchants of Death*. The wartime profits during WWII were duly noted by all industrialists, including the president of General Motors, Charles Wilson, who suggested continuing such an alliance. Despite the calls for disarmament from the war-weary public, the Truman administration obliged by depicting the rivalry with the Soviets as an imminent threat.[620] On many occasions since 1946, the Soviets have asked to ban atomic weapons, which the US government repeatedly declined. When the Soviets accepted the 1954 Franco-British plan for nuclear disarmament to Washington's surprise, it was the American negotiators who left the table. Even their request to join NATO was denied to ensure the existence of that "Great Red Enemy" to justify the enormous US military expenditure. It is similar to convincing someone of an impending alien invasion to have him buy an expensive "alien insurance," and then using the lack of such invasions as proof of its effectiveness while pocketing the money.

In a rare moment of truth, President Eisenhower sighed: "Every gun that is made, every warship launched, every rocket fired, signifies in a final sense a theft from those who are hungry and are not fed, those who are cold and not clothed." Yet, each politician played a scripted role in creating the mass hysteria that allowed for much of the absurdities that dominated the rest of the 20th century. The post-war Truman Doctrine was comical in stating the goal to "free peoples who are resisting attempted subjugation by armed minorities or by outside pressures." Its immediate demonstration in Greece and everywhere else was the armed subjugation of the majority by the dominant US global pressure that none of those countries have recovered from. Who have they not affected?

Just before the 9/11 attacks, Air Force Colonel Robert Bowman confessed: "We are not hated because we practice democracy, value freedom, or uphold human rights, [but] because our government denies these things to people in Third World countries whose resources are coveted by our multinational corporations…Instead of sending our sons and daughters around the world to kill Arabs so we can have the oil under their sand, we should send them to rebuild their infrastructure…we should do good instead of evil."[621] While we rightly chant "Never Forget" and commemorate the 2,977 lives lost in the Twin Tower attacks, it is important to use that tragedy as a lens through which to view the immense suffering we have inflicted on others worldwide. Until we recognize the sanctity of every human life, similar violations will continue under various excuses both domestically and abroad.

Our government and politicians would have continued all of these wars indefinitely with full media support had they never faced public outcry and protests. It is in their interest as they have everything to gain from such conflicts with little to lose. When the people refuse to participate in their aggressions, they are punished and jailed with the full support of the judicial system. The Vietnam War and our continued support for Israel serve as a poignant example of our democracy's flaws. In 1941 A. J. Muste explained that the problem after the battles are over lies with the victor: "He thinks he has just proved that war and violence pay. Who will now teach him a lesson?" Therefore, the Allies came out of WWII chanting "Never again," only to immediately use the same Nazi tactics to build concentration camps in Kenya.[622] When a group of West African soldiers fighting for France asked for their wages after the war, they were all taken to Camp Thiaroye and shot dead.[623]

Numerous examples continue as we fail to recognize the anger of Afghans after helping monsters like the Mujahideen to power. When such projects inevitably fail, we carpet bomb the entire country to out-terrorize them all. President Carter's national security adviser, Zbigniew Brzezinski, outright stated the intention in Afghanistan in the '80s was to "give the USSR its own Vietnam" by drawing them into a quagmire.[624] In that process, the US helped overthrow a democratic Afghan government to empower extremists who served its purpose. The CIA even printed jihadist textbooks in Pashto and Dari in Nebraska and distributed them all over Afghanistan.[625] "One such edition declared: 'Jihad is a kind of war that Muslims fight in the name of God to free Muslims...if infidels invade, jihad is the obligation of every Muslim.' An American text designed to teach children the Farsi alphabet began: *Aleph* [is for] Allah; Allah is one. *Bey* [is for] Baba (father); Father goes to the mosque. *Tey* [is for] Tofang (rifle); Javed obtains rifles for the mujahedeen. *Jeem* [is for] Jihad; Jihad is an obligation. My mom went to the Jihad."[626]

When the Mujahideen fought against the Soviets, they were labeled as "freedom fighters," whom President Reagan compared to America's founding fathers.[627] These same militant warlords turned the US-supplied weapons on their own people following the Soviet expulsion. Their atrocities during the civil war directly led to the formation of the opposing Taliban party to restore some peace and justice. The name means *students* who saw no option other than to take up arms to defend suffering civilians, naturally gaining popular support. Erstwhile Mujahideen warlords then formed the Northern Alliance, which controlled less than 40% of the country. They invited bin Laden to destabilize the majority Taliban rule, as Al-Qaida's Wahhabi base differed from the Taliban's Sufi philosophies to the point of open animosity. In fact, the Taliban government not only agreed to hand him over on several occasions but even warned the US of the terrorist attacks, which were ignored.[628] The irony of the US invasion following 9/11 was when the Taliban were replaced with the Northern Alliance in power. When Brzeziński was asked if he had any regrets, he replied: "What is more important...Some stirred up Muslims or the liberation of Central Europe and the end of the Cold War?"[629] There are at least three false premises masterfully embedded within that last statement.

Afghanistan has been called "the Graveyard of Empires," except for Islam, which has been there since its inception. Of note, bin Laden's stated goals paralleled Brzezinski's in that he sought to provoke the US into a prolonged ground assault. Not learning from history, America plunged into the same quagmire, resulting in two decades of inexplicable tyranny. The eventual defeat was a matter of perspective, as trillions of taxpayer dollars flowed into the pockets of the warmongers as planned, evident from the rising stocks of invested companies like Raytheon, Lockheed Martin, and General Electrics, among others. Richard Barnet's book *Roots of War* highlights the irrationality of empire-building, revealing how the cost of maintaining an empire's foreign interests outweighs the benefits. Economist Thorstein Veblen pointed out the difference in the distribution of that cost to the average taxpayers. The profit is enjoyed only by the privileged, who hypnotize the average citizen into sharing "our" goals.[630] But what interest does an average person have in foreign lands that they cannot even name or place on a map?

A closer look at the financial portfolios of those who initiate and perpetuate wars exposes their real motives. For example, Dick Cheney retired early as the CEO of Halliburton with a severance package of $33.7 million after his VP nomination in 2000.[631] Upon taking office, he manufactured consent for wars that awarded his former company over $39.5 billion in contracts in Iraq alone by 2013, mostly without competing bids. Now, that is an excellent return on investment. Similar private and public firms received over $138 billion of US taxpayer money for government contracts during that war.[632] And then there's Trump and his privatization of nearly everything, including the distribution of aid during a genocide that is also funded and supplied by America.

Only 5.4% of the $557 billion that Washington spent in Afghanistan between 2001 and 2011 went to development or governance, while the rest went into the pockets of private contractors, politicians, and other major corporations, who were outraged at the news of ending the occupation.[633] The claim of building "many schools" with "40% female students" was nonexistent in 80% of cases.[634] Similarly, the claim of providing 85% of Afghans with access to healthcare only meant the *possibility* of having at least one facility per district, most of which were, in reality, nonfunctional.[635] "Throughout the south, the US military supported showpiece projects—a new well or a refurbished school, in some cases even whole model villages," reports Gopal. "But if the south was dotted with Potemkin villages, Afghanistan itself had become a Potemkin country, built almost entirely for show."[636]

Then the US left abruptly, just like the Brits before, after decades of unjustified terror costing over a million undisclosed deaths, and $8 trillion of taxpayer money, calculating to $24,136 per capita.[637] Imagine if the government had offered every household of five $100,000 in exchange for not murdering a million innocent civilians worldwide, would you take it? If it sounds like a no-brainer, then you should be as apoplectic by the contrary. That money ended up in the off-shore accounts of a few elites, who vociferously fight even the most minor social service programs benefiting actual taxpayers. Had that enormous sum been invested within the country, we would have solved all of our domestic issues and stood taller in the global community. Yet, their greed and arrogance continue to deceive a country divided and fragmented at the brink of collapse.

So He caused hypocrisy to plague their hearts until the Day they will meet Him, for breaking their promise to God and for their lies. (al-Tawbah 9:77)

The US suffers from selective amnesia and forgets that it fomented many coups, like the one against Muhammad Mossadegh, the democratically elected President of Iran in 1953, only to replace him with a monarchy and secure control of Middle Eastern oil. Mossadegh's pitfall was his strong principles of establishing democracy and listening to the people's demands for restoring Persian control of their resources, which spells a suicide note for any non-American government. Roosevelt's grandson showed up in Tehran with sacks of money to fan public opinion in events rivaling Hollywood villainy.[638] Our government even exempted oil companies from antitrust laws to force them to take over Anglo-Persian Oil.[639]

American corporations and oligarchic politicians have an extensive history of aiding counterrevolutionaries worldwide in their unrelenting support for capitalism and maintaining an elitist class disparity.[640] They helped Iran develop nuclear programs until the Shah's abusive rule resulted in the rise of Ayatollah Khomeini and Iran's revolution of 1979. Despite continued hostility towards Iran, the country has managed to remain one of the most democratic in that region, even surpassing Israel's apartheid regime. This is an impressive feat given the incessant attempts to destabilize their government, such as the arming of Iraq to invade them within a year of their revolution. But the gray zone of world politics was highlighted by Israel supplying arms to Iran to fight Iraq, even when the US withheld due to the hostage crisis.[641] While the US and Britain's war crimes escape mainstream narrative, they are detailed in many scholarly works like *The U.S. Press and Iran*.[642] Like its idolized past empires, the current Western mega-empire continues to look towards the honeypot along the Eastern Mediterranean and beyond. Ironically, many Orientalists at the turn of the 20th century—like T. E. Lawrence, Paul Valéry, Sylvain Lévi, etc.—saw the writing on the wall and expressed, through their usual racist rhetoric, how the Orient would sooner or later overwhelm Europe if not appropriately materialized.[643]

With so much outside interference, it becomes impossible for a country to evolve into any meaningful existence other than authoritarianism. It is not an apologia but a fact supported by social and political sciences. Despite our biases, Khomeini was not factually incorrect in his accusations: "The preachers they planted in the religious teaching institution, the agents they employed in the universities, government educational institutions, and publishing houses, and the orientalists who work in the service of the imperialist states—all these people have pooled their energies to distort the principles of Islam. As a result, many persons, particularly the educated, have formed misguided and incorrect notions of Islam."[644]

At the same time, the global plunder is packaged with rebuilding efforts by Christian aid organizations, which, regardless of intent, can be seen as another Crusade to conquer and convert. Those skeptical about the religious motives of such foreign policies must recall Europe's origin as a direct counterrevolution to Islam, which arguably never ceased. As Aslan comments, "It would seem, therefore, that the biggest obstacles in the path to creating a genuinely Islamic democracy are not the Traditionalist Ulama or Jihadist terrorists, but, perhaps more destructively, those in the West who stubbornly refuse to recognize that democracy."[645]

Never will the Jews or Christians be pleased with you, until you follow their faith. Say, "God's guidance is the only [true] guidance." And if you were to follow their desires after [all] the knowledge that has come to you, there would be none to protect or help you against God. (al-Baqarah 2:120)

President Eisenhower referred to the Middle East as "'the most strategically important area in the world,' 'a stupendous source of strategic power' and 'probably the richest economic prize,'...a prize that the United States intended to keep for itself and its allies."[646] The US has followed in the footsteps of its maternal British Empire, which saw no issues invading Baghdad in the spring of 1917 with the same goal. As Britain's grip on the dismantled Ottoman Empire started to slip, it aggressively divided up land on maps that overlooked their practicality. Borders were drawn around provinces with different influences and complex historical rivalries to secure Mesopotamian oil fields. "Basra looked southwards towards India and the Gulf; Baghdad was closely linked with Persia; Mosul naturally connected to Turkey and Syria," explains Frankopan.[647] The level of concern was displayed in Lord Hardinge's letter: "It really would not matter if we choose three of the fattest men from Baghdad or three of the men with the longest beards who would be put up as the emblems of Arab rule," as long as they had their control on oil.[648] Thus Iraq was created, a Shi'a majority country with a Sunni King implanted from the Saudi royal family, allowing Brits access to their oil.[649] It was much cheaper than the previous colonial occupation, especially considering Britain's surmounting post-war debts. Similarly, Lebanon's borders were gerrymandered by France to give the Maronite Christians power over Muslims.

Colonialism transitioned to neocolonialism, which recruited the US as its champion—described quite astutely as a "condominium empire" by Parenti promoting rentier economics.[650] In fact, the American Empire invaded places for much less in its infancy. It annexed hundreds of small islands across the Caribbean and the Pacific in the 19th century to feed its appetite for bird feces. President Fillmore even sent a battleship risking a war with Peru in 1852 in hopes of scraping that guano off their coast.[651] While most of these islands eventually were forgotten—once leading to our army embarrassingly invading an island it had already annexed—some key ones became essential for future CIA operations and military stations, providing material for many Bond movies.

Although the US initially praised Saddam's rise as a charismatic hitman, it soon became wary of his ambitions. It did not take long for our government to lose his trust through the usual masterplan of playing both sides for short gains. President Reagen tried to buy him back in 1983 by sending Donald Rumsfeld, who downplayed Saddam's regular use of chemical weapons to avoid tension.[652] In a twisted ploy, Saddam was nudged by the US into invading Kuwait in 1990 only to be snagged by a thirty-four-country coalition against him. The wars of those two decades wasted away Iraq's infrastructures, resources, and an entire generation of youth, as symbolically demonstrated on the Highway of Death. Although President papa-Bush trained Iraqi nuclear engineers for advanced weapons production, with perfect schizophrenia Iraq was illegally invaded in 2003 with false nuclear claims. The real motives became apparent when President son-Bush demanded Congress to allow permanent stationing of US forces to ensure "United States control of the oil resources of Iraq."[653] While the father drew his inspiration from "America, as Christ ordained," the son only completed the capitalist "Crusade" as his "mission from God."[654]

Ever since, American bases on Iraqi oil fields have provided a steady supply of stolen sweet crude, just as they have in Syria through similar maneuvers. It is not a coincidence that such drawn-out terrorism in that region resulted in an unnatural selection of extremism and fundamentalism. All of it was justified by the Neocon movement of Leo Strauss (1899-1973 CE) and his students, like Paul Wolfowitz.[655] Remarkably, a survivor of Nazi brutality gave rise to a similar Machiavellian movement directed against another Abrahamic faith. Perhaps it is their exposure to cruelty that turned them into their oppressors, which is why Moses asked his people to seek refuge against such trials (*Yunus* 10:85). The supposed reverse side of this is the neoliberal push to force open the entire world to capitalism. It is often difficult to distinguish between them, proving their complementary relationship masked by seemingly divergent foreign policies.

The Project for the New American Century (PNAC) think-tank was established in 1997 to map the road to Pax-America in a post-Soviet era. A list of countries was created that needed to be dismantled in that effort, along with a detailed plan, which was even stated in writing: would not be realized without the propulsion from a catastrophic event. Of the eighteen people signing that document, ten soon went on to serve the Bush administration, including the architects of the subsequent foreign policies—Dick Cheney, Donald Rumsfeld, and Paul Wolfowitz.[656] Professor Rebecca Gordon lays out the legal case in her book *American Nuremberg: The U.S. Officials Who Should Stand Trial for Post-9/11 War Crimes*. While it is easy to get lost in these name-calling games, one must be reminded that right and wrong have been ultimately made clear to us. It is typically the latter that necessitates circular arguments, rationalization, and discussion. The truth can be summed up by the much simpler Prophetic dictum: "There should be neither harming (*darar*) nor reciprocating harm (*dirar*)" (*40 Hadith Nawawi* #32).

Even a brief study of our history reveals events that unravel our national diagnosis of paranoid schizophrenia. It has become a right of passage for the president to pick a Muslim country to attack after taking office, which is a common tactic throughout the animal kingdom used to announce one's dominance. Besides, all the efforts of the enormous military-industrial complex are fruitless if the weapons and bombs collect dust. Therefore, the US had little choice but to become the biggest arms dealer in the world to protect the economy, as war is its major global export.[657] One must ask why the first suicide bombing in Iraq's history was after the US invasion in 2004 when it had been under Muslim rule since the first Caliph Abu Bakr? Such desperate measures are always a response against oppressive regimes.

According to a 1995 U.N. Food and Agriculture Organization (FAO) report, sanctions in the '90s led to the death of 567,000 Iraqi children under five, resulting in several resignations in protest. When asked about it, Secretary of State Madeleine Albright responded: "We think the price is worth it."[658] The brutal nature of sanctions as collective punishment often hides the active sabotage of civilian infrastructures. Those aware, like the former CIA Station Chief in Kabul, Graham Fuller, hold the US directly responsible for the rise of ISIS and other extremist groups worldwide.[659] While we boast of ousting brutal dictators like Saddam and Gaddafi, far worse genocidal war criminals like Bush, Kissinger, Rumsfeld, Obama, and Biden escape the same fate. There is national amnesia regarding their atrocities which are quickly forgotten as the perpetrators are turned into warm and fuzzy teddy bears appearing on morning talk shows.

America not only deals with terrorists but sits at the head of that entire organization. The country's long history of torturing prisoners and natives is nothing new. It was exemplified at Wounded Knee and in the Philippines by General Jacob Smith and Major Glenn, with the full support of President Theodore Roosevelt. As a Confederate colonel from Georgia remarked: "I fought through the Civil War and have seen men shot to pieces and slaughtered by thousands, but the Cherokee removal was the cruelest work I ever knew."[660] For such work, twenty soldiers involved in the massacre of three hundred Sioux were awarded the Congressional Medals of Honor, and a monument was erected at Fort Riley for the soldiers who died from friendly fire. Roosevelt epitomized the country's attitude towards conflict in a letter to a friend in 1897: "In strict confidence...I should welcome almost any war, for I think this country needs one."[661] His violent racism extended beyond people of color, as he wrote his sister that a mob lynching of Italian immigrants in New Orleans was "rather a good thing." Such extreme character traits often pervade all aspects of an individual's behavior.

The Spanish-American War serves as a darkly comical example, as depicted in its official US military veterans seal. It shows a desperate native submitting to an armed US soldier and a sailor, with a typical battleship diplomatic backdrop. Just when the natives were about to defeat Spain, America swooped in at an opportune moment, claiming its never-ending humanitarian plight, only to carve out the territories (e.g., Cuba, Puerto Rico, and the Philippines) for itself. To their utter dismay, the betrayed natives were wholly excluded from the negotiations. The Spanish governor-general even stated his willingness "to surrender to white people but never to Niggers."[662] Throughout history, the majority of global aggression and ebullient slaughter have been directed at minorities. Even though the US fought both Germany and Japan during World War II, the latter ended up in domestic internment camps and bore the devastation of the atomic bombs.

Historian Ken De Bevoise notes that America's exuberant military glory in the Philippines alone came at the cost of 775,000 local casualties over five years. When Muslims of the Moroland resisted in March 1906, it peaked at Bud Dajo, where General Leonard Wood killed thousands "like dominoes under machine-gun fire...'We abolished them utterly, leaving not even a baby alive to cry for its dead mother,' wrote a bitter Mark Twain, privately, 'This is incomparably the greatest victory that was ever achieved by the Christian soldiers of the United States.'"[663] The famed General Pershing only reenacted the scene in June 1913 in Bud Bagsak. The army's first twelve chiefs of staff served in the Philippine War, and twenty-six of the thirty generals in the Philippines received their training slaughtering civilians in the Indian wars.[664] In summary, we liberated those islands from Spain's brutality by massacring their inhabitants.

The movement of soldiers in history always leaves behind a trail of depredation, rape, murder, and savagery, with few exceptions. This chilling reality was demonstrated by the gangrape of 14-year-old Iraqi child Abeer Qassim Hamza al-Janabi and the murder of her family by American liberators on March 12, 2006. Furthermore, American soldiers have been reported to rape Japanese minors at the Okinawa base even now.[665] For one such story, hundreds likely remain untold and unreported.

When we condemned the "Turkish-backed" Syrian rebel groups for their war crimes against the Kurds, we forgot to mention that the US had armed them for years leading up to those events.[666] Our abandonment of the Iraqi Kurds in the '70s led to their massacre over several decades, which we also aided by supplying arms to Saddam. Kissinger stated in a Congressional inquiry on that atrocity: "Covert action should not be confused with missionary work."[667] Such covert operations include the 1985 car bomb outside of a busy mosque in Beirut just as worshippers were leaving from the Friday prayer, orchestrated by the CIA with the help of Britain and Saudi allies. While their intended target escaped, it managed to kill 80 people, wounding another 256, including infants, children, and women.

Who remembers the Libyan Arab Airlines Flight 114 shot down by the US-supplied Israeli jets in 1973, killing all 110 passengers? Or the downed Iran Air civilian Flight 655 in July 1988 by an SM-2MR surface-to-air missile fired from USS *Vincennes* just for "the opportunity to show [them our] stuff."[668] All 290 passengers were killed while the commander and the officer in charge were awarded the US Legion of Merit award for their "exceptionally meritorious conduct in the performance of outstanding service."[669] Israeli military historian Martin van Creveld remarked that after witnessing how the US invaded Iraq, the Iranians would be crazy for not building nuclear weapons.[670] However, most global agencies have already dismissed any such ambition on Iran's part. Both Ayatollahs gave *fatwas* against nuclear weapons as antithetical to the core values of Islam. The nuclear program was pursued only for their basic energy needs as some of it is even needed for routine medical treatments, which America opposes to continue Iran's dependence on foreign corporations for commodities. Professor John Ghazvinian clarifies much of this in his book *America And*

Iran, along with the nuances of this propagandized conflict. It is through America's own insecurities from its violent history that it finds such truths unpalatable.

In reality, the only Middle Eastern regime with nuclear weapons is Israel, which it secretly developed with the help of France in the '50s. The Dimona project, as it was ironically called, was an embarrassing American intelligence failure for nearly a decade, followed by the endless lies and coverups from Israeli officials claiming the reactor site to be an ever-changing textile plant to a weather station.[671] The Kennedy administration was the only time some pressure was placed against Israel's unilateral aggression in the region, often at America's expense. JFK also attempted to register AIPAC as a foreign entity. Unfortunately, it was short-lived due to his assassination, which has Mossad's fingerprints all over it from recently declassified documents. Such "conspiracies" are only evident from the Israeli history of the assassination of British minister Lord Moyne in 1944, the bombing of the King David Hotel in 1946, the assassination of UN mediator Folke Bernadotte in 1948, the attack on USS Liberty in 1967, and possibly even the twin tower attacks.

Uncle Sam had its hand in destabilizing every Middle Eastern nation over the last century. A simple Google search yields more than eighty countries where it played overt and covert roles in a coup, often replacing a democratic government with a terror regime. US troops entered Cuba (four times), Nicaragua (three times), Guatemala, Panama (six times), Costa Rica, Mexico (three times), and Haiti (twice) between 1903 and 1934 to ensure "political financial stability."[672] With a neighbor like us, who needs enemies? Thus, our foreign policy was colorfully stated by FDR: "He may be a son of a [female dog], but he's our son of a [female dog]."[673] Right after WWII, the US imposed the "Economic Charter of the Americas" to eliminate economic nationalism for its neighbors. Guatemala has been a continuous horror chamber since the US helped overthrow its parliamentary government in 1954. US military aid was crucial to the right-wing brutalities in El Salvador, Indonesia, Argentina, Brazil, Malaysia, Zaire, and Israel among others.[674] The current portrayal of Venezuela is also a decades-long propaganda effort, as detailed in *Extraordinary Threat* by Justin Podur and Joe Emersberger.

When the democratic government of Chile under Salvador Allende attempted to take control of their national resources through social and economic reform, the Nixon administration succeeded via a military coup on what is aptly regarded as the first 9/11, 1973. The subsequent dictatorship planted by the US along with the "Chicago Boys" economists resulted in such horror that it served as an example to all "foreigners [who] are out to screw us [out of our foreign investments]," boasted Nixon.[675] Even after the Watergate scandal and Nixon's resignation, none of the domestic media had the guts to say what Claude Julien of *Le Monde Diplomatique* noted in 1974: "The elimination of Mr. Richard Nixon leaves intact all the mechanisms and all the false values which permitted the Watergate scandal."[676] Kissinger kept his job along with the same foreign policies, the same game, and corporate players. The next president pardoned Nixon right away, which protected him from any accountability and allowed him to retire peacefully with an enormous pension.

America continues to punish and make an example of Cuba for daring to go against its predatory foreign policies through a legacy of state-sponsored terrorism (e.g., the Bay of Pigs invasion and Operation Mongoose). It protected terrorists like Luis Posada Carriles, who brutally attacked civilians, including bombing a Cuban Airline and killing 73 passengers. A point of consideration for all is whether harboring such criminals in America also gives other nations the right to invade for extradition. Although these events seem too far removed to compete for public interest or attention, they are done in our name, making us shared criminals. Like the recent US-backed military coup in Honduras that directly exacerbated the fleeing of its natives since 2009.[677] Then to see the pathetic aggression of some Americans to the endless refugees arriving at its doors in attempts to escape the hell it created for them for centuries further makes any intelligent citizen want to hide in shame.

During this time, many different cabinets have come and gone with contrasting foreign policies, which have, in practice, differed minimally. None of it represents any democratic principles. Even during the El Salvador affair in 1982, only 16% of the sampled population supported Reagan's military activities.[678] With the endless protests of hundreds, even thousands at times, how much does it ever affect foreign policy? Indeed, a Princeton University research confirmed this inequality in our democracy concluding that public opinions or interests have no impact on our government.[679] The atrocities committed by Genghis are well-known, but they pale in comparison to the brutal and indiscriminate slaughter of 214,000 civilians and the destruction of two cities in August 1945 by a lesser-known war criminal. Dostoevsky once mused, "Have you noticed that the most refined bloodletters have almost all been most civilized gentlemen, beside whom the Atillas and Stenka Razins often look like mere amateurs?"[680]

Today's world powers carry out similar 9/11's routinely, all around the globe. While they may avoid punishment in this life, there is a momentous Day when they will be brought to justice. Even their escape on earth is a mirage, as their personal lives are often fraught with strife, for there is no barrier between the cries of the oppressed and God (*Sahih al-Bukhari* 2448). "Do the corrupt at heart assume that God will not expose their malice?" asks God (*Muhammad* 47:29). Nicolas Davies has documented 35 countries where the US has supported fascists, drug lords, and terrorists since 1945, making the CIA the worst terrorist organization in history.[681] Its "Operation Phoenix" in Vietnam secretly executed over 20,000 civilians without trial, simply on suspicion of communism. Its constant, aggressive interference demonstrates a lack of intelligence noted even by its own personnel.[682] The CIA's unilateral exceptionalism also extends to cyberspace, as seen with the Stuxnet virus against Iran.

In places where the US is hesitant to intervene directly, many dependent allies are eager to meddle on its behalf. One Israeli writer noted, "Consider any third-world area that has been a trouble spot in the past 10 years and you will discover Israeli officers and weapons implicated in the conflict—supporting American interests and helping in what they call 'the defense of the West.'"[683] In return, Washington blindly supports and supplies their ongoing genocide while skimming off the struggling taxpayers. Greater America is in everyone's backyard, with over 800 overseas bases allowing its neo-imperial coercion. While the average American remains unaware, they are still affected as bin Laden explicitly stated the Twin Tower attacks were a retaliation for such bases, also confirmed by military analyst Robert Kaplan in his book.[684]

While we may mock the absurdities of the North Korean leadership, we overlook the devastation caused by the bombing of dams during the Korean War and the joy expressed at the sight of them drowning in American media. With their nuclear capabilities, it is now difficult to bully them around, so we hurl names across the playground like "Axis of Evil." When we lay siege to that entire country by blocking textile exports, it is the poor working class that goes hungry; our blockade on metal imports also makes civilians suffer, as hospitals are barred from basic metal instruments like surgical blades. Yet, we justify these sanctions under the guise of "humanitarianism," which is quite baffling.

Although we may disagree with some of our adversaries' methods, we cannot disregard all of their grievances against us. A 2010 survey found that the general European population viewed Israel as the greatest threat to world peace, while only 10% of Egyptians considered Iran a threat.[685] According to leading Western polling agencies like WIN and Gallup International, the US remains the greatest threat to world peace.[686] It has been the biggest terrorist on the planet for centuries, with American Political Science Association president, Robert Jervis, echoing Samuel Huntington's statement that "in the eyes of much of the world, the prime rogue state today is the United States."[687] This country has been in constant wars for almost all, except 11 years, of its entire existence since 1776, with its armies deployed abroad 211 times in 67 countries since

1945.[688] For such a nosy empire, globalization creates a void of a well-defined enemy to focus its Orwellian propaganda.

The global "War on Terror" provides a brilliant solution by painting the entire Muslim world as the *invisible enemy*. Ultimately, as long as the people are kept distracted, they could care less about world events. "The mind would rather amuse itself than heal itself, making philosophy into a diversion when it is really a cure," noted Seneca.[689] His writings described a world identical to today's hedonism. Stoics like him attempted to provide a way to live meaningfully during chaotic Roman times with the abandonment of teleology, which is the reason for its recent popular revival.[690] "To make a name for yourself in this crowd, you need to combine extravagance with notoriety. In such a busy town, ordinary vices don't get reported."[691]

Today's competition for attention and clicks makes us forget that anything *viral* has the potential to plague. We are the proud, cheering Romans distracted by the gladiator games, oblivious to the ongoing horrors at the empire's penumbra. After returning from such an event, Seneca wrote to his friend to avoid all such crowds for the devastating effects of herd mentality that can make even a rational man scream for blood. We celebrate victory and our veterans against classic teachings like: *Those who celebrate victory are bloodthirsty, and the bloodthirsty cannot have their way with the world.*[692] Similar rage today instantly goes viral with global consequences that are impenetrable to reason.

When true values are stripped from people, their misplaced loyalties are easily exploited, similar to Carl Jung's proposed archetypes. Pride is a wolf disguised in sheepskin and promotes ignorance commonly shared by the mindless. We must remember the *original sin* of pride and arrogance that brought about the world as we know. God commands: "Do not strut arrogantly about the earth: you cannot break it open, nor match the mountains in height" (*al-Isra'* 17:37). It is this pride that led one of Noah's sons to dismiss the warnings and physically climb to reach his metaphorical mountain of arrogance; yet, he too drowned with the rest of his nation.

Our pride sets us in a similar predictable trajectory unless constantly kept in check with humility and intelligent rationalization. "We have destroyed even mightier generations before," warns God (*Qaf* 50:36). There are things that bring humanity together and things that divide. Blind nationalism and patriotism belong to the latter group and must be approached with caution. As Hugo of St. Victor said in *Didascalicon*, the man who finds his homeland sweet is still a tender beginner, while he to whom every soil is as his native one is already strong. But the perfect person is the one to whom the entire world is a foreign land.[693]

CENTER ALIGN

We have made you [believers] into a just community [middle nation], so that you may bear witness [to the truth] before others and so that the Messenger may bear witness before you. (al-Baqarah 2:143)

I: What Now?

If the historical bombardments of the previous chapter trouble you, it is a sign of your humanity. But now, what do we do with all this knowledge? Maintaining a healthy balance is generally the best approach, as deviating can lead to extremism on either side of the spectrum. While individuals may be able to slip by without staying on that path, civilization cannot afford such missteps. When a society leans towards a side, it creates a force that obeys Newton's third law, and the pendulum must swing away. Each extreme represents only a temporary state and if the momentum becomes too great, the entire system can destabilize and break. At the same time, the more momentum it gains, the more difficult it becomes to bring it back to the middle without an overpowering force.

Then again, what is civilization but a collective of its individuals? Its imbalance only reflects the sum-over histories of the collective. If an individual leans too far to one extreme, another must go to the other to maintain overall balance. While this may technically resemble equilibrium, in practice, it leads to a polarized society. As we seem to be living in one right now, this apparent "stability" is deceptively volatile, where all it takes is a few to stray for the entire society to crumble. Furthermore, seeing the world in a binary way distorts reality and obscures the true complexity of issues along the spectrum. It brings us back to the question of whether individuals can truly afford to deviate from the middle. The rational answer would then be: not without dire consequences.

And do not turn your nose up to people, nor walk pridefully upon the earth. Surely God does not like whoever is arrogant and boastful. Be moderate in your pace. And lower your voice, for the ugliest of all voices is certainly the braying of donkeys. (Luqman 31:18-9)

Take racism, for example, which Toni Morrison calls a distraction from the actual societal diseases of class and economic disparities. Even when the elites and the politicians jump on various social justice bandwagons, they sidestep larger issues that plague our communities. Extreme views are not sentinel events but rather personality traits that manifest in various ways. Straying from that lagom can cause even the most righteous deeds to be performed wrongfully. In everything we do, whether it be love, hate, happiness, sadness, entertainment, play, work, pride, anger, piety, defiance, activism…it is crucial to find a middle balance that separates vice from virtue.

Accordingly, there are many Prophetic teachings against extremism and Qur'anic commands of adhering to the middle. Interestingly enough, even the ancient Greek and Hebrew roots of the word "sin" means *missing the mark*, or simply deviating from the center. Hence, Jesus preached that the way to enter the kingdom of heaven is by becoming like children with pure *fitras (Matthew* 18:3), for it is only thereafter that we deviate. Islam teaches us to train ourselves (i.e., our *ego, nafs*) to find that steady state, where we evolve from an appetitive self (*nafs ammarah*) to a tranquil state (*nafs mutma'innah*). It enables us to achieve moderation like courage, rather than the extremes of cowardliness and aggression; generosity over stinginess and extravagance; dignity over timidity and narcissism, etc.

A similar concept in Hinduism describes creation as having three primary qualities or *gunas: sattva, rajas,* and *tamas.* Its sacred texts also demand mastering temperance in all things. Of course, if it was easily achieved, streets would be full of angels and history books devoid of conflicts, as Rumi said: "The angel is free because of his knowledge, the beast because of his ignorance. Between the two remains the son of man to struggle."[694] Much of today's discourse—such as the ones around gender and sexual identity—fails to evolve from the appetitive self, which is instead championed. It creates a peculiar paradigm blindness and sets false premises from which all further discussions and intellectualization become misguided and bizarre.

The ancients saw philosophy as a treatment for the soul, with significant theological overlap that made it more practical than its modern abstraction. Aristotle repeatedly stressed in *Ethics* that *virtue is a mean between the extremes of defect and excess.* Socrates conveyed a similar philosophy to the Stoics, all of whom were at variance with their surroundings. Despite their popularity, the fruits of their laborious struggle to improve the lives of their kith and kin never truly bore. In contrast, the Prophet's balanced philosophy, with its divine blend of genres, has proven to be miraculously transformative for all who came in contact with it. While it does not conquer all external conflicts—nor was it meant to—it remains a unique blueprint for humanity.

God holds each individual responsible for his intentions and efforts, rather than their material success or failure. This is especially critical when studying history, which is laden with numerous atrocities, only a fraction of which have been highlighted in this book. It is easy to get lost in that darkness and lose sight of the divine light we should be cultivating within ourselves. The balance is tipped by either focusing too much on earthly matters, which can discourage us from our individual efforts; or ignoring these matters altogether, which can blind us to the powers at play and make us vulnerable to their schemes. As the Prophet advised, a believer is not bitten from the same hole twice (*Bukhari*).

Identifying and facing problems is the first step to solving them. As George Santayana famously said, "Those who cannot remember the past are condemned to repeat it." Peter Lamborn Wilson added, "Those who understand history are condemned to watch other idiots repeat it." Ultimately, we cannot stop the wheel of history from turning even if we feign ignorance and become victims of apathy. Hence, Imam al-Ghazali stressed the importance of recognizing which of our attributes are accidental versus essential. If we occupy ourselves with our animalistic attributes—such as eating, sleeping, fighting, etc.—then we devolve down to their level; if we are busy causing mischief in guile and deceit, we act more like the devils; but our potential is of angelic stature if we only rise through our contemplation of God's beauty and balance ourselves between our other two attributes by making one our steed and the other a weapon.[695]

As we continually deprive each other of God-given rights, various noble movements try to restore the balance, but inevitably tip over through our vices. That has always been Satan's gambit starting with his convincing our parents to disobey God to reach immortality and permanence in their paradise. Today, Locke is credited with the revival of liberalism, whose principles of life, liberty, and property were all denied during the European Middle Age. However, that loss came through the corruption of Jesus's message, which the Prophet had already restored in Arabia in the 7th century. He commanded: "Verily! Your blood, property, and honor are sacred to one another...It is incumbent upon those who are present to inform those who are absent because those who are absent might comprehend better than the present audience" (*Sahih al-Bukhari* 67).

In contrast, Locke's movement stripped of that divine balance led to an all-out sprint away from religion, which even goes against his core values. He saw *evil* as having an overpowering effect on moving our desires than *good* because the struggle for a greater good may not always translate to personal happiness. While we all desire to be happy, the satisfaction from a desired action is incumbent upon whether what we think as good is truly a part of our actual happiness. "The result of our judgment upon that examination, is what ultimately determines the man, who could not be *free*, if his *will* were determined by anything, but his own *desire* guided by his own *judgment*," explained Locke.[696]

As for our God-given rights, we must realize that anything *given* can also be taken away, which is why God refers to us as His *slaves*. It is a term of endearment referring to our complete dependence on our Creator, who declares: "O My servants! I have forbidden *dhulm* (oppression) for Myself, and I have made it forbidden amongst you, so do not oppress one another" (*Sahih Muslim* 2577). When we fully submit to this fact, we enjoy God's promise of protection from the whispers of the devils (*al-Hijr* 15:42). Rebellion against God only violates those rights, as demonstrated through our disgraceful history of slavery. True freedom from the enslavement of falsehood, emotions, desires, and anxiety is achieved through complete submission to God alone. Unfortunately, today's world embodies such enslavement, which is the primary source of all of our anguish. "So if we see someone who is unhappy or miserable, we can know, with confidence, that person is not free," taught Epictetus.[697]

The Qur'an has a remarkable story in which God honors al-Khidr by referring to him as His slave (*al-Kahf* 18:60-5), whom Moses sought as a teacher. Although Moses was the most knowledgeable person of his time in terms of Revelation, he was humbled by al-Khidr's knowledge of Reality demonstrated through his seemingly outrageous worldly acts. The meeting of these two *oceans* of knowledge ultimately presented three manifestations of divine mercy that even tested Moses's prophetic patience. While al-Khidr was blessed with such insight, the rest of us must have faith in God's plan, for all of our reactionary actions stem from impatience with divine wisdom. "God's Judgment is coming, so do not ask to bring it on sooner. Glory be to Him! He is far above anything they join with Him!" (*an-Nahl* 16:1).

It is comforting to know that even the worst injustices of the world are part of a greater plan that we cannot fathom during our limited presence on Earth's timeline (*Ibrahim* 14:46). The Prophet explained that sometimes God helps His religion with a corrupt man (Sahih al-Bukhari Book 56,

Hadith 267). Even those who deny God are unknowingly following the divine script. Everything is recorded and accounted for. "Did I not tell you that you would never be able to bear with me patiently?" reminds God through al-Khidr (*al-Kahf* 18:72). "Verily man is impatient by nature" (*al-Ma'arij* 70:19); "And how can you be patient with what is beyond your [realm of] knowledge?" (*al-Kahf* 18:68). Our God-given rights are meant to protect us from each other in our aggression, but not to be taken unchecked. In contrast, the liberal application of Locke's declaration was a departure from God and more in line with extreme individualism.

God reminds us that our life, liberty, and property belong to Him and must be managed according to His laws. We must practice perfection in improving ourselves and tolerance in dealing with others. Although Caliph 'Umar was known for his strictness, during the famine of ar-Ramadah, he suspended the prescribed *shari'ah* punishment for theft, realizing the sociopolitical issues that may force one to steal for survival. Such precedence shows the pious predecessors' understanding of God's mercy in balancing their shortcomings. When we deviate from that in a search for *absolute freedom*, we only trade our slavery from the Almighty for our desires. Those *inalienable rights* are given to us by God, and denying Him results in a forfeiture of those rights, which is then reflected in our devilish actions.

God created the heavens and earth for a true purpose: to reward each soul according to its deeds. They will not be wronged. [Prophet], consider the one who has taken his own desire as a god, whom God allows to stray in the face of knowledge, sealing his ears and heart and covering his eyes—who can guide such a person after God [has done this]? Will you [people] not take heed? (al-Jathiyah 45:22-3)

If we picture the timeline of Muslims since Adam as a straight line through Noah, Abraham, Moses, Jesus, and Muhammad, a Jewish saga splits around the time of Jesus and becomes somewhat dotted following the destruction of Jerusalem in 70 CE. Christianity then struggles for survival through the first few centuries, perhaps re-emerging as a separate line after the Council of Nicea and paralleling the Muslim timeline as Roman Christianity until the 8th century. If we compare the history of these lines, one appears to stay closer to the middle—the peace and justice as preached by the prophets. Meanwhile, these values were submerged in the dense forests and swamplands of what was yet to become Europe, which gradually defined its identity in opposition to the Andalucian civilization beyond the Pyrenees. When they adopted a version of Christianity that broke away from the Byzantine Church, they showed little regard for the divine values that underpinned the original gospels. This theological darkness from its conception would have a profound impact on Europe's future, setting it on a trajectory that diverged sharply from a civilized middle. Thus, from an Islamic perspective, there have always been two Christianities: the original gospel preached by Jesus, the messenger conforming to Islam; and the Pauline version that gradually transformed into Western Christianity and the current Bible.[698]

God typically sends messengers when His message is on the verge of complete corruption to preserve continuous guidance for humanity. The century leading up to the birth of the Prophet was particularly ominous, marked by global calamities that foreshadowed the loss of the original message of Jesus to the Pauline Church. Historian Michael McCormick has deemed this era *the worst time to be alive* due to some lesser-known global calamities. In 536, a mysterious fog blanketed the world for 18 months, blocking sunlight and initiating the coldest decade of the previous 2300 years. Procopius, a Byzantine historian, described it in chilling terms: "For the sun gave forth its light without brightness, like the moon, during the whole year." Setting aside the theatrics, the practical consequence was global crop failure and famine, which forced people to consume anything they found, including rodents. Unsurprisingly, the next stop was the bubonic Plague of Justinian, which wiped out half his mighty empire.[699] It may have also triggered the famine and decline of the contemporary Teotihuacan civilization halfway across the globe in central Mexico.

Following that plague, all of Christendom remained in darkness until the enlightened ideas from Muslim lands were translated and brought back to Europe, reminding them of their forgotten liberties. These ideas immediately challenged their religious establishment, which had acted more like feudal warlords by removing people's access to religion and free thought. The greed and corruption within the Church eventually caused people to lose faith and become disillusioned, as Desiderius Erasmus (1466-1536 CE) observed: "It will be pretty to hear their [Church and the monastic order] pleas before the great tribunal: one will brag how he mortified his carnal appetite by feeding only upon fish: another will urge that he spent most of his time on earth in the divine exercise of singing psalms...but Christ will interrupt: 'Woe unto you, scribes and Pharisees...I left you but one precept, of loving one another, which I do not hear anyone plead that he has faithfully discharged.'"[700]

That corruption did not spare many popes, patriarchs, or even saintly figures like Mother Teresa.[701] A recent survey discovered that between 2001 and 2006, 85% of Roman Church dioceses in the US experienced embezzlement of funds.[702] Such exposure pushes people away from religion, placing the burden of blame not on their blind faith but on God, just like the devil before. Arguably, one's loss of faith is only a testament to a lack of proper acquaintance with God from the outset. Kierkegaard went so far as to consider the Church "the very antithesis of Christianity."[703] As a result, the West gradually turned away from religion altogether when that system failed, and sought secular solutions. However, their solutions based on false premises took them further from the truth. During the rise of secularism, instead of seeing the actions of the accused as the problem, people sought to make that same greedy philosophy universal. They went on a *jihad* to sever all ties with divinity and redefine a societal structure and even morality without a clear *telos*. Instead of restoring balance, the scale was tipped too far in the other direction, where decisions are now based solely on rationalization, which can be as subjective as our caprice uncaged from divine limitations.

For instance, the founders of America were apoplectic when they felt misrepresented at the King's court, but their *rational* solution did not provide representation for all Americans. The 1776 Maryland constitution required a person to own 5,000 pounds of property to run for governor, with similar laws effectively excluding 90% of the population from holding office. This type of gross inequality is by design and consistent with Locke's natural right doctrine.[704] The Royal Proclamation of 1763 forbidding any further indigenous land grab beyond the Appalachian Mountains outraged the colonists following the French and Indian War. Elite colonists with significant investments in that Indian land, like George Washington, were quick to take up arms. This makes the American fight more accurately resemble a counter-revolution to Britain's anti-slavery movement, as endorsed by historian Gerald Horne.

Historian Carl Degler pointed out that "no new social class came to power through the door of the American Revolution. The men who engineered the revolt were largely members of the colonial ruling class."[705] Nearly three-quarters of the signatories of the Declaration of Independence held colonial office during British rule. Merely days after the aristocrats declared war, the Boston Committee of Correspondence ordered a mandatory military draft for the poor, which could be substituted by the rich, causing the poor to scream "Tyranny." Only a third of the population supported the Revolution per John Adams's own estimates. The subsequent laws mandating military enlistment—of all males between sixteen and sixty in Connecticut, for example—appear less democratic than the popular misconception.

George Washington, the wealthiest man in America, was so disgusted by the peasants in his militia that it nearly cost him the war. He referred to them as "an exceedingly dirty and nasty people, an unaccountable kind of stupidity in the lower class of these people."[706] Unsurprisingly, the class disparity continued within the revolutionary army, leading to frequent uprisings such as the Fort Wilson riot and the Pennsylvania Line Mutiny.

The First Company of Philadelphia Artillery in 1779 even complained against "those who are avariciously intent upon amassing wealth by the distribution of the more virtuous part of the community."[707] The morale was so low that the Americans lost the first battles until the tide was turned by a dominating French intervention.

Following the revolution, President Washington instructed Major General John Sullivan "to lay waste to all the settlements" around the Haudenosaunee. "…[Indian] country may not be merely overrun but destroyed…you will not by any means, listen to any overture of peace before the total ruin of their settlements is effected…and in the terror with which the severity of the chastisement they receive will inspire them."[708] Even before the writing of the Constitution, the Continental Congress produced the Northwest Ordinance, which served as a blueprint for grabbing the British-protected Indian Territory by violently cleansing its indigenous population.[709]

They wrote about *all men* being *equal*, while sitting in their plantations, claiming Locke's ideals. Perhaps even telling the house slave to fetch the next bottle of ink. But words are tricky things that do not always reveal the true intentions lying between the lines. Locke's Calvinism shaped much of his ideas to the point that even his written constitutions for the Carolinas in the 1660s turned out to be a feudal aristocracy run by slave owners. Historian Carl Bridenbaugh's work reveals a clear class system set in place in the early colonial days that "eagerly sought to preserve in America the social arrangements of the Mother Country."[710] The colonial oligarchs controlled the peasant population through business, politics, religion, and marriage alliances, though their grip on power gradually loosened with the widening disparities.

That stress was cleverly alleviated by legislating a race wall that separated angry poor whites from rebellious slaves. Their intentions were as diverse and complex as human nature, contrasting the simplistic myth of a fight for freedom and equality. The elite colonists diverted the tumultuous class tension towards the British in a masterful play of patriotism crafted by Thomas Paine in 1776. Ironically, Paine's reference to the Norman conquest of 1066 also describes a settler takeover of native lands: "A French bastard landing with an armed Banditti and establishing himself king of England against the consent of the natives, is in plain terms a very paltry rascally original. It certainly hath no divinity in it."[711] Even by their standards, it is just *Common Sense*.

Then it should come as no surprise that Texans only revolted against their former Mexican government when their black president abolished slavery. We should certainly *remember the Alamo* for what it was: rebel slaver's standoff against their government's manumission.[712] The annexation of Texas to California was another blatant US aggression confessed by a participating Colonel Ethan Allen Hitchcock in his diary.[713] Henry David Thoreau was jailed for his protest against the Mexican War, which later led to his lecture on "Civil Disobedience." His friend Ralph Emerson shared his antiwar sentiment but considered it futile to protest. They were both right. History broadens our minds and allows us to diagnose the problems of our time. Such retrospection is not to play the blaming game, nor to dismantle all current systems in place, but to honestly study our past in hopes of balancing a just future.

The lack of true representation in our government was not accidental but rather masterfully planned. As John Jay, the president of the Continental Congress, stated: "Those who own the country ought to govern it."[714] "Or as Madison put it, power has to be in the hands of the wealth of the nation, the more responsible set of men who sympathize with property owners and understand that you have 'to protect the minority of the opulent against the majority.' The rest of the population has to be tamed to make sure they can't do very much," explains Chomsky.[715] This racial and economic undertone dominated all actions thereafter, with two-thirds of the eighteen American presidents between 1789 and 1877 owning slaves.[716]

Four groups were not represented nor protected in the Constitutional Convention: women, men without property, slaves, and indentured servants. It provides context when interpreting "all men" within its texts. Protests and riots by the marginalized were common during the early days of the new republic, as exemplified by Shays' Rebellion of 1786, resulting in Samuel Adams' Riot Act and the suspension of *habeas corpus*. While the economic goal of the Constitution in protecting the interest of the wealthy was noted by early historians like Charles Beard (1874-1948 CE), its promotion as a work of genius by wise and honest men within the country's education system seals young minds to any alternatives. Its sacred status was debunked within a decade of the First Amendment, with the legislation of the Sedition Act in 1798 limiting freedom of speech and press. At the same time, the American Constitution does just enough for small property owners to create a healthy middle-class buffer against the marginalized.

Those glorified men understood liberalism as it applied to *them* eccentrically, which explains the irony of Jefferson writing the Declaration of Independence and continuing to have an enslaved child for personal pleasure. Perhaps he should have been punished according to his state's laws for "abusing himself to the dishonor of God and shame of Christians, by defiling his body in lying with a negro."[717] The apologist's excuses are just as anachronistically damning as their ignorance. At least, these men could have refused any part in the institution that they so "abhorred," regardless of the consequence or endless justifications in the aftermath. But they did not, and their moral failings continue to haunt America. Seeing America's moral plight abroad, early mixed-race Louisianians protested their disenfranchisement. "'Do political axioms on the Atlantic become problems when transferred to the shores of the Mississippi?' they asked on a trip to the capital. Jefferson shrugged his shoulders and did nothing."[718]

Jefferson later confessed: "Can the liberties of a Nation be secure when we have removed a conviction that these liberties are the gift of God? Indeed I tremble for my country when I reflect that God is just: that his justice cannot sleep for ever." Such noble words do not excuse one's hypocrisy as God warns: "There is the one who is miserly, who is self-satisfied, who denies goodness—We shall smooth his way towards hardship and his wealth will not help him as he falls" (*al-Layl* 92:8-11). Today, we may be physically free, but we remain shackled by the invisible chains of capitalism and imperialism. The plantation owners have been replaced by billionaire masters like the Rothschilds, mythical figures we only read about on the news. We are grateful for the scraps they send our way and continue to slave away at their machine to profit only for them, forgetting all of our expandability in their eyes. Just as the high command was informed of the American POWs at Nagasaki prior to the bombing; the cold response was: "Targets previously assigned for Centerboard remain unchanged."[719] In times of relative peace, it all seems fine; but at the slightest disquiet, the masters on top separate perfunctorily to send us to the front as the first line of defense. We saw it all unfold before our eyes during the COVID-19 pandemic.

The same divide-and-conquer policy employed abroad is also ingeniously deployed at home to maintain control. The middle class is taxed to relieve the poor, creating resentment and keeping the majority split. Even during desegregation, poor black students were bussed to impoverished white schools with violent outcomes, while keeping the affluent schools untouched. The politicians will breathlessly canvas around helping the poor but vote against social services and welfare *ad nauseam*, passing bills to shift taxpayer money to themselves and their friends through big corporations. At any sign of distress, they will just bomb another country with their controlled media to manufacture consent and divert the mob's attention elsewhere. The problems are not the immigrants and minorities taking the poor Americans' jobs, but the industry's greed, moving jobs overseas to maximize margins at any cost.

In a capitalistic society driven by individualism, justice will forever remain a concept to be fought and debated over but never truly achieved. Guru Granth Sahib, the holy scripture of Sikhism, astutely observes that it is wealth rather than religion or race that divides us as human beings (GG: 417). Unfortunately, there is no system devoid of such elite dominance in the domain of human conception. The very principles that underpin capitalism are inherently Darwinian, designed to unnaturally exploit and prey upon the vulnerable. While we may all have certain inalienable rights bestowed upon us by a higher power, these rights cannot come at the expense of others. If one person's freedom is allowed to impede upon the well-being or existence of another, then we cannot truly say that all men are created equal. If my freedom denies the right for another to exist, then none of us are indeed free. We arrogantly reject divine laws with various rationales, only veiling our selfish motives and rebelling against the ultimate King of the universe.

II: Sirat al-Mustaqim

God has given some of you more provision than others. Those who have been given more are unwilling to pass their provision on to the slaves they possess so that they become their equals. How can they refuse to acknowledge God's blessings? (al-Nalh 16:71)

For believers, the divine diagnosis is clear but to secular intellectuals, God's remedies are worth little more than an eye roll. All of their proposed alternatives are ignorant of the timeless flaw of "original thought." For instance, Russell defined *ethics* as "the motive or state of mind of the agent." Unbeknownst to him, this is the first measure of Islamic jurisprudence, as stated by the famous Prophetic dictum: "Actions are [judged] by their intentions" (*Sahih al-Bukhari* 1). Russell went on to clarify that "acts inspired by certain emotions are good, and those inspired by certain other emotions are bad."[720] This parallels Muslim beliefs about the whispers of the angels and the devils. These realizations appear to be rationally deducible (although infrequently), but they have been clarified through divine inspirations throughout our existence. Hence, the periodical re-emergence of these ideas is not as original as it may seem.

When we appreciate the middle balance of Islam, all secular wisdom worth a neuron seems to state the obvious. Russell's rule for reaching an ethical balance is to *act so as to produce harmonious rather than discordant desires*.[721] Accordingly, love is logically better than hate, but one cannot be commanded to love, which demands a better understanding of desire. He described desire as a product of naive disposition, education, and present circumstances, of which only education can shape desires to conform habitually to social benefit in a self-satisfactory manner. While other animals can also speak, our ability to write and learn from our writings distinguishes us from the rest. Thus, "Read! And your Lord is the Most Generous, who taught by the pen—taught humanity what they knew not," was the opening revelation to humanity from God (*al-'Alaq* 96:3-5).

Chances are, even your most recent argument was a result of failed communication, which is a two-way process where both sides must demonstrate artful mastery to be successful. Our failure to communicate becomes a barrier to intelligent discussion and resorts to force. Then we fail to live as friends and are unable to flourish, resembling our current state, where "we are constantly oppressed by every sort of dread, and checked in every movement by suspicion," wrote Adler. He questioned the soundness of our liberalism and whether we truly understood the origins of liberty and its limits, as all the different aspects of freedom are based on freedom of thought. "Without it, freedom of speech is an empty privilege, and a free conscience nothing but a private prejudice," he explained. "Without it, our civil liberties can be exercised only in a *pro forma* way, and we are unlikely to retain them long if we do not know how to use them well."[722]

The professional and intellectual goal is not to tell people what to do but to rethink new possibilities by breaking away from overconfidence cycles.[723] The key is to educate and train ourselves to consistently desire good, which cannot be achieved simply through positive reinforcements, moral exhortations, or explicit instruction. Russell explained that it can only be achieved through social institutions that merge our varying interests and education that habituates individuals to desire harmoniously with their neighbors.[724] This again resonates with the Islamic way of life, which gives us a divine prescription for habituating our desires (*nafs*) towards good.

Current global conflicts can be seen as a failure to achieve this ethical balance due to politics and malice. Today, an overwhelming promotion of global hatred towards the oppressed is achieved through powerful propaganda silencing their screams through bad education. To clarify such matters, we must educate ourselves against all external pressures to desire that which serves humanity best. Russell continued: "Desire for power over other people is a potent source of conflict, and is therefore to be discouraged; a respect for the liberty of others is one of the things that ought to be developed by the right kind of education...The conclusion may be summed up in a single phrase: *The good life is one inspired by love and guided by knowledge.*"[725]

We cannot cure a pathologic process by only treating its symptoms. Still, in misguided efforts, we try to alleviate the symptoms of our diseased society at face value. We try to fix racism by making laws to desegregate, but without bringing people's minds out of the darkness, ignorance remains just as prevalent in people's hearts. We attempt to fix economic disparity through taxation, yet fail to bridge the gap between the rich and the poor, resulting in accusations of socialism, bailouts, and unemployment. History teaches us how such externally forced solutions inevitably fail as they lack internal training and reeducation. Symptomatic relief alone allows the underlying pathology to pester and prevail—cancer always wins. This vital lesson was missed by many who have tried to crush extremism forcefully without addressing its root causes. "Fundamentalism is impervious to suppression," writes Aslan. "Counter it with cruelty, and it gains adherents...Respond with despotism, and it becomes the sole voice of oppression."[726] The Prophet warned that no one flirts with extremism but is eventually consumed by it and advised a middle path for his followers (*Sunan Abi Dawud* 4612). It may be the viper we are forced to lie with due to our failure to secure peace and justice for our fellow humans.

He has raised up the sky. He has set the balance so that you may not exceed in the balance: weigh with justice and do not fall short in the balance. (ar-Rahman 55:7-9)

Education is one side of the equilateral triangle that buttresses knowledge and wisdom, which can be gained independently of one another without reaching the goal. Educator John Taylor Gatto criticized our current system for not finding "a better way to do things than locking children up all day in cells instead of letting them grow up knowing their families, mingling with the world, assuming real obligations." Both knowledge and wisdom can be gained through observation of our surroundings with time. Education attempts to make that process more efficient by building on the knowledge we already have from others. It is more than just hoarding information with a certificate of proof from prestigious institutions or the speech of a caged parrot.

While Malcolm X's physical restraint in the prison library helped him free his mind, many of us roam free with our imprisoned minds. Aristotle defined the highest level of wisdom as *knowledge of all things* predicated on our familiarity with the One who is *All-knowing*. Awareness of God then ties back to our awareness of ourselves, reaching enlightenment according to Lao Tzu. Today's scientific emphasis on the *how* without a proper understanding of the *why* falls short of this time-tested understanding. The classical Arabic definition of *wisdom* is meaningful knowledge that is beneficial *and* acted upon. Merely obtaining knowledge without its internalization and manifestation through wisdom blunders proper education. There are many widely read ignoramuses today who even go so far as to criticize the words of God in the Qur'an in a *sophomoric* way of its original Greek meaning. God compares such people to a donkey carrying books, not benefiting from its burden (*al-Jumu'ah* 62:5). The picture painted by such *ayats* makes even my researched facts resemble a terminally ill physician who dispenses medicine yet cannot heal himself. "When you want to preach to people, [first] preach to yourself," God said to Jesus. "If you respond to your own preaching, then preach to others; and if not, be shy from Me."[727]

Imam al-Ghazali's works are remarkable in their balanced understanding and wisdom. Often wrongfully blamed for the decline of the Islamic Golden Age for his criticism of philosophers like Ibn Sina, his opposition was mainly towards the peripatetic and the occultist schools of philosophy, and those tipping the balance of practical spirituality and philosophical reasoning. Even the most notable philosophical works reveal verbose discussions on minutiae that are only made relevant through the time spent writing, reading, and discussing them. What more can be said about it than what had already been written by Seneca two thousand years ago?[728] Aristotle recommended that we only deliberate about things in our power, which even he failed to adhere to on many occasions.[729] Often, their vague, incomprehensible jargon is self-contradictory, which is later praised through projected theories derived from the denial of bewilderment.

Al-Ghazali still recognized the importance of that aspect of knowledge to be able to legally defend one's faith, as failure to do so might lead to violent measures. Ibn Taymiyyah noted in *ar-Radd 'ala al-Mantiqiyyin* (The Refutation of the Logicians) that logic does not benefit the ignorant and is superfluous for the intelligent. Ibn Khaldun also praised the philosophical methodology in his *Muqaddimah* despite the errors of the philosophers. Al-Attas attributes the steady decline and misguided scholarship since the Islamic Golden Age to a loss of *adab*, which he defines as the recognition of excellence and virtue with love, respect, and humility.[730] As for God's promise: "I will keep distracted from My signs those who behave arrogantly on earth without any right, and who, even if they see every sign, will not believe in them; they will not take the way of right guidance if they see it but will take the way of error if they see that. This is because they denied Our signs and paid them no heed" (*al-A'raf* 7:146).

Accessibility of knowledge today gives rise to pseudo-intellectuals who force their ignorance upon the masses by their degrees. Interestingly, a recent study found that individuals with higher IQs are more prone to stereotyping and biases due to their enhanced pattern recognition abilities.[731] Another found them to also have difficulty changing their minds when presented with newer information.[732] Thus, we see educated people siding with the most corrupt and delusional beliefs. "They divided, out of rivalry/jealousy, only after knowledge had come to them, and, if it had not been for a decree already passed by your Lord to reprieve them until an appointed time, they would already have been judged. Those after them, who inherited the Scripture, are in disquieting doubt about it," clarifies God (*Ash-Shuraa* 42:14).

It becomes even more dangerous when we start to believe our biases, losing sight of reality. Then it becomes difficult to assess if those like Sam Harris are simply racist masterminds or incontinent bigots. The result is an incurable disease when the carriers are asymptomatic and unwilling even to wear a mask. Similar to Anton-Babinski syndrome, where blind patients deny their vision loss through confabulation. A spectrum of similar behavioral patterns can be observed all around us today. Rather than recognizing blind spots, the affected individuals only publicly display their underlying pathology. We are all a product of our childhood; some are victims of their upbringing. Perhaps this book can also be seen as a similar expression of personal experience with third-world oppression and first-world racism.

Darwin observed that "ignorance more frequently begets confidence than does knowledge." For each such saying, there are often contradictory maxims, all of which have real-world merits. Sun Tzu's classic manual is full of contrasting aphorisms targeting a literal balance, often at the cost of practicality. One, in particular, seems to nullify the rest: *Therefore victory in war is not repetitious, but adapts its form endlessly*.[733] True knowledge and wisdom, however, are demonstrated through the humility of their possessors, who do not yield them as weapons. The Prophet further warned: "Whoever seeks knowledge so he can contest with fools, vie with the scholars, or attract attention toward himself, occupies his seat in the Fire" (*Mishkat al-Masabih* 225, 226).

The best teachers are those who acknowledge the impossibility of knowing everything. The Prophet was once asked a simple question: what are the best and worst places on earth? He could not be faulted for answering to the best of his ability, as he was the most knowledgeable of men. However, he demonstrated humility by deferring until he asked Archangel Gabriel, who also deferred until returning with the divine answer (*Mishkat al-Masabih* 741). Their humility left a legacy of students prepared to face any obstacle with an impact that continues to be felt today.[734]

Montaigne spoke of "an abecedarian ignorance that precedes knowledge, and a doctoral ignorance that comes after it." The arrogance of humanity is demonstrated through its Dunning-Kruger effect, taking pride in our recent progress, creating a false sense of mastery. We become trapped in a beginner's bubble of ignorance, which becomes the staunchest enemy of justice in the wrong circles. Even the famed philosophers were not immune to it, as detailed by MacIntyre in *After Virtue*. Thus, God warns: "O you who believe! If an evildoer comes to you with any news, verify it, lest you should harm people in ignorance, and afterwards you become regretful for what you have done" (*al-Hujurat* 49:6).

The confusion between ignorance, hate, and freedom of speech arises from misinterpretation of the First Amendment. This is similar to the misinterpretation of religious text, as some often treat the Constitution with comparable regard. Supreme Court Justice Oliver Holmes shaped much of the First Amendment in the early 20th century through his dissenting opinions. Initially an opponent of free speech from his Civil War experience, he coined the *free marketplace of ideas* through his first dissent in *Abram v US* in 1919. It was a time when President Wilson condemned political activist and presidential candidate, Eugene Debs (1855-1926 CE), to a ten-year prison sentence for even questioning the motives for entering WWI. Justice Holmes had previously upheld the Espionage Act in 1917 by his famous analogy of *shouting fire in a theater and causing panic*, which was technically incorrect. A more accurate analogy of the inciting anti-war publication of Charles Schenck would be *truthfully informing those buying theater tickets of a raging fire inside*.[735] Nevertheless, a reasonable standard was then set by the 1969 Supreme Court case in *Brandenburg v. Ohio*, which granted freedom of speech until it was directed at producing criminal acts.

While *absolute* freedom of speech is a commendable ideal, its caveats are demonstrated in today's disinformation epidemic. A 2019 MIT study showed that the spread of false information is six times faster than truth on social media, as the virtual world appears to be a much better stage for the devils. Al-Sulami (937-1021 CE) was one of the earliest psychologists to diagnose: "Among the infamies of the soul is that it never prefers the truth, and worship is contrary to its nature and disposition. Most of this is derived from pursuing caprice and chasing desires."[736] This disproportionate demand for freedom of speech over the public's right to the truth is warned against by God: "Do not follow blindly what you do not know to be true: ears, eyes, and heart, you will be questioned about all these" (*al-Isra'* 17:36).

One of the primary points of criticism and intellectual etiquette for all things read or heard is asking: *Is it true?* And *What of it?* Unfortunately, this crucial etiquette has been neglected as a criterion of excellence. To make matters worse, "Books win the plaudits of the critics and gain widespread popular attention almost to the extent that they flout the truth—the more outrageously they do so, the better," noted Adler.[737] It extends to all audio and visual materials—including newspapers, TV, podcasts, and social media platforms—where things are judged, praised, or condemned without any attention to their veracity.

On the other hand, our increasing need for "proofs" gets exploited without notice. Using standard statistical techniques, a thriving sector —including advertisers, politicians, pundits, pollsters, and others—crafts mathematical falsehoods to manipulate our thoughts and actions.[738] "But man is so addicted to systems and to abstract conclusions that he is prepared deliberately to distort the truth, to close his eyes and ears, but justify his logic at all cost," wrote Dostoevsky.[739] The COVID-19 pandemic was a quintessential example, where the truth was readily accessible, but the spread of disinformation was disastrous to the global response. A significant portion of the population was violently willing to believe a conspiracy on a global scale than the visible truth at local hospitals. It was a peculiar manifestation of collective denial and radical postmodernist skepticism (i.e., Foucault and Lyotard's *blurring of boundaries*).[740] Greedy politicians displayed alacrity to accept population deaths to protect their pockets—forever worshiping mammon as foretold by Ambrose Bierce (1842-1914 CE). Some elites even propagated disinformation to benefit personal agendas in their continued globalization exploits and the resorption of wealth from the subaltern.[741]

Meanwhile, those in the center threw their hands down in frustration and dismay, unable to bring either side to the middle—embodying W. B. Yeats's line, "the centre cannot hold." Giving up is an inspiration from the devil, as his name *Iblis* is rooted in the Arabic words for despair. Even in defiance, he recognized God as his lord but blamed Him for his shortcomings. "And then Iblis said, 'Because You have put me in the wrong, I will lie in wait for them all on Your straight path: I will come at them—from their front and their back, from their right and their left—and You will find that most of them are ungrateful" (*al-A'raf* 7:16-7). What differentiates us is the Adamic example of persistence in seeking God's forgiveness and struggling to improve after faltering. Hence, the first *ayat* of the Qur'an and every Muslim prayer is a declaration and reminder of our gratitude to God. Otherwise, blaming others, including the devil, without realizing our shortcomings and taking active steps toward correction only feeds the devil's ego.

This book discusses a fair amount of political matters, but we must be cautious not to overlook their nuances by making sweeping generalizations. The optimal level of involvement in politics for individuals has always been widely debated, with even the most righteous differing along the spectrum but with *adab*. Retrospective commentaries on past events are much easier than real-time assessments, where inevitably contrasting stances are held by even the most knowledgeable. The balance lies in accepting our differences as long as honest intentions of promoting a just society are maintained. There remains a unique equipoise between the entanglement of worldly politics and apathy for each individual's success.

Sometimes even those who appear to be on the "right side" are overpowered and humbled in divine wisdom, just as it is also possible for both sides of a conflict to be virtuous.

While our individual sins may manifest as trials and tribulations in our personal lives, the punishment for global injustice and rampant debauchery is communal, as mentioned by God: "As for the perverse at heart, each new sura adds further to their perversity. They die disbelieving. Can they not see that they are afflicted once or twice a year? Yet they neither repent nor take heed" (*al-Tawbah* 9:124-126). Although our best efforts may fail to change the world without, we are still the masters of the world within. At the very least, we can educate and train ourselves to see the world clearly and purify our hearts where true peaceful balance ultimately resides.

The Prophet said (about the end of days): "Years of treachery will come over people in which liars are believed, and the truthful are denied, the deceitful are trusted, and the trustworthy are considered traitors, and the al-Ruwaybaḍah will deliver speeches."

It was asked, "Who are the al-Ruwaybaḍah?" The Prophet answered, "Petty men with authority over the common people." (Sunan Ibn Mājah)

GLASS CASTLES

You may dislike something although it is good for you, or like something although it is bad for you: God knows and you do not. (al-Baqarah 2:216)

When we delve into the history of the Occident, much of its pride dissolves into a tale of lies and deceit. The once-shining empires are revealed to be nothing more than colored plastic duct-taped over the foundation of exploited people. Its proverbial closets are filled with not just skeletons but graveyards of all who came in its way. Selling its harrowing tale requires layers upon layers of revisionist history, elevating its exceptionality above all. This pathology is fittingly reflected in the Winchester Mystery House, serving as a metaphor for our government and society.

Chinua Achebe once said, "Until the lions have their own historians, the history of the hunt will always glorify the hunter." Unsurprisingly, the history books in our schools are quite embarrassing to read, and most people are too ignorant to know the difference. Little is mentioned about the Japanese internment camps in the Philippines and Hawaii or the treatment of the Alaskan Aleuts during WWII. Just like the revered Venetian glass that turns out was stolen from Syria following the Papal embargo in 1291. "All the World's a Stage" for us, but even Shakespeare's existence cannot be authentically corroborated. Just as our patriotic song, "America the Beautiful," defies geographic realities in its hyperbolized native crops and domesticated animals stretching from sea to sea.[742]

These harsh criticisms of the West seem biased and berating, but they are necessary to even the playing field. All civilizations make hideous mistakes and also "do great and beautiful things," as Du Bois wrote. "And shall we not best guide humanity by telling the truth about all things, so far as the truth is ascertainable?"[743] World history has been lopsided for so long that we need to shift focus to its victims, not to point fingers, but to learn from our mistakes. Bestsellers like Bryson's *A Short History of Nearly Everything* are odes to brilliant European minds while completely ignoring their Muslim influences. This trend of refutation was initiated by Jamal al-Din al-Afghani in 1883 through his open letter in response to Ernest Renan's lecture on "Islam and Science."[744] While perfectly valid, it is not meant to downplay or deny the staggering advancements in the Occident following the Islamic Golden Age. It only highlights the deliberately ignored Muslim contributions to natural scientific evolution, which have indeed since diminished. It is up to us to contemplate and identify the factors that have resulted in such a demise of intellectual curiosity if we are to revive that vigor repeatedly demanded by God in the Qur'an.

The general historical trends discussed here have been nuanced in numerous in-depth studies on each subject matter, but by no means are meant to indict an entire civilization, most of whom are unaware. All of this also risks being labeled as a synecdoche of anti-Westernism. The Western worldview, however, is a relatively recent one only dating back to the age of colonization. In contrast, Islamic traditions can be traced back through the Golden Age polymaths to the classical Greek philosophers. Plato and Aristotle were taught in Baghdad long before Britain, perhaps giving the West more claim to Andalusian Averroes than the Eastern Plato, whose legacy spent nearly half a millennium under Ottoman rule. Virtually all that has come down to us from the classical period is owed to Muslim scholars, who are intricately bound to the West for its entire existence. Therefore, our history learning needs to be predicated on correcting cultural misconceptions that have been deeply ingrained in our collective consciousness for centuries.

Those [disbelievers] before them [secretly] planned, but God has the ultimate plan. He knows what every soul commits. And the disbelievers will soon know who will have the ultimate outcome. (al-Ra'd 13:42)

Today, the finger is always pointed at Islam, as it is constantly painted as a violent and intolerant faith by Islamophobic hatemongers to further their political agendas. Books and academic articles that echo the virulent anti-Islamic polemics of the Middle Ages and the Renaissance continue to be published. Virtually anything can be written or said about Muslims without challenge or demurral, unlike any other ethnic or religious group. As a result, Muslims are psychologically forced to lead furtive lives in places they consider their homelands, despite being deeply woven into the nations' entire histories.[745] Ironically, almost everything Islam is accused of is far more prevalent in the accusers. Islamic property rights for women were only granted to Western women a few generations ago.

Similar misconceptions about Islam stem from Orientalism, an institution weaponized by colonial scholars to propagate their cultural and religious prejudices. Accordingly, Islam is misreported as a belligerent, bellicose, backward, Third-World religion of oppression and fanaticism through a poor translation of the Qur'an. Sadly, even some Muslims who are more knowledgeable about secular Western dogma than about their rich Islamic traditions propagate such misconceptions. As explored in previous chapters, Western secularism developed as a countereffort against religion in general, and as an offensive against the triumph of Islam. "Thus, we have weak Muslims and weak and dangerous leaders whose comprehension and knowledge of Islam is stunted at the level of immaturity; and because of this Islam itself is erroneously made to appear as if 'undeveloped' or 'misdeveloped' or left to 'stagnate,'" explains al-Attas.[746]

Today, any act of violence is by default "Islamist terrorism" until proven non-Muslim, and then everyone suddenly loses interest. He becomes a "troubled individual" or a "lone wolf," among other excuses for his privileged behavior. Islam, as practiced by Muslims worldwide, is self-evident of the inherent peace, tolerance, and sanctity for human life that are at the core of God's commands in the Qur'an and the teachings of the Prophet. Though many accusers are aware of this, those buying into their propaganda are often ignorant people with little knowledge. God warns them both about Judgment Day: "When those who have been followed disown their followers, when they all see the suffering, when all bonds between them are severed, the followers will say, 'If only we had one last chance, we would disown them as they now disown us.' In this way, God will make them see their deeds as a source of bitter regret: they shall not leave the Fire" (*al-Baqarah* 2:166-7).

Islam is fair and God allows one to defend when attacked (*Riyad as-Salihin* Book 11, Hadith 73).[747] Therefore, we do not argue to be crass or polemic, but to review historical facts that may shed light on their smearing. Western cultures' *holier than thou* recalcitrant attitude must be exchanged for one of recognition of guilt, as "the story of the new world is horror, the story of America is a crime," confesses Professor Byrd.[748] Any chance of solving the problem would require paying attention to all its sources and dealing with them effectively. When one comes to the table with the usual arrogant Western attitude, no real effort is made toward remediation. That admission of guilt is the one thing the devil refused to do and swore to sway us from.

Interreligious dialogue on such premises is also futile. Even psychologically, the rethinking process is most effective when initiated by the offender, rather than the victim.[749] It allows us to heal together and act in a genuine, neighborly manner on our shared planet. Polarizing issues, such as racism and bigotry, are nonbinary and dynamic, as we can harbor prejudice at one moment and not the next. Their effects are not ubiquitous, nor is it a *common* experience that is shared equally. This is not to say that people of color cannot be racist, nor that non-minorities can never opine over such matters. Only that it requires extrinsic aid for those unexposed to fully comprehend the issues without deviating to the opposites of denial or labeling it as the postmodernist default. Unfortunately, this is a challenge in today's world of fragmented morality where individuals no longer take any general ethical responsibility.[750]

No major world religion preaches hate, only hateful people. Ultimately, it is not one's religion that makes them violent or peaceful, but their adherence to the universal values of peace and tolerance that distinguish them from those who promote injustice. All the different world religions should instead "compete with one another in doing good" (*al-Ma'idah* 5:48) to make this world a better place. Anyone deviating from this end goal is missing the point, regardless of their color or claimed faith. We must shift towards desecularization and bring true religious values back to our education and practice. "[In time] God may bring about goodwill between you and those of them you [now] hold as enemies. For God is Most Capable. And God is All-Forgiving, Most Merciful" (*al-Mumtahinah* 60:7).

Life in the West is still far safer than in most places on Earth. Albeit most global issues directly result from its predatory foreign policies, the better quality of life here is undeniable. The ability to even write a book criticizing the government is a rapidly disappearing luxury in most of the world. Today, justice and fairness are more achievable concepts in the West than its counterparts. So what does it all mean for the average apolitical Westerner, to whom it all seems unrelatable, past events? Is it fair to make such broad generalizations and paint everyone with the same brush?

Let us consider the *average man* throughout history, who is generally good-natured, peaceful, and primarily concerned with providing food, shelter, and safety for himself and his family. His benign circle of influence does not extend far beyond his family and friends. His thoughts and aspirations rarely go above that, with little concern for global events or historical anecdotes. Therefore, it is infuriating for him to see violent, angry faces on TV burning his nation's flag and threatening his peace. He trusts his media and government when told about these animalistic, uncivilized savages waiting to come into his home and raise havoc. It is especially challenging when these people do not even look or sound like him. His media never informs him about his government's crimes around the world, nor is he taught the truth in his textbooks. He has no reason to distrust his kinsmen, so he will take the bait and vote for those who promise to deal with these foreigners harshly and keep them out of harm's way by any means necessary.

While this average man is not a bad father or husband, his ignorance makes him an accomplice in the massacre of humanity. His misunderstanding of the same basic needs of another average "foreigner" causes him to wish ill upon someone ultimately not so different from him. Most of our daily interactions reveal overwhelming decency among the general population, which is often not represented through the actions of our leaders. We often naively expect the politicians to demonstrate similar humanity, which they had abandoned long ago on their path to power. They exist in their echo chambers in an alternate reality. It brings us back to the discussion of the responsibility of intellectuals and the public, as proposed by Dwight Macdonald and Noam Chomsky.[751] When we think of the world, we do so first as a Westerner, framed by our Western upbringing and education. Our worldview is therefore inherently biased by our position of power, with our government's continuous political interests and involvement in the Orient since the time of Homer.[752] As a result of the Occident's history of aggression, the average Westerner is responsible for correcting their default, prejudiced view if he is to opine over such matters.

Some in the West are fully aware of this and are actively drawing attention to topics that are often considered taboo by others. Unfortunately, those voices are a rarity and inaudible, *sotto voce* amidst the rhetoric. Those who claim to be "neutral" often harbor malice, as their silence amounts to passive approval. Some are completely deaf, dumb, and blind, waving flags and assault rifles, unembarrassed to flaunt their bigotry. A glance at them makes any reasonable person lose hope for the future of humanity. Discussions with them remind us of God's illumination: "Calling to disbelievers is like a herdsman calling to things that hear nothing but a shout and a cry: they are deaf, dumb, and blind, and they understand nothing" (*al-Baqarah* 2:171). The caveat is that we cannot see into their hearts or predict their future. Thus, it is essential to assume that everyone has the potential to believe and continue our efforts to spread peace and justice.

The Prophet said: "Whosoever of you sees an evil, let him change it with his hand; and if he is not able to do so, then [let him change it] with his tongue; and if he is not able to do so, then with his heart—and that is the weakest of faith." (40 Hadith Nawawi 34)

Bigotry often stems from a fear of losing one's identity when confronted with change, which ultimately is a construct that defines one's self-understanding in contrast to *others*. When that self-realization or identity is threatened, it promotes chauvinism and xenophobia. Any attempts at change are more compelling when framed from a perspective of continuity that allows one's identity to endure despite evolving strategies.[753] The prevalence of extreme views is also overemphasized by disproportionate media coverage.[754] While it makes for sensational news, it obscures the balanced middle and dampens their motivation for change.

Many sympathizers, drawn to goodness, can see through the propaganda. Dr. Dirks, an ordained minister, speaks of such a coterie within the priestly who identify as "atypical Christians."[755] There have always been souls like Masaccio, the first Renaissance painter, who secretly painted the shahada around Mary's halo in his Triptych of San Giovenale in 1422.[756] Even Goethe—considered the German Shakespeare—famously wrote: "If Islam means, submission to God/ We all live and die in Islam." His moving tribute to the Prophet in "Mahomet's Song," as well as his veneration of Islam throughout his life, is noteworthy.[757] God confirms: "Indeed, there are some among the People of the Book who truly believe in God and what has been revealed to you [believers] and what was revealed to them. They humble themselves before God—never trading God's revelations for a fleeting gain. Their reward is with their Lord. Surely God is swift in reckoning" (al-'Imran 3:199).

Right and wrong have been made clear to us, and we have been cautioned about respecting the gray areas as the sanctuary of God and His prohibitions. "Truly in the body, there is a morsel of flesh, which, if it is whole, all the body is whole, and if it is diseased, all of [the body] is diseased. Indeed, it is the heart," said the Prophet (*Sunan an-Nasa'i* 4453). Much more unites humanity than our manufactured differences through arrogance, avarice, and jealousy—all diseases of the heart and the soul. It is not coincidental that our gradual emphasis on the heart as nothing but an organic pump and dismissal of the soul has led to a promotion of such diseases, which bring us down to the level of animals, only following caprice. "Your enemy is not the one you are relieved from if you killed him," said Hasan al-Basri. "Rather, your true enemy is your own soul, between your two sides" (*Tahdhīb al-Āthār Musnad 'Umar* 2/812). Thus, after returning from a campaign, the Prophet remarked that he had returned from the lesser *jihad* to the greater—referring to the struggle of our daily lives to battle our *nafs*.

We become humans by looking into our hearts honestly and being our own judges. We need to become spiritual healers of ourselves to first diagnose such illnesses within us and then work on the remedy. These illnesses ultimately destroy our inner peace and happiness, making us see the world negatively and creating insecurities and loneliness. Our opinions of others only serve as our heart's mirror. If our religion tells us to be unjust, we need to reevaluate our faith. If our beliefs lead us astray, we must correct them. If our leaders preach immorality, we need to force them out and hold them accountable. If our speech and hands harm someone, we need to practice silence and restraint. If we fail to act like humans, we need to be constrained like animals, for the hate that appears to unite the devils also fuels their own hells.

When we find hate in our hearts, we must acknowledge its evil etiology. Followers of all faiths must study them thoroughly with an open mind as their future depends on it. We must question the motives of those who tell us otherwise before turning into puppets of a larger political game. The last perfect man on earth passed away in the 7th century, and everyone else thereafter has personal reasons for their worldview. For me, it is the hope of illustrating one of the many sides of the human experience. It is up to you to scientifically consider these propositions and decide if there is any good in them. Anyone reading solely to cavil and refute is completely missing the point. We did not choose our birthplace and could have been born in a culture we hold to be our antithesis. Our emotional identity is often based on arbitrary animosities displayed even in sports rivalries. We owe it to *them* to learn about their struggles, just as we would like them to understand ours. Through such understanding and building steady personal relationships, commonalities between all *average men* become apparent. Such concepts have been also proven through psychological experiments for those who require data.[758]

A sound education system is critical to teach citizens of a true democracy first to understand, and then participate responsibly. Those who stand to lose from this would naturally conspire to maintain an uneducated and confused population, which is then easily controlled through vitriol, rancor, and rage. The price paid for that lousy education is also reminiscent of the famous saying of John Adams: "There are two ways to conquer and enslave a nation. One is by the sword. The other is by debt." It is achieved domestically by placing the educated under a burden of inescapable debt to enslave them for life and prevent social mobility. As a result, education itself has shifted from the liberal arts to the servile to fuel the ever-growing economic disparity.

Psychologists have found that the *common identity* concept is only effective in bringing people together in emergencies. Even when we identify with an antagonist through dialogue, we make an exception for *that* individual without changing our stereotypes for the entire group. Although some stereotypes may have a real-life basis, studies have consistently shown them to be increasingly inaccurate when held towards an antagonistic group with different ideologies.[759] Psychologist and Holocaust survivor Herb Kelman encountered this dilemma in his attempt to bridge the Israeli-Palestinian conflict.[760] I have also experienced it personally in post-9/11 America when referred to as "one of the good ones."

Building interpersonal connections is made increasingly difficult by today's disproportionate access and spread of disinformation. Although the current global picture may seem like a losing battle, we must continue our personal rethinking process and encourage conversations within our circles of influence. A broader and lasting reversal of stereotypes only takes place when we counterfactually rethink through the silliness of animosities and their real-life consequences.[761] Musician Daryl Davis has shown incredible transformations through similar engagements with long-time Klan members, highlighting the issue of our minds' inability to question our core values.[762] Many of our deeply held beliefs are cultural truisms that are rarely probed.[763] Think of all of your currently held stereotypes and ask yourself: what would it take for you to change your mind? If the answer is "nothing," then that belief is more like a *cult* for you, and you are not thinking like a reasonable *scientist*.

Today's anti-vaccine rhetoric runs along the same spectrum of psychological immunity to common sense. We have the *Library of Babel* at our fingertips and simply need to care enough to search for the truth. Similarly, if one has any negative connotation about Islam, he owes it to himself to read the Qur'an, for the secrets it holds for him might change his life. Islam's blueprint for social justice inherently clashes with those who benefit from the unjust *status quo*. It is refreshing to see Western scholars like Robert Briffault, Richard Bulliet, Juan Cole, and Anna Moreland bring a fair Western voice to the table as well as the commendable efforts of Evangelical pastor Bob Roberts, who truly portrays the loving message of Jesus. They demonstrate a similar objective methodology as al-Biruni in his efforts in India. Even at a cellular level, we need constant reassurance and care from our neighbors to flourish and avoid apoptosis. It is that level of mutual respect and understanding that would make most of the current world's problems solvable.

And when Our Clear ayats are recited to them, you will notice a denial on the faces of the disbelievers! They are nearly ready to attack with violence those who recite Our ayats to them. Say: "Shall I tell you of something worse than that? The Fire [of Hell] which God has promised to those who disbelieve, and worst indeed is that destination!" (al-Hajj 22:72)

Each of us is afforded the luxury of becoming informed citizens, allowing the gifted individuals to expand their circles to lead fellow countrymen. At the very least, we can actively change ourselves to become free thinkers, raise awareness within our families, and be the voice of reason for the ignorant within our inner circles. The average person's visceral reaction to terms like *terrorism* and *extremism* and their strategic association with *Muslim terrorists* and *Muslim extremists* is not accidental. It has a reproducible classical conditioning response and reflexively evokes a similar subconscious disgust upon mere introduction to a Muslim.

There is similar dishonesty from a belligerent intellectual circle, whose sole aim is to manipulate public opinion through superficially academic "screeds bearing screaming headlines about Islam and terror, Islam exposed, the Arab threat, and the Muslim menace," noted Said.[764] As a rule, the same actions of a non-Muslim are not prefaced with similar Christin-, Jewish-, or atheist- prefixes. The purpose here is to raise awareness about historical events, which sheds light on current global politics. It is not to justify anyone's wrong actions nor to play into whataboutism or tu quoque logical fallacy. We need to focus on issues that we have the power to change and refrain from discussing matters outside our control or foreign nations until we address our domestic affairs.

We must first identify our wrongdoings—both at individual and national levels—and use our democratic powers to hold our politicians responsible. Of course, they would want nothing but for us to shift focus on everything else as a routine magician's misdirection. We must recognize such tactics, displacing our emotions following a tragedy to bring down decades of terror on millions of civilians to aid their political agendas—and ultimately, their pockets. We must put an honest effort into putting ourselves in others' shoes. Only then would we understand the anguish of another *average man* turning the corner to hear the screeching sound of an airstrike on the house where he had just left his wife and kids. Those of us with children should feel the agony and helplessness of a parent shielding his terrified child with nothing but his arms against showering bullets and bombs. While he has physically failed to protect his family from humanity's cruelties, the rest of us have truly failed him in morality.

What would we do to make those responsible pay if we were in his shoes? How would we feel about those remaining silent and careless about their government's ineffable crimes affecting us? What excuses would we make for them? How can we achieve peace through war? Instead, it is just another *average man* who becomes the casualty of inexplicable hate and fails to provide his family with the same basic human rights. Genuine compassion comes from seeing all humanity on an equal footing with an equal right to desire happiness. Our equal right to fulfill those aspirations should create a sense of familiarity with even those on the other side of the planet, regardless of whether we view them as friends or foes. Collectivism and generalization lead to hateful rhetoric and injustice. God warns: "O believers! Stand firm for God and bear true testimony. Do not let the hatred of a people lead you to injustice. Be just! That is closer to righteousness. And be mindful of God. Surely God is All-Aware of what you do" (*al-Ma'idah* 5:8). Although a fair amount of general terms have been used in this book, it is done as a reporting tool rather than a broad discriminatory accusation. While we all feel the need to clarify the tenets of our beliefs, interfaith dialogues should take a backseat to the larger goal of interreligious cooperation through socio-political and economic justice.

Muslims cannot afford ignorance as God commands us to be knowledgeable. How can we claim to believe without reading and understanding God's words in the Qur'an? The trials and tribulations of our times can be best deconstructed by reading the *eternities*, as advised by Henry David Thoreau. All of our external and internal conflicts directly result from our distance from the Qur'an, within which lies their remedy. Many misconceptions Muslims have about their faith are often osmosis of Occidental obloquy, which fall apart when one approaches the Qur'an with pure intention. Dr. Cleary deemed it a "necessary step toward the understanding and tolerance without which world peace is in fact inconceivable."[765]

The Qur'an is the ultimate instruction manual that the Creator has bestowed upon us. To benefit from it, we must start by first improving ourselves through consistent observance of our obligations and avoidance of prohibitions. Imam al-Haddad (1634-1720 CE) advised us to then extend this practice in succession to our immediate family, neighbors, city, country, and beyond.[766] Unfortunately, some people skip these necessary steps and jump to "change the world" without correctly understanding Islam and implementing it in their own life with *ihsan* (excellence). The resulting chaos then only reflects the state of their own minds and reason.

During the time of the Prophet, the Quraysh's strategy was to prevent people from hearing the Qur'an to stop it from affecting their hearts. "And said those who disbelieved, 'Do not listen to this Qur'ān, and make noise during its recitation, so that you may overcome'" (*Fussilat* 41:26). Today, we make similar *noise* by immersing our senses in endless entertainment, which creates an impenetrable layer of ignorance around our hearts. The Romans, at their height, used bloody gladiator games as entertainment where foreign prisoners and nature were violently subdued. While this speaks volumes regarding the state of their inhumanity, a perusal of the top movies, TV shows, and games today demonstrates a similar display of immorality, if not worse. Consequently, even when we hear the Qur'an's recitation, we find its message confusing and incomprehensible.

When the Crusaders attacked the "Saracens" indiscriminately, Muslims were divided into Umayyads, Abbasids, Fatimids, Shi'as, Seljuks, and so on. As they continue to attack us today, we keep adding to that narcissism of small differences, with even more national and ethnic divisions as our worst enemy. Indeed, that is the one path of destruction that was left open for the *ummah* by God (*Sunan Ibn Majah* 3951). "They do not break their covenant with God and His Messenger, but God will enable their enemies to overpower them and take some of what is in their hands," warned the Prophet. "Unless their leaders rule according to the Book of God and seek all good from that which God has revealed, God will cause them to fight one another" (*Sunan Ibn Majah* 4019). All prophets preached a peaceful message of love and obedience while maintaining a life in accordance with God's laws. They left the judgment up to Him. This should be the overall take-home message guiding the rest of our actions. When we face backlash, we are again reminded: "Never have We sent a warner to a community without those among them who were corrupted by wealth saying, 'We do not believe in the message you have been sent with.' They would say, 'We have greater wealth and more children than you, and we shall not be punished'" (*Saba* 34:34-5).

Islamic creed asserts God's oneness and the prophet Muhammad as his final messenger. Loving the Prophet is as essential to our faith as our love for God and His message. Since love is directly related to familiarity, we cannot fulfill our obligation to the Prophet without studying his life (*seerah*) and his traditions (*ahadeeth*). Such love can elevate us to the level of Imam Ahmad Ibn Hanbal, who forgave his jailer *before* every whipping to avoid displeasing the Prophet on the Day of Judgment (for being the cause of another Muslim's punishment). It is incredible how there is an authentic Prophetic tradition for nearly all pearls of wisdom we come across in our lives. He taught: "Charity does not decrease wealth, no one forgives another except that God increases his honor, and no one humbles himself for the sake of God except that God raises his status" (*Sahih Muslim* 2588). Yet, these lessons go unnoticed due to mainstream misdirection and unfamiliarity.

Although Islam strives for perfection, like any faith, most Muslims (including myself) fall short. Insults and heinous charges against our loved ones deeply disturb us, just like anyone else. When someone denigrates the Prophet, whom we are supposed to love more than ourselves, it hurts us even more (*Sahih al-Bukhari* 6632). As Chomsky notes, publishing cartoons that ridicule and humiliate people is akin to an immature adolescent prank. "And it's really vulgar when you're attacking people whom you're grinding under your jackboot."[767] The same French magazine even went so far as publishing deplorable cartoons mocking over fifty thousand Muslim deaths following an earthquake in 2023.

Muslims do not have to apologize for the crimes of deranged criminals who identify as Muslims any more than Christians should have to for the crimes of other Christians. The world becomes far less complicated once we treat each other fairly. No one's freedom of expression should extend beyond the limits of the commonsensical dignity of others' freedom of life, liberty, and property. God also commands: "[O believers!] Do not insult what they invoke besides God or they will insult God spitefully out of ignorance. This is how We have made each people's deeds appealing to them. Then to their Lord is their return, and He will inform them of what they used to do" (*al-An'am* 6:108). None of our stated freedoms are without limits but must be practiced with mutual respect. Otherwise, we risk creating an unlivable anarchy devoid of civility.

As the Prophet said, "Righteousness is in good character, and wrongdoing is that which wavers in your soul, and which you dislike people finding out about" (*Sahih Muslim* 2553a). Muslims must resist being reactionary and acting in an unIslamic manner. True intellect (Arabic, *'aql* عقل) demonstrates restraint, and the best *dawah* is the excellent character of a Muslim, which will carry the most weight on the Day of Judgment (*Jami` at-Tirmidhi* 2003). We should avoid actions that may discourage others from Islam. Instead, we should strive to emulate Hamza Ibn Abdul-Muttalib, who became a devout Muslim upon learning the news of his tribesmen disrespecting his nephew.[768] The *Islamic Manners* outlined by Shaykh Abdul Fattah Abu Ghudda demonstrates the excellence we can achieve in civil society, although it is infrequently observed in our daily lives. Still, it provides hope by giving us something to aspire to and inspiring others through the process.

True love of God would naturally offend any pious soul facing blasphemy. It infuriates God infinitely more, as He says, "The disbelievers say, 'The Lord of Mercy has offspring.' How terrible is this thing you assert: it almost causes the heavens to be torn apart, the earth to split asunder, the mountains to crumble to pieces, that they attribute offspring to the Lord of Mercy. It does not befit the Lord of Mercy: there is no one in the heavens or earth who will not come to the Lord of Mercy as a servant—He has counted them all: He has numbered them exactly—and they will each return to Him on the Day of Resurrection all alone" (*Maryam* 19: 88-95). Shortly after the Trinity was made the official doctrine, Nicea was devastated by two major earthquakes that left the prosperous city in ruins. Nonetheless, God demonstrates infinite Mercy by allowing such offenders to roam freely and continues to provide them with sustenance. Furthermore, God instructed His most beloved messenger to be patient against such provocations (*Qaf* 50:39). If we act differently in our anger, we risk exposing ourselves to God's wrath, which may deprive us of His Mercy. Thus, God closed the discussion with: "We know best what they say. And you are not to compel them [to believe]. So remind with the Qur'an [only] those who fear My warning" (*Qaf* 50:45).

Although it may be tempting to point fingers at others for the current state of the Muslim world, it is essential to recognize our role in contributing to these issues. Indeed, God tells us that believers will certainly hear many hurtful things from both people of the book and other paratheists. The divine solution is to be mindful of God and respond with patience and wisdom (*ali 'Imran* 3:186). Today, one in five individuals worldwide is Muslim, providing ample opportunity to showcase the true message of Islam through our actions beyond all propaganda. We must learn from the historical lessons and *cast down our buckets wherever we are*. Islam flows through people's minds like a flash flood down a valley, with all the filth foaming up to the surface and washing away. "This is how God compares truth to falsehood. The [worthless] residue is then cast away, but what benefits people remains on the earth. This is how God sets forth parables" (*al-Ra'd* 13:17).

Similarly, we must learn from the Prophet's exceptional character and conduct throughout his life. He brushed off hatemongers by reminding them that his name, Muhammad, means praiseworthy, indicating that they could not be referring to him. He also warned that those who go to either extreme in loving or hating him would be doomed on the Day of Judgment (weak chain, *Musnad Ahmad* 1376). We can only dream to aspire to his standard, usually falling short and writing books about it. To some degree, we only substantiate the insults against his perfect character by reacting and engaging in such fatuity. As Shaykh Mikaeel Smith reminds us, engaging with the ignorant is like wrestling a filthy pig—everyone becomes dirty and only the pig enjoys it. Therefore, we must learn to ignore the ignorant and avoid comment sections.

A FATEFUL INTERLUDE

The Prophet's words resonated even more deeply amid the pandemic: "The plague is a punishment sent by God on whom He wished, and a source of mercy for the believers." Those who remain patient in times of crisis and trust in God's plan are rewarded with the honor of a martyr (*Sahih al-Bukhari* 3474).

On a scorching summer day, after a long and tiring shift treating COVID patients, I returned home with quarantined spirits. My wife greeted me with our fussy two-month-old daughter, while our boys were running around, trying to burn off their excess energy. As I took our daughter from her, I prayed that I would not inadvertently expose my family to the virus, as was the *usual* daily mental routine.

After a while, I brought the baby back to my wife to pray the afternoon prayer. I found our two-year-old with her upstairs, waiting for his snack. She offered me to either keep the baby or take the toddler downstairs, and I chose the latter. He skipped around impatiently while I prayed, and loved the suggestion of going to the backyard for a change. So we both went to the kitchen, grabbed his snack, and just as we were about to step out through the kitchen door, I noticed that my slippers were missing from their usual place. Somewhat annoyed, I walked across the kitchen towards the garage to look for them. As soon as I opened the door to the garage, I was suddenly engulfed in thick smoke, making it difficult to breathe. Through its darkness, I saw a fire raging from the corner, clawing under the gas tank of my parked car.

Panicking, I yelled for my wife to leave our bedroom with our infant, directly above the garage. Pushing our toddler into the kitchen, I rushed to grab the fire extinguisher under the sink. While breaking the yellow seal, I realized I had never operated one before and prayed for it to be functional and intuitive. As I plunged into the smoke, something exploded! I feared it was the gas tank but realized my limited choice, so I proceeded with blindly spraying and approaching the fire in the corner. In what felt *much* longer than a few seconds, I covered the entire section with white foam. Then I quickly backed the car out of the garage and watched the dark smoke rising above our bedroom. After the smoke cleared, the cause of the fire became apparent. "IT WAS THE HOVERBOARD!" The boys had just rediscovered it and decided to charge it in the garage. The outlet was utterly charred, and the fire had started climbing up the plywood onto our bedroom floor.

Even to this day, I am unable to explain how I instinctively walked into that fire at the precise moment, preventing it from trapping us in our rooms. The older boys would have been unaware in the basement with their headphones on. It was as if an invisible force was guiding me, leading me subconsciously to exactly where I needed to be. As I reflect on that day, I am reminded of the value of each passing moment. When I consider the different ways that day could have played out, I am ashamed of how much I take for granted in life. My complaints upon the slightest distress are almost instantaneous; how could I even begin to show my gratitude for the rest? If I ever had a flat tire or a fender-bender on my way to work, I would probably complain for an entire week. Then in comparison, how much should my appreciation be in proportion to all the days I return home without incident, passing by others less fortunate along the way?

"Surely God is ever Bountiful to humanity, but most people are ungrateful" (*al-Baqarah* 2:243). In such brief pauses in our otherwise comfortable state, we neglect the ever-constant mercy of God that those trials are meant to signify. Cicero considered gratitude to be the *mother of all virtues*.[769] Seneca wrote an entire treatise *On Benefits*, describing ingratitude as one of our most common vices. A recent study in *Harvard Business Review* found that most employees complained more than ten hours a month at work, with a third of them complaining for twice that amount.[770] Complaints are indeed pathways towards ingratitude and ultimately *kufr* (unbelief), as it is truly impossible to claim our love and appreciation for God, or anyone for that matter, without gratitude (*Sunan Abi Dawud* Book 43, Hadith 39).

But what exactly should we be grateful for, wondered Kierkegaard?[771] If it is only what we discern as good, it lowers our relationship with God to our likeness and finite knowledge of discernment. Even when we determine something to be "bad," it is still good in a greater sense of the infinite (*al-Baqarah* 2:216). When we truly internalize that concept, we arrive at the gate of gratitude for all and everything beyond any discrimination, which lies at the heart of the Arabic saying: *Alhamdulillah 'ala kulli haal*— الْحَمْدُ لِلَّهِ

.عَلَى كُلِّ حَال

Constructive criticism is much more effective, while constant complaining can lead to annoyance and hinder mental growth and well-being. To break the habit, Pastor Will Brown of Kansas City created a challenge that required participants to go twenty-one days without complaining. On average, it took participants four to eight months to complete the challenge.[772] The Stoics saw complaining as unharmonious to the natural order and found beauty in one's acceptance of *amor fati* (love your fate). Interestingly, Marcus Aurelius's writing in this regard almost resembles a Sufi prayer with the exchanges of a few words:

> Every thing that is harmonious with you, oh Universe, suits me also. Nothing is too early or too late for me that is timely for you. Everything that your seasons bring is fruit for me, oh Nature. All things are from you, in you, and all things return to you. (*Meditations* 4.23)

This reminds me of two friends I lost in a house fire over a holiday weekend. When the fire marshals found their remains, they were just a few feet away from the door.

Each person has guardian angels before him and behind, watching over him by God's command. God does not change the condition of a people unless they change what is in themselves, but if He wills harm on a people, no one can ward it off—apart from Him, they have no protector. (al-Ra'd 13:11)

Now several years following that fateful day, I wonder how much it truly impacted my life. Have I taken my countless *second chances* for granted and fallen back into the typical routine of a distracted life? God describes gratitude as the opposite of *kufr*, and we all fall short of it; He promises not to burden us with trials that are beyond our capacity to bear (*al-Baqarah* 2:286). As such, the prophets were tested the most, followed by "the righteous, some of whom were tested with poverty until they could not find anything except a cloak to put around themselves. One of them rejoiced at calamity as one of you would rejoice at ease," reported the Prophet (*Sunan Ibn Majah* 4024). Often, we make the mistake of trading our afterlives for fleeting worldly pleasures. God warns in the Qur'an that some people worship Him only on the brink of faith, content when they receive blessings but quick to relapse into disbelief when tested with trials, thereby losing out on both this world and the Hereafter. This is the ultimate loss, as they call upon those who cannot harm or benefit them and stray far from the path of righteousness (*al-Hajj* 22:11-13).

Our problem lies in the assumption, both conscious and subconscious, that our lives on earth are everlasting despite all evidence to the contrary. It leads to grief and disappointment that become intolerable when coupled with that mindset. Similar to the Islamic tradition, the Stoics suggest that viewing everything as a loan rather than a possession can alleviate the inevitable loss.[773] God reminds us: "We will certainly test you with a touch of fear and famine and loss of property, life, and crops. Give good news to those who patiently endure—those who say, when afflicted with a calamity, 'We belong to God, and to Him, we shall return.' They are the ones who will receive God's blessings and mercy. And it is they who are [rightly] guided" (*al-Baqarah* 2:155-7).

THE UNTRACEABLES

We relate to you such accounts of earlier towns: some of them are still standing; some have been mowed down; We did not wrong them; they wronged themselves. Their gods, which they called on beside God, were no use to them when what your Lord had ordained came about; they only increased in their ruin. Such is the punishment of your Lord for towns in the midst of their sins: His punishment is terrible and severe. (Hud 11:100-2)

Thank you for persevering through these choppy waters and overcast skies on our journey. You may be wondering where we are headed and if a storm is on the horizon, but it's worth knowing that the sun always shines, even when dark clouds dim our perspective. I am no preacher nor a prosecutor, but the scientist in us often pushes us to seek a secular route to avoid being perceived as such. Some readers may have already found the religious references unappealing, especially if they are unsympathetic.

One of the primary purposes of our discussion is to refamiliarize ourselves with the divine and prophetic traditions. Discussions like this can take the form of dogmatic theology, which can be problematic for some, even temporarily, to accept the propositions. Recognizing this natural predisposition can help us overcome and fully internalize the rhetorical conclusions that are otherwise natural. As we continue to lay the foundations of our understanding, let us rethink the origins of such preconceived notions and explore their validity. Like sailors on the ocean, the constant changes around us can only be navigated and conquered through the faithful eternal.[774]

Historians have a legacy of dismissing religious texts as evidence, citing the lack of corresponding archeological proof to appease their scientific appearance. Anthropologists and archeologists join them in either rejecting theological claims or searching for correlating evidence. Here we will explore why both of these approaches are inherently flawed. It is not meant to validate Islam by science, as such validation is irrelevant and misguided. Assigning modern meanings to the original Arabic words in the Qur'an for contemporary translation and then using that as evidence is also problematic. Submission to God automatically makes His words in His book and His messenger above all with absolute veracity. Thus, God's statement of sending the Qur'an and His messengers as a guide and mercy for humanity takes precedence over all misconstrued attempts of misinterpreting both (*al-Jathiyah* 45:20).

The secular view is not necessarily enlightened but a restrictive outlook that ignores natural evidence. It reflects cultural conditioning that assumes science to be *the final arbiter of truth*, taking after the analytic tradition of Quine. This separation of various "sciences" from religion is a relatively recent movement, as most historians and scientists were religious clergy for the better part of our existence. Their attitude towards nature and understanding of causality in terms of providence and fate allowed them to see how humans fit into the picture to derive their scientific theories. Einstein recognized it as "the cosmic religious feeling, [which] is the strongest and noblest motive for scientific research."[775]

Quine's assertion is also erroneous, as *truth* has long ago ceased to be the goal of science, which is not to say that it was replaced by falsehood. As science evolved from various classical philosophical fields, its pursuit became knowledge itself, which is not necessarily tied to an end—for better or worse. The search for truth remained with philosophy and has since been reduced to linguistic obscurities devoid of its scientific material side and *telos*. A Muslim reader may understand it as a separation of *deen* from *dunya*. The latter refers to the worldly life derived from the Arabic root *dana*, meaning something brought near. It is necessarily linked to *deen* —commonly translated as "religion" or the afterlife, but also signifying *indebtedness* and *submissiveness* to God—which was exemplified in the City of the Prophet. Thus, it was named al-Ma*deen*ah from the same Arabic root, where the Prophet served as the judge and the governor—a *dayyan*. Accordingly, *deen* can only be fully realized within human interactions in a community through its governance.

The eternal pairing and contrasting nature of God's creations are reflected here by *dunya's* counterpart *al-akhirah*—the life hereafter. The Prophet emphasized that neither can be fully realized without the other.[776] Unfortunately, modern scientific investigations and their proponents are stuck in their material levels without ever fully maturing into their cosmic perfection, as metaphorically illustrated by Ibn Tufail's Hayy. Ubiquitous examples of this transition include the pursuit of nuclear and synthetic research that brought us to the present state of world affairs without any foresight or direction.

During the Enlightenment period, this particular shift was troublesome to the critics of Darwinism, who were otherwise quite familiar with its evolutionary aspects.[777] It was distinct in its departure from its predecessors' goal-directed theories, where evolution was a divinely guided process toward a perfect end. Darwin divorced his theory from all religious ties, leaving evolution to happen for its own sake from natural selection. Since then, all sciences have pursued a secular understanding of natural phenomena without any attention to their philosophical or metaphysical *truth*. Our recent technological advancements have moved us away from the old Socratic-Platonic-Aristotelian logic to the new mathematical-propositional logic of Nominalism.[778] This secularization of knowledge directly affects our thought process, where it exerts its "scientific methodology" in a contradictory manner—for how can any such knowledge gained without regard for a creator be used against God?

We have explored the forces that motivated secularization and the gradual development of secularism as a religion throughout this book. While some secularists are cognizant of this, most are unaware of their dogmatic practices, which often defy logic and a rational thought process. It is similar to the very trends that had initially caused them to separate. Thus, history continues to repeat as we become mere puppets of the devils, whose gambit is the true force behind all movements away from the divine. The bias toward subjectivity is not unique to history but an inherent characteristic of all sciences and acquired knowledge to a degree. The more scientifically we scrutinize our knowledge, the more it becomes apparent how little we know. Although "science" is often used as the benchmark of veracity, it is just another word, substantiated only by proof. "But you cannot go on 'explaining away' for ever: you will find that you have explained explanation itself away," explained C. S. Lewis. "The whole point of seeing through something is to see something through it...To 'see through' all things is the same as not to see."[779]

Since time immemorial, we have been trying to make sense of the unpredictability surrounding us by defining and categorizing it through our linear thought processes. The difficulty has always been that life and all natural processes are nonlinear, which inevitably leads to intellectual frustration. Thomas Kuhn's work as a philosopher and historian of science is noteworthy in explaining the natural evolution of all sciences as developing *theories* to explain natural phenomena. The process results in many theories until the most experimentally reliable one becomes a *paradigm* that boxes in a field and guides its future development.

What exhausts normal science is determining significant facts and then matching them with theory for its articulation.[780] It is, however, erroneous to apply this method outside of a paradigm where its defined parameters no longer hold.

Paradigms come at the cost of restricted vision for those educated within, who further solidify it through research and results conforming to itself. It naturally leads to paradigm blindness, where things outside the paradigm are discouraged—often aggressively. Those within the paradigm forget that the entire science was born within nature without ever creating any novel phenomenon. Normal science consists of such paradigms developed within the natural world of God, which makes the denial of the Creator by any adherents of paradigms unnatural. It is akin to asking software to perform a task beyond the limits of its source code. All natural or physical laws are limited by that initial boundary conditions and constants, which made Michael Polanyi confess: "Physics is dumb without the gift of boundary conditions forming its frame."[781]

Nevertheless, they slip into the pitfall of stepping outside their boundary and abrogating things unexplained by their paradigms—the natural world outside their box. The dilemma then becomes whether to surrender to divine sources for unexplained things or to double down on our ego and follow it blindly. Hence, David Hume (1711-76 CE) criticized reason as a slave of passion, which only aspires to mask our inner desires. It makes our reliance on reason alone illogical, which has inevitably driven its slaves to insanity throughout history. Therefore, Feyerabend methodically declares *Farewell to Reason*, and its distorting "false consciousness."[782] To snap out of such ignorance requires stepping outside our self-created epistemological boundaries and expanding our awareness of the entire natural world that lies beyond our described knowledge.

Numerous nations before us have followed a similar path away from divinity, including the people of Rass, 'Ad, Thamud, Noah, Lot, Pharaoh, Jethro, Tubba', and more. "In their stories, there is truly a lesson for people of reason. This message cannot be a fabrication, rather a confirmation of previous revelation, a detailed explanation of all things, a guide, and a mercy for people of faith," declares God (*Yusuf* 12:111). The fall of all civilizations can be seen as *falling* from God's grace and can take two separate paths: one leading to the decline of society with surviving remains versus the total obliteration of a nation with no traces. The latter is an exceptional, exemplary case where a miracle of God through a prophet is demanded and subsequently rejected. The only reason we even know of this latter group is from their mention in scripture. Between them lies a spectrum with one side demonstrating civilizations undergoing social and moral cycles with some cumulative technological evolutionism. Therefore, it is impossible to prove the opposite end of the spectrum due to their *total obliteration without any trace* or archeological remains.

For example, many have attempted to find evidence for or against the Noachian deluge with differing theories. If Noah's people were among those destroyed *without a trace*, then human history would naturally fall into the dyad of pre- and post-Flood. The geographical extent of the Flood has several possibilities that may explain the dilemma many geologists observe. While the Judeo-Christian support is for a Universal Flood, Muslims have traditionally believed in a more localized Flood, as evidenced by early uniformitarians like al-Biruni. Nonetheless, if we accept the Flood to have caused total destruction, it may be irrational to look for evidence of the affected ones. Their complete obliteration (except those on the Ark) would destroy all evidence, making them untraceable. The only signs we would be left with are that of the Flood itself and possibly the Ark, as mentioned in the Qur'an (*al-Qamar* 54:15).

Similarly, geological records indicate a catastrophic seismic event occurred around the 2nd millennium BC along the Great Rift Valley fault line. Its epicenter near the southeastern Dead Sea correlates with the location and time of the destruction of Sodom and Gomorrah. Before the earthquake, the region was a fertile valley with the Jordan River flowing into the Gulf of 'Aqaba through a fecund valley chosen by Lot for his pasture. The earthquake overturned that valley and buried it under an extended lake, cutting it off from the river, becoming the Dead Sea, and leaving no trace of its previous inhabitants. This cataclysmic seismic event would have been felt by Abraham, standing only 36 miles away in Hebron. He may have even seen the smoke rising from the expelled magma over the eastern horizon.[783]

When We decide to destroy a town, We command those corrupted by wealth [to reform], but they [persist in their] disobedience; Our sentence is passed, and We destroy them utterly. How many generations We have destroyed since Noah! Your Lord knows and observes the sins of His servants well enough. (al-Isra' 17:16-7)

What about all the other seemingly "unrealistic" stories and claims within the scripture? All three Abrahamic faiths speak of the earlier people being taller and living longer lives. According to the Qur'an, Noah lived for over 950 years. *Genesis* reports Adam lived for 930 years, and his successors lived hundreds of years down to Abraham, who lived 175 years. Biblical sources and *ahadeeth* describe Adam as 60 cubits tall (roughly 30 meters or 100 feet), although there are differing opinions regarding whether he retained the same height upon his descent to Earth. Critics use such scriptural assertions as their points of debate. Many notable scholars, including Muhammad Yunus Jaunpuri (1937-2017 CE), raised the possibility of mistaken attribution of rabbinic/biblical stories through some early converts. The *matn* (content) criticism of hadith in this regard is worth mentioning but beyond the scope of our discussion.[784] It even raised skepticism—not in terms of faith but the source of such stories—within the earliest of the most sincere scholars like Ibn Hazm (994-1064 CE) and Ibn Khaldun, the former just leaving it as something we cannot definitively corroborate. These are undoubtedly complex issues that have been debated exhaustively for over a millennium. Those rejecting even the Qur'anic narrative often present the lack of skeletal remains as evidence against their existence. Science appears to diverge from scripture and attempts to reconcile the two often involve separating them in seeking a secular path. It raises the age-old question of whether the absence of evidence serves as evidence of absence.

Perhaps our faith in science is less scientific than our faith in divinity, as it is essential for science to keep an open mind to allow for the forever-evolving pieces of the puzzle to fall into place. David Berlinski points out that even within mathematical physics, theory determines the evidence, not the other way around. What is considered acceptable evidence also varies depending on the person and their background. Furthermore, "neither the premise nor the conclusions of any scientific theory mention the existence of God," fact-checked Berlinski.[785] Embedded deep within the evolution of natural science are paradigm shifts based more on future promise than past evidence. All noteworthy scientists have revolutionized their fields by placing more faith in a new paradigm and defying the facts at hand.[786] According to Feyerabend, *facts* ultimately depend on what people choose to believe, and the only principle that can be defended under all circumstances is that anything goes.[787] Essentially, all *facts* are lived experiences, making them subjective by definition. Even stating *facts* like the time of day would be impossible without a conscious experience. Similar subjectivity applies to *all* of human epistemology, while divine knowledge always supersedes it untouched, even when our interpretations of it vary.

Kuhn explained how the outdated past scientific myths can still be produced today through the same scientific method that led to our present knowledge.[788] Countless *facts* we readily accept today were until recently nonexistent. A flat earth was simply a fact for thousands of years (unfortunately, some still hold that belief) even when God says: "As for the egg-shaped earth, He spread it out as well" (*an-Nazi'at* 79:30). Interestingly, some motifs of the solar system in the Valley of the Kings near Luxor depict the sun's rays falling on a spherical earth. Although Aristotle (384-22 BC) entertained the possibility of a round earth in his book *On the Heavens*, he still held a geocentric model of the universe. Eratosthenes (276-194 BC) calculated the earth's circumference in Alexandria a century later, which astronomers continued to use for centuries, despite its irreconcilable mathematical flaws. Proposing something different would have required one to bet their own life as the scientific community and the Catholic Church would deem it heretical. Although the truth became evident to Nicholas Copernicus (1473-1543 CE), he made his heliocentric proposition anonymously fearing retribution and ex-communication. Technically, a similar proposal was made by Aristarchus of Samos (310-230 BC) two millennia prior. Still, the scientific community refused to accept his dissent for centuries until Galileo Galilei (1564-1642 CE), who was then deemed a heretic by the Church and placed under house arrest for the rest of his life. Others were not as fortunate, as Giordano Bruno was burned at the stake in 1600 for even proposing an infinite universe.

Are the disbelievers not aware that the heavens and the earth used to be joined together, that We ripped them apart, and that We made every living thing from water? Will they not believe? And We put firm mountains on the earth, lest it should sway under them, and set broad paths on it so that they might follow the right direction, and We made the sky a well-secured canopy—yet from its wonders they turn away. It is He who created night and day, the sun and the moon, each floating in its orbit. (al-Anbiya' 21:30-4)

While the Islamic Golden Age exhorted open-mindedness, the contemporary Catholic Church was vehemently intolerant of such ideas.[789] Contradictory scientific discoveries further fueled an antagonistic relationship between the Church and the scientists, greatly influencing the latter to abandon creationism. They were also routinely persecuted by the Church and executed in public.[790] The subsequent Enlightenment period in Europe was a retaliation against the Church's control of the intellectuals, resulting in the empiricists' "Age of Reason," which was rather an *irrational* denial of God's existence. Their fanaticism was demonstrated through their overemphasis on reason and rationality, which ultimately led to their failure.[791] Had the Church been more supportive of scientific findings, one wonders if history would have been different.

Discussions of the European Enlightenment tend to overlook Oriental influences and notable failures of revolution, wars, oppression, and impatience. Gustave Flaubert (1821-80 CE) satirized the messianic attitude of the European scientific movement in *Bouvard et Pecuchet*, which is ultimately not different from its religious counterpart.[792] Scientific methods are plagued with arrogant views that are often worse in their assumption of "rational" superiority. Yet, in viewing the Orient, both religious and secular scholars demonstrated the same bigotry, only with differing terms and rationality.

In contrast, "antagonism between religion and science such as that familiar to Westerners is foreign to Islam," noted Dr. Cleary.[793] The Qur'an alludes to the creation of the universe from a single *Word*: "[God is] the Originator of the heavens and the earth! When He decrees a matter, He simply tells it, "Be!" And it is!" (*al-Baqarah* 2:117). We typically understand *words* as spoken, heard, written, and read—all of which are only a matter of convention. A *word* can otherwise be anything that conveys or initiates a message.[794] The existence of language pursues God's infinite knowledge and forever falls short of capturing its true breadth. Now, what that *Word* means in a divine arena is beyond the scope of our understanding, as evident from our study of the universe, and closer to the concept of *logos*. One of its many implications is that even the verb "to be" that initiates all acts from nothing is itself a creation of God. Thus, linguistics has been a focus of Islamic scholarship since the 7th century with a rich tradition. It has only recently gotten the Western philosophical attention it truly deserves with the rise of linguists. However, it quickly took a sharp left turn with the postmodernists due to a lack of divine oversight.

Our current understanding of the universe is so widely accepted that it sounds inconceivable to learn about the beliefs that have prevailed for most of history. We have just recently discovered dark matter, which we now estimate to comprise up to 95% of the universe. As we still do not understand dark matter, it places our actual knowledge below 5%—realistically much less, as we do not fully understand how our minds work. We continue to discover astonishing natural phenomena like the migrating veeries' accurate prediction of the hurricane season months before any meteorologist.[795] Then what does it say about the One who created them and guides them while we are unaware?

Even a yeast cell is created with as many components as an airplane fitted into a sphere of a few microns width, which can then reproduce independently. Every time we learn something new proves our prior compound ignorance. To have strong convictions about our knowledge at any given point only proves our ignorance of epistemology. When the Prophet returned from his Night Journey (Arabic: الإسراء والمعراج, *al-'Isrā' wal-Mi'rāj*), his critics balked at the thought of traveling from Mecca to Jerusalem overnight, which generally took months camelback. Now it is barely a two-hour flight. Similarly, his reference to the 360 joints in the human body was miraculously ahead of its time (*Sahih Muslim* 1007). The answers to similar dilemmas regarding the Qur'an and *hadith* may someday become common knowledge. Our lack of understanding today only reflects the limitations of our intellect and nothing more.

Humility and tolerance are the signs of a truly knowledgeable person, while their absence is mutually evident. When scientific discoveries confirmed the feasibility of prehistoric earth's ability to support larger organisms, suddenly, our previous doubts fell within the realm of acceptable possibilities.[796] The same higher oxygen content that enabled the evolution of giant placental mammals could have also supported humans of large stature.[797] Even if we never find any skeletal proof of such humans, we cannot positively deny their existence with certainty, the same way we cannot disprove scripture. "What we observe, to a limited extent, is what happens, and we can arrive at laws according to which observable things happen, but we cannot arrive at a reason for the laws," explained Russell. "If we invent a reason, it needs a reason in its turn, and so on."[798] It is akin to watching endless dominos falling and concluding it as an eternal process without a first domino. Therefore, it is illogical to abjure the *unknown* based on what we *think* we know, for ultimately, we all operate only through pattern recognition. Our scientific data enhances this process, which can often be confused with the "truth." "But nothing is ever 'true,' except under certain circumstances, and then only from a particular viewpoint, characteristically unstated," explained Dr. Hawkins.[799]

It is God who raised the heavens with no visible supports and then established Himself on the throne; He has subjected the sun and the moon each to pursue its course for an appointed time; He regulates all things and makes the revelations clear so that you may be certain of meeting your Lord. (al-R'ad 13:2)

There are examples like air and gravity that we cannot see directly but know to exist by their effects and secondary signs. We live in the internet age, where tons of data can be sent and received through thin air almost instantly. Similarly, we acknowledge the existence of God through His secondary signs, such as a germinating seed. For Imam al-Shafi'i, it was the leaves of the mulberry tree that "have the same taste, color, smell, and form but when silkworm eats from it it gives silk, when the bee eats from it it gives honey, when the sheep eats from it it becomes fat and milk increases in its udder, and when the gazelle eats from it it nourished itself and gives musk." Although Rodin is no longer alive, we know he sculpted the Thinking Man without him having to be present beside the statue to confirm it to visitors. Then how can the thinking men in the flesh so readily accept that something as big as the universe came about on its own, where the signs of the Creator are all around us? Such arguments resemble the old joke of a fish that asked its friend if he was grateful for water, only for the friend to reply, "What is water?" Scientifically, those making such arguments must provide evidence for their null hypothesis and deviation from natural logic. "The worst creatures in God's eyes are those who are [wilfully] deaf and dumb, who do not reason" (*al-Anfal* 8:22).

Returning to the archeologist still digging: often, the "evidence" is fragments of pottery, bones, tools, or art, from which an educated inference is made. The theories remain subjective, as embarrassingly demonstrated by the Pedra Furada rock shelter in Brazil. Carbon dating has its margin of error, and archeological sites do not always resemble a neatly sealed time capsule.[800] Psychological studies also reveal that complete objectivity is impossible for any human being. Consequently, differing hypotheses arise from the same dig that are still easier to accept for some of these experts than scripture. The objective artifacts remain simple ruins, while the proposed events surrounding them are only a construct of the expert's imagination.

This is not to swing to the opposite, extremely cynical stance of radical postmodern skepticism, but to highlight the caveats of our epistemology to balance our confidence and doubt. Humanity's understanding is like a single-celled amoeba, slowly progressing as its pseudopods of *movements* pull it in different directions. Many radical thinkers and views emerge like microfilaments within these movements to test new territories. Whether these pseudopods lead to a better environment or the organism's death remains the subject of retrospective speculation for the opinionated. But what does it say about the amoeba when it starts to deny the existence of far-away galaxies or God based on the sense data it receives from its pseudopods?

Imagine future archeologists digging up our graves a millennium from now, as we live through the apparent pinnacle of our existence. What would their imaginations tell them about our decayed bones wrapped in cloth or a casket? Ian Tattersall commented on the scarcity of fossil records representing 500,000 years of hominoids, saying that it could all fit in the back of a pickup truck. In comparison, something as short-lived as our civilization would not leave a significant archeological footprint as we represent a speck of humanity's entire existence. "But perhaps above all... Scientists have a natural tendency to interpret finds in the way that most flatters their stature," reminds Bryson. "It is a rare paleontologist indeed who announces that he has found a cache of bones but that they are nothing to get excited about. Or as John Reader understatedly observes in the book *Missing Links*, 'It is remarkable how often the first interpretations of new evidence have confirmed the preconceptions of its discoverer.'"[801]

We are fascinated by the stories of the pharaohs and their impressive pyramids. Yet, what survived the test of time is only a tiny fraction of their vast empires. The elements that caused the rest of it to fade could have erased it completely. If it was all gone, experts would have brushed off the correlating stories in the Qur'an as fables. It would be unfathomable to believe that people five millennia ago were capable of building massive pyramidal structures with impeccable precision. Is it random that only certain structures somehow managed to survive while the rest were utterly obliterated? Then, how can we claim that what remained is simply serendipitous? Indeed, the discovery of the first mummy in 1881 only emphasized its miraculous mention in the Qur'an, where God informs us of preserving the pharaoh's body as a sign for posterity (*Yunus* 10:90-2).

If science claims to be driven by laws that must be proven without bias, archeology and human history will not make the cut. Subjectivity can be found in all of our sciences that we naively accept as undeniable truth. Even in hard sciences like physics, it is impossible for two scientists to observe the same phenomenon.[802] We will further explore how all of our acquired knowledge is subject to errors in a later chapter. Before my writings, there was little external evidence of these thoughts to differentiate me from a Cro-Magnon. Arguably, the latter left behind more evidence of tallied bones and artifacts to make my remains appear less intelligent to future experts. Had God not informed us of teaching Adam everything, we would have similarly given little credit to Adam's intelligence (*al-Baqarah* 2:31), reducing him to a primitive caveman.

Our misconceptions arise from four common gaffes: 1) a failure to differentiate between subjectivity and objectivity, 2) disregard for the inherent limitations of context in basic design and terminology, 3) poor understanding of consciousness, and 4) misunderstanding causality.[803] It is illogical to dwell on hypotheses regarding past events while simultaneously dismissing theological references as historical evidence. The preservation of the Qur'an over 1400 years confirms its authenticity, and its completeness makes it a far superior source than any of its contenders. Its primacy as divine wisdom makes it the ultimate filter through which all knowledge must be vetted since anything the human mind can conceive is, by definition, subjective. Proper understanding is achieved by examining data with the right context to avoid the errors of functional savants.

To think that God would command us to obey Him and His Messenger (al-'Imran 3:32) and not ensure the preservation of both the Qur'an and *sunnah* is ludicrous. Those who question their authenticity are either ignorant or have an ulterior motive. The Islamic tradition of a chain of transmission (Arabic: إسناد *'isnād*) is the earliest form of fact-checking. "The *isnad* is from the religion; were it not for the *isnad*, anyone could say anything they wanted," stressed Abdullah Ibn al-Mubarak (726-97 CE). Even if a single person in a chain of narration was missing or found to have character flaws, the *hadith* was classified as "weak" or dismissed. This process is more critical than any peer-reviewed scientific publication of today. We understand its importance as we see the dangers of misinformation. The irony lies in the oxymoronic concept of an "original thought," as even *that* has been contemplated by many in the past. Shaikh Hamza Yusuf takes it even further and reminds us that every expressible knowledge has an *isnad* that can ultimately be traced back to one of two sources: if one cannot trace his source of knowledge back to God, then it is likely inspired by the devil.

All criticisms fall apart when one looks into the matter, but are still flung around from a long tradition of Orientalism. These oft-repeated lies from "experts" are then taken as facts by laypeople to substantiate further their fallacies. Swiss metaphysician Titus Burckhardt (1908-84 CE) found these accusations diabolical through his investigation. He identified the reasoning of most critics as: "If you bring me no proof it is because you are wrong, but if you do bring proof it means you need it, and so again you are wrong. How can these orientalists believe that countless Muslim learned men—men who feared God and hell—could have deliberately fabricated sayings of the Prophet? It would lead one to suppose bad faith to be the most natural thing in the world, were it not that 'specialists' have almost no feelings for psychological incompatibilities."[804]

While other scriptures may not live up to the same standard, they are still the most well-preserved artifacts from our ancient world. Their differences can be a matter of debate, but their similarities can strengthen each other as proof. If three witnesses in a court of law with differing motives give conflicting accounts, they can be dismissed; however, if all three agree on specific events, the case is solidified. It is also a well-developed concept in the Islamic sciences known as *tawatur* (Arabic: تواتر), where the multiplicity of an event confirms its authenticity. The clearest example is one's birth, which he does not remember, but knows as the undeniable truth based on the few people present at that moment to narrate it thereafter, making it *mutawatir*.

There are examples in etymology and philology with words like *Eden*. The

Bible describes it as the garden of God where Adam and Eve originally resided after their creation. This word appears in ancient Akkadian as *edinnu*, from the Sumerian *edin* dating back to the 8th century and 3rd millennia BC. This is also related to the Arabic *'adan* as another name for paradise in the Qur'an, which also has a similar root in Aramaic. The story of Eden can be traced outside the scriptures back to an ancient Mesopotamian myth of a kingly primordial man placed in a divine garden to guard the Tree of Life. While these can be brushed off as coincidence or cultural plagiarism, if one connects the dots accurately, they would serve as evidence pointing towards the main event.

Similarly, the Great Flood is a recurring theme in almost all ancient cultures, including the Popol Vuh of the Quiche Maya.[805] While some may dismiss Noah's Flood as just another fable borrowed from preexisting traditions, a more logical deduction would solidify the actual Flood based on the widespread prevalence of that story across cultures. It is improbable that all cultures would have their own original stories about a deluge had there not been a single root source event. This brings up the concept of *tawatur*, where the high number of narrators from the beginning to the end of the chain and the narration passed through seeing/hearing make it impossible for that many people—at times from opposing factions—to conspire to form one unified lie.

This hypocrisy of the scientific community was noted by Imam al-Ghazali a thousand years ago, who explained that those same scientists readily rely on the findings of other experts in the field unquestioningly. In this case, the prophets and messengers are the ones experienced in revelation, and by following their path, we can perceive some of it by direct vision. Al-Ghazali drew a parable of the sick man who may dismiss a cure for his lack of personal experience with the remedy.[806] Locke echoed the same and wrote: "He that will not eat, till he has demonstration that it will nourish him; he that will not stir, till he infallibly knows the business he goes about will succeed, will have little else to do, but sit still and perish."[807] And therefore, today, we perish.

A Great Flood that destroyed *without a trace* would leave us with no remains of our predecessors. There would be no giant skeletons to find. The belief in scripture that leads one to search for such evidence is the same that hints towards its nonexistence. Somewhere embedded within this dilemma is faith. God reminds us, "Among them are some who [appear to] listen to you, but we have placed covers over their hearts—so they do not understand the Qur'an—and deafness in their ears. Even if they saw every sign, they would not believe in them. So, when they come to you, they argue with you: the disbelievers say, 'These are nothing but ancient fables,' and tell others not to listen, while they themselves keep away from it. But they ruin no one but themselves, though they fail to realize this" (*al-An'am* 6:25-6).

Religion is not only a matter of passion, as Kierkegaard would have it, for God repeatedly appeals to our reason. God's existence is also a matter of common sense and rational reflection. Maxime Rodinson pointed out that the verb *aqala* (Arabic: to connect ideas, reason, and understand an intellectual argument) appeared about fifty times in the Qur'an. God appeals to our reason thirteen times: *a fa-la taqilun* (have ye then no sense?); and criticized the disbelievers as a people of no intelligence, persons incapable of intellectual effort like the lower class of animals.[808] This "harmonious interplay of faith and reason is an essential aspect of the Qur'an that appeals to the post-Christian secular mind," wrote Dr. Cleary.[809] Humankind is commanded to come to Islam through their intellect and an open heart, not through their personal biases and blind faith (fideism). This is one thing that nearly all Orientalists agreed upon. Otherwise, even to the learned, God's message would appear to be "a wearisome confused jumble, crude, incondite; endless iterations, long-windedness, entanglement—insupportable stupidity, in short."[810]

It would have been natural for Noah's children to pass down bedtime stories of their ancestors who lived over a thousand years and were *as tall as trees*. The stories then spread across the earth and evolved into unique regional fables separated by time and isolation. The farther removed from the actual events, the more fantastical the stories became. Tall predecessors evolved into giants living in a distant world connected to ours by a beanstalk. Climbing down to a world of smaller beings sounds strangely similar to Adam's descent to Earth. The longer lifespan evolved into tales of immortals and fountains of youth. The *people of the cave* —or the man in *al-Baqarah* 2:259—similarly evolved into stories like Rip Van Winkle. The tree of Eden and Eve's descent unto Earth became the Haudenosaunee sky woman. These are just a few examples in scripture where parallel connections can be made between stated events and existing fables worldwide. Those denying the scriptures would appear to ignore this logical conclusion and evolution.

THE WORLD OUTSIDE THE CONE

As for the believers, they know that it is the truth from their Lord. And as for the disbelievers, they argue, "What does God mean by such a parable?" [Through this test], He leaves many to stray and guides many. And He leaves none to stray except the rebellious. (al-Baqarah 2:26)

Believing in creationism today is stigmatized as outdated and backward, which puts the believer on the defensive. There is some consolation in the Prophet's foretelling: "Islam began as something strange and will go back to being strange, so glad tidings to the strangers" (*Sunan Ibn Majah* 3986). Contempt towards religion from those considered the most educated approaches fanaticism in their refusal to even consider the possibility of God's existence until scientifically proven otherwise—which is inherently impossible. Still many popularly paraded titles—by Richard Dawkins, Victor Stenger, Taner Edis, and Christopher Hitches, among others—claim to prove just that. Instead, they all offer some scientific observations followed by much conjecture, demonstrating their willingness to believe just about anything but God. Both sides attempt to justify their stance based on limited available knowledge, and when reasoning fails, many reject scripture or science altogether, thus defaulting on ignorance. But is it even possible to separate creationism from evolution and science from scripture?

The West's antagonistic history with the Catholic Church gradually backfired in a push toward secularism. The reproach from the proud, prodigious atheist bulk has since become intellectual bullying, not too different from the Church's religious fundamentalism. In that regard, militant atheism can be seen as a reaction to the history of religious violence. It is arguable how successful they have been in achieving secularism, which is defined by a separation of state built on the Occidental definition of *religion*. At the very conception of this relationship with the coronation of Charlemagne by Pope Leo in 800 CE, there was an embedded ambiguity that dominated European power politics between the Church and the state. Religion as a distinct entity—separated from politics, economics, and other aspects of life—is a categorization developed in the 4th and 5th centuries CE. Historian Daniel Boyarin argues that it was an act of early Christian self-definition against eventual Rabbinic Judaism, as a forced partition between the two. Otherwise, religion played a vital role in all aspects of life for most of our history, and arguably, it continues to do so even when we charge to be "secular," because all of our thoughts and actions are always guided by a deeper code of belief.

Philosophical reasoning and logic dictate that if subject A believes premise *p*, he will act in a way that will achieve his ends if *p* is true.[811] Conversely, one's true beliefs are revealed by their actions, which provides perspective on God's criticism: "Do you not see how they rant in every field, only saying what they never do?" (*ash-Shu'ara* 26:225-6). Secularism is often distinguished from secularization, presenting the latter as a better ideology that politically protects minorities. In reality, both are closed metaphysical worldviews that function very much like a new religion, as Protestant theologian Harvey Cox explains.[812] The academic distinction between secularism and secularization also disintegrates upon dissection as two sides of the same token.[813] Therefore, the secular ban on the hijab in Turkey by Mustafa Ataturk was not too different in concept from the state-enforced hijab in Iran. It is the sardonic twist of secularism, where its proponents viciously turn it into another religious fundamentalism, proselytizing science as the only good thing worthy of absolute devotion and faith. Their aggressions sharply contrast their claims of tolerance when facing anyone with differing views.

In the 1980s, secularism became controversial in Tennessee and Alabama when parents challenged the constitutionality of school textbooks preaching the "religion of Secular Humanism." Supreme Court Justice Tom Clark wrote for the majority in the 1963 case *Abington vs. Schempp* that schools cannot endorse any particular religion, including the "religion of secularism."[814] Theologian John Cobb (1899-1952 CE) went further and referred to the new American religion as *economism*. All of it is essentially a declaration of war against divinity, saying: we no longer wish to live our lives to fulfill Your wishes, but only ours (thus, by default, Satan's).

Ironically, an honest pursuit of secularization would also entail separating the state from contemporary unorthodox religions, including capitalism, scientism, and even secularism.

We forget that this nation was built on Judeo-Christian (i.e., Protestant) values serving as the religious foundation of America's political system. This fact was noted by Alexis de Tocqueville two hundred years ago and is still evident today through anti-abortion laws. (Of note, the Prophet also mentioned widespread abortion as one of the signs of the end of days (*Muṣannaf Ibn Abī Shaybah* 37297).) Over the centuries, the gradual push toward secularizing has tipped over to unbalanced secularism, resulting in our current confused state, far from the intended goal. Philosopher Allan Bloom argued in *The Closing of the American Mind* that secularism was a complete failure, producing closed-minded individuals by omitting religious and cultural perspectives. Professor Harold Bloom saw the Western Canon as anything but social salvation, warning that if we read it solely to form our social, political, or personal moral values, we would become monsters of selfishness and exploitation.[815] He was incorrect in assuming that to be a *potential* threat, as our history places us well into the resulting inequality and wealth disparity while simultaneously wondering how we got here.

We have created man for toil and trial. Does he think that no one will have power over him? He may say [boastfully]: Wealth have I squandered in abundance! Does he think no one observes him? (al-Balad 90:4-7)

Abraham asked the same question to his idol-worshiping nation regarding who had more right to a peaceful and secure future, and God answered: "It is those who have faith, and do not mix their faith with idolatry, who will be secure, and it is they who are rightly guided" (*al-An'am* 6:82). Idolatry here extends beyond the worship of material objects to nonmaterial icons as well as ideologies. The trials and tribulations of life often cause people to question their purpose, and the frustration of not being in control can lead to the denouncement of creation. Religious persecution, in particular, serves as low-hanging fruit for those on a *jihad* against God. While ordinary people remain religious and virtuous, the world leaders responsible for large-scale atrocities throughout history lacked both. Still, secularists employ circular logic to deny God's existence and then use the willful transgressions of others against His commandments as their evidence. To their annoyance, the overwhelmingly nonreligious 20th century unleashed limitless scientific possibilities that enabled the secular brutalities of Stalin, Hitler, Mao, Pol Pot, and various American and Israeli presidents.

Berlinski explains the concerning updated hypothetical syllogism, where: a) *if God doesn't exist, then everything is permitted*; b) *if science is true, then God doesn't exist*; c) *if science is true, then everything is permitted*. The latter trend is substantiated by our recent history, some of which were explored in the previous chapters. The common denominator among the perpetrators of all such monstrosities is their lack of belief that God is watching their actions.[816] God reminds us: "If God were to hasten on for people the harm [they have earned] as they wish to hasten on the good, their time would already be up. But We leave those who do not expect to meet Us to wander blindly in their excesses" (*Yunus* 10:11).

Kierkegaard likened life to a play where each of us gets to act in various roles, but when the curtain falls at death, "the one who played the king, and the one who played the beggar, and all the others—they are all quite alike, all one and the same: actors."[817] Psychoanalyst Carl Jung believed that at death the self is fully realized. By returning to mysticism, he bridged the secular gaps in the Freudian materialistic view of the psyche, finally making it more applicable to real life. Ultimately, all questions come to a sharp halt at death, beyond which we can only speculate. Only God can provide a credible perspective, as the outside view is nearly impossible while occupying our spacetime. "[Ultimately,] with the throes of death will come the truth. This is what you were trying to escape! And the Trumpet will be blown. This is the Day [you were] warned of. Each soul will come forth with an angel to drive it and another to testify. [It will be said to the denier,] 'You were heedless of this. Now We have lifted this veil of yours, so Today your sight is sharp!'" (*Qaf* 50:19-22). Without the outer perspective provided by God, all secular understanding—however advanced—remains incomplete and in the dark.

Our mere existence becomes spiritual the moment our spirit is blown into the body. While that made Adam sneeze and say *alhamdulillah* (*Jami` at-Tirmidhi* 3367), today, some would rather abjure the existence of souls and remain ungrateful. Pursuing secularism then would be equivalent to the separation of the soul and the body or death, which is evident in all secularists. Many philosophers have tackled the mind and body dualism since antiquity without fully satisfying the world with a solution to *res cogitans* (the mind) and *res extensa* (the body) Cartesian dilemma. Even Sigmund Freud's psychoanalysis of the conscious ego's suppression of unconscious desires can only be manifested through a soul's presence in an individual's driving seat. Contrary to the conscious mind of the rationalist, the soul is not synonymous with our conscious self (i.e., Arabic: 'aql, عقل), as the latter is a gradual development philosophically evident through our memories.

The Traditional Islamically Integrated Psychotherapy (TIIP) model identifies the distinct aspects of our psyche much better than their secular counterparts. Accordingly, the enveloping term *soul* includes four distinct aspects: *ruh, qalb, nafs,* and *'aql*. Understanding these components is critical to avoid neglecting certain aspects of our souls. Recent overemphasis on our reason (*'aql*) and desires (*nafs*) with complete denial of the rest is a major force behind our current imbalanced state. It is not that we completely ignore these concepts, as we often refer to our soul or heart with respect to desires but neglect them in other matters. Even when we desire something, rationalizing the options and their consequences, our heart (*qalb*) often moves towards one option, ultimately making the final decision. All of this then affects our spirit (*ruh*). Ignoring the power of our hearts can let our desires overpower our reason into actions that will gradually lower our spirit to a state that modern medicine and psychology would fail to diagnose or alleviate. Thus, 'Ali Ibn Abi Talib referred to the heart as the leader of a person, constantly pulling him to the direction it is accustomed to: a direction of subconscious habit.

The boundary between our conscious and subconscious worlds is not as well defined as some would have us believe. While some conscious experiences are easily remembered, the absence of memory does not necessarily indicate a lack of prior experience. We routinely forget many such experiences and have no recollection of events before a certain age, limited by our organic brain and its development. The distinction between our soul, mind, and body is similarly indistinct, with significant overlap. Behavioral kinesiology studies find our bodies responding accurately even when the conscious mind is unaware of the stimuli. Thus, our souls appear to belong more subconsciously, connecting our material bodies to a timeless realm. They utilize our sense perceptions to achieve intellect, which raises us from the level of animals to the blessing of Adam. We can even become those whom God blesses exceptionally by mastering that spiritual awareness to the point of intellect beyond any sensory input.

The soul's connection to the eternal, timeless world can be exemplified by the simple act of catching a ball. As a thrown ball approaches, we subconsciously use our past experiences to predict its future location and move our limbs accordingly. The physics of it can dilute or even eliminate the miraculous nature of such ordinary occurrences. But we must remind ourselves that science only attempts to explain everyday miracles, which should never downgrade their subconscious experience. In a way, our souls transcend the spacetime we occupy to peek into the immediate *future* that has yet to manifest. Our brains function as hard drives for memories that our souls use for tasks that are even higher than the so-called *higher cortical functions*. Al-Kindi took it further to explain how a pure soul can similarly look into the future during sleep and make those events available to the brain as prophecies.[818]

Perhaps this is why we cannot remember a time before our souls entered our bodies in the womb, making our *fitra* (innate nature) resemble the soul's prior residual experience (i.e. Plato's *anamnesis*). Similarly, our memories of this life may blur in the afterlife, until the body itself testifies for all of its earthly actions. In fact, this view was held by Plato in *Phaedo* as well as al-Kindi in *On the Intellect*.[819] Like the rest of the animal kingdom, we also share an innate attachment to our mothers during early development, which shapes our worldview, trust, and relationships for the rest of our lives.[820] The Arabic term for the womb, *raham*, is related to *rahma*, which means mercy. It is also one of the names of God, *ar-Rahman*, the Most Merciful. This linguistic connection hints at our soul's and *fitra's* dependence on a conscious relationship with God. Without that trust, His presence or absence has little significance in our worldly activities. The reverse is also demonstrated in the gradual secularization of the Occident over the last few centuries, eventually culminating in the Nietzschean cry declaring "god is dead" and its manifestation into nihilism.

One thing is clear in this ocean of conjectures: the body cannot exist bereft of the impetus soul, that *oomph*, or whatever you may call it. Our limited understanding of the soul is demonstrated by various subpar solutions provided by many, including an entire treatise by Aristotle. Cartesian philosopher Nicolas Malebranche (1638-1715 CE) later made God the *causal power* between the mind and the body with the doctrine of occasionalism, which was then dismissed by the materialists, claiming the mind to be nothing more than the brain.[821] Similar scientific attempts to explain our world are based on various associations, which are, at best, deductive assumptions, but often mistaken for undeniable causality. The pitfall and crux of reasoning have always been this mistaken correlation of association with causation. The latter itself is a poorly understood concept in philosophy, pointing us back to God's reminder in the Qur'an: "And they ask you [O Muhammad] concerning the rooh [the spirit]. Say: 'The rooh is one of the things, the knowledge of which is only with my Lord. And of knowledge, you [mankind] have been given only a little'" (*al-Isra'* 17:85). For those interested in exploring causality in greater depth, Imam al-Ghazali's works *Shifa' al-Ghalil* and *Asas al-Qiyas* offer masterful insights.

As medical science advances in keeping our physical body alive, the distinction between life and death becomes increasingly blurred. Ultimately, it is of little consequence whether we favor Cartesian dualism, Spinoza's rational pantheism, Leibniz's monad, Schelling's transcendental idealism, or any of the numerous other convoluted theories, for the truth of the matter will always be a knowledge of the unseen. Ibn Sina once lamented that, despite reading Aristotle's *Metaphysics* to the point of memorizing it, he still could not comprehend its contents.[822] By voluntarily delving deep into what God warned against, they all eventually struggled with free will. Some even rejected it with glaring irony. As God asks rhetorically: "You argue about some things of which you have some knowledge, but why do you argue about things of which you know nothing? God knows and you do not" (*al-'Imran* 3:66).

Imam al-Ghazali described the soul as a traveler visiting a foreign land to shortly return home, echoing a hadith with the same message. We can get a feel for it by closing our eyes and muting all other senses while focusing our thoughts just on our existence in the present moment. It is similar to Ibn Sina's floating/falling man thought experiment, which he presented as a philosophical proof of the soul. The soul's origin beyond our universe makes it immortal and not a substance of this world, where things are not as indestructible as classically assumed. There lies the connection between the soul and divinity, which makes one's denial of one eventually result in a disregard for the other.

Recalling the epistemological premise of knowing a thing through its opposite reveals the reality of God always remaining unthinkable. His unity makes it impossible for Him to have an opposite in substance. Thus, our souls also remain unknowable and misunderstood by extension for "both intelligence and its objects are finite."[823] Russell described philosophy as piecemeal and provisional, like science, while the final truth belonged only to heaven.[824] He later concluded that the entire question of personal immortality or soul is beyond the scope of philosophy and best left to revelation.[825] We can only deduce that the soul is a creation of God, and our awareness of it comes from self-discipline and perseverance on the righteous path. It is impossible to say anything substantial about things that originated beyond our universe based on our scientific observations from here within *the box*. Thus, divine matters involving knowledge and criticism of ourselves from the outside must be left to religion.

So we come to the only option of trusting God, who reveals that all His creations possess a subjective presence that goes unnoticed by ordinary humans. "The seven heavens, the earth, and all those in them glorify

Him. There is not a single thing that does not glorify His praises—but you [simply] cannot comprehend their glorification. He is indeed Most Forbearing, All-Forgiving" (*al-Isra'* 17:44). Most native cultures attribute similar consciousness and *being* to all things living or otherwise. The secular bias of the scientific community pushed humanity away from this timeless norm, resulting in a materialistic view that has had disastrous environmental consequences. However, the truth becomes apparent to those who look with a clear mind.

Nuclear physicist Ernest Rutherford once exclaimed: "An electron would have to 'know' beforehand to which orbit it was going to jump. Otherwise, it would not emit light with a single, definite wavelength when it starts its leap."[826] Wolfgang Pauli's exclusion principle also echoed the same at a subatomic level. Quantum theory predicted that particles have a characteristic spin that pairs with a sister particle in opposite directions, regardless of the distance between them. This was proven in 1997 at the University of Geneva, where photons separated by miles reflected an immediate change in the spin of one particle, matching the induced change in the other. This violation of the special theory of relativity has yet to be resolved. Apparently, these inanimate objects demonstrate a stronger consciousness of their souls than the living beings they compose. A lack of free will makes their natural function an act of glorification of their Creator, which perhaps makes them animate.

Our current materialistic understanding correlates the size of an animal's brain to its mental capacity to the point of excluding the possibility of higher cortical function in simpler creatures, as displayed by the ant or the bird in the Qur'an (e.g., *An-Naml* 27:18, 22-6). However, giving the Creator of all life the benefit of doubt would attribute the source of all thoughts to one's soul, where the brain becomes analogous to the hard drive of a computer to its operator. Accordingly, the inactivity of the brain in functional imaging studies would mean little to the subconscious awareness of an individual in a coma. Our infatuation with intellect blinds us to these spiritual truths that govern the universe. Only by purifying the heart can we regain the intuition and insight needed to recognize God's commands in all things. Those who refuse to submit are still subjected to the physical laws of the universe, revolving along with the planet they miraculously occupy. Hence, humanity is commanded to submit to God's will and physically revolve around the Ka'ba counterclockwise. This circumambulation from an aerial view is almost inseparable from the iron filaments surrounding a magnetic cube. It serves as an unmistakable reminder of the Creator, which is also why the door of repentance will close with its reversal—the sun rising clockwise from the west (*Sunan Abi Dawud*

2479).

Have they not traveled throughout the land so their hearts may reason, and their ears may listen? Indeed, it is not the eyes but the hearts in the chests that grow blind. (al-Hajj 22:46)

Stumbling back, some find themselves questioning the origin of life itself. If no soul enters a body and brings it to life, how do we define our identity? In fact, our entire body replaces itself every seven years at a cellular level. Moreover, life cannot simply be our physical existence, for a significant portion of the body can be surgically separated without the entire *being* vanishing into a void. If the lower half of the body was amputated, life is not duplicated nor is it diminished. Is it then the heart and the brain that define life—the "crucial" organs responsible for our physical existence? Then what happens when we have a heart attack or a stroke and a portion of that critical organ fails? Do we become lesser beings? How do we then define a heart transplant?... It would be interesting to study the changes in one's subconscious preferences with a new heart and its correlation with the donor.

The denial of an afterlife abruptly breaks the logical progression of events. The usual alternative is that we cease to exist, which then begs the question: what exactly separates the living from the dead? Indeed, death is not simply the absence of consciousness, as the body can maintain autonomy when the soul departs during sleep. Perhaps this is how a martyr is spared the pain of his corporeal sacrifice (*Riyad as-Salihin* Book 11, Hadith 39). These questions are often asked with a preconceived premise of causality that can predetermine the accuracy of the answers. Even a simple medical statement of a patient regaining consciousness presumes it as nothing more than a material function of the brain, turning it into "a mundane physical phenomenon, a self-evident priority for experience about which nothing more needs to be said," noted Dr. Hawkins.[827]

Devoid of the soul, we are left with a reluctant explanation of life coming from nothing and death being the sudden oblivion. Then comes the associated existential crisis with a laundry list of moral and philosophical dilemmas that follow as an unavoidable package deal. Russell concluded that "philosophical errors in common-sense beliefs not only produce confusion in science, but also do harm in ethics and politics, in social institutions, and in the conduct of everyday life."[828] Such deviation from common sense plagues our society at every level, bringing us down to the same level as animals or plants, and equally perishable. Some claim God to be above any need for our worship, ignoring His revelation telling us to turn to Him for every need. Al-Ghazali used the same parable of a sick man to clarify that, ultimately, the remedy does not matter to the doctor. However, the patient only destroys himself by his disobedience.

If there is no point in existence, then why exist at all? In the Qur'an, God presents our existence as the most straightforward, self-evident confirmation of Him. Charles Lyell developed the scientific principle of explaining the past through causes available in the present, as stated in the subtitle of his magnum opus, later employed by Darwin. Although evolutionary biologists since then have rather aggressively pushed forth their neo-Darwinian dogma, all of their laboratory experiments along that hypothesis are *always* the result of intelligent human design—not random events.[829] That is the strongest evidence for the mystery behind the origin of life that the neo-Darwinian theory has failed to explain to date. To be present now and deny our purpose is to deny our existence, which is absurd. Kierkegaard considers all such philosophical and scientific attempts to prove God's existence inherently foolish.[830] Concerning God's immanence, Ibn 'Ata' Allah said, "When did He disappear that He needed to be indicated?"[831] This absurdity is highlighted in a famous dialogue between Imam Abu Hanifa and an atheist traveler, illustrating the comical nature of such debates.[832] Imam al-Ghazali would argue that people in that state of mind are so far gone in error that there is no point in even debating. There are even potential harms of such discussions, which prompted Hasan al-Basri to say: "As for me, I know my religion; if you have lost yours, then go and look for it."

To further beat this soulless horse, let us picture a ball rolling from point A to point B. If we define A as the ball's sudden appearance and B as its sudden disappearance, then the path it takes in between becomes inconsequential in the grand scheme of things, sort of a unidimensional event. While we may discuss the path for the sake of it, it ultimately holds no weight. However, if we extend the ball's history beyond these two points, the trajectory it takes before reaching point A affects its course between A and B, and the path it takes from A to B determines the ball's destination thereafter. Suddenly, we have a multi-dimensional picture that resembles the world we live in. Without these additional dimensions, any discussion of the path between A and B becomes irrelevant.

Following the same logic, morality without the presence of an afterlife cannot hold ground and is not worth debating or defining. Any such discussion is merely a waste of time and effort, reflecting the unidimensionality of one's intellect. Macintyre's works on this point are noteworthy in recent times. He wrote, "Since the whole point of ethics—both as a theoretical and a practical discipline—is to enable man to pass from his present state to his true end, the elimination of any notion of essential human nature and with it the abandonment of any notion of a *telos* leaves behind a moral scheme composed of two remaining elements whose relationship becomes quite unclear."[833]

At first glance, this may resemble the teleological view of natural things that philosophers like Aristotle discussed—a view that defines beings by their end—and subsequently taken to another practical extreme by Niccolo Machiavelli. However, that is also half the picture and ignores the equally important path leading to the end. Our *essence* or struggle in real-time is shaping and constantly changing the topography of the path to the end, which will ultimately define our *nature*. They are inseparable and far too complex to be defined by a single reason or be described as purely deterministic, as presumed by Democritus (460-370 BC). Thus, Ibn 'Alawi al-Haddad (1634-1720 CE) advised, "The one with intellect should not address the fool. For if he addresses him at his level, he would be wasting his intellect and disgracing his honor, and if he addresses him at [the fool's] level, he would be emulating ignorance and counted amongst them. God says, 'Hold onto forgiveness and command the good, but turn away from the ignorant.'"[834]

All things in the universe have a natural purpose that they strive to fulfill. "God created the heavens and the earth for a true purpose, He shaped you and perfected your form. And to Him is the final return" (*at-Taghabun* 64:3). It is remarkable how close our intellect can bring us to the truth, yet reason alone without divine guidance carries us away to extremes, only grazing its periphery. Why would it not, as to think is to be subjective? This was at the core of St Augustine's (354-430 CE) philosophy, who interestingly was a pre-Islamic African convert to Christianity (Islam?) from Algeria. He saw both philosophy and religion as quests for the truth, but the former as an inferior pursuit.[835] Today's sciences see neither religion, philosophy, nor truth as their goal. Thus, the Prophet compared our reason to sorcery, as it can even justify the clear wrong (*Sunan Abi Dawud* 5009).

Without ties to the Creator, the creation is cut to a freefall. Deprived of a tangible consequence, it becomes futile to argue any level of ethics. Indeed, today we have nearly lost both theoretical and practical understanding of morality, which is evident from the current state of world affairs.[836] The dichotomy of good and evil—the bottom line of our history—only exists because of an associated afterlife. There is absolutely no logic behind such debate without the recognition of a superior being representing ultimate justice. That is not to say that individuals cannot be moral without religion, nor that religiosity automatically makes one moral. Only religious beliefs with attached consequences provide a firm base for such ethics for even those who internally struggle with virtue. Without that anchor, all ethical discussions become relativistic on ever-shifting grounds, examples of which unfortunately surround us today.

Is it then surprising that throughout history, the rise of disbelief has always coincided with a decline in ethics and justice, leading to the eventual downfall of civilization? Ibn Khaldun discerned that those in power are the usual perpetrators of injustice, as they can escape worldly repercussions.[837] Otherwise, crimes met with punishment are not necessarily injustices, *per se*. Hence, Islam censures injustice to encourage those in authority to exercise self-restraint, which disappears altogether in a society without religion. "My point is that those who stand outside all judgments of value cannot have any ground for preferring one of their own impulses to another except the emotional strength of that impulse," explained C. S. Lewis.[838]

We can debate and say many things on the surface but cannot escape the deeper truth. Such discussions today take the form of radical skepticism with a splitting-hair discourse of minutiae that are as disorienting as pointless. Skepticism can be a powerful tool to check our cultural and societal misconceptions. However, when we question everything, we direly need a superseding measuring stick to keep us tethered to sanity. When we denounce God, we also renounce any existence of a meaningful life for ourselves. The result is the curse of immorality and injustice while we scream into our manufactured void by sticking our heads into the sand. As the unnamed poet said, injustice is a human trait: If you find a moral man, there is some reason why he is not unjust.[839]

Such ethical incontinence only gradually soils our souls. "Immorality never appears among a people to such an extent that they commit it openly, but plagues and diseases that were never known among the predecessors will spread among them," warned the Prophet (*Sunan Ibn Majah* 4019). As we are plagued with such illnesses while denying the existence of our souls and God, we desperately look for answers in psychology. Ironically, it is a field entirely devoted to our *souls* with its Greek roots in the *psyche*. Maybe a revaluation of our epistemology is warranted today to correct some deeply held misconceptions. Instead of using our limited knowledge of psychology to derive the benefits of revelations like *al-Fatiha*, we should use the divine wisdom within its *ayats* sent as a cure for humanity and improve our understanding of the human mind (*Sahih Muslim* Book 39, Hadith 89).

If we backtrack even further, we arrive at the Big Bang, claiming the entirety of this universe was created from nothing, for nothing, only to return to the same. This contradicts Newton's first law, which states that an object will remain unchanged unless acted upon by an *external force*. Arguably, these basic physical laws of the universe may not have existed before the Big Bang—the "outside of the box" scenario. Theoretical physicists would further dismiss the prevalence of Newtonian physics at the singularity, where quantum theory prevails (more on that later). Still, all of our sciences and mathematics halt at the singularity and fail to explain preceding events for reasons already discussed. Nevertheless, like all things within the universal "box" bound by these laws, our physical selves cannot be exceptions. Our appearance and disappearance cannot be unless *acted upon by an external source*. It is similar to Thomas Aquinas's (1225-74 CE) "Five Ways," but with a crucial difference: God is not simply the Unmoved Mover of Aristotle, but movement itself. In this context, our souls can be seen as the *unmoved mover* of our physical selves, endowed with the essence of God's eternal realm. Of note, the "Five Ways" have their roots in the Islamic *Kalam* cosmological argument, which has continuously influenced theologians such as William Lane Craig, who wrote a book with the same title.

The abruptness of the secular claims also gainsay the first law of thermodynamics—energy can neither be created nor destroyed. Our creation is akin to the birth of the first man and the universe, as we are all infinite pieces of a larger puzzle. Even the notion that we came from *nothing* implies an external power that created us from nothing, disrupting the natural order that governs our physical realm. Those aware of the *light-cone* concept of special and general relativity should also reach the same conclusion. In simple terms, it represents the path of light originating from a single *event* (e.g., the birth of a star) and traveling through spacetime in all directions. This creates a conical shape on a multi-dimensional spacetime graph. As nothing in the universe can travel faster than the speed of light, our *absolute future* lies within the upward-facing cone with respect to time, while our absolute past lies within the downward cone (see figure on the left).

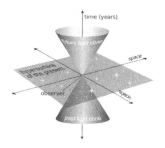 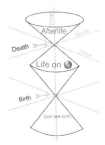

One can view the death of a person as a similar *event*, defined as any occurrence in a single point in space (delineated by three agreed-upon coordinates) and time. Through the light-cone concept, the event of death marks the beginning of a new cone from which a new *absolute future* of that person emerges. By definition, the past-cone represents the moments leading up to the person's death, going back to their birth as the previous *event*. Within these two *events* lies the person's life on earth. To view life and death as anything other than a continuum of this spacetime paradigm contradicts our current understanding of the universe, rendering atheism an ignorant and unscientific stance.

Consider a glass of water slipping from your hand and shattering on the floor. Some might dismiss this event as meaningless, but that is only looking proverbially at the glass half-full. Could you reproduce the same pattern with another attempt? While the water has the *potential* to spill anywhere until it hits the ground, a specific pattern of spillage emerges after the impact. *This* pattern is no longer random but a precise and describable reality. Since the drops do not spill everywhere at the same time, the exact spread becomes predetermined and within the space-light-cone of the glass, eliminating all other possibilities from its absolute past. This predetermination gives it and everything else that follows within its light-cone a purpose. Denying this does not erase the predetermination; it simply reveals one's lack of understanding.

The hypocrites and those who have sickness in their hearts said, "These people [the believers] must be deluded by their religion," but if anyone trusts in God, God is mighty and wise. (al-Anfal 8:49)

From a pragmatist's standpoint, philosophical debates can be resolved by evaluating the best possible outcome of competing answers. God is Most pragmatic in asking: "What harm would it do them to believe in God and the Last Day, and give charitably from the sustenance God has given them? God knows them well" (*an-Nisa* 4:39). Hence, William James (1842-1910 CE) deemed the issue of religion to be both *forced* and *momentous*.[840] A life with a belief in God—providing various positive effects in discipline, motivation, and character—is a far better choice than one without; the latter also risks eternal damnation if one loses the bet in the hereafter.

Essentially, science also brings us back to creationism, and why should it not? Since God created everything, all things within should only point towards the source, similar to the Turkish Sufi scholar Fethullah Gülen's proposition. Even in theoretical physics, the most abstract of all sciences, everything points to the singularity where all of our paradigms and knowledge break down. What is that singularity but just another secular synonym for God? This had been the traditional Muslim approach to science, where "In Islam, as in no other religion, the performance of various aspects of religious ritual has been assisted by scientific procedure," remarks historian David King.[841]

In 1949, Kurt Godel showed mathematically that it is impossible to prove all factual statements, even if we limit it to just arithmetic (Skeptics must refrain from celebrating just yet). Our inability to logically explain the soul and other uncertainties only reflects our lack of understanding and intellect. However, to derive an absence of overall purpose from this and reject the presence of a creator is illogical. Some go to extreme lengths to invent new ideas like the Gaia hypothesis only to redefine what God had already revealed since the beginning of our existence. Our limited understanding of creationism still is the overall image containing several shades of science, which makes it impossible to separate them and still get a complete picture.

THE BLIND SCHOLAR

Whoever desires the harvest of the Hereafter, We will increase their harvest. And whoever desires [only] the harvest of this world, We will give them some of it, but they will have no share in the Hereafter. (ash-Shuraa 42:20)

Our individualism goes in concert with secularism and promotes a departure from spirituality through contrasting idioms. Then we are left with atheism becoming the largest growing "religion" in the world, but there truly is no such thing as atheism, only self-delusion. We all worship something, whether it be our desires, values, or priorities, and when we turn away from God, we become enslaved to these things instead. This is not to say that all atheists are immoral and hedonistic, as statistically, that can be said of organized religions with a higher prevalence. Most complaints against organized religion are undeniable, and criminal activities of many "people of faith" are commonly highlighted as evidence against religion. It is worsened by a lack of accountability or even outright protection by certain influential organized religions, leading to the association of their crimes with their stated belief.

We are all imperfect beings and our actions are a reflection of our inner beliefs rather than what we claim. Criminals of any hat can go untouched by the ideals, just as corruption within religious institutions, revealing nothing more than the darkness of their free will. Occasionally, even scientists falsify or manipulate data for various personal gains. That deviation from the scientific method is a personal choice but cannot be used as some "proof" against science. Recurrent instances of scientific dishonesty from an institution would indicate an institutional problem requiring further investigation with root cause analysis. However, anyone taking such examples to make a case against science altogether would be depriving himself of its overwhelming benefit, which in and of itself does not force our actions.

We have surely set forth in this Quran every [kind of] lesson for people, but humankind is the most argumentative of all beings. (al-Kahf 18:54)

Einstein argued that morality can be based on sympathy, education, and social ties without needing a religious foundation. He wrote, "Man would indeed be in a poor way if he had to be restrained by fear of punishment and hopes of reward after death."[842] Now a century later, we live in the most secularly educated world in history with declining global religiosity, and the only truth remaining seems to be our *poor way*. According to Ibn Khaldun, it is only one's inherent restraint that safeguards his fortitude, which is otherwise lost through external restraints like fear, punishment, and education. Religion liberates men from these external restraints and provides inner understanding and guidance, which for Ibn Khaldun was the secret to the success of the Prophet and his companions —something Einstein failed to appreciate even with his documented IQ.[843] Accordingly, Ibn Ashur attributed religio-spiritual self-restraint as the highest significance in Islamic jurisprudence (i.e. *shari'ah*).[844] God appeals to our reason: "As for the disbelievers, their deeds are like a mirage in a desert, which the thirsty perceive as water, but when they approach it, they find it to be nothing. Instead, they find God there [in the Hereafter, ready] to settle their account. And God is swift in reckoning. Or [their deeds are] like the darkness in a deep sea, covered by waves upon waves, topped by [dark] clouds. Darkness upon darkness! If one stretches out their hand, they can hardly see it. And whoever God does not bless with light will have no light!" (*an-Nur* 24:39-40). This final aspect of the blessing of guidance is crucial, and we cannot be grateful enough for it. We can see its absence in even the most brilliant minds who fail to take that final leap of faith.

Richard Dawkins, one of the most outspoken atheists of our time, writes: "When I lie on my back and look up at the Milky Way...I am overwhelmingly filled with a sense of almost worship...sort of abstract gratitude that I am alive to appreciate these wonders."[845] Similarly, Nietzsche found himself immersed in a *perfect day* filled with profound gratitude, forcing him to ask: "How could I fail to be grateful to my entire life?"[846] This is the same question God repeatedly asks, especially in surah *ar-Rahman, The Beneficent*. That feeling of *worship* and *gratitude* is indeed a remnant of our *fitra* (i.e. innate nature), but only a firm belief in God and the afterlife can motivate meaningful personal change. That is all we can hope to achieve, while the wheel of history turns along its predestined course. Though other *things* can fill that gap, only God's pleasure can withstand the assaults of our desires.

The only sure thing in life is death, making eternal paradise a motivator for all. *But why should this view have any weight against all the secular experts'?* Such hesitations were certainly an obstacle to even contemplating these ideas but outweighed by today's overwhelming lack of intellectual *adab*, etiquette, and dishonesty. The fictitious use of the term "expert" along with its kindred was masterfully investigated by MacIntyre, explaining "how in the social world of corporations and governments private preferences are advanced under the cover of identifying the presence or absence of the finding of experts...The effects of eighteenth-century prophecy have been to produce *not* scientifically managed social control, but a skillful dramatic imitation of such control. It is histrionic success that gives power and authority in our culture."[847] It is like a blind scholar who spends a lifetime studying calligraphy and becomes an expert but cannot fully appreciate its elegance to the same level as a layperson with sight and a receptive heart. While only God can look inside our hearts and judge, we must use our reason to choose what serves us best in this life and the hereafter. Ultimately, God is still more deserving of our blind faith than any human.

Atheism is typically initiated by a fallout with God, leading to a desire for freedom from religious responsibilities and obligations. If an atheist truly did not believe in God, why would he concentrate so much effort and energy on going on a lifelong war against Him? Auguste Comte (1798-1857 CE) realized this dilemma and proposed abandoning God and all things related. Unfortunately, it is easier said than done, as even the most militant atheist cannot help but reflexively appeal to God in moments of despair from the remnants of his *fitra*. Driven by conniving whispers, their masked liberation gradually transforms into unique loneliness when even the devil deems the subject unworthy of pursuit. "I came to the harsh realization that my universe had become a prison, a place to hide," confessed an ex-atheist. "But I had no idea what I was running from. It was not so easy being a god, after all!"[848]

As for the theist and the deist, God simply asks: "Does man think that he will be left without purpose/guidance [after he was created]?" (*al-Qiyamah* 75:36). If we momentarily ignore linguistic boundaries, even the word *Maker*—phonetically resembling the Arabic *makar* (مَكَر, e.g., *al-Naml* 27:50), meaning to plot or make plans—appears to linguistically relate all of creation to an inherent purpose. God further challenges: "Anyone who thinks that God will not support him in this world and the next should stretch a rope up to the sky, climb all the way up it, and see whether this strategy removes the cause of his anger" (*al-Hajj* 22:15). Agnosticism, on the other hand, is an acknowledgment of one's incapability to comprehend God. Today it serves as a politically correct answer of plausible deniability, perhaps foreshadowing the same answers that will be given upon entering the grave to al-Munkar and al-Nakir (*Mishkat al-Masabih* 130). Few are as brilliant as Einstein, but there is a difference between not understanding quantum physics and saying it cannot be proven.[849] Even he struggled with the quantum world's uncertainty of a universe where certain things are forever unknowable. The recent era of theoretical physics, string theories, M-theory, Kubo-Schwinger-Martin condition, etc., only made it clear how little we truly know. God highlights this in profound simplicity through the opening letters of twenty-nine surahs throughout the Qur'an known as the fawātih (Arabic, فواتح) whose meaning is only known to God. For us, they signify a meaning even at the level of letters that we are unaware of.

Russell observed that what passes for knowledge in ordinary life suffers from three defects: it is cocksure, vague, and self-contradictory.[850] Over the years, many logical explanations for God's existence have been proposed by notable figures, such as St. Anselm, St. Thomas Aquinas, Rene Descartes, and Norman Malcolm. Malcolm's argument was unique in its default position on God's existence until definitively proven otherwise, which is inherently impossible. How can we say anything in confidence about God, who cannot be perceived through sensory perceptions that our reason is based on? Aristotle described all scientific knowledge as a derivative of first principles, which can only be grasped through intuition. Therefore, as God is the first principle of everything, He can never be understood scientifically, philosophically, or through induction.[851]

We describe our vast universe as chaos, yet marvel at the precision of its order. Even Morrie, a lifelong agnostic, confessed in the end that the universe is too harmonious and grand to be accidental.[852] Thus, Rumi said: "Think not that there are no travelers on the road, or that those of perfect attributes leave no trace. Just because you are not privy to the secrets you think that no one else is either."[853] This thought process originates from one's individualism and egotistical concept of being able to master *all* knowledge. We repeatedly see cognitive dissonance among intellectuals like Bryson, who summarizes the cellular miracle as just *random, frantic actions* without any thought process, happening so *smoothly and precisely* in harmony to avoid our notice.[854] One cannot logically claim all of it to be *random* and *precise* simultaneously. Those two things are oxymoronic.

Such cognitive distortion is also reflected in evolutionary theory, where natural selection is explained as a random process, while sexual selection, lying at the center of it, is anything but random. The precision and harmony would rather be self-evident of the perfectness of the Creator guiding everything, even at the cellular and atomic levels. As prominent mathematicians and computer engineers point out, random changes in any system or software only lead to degradation and functional destruction over time.[855] Only recently we discovered the hidden coherence within seemingly random erratic events, as demonstrated by Edward Lorenz's Butterfly. "Surely in the heavens and the earth, there are signs for those who have faith," declares God (al-Jathiya 45:3). Thus, Newton observed in his *Principia*: "The most beautiful system of the sun, planet and comets could only proceed from the counsel and dominion of an intelligent and powerful Being."

Relying solely on logic and reason has its caveats. Al-Ghazali warned that if our faith is based on some careful logical argument or proof, it can also be lost by an equally well-ordered argument instilling doubt.[856] Signs of divine intervention and design are all around us, even in the million types of protein in our bodies. Each of these proteins is a miracle, as by the laws of probability "the chances of a 1,055-sequence molecule like collagen spontaneously self-assembling are, frankly, nil."[857] This combinatorial inflation problem has been convincingly demonstrated by mathematician David Berlinski among others. By similar probability, neither should our planet, sun, oceans, atmosphere, or even ourselves with the limbs we use to charge against their Creator.

Meanwhile, individuals continue to put some water and elements in a flask with sparks, creating a green broth of a few organic compounds, to rid themselves of the need for a Creator. Many brilliant minds similarly dismiss God's creations' overwhelming beauty and precision by highlighting various bodily complications or seemingly bizarre phenomena like Darwin's Ichneumonidae or Sam Harris's whale teeth.[858] These critics demand absolute perfection on earth—as they understand and define it —without ever putting forth any effort to earn God's promised Paradise, where perfection awaits. Alexander Pope diagnosed it back in his time writing: "Call Imperfection what thou fancy'st such, Say, here he gives too little, there too much; Destroy all creatures for thy sport or gust, Yet cry, If Man's unhappy, God's unjust."[859] Such pathology is a competition between intellectual narcissism and laziness. These critics rarely do anything to help humanity beyond taking misguided shots at God from their armchairs.

Ultimately, "above everyone who has knowledge, there is the One who is all-knowing" (*Yusuf* 12:76). Plato's (427-347 BC) "Allegory of the Cave" famously set the foundation for the different levels of knowledge, where *noesis* (intuition/faith) ultimately trumps both reasoning and sensation. Although our perception is the foundation for all knowledge, we have to be cognizant of its uniqueness due to the organic processes of our brains and senses, revealing little about the true form/nature of things. Reason and perception can be deceiving and lead to false conclusions if not handled carefully. Thus, our five senses must be consciously controlled for our preservation, just like the five horses drawing Prince Arjuna's chariot. Similar to our reflections in a mirror, which we have learned through experience as not another version of us on the other side.

Unfortunately, ever since the abandonment of Platonism, most postmodern philosophies and scholarship aspires to the materialistic line, achieving only the primary *intelligibilia* of Ibn Khaldun—limiting intellect to the boundaries set by sensory perceptions, imagination, memory, and estimative power according to certain rational rules.[860] While the philosophical reasoning of the blind and the deaf may seem inaccurate to the eyes and ears of another, those with all the senses may still be missing other unknown senses that limit their reason from reaching a higher level. Hence, the Prophet advised us to seek God's refuge if we hear a dog barking or a donkey braying, for they can see beyond our capabilities and into the realm of the devils (*al-'Adab al-Mufrad*, Book 51, Hadith 1233). Through mastering the sense data, one can achieve the level of *spiritual intellection* —a level reached by God's messengers—where an innate intuition replaces the former. If truth is not found immutably in the physical world, it must be achieved through eternal sources that come through God's messengers. Ignoring God's guidance results in a void that philosophers and scientists try to fill in their attempts to provide a blueprint for existence. Nevertheless, in all recorded history, they have only repeatedly proven God's declaration that: "Even if all mankind and jinn [including devils] came together to produce something like this Quran [and its guidance], they could not produce anything like it, however much they helped each other" (*al-Isra'* 17:88).

Keeping with his Theory of Forms, Plato tried to provide us with a quintessential society in *The Republic* but failed to incorporate the human diversity and pluralism that ails every nation. Admittedly, his solution was only supposed to be an ideal form, which still resembles an elitist totalitarian regime, a system that has failed numerous times in history.

Perhaps Plato's error was rooted in his focus on *things* rather than *change*, which led him "to write the mathematics of the *shape* of atoms, rather than the mathematics of their *movements*," criticized Rovelli.[861] Still, his reasoning for the empiric world and innate knowledge allowed him to get a firmer grasp of the soul and body dualism than others.

Similarly, Thomas More's (1478-1535 CE) vision of a *Utopia* became oppressive like the Maoist and Cambodian regimes.[862] Locke's Fundamental Constitutions of the Carolinas in the 1660s resulted in a feudal aristocracy leading to quick rebellions. He also admitted in *The Second Treatise of Government* that his proposed liberal economics would create pervasive inequality to an unlimited disparity.[863] Jean-Jacques Rousseau's (1712-78 CE) *The Social Contract* turned into a totalitarian state, forsaking any notion of individual rights, similar to Jeremy Bentham's (1748-1832 CE) utilitarianism. When Lenin became disgruntled and caught between the leftist Marxists and the corrupt democracies, he ignored Trotsky's objection to the concentration of power into an elite. It played right into the hands of an opportunist Stalin, whose failures and paranoia need little mention. Thus, Marxism had to be reassessed by neo-Marxists like Gyorgy Lukacs (1855-1971 CE) and others from the Frankfurt School, infused with consciousness and individualism. These socialist ideas played a significant role in developing 20th-century Third World ideology and today's postmodernism.

Even good ideas and intentions are inevitably harnessed to further the ambitions of the wily opportunists to no avail of the impoverished. We have seen the peasantry aid many such movements, allying with the elites, to ultimately be suppressed under various compromised ideologies that only maintain social hierarchy like Arab Socialism, African Socialism, Sarvodaya, or Nasakom.[864] On the other hand, today's liberalism with its Kantian roots has also failed due to its false premise of the elevation of individual autonomy, as argued by Professor Deneen in *Why Liberalism Failed*. Jesus said, "Therefore, by their fruits, you will know them" (*Matthew* 7:20). If we judge these philosophies by their outcomes, then the resulting disastrous consequence of those movements should suffice. These ideas arise from a dissatisfaction with the world order and a plan to change, which often hide the fact that many such movements are based on dissident Western intellectuals who failed to materialize a viable political ideology at home. Their utopianism is often removed from the realities of daily life, politics, and governance. In essence, it is a real-world manifestation of the Orwellian *Animal Farm*, which Muslim leaders and thinkers must recognize to counter the rise of nihilistic violence.

Similar Islamic works like *Al-Ahkam as-Sultaniyyah* by Imam al-Māwardī or even Imam al-Juwaynī are also idealistic without any successful practical implementation in history. Most mainstream Islamic movements today lack a detailed plan or a comprehensive understanding of the world. While the Islamic way of life provides the best blueprint for our life on earth, classical Islamic political theory never viewed it as a utopian movement. This makes it *okay* even if we do not accomplish our goals in this temporal life, for the Qur'anic focus is more on the struggle that "culminates in a successful meeting with the Divine (84:6)."[865] Any movement for a better society on earth cannot violate the sanctity of civilian life and the protection of the public sphere, which completely goes against the limits set by God.

Such intellectual guidance from a belief in God and an afterlife is aided by our *fitra* (i.e. innate knowledge), which sets us on the straight path (Arabic: الصراط المستقيم). God describes it as our natural disposition that is only corrupted after birth (*ar-Rum* 30:30). "No baby is born but upon *fitra*. It is his parents who make him a Jew or a Christian or a Polytheist," said the Prophet (*Sahih Muslim* 2658). Children with unspoiled *fitras* ask the most simple—yet splendid—questions that grownups overlook. That "childish" curiosity separates most great thinkers from the rest, who have lost their innate connection to the spiritual realm. While empiricists like Locke argued against innate knowledge, our current understanding places us in Schrodinger's world of uncertainty, where the duality of particle-antiparticle pairs and electrons in the atom is an accepted reality.[866] It is similar to our understanding of causality, where all natural phenomena have a cause leading back to the first cause, which is *uncaused*. From that perspective, various Prophetic teachings refocusing our intentions to think of God as the only cause of our pure actions come to light.

Our *fitra* is perhaps a more advanced form of imprinting seen throughout the animal kingdom, popularized by Konrad Lorenz (1903-89 CE) and Thomas More's *Utopia*. Plato also discussed this concept through Socrates' dialogue in *Meno*, where he argues: "Then if the truth of things is always in our soul, the soul must be immortal; so that what you do not know now by any chance—that is, what you do not remember—you must boldly try and find out and remember?"[867] Subsequent philosophers, including Ibn 'Abd al-Barr of Cordoba (978-1071 CE), Ibn Taymiyya, and Noam Chomsky, refuted the concept of a *tabula rasa*.[868] What they describe as innate knowledge is our *fitra*, which creates the initial urge to seek the divine as the primordial state of humanity until our egos carry us astray. Therefore,

God reminds: "(Recall) when your Lord brought forth their progeny from the loins of the children of 'Ādam, and made them testify about themselves (by asking them,) 'Am I not your Lord?' They said, 'Of course, You are. We testify.' (We did so) lest you should say on the Day of Judgment, 'We were unaware of this" (*al-A'raf* 7:172).

Dr. Lang relates it to his initial yarning for listening to the Qur'an in a language he did not understand, similar to a mother's voice comforting a baby.[869] While simpler creations rely heavily on imprinting, our intellect enables us to defy it. If our conscious, perceptive selves are corrupt, it drags the subconscious to iniquity against its will/*fitra*, being the loudest voice in control. Had it not been for—yet even with—our *fitra*, we would complain about the unfairness of being held responsible for our sins. Thus, free will is provided with the tool of reason and innate guidance from our *fitra* to navigate our way through life. That is the connection between the four levels of Plato's and Aristotle's epistemology, which allows us to elevate stepwise to the ultimate knowledge of the objective truth.

While our *fitra* makes us think of naked Amazonians as primitive and uncivilized, some willfully abandon clothing and modesty, claiming Dionysian "progress." Ibn Taymiyyah gave the example of milk, which all infants are born to yearn for its natural health benefits.[870] Later in life, we corrupt our taste for such wholesome food and instead desire that which is harmful. When both milk and wine were presented to the Prophet during his Night Journey, he chose the former and was congratulated by Gabriel that he was guided to the *fitra* (*Sahih al-Bukhari* 4709). Without the divine light, our innate knowledge and *fitra* can certainly go unnoticed by onlookers and disproven through our actions. However, to use the reverse logic—that if our actions do not reflect our *fitra*, it must not exist—is a fallacy of syllogism.

He makes Satan's insinuations a temptation only for the sick at heart, and those whose hearts are hardened—the evildoers are profoundly opposed [to the Truth]. (al-Hajj 22:53)

Our *fitra*'s connection to the soul makes them both difficult to comprehend and seem non-existent to those out of touch with their spirituality. When our souls separate momentarily from the body during sleep, an autonomous state takes over, and our innate nature dominates. Our conscious selves often cannot recall our experiences during that state, which we call dreams. Still, some with a keen sense of spirituality can attain knowledge of the unseen through their dreams. The Prophet once said, "My eyes sleep, but my heart remains awake" (*Sahih al-Bukhari* 1147). Just because the rest of us cannot sense at that spiritual level does not prove its nonexistence along the same logical flaw of syllogism and deterministic linear sequence. If our earthly memories are physically stored within the hard drives of our brains, how can we recall any innate knowledge tied to our souls? It would be similar to looking for the thought process behind this sentence on my laptop's hard drive. The fallibility of memory, in general, can be demonstrated through many logically irrefutable fallacies, such as the world being created just minutes ago, complete with all our memories and records (i.e. Ockham's Nominalism). Therefore, Antoine Arnaud's (1612-94 CE) view of logic ultimately being a tool of thought and rhetoric, rather than a universal law, appears more accurate.[871] Ultimately, all such ideas—about human understanding, empiricism, simple vs. complex ideas, primary vs. secondary qualities, etc.—are theoretical arrows shot blindly at God's eternal knowledge, hoping to hit the mark.

Locke's denial of innate knowledge led him to formulate various incorrect assumptions that have since been refuted. Similarly, his theory of identity was disproved by Thomas Reid (1710-96 CE) using transitivity of identity. His challenge of Molyneux's Problem ignored the power of the subconscious, which is now a well-studied phenomenon. Billions of dollars are invested today in its application in consumer behavior. Refuting such entanglement is not the scope of this book nor worth the time and effort. It is unsurprising that following similar delusions, some, like Hume and Quine, completely denied God's existence. The miserable status of such philosophers is reflected in their worldview, which highlights the other classical definition of *fitra* as "misery and happiness" attributed to Imam Ahmad Ibn Hanbal. Ibn Taymiyya then connected it back to our *fitra's* disposition with God, which determines its success and happiness in earthly and afterlives.[872] A remarkable summarization of these concepts is also seen in Krishna's advice to Arjuna in Bhagavad Gita (Ch. 16).

If we were to take these empiricists at their claim and only accept knowledge gained from senses, humanity would never make any meaningful progress. Every experience gained from our predecessors would have to be rejected at the turn of every generation and re-experienced to confirm its validity while carving out a unique layer in Dante's Hell. There comes a point when it is difficult to continue reading such delusions and shake heads with al-Ghazali.

> On the gist of philosophy: what is blameworthy in it, and what is blameless; what doctrine lays its proponent open to the charge of unbelief, and what doctrine lays him open to

> the charge, not of unbelief, but of innovation; and an expose of what the philosophers have stolen from the sayings of the men of truth and mingled with their own errors together with those truths; and how souls come to feel an antipathy for those truths; and how to extract the unadulterated truth from amid the counterfeit and spurious views found in the aggregate of the philosophers' teaching.[873] [al-Ghazali]

To battle ignorance effectively, we must arm ourselves with all the available resources. Combining our senses, philosophical reasoning, and revelation without compartmentalizing is a more accurate approach to obtaining ken. Otherwise, we are just setting ourselves up for failure. Plato's philosopher in the cave ignoring the world outside would eventually become blind like the rest of the cave dwellers in a Darwinian world. Even Philo's Platonic reinterpretation of the book of Moses—as God first created man as a form in His mind as *logos*—is limited by the anthropomorphic assumption of God's *mind*.

We cannot always rationalize everything we sense or sense everything that we can rationalize. Attempting to do so is a syllogistic induction, which later Freudians called *rationalization*.[874] It is just another version of classical conditioning. Like physiological induction, scientific induction is also a frequent source of error. Georg Hegel's continuous chain of synthesis of thesis and antithesis into a new truth may someday bring us to the absolute truth, but how many generations would perish in between believing falsehood that has yet to be disproven? The truth will always remain so, even if unseen by the blind scholar in the cave and all those who followed him in arrogance. It can only be clarified by those in direct communication with divinity, possessing true wisdom of both intuition and deliberation. The secular view rather ironically dismisses this prophetic wisdom for the opinions of various philosophers, intellectuals, and scientists—ultimately elevating them to the same "prophetic" level of their "religion." While much of their secular deliberations sustain, without that divine intuitive guidance, it becomes a gamble to determine when they veer off the correct path.

The world of philosophy then becomes a sphere of conceited intellectuals stroking each other's egos through endless cycles of refutation and confirmation, all to construct unintelligible alternatives to revelation. In contrast, the Qur'anic explanations are beautiful in their profound simplicity. God provides timeless clarity to age-old questions that can be taken at their face value or for deeper contemplation to the seeker's satisfaction. "We will show them Our signs in the universe and within themselves until it becomes clear to them that this [Quran] is the truth. Is it not enough that your Lord is a Witness over all things?" (*Fussilat* 41:53). The only requirement is pure intentions and faith, for the embarked journey is promised to be divinely guided. "This is God's promise, and He does not go back on His promise. But most people do not know" (*ar-Rum* 30:6).

Despite an Omnipotent Creator sending messengers to directly tell us how He "taught by the pen" (*al-'Alaq* 96:4), some try to argue instead that the pen does not exist, like Arthur Schopenhauer (1788-1860 CE).[875] He started on the right course but took a sharp turn concluding that our struggles can ultimately be overcome by realizing that we are merely slaves of the *universe* freed by death, paving the road to suicide. Or we can just accept God telling us that we are *His* slaves and to live by His ideals, which holds profound wisdom for the sensible. Even after thousands of years of effort, philosophers and psychologists have yet to fully understand how we learn the exact meaning of all the penned languages and symbols of the world. This makes it another divine miracle, as Ibn 'Arabi identified the utterance of words with life since we breathe letters into existence.[876] It begs the question of whether beings without language are even capable of thought.

Although this discussion may seem strictly philosophical, we can see deviations from logic manifesting in the public sphere throughout history. The translation and revision of classical philosophy by Muslim scholars of the Golden Age left their marks on the Mu'tazilites, who caused significant suffering to the *ummah*. Similarly, their rediscovery in the West resulted in reformation along with the rise of individualism and secularism. While the Ash'aris countered the Mu'tazilites in the Muslim world, the latter's counterpart in the West went intellectually unchecked. This resulted in an unbalanced rise of philosophy with strict adherence to science as the ultimate truth.

Science is an art of probability, for every inference is inductive. All knowledge gained from this methodology is at best *probable*.[877] Each group got some things right and others wrong, but all demonstrated degrees of intolerance. While any dive into a field of science only reveals the little that we have truly uncovered, most scientists refuse to submit to the vastness of the unknown out of intellectual arrogance. Their ideas are not inherently blameworthy; rather, it is their misinterpretation that leads people astray. They can be reinterpreted through a divine measuring stick to separate the truth from falsehood. Hence, God calls the Qur'an *al-Furqan*, the standard to discern between right and wrong as well as the real and apparent good. Otherwise, the traps set within the secular world can make a careless navigator easily succumb to his demise.

Instead of focusing on the skill to discern the ever-increasing available knowledge, today's push is towards reducing and *leveling*, where all things are made equal. Even here, a noble concept is used injudiciously without *discernment*, further emphasizing the main problem. In truth, no two things are equal: darkness and light, night and day, virtue and vice, male and female, and so on. "Claiming to liberate the individual from embedded cultures, traditions, places, and relationships, liberalism has homogenized the world in its image—ironically, often fueled by claims of 'multiculturalism' or, today, 'diversity,'" writes Professor Deneen. Instead, "liberalism has left the individual exposed to the tools of liberation —leaving us in a weakened state in which the domains of life that were supposed to liberate us are completely beyond our control or governance."[878]

The Prophet said: "At the end of this ummah, there will be a collapse, transformation, and Qadhf." 'Aisha asked: "Will they be destroyed even while there are righteous among them?" He said: "Yes when evil is dominant" (Jami` at-Tirmidhi 2185)

There lies the scholarly debate on their value and permissibility. The schism that divided Aristotle's and Plato's concept of the *essence* was merged by Ibn Sina in his famous thought experiment of the floating/falling man. He argued that even with complete sensory deprivation and lack of prior experience, one would be fully aware of his existence (i.e., his essence/soul). This was derived from his faith and being a true polymath, suggesting self-awareness as fundamental to existence. Bereft of that level of understanding, we are left with the schism created by Plato and Aristotle and stuck in spacetime. The "Allegory of the Cave" found its way into Ibn al-Nafis's (1213-88 CE) island, where an individual equipped with philosophical reasoning and all the senses could discover God logically. Wilhelm Schmidt (1868-1954 CE) showed in his twelve-volume magnum opus, through extensive cataloging, that all primitive religions indeed believe in *one* god. It disproved prior evolutionary anthropologists' claims of religion beginning with animism, which were made without comparable evidence or research (e.g. works of Edward Tylor (1832-1917 CE) and John Lubbock (1834-1913 CE)).

Ibn Sina's Falling Man has floated through history, leaving a mark on many similar philosophies, including Descartes's *cogito ergo sum*. Although

Western philosophy often champions Descartes as the first modern philosopher, his questioning of intellectual truths curiously parallels al-Ghazali's writings from five hundred years prior. Descartes doubted everything except for self-observation, but even that was later refuted by many. Russell, on the other hand, blamed him for introducing a subjective bias into modern philosophy by saying, "I think."[879]

In fact, all philosophical trends result from the intellectual community's reaction to their prevailing environment. Take the empiricists crawling out of the Middle Ages with a *tabula rasa*, and the liberals working through the revolutions of the Enlightenment and diving straight into industrialization, which generated the evolutionists' cry for survival and the materialists' struggle to stay fit. The inevitable global conflicts for power then gave rise to the existentialists through the sheer brutalities of the World Wars. Then we arrived at a complete reversal of Aristotelian ethics by Jean-Paul Satre (1905-80 CE), claiming: "Since there is no God or designer to give man a purpose, it is up to the individual to choose the life they think best."[880] Eventually, all culminated in the desperate helplessness of this nuclear era, with nihilism becoming the dominating theme. The postmodernist turn since Foucault, Derrida, and Lyotard unleashed radical skepticism, taking liberalism to today's stale-mated identity politics. Instead of applauding such deviations, a more pragmatic focus would be a psychoanalysis of all the philosophers in history. Some of them were even institutionalized by the end of their careers, like Nietzsche. Yet, their chaotic philosophies are later adopted as solutions for humanity, overlooking the divinely guided examples of prophets and messengers.

The destiny of man placed within himself in a radical state of freedom does not translate to optimism. It engenders despair as demanded by the hopelessness of that manufactured divine abandonment. The concept of life as endless choices defining us can also be used to sum up religious dogma. Most philosophical trends overemphasize certain aspects of the human condition that have accompanied us since Adam. They are unbalanced reactions to environmental pressures, often becoming movements rebelling against divinity through yet another devilish delusion. Why, then, have so many intelligent thinkers failed to come to this same conclusion? Perhaps their qualms against divinity lie with their realization of the inconsistencies within their faiths—including secularism.

The Qur'an maintains to have come to replace the previously corrupted scriptures. From a Biblical perspective, this can be directly traced back to the Councils of Nicea, which began in 325 AD. Dragooned by Emperor Constantine, there was little unity among the participants, also excluding many dissenting sects. Constantine's motivations for conversion were more complex than what the empire's biographers portrayed. In fact, contemporary monuments, coins, and inscriptions depict him as a supporter of the cult of the Under Defeated Sun (i.e., *Sol Invictus*).[881] In his final act, he prematurely celebrated his plans to invade his life-long enemy with a public humanitarian plight: to save the persecuted Persian Christians. This led the Christians of Persia to celebrate with him publicly, welcoming an immaterialized invasion, which resulted in their massacre by Shapur II.

During those Councils, the original message of Jesus was changed to make the religion more palatable.[882] The minority concept of Trinity, coined by Tertullian of Carthage, and the nature of the son was then solidified as the official doctrine.[883] Curiously, Dr. Hawkins's kinesiology research found that *the level of truth* of Christianity dropped significantly right after those Councils due to the misinterpretations of Jesus's teachings.[884] Doctrinal formulations like the Nicene Creed resemble Greek philosophy because they *are* derived from it.[885] Similarly, Plato's universal form of man directly influenced later Christian theology, but would be more accurately applied to the creation of all of humankind from the perfect Adam. The revised Christian alternative became the opposite of Islamic *tawhid*, commonly known as *shirk*, which is the greatest sin that takes one outside of the folds of a believer. It is not simply polytheism but any obscuration of God's oneness that is unacceptable in Islam.

Of course, a complete discussion of Jesus's message, its realization by various disciples, and the standardization of the Bible is a much larger topic and has already been studied by many. Nevertheless, the alterations raise demur about the Bible's authenticity, which is apparent to many. That was the driving force behind the various reformation movements since the Middle Ages. A graduate of the Harvard Divinity School and a former Methodist priest writes about his own seminary experience to be conflicting, which he could only resolve through his subsequent study of the Qur'an.[886] Simple examples, like God clarifying that the creation of the heavens and the earth *did not* cause Him any fatigue to require "resting on the seventh day," frees Him from such anthropomorphic frailties of the Bible (*Qaf* 50:38; *Exodus* 31:17).

Do they not know that God is aware of what they conceal and what they reveal? (al-Baqarah 2:77)

The Qur'an is unique among other scriptures because it represents God's words in a first-person narrative, while the Old and New Testaments represent oral traditions that are more comparable to *ahadeeth*, albeit with notably differing motives. It is stated in the *New Oxford Annotated Bible with the Apocrypha*: "Why, how, and when the present books of the New Testament were finally gathered into one collection are questions difficult to answer because of the lack of explicit information."[887] Notwithstanding the ambiguity of what is meant by the Torah, the Pentateuch, and the Mishnah were not written down until the 1st-2nd century CE. According to the Jewish Historical Institute, the Talmud (i.e. Mishnah and Gemara) dates to the 3rd-8th centuries, while the oldest extant edition of the Babylonian Talmud is from the 14th century. "In the light of this we now know that in some instances what was thought to be Jewish haggadic influence in an Islamic text might well be quite the reverse," writes Norman Stillman. "Careful analysis of particular narratives may show that, in contrast to the assertions of previous generations of scholars, the Quran simply does not consistently reflect the direct derivation of biblical data from Jews or a straightforward assimilation of rabbinic midrash," added Professor Pregill. "Rather, the opposite may be the case, namely, that Jews quite likely 'borrowed' from the Quran, or even from later Islamic literature."[888] Professor Nicolai Sinai also makes a similar case in his recent study in *The Qur'an's Reformation of Judaism and Christianity*.

If we were to scrutinize the gospels through the same stringent science of hadith authentication, most of them would not pass muster. For instance, of the 600,000 ahadeeth examined by al-Bukhari, only 2,602 made it to his *Sahih* collection. Today's secular and scientific work would not meet the standards of the Islamic traditions either. Another point to note is the loss of any work's original meaning upon translation. Even the best efforts alter the primary source by contextualizing words and phrases having different meanings in different times, cultures, and languages. Hence, no translation is *indeed* the Qur'an and all Muslims are exhorted to learn and read it in its original Arabic.

Among the many embedded miracles in the Qur'an that are lost in translation is its unique style, which is noted by all who study Arabic. Its revelation over twenty-three years in that distinctly divine style simultaneously differed from the rhetorical style of the Prophet, as noted by his companions and recorded for posterity through *ahadeeth*. God stresses this point by telling His messenger: "Say, 'If God had so willed, I would not have recited it to you, nor would He have made it known to you. I lived a whole lifetime among you before it came to me. How can you not use your reason?'" (*Yunus* 10:16). As a result, those who truly study the Qur'an and *ahadeeth* inevitably end up getting closer to God and their spirituality. Such transformations are exemplified in the writings of Orientalist Ignac Goldziher (1850-1921 CE), who by the end of his career seemed to proclaim his submission, stating that Islam is the only religion to fully satisfy philosophical minds.[889]

The resulting oral tradition—preserved by the *qurra*—and its broad prevalence in people's minds at any given time guarantees its authenticity. The Qur'an was also written down during the lifetime of the Prophet and then collected into its current form by the first Caliph Abu Bakr.[890] That was successively passed down until canonized by Caliph Uthman with the consensus of the *huffaz*. The often criticized elimination of the other "variations" by Uthman only reflected the minimal changes that existed due to the different Arabic dialects, which had no significant deviation from the meaning. Even Orientalists like Gibb (1895-1971 CE) professed the Qur'an's authenticity as "preserved with scrupulous precision."[891] (Still, his knowledge of Islam was overshadowed by his deeply ingrained Western superiority complex demonstrated elsewhere.[892])

Therefore, the discrepancies between the Qur'an and the other texts expose the latter's alterations, which fueled much of the intellectuals' skepticism. With every new scientific discovery, another Biblical contradiction emerged, making it difficult for Christianity to survive the Enlightenment. As philology developed, new knowledge of Sanskrit outdating Hebrew also questioned the Biblical story of language, causing many like Ernest Renan (1823-92 CE) to replace his Christian zeal with science.[893] The Catholic Church's history of corruption, retaliation against intellectuals and scientific discoveries, further diminished its credibility over time. While this could have been disregarded as a mortal matter, the Church's claim as the sole religious authority turned it into a battle between the intellectuals and God. As a result, those seeing the contradictory facts had little choice but to go against the Church, which meant for them to go against God.

One must wonder, would they have felt the same way with proper knowledge of the Qur'an? If their religion did not push them away from God, would we have arrived at the godless world of today? These crucial questions are ignored by most, including reputable philosophers of science like Stephen Miller in his commendable attempt to bring God back into science. Even Stephen Hawking entertained the possibility of a Creator in his books but failed to take that final leap of faith. Al-Ghazali commented on such cognitive bias and the Dunning-Kruger effect a millennium ago. While these mathematicians, scientists, and philosophers master their corresponding fields of expertise, it says nothing about their acumen in religious matters. However, their study of seemingly solid facts engenders confusion in those later exposed to their methods. Marveling at their precision and genius proofs results in the false assumption that all of their opinions have the same lucidity and apodeictic solidity. Their unbelief makes others follow out of pure conformism, asserting: "If religion were true, this would not have been unknown to these philosophers."[894]

"A scientific theory is just a mathematical model we make to describe our observations: it exists only in our minds," confessed Hawking.[895] Ultimately, we are only humans limited by our shortcomings. While browsing through brilliant theories seemingly effortlessly, many come close to the conclusion that the complexity of it all only points to a Creator. Yet, they shy away from it *ad nauseam* through inherent biases and whispers to fight creationism. Aristotle argued that when a scientific man of practical knowledge comes to the wrong conclusion through his deliberations, he only demonstrates a failure of true wisdom and apprehension.[896] Another reader with confirmation bias towards the opposite can read the same arguments and come to a completely different interpretation. Or perhaps it is desirability bias. In any case, it is ultimately our faith that brings us out of the cave to the world of the objective truth. Thus, God reminds: "Say (O Prophet), 'Consider all that is in the heavens and the earth!' Yet neither signs nor warners are of any benefit to those who refuse to believe" (*Yunus* 10:101).

HOW TO UNLEARN

When God sent them a messenger confirming the Scriptures they already had, some of those who had received the Scripture before threw the Book of God over their shoulders as if they had no knowledge. (al-Baqarah 2:101)

Mental rigidity has always been the crux of human history as we struggle to contemplate unfamiliar concepts. Its etiology is multifactorial with deep psychological roots, for questioning deeply held beliefs threatens one's identity. Psychologists call it cognitive laziness, where we prefer old views over actively grappling with new ones to improve our intellect.[897] A structured education can counterintuitively propagate such constraints on the mind and result in mental incarceration. When the mind becomes inflexible, it hinders learning and developing one's thought process, for "truth" is whatever we are subjectively convinced of. Postmodernity hyperbolizes this to the culmination of individuals claiming their delusions as their own "versions of the truth" rather than trying to correct their misconceptions. It has led to the acceptance of many unfounded and impractical beliefs that are not even intellectually provable.

On the first day of medical school, one lecturer's opening statement was that much of what we were about to learn would be proven wrong within our careers. We were advised to embark on that mindset and continue our post-graduate education to serve our patients best. Unfortunately, most fall short, as studies have shown that many physicians' peak medical knowledge corresponds with the year of their graduation. Even if one does not actively pursue knowledge, it is crucial to keep an open mind to allow potential osmosis. Wisdom ultimately reflects the malleability of the mind to new ideas. However, there is a caveat against indiscriminate open-mindedness without first acquiring a firm anchor.

The history of astronomy provides a good example of the dangers of inflexibility. Before the invention of the telescope, astronomical discussions were mostly philosophical, and many misinterpretations were derived from mythical religious beliefs. Subsequent Muslim scholars made remarkable discoveries through their improved scientific methodology during the Golden Age. Abd ar-Rahman al-Sufi described the Andromeda galaxy in 964, centuries before the invention of the telescope, which was itself based on Ibn al-Haytham's groundbreaking work in the *Optical Thesaurus*. These discoveries influenced the works of later scientists, including Da Vinci and Kepler.[898] Al-Biruni calculated the Earth's rotational axis and its orbit around the sun as early as the 11th century. Nasir al-Din al-Tusi's couple (1201-74 CE) replaced Ptolemy's equant, which was employed by Ibn al-Shatir (1304-75 CE) and Copernicus to derive their geocentric and heliocentric models. Still, the Catholic Church refused to update Ptolemy's problematic equant, violently holding on to its Aristotelian theology. A contemporary Muslim scholar, Imam al-Qarāfī (1228-85 CE), noted that inflexibility concerning scripture is always misled and misleading.[899] It was demonstrated through the Church's fierce resistance to contradictory scientific discoveries. Even Kepler was forced into exile from Graz to avoid execution by the local Catholic archduke, who vowed to "make a desert of the country than rule over heretics."[900]

God revealed in the 7th century Qur'an: "I swear by the receding stars which travel and hide [e.g., black holes], and the night as it falls and the day as it breaks! Indeed, this [Quran] is the Word of [God delivered by Gabriel] a noble messenger-angel, full of power, held in honor by the Lord of the Throne, obeyed there [in heaven], and trustworthy" (*al-Takwir* 81:15-21). These concepts of an expanding universe and the Big Bang were only developed in the 20th century, which Stephen Hawking considered as one of the greatest intellectual revolutions.[901] All the while, he failed to give similar weight to its mention in the Qur'an. Although these ideas did not make much sense to the early Muslims, their faith demanded simply accepting it as nonlinear *knowledge of the unseen* (Arabic: علم الغيب) from the all-knowing Creator. Of course, many (outsiders and insiders) criticized these ideas as contemporary science disagreed, but how foolish do they seem now in retrospect?

Hubble is credited with the 1929 discovery of the red shift of the color spectra of stars through the Doppler effect. This phenomenon had previously been observed by Vesto Slipher in Arizona, demonstrating that stars were moving away from us in proportion to their distance. Suddenly the focus was shifted back to creationism as that discovery pointed to a singularity as the beginning of everything, as stated in scriptures for millennia. This was accepted rather favorably by the Catholic Church, issuing an official doctrine of support in 1951. The pushback now came from the scientific community, as they retaliated with opposing theories to creationism. Many subsequent failed attempts were made by prominent scientists like Herman Bondi, Thomas Gold, Fred Hoyle, Evgenii Lifshitz, and Isaac Khalatnikov, to name a few. Evidently, in this battle of egos, both sides demonstrated similar tendencies towards closed-mindedness throughout history. Even Pythagoras and Plato attempted to suppress the dissenting and contradictory views of their contemporaries.[902] Nonetheless, the truth remains grounded in the middle of this tug-of-war as newer discoveries are made, which makes it essential to remain honest and humble while staying firm on eternal knowledge.

Psychological research shows that our learning is conditional on our humility in realizing that we have something to learn.[903] Our beliefs act like goggles that we use to see the world. We often become hostile and defensive when our beliefs are questioned, as it jeopardizes our sense of identity. Psychologist George Kelly found such feelings to be even more pronounced when one knows the belief under attack to be false, making him further dig in his heels to defend at any cost.[904] The general disregard for Islamic knowledge today suffers from this pathology. According to Dr. al-Attas, the remedy is *Islamization*, which involves "the liberation of man first from magical, mythological, animistic, national-cultural tradition opposed to Islam, and then from secular control over his reason and his language."[905]

Outdated Newtonian dogma continues to be taught as hard facts in our schools as we struggle to see past Newtonian *absolute time*. Instead, the world is better viewed as continuously changing events relative to regular recurrences. Quantum gurus today find it more convenient to refer to time with respect to recurring natural phenomena such as the phases of the moon or the sun.[906] After strutting the gaudiness of Newtonian physics for centuries, we are now faced with a renewed appreciation for *ayats* like: "We made the day and night as two signs. So We made the sign of the night devoid of light, and We made the sign of the day [perfectly] bright, so that you may seek the bounty of your Lord and know the number of years and calculation [of time]. And We have explained everything in detail" (*al-Isra'* 17:12). Of note, Bryce DeWitt and John Wheeler discovered a mathematical equation for quantum gravity in 1967 without a time variable. It signifies our existence relative to one another and beyond the boundaries of absolute time. Essentially, it is our interactions with our surroundings that define us. This interaction even reaches a subconscious level of a possible shared collective "database of consciousness," similar to the proposition of Carl Jung. It explains the simultaneous emergence of similar ideas in waves globally, arising independently within minds worlds apart.

Paul Feyerabend, in his book *Against Method*, argued that science is not a customary, but an epistemologically anarchic enterprise. He passionately refuted the role of the scientific method in any major discovery, claiming that they were intuitive and their scientific methods only developed in retrospect to aid in understanding. Shaikh Hamza Yusuf cites Nobel laureate chemist Linus Pauling (1901-94 CE) as an example, who came upon his discovery during a febrile haze. We still do not know what really happened when Newton quarantined himself in Woolsthorpe Manor during the summer of 1663 before his big discovery. It conforms to Plato's highest level of *intelegibilia* and the orthodox view of our instincts as superior to reason. It is not to overlook their life's pursuit, for great intuitive moments only favor those seeking the truth. Perhaps that is why both Feyerabend and Shaikh Yusuf's propositions sound similar to Aristotle's description of wisdom as a combination of intuition and deliberation.[907]

Before hastily dismissing something as irrational or illogical, it is crucial to pause and examine our motives. Our *rational* line of logic can be deeply irrational, as demonstrated through numerous examples and research. Most of our understanding of *causes* is observed sequences of events that belong to a spectrum of exemplified instances. Thus, Russell pleaded to remove all notions of compulsion or force, which is much easier said than done, as we often confuse objectivity for subjectivity.[908] When intellectualizing, we become obsessed with theories and concepts, overlooking the subjectivity of *all reason* based on human perceptions. Our sense data only provides a massive amount of information without any objective guidance to the truth. Rational thinking, like mathematical proofs, can make even the most absurd statements convincing.[909] God compares such ignorance to the one who covers his ears at the sound of thunder to protect himself from lightning (*al-Baqarah* 2:19-20).

Numerous noteworthy scholars of the past have repeatedly demonstrated this flaw, as even Aristotle's *Metaphysics* is plagued with confidence that failed to withstand the test of time. Much of their commonly held beliefs sound mythical today—as mentioned earlier, but not limited to astronomy —raising the benefit of their study. It is humbling to read Aristotle's critique of the "modern philosophers and their predecessors" with the conclusion:

"But into the subtleties of the mythologists it is not worth our while to inquire seriously; those, however, who use the language of proof we must cross-examine and ask why, after all, things which consist of the same elements are, some of them, eternal in nature, while others perish."[910] Dr. Hawkins dove into this pitfall when attempting to contextualize the complexity of human consciousness. His belief in kinesiology defined his identity over time, which can be a downward spiral to intellectual incarceration. We can avoid it by basing our identities on our values rather than our beliefs. God provides us with timeless values for humanity that define our identity as Muslims. Our beliefs on how to translate those values reflect the fallible interpretation of God's message, which can change over time without jeopardizing our core principles. Otherwise, basing our identity on beliefs or interpretations can cause us to deviate from the core values of Islam in our misconstrued preservation of identity.

Humans, being rational animals, cease to be when acting irrationally. It serves one better to look at all knowledge as divine versus discovered. The former is known through revelation, while the latter represents all of our scientific theories and observations. They can also be described as external versus internal knowledge, where the latter encompasses all acquired knowledge that ultimately cannot be turned against the external. In the Qur'an, God makes this distinction by referring to one as the knowledge of the heart and the other as belonging to the mind. The latter is only praiseworthy when it increases the former in faith. The Qur'an's origin beyond our universe serves as the external objective sieve for all discovered knowledge. We can use God's gift of reason to explain His creations, but not to deny Him. Thus, 'Ali Ibn Abi Talib advised knowing the truth by its adherents, not the speaker. Today's overemphasis on secular education deprives one of this crucial framework and guidance.

As we discussed in the prologue, in our attempts to simplify education we have gradually broken it down into various categories, which we study individually and independently, without ever integrating them back into an ontological unity. The inevitable outcome is misdirected intellectuals on a *jihad* to free the world of divinity, which only invites the devil to fill the void. It can be argued that any opinion without a deep knowledge of Islam (in its broadest definition) is tantamount to compound ignorance. Without that external guidance, all internal derivatives may deviate from a clear purpose and lead to blasphemous alternatives. For example, revelation asserts the infallibility of God's messengers as all of their actions are divinely guided. If some acquired knowledge reports questionable recounts of some messengers, it would naturally reflect an error on the part of the reporter for whatever the motive may be. Deprived of such guidance, one may view all biased sources with equal footing to taint the characters of such noble men, leading to a corrupted image of God, which provides ammunition for cynics. Hence, a secular view is not as neutral as often mistakenly assumed, and it leads to severe errors in judgment, as evident in *realpolitik*.

> *The Prophet said: "At the end of time there will come a people young in years, foolish in minds, reciting the Qur'an which will not go beyond their throats, uttering sayings from the best of creatures, going through the religion as an arrow goes through the target." (Jami` at-Tirmidhi 2188)*

All acquired knowledge ultimately represents our subjective understanding of the world, whose fragility can be seen among those lacking some perception, such as hearing or eyesight. Yet, we are often unwilling to entertain the slightest variations of ideas, let alone contemplate those that may alter our perspective. It is a highly prevalent pathology known as *paradigm blindness*, which also becomes an obstacle to attaining spiritual truth. "If we are to arrive at pure spiritual truth, we must put away, for the time, knowledge which has been acquired by external processes and which too often hardens into dogmatic prejudice," urged al-Ghazali.[911] This concept was shown in a classic study in 1949, where subjects repeatedly failed to detect abnormalities that deviated from their prior knowledge.[912] Similarly, habituation of perception was demonstrated by Stratton in 1897, where subjects wearing inverting lenses soon adopted their vision to normal orientation.[913]

Our naive realism is, at best, subjective knowledge that is inherently incapable of reaching the level of divine knowledge through rationalization and logic. We must practice patience because historically discovered knowledge has evolved many times over, eventually conforming to the divine. All of our sciences are an ever-evolving process of trial and error, making any absolute faith in them more inconsistent than any accusations against a belief in a God who has been the same since the beginning. Immediately jumping on the bandwagon of discovery and renouncing divinity is extraordinarily shortsighted and demonstrates obstinance.

At the same time, given the availability of multiple scriptures, it behooves one to study their inherent and historical validity to follow the most accurate guidelines. The alternative is blind faith, which rarely leads to any favorable outcome. The nourishment of an entity is tied to its place of origin, its *home*, and its kin. Just as fire feeds on fire, water flows from itself. Our bodies, made of earthly elements, are similarly sustained by sources within our universe and returned to Earth after death. Likewise, our souls, originating from heaven, need their sustenance from ethereal sources. The Qur'an serves as this nourishment, which God describes as being *sent from above* (*Ya-Sin* 36:5). Its power has been noted by nearly all who study it deeply, resulting in a high level of scholarship since its revelation. Even the concept of a dictionary arrived from the early Islamic scholars' efforts to preserve the classical Arabic language. Through this connection to divinity, the soul is delighted and achieves peace, further aided by our proximity to those in service to God—whether a pious person or a contemplative walk through a forest.

When our attention is consumed by terrestrial matters, our souls become malnourished and demonstrate their cachexia through our overall malaise. "Liberating" ourselves by claiming freedom from the divine guidelines only creates a void with incessant failed attempts of replacements. It is evident in all such *liberals* through their rituals and devotional icons—whether it be sports, consumerism, or entertainment. "Don't you see that a madman has physicality but no discernment?" pleaded Rumi, "Discernment is that subtle concept that is inside you, but night and day you are occupied with nourishing that physical being indiscriminately."[914] If we constantly feed the steed of our physical bodies and our worldly desires, we imprison our souls from reaching their angelic statuses like Majnun and his camel. Thus, poet 'Urwa ibn Hazam said: "My camel's desire is behind me, while my own desire lies ahead: Truly she and I are at odds."[915]

In *Fihi ma fihi*, Rumi spoke about prophet Yusuf's friend giving him a mirror as the most befitting gift for the possessor of his beauty. Similarly, the most appropriate gift we can offer God from our sojourn in this world is a pious soul and a polished heart that reflects His magnificence.[916] That state is achieved through the practices prescribed by the Prophet, who served as a divinely trained physician for our souls. The remedies include prayer, where the *sujood* is twice as much as the *ruku'*, and the *fajr* prayer is half as long as the *dhuhr* prayer, among others. This prescription is not coincidental, but its significance is beyond the scope of any rationalization and can only be knowable through prophecy.[917]

The purpose of education is to plant seeds of curiosity and provide the mind with tools to think. A crucial part of any education system should then also teach and emphasize the ability to unlearn. Simply memorizing facts without learning the skills to process them is like shoving food down one's throat without ever learning to produce new products. When removed from the buffet, this person is doomed to starvation. Socrates challenged even the most common things to show how little we truly know and demonstrate the dangers of blind faith. Hence, most revolutionary theories in science came from young scientists who were not emotionally attached to the *status quo* and were sometimes outsiders to the field they transformed. Dalton reconfigured the entire atomic theory of chemistry from the questions he asked as a meteorologist.[918] His lack of preconceptions, unlike contemporary chemists trained in the field, allowed him to shuffle the available pieces of the puzzle innovatively. Still, the answers he developed at the very end of his career came from questions he never asked during his early years, contrary to the chronology portrayed in most textbooks.[919]

The suspension of critical thought is indeed the spiritual death of an individual. Although the ability to rethink is a crucial cognitive skill for survival in our turbulent world, *thinking* has significantly diminished in modernity. Most of our inputs—whether from the TV, internet, or streaming services—are presented in preformed packages where the thinking has already been done for us. The packaging is so effective that we are rarely aware of the manipulation that takes place. In the backdrop of all the arguments about God and destiny, an entire field of research and industry exists to predict and manipulate our opinions down a predetermined path. When prompted, we regurgitate that opinion and act accordingly without requiring any original thinking.[920] For those rejecting God, the resulting regretful thoughts are certainly promised to be a source of recurrent pain and anguish (al-'Imran 3:156).

Information is now considered the most valuable commodity, and as a result, large companies compete for our attention using any means necessary. We are constantly bombarded with propaganda and subliminal messages, both in our physical and virtual lives, to manipulate our every action. All the while, we flail around as satisfied puppets, thinking that we are exercising our polluted concepts of liberty. How we arrived here is quite riveting. In the early 20th century, Americans became increasingly paranoid about "brainwashing" due to the amount of propaganda being used to explain the world's hatred towards the US. It was also used to explain why some American soldiers turned against their own during the Philippines and Korean Wars. Although these soldiers often went rogue after realizing the immorality of the whole mess, the US's exceptionalist self-image made it unfathomable to admit or believe that the locals would voluntarily fight to defend against invaders. Ironically, the government sought help from the advertising industry to help counter-wash the natives from defending themselves in Vietnam.[921] When the massive amount of airdropped leaflets with coupons failed to achieve the desired effect, the soldiers played tapes of supposed Viet Cong ghosts agonizing in hell in their forests to scare the villagers to death.[922] History often outdoes most fictitious stories, which only attempt to take inspiration from it.

Psychologists now emphasize the importance of detachment from the world in achieving clarity, which was advised in many Prophetic narrations. "Be unattached to this world, and God will love you; and be unattached to what people possess, and they will love you," said the Prophet (*40 Hadith an-Nawawi*, #31). Emotional attachment to our beliefs inevitably leads to closed-mindedness, which prevents even the most aware individuals from transparency. Separating our opinions and beliefs from our identity allows us to evolve and change in a meaningful manner without feeling threatened. In our perpetual daily *war*—the Islamic greater *jihad*—the classic Taoist teaching comes alive, as "it is the unemotional, reserved, calm, detached warrior who wins, not the hothead seeking vengeance and not the ambitious seeker of fortune."[923]

Spoon-fed knowledge is ineffective, as the path to wisdom is a two-way street. The source of knowledge is as important as the attitude of the seeker. Unfortunately, we are gradually losing both the etiquette of teaching and learning, with an imbalanced top-down attribution of ignorance to a failed education system. Proper education is only obtained when an honest teacher guides a student through a path he seeks out for himself and climbs to his zenith. If the student lacks that hunger for knowledge, even the most experienced attempts would be fruitless. Education is a mutual process, similar to motivational interviewing; when done right, both the teacher and the student gain from it, as no one can ever reach the ceiling of change. True knowledge is liberating beyond any degree on a piece of paper, as demonstrated by Malcolm X, who learned the folly of knowledge without purpose during his early years in the prison library. We know many who can quote endless facts about sports statistics or other random events with no deeper purpose. Therefore, the Prophet advised us to ask God for beneficial knowledge and seek refuge from the rest (*Sunan Ibn Majah* 3843).

Knowledge gained from others represents a filtered version. Often there are more than just two sides to a story and the picture becomes clearer when the sources are eclectic. Just as diversifying one's portfolio secures material investments, diversifying the sources of knowledge secures our emotional investment, bringing us closer to truth and wisdom. Conformity and herd mentality only make us inherit others' biases and sheepishly repeat them. Developing a framework to evaluate knowledge is an exceptionally powerful tool. Al-Ghazali stressed in *Path to Sufism* (*al-Munqidh min al-Dalal*) the importance and permissibility of obtaining beneficial knowledge from *any* source—with the caveat of understanding the source's motivations. Al-Kindi also echoed the same, "For him who seeks the truth there is nothing of higher value than truth itself." It only becomes dangerous when we demonstrate borderline personality traits by either taking *everything* from an earthly source as the absolute truth or rejecting it *all* because of a particular dissent or disagreement. It is also injudicious and irresponsible to learn about one's physical and ideological enemies from his kin. The result is intellectual monolingualism: fluency in one tradition while being unaware of the existence of others.[924] To obtain the most accurate understanding, one must fight inner biases and actively listen to the other side's arguments from *their* scholars. Only then can we avoid becoming victims of group polarization.

When it comes to history, we only have limited insight to fully dissect why people repeatedly allow oppression, tyranny, and diversion from justice, even with the benefit of hindsight. Islamic ideals are first and foremost set on building an egalitarian society based on the virtues of peace and justice, as exemplified by the Prophet's development of his community in Medina.[925] His examples, such as leaving an elderly blind man in charge of the city when he left on a campaign, are unmatched. While others thereafter tried to recreate the same model, even with the best intentions, they inevitably failed due to internal corruption. Although optimism is at the core of Islam, realistically, this resembles the story of Sisyphus. Albeit under earthly conditions, even the latter's boulder and hill would eventually erode down to a pebble on a plain in a relative "minute" of eternity. A poem by Mirza Ghalib (1797-1869) comes to mind: "All your life, O Ghalib, you repeated the same mistake: your face was dirty, but you kept obsessively cleaning the mirror!"

The Prophet invested a significant time molding the characters of his companions, who then became instrumental in maintaining his community. Once that generation was gone, we immediately saw the lack of that *divine ingredient* in all those who followed, continually demonstrating their humanness through their shortcomings. Although there are periods when different fringes try to sway the ummah, the majority seems to have unmovable inertia, similar to a weak Prophetic tradition (*Sunan Ibn Majah* 3950). Sometimes this inertia almost appears to be a fault when the gradual corruption of religion and communities is tolerated without immediate action. Perhaps the lesson is that the best action is often inaction to avoid being reactionaries. Accordingly, the Prophet alluded to such a time of turmoil when the lesser act would be a preferable refuge (*Sahih Muslim* 2886a).

Dr. Yasir Qadhi advises a path of gradual pragmatism, which may provide the most balanced approach. For all the divisions and movements within the ummah, how can any be justified without Prophetic precedence or support for such extremes? "Indeed, in the Messenger of God you have an excellent example for whoever has hope in God and the Last Day, and remembers God often" (*al-Ahzab* 33:21). Unsurprisingly, we saw the rise of many fringe movements even in the early Islamic empire at its penumbra, resulting from a suboptimal understanding of the core message and values of Islam. The Kharijites, intending to "restore" Islamic ideals, failed to see the irony of deviating from God's mercy and the Prophetic tradition of tolerance. Their extremism led them to the cardinal sin of the murder of even those closest to the Prophet, while the majority failed to change the course of history. Seldom do we succeed in controlling the masses as even 'Ali and 'Aisha could not divert the bloodletting of thousands of pious souls at the Battle of the Camel from the conspirators on both sides.

An entire city of Kufa stood by as the family of the Prophet was brutally murdered and then crucified around town by Yazid Ibn Mu'awiya's army. Even though the later Abbasid rule chimed in the Islamic Golden Age, it was at the cost of the persecution of many. Their treatment of the Umayyads and the fissiparous bloodshed ocring their legacy could not have been further from the Prophet's teachings. Examples of this type of fanaticism can be seen on both sides of the religious-secular line, where even traditionalists like al-Ghazali decried his contemporary ulama's assertion that only their particular interpretation was the correct one.[926] In the heat of the argument, we all forget our humanness and become prone to intolerance, driven by the whispers of Satan fueling our egos. When we demonstrate such rigidity and fall shy of the tolerance evident in the Prophetic *sunnah*, we deprive others of God's mercy, which only serves to bring His displeasure unto us.

Interpretation (Arabic: اجتهاد ijtihād) ultimately defines religion, making the Islamic way of life vulnerable to exploitation, perhaps even more so due to its superior ideals. Setting aside the outside propaganda, Islam, at its core, promotes a peaceful, nonviolent, nonaggressive society: "God wants ease for you, not hardship" (*al-Baqarah* 2:185). This ideal society must respect its neighbors' sovereignty and promote antimilitarism while walking a thin line between strength and bellicosity. The problem is that any society that even comes close to these ideas becomes ripe for the picking by those experienced in imperialism. Few come close to these ideals, while most only compete in the struggle for power dominance. Even when various movements attempted to "restore" Islam, the lack of understanding was evident through their fanaticism, which was often rooted in cultural misconceptions. The Islamic *way of life* is primarily for individual salvation and must begin with a proper understanding and implementation *internally*. It is that selfish preference for what is best for one's salvation and the afterlife that we must seek the noble, selfless path in life, which was also how Aristotle understood ethics.[927]

Forceful *external* implementation of religion inevitably fails by deviating from the Islamic core principles of peace and tolerance. Thus, Imam Ṭāhir bin 'Āshūr (1879-1973 CE) stressed in *Revelation and Illumination* that God's prohibition of compulsion in faith (*al-Baqarah* 2:256) abrogates all rulings on religious fighting because of its assertiveness.[928] This lesson was not heeded by Muhammad Ibn Abd al-Wahhab (1703-92 CE) and his followers in Arabia, who committed senseless massacres in the name of Islam.[929] Their actions were exploited by the ambitious Muhammad Ibn Saud (1710-65 CE) and, several generations later, by his heir Abd al-Aziz's alliance with the shrewd British Empire.[930] A new Kingdom was ushered in with significant casualties, reimposing Wahabism in exchange for British access to their resources.[931]

Facilitated by the oil economy, Wahhabism spread like a grease fire through the Muslim world. However, fundamentalism is inherently a reactionary movement that cannot remain tied to power.[932] Thus, the Wahhabi-turned-Ikhwans soon found themselves at the receiving end of a massacre in 1929 by the same King they had empowered, who was now Westoxified and knighted by the Queen he served. "Whoever assists an oppressor, will one day be tested by that oppressor," warned Ibn Taymiyyah. This pattern continued, with the US entering the picture, when FDR and King Abdul Aziz formed a relationship on Valentine's Day 1945. As long as the US was given access to Saudi oil and Zionism, they could enjoy the backing of the American military-industrial complex and advanced weapons.

And when We let mankind taste of mercy after some adversity has afflicted them, behold! They take to plotting against Our Ayat [proofs, evidences, lessons, signs, revelations, etc.]! Say: "God is more Swift in planning!"

Certainly, Our Messengers [angels] record all of that which you plot. (Yunus 10:21)

The common misconception of the stagnation of Muslim intellect since Ibn Rushd is another myth perpetuated through the Occidental ignorance of all things thereafter. This is aided by the dense history of European warfare since the Islamic Golden Age, overshadowing the relatively uneventful and peaceful conditions in Muslim lands. Ironically, historian al-Mas'udi (896-956 CE) attributed the loss of the ancient Greek and Roman sciences to their adoption of Christianity, but today, the West projects a similar sentiment onto the Islamic world to conceal their exploits.[933] There were growing concerns among the traditionalists at the end of the 4th century AH about the political and general manipulation of *ijtihad* in corrupting Islamic values. From it emerged the *taqlid* movement, which preached a strict adherence to the deductions and interpretations of the 1st generation of jurists. "Needless to say, this was in direct opposition to the teachings of the early doctors of Islamic law and the founding fathers of the schools of jurisprudence," notes Professor Mumisa.[934] Much of the later criticism of the fossilization of Islamic thought can be attributed to the subsequent *taqlid* regimes and their inevitable countermovement of reform (*tajdīd* Arabic: تجديد) over the recent century.

For much of history, fundamentalists were not Muslims but Christians in a closed-minded Europe—arguably, they still are.[935] Once the battles were fought, Islam promoted peaceful civil societies focused on worship and egalitarianism—a concept foreign to those engaged in endless wars. The sleeping giant was eventually awakened by colonial exploitation, which unleashed political fervor worldwide. Jamal ad-Din al-Afghani (1838-97 CE) attempted to revive Islamic socio-political ideology in Egypt after witnessing British tyranny in India. He turned out to be one of the most influential figures of the century across the Muslim world. But power corrupts even the noblest of men, not divinely protected like the prophets and messengers. Although the *ulama* can aspire to be the inheritors of the prophets, they remain as fallible and humanly corruptible as the rest of us. Expertise in religious sciences does not make one a good politician, and vice versa.

For instance, Ghazi Amanatulla Khan (1892-1960 CE) was the first to successfully expel European colonialism in forming a sovereign nation of Afghanistan in 1919. Then the Deobandis from India overthrew him in 1929 with British help, resulting in the undoing of all of the decade's progress within a year. Sure, much of that secular progress was a misguided reaction to the prior centuries' stagnation. Still, the fundamentalism of the Deobandi's Wahabi roots caused destabilization and suffering of the masses that have yet to resolve. Therefore, all post-prophetic claims of "divine guidance" and absolute obedience should be approached with extreme caution, if not avoided altogether. The *ulama* are still crucial in our understanding of Islam, as its entire scientific breadth cannot be fully unpacked without a lifelong study. Unfortunately, many individuals undertaking such a long journey come out with a rigid worldview resulting from institutional traditions and unfamiliarity with a pluralistic environment. Deeply rooted cultures attributed to the *salaf* end up overshadowing the overwhelmingly tolerant Prophetic teachings, resulting in intellectual slump and encaged curiosity due to the fear of innovation (*bid'ah*, Arabic: بدعة).

Not all innovations are unsavory, and the doors to *ijtihad* are left open in divine wisdom for Islam to provide solutions to ever-changing times.[936] While such endeavors are best left to the scholars, it does not absolve the layman from pursuing his own religious education. A balanced approach with an individual pursuit of spirituality and knowledge with the guidance of pious *ulama* is key to the practical implementation of Islam. Hence, al-Afghani and Muhammad Abduh's Pan-Islamism—with the exclusion of the *ulama*—was doomed from the start. Abduh's reluctance to place secular power in the hands of the *ulama* was not unjustified, as history repeatedly demonstrates that those well-versed in religion are not necessarily good leaders. Moreover, it is a monumental task to unite all Muslims under the banner of Islam with today's global diversity. To localize this difficulty, the *Salafiyyah* movement under Sa'd Zaghlul (1859-1927 CE), Sayyid Rashid Rida (1865-1935 CE), and Sati al-Ḥusri (1880-1968 CE) became Pan-Arabism, which also was ill-fated for its exclusivity. Islam's success and strength have always been its unification under a raceless, colorblind ideal. Attempted division of Muslims for ease overlooking this key factor eventually fails without exception and aids its enemies in the process.

Inspired by al-Ghazali, Hasan al-Banna (1906-49 CE) appealed to the Muslim Brotherhood through social activism against colonial oppression, which quickly became enough of a threat to result in his assassination in 1949. It is surprising to see his ignored appeals to al-Azhar's *ulama* given their pivotal roles against nearly all unjust regimes of the past—including the French, the British, and Abd al-Nasser—often suffering heavily at the hands of tyrants like Napoleon. Perhaps it only reflected their maturity through prior experience. While revolution is not everyone's cup of tea, the inherent sociopolitical aspect of Islam makes it impossible for Muslims to remain utterly apolitical during oppression and injustice, as emphasized by Asghar Ali Engineer's (1939-2013 CE) liberation theology. Then what is the solution?

The Prophet said: "After me, there will be rulers: whoever enters upon them and condones their lies and supports them in their oppression, then he is not from me, and I am not from him. And he shall not drink with me from the Hawd." (Jami` at-Tirmidhi 2259)

We have witnessed failed theocracies where the command of God to not make religion difficult for the people was ignored. Secularism is also problematic as it creates room for injustice from a lack of divine oversight. Colonial rule was gradually expelled throughout the Islamic world only to be replaced by poorly planned, corrupt authoritarianism. Under the banners of monarchy, autocracy, democracy, and more, these regimes have only fueled further extremist movements out of desperation. The role of foreign powers in their asymmetric support for radical Islamic fundamentalism also cannot be overstated. The US, and Great Britain before it (among others), have significantly contributed to the rise of fringe groups in their efforts to destabilize and prevent national sovereignty from interfering with their foreign investments.

These betrayals often resulted in even their biggest supporters becoming their staunchest enemies, as portrayed by the life of the Puerto Rican nationalist, Dr. Pedro Albizu Campos (1891-1965 CE). Similarly, Sayyid Qutb (1906-66 CE), a contemporary activist halfway across the globe, was not wrong in his diagnosis of the West's "materialistic attitude" and "evil and fanatical racial discrimination," which rapidly spread through the Muslim world, dubbed "Westoxification."[937] The apolitical activism of the Muslim Brothers ended with Qutb's imprisonment, which turned him political. A decade of torture and confinement taught him that those who usurped the authority of God and caused oppression would not be changed merely through preaching.[938] While vehemently criticizing communism, his eventual solution in *Milestones (Ma'alam fi al-Tariq)* ironically paralleled Marxist ideology.[939] These issues typically arise at the far reaches of empires, where the rights of the inhabitants are neglected and remain unknown to those living routine lives on the mainland. While Qutb's ideas of an Islamic state were noble, they still overlooked the human factor. Perhaps his unity of "the realm of earth and the realm of heaven in one system" should be focused primarily at an individual level. Devoid of that self-annihilating aspect of Islam, we have gradually arrived at a world without a leader of a fractured ummah, and without a single country devoted to upholding the peace and justice that would make them Islamic.

The Prophet said: "A Muslim is he from whose hand and tongue the Muslims are safe" (*Sahih Muslim* 41). Today, we see some Muslims shedding Muslim blood while others rejoice at their misfortune without remorse or sparing them from their virtual tongues. The Prophet was asked about such a time, and his advice for us was to have a tenacious grip on the roots of Islam until death found us in that state (*Sunan Ibn Majah* 3979). Instead, we are witnessing various revolutionary movements, some even claiming to be Islamic, deviating drastically from the most basic principles of Islam. The resultant chaos is inevitable when some succeed in overthrowing one regime for another far worse, surrounded by the watchful eyes of the vulture elites.

And relate to them [O Prophet] the story of the one to whom We gave Our signs, but he abandoned them, so Satan took hold of him, and he became a deviant. If We had willed, We would have elevated him with Our signs, but he clung to this life—following his evil desires. His example is that of a dog: if you chase it away, it pants, and if you leave it, it [still] pants. This is the example of the people who deny Our signs. So narrate [to them] stories [of the past], so perhaps they will reflect. (al-A'raf 7:175-6)

Access to knowledge has never been easier in human history. One can become an expert on a topic within days from the comfort of his bed. This can potentially elevate us to the status of the companions of the Prophet, whose understanding of God's message was reflected through their actions both internally and externally. As the *ummah* spread exponentially from Medina, that understanding of Islam was diluted enough to allow Satan's predatory tactics to engulf us back into *jahiliyyah*. God warns us against such grave missteps of ignoring divine wisdom in pursuing our desires. Only by baptizing ourselves in that ocean of knowledge at an individual level can we truly come out of that darkness. It is only through its expression in our actions can we achieve a peaceful and just community. While our current access to knowledge is unprecedented, it can be dangerous without the necessary prerequisites and guidance for internalization. It is like plunging into an ocean without navigation, hoping to make it unharmed to the other side.

Not all knowledge is beneficial, as imagined through the Nazis winning the nuclear race during WWII. Arguably, that knowledge was not beneficial for the rest of the world either given its aftermath. Islamic scholarship recognized this fact and divided the pursuit of knowledge into two categories with the final goal of becoming a good citizen of the Kingdom of God. It gives the pursuit of knowledge a noble purpose. The knowledge of essential prerequisites is made obligatory for all (*fard 'ain*), while the knowledge of the higher levels is only obligatory upon the qualified, virtuous individuals (*fard kifayah*). Although the latter man may also be a good citizen, a good citizen may not necessarily be virtuous. Past scholars would refuse to take students who had not reached a certain level of wisdom through action due to the dangers of such knowledge in the wrong mind. It is similar to the prerequisite courses often required for higher-level learning at our universities today. However, the latter falls short of distinguishing between the characters of those pursuing advanced studies. Therefore, we see many learned individuals with nothing but misguided evil intent, using their knowledge and skills to spread corruption. For that power, they will indeed face more stringent accountability from God on the Day of Judgment.

The Prophet routinely sought God's refuge from knowledge that did not benefit, and we can see the wisdom behind it. Unfortunately, today, most of us actively seek barren knowledge while the truth remains buried in obscurity in plain sight. We must master the skill of unlearning and shedding deadweight in our pursuit if we are to remain afloat. God commands us to seek knowledge and contemplate his signs in the Qur'an, just as he commands us to pray, fast, and give *zakat*. Therefore, the Muslim mind must constantly be in search of knowledge like Imam Ahmad Ibn Hanbal, "with the ink-pot to the grave!"

HOLY TIME

By the [passage of] time! Surely humanity is in [grave] loss, except those who have faith, do good, and urge each other to the truth, and urge each other to perseverance. (al-'Asr 103:1-3)

Our discussions on history and life are inextricably linked to time, whose creation is so essential that our Creator swears by it. Its constant depletion is the only surety of our shared experience, serving as our test, our onus, and our reward on earth. As we exist because of it, we must die to be free from its constraints.

Since our first conscious existence, keeping track of time has become crucial, relying on the day and night cycles to calculate the months and the years. Perhaps Adam's initial lessons included this knowledge: "God decrees that there are twelve months—ordained in God's Book on the Day when He created the heavens and earth—four months of which are sacred: this is the correct calculation" (al-Tawbah 9:36). It is now evident that this applies only to earth's inhabitants and would be different had we been anywhere else in the universe. It highlights our planet's uniqueness in this vast universe, parallelling the classic anthropic principle.

The seven-day week likely originated from scripture as well, through the creation story of the universe. Sunday and Monday are named after ancient Babylonian sun and moon idols, which Emperor Constantine adopted into the Roman calendar in 321. The remaining days have an Anglo-Saxon origin from Teutonic mythology: Tuesday from Tiu or Tyr; Wednesday from Odin or Woden; Thursday from Thor; Friday from Frigga; and Saturday from Saturn.[940] Interestingly, the ancient Egyptians had a ten-day week based on a lunar cycle. One of their sundials from 1500 BC provides the earliest recorded day divided into twelve equal segments between sunrise and sunset, based on their duodecimal counting system. They also divided the night into twelve segments based on a complex astronomical system, resulting in a 24-hour day.

It is He who made the sun a shining radiance and the moon a light, determining phases for it so that you might know the number of years and how to calculate time. God did not create all these without a true purpose; He explains His signs to those who understand. (Yunus 10:5)

This measure of time as a function of *change* (of the sun or the moon) influenced many, such as Aristotle, in shaping their philosophy. Hipparchus further standardized it between 147 and 127 BC by dividing the entire day into 24 equinoctial segments to ease theoretical calculations. Most people continued to use the unequal system for daily functions until the popularization of mechanical clocks in the 14th century. Although Europe is credited for its invention, Caliph Harun al-Rashid's gifts to Charlemagne in 799 remarkably included a mechanical clock with twelve horsemen galloping out to announce the hour.[941] The exact origin of 60 minutes and seconds is unknown, but the sexagesimal system has been used since the early Sumerians from 2000 BC. In 1967, the second was redefined as the duration of 9,192,631,770 energy transitions of the cesium atom for ultimate precision. That only lasted a few decades until the theory of time dilation was experimentally proven: four cesium-beam clocks were taken on a flight around the world to demonstrate the variability of seconds, proving prior predictions of Einstein and Carl Sagan.

Einstein's theory, in particular, revolutionized our understanding of time by reinstating it as another dimension to our three-dimensional world, otherwise defined by length, width, and height. Since then, space has been determined by three coordinates plus time, which overwhelmingly constrains our imagination, making it difficult for us to envision existence in any other way. Even if we draw a dot on a piece of paper or a line to represent 0-D and 1-D, both would have three dimensions at a microscopic level. Moreover, none of the other dimensions are perceived outside of a moment in time. Our continued being and subjective reality are defined by the time we inhabit, much like fish in water. Without time, physical existence becomes unintelligible, while the other dimensions lose their value. Perhaps this is why the Prophet related time's duration with God and forbade cursing eternity (*Sahih Muslim* 2246).

Time is not simply "another dimension" but the central construct that guides everything around us. However, as a prominent physicist explains, our understanding of time is like holding a snowflake: it gradually melts away as you study it.[942] Looking at a night sky, for instance, reflects the past based on the time it takes for light to travel from its distant sources. Our perceptions also take some time to be sensed, relayed through our neurons, and finally interpreted by the brain, making our entire conscious existence a past event and blurring the lines of *present* reality. The concept of *true* time is a relatively recent invention derived from Newton's *Principia*, which turned out to be erroneous. Leibniz and others contested it and defended the traditional concept of time as an order of events. He was even said to have dropped the *t* from his name (Leibnitz) to emphasize his rejection of the absolute Newtonian time *t*.[943]

In Islam, it is generally understood that the six days mentioned in scripture (e.g., *Yunus* 10:3) for the creation of the heavens represent different stages rather than literal 24-hour days. This is evident from our astronomical observations, where the length of a day varies drastically based on the planet, solar system, and galaxy. For instance, a day on Saturn lasts 10 hours and 42 minutes, while on Mercury, it lasts 1407 hours and 30 minutes. A day essentially signifies the time between darkness, which can have many meanings in the creation context of this universe. Similarly, the creation of the heavens is not synonymous with our universe, as God mentions creating seven heavens, with only the lowest decorated with stars (*Fussilat* 41:12). Interestingly, the Prophet (in a weak narration) further characterized it as a *preserved canopy* whose *surge is restrained* (*Jami' at-Tirmidhi* Vol. 5, Book 44, Hadith 3298). Our universe with all the stars and galaxies only represents the lowest of these *heavens*, and the contents of the outer six will forever remain beyond our imagination.

Before we get carried away talking about the universe, it is worth reminding ourselves of the cold, hard fact that we barely know the contents of our solar system, the breadth of which makes it impossible for us to even represent it to scale. The vastness of our universe makes it appear neverending, as once assumed by Alexander Friedmann (1888-1925 CE) and supported by the works of Arno Penzias, Robert R Wilson, Robert Dicke, and Jim Peebles. It is estimated that if each planet represented a grain of sand, all of the sand on Earth would likely amount to the number of planets in our galaxy alone. Similarly, there are just as many galaxies in our universe containing an unimaginable number of stars—but still not to be confused for an *infinite universe* as was once believed by Newton. It gradually became evident that it is impossible to have an infinite static model of the universe where gravity remains a force of attraction.[944]

God declares, "[He is the One] Who created seven heavens, one above the other. You will never see any imperfection in the creation of the Most Compassionate. So look again: do you see any flaws? Then look again and again—your sight will return frustrated and weary" (*al-Mulk* 67:4). Although this apparent *infinity* makes it challenging to visualize the total seven layers of heaven, its finity ultimately makes it possible. The concept of Euclidean spacetime, where there is no difference between the time direction and directions in space, with *imaginary time* describes the universe as finite. It is similar to the surface of the earth, where one can sail on without ever coming to an end, which explains our universe's "endless" appearance. It also helps to visualize the additional six *heavens* as spheres similar to the layers of an onion or the orbitals of an atom. Any doubt regarding these seven layers should be buried with its kindred and accepted in faith as divine knowledge of the unseen. "God is the One Who created seven heavens [in layers], and likewise for the earth. The [divine] command descends between them so you may know that God is Most Capable of everything and that God certainly encompasses all things in knowledge" (*at-Talaq* 65:12). The emphasis here is on the revelation of the earth's seven layers to an unlettered Prophet in the 7th century.

Although enlightened philosophers scrutinized the Catholic Church's adaptation of an eternal Aristotelian universe, later recognition of a finite universe did not satisfy their successors either. Hawking, among others, used this discovery to further limit God's role in the affairs of the universe, going so far as even to question His place.[945] Perhaps even then the *place for the Creator* is to say, "'Be!' And it is!" (*al-Baqarah* 2:117). His acceptance of the possibility of the creation of the entire universe by an outside agency within which we reside makes any further denial or limitation of the Creator's power illogical. Linguistic philosophers like Moritz Schlick and Ludwig Wittgenstein would even argue that discussing *when* God created the universe is meaningless, as it cannot be proven through any human experience. The *instantaneous* creations of God are different from our relative spacetime, similar to the inflation theory. God declares, "We built the universe with [great] might, and We are certainly expanding [it]" (*adh-Dhariyat* 51:47). Edwin Hubble described the singularity as the universe being infinitesimally small and infinitely dense, which pretty much translates to *nothing*. As our physical parameters approach infinity at the singularity, it only signifies the infinite potential conveyed through even a simple *word* of God. Rejection of this sudden appearance of the universe as anything but an act of creation does not preclude a Creator but only places limits on our intellect.

Penzias famously remarked, "The best data we have are exactly what I would have predicted, had I nothing to go on but the five books of Moses, the Psalms, and the Bible as a whole."[946] Idolizing brilliant minds for theorizing the origin of the galaxies from clouds of gas after the Big Bang demands more admiration of the Qur'anic *ayats* like, "Then He turned to the sky, which was smoke—He said to it and the earth, 'Come into being, willingly or not,' and they said, 'We come willingly'" (*Fussilat* 41:11). The logical hypothesis based on chronology would then be Hawking's plagiarism of these Qur'anic answers provided a millennium ago, followed by an audacious attempt to take all the credit by dismissing God's existence. Interestingly, some of Hawking's more rational thoughts echoed Ibn

Rushd's *Tahfut al-Tahafut* (*Incoherence of the Incoherence*). Despite coming so close to the answer, some, like Edward P. Tyron, posit that our universe is a coincidence resulting from additional "failed attempts." Others, inspired by such "modesty," like Alan Guth, conclude that its creation is an unlikely event.[947] In *The Theory of Everything*, Hawking reiterated his beliefs nearly verbatim fourteen years later, showing no progress in his wisdom. While he demonstrated scientific knowledge, he was deluded by the infamy of many who lack the intuitive reason to achieve wisdom in the classic Aristotelian form.[948]

Their thought process correlates with the explanation of Nobelist Sir John Eccles, who described the brain as the receiver of the mind's existing energy patterns. The mind then becomes nothing but the thoughts of our souls with its various influences. We confuse them as our own in vain by ignoring the angelic and devilish whispers. "Genius, on the other hand, commonly attributes the source of creative leaps of awareness to that basis of all consciousness—which has traditionally been called divinity," explained Dr. Hawkins.[949] While the Big Bang ended Aristotle's eternal universe, it speaks volumes about those in the past who lost their faith by siding with his philosophies. Such blind faith in *logic* is yet another form of fundamentalism that was fought by the likes of al-Kindi.

Our misconceptions about time are also projected onto other time-dependent phenomena, such as free will, fate, and predetermination. Christian theologians struggled with these concepts for centuries, and the Nestorians then introduced this dilemma to the Mu'tazilites.[950] Ibn Sina's solution was through determinist ontology, "where every event in the created world is by itself contingent (*mumkim al-wujûd bi-dhâtihi*) yet also necessitated by something else (*wâjib al-wujûd bi-ghayrihi*)."[951] This provided a reasonable interpretation of God's predetermination, later adopted by Imam al-Ghazali. Ibn Taymiyya then related our *fitra* to predetermination in his epistle, stating: "Every child [is born] with what is known according to God's foreknowledge of what he is going to become [lit., that he goes to]."[952] In his other works, he described predetermination as more like divine guidance, writing: "Human beings [are created] with fiṭra, and they meet happiness and misery, which were ordained according to God's foreknowledge. That does not indicate that they are without a complete fiṭra at birth, [a fiṭra] which would have led to belief, were it not for the obstacle (that is, the conversion of newborns to Judaism and Christianity by their parents)."[953] This predetermination in the form of divine guidance is not arbitrary but ultimately follows our individual choices (*al-Baqarah* 2:26). It all hinges on our understanding of our universe and spacetime.

Locke attributed our sense of duration to our *reflection on the train of the ideas* we observe in succession—echoing the philosophy of Plotinus's Neoplatonist cosmology from the 3rd century.[954] He understood time as our perception of the sequence of events surrounding us. It helps us understand free will and its consequences as a direct result of time's manifestation through our successive individual choices. For beings without free will, there is no relative importance of time; nor can we practice free will without any available choices in frozen time, which would obviate the need for any accountability or an afterlife. Al-Raghib al-Isfahani, an 11th-century scholar, defined *qadar* and *taqdir* as "the making manifest of the measure of a thing" or simply "measure," signifying the divine laws that regulate and balance creation.[955] Perhaps this is a *measure* of time or *time* itself.

Most confusions and contradictions in this and similar curiosities arise from erroneous premises of the questions themselves, which assume God's existence in a similar spacetime as ours. Their historical roots lie in classical Greek and Persian philosophies that crept into early Islamic (and Christian) interpretations of *qadar* and *kasb*. Although remarkably brilliant for their time, they require reinvestigation as they predate our revised understanding of spacetime. *Predetermination* and *destiny* are concepts based on time, which is itself a creation of God. As we cannot conceive of an existence outside the bounds of time, we inevitably encounter logical fallacies when trying to reason on this path. Even the slightest errors in the premise can result in grossly incorrect answers, as seen before. The theological differences between the Mu'tazilites and Ash'aris regarding the sequence of events from God's will and human actions, as stated in Abū al-Ḥasan al-Ash'arī's treatise, dissolve when God's timeless realm is considered.[956] It further strengthens Ibn Taymiyya's assertion that divine knowledge does not equate to predetermination; instead, it is the divine will that is causative.[957] A striking example of free will and predetermination in the Qur'an was illustrated in real-time with the revelation of the surah *al-Masad*. In it, God condemns the Prophet's uncle Abu-Lahab (and his wife) for his outrageously persistent animosity towards His messenger. As one of the staunchest enemies, all he had to do to disprove revelation was to briefly accept Islam, resulting in his complete forgiveness per God's promise. Yet, they persisted in willfully fighting against Islam and fulfilling their destiny similar to the devil. Perhaps the devil also has until Israfil blows the horn to change his mind and repent, limited only by his anger and arrogance.

God refrains from telling us how the heavens were created, which is beyond human comprehension. Still, He asks us to wonder about His wonders (*Nuh* 71:15-16). Indeed, the Big Bang could be the *how*, but we must trust in

God's *why*. Hawking confessed to the lack of scientific evidence for many expert theories, which we only believe *on the grounds of modesty*.[958] Then why can't we believe in God on similar grounds? Does God not deserve more benefit of the doubt than a fellow man? At least physicist Gerald Schroeder seemed open to such possibilities.[959] All of our deductions about the beginning of time and the universe are based on our living experience with spacetime, which cannot be projected onto the Creator. If we cannot even contemplate a realm beyond spacetime or the singularity, how can we ever understand God? How can we explain that which precedes the existence of language and reason? Thus, the *void* we designate it with only reflects our knowledge of that infinity.

Time likely came into existence alongside the Big Bang, because an expanding universe requires its existence. As with all things that have a beginning, time must also end, which is why the discovery of an expanding universe in the 20th century solved many scientific debates. Suddenly, Kant's contradiction became baseless as his argument was presumed on *absolute time*. He paved the way for scientific materialism by undermining the logical syllogism of the Kalam cosmological argument by introducing skepticism in the universe having a beginning.[960] "Kant has the reputation of being the greatest of modern philosophers, but to my mind he was a mere misfortune," rebuked Russell.[961] This misfortune was shared by Newton in his *Principia Mathematica*. We forget that even scientists are people with common flaws and cognitive biases. Newton, among his oddities, once even inserted a needle into his orbit to see how far it would go before reaching the back wall. In his lesser-known works, he calculated the second coming of Christ to be in 1948.[962] Nevertheless, he conformed to Arianism and rejected the divinity of Jesus, concluding: "The revealed documents gave no support to the Trinitarian doctrines due to late falsification. The revealed God was one God."[963]

So we end up with a starting point/*event* for *time* itself within the spacetime paradigm directed toward the first light-cone of the absolute future. Any discussion of God or anything outside of this cone or preceding it would be irrelevant and impossible. Although this makes time seem like a vector, its directionality becomes ambiguous in a deeper study. For the sake of discussion, if we allow the physical definition of a vector, time must also have a magnitude and a direction. All living things exist at a specific point within this vector, facing their absolute future and their backs against their absolute past. Now imagine standing on a conveyor belt at an airport terminal, looking directly down at your feet—such is our existence at this moment in spacetime. We cannot see our future or past, and deduce a beginning and an eventual end but are uncertain about the exact when and where. We are the object in this uncertainty principle—unable to know our precise location in time or our momentum.

That uncertainty principle applies not only to electrons but to all aspects of our lives. As long as we are aware of our precise existence in the current spacetime, we cannot make any assumption about God with certainty without Him telling us through His messengers. Just as locating an electron changes its velocity, we cannot effectively change our future course without thoroughly studying where we are today and how we arrived here. The atoms that make us hold clues to the nature of God, as even electrons can be described as being simultaneously everywhere and nowhere. If that is what we have scientifically come to believe about the tiniest constituents of our universe, then what about the One who created it all? When asked how to envision an atom, Heisenberg himself replied, "Don't try."[964] Yet, we refuse to take God's word about Himself and try to envision him in various forms and idols. God asks: "Are they, then, seeking a religion other than that of God, while to Him alone submit all those in the heavens and the earth, willingly or unwilling, and to Him they shall be returned?" (*al-'Imran* 3:83).

The problem lies with our definition of *eternity* as an endless, infinite time. A better definition might be the absence of time (as we know) altogether. Death is somewhere in between that carries us to a different dimension with its separate spacetime cone, an existence unlike anything we have experienced in a parallel realm. Our fabric of time has already been shown to have measurable differences with varying dimensions. Special relativity proved the effect of gravity and speed on time, which makes physicists today refer to time more like a legion, differing in every point in space.[965] Where our souls go after departing our bodies is knowledge of the *unknown*. If the soul remains within our universe until the Day of Judgment, it will experience a spacetime continuum relative to the gravity of its realm. The perceived time to the end for all individuals living or dead would vary depending on their location in spacetime. This may be the variability implicated in: "When the trumpet is sounded and We gather the sinful, sightless, they will murmur to one another, 'You stayed only ten days [on earth]'—We know best what they say—but the more perceptive of them will say, 'Your stay [on earth] was only a single day'" (*Ta Ha* 20:102-4).

Hubble's description of the Big Bang implied a proportional increase in mass and its effect on time (based on $E=mc^2$) near a singularity. Beyond the Big Bang, we enter a realm where time (and space) may not exist. Without a time vector, concepts such as "beginning," "end," and any time-defined notions no longer hold. That causes the vector to suddenly collapse into a single dot or perhaps nothing we can describe. Suddenly, it is easy to appreciate the silliness of questions like: *Where did God come from?* Or *What was there before God?* as they are asked with time as a frame of reference. It is logically impossible to have a materialistic explanation beyond a point where matter no longer exists. Muhammad Asad (1900-92 CE) wrote, "What men conceive as time has no meaning with respect to God because He is timeless, without beginning and without end, so that 'in relation to Him A day and a thousand years are alike.'"[966] This understanding of God prevailed among Muslim scholarship centuries before our current theories of time.

If we imagine our experiences as suspended video footage along that time vector, jumping out of the bounds of time makes all of those moments collapse into a single point or tableaux. Suddenly, everything appears superimposed in front of us, with their timestamps. From here, we can see what any being is currently doing, ever did, or will do without really affecting their actions. Even that notion of seeing their entire life having any effect on their free will would be a silly one—although it could if an Omnipotent being willed. Thus, the concepts of free will and destiny come together in harmony without contradiction. "In the space-less realm of light of God, the past, present, and future do not exist," said Rumi in *Masnavi*. "Past and future are two things only in relation to you; in reality they are one. Thy thought is about the past, and future; when it gets rid of these two, the difficulty will be solved."[967]

"People like us who believe in physics know that the distinction between past, present and future is only a stubbornly persistent illusion," echoed Einstein.[968] That is not to support either eternalism or presentism, but to provide perspective to how a billions of years old universe could be seen as a *six-day* event, as well as our entire evolutionary process as a "blink of an eye" (*al-Qamar* 54:50). Even the criticism of the Qur'an's nonlinearity becomes evidence for its eternal divine source. Scientists had to wait for today's advanced computers to decipher the hidden patterns within previously deemed *incoherent* cosmological data. These patterns were predicted and confirmed by nonlinear mathematical equations explaining various "random" natural phenomena. Most natural processes owe their beauty and richness to nonlinearity, which mathematicians avoided for a long time due to their complexity.[969] Sofia Kovalevskaya (1850-91 CE) was one of the few willing to tackle the spinning top problem, which showed the unpredictability of determinism. Henri Poincare called this *chaos*, which is still rather deterministic in the short run. Their extreme sensitivity to small changes only gives them the appearance of "randomness" to imperceptive observers.

Entities that exist outside of time constraints would not only be able to see all of existence (with God's permission) but also discern the patterns within the nonlinear *randomness*. Hence, the angels immediately saw upon Adam's introduction the mischiefs his offspring would cause, even before Adam and Eve were sent down to earth (*al-Baqarah* 2:30). Our soul's origin in that eternal/timeless realm keeps our material existence connected to it. Some can temporally achieve a state of timelessness through God-consciousness (Arabic: تقوى *taqwā*), whereby a sense of *presence* is reached. The prophets attained this level of connection by exchanging their corporeal and spiritual humanity for *angelicity*, which enabled them even to receive revelations from that timeless realm in a flash.[970]

Time's variability extends beyond the spiritual realm into the physical, where it passes faster in the mountains than at sea level.[971] It is often illustrated by the twin paradox, where one twin traveling in a spaceship would age less than the earthbound sibling after a few decades due to the effect of gravity on spacetime. Despite this difference, both twins would perceive time similarly since the laws of physics would *feel* unchanged to both. This raises the dilemma of "real-time," which ultimately is inconsequential, as we are more concerned with time as a vector than its duration. What matters most to us are our past and future, cause and effect, pain and suffering, and so on.

St. Augustine concluded in Book XI of the *Confessions* that "it is within my mind that I measure time. I must not allow my mind to insist that time is something objective." This notion was deemed heretical by the bishop of Paris, Etienne Tempier, in 1277. Vierordt's law highlights this memory aspect of time in perception. Since the only measurable truth to our existence is the present, our concept of time is ultimately brought to life by our memories, which provide a direction based on past experiences. Time means something different to each of us, even if it measures the same on a conventional scale. We may sit next to each other, yet perceive a different experience of time. While this may sound brilliant today, it was laughed at by the Quraysh upon learning about the Prophet's journey to Jerusalem, then up through the heavens, and back in a single night. The only laughable matter, it seems, is our confidence in our knowledge of spacetime.

Gravity has a more significant impact on time with denser objects. Larger masses slow down time around them more than smaller ones based on the structure of the spacetime fabric they occupy. This is why the Earth slows down time more at sea level than in the mountains. It would have been even more prominent at the Big Bang, which is similar to the singularities we now associate with black holes. Hawking explained it through the scenario of an *intrepid astronaut* on a collapsing star sending a signal back to his orbiting spaceship every second. As the star approaches the critical radius, each subsequent signal takes exponentially longer to arrive at the spaceship until the gravitational field becomes too strong for any subsequent signal to escape.[972]

Suppose we were to reverse the signal being sent every second from the spaceship down to the fearless astronaut. As the gravitational field around the astronaut became stronger, each successive signal would arrive quicker. Among the signs of the end of time foretold by the Prophet was time passing quickly, an overall decrease in true knowledge, and an increase in miserliness and bloodshed *(Sunan Ibn Majah* 4052). The passage of time here may be a matter of perspective, as noted by Vierordt's law, or it may relate to the effect of a stronger gravitational field on time itself. Due to our leaky atmosphere, the Earth is getting slimmer with time, along with its gravitational pull.[973] This makes the latter scenario only possible through the Earth's overall proximity to an even larger mass, which would certainly lead to the death kiss for humanity.

To add to the confusion, time is also affected by an observer's speed. Using Maxwell's equation for electricity and magnetism, Einstein calculated that a moving object experiences a shorter time duration than a stationary object. Meaning that time contracts for objects in motion, for whom time passes more slowly. Such individuals would age less, their watches would mark less duration of time, their plants would take longer to germinate, and they would ultimately have less time to think.[974] This theory was demonstrated in the 1970s using advanced watches on airplanes, as mentioned earlier.[975] Therefore, time is a highly subjective phenomenon that depends on a specific individual, at a specific point in spacetime, and at a specific speed, which loses meaning for any other observer or location. Then what do past, present, and future even mean? "The Truth of the matter is that we need to give up asking the question," confessed Rovelli, because it is all an illusion and "an illegitimate extrapolation of our own experience."[976] Thus, the concept of the present time starts to disappear in the world of theoretical physics, although that is all that matters to us individually.

We are now aware of the giant black holes at the center of every galaxy that holds it together, called quasars. Perhaps our end may come from the adduction of the arms of our Milky Way to its nucleus. The laws of physics we are used to are based on our current location in spacetime. Although these laws would remain the same in principle even if we gradually moved closer to a black hole, their manifestation under such a strong gravitational force would be unlike anything we are accustomed to. It would be as jarring as seeing a night sky with multiple moons, which Saturn has over eighty. Being in such proximity to an event horizon would distort our spacetime fabric in ways to open the sky up to various portals, as mentioned in the Qur'an. "A Day when the Trumpet will sound and you will come forward in crowds, when the sky is opened and becomes wide portals" (*an-Naba* 78:18-9). Maybe through those portals, all the Angels would come down to carry out their orders.

The Day that We roll up the heavens like a scroll rolled up for books [completed] —even as We produced the first creation, so shall We produce a new one: a promise We have undertaken: truly shall We fulfill it. (al-Anbiya' 21:104)

Earth's gravity anchors our feet to the ground and keeps us from drifting into space. But what if a more powerful force, like a black hole or a massive planet, were to override it? The combined arithmetic would sweep us off our feet before the collision. Eventually, our mighty sun would cool down according to the natural process of its hydrogen and helium fusions as God promised: "When the sun is put out" (*at-Takwir* 81:1), turning into a red-giant like "molten brass" (*al-Ma'arij* 70:8), consuming everything in its path, including earth.[977] "When the sun and the moon are brought together" (*al-Qiyamah* 75:9), the enlarging gravity and heat will cause the oceans to "swell/flare-up" (*at-Tur* 52:6). Other merging galaxies would result in intergalactic space appearing as if "the sky is stripped away" (*at-Takwir* 81:11). While today's astronomers estimate such events to be billions of years into the future, nothing really can stop its acceleration if willed by the same creator who made it all appear from nothing.

Similarly, the mountains and rivers pinning the earth's crust would float away under the influence of a stronger external gravitational pull. "What will make you realize what the Crashing Blow is? On a Day when people will be like scattered moths and the mountains like tufts of wool, the one whose good deeds are heavy on the scales will have a pleasant life, but the one whose good deeds are light will have the Bottomless Pit for his home—what will explain to you what that is?—a blazing fire" (*al-Qari'ah* 101:3-11). If that defines our end, the resulting colliding masses will form an expansion large enough to accommodate the resurrection of all of humankind. Its environment would be extremely violent, similar to that we see near an event horizon. "One Day—when the earth is turned into another earth, the heavens into another heaven, and people all appear before God, the One, the Overpowering" (*Ibrahim* 14:48). And the *time* of that expansion would feel like nothing we have experienced before.

God's creation of time frees Him from its bounds, which is highlighted by various *ayats* like: "They will challenge you [Prophet] to hasten the punishment. God will not fail in His promise—a Day with your Lord is like a thousand years by your reckoning" (*al-Hajj* 22:47). We cannot understand His magnificent existence and are better to refrain from such questions for their lack of benefit. Otherwise, it can be a source of heartache for many causing them to leave the faith. That submission can be a blessing of peace, similar to one of the fundamental creeds of *Ahl al-Sunnah wal Jamā'ah* (in *Al-Aqeeda Al-Tahawiyah* by Imam Tahawi (853-933 CE)). Our purpose is to exist in our gifted time. The *why* is beyond our understanding regardless of how we feel about it. The *how* we can surmise from our sciences. We are tested with allotted time and accountability at the end followed by a grand prize. Without accountability, none of it makes sense nor is it relevant. Heaven and hell may also be in a realm outside of time, which makes it nearly impossible for us to understand *eternity*. For some, the idea of an eternal afterlife is difficult to fathom and "silly." They wonder how it is possible to live forever without experiencing hunger, fatigue, or boredom. Yet, the same people pursue similar heavenly conditions in their temporal earthly lives. "As for those who do not believe in the Hereafter, We have certainly made their [evil] deeds appealing to them, so they wander blindly" (*an-Naml* 27:4).

The entire concept of causality disappears in a realm without time. Eternity, as an absence of time, eliminates all time-dependent bodily needs and pains. In such a place, it is existence, unlike anything we have experienced where everything simply *is*. We can compare that noumenal world to our sleeping state. "God takes the souls of the dead and the souls of the living while they sleep—He keeps hold of those whose death He has ordained and sends the others back until their appointed time—there truly are signs in this for those who reflect" (*az-Zumar* 39:42). During sleep, our physical bodies remain within the earth's spacetime fabric, but our souls enter an ethereal realm. Sometimes we have long, elaborate dreams only to wake up to realize that we have merely dozed off for a few minutes. Our experiences in this dissociative extracorporeal state are so vivid that we may wake up in fright or with a lingering smile. In our dreams, we get a glimpse of the limitless possibilities of heaven, where all we have to do is think of a thing, and voilà! Instantaneously we are flying or eating the pheasant that flies by. Also, the terrors we experience can seem never-ending, only ceased by God's merciful awakening.

On the Day the Hour comes, the guilty will swear they lingered [on earth or in the grave] no more than an hour—they have always been deluded—but those endowed with knowledge and faith will say, "In accordance with God's decree, you actually lingered till the Day of Resurrection: this is the Day of Resurrection, yet you did not know." (ar-Rum 30:55-56)

The unimaginable complexity of our universe always hanging over our fragmented theories to explain different aspects of the entire picture is like the blind men describing al-Ghazali's elephant. The caveat of these discussions is demonstrated in Hawking's "Arrow of Time," where he deviated drastically from logic. In physics, the only directionality of time is observed in the thermodynamic principle: heat cannot pass from a cold body to a hot body. It was noted by Sadi Carnot (1796-1832 CE), the grandfather of the former President of France—both of whom were interestingly named after the Persian poet Saadi Shirazi. In contrast to heat, for instance, a falling ball can rebound back up. It led Rudolf Clausius (1822-88 CE) to derive *entropy*, later forming the second law of thermodynamics, which hides an entire world within its simple equation ($\Delta S \geq 0$). This characteristic of heat is the *only* observable law of physics that differentiates the past from the future, which Hawking refers to as the thermodynamic arrow of time.[978]

Hawking's attempt to break the arrow of time into a thermodynamic component—along with the proposed psychological and cosmological arrows of time—is flawed. His example of a box of puzzle pieces with only one orderly state (where the pieces fit) compared to many disorderly states ignores Newton's first law, where the box would remain unchanged without outside interference (i.e., someone shaking the box). Time would not point to an increased entropy without external energy. Just as energy is needed to create order, it is also needed to create disorder. The thermodynamic arrow of time (i.e., entropy) would cease to exist without outside interference, while the psychological and cosmological components would remain unchanged. They may even change direction if an outside force who had created its laws in the first place willed.

And when it is said to them, "Do not spread disorder on the earth", they say, "We are nothing but reformers." Beware, it is, in fact, they who spread disorder, but they are not aware. And when it is said to them, "Believe as people have believed," they say, "Shall we believe as fools believe?" Beware, it is, in fact, they who are the fools, but they do not know. (al-Baqarah 2:11-3)

Another commonly cited example is gas particles of different temperatures or pressures moving to equilibrium in a closed compartment, resembling Feynman's sum-over-histories. Yet, if the particles were stationary (e.g., at absolute zero temperature), there would be no increase in entropy over time. Entropy itself is not the law of the universe but rather a consequence of a change in the energy state of an environment, which still maintains conservation law. Similarly, Murphy's law is just a theory that manifests only in the presence of an *external force*. The more logical observation is that the universe is set on a baseline level of order, which is only made disorderly when acted upon. Hawking himself confessed to the statistical nature of entropy, citing the example of black holes, which is also rather presumptuous of our knowledge beyond the event horizon.[979]

The Austrian physicist Ludwig Boltzmann (1844-1906 CE) was closer to the truth in concluding that entropy only exists when we look at the world in a *blurred* manner. Meaning that the initial *order* we perceive is just one of many particular ways of observing our surroundings. If we consider all the infinitely other ways things can be ordered, we would see no overall change in entropy. Considering all the microscopic details of the universe, even this thermodynamic characteristic of time differentiating between past and future becomes blurry.[980] Hence, the previously assumed "thermodynamic time" lacks direction and is simply a phenomenon.

Our framing of these natural phenomena in a skewed manner has real-life implications, as seen with Darwinism. While questioning the disorder that consumes our world, *entropy* excuses us from the individual choices we make as solitary human particles colliding with other humans throughout our lives. Thus, God commands: "...and do not go about the earth spreading disorder" (*Hud* 11:85). While we can make our interactions orderly, acting unjustly results in an unequal transfer of energy, with one side gaining more from the interaction. Conservation of resources is neglected when the top 1% own more than half the world's wealth. All of it creates a chain reaction or ripples in our spacetime fabric, resulting in more disorder and chaos, which is still deterministic. Instead of taking responsibility for our actions at an individual level that caused this chaos in the first place, we take the easier route by blaming the entire system and calling it the *law of thermodynamics*. It is as if we are reverting to a fatalistic view of determinism rather than taking control of our fates, as Ibn Taymiyya and Ibn Qayyim al-Jawziyya had advised.

Similarly, rewriting our history as a product of only environmental factors tries to vindicate us of the ghastly individual choices made in the past. We are a product of our history, birth, environment, knowledge, choices, resources, and beliefs expressed through our free will. For instance, Charles Savage's savagery in the Fiji Islands in 1808 demonstrated his free will, not merely a display of superior weaponry. Such deviation from logic conveniently buries the truth and leads to more illogical questions like: why would God even allow such disorder to occur? Well, if He did not, there would be no such thing as *free will*, and we would all be angels. Thus, some historians argue that it was not simply superior technology and numbers but a willingness to massacre entire nations to claim their resources that dominated the recent success of the West.[981]

God commands, "Do not spread corruption in the land after it has been set in order" (*al-A'raf* 7:56). The latter portion of the *ayat* highlights God as the ultimate source of order, and our role is simply to avoid disrupting it. Thus, entropy is an act of our free will. Debates on solving global problems such as climate change, poverty, and wars focus on human solutions, which fail to produce any meaningful change to the cascading chaos. With arrogance and false pride, some individuals deny God's existence and assume control, trying to fix it but failing miserably and causing more harm. While the prophets and sages of the past sacrificed selflessly for individual salvation, today's leaders do not hesitate to sacrifice individuals for some "greater good." If we focused on just stopping all present actions that spread corruption and disorder, with God's endless Mercy, perhaps the problems would naturally solve themselves. It is suggested by the rest of the aforementioned *ayat*: "And call upon Him with hope and fear. Indeed, God's mercy is always close to the good-doers" (*al-A'raf* 7:56).

Even simply listening to each other without judgment can achieve more than our best plans, as demonstrated through Betty Bigombe's interactions with Joseph Kony. God provided us with twice the amount of ears than tongues to encourage us to become better listeners. However, most of us listen only to reply, not to understand. Those who had the fortune of interacting with the Prophet unanimously praised his charisma and intense listening skills. This book can also be criticized as yet another "righting reflex" of our desire to fix and provide answers. Perhaps what is better to avoid with speech can be sidetracked in writing, as we have ten times more fingers. Underneath it all lies a shared empathy and concern for humanity, which is ultimately the force that moves mountains. In all of our endeavors lie critical choices of determining what is essential and what is ignorable, with the danger of falling into intellectual dishonesty. Our disputes often arise from failing to see beyond the world of phenomena and mistaking servants of the lowest rank for the king. Although the laws of phenomena are constant for science, they remain slaves to their true Master.[982]

What is time and entropy but another illusion of relativity and perception? Even the marvelous planetary orbits are objects traveling straight in curved spacetime. It is all a matter of perspective at the end of the day. Looking down on an ant colony may appear disorderly, but a deeper observation would reveal the purpose of every movement. My wife describes my office as entropic, while for me everything is in its due place. To the astronaut at the space station looking down, all the individual human movements down on Earth may also look random and disorderly. However, down here, we would argue otherwise. What we perceive as a disorder only indicates our lack of understanding of the order in plane view. The chaos then remains in the mind of the beholder.

The life of this world is merely an amusement and a diversion; the true life is in the Hereafter, if only they knew. (al-'Ankabut 29:64)

THE QUARKS THAT MAKE US

[He is the One] Who has made the earth a place of settlement for you and the sky a canopy; and sends down rain from the sky, causing fruits to grow as a provision for you. So do not knowingly set up equals to God [in worship]. (al-Baqarah 2:22)

Humanity's observation of the physical world and cosmos has long provoked contemplation about the existence of a Creator and our purpose. Theological discussions inevitably lead to metaphysical inquiries, which can raise apparent dilemmas that remain unsolved due to the limited overlap between these fields. The vast amount of available information makes it challenging for anyone to be a polymath like in the old times. Nevertheless, modern Western neo-*religion* includes non-denominational entities such as secularism, science, and quantum theory with their existential push against divinity. Here we will present some insights into topics that may offer some resolution to these curiosities.

First, there is a caveat of reading too much into the ambiguous Qur'anic *ayats* and *ahadeeth*. The natural process of *hadith* transmission often resulted in the availability of versions from different narrators, whose main goal was to relay the gist of the message with slight variations in the exact wording of the Prophet. Most Arabic words have a range of projected meanings and cannot be translated without losing some of their essence. Ultimately, the purpose of the Qur'an and *sunnah* is not to educate us in history and science but to spiritually guide humanity in morality and action. These discussions are done only to increase our faith but can never be used to counter God: "It is God who has sent this Scripture down to you [Prophet]. Some of its *ayats* are definite in meaning—these are the cornerstone of the Scripture—and others are ambiguous. The perverse at heart eagerly pursue the ambiguities in their attempt to make trouble and to pin down a specific meaning of their own: only God knows the true meaning. Those firmly grounded in knowledge say, 'We believe in it: it is all from our Lord'—only those with real perception will take heed" (al-'Imran 3:7).

For most of human history, scholars were both scientists and philosopher-theologians. It was not until the European Enlightenment that they began to separate due to the adversarial stance of the Catholic Church against rapid scientific advancements. As science became more technical and mathematical, it became difficult for theologians and philosophers to keep up and explain the *why*. By the 20th century, philosophers "reduced the scope of their inquiries so much that Wittgenstein, the most famous philosopher of this century, said, 'The sole remaining task for philosophy is the analysis of language.' What a comedown from the great tradition of philosophy from Aristotle to Kant," criticized Hawking.[983]

It is not as much of a *comedown* when one analyzes the impact language has in the current world compared to theoretical physics. Words now defy gravity and rise to the clouds, traveling faster than light around the world, pushing to redefine the laws of the universe and its fundamental truths. It led some recent scientists to pick up the reins in their attempts to bring philosophy back into science, which inevitably takes an atheistic turn given their cognitive biases. By challenging God's existence, scientific materialists widen the schism between Hume's differentiation between *ought* versus *is*. Science aims at explaining what *is*, without any supernatural appeal of what *ought* to be. The atheistic intellectual dismissal of the supernatural only opens the door to limitless immorality left at the discretion of the individual.

Gravity was likely Adam's first impression on Earth, which Newton described in *Principia Mathematica* as an attractive force between two masses, inversely proportional to their distance. Einstein clarified by calling it a consequence of masses moving straight in a curved spacetime caused by an uneven mass distribution. Hawking then gave it negative energy with respect to conservation, as it requires energy to move two masses away from their gravitational attraction. While this force was manifest to many planted on earth since Adam, Newton formulated the mathematical relationship of this attraction. He achieved that quandary by solving the mathematics of a curve through his most notable invention, calculus. This new field of mathematics took its name from the pebbles ancients once used for counting. Coincidently, both fathers of modern calculus—Newton and Leibniz—in the end suffered tremendously from fatal bladder and renal calculi.[984]

Russell reminds us that physics is mathematical not because we know so much about the physical world, but because we know so little.[985] It is only through discovering its mathematical properties that we can appreciate it. While we have made great strides in understanding the universe through equations like $F = G\frac{m1m2}{r2}$, we have yet to fully grasp the true nature of gravity. In fact, Newton's refusal to define gravity irritated Leibniz so much that he accused Newton of giving "refuge to ignorance and laziness by means of an irrational system which maintains not only that there are qualities which we do not understand—of which there are only too many—but further that there are some which could not be comprehended by the greatest intellect if God gave it every possible opportunity."[986] Although this force applies to *every* mass in the universe, we still struggle to comprehend how it manifests qualitatively between two people, getting weaker with distance. How would that *attraction* feel emotionally as we bridged the gap between us? If this force is inherent to every *body*, is it related to its *essence*? How would gravity then relate to our souls, both belonging to the *unseen* world?

Gravitational pull appears to act through invisible "strings" of the spacetime fabric, causing it to distort accordingly. This results in an intricate relationship between time and gravity, as all *bodies* slow down time around them proportional to their masses, causing lighter objects to *fall* into them. In interplanetary space where time is uniform, objects float instead of falling. Essentially, two masses interact by each gravitating towards a slower spacetime—just as time appears to slow down when one is with the beloved. Our feet adhere to the ground when we walk because time passes slower at our feet than at our heads.[987] Perhaps this helps us to think faster than moving to action, as all things constantly gravitating to a slower spacetime metaphorically remind us to be more *present* in the moment. Suddenly, phrases like "out of sight, out of mind" and "tree-hugger" take on new meanings.

While philosophy evaluates our scientific knowledge, religious interpretation of the entire thing is also critical, particularly for Muslims. Our covenant with God demands an upward path against gravity and our natural animalistic disposition. While our conscious lives are spent materially bound to earth, our initial development takes place in a floating state of the amniotic fluid. We find comfort in reverting to that state of weightlessness, away from the stresses of the material world that drag us down. Physically, we imitate it through zero-gravity beds, while spiritually, we seek it by detaching ourselves and our egos from all terrestrial attachments. That intrauterine state of unity with our mothers only mimics our soul's unity with its creator, leading our *fitra* to seek it during our earthly lives. Contemporary psychologists believe that subconscious "oneness" permeates our adult interactions and expressions of love. By harmonizing with others, we manifest a force of attraction that recreates the magical *feeling of omnipotence, as if all things are possible.*[988] This feeling of love may just be a manifestation of the gravitational force of attraction that is also innate to us, like our *fitra*.

He has the keys to the unseen: no one knows them but Him. He knows all that is in the land and sea. No leaf falls without His knowledge, nor is there a single grain in the darkness of the earth, or anything, fresh or withered, that is not written in a clear Record. (al-An'am 6:59)

Just when we start to understand gravity, quantum mechanics reshuffles the deck with its complexity. At the quantum level, gravity is just one of many forces grouped into four categories according to their strengths: gravitational, electromagnetic, weak, and strong nuclear forces. Gravity is unique in its *attraction* and prevalence over long distances. Sometimes it is described as matter particles being affected by *spin-2 particles*, also known as gravitons with no inherent mass, allowing them to be carried out over a long range. The gravitational attraction between two masses is then pictured as the virtual exchange of gravitons between these masses behaving like waves.

How would these exchanging gravitons feel between perceptive creations like ourselves? When we touch an object, the nerve endings at the end of our fingers fire signals that, combined with our other senses, create an emotional and physical response. Similarly, gravitons must have some effect on our sensory receptors. While detecting such a weak force would be nearly impossible, the quantum theory argues against excluding such a possibility. Just as our existence within the gravitational sea makes us unaware of its effects, our soul's residence within the body makes us neglect their separate identities. Nevertheless, our organic senses can directly affect our soul's connection to the metaphysical. While physics is our best attempt to understand our surroundings, devoid of a unified theory of the universe, we remain in the dark about the true nature of the things we define.

In light of our current discussion, classic texts start taking a new life. What if the force of gravity is simply an aspect of pure souls moving and exerting their willpower on others? Al-Ghazali suggested that an exceptionally spiritual soul's power over the body may even extend to other bodies, helping them recover from an illness, or that their remembrance of a person may manifest into a spontaneous visit. A pious soul's connection to the unseen world may even allow its possessor to achieve intuitive learning that others pursue laboriously.[989] The well-documented placebo effect may also be the manifestation of the soul's faculty over the body. The possibilities are limitless and only relative to one's level of consciousness.

Einstein's theory of relativity described planets as moving in a straight line to their nearest destination in a curved spacetime, which gives the appearance of an orbit to a faraway observer. Relatively speaking, time is not a linear phenomenon but a stacked collection of events, similar to how motion pictures are made from stacked images. It further roils our concept of *force* and *causality*, as discussed briefly earlier. What appears to us as a sequence or causality is a subjective interpretation of our perception relative to our location and should not be confused with compulsion or force.[990] Meaning that the recently described gravitation "strings" that the sun presumably uses to rotate the planets around are also illusions of perspective, according to Einstein.

The theory of relativity breaks apart all notions of scientific causality that we infer in our logical, secular thought process. We are thrown back to God's mercy regardless of our feelings. Our understanding of all forces is based on sensory inputs on earth, and to describe heavenly bodies similarly is an anthropomorphic misconception. Causality may only be our perceived understanding of the succession of events through spacetime, which varies from differing perspectives. For example, bees see the world in the UV spectrum, and snakes "hear" by sensing vibrations. Their worldview based on their senses would be relatively different from ours, just as ours would be from the actual *reality* of things. No matter how advanced we become, we will never be truly logical. Then where do we go from here without the absolutism of God? What appears to us as gravity or any described *force* is rather successive changes of the position of matter taking the easiest path through a non-linear spacetime, perhaps to fulfill God's command: "We will ease his way towards ease" (*al-Layl* 92:7). Then, through the reversibility of causal laws, what else explains everything but simply as acts of God and his simple decree of "Be!"? Interestingly, a similar deconstruction of causality was also proposed through the conversation between Krishna and Prince Arjuna in Bhagavad Gita (Ch. 3).

Beginning with Aristotle's four earthly elements, we have gradually uncovered more elemental particles such as atoms and their constituents. Recent technological advancements have allowed us to build powerful particle accelerators at ever-smaller wavelengths of energy, leading to the discovery of even more elemental forms like bosons and quarks. Over 200 subatomic particles have been identified without a complete understanding of their roles in the universe. For pragmatists such as Ernst Mach and Quine, these unobservable posits may "have no greater epistemological footing than 'Homer's gods.'"[991] Such extreme pragmatism often defies reality, like the falling man in terminal velocity, claiming to be fine until coming into contact with the ground. The exploration of smaller particles may turn out to be a bottomless pit, resembling a universe of its own, with local equivalent galaxies of ever smaller particles that are themselves tiny universes, endlessly both up and down, as Carl Sagan suggested.

Each of us is also a little universe, living through its chaotic precision. When Rutherford discovered the atom's nucleus in 1910, he became perplexed by the surrounding emptiness, not unlike the emptiness of space. The nucleus is now understood to be only one-millionth of a billionth of the total volume of an atom—if one can even imagine that. Despite everything around us being composed of such "empty" atoms, we still *see* things as solids and liquids. It is a miracle that when we sit on a chair, we do not just fall through (and keep falling) like the neutrinos from the sun passing through us at all times. Instead, we remain levitated about one angstrom above the chair, repelled by our electrons. As I type these letters, none of my fingers are actually touching the keys on the laptop, but my brain perceives it through its lifelong conditioning. When we look at an object, we only see the reflected light of its atom hitting our retinas. Our actual surroundings have never been observed by anyone alive, confirming the philosophical doubt of yore.

God reminds us: "The life of this world is but the comfort of illusion" (*al-'Imran* 3:185). Perhaps Aristotle and John Duns Scotus were right: we only experience the forms/qualities of things rather than their substance. Although substance, as classically understood, falls apart in light of the spacetime paradigm, it aligns perfectly with Rumi's view of the afterlife. He described the afterlife as the realm of substance and our earthly lives as the realm of form. Like all Muslims, he preferred the substance of the afterlife, which can only be reached through our worldly form. It has profound implications for our concept of knowledge and worldview, which has been gradually skewed since birth.

When a baby is born, although his sensory organs are fully formed, without the necessary connections between those organs and his cortex, he senses a drastically different world. What he senses is somewhat ambiguous, as all his receivers are flooded with a sudden overload of terrestrial inputs. The initial adaptive process of our substantial soul with its newly acquired physical form is complex, where physical stimuli are filtered by biological sensory organs and then translated through physiological pathways to be finally interpreted by the brain. That final product is what we consider knowledge and understanding our arrival at it makes its subjectivity evident. How each of us came to know the color green is likely different from everyone else, with some similarities that allow us to understand each other, yet with enough difference to make it unique. Accordingly, each of us views the same world differently based on our personal preformed connections, both organic and psychological. Therefore, all acquired knowledge is inseparable from introspection and, at best, personal opinions.

This consideration of our mind reveals the fragility of *matter*, as introduced earlier by the quantum perspective. The all-too-familiar blue sky becomes our brain's interpretation of sunlight refracting through the atmosphere, which may not reflect its actual substance. Our memories are stored in the hard drives of our brains, and our souls attain that memory and knowledge through our physical bodies. Whether our souls require our senses to perceive is debatable and higher levels of spirituality aspire to rise above it. Our bodies may serve as merely training wheels for our soul's ascension to maturity, and what we secularly learn is only the consensus of our sensory perceptions thus far into our history based on the law of association. However, the Truth remains out there, some of which have been revealed by the mercy of God.

Russell posed the question: *If what we see is as mental as our seeing, why distinguish between the two?* It is this realization that separates one from the extremes of nihilism. Philosophers and theologians since antiquity—including Thomas Aquinas, William of Ockham, Descartes, and Kant—have struggled with this distinction between essence and existence. We categorize everything in neat little boxes to explain our surroundings through reason and intellect, driven by an inherent urge to name everything to rid ourselves of the fear of the unknown. Aristotle made an audacious attempt even to name it all in his *Categories*, as an inability to define can lead some to complete denial of the *unseen*.

Physicist Carlo Rovelli considers this *grouping* a key factor in defining our identity. Even our attempts at artificial intelligence ultimately rely on the distinct categories of zeros and ones. However, the more we learn about our world, the more it becomes apparent that nothing in our universe is linear or categorical. Our journey here has been to demolish these preformed compartments in our thinking and show the beautiful interweaving surrounding us. Once we free our minds, we can see how little substance remains in the accidental world of metaphysics. Islamic ontology cannot be explained through Plato's or Aristotle's metaphysics, nor anything that came thereafter, as it predates them all to the creation of the universe. Islam denotes a way of life of *submission* to the revelation, which cannot be put into any further category. Hence, any adjective around Islam only demonstrated a complete departure from it.

Everything is *granular*, fluctuating through their statistical probabilities, even at the quantum level. Although we learn an electron's mass and charge in our introductory chemistry courses, in reality, they are both unknown. Knowledge and substance seem to fluctuate at this level as *matter* appears and disappears like the Cheshire cat. All of this is championed by the uncertainty principle and observer effect, stating that the more accurately we measure something, the more we alter it, rendering our measurements invalid. In other words, as our margin of error for one physical quantity approaches zero, the uncertainty of its dependent quantity approaches infinity. Our theories and estimations only work as long as we stay a certain critical distance away from the object of interest in a process called *renormalization*, which earned Feynman his Nobel prize. In quantum field theory, renormalization attempts to tackle the problems of infinity and zero, just like many similar tricks by mathematicians of the past. Still, both infinity and zero continue to re-emerge even with our most brilliant avoidance attempts, as we will see in the next chapter.

At the quantum level, time is also reduced to its smallest component, and classical debates regarding its duration and linearity are plentiful. St. Bede (673-735 CE) introduced the granularity of time in the 7th century in his work, *De Divisionibus Temporum* (On the Division of Time).[992] Maimonides described time as composed of its smallest components, which cannot be further subdivided because of their short duration.[993] One can only imagine the stimulating discussions he had with his teacher, Ibn Rushd, on this topic. Today, quantum gravity offers a Plank space and time, which is very *blurry* at its most basic level, according to loop quantum gravity. Fluctuations here translate to quantum superpositions of time, where the distinctions between past, present, and future appear to disintegrate. This should not cause despair, for we do not live at a quantum level defying Zeno's Paradox of the Arrow (let us not get into that...just forget it was even mentioned).

Humans can barely perceive time down to a tenth of a second. We can observe the accelerating blades of a helicopter up to the limit of our perception, beyond which the blades become blurry and our brains only perceive *an object in motion*. That is how God created us, and He confirms by telling us: "The life of the world is but a matter of illusion" (*al-Hadid* 57:20). As all things become *blurry* in the quantum world, we are forced to view the world not as a collection of things but only as a collection of events. Each of these events is momentary with the inevitable *change* that defines our existence. Your reading of this text resulted from a sequence of events that extend to the limits of your memory. Similarly, wars result from selfish choices that lead to catastrophic suffering, and waves are a tug of war between air and water molecules, a dance between the seen and the unseen worlds. God brings our attention to this *change* that dominates our earthly lives, where the only things everlasting are our deeds and the Afterlife.

In this universe of microscopic quantum events, we only feel the weak gravitational force at every step. If we broaden our view, the forces affecting us at an individual level seem to matter less when viewed from the perspective of an entire body of people. Yet, our individual existence is preserved through the differences that prevent us from becoming a uniform *soup*, as in Pauli's exclusion principle. Just like the quarks that make us, complete uniformity of all the individuals in a society would be the collapse of that civilization. "People, We created you all from a single man and a single woman and made you into races and tribes so that you should get to know one another. In God's eyes, the most honored of you are the ones most mindful of Him: God is all-knowing, all aware," reminds God (*al-Hujurat* 49:13).

Despite all the perceived interspecies and intraspecies differences—as well as between us and inanimate objects—we are all made of the same basic building blocks. These identical atomic and subatomic particles divinely combine in different arrangements to form all that we can sense as different. While individually, we appear to follow every possible path in life, humanity is more like Feyenman's *sum-over-histories*. At any given point, this history can be characterized by the size of the wave of its movement and its position in the cycle of civilization. Otherwise, history appears to be "just one damn fact after another" from a myopic perspective.

Although the overall history of humanity may resemble a sinusoidal cyclical pattern, its smoothness only approximates the jagged edges hidden within. While scientists explain the physical laws of the universe, only the prophets and messengers of God can tell us about its metaphysical laws. Their purpose is to warn against jumping out of our earthly lives without a parachute of good deeds and a pious soul (Arabic, النَّفْس المُطْمَئِنَّة), so we do not become victims of misunderstood forces.

BLINDING LIGHT

God is the Light of the heavens and earth. His Light is like this: there is a niche, and in it a lamp, the lamp inside a glass, a glass-like a glittering star, fuelled from a blessed olive tree from neither east nor west, whose oil almost gives light even when no fire touches it—light upon light—God guides whomever He will to his Light; God draws such comparisons for people; God has full knowledge of everything. (al-Nur 24:35)

Theories in physics rest on the assumption that the speed of light in a vacuum is constant, set at 299,792,458 meters per second. It has long been believed that nothing can travel faster than light, except for the recently discovered phenomenon of quantum spin. The spacetime-cone model mentioned before is a graphical manifestation of that boundary demarcating the limits of our knowledge and existence. These limits have led us to ponder whether there can be even any beauty without light.

How we see and sense our visible world is a learned adaptive phenomenon. Throughout this book, we have repeatedly emphasized this fact to overcome our paradigm blindness. At birth, when a child first opens his eyes, the terrestrial brightness is initially blinding through his clear lenses, which gradually change color to filter light. Without the neural connections from his retina to his visual cortex, sometimes his visual stimuli make him *hear* or even *taste*, as often detected in EEG (electroencephalogram) studies. As newborns, we also hear a deafeningly noisy world, which our brains gradually learn to selectively mute for a more controlled sensation. We can appreciate the temporary adaptation to similar muting after returning from a loud monster truck event or concert.

A few months after birth, our sensory functions switch from a subcortical to a cortical level that defines our advanced being. Perhaps it is also when our pure *fitras* are introduced to their terrestrial influences, marking the beginning of their conditioning. This switch is often displayed by an infant's prolonged stare at his mother. His apparent infatuation is instead a momentary loss of oculomotor function in a phenomenon known as *sticky fixations*. Of course, leave it to science to destroy even the magical world of parental bonding. Nevertheless, we gradually adapt to our new environment and learn to sense the world not as it truly is but only as a filtered version that is quite different from *reality*. As a result, all the things we are so sure of and *know* to be *true* are simply leaps of faith. All perceived knowledge is subjective like an amputee's phantom limb.

Physicists have long debated whether light behaves more like a particle or a wave. We now understand that it exhibits both characteristics, known as wave-particle duality in quantum mechanics. At this point, even the staunchest atheist scientist would have *faith* in his assertion that a single photon behaving like a wave would travel *simultaneously* through two slits. Light is so unique that a single theory cannot even explain it. Einstein predicted that light behaves like a particle under the influence of gravity, which was later confirmed by Arthur Eddington during a solar eclipse in 1919. Recently, scientists were able to cool atoms to a few millionths of a degree above absolute zero, which remarkably made them forget their identities and clump together to form the Bose-Einstein Condensate. Physicist Lene Hau then used that medium to stop light in its tracks, trapping it in a solid and releasing it later at a different place and time. Its significance starts to unfold when we realize that all we see as "real" is simply light that hits our retinas from a source.

Then there is the observer effect suggesting that matter acts differently when seen versus unseen. It was experimentally demonstrated in the aforementioned double-slit light experiment, where placing a camera to watch photons exiting a double-slit changed their behavior. Perhaps there is a correlation here with the Prophetic advice to cover our food and drinks, as well as his many related miracles demonstrating their blessings (*Sahih al-Bukhari* Book 74, Hadith 50). As pure energy is an interaction between light and matter, perhaps its fluctuation at the quantum level allows for multiplicity according to divine will. What that entails in a macroscopic world is only a matter of perception. The question for the quantum theorists would remain what causes these fluctuations between existence and nonexistence other than the will of God?

Although we perceive light only when it enters our senses, it has been constantly present since the Big Bang, directed at us from all directions. This phenomenon gives us the illusion that we are at the center of the universe, but all the trajectories of light can be traced back to a single origin in Euclidean spacetime. That singularity at the Big Bang contained the entire universe within an infinitesimally small space, which amounted to *nothing*. Such contradictions and dualities are a constant theme that has plagued humankind since we learned to think. The resultant infinite density of the singularity created an event horizon similar to those we now associate with black holes, where not even light escapes (as far as we can see).

The Big Bang would have appeared as an absolute void until it grew to a size where the density and the sum of its gravitational attractions were low enough to allow an explosion of light to escape. This *outside* observer would be an anomaly to the spacetime-cone but would have suddenly found himself surrounded by a rush of an expanding universe zooming past him. The rest of us can still watch this phenomenon on our TVs manifesting as about 1% of the static noise, or hear it on the radio as static. This discovery was instrumental in disproving the steady-state theory of cosmology, which was, for a moment, contradictory to revelation.

In the Qur'an, God describes himself as the *light* of the heavens and the earth, and everything that He creates to sustain life reflects some of that *light*. The sun is an example, sustaining everything that feeds our physical bodies. Light takes about eight minutes to reach us from our sun and makes life as we know it possible. It is the quintessential ingredient that brings a seed to germinate similar to perhaps how our bodies would also be resurrected on the Day of Judgment. Astronauts in orbit note a remarkable 400 degrees Fahrenheit temperature difference at every sunrise —happening every 90 minutes for those in the international space station. Light also affects us psychologically, as we can feel its absence during a lunar eclipse, and its warmth makes us feel happy by synthesizing vitamin D in our skin. To this effect, many organisms have developed kleptothermy, which even manifests in human behavior. Research in this field by psychologist Hans Ijzerman correlates diversity in human interactions with improved thermoregulation.[994] Meaning that the more we interact with people of different ethnicities and socioeconomic backgrounds, the warmer and happier we feel.

Similarly, the warmth of the divine *light* is felt in our souls through our *fitra's* innate affinity for beauty and goodness. Our confusion around these concepts emerged relatively recently following the European Enlightenment, which rather benightedly redefined human nature as inherently selfish and violent. Perhaps such misconceptions—popularized by Thomas Hobbes, George Santayana, Sigmund Freud, Robert Audrey, Konrad Lorenz, and others—only reflect their inner selves. Fortunately, more recent research has debunked these delusions, with the 1986 Seville Statement on Violence signed by leading scientists reinstating: "It is scientifically incorrect to say that we have an inherited tendency to make war or act violently. That behavior is not genetically programmed into human nature."[995] Studies by Daniel Batson, Nancy Eisenberg, and Linda Wilson have even found altruism to be a baseline human tendency, bringing us back to the divine *light*. Nonetheless, centuries of misdirection resulted in endless wars that overlooked the elite's planning and plotting that deviated from the general population's natural, peaceful state.

While divine *light* is spiritually enlightening, we are blinded by physical light and unable to bear its brilliance. Even Newton attempted to stare directly at the sun rather unsuccessfully among others in history. As if all things beyond are kept away from us in every possible way. When Moses requested to see God, he was reminded of its impossibility. His sight was redirected at a nearby mountain, which instantly vaporized at even a veiled exposure to God's light (*al-A'raf* 7:135). Similar limits set by light led Roger Penrose to propose the cosmic censorship hypothesis, stating that singularities produced by gravitational collapse only occur in black holes, where an event horizon hides them.[996]

Such limits make God knowable only through our *inability*, as God's unity makes it paradoxical for Him to have an epistemological opposite. Nonetheless, we can still appreciate His opposite in form or attribute, where His light is reflected through His creation of the dark void.[997] Many literal and figurative implications of the divine light have been discussed in depth throughout Islamic scholarship. It is an all-encompassing light beyond our typical understanding, only described to give us an idea out of divine wisdom. Anything beyond is above human comprehension, similar to all things behind an event horizon. The benefits of such discussions are doubtful and potentially harmful. As even a filtered glimmer of the divine light made the mountain crumble, overthinking it will likewise fry our brains into absurdity.

The Prophet warned: "The devil comes to one of you saying, 'Who created this? Who created that?' even saying, 'Who created your Lord?' When he gets that length, the man should seek refuge in God and stop thinking about it" (*Mishkat al-Masabih* 65). He also advised us to leave the things that make us doubt, for the truth is recognized by the tranquility it brings to our hearts (*Jami` at-Tirmidhi* 2518). Nothing within the created realm can do justice to understanding or describing God's Eminence as emphasized by Pseudo-Dionysius the Areopagite. Thus, we are stuck with our limited imagination and language to express Him and forever falling short because all adjectives are inherently meaningless as God is neither substance nor accident.

> "Imagination does not reach Him," stressed the Egyptian theologian al-Tahawi (d. 933), "and understanding does not comprehend Him." God is, in other words, wholly Other:

the *Mysterium Tremendum*, to borrow Rudolph Otto's famous phrase. God is, according to the Sufi master Ibn al-Arabi, the *only* being with real existence: the *only* reality. For al-Ghazali God is *a'-Awwal*, "the First, before whom there is nothing," and *al-Akhir*, "the Last, after whom there is nothing." Al-Ghazali, it must be understood, is making neither an ontological nor a teleological argument for the existence of God; God is neither Thomas Aquinas's "First Cause," nor Aristotle's "Prime Mover." God is the *only* cause; God is movement itself.[998] [Aslan]

Those who still push the limits of these questions may find some answers in mathematics, which in the scope of human knowledge may seem as factual as our existence. The origin of the numeric system is perhaps rooted in the creation of the first man as *one* by the One and only, with the next numeral, two, making the following numbers possible through Eve. Hence, al-Kindi *On First Philosophy* argued against *one* as an integer at all, but a principal source of numbers.[999] Arithmetic and algebra then became necessary for us to explain our surroundings, starting with simple daily functions and evolving to more complex logical formulations enabling empiric thought. Mathematics became a written numerical language without the emotions of rational men. All of it is essentially based on simple logical principles used to predict future outcomes, which were then stuck in the complex geometry of curved surfaces for two millennia. That was finally overcome through calculus with the help of infinity and zero, which made all modern innovations possible, from space travel to cell phones. If you must ask *how*, find your nearest applied mathematician and brace for an earful.

First, the power of zero was used to overcome the infinity of a circle. An ingenious method was developed by assuming the circle as a polygon whose sides could be added to an approximation to calculate its circumference. The more sides given to the circle, the more accurate the approximation of the circumference, to the point that a circle with an infinite number of sides would have a circumference with zero margin of error. However, no matter how many sides are added, the limit set by infinity cannot be truly reached, similar to the paradox of approaching a goal by walking half the distance in between, as famously put forth by Zeno. Our rational logic is limited by this concept of infinity, and attempting to extend beyond it creates logical fallacies such as dividing by zero. For instance, if a polygon indeed had an infinite number of sides to mimic the smoothness of a circle, the length of each side would be zero. The circumference of that circle would then be the summation of all the zeros, which is still zero and would also be the case with circles of *all sizes*. Clearly, this is illogical, and for similar reasons, Aristotle forbade the use of completed infinity in mathematics and philosophy.[1000]

It illustrates the logical conundrum of attempting to understand God through our reason, which is caged by His limits of infinity and nothingness. The forever remaining *half distance* of Zeno can only be filled by a leap of faith in infinity, which simplifies all other complexities. Our natural gravitation towards infinity is yet another sign of our *fitra's* eternal connection to God. Interestingly, the *unveiling* process of some Sufi traditions takes the seeker first to a feeling of *combination* with all existence, where a state of oneness is reached. It is then advanced through *differentiation* of existence to reach the level of a competent gnostic.

More absurdity arises when we treat zero as a number (i.e., *nothingness* by logic) despite violating the axiom of Archimedes. Its dilemma is clarified by spelling out the problems of multiplying or dividing any number with zero. Since zero represents a void of nothingness, it inherently cannot participate in any logical concept of *increasing* or *decreasing* a real number. The use of zero in other real numbers like 10 is simply a placeholder and does not apply. Therefore, the acts of *multiplication* and *division*, just like *addition* and *subtraction*, require real numbers or definable quantities. Otherwise, any assumption based on that violated premise leads to situations where *anything* in the universe can be "proven," whether true or false.[1001]

The confusion lies in assuming zero is something less than one and infinity is a "large number" when both are indefinable. They are more similar than opposite ends of some logical spectrum. Even the shape of 0 unintentionally twists it to ∞, demarcating the opposite poles of the Riemann sphere. The introduction of negative numbers allowed zero to fall between 1 and -1, giving it the appearance of a false existence beyond its historic placeholding purpose. In reality, even negative numbers are somewhat difficult to explain. For example, if you have 2 apples and I take away 3, simple arithmetic would say that now you have -1 apple, which could be explained as you owing one. But how can I take away more than what you possess? How can you have a negative apple? In terms of the number spectrum, that would require you to go through an indefinable zero-void to get to that side of anti-logic, which may make sense on paper but is absurd in real life. This absurdity then allows for the ever-increasing wealth disparity by normalizing similar unjust transactions.

While the "number" zero helps us to perform calculus better, the concept of zero is infinitely complex. Seife writes that even "calculus, at its core, defied the logic of mathematics. Scientists have taken a leap of faith to accept it as the language of nature, despite the trouble they encounter with logic every time they deal with the infinite or zero.[1002] This is solved by deconstructing back to calculus's logical roots, where the incongruity between zero and infinity tells us that divinity cannot always be proven by rationality. Sometimes it also requires a leap of faith. Trying to remain *rational* in a literal mathematical sense once drove Pythagoreans to homicide. They feared the power of zero when they realized the literal *irrationality* of their golden ratio. Aristotle developed his metaphysics on a similar disregard for infinity and derived his concept of the *prime mover* based on an eternal universe. The Catholic Church adopted his metaphysics to prove divinity, but this caused inconsistencies with the Bible's references to God's creation from *nothing*, forcing Christian authorities to pick a side. Unfortunately, they picked the wrong one. Christian scholars feared the void so much that they even changed the Bible to match Aristotle's views.[1003] Soon, even Aristotle's misogyny and racism permeated through Church doctrines.

Meanwhile, the father of calculus, Newton himself had to make mathematically unconventional assumptions in developing his method of fluxions. That leap of faith allowed him to formulate his life's work that produced results acceptable to the scientific community. Although Einstein owed his success to the same principles of calculus, his departure from it to maintain a static universe resulted in his self-proclaimed "biggest mistake" of the cosmological constant. In all the natural laws that calculus has since inspired, there is nothing curious or coincidental about nature's predictability through equations, but rather our innate connection to them through a blend of logic and faith. Then why is it that after reaping the benefits of such advances, some are now eager to abandon this faith? Those who study history would undoubtedly see this departure nullifying all of the logic built upon that very foundation of faith.

Newton's dirty tricks of making zero and infinity vanish from his equations continued to vex subsequent mathematicians. Some, like D'Alembert, provided solutions by eliminating zero from the equation and imposing limits to seal the logic of calculus. The reader may relate this to the cosmic censorship hypothesis, where anything approaching the void and infinity is beyond our rational scope. Nevertheless, scientists and mathematicians in recent times have persisted in their pursuit to banish infinity and zero. The theoretical hope is that once they succeed, they will finally comprehend the laws of the universe. Some seek it to understand God, while others to nullify Him.

Ironically, the reality of their defiance is that they are striving for a goal that itself approaches infinity, much like Zeno's Paradox. "The theories that unify quantum mechanics and general relativity, that describe the centers of black holes and explain the singularity of the Big Bang, are so far removed from experiment that it might be impossible to determine which are correct and which are not," confesses Seife.[1004] Even Hawking admitted the impossibility of proving such theories based on logistics. A particle above the Planck energy of 1019 GeV would have a mass concentrated enough to sever itself from the rest of the universe and form a black hole.[1005] To generate energies even closer to it would require a particle accelerator bigger than our solar system.

Others sought to evade this issue by transforming a zero-dimensional point into a one-dimensional string, giving birth to string theory. This and other related physical and mathematical concepts of the last century became exponentially complex, all in futile attempts to secularize knowledge. For instance, at least ten total dimensions are necessary to make string theory work. Then came M-theory with its eleven dimensions. Seife acknowledges the mathematical precision of such theorists and cosmologists but admits that their theories are as useless as Pythagorean philosophy and can be utterly wrong.[1006] Just as Alexander Vilenkin once contended that quantum cosmology is ultimately not observational science but philosophical conjectures at best.[1007] Their experts fail to realize that their attempts to cage their hearts with numerical language prevent them from benefiting from their acquired knowledge. Although many of them excel in thought and mind, their brilliance is akin to that of an Olympic athlete who still cannot prevent his physique from deteriorating and perishing.

The Qur'an is often referred to as the *light* sent down to humanity during its metaphorical darkness and spiritual death. Its message illuminates the minds of those who approach it with an open heart. As predominantly visual beings, our perception and knowledge are drastically limited in the absence of light. Without it, even a tropical paradise would be frightening in pitch-black darkness. Our best attempts to manufacture artificial light would fail to bring out the same beauty. One of the first things astronauts must acclimate to in outer space is the jarring reality of a black sky during "daytime." Similarly, a world experienced without divine light is frightening, and the resulting darkness obscures its true meaning. Once we allow the divine light to shine through us, the resultant luminescence of our souls is uncontainable.

The strength of our soul's connection to God is reflected in its luminescence, which will become visible on the Day of Judgment (al-Hadid 57:12-3). There are some prominent Sufi elements to this line of thinking. While Sufism is just another aspect of spirituality, like all things, it can also lead astray from the middle balance. The spiritual language of the Sufi is often misconstrued by those uninitiated, which has historically incurred the wrath of theologians. In *Ihya-ul-Uloom*, Imam al-Ghazali repudiates its extreme forms that deviate from the Islamic middle, while much of his sentiments actually favor mysticism. The Sufis maintain the ontological unity of God and see His immanence in His creation. "Whatever notion you have of God," said Rumi, "He must be something like that because He is the creator of all your notions."[1008]

This divinity in the creation theme reaches an extreme level in Hinduism and Buddhism. Yet, the original Vedic texts contain profound expressions of *tawhid*, such as the Yajurveda's declaration that God is "imageless and pure" (40:8). In the Bhagavad Gita, Krishna reproaches those who confuse the Creator with the created objects of worship (Ch. 7). The Mughal scholar-prince Dara Shikoh (1615-59 CE) found the *Upanishads* to be more sagacious than his study of the New and the Old Testaments, and the reference to "secret scriptures" in the Qur'an to be more applicable to the *Upanishads*, which the Brahmans hold in secrecy.[1009] Moreover, there are many traces of the Islamic creation story within the Rigveda—one of the four sacred Hindu texts dating to 1500 BC—which would be natural from its revelation since Adam to all nations.

According to the Rigveda, at the beginning of creation, "there was neither non-existence nor existence: There was no realm of space, no sky beyond it." This resembles a sentence from Hawking, which also conforms with Abrahamic metaphysics. The hymn then provides a poetic description of the void and infinity: "Darkness there was: at first concealed in darkness this All was indiscriminated chaos." This echoes the more accurate translation of the first sentence of the Bible: *At the outset of creation, there was chaos*. The subsequent verses resemble the famous fabricated hadith of "A Hidden Treasure" that is often quoted in Islamic mystical circles: "All that existed then was void and formless...Thereafter rose Desire in the beginning, Desire, the primal seed and germ of Spirit."

The hymn continues with a description of the sages who searched with their heart's thoughts and discovered the kinship of existence with non-existence. "Transversely [across the universe] was their dividing line extended: what was above it then, and what below it?" This division of creation from the original chaos theme reappears in the Abrahamic faiths and Babylonian mythology and is consistent with the current cosmological hypothesis. Perhaps a prophetic figure asked the next rhetorical question: "Who verily knows and who can here declare it, whence it was born and whence comes this creation? The gods are later than this world's production." This last verse can almost be placed on the tongue of a prophet making a case against polytheism. "Who knows then whence it first came into being? He the first origin of this creation, whether he formed it all or did not form it, whose eye controls this world in highest heaven, he verily knows it."[1010] God also asks us similar questions in the Qur'an, as none of us were there to refute His provided answers.

Zoroastrian texts similarly describe one god (*Ahura Mazda*) founded by a prophet Zardosh/Zarathustra around the 6th to 12th century BC. He commanded his followers to pray five times a day, similar to the Muslim five daily prayers. His description of God and the afterlife in *Dasatir-i-Asmani* sounds nearly verbatim to numerous Qur'anic *ayats*, raising the possibility of fire worship as a later corruption of the general theme of God's divine *light*. If someone saw (or heard of) Moses communicating with God through the fire within a bush (*Exodus* 3), they could have mistaken the flames for the actual Creator. Indeed, Zardosh was commanded to climb a mountain around the age of forty for an audience with the creator, just like Moses, and there he received a message for humanity regarding the oneness of god. Zardosh's surviving vision of Judgment Day (*Frashokereti*) describes people walking across a bridge towards the afterlife, where their deeds are weighed, similar to the Islamic description of the Day and *as-Sirāt* (Arabic: الصراط).[1011] After the accounting, all devotees of Ahura Mazda would proceed to an everlasting garden called *pairidaeza* in Avestan, which in modern Persian became *firdaws*. He even foretold of a prophet *Saoshyant* (mercy for the worlds) who would be the *Astvat-Ereta* (the gatherer of all nations), which are the descriptions of prophet Muhammad in Islam.

Judaism shares not only a similar creation theme with Hinduism but also an extreme orthopraxy by placing a heavy emphasis on their *shari'ah*. Christianity, on the other hand, struggled with the divine light's connection to the Holy Spirit and Jesus's miraculous birth and eventually created the concept of the Trinity. Its inherent contradictions led to the formation of various sects based on their interpretations. Montanist Christians, like Tertullian, believed in Jesus's divine *quality* but in a different *quantity*; Modalist Christians saw it as three successive modes of the Father, the Son, and the Holy Spirit; Nestorian Christians believed in separate human and divine natures of Jesus; Gnostic Christians, especially Docetists, believed him to be full divinity, only appearing to be human; and the Arians rejected the entire Trinity.[1012]

In Islam, the Holy Spirit refers to Archangel Gabriel, who was tasked with communicating God's revelation to His messengers and is simply a creation from *light*. God's command—described as a word (i.e., Be!)—communicated to Mary via the Holy Spirit, resulting in Jesus's miraculous birth. Through the same Holy Spirit, God clarifies: "People of the Book, do not go to excess in your religion, and do not say anything about God except the truth: the Messiah, Jesus, son of Mary, was nothing more than a messenger of God, His word, directed to Mary, a spirit from Him. So believe in God and His messengers and do not speak of a 'Trinity'—stop [this], that is better for you—God is only one God, He is far above having a son, everything in the heavens and earth belongs to Him and He is the best one to trust" (*al-Nisa'*

4:171).

Within the Abrahamic faiths, we see a miraculous progression: first, a birth without any parents (Adam); then, a birth without a mother (Eve); and finally, a birth without a father (Jesus, al-'Imran 3:59). Imagine Jesus's frustration after struggling his entire life to revive God's message, only to be turned into an idol soon after his ascension. It was probably similar to Moses's rage when he found his followers reverting to idol worship within days of his ascension to the mountain. In fact, all things people worship other than God reduce down to what they see around them, a practice God never sanctioned (Yusuf 12:40). Such innovations are only substantiated by complex myths and fables that sharply contrast the elegant rationale for one God.

Interestingly, various past philosophers like the Buddha and Confucious were also idolized after death. In his *Kitab al-Milal wa al-Nihal* (The Book of Religions and Sects), Imam al-Shahrastani (1086-1153 CE) included Buddhists among the Sabians and noted some commonalities between the Buddha and al-Khidr (*al-Kahf* 18:60-82). Ibn 'Ajiba in *al-Bahr al-Madīd* commentary also mentions a *hadith* where the Prophet described al-Khidr as "the son of a king who desired that his son inherit his throne, but he refused and fled to a secluded island place where they could not find him." This is similar to the description of Gautama Buddha, whose lucky color was green, as is "the Green Man" a literal translation of al-Khidr in Arabic. In his Qur'anic commentary, al-Alusi (1802-1854 CE) reports that Abu Nu'aym al-Isfahani (947-1038 CE) described al-Khidr as the Buddha in India. Ibn Kathir's (1300-73 CE) narrations of al-Khidr's parting advice for Moses in *Qasas al-Anbiya* are also remarkable, as some of them closely resemble various teachings attributed to Buddha. These teachings include being beneficial wherever you go and never causing harm, being joyful and radiant, never being angry nor going without purpose, and leaving disputation.[1013]

While it is narrated that God sent 124,000 messengers to humanity over the years, only 25 of them (perhaps 24) are named in the Qur'an. God tells us: "There are messengers whose stories We have told you already and others We have not" (*an-Nisa* 4:164). The vast majority of these messengers remain unknown across different cultures and eras, and statistically, many of the ancient religions, philosophies, and fables around the world are just derivatives of those messengers' messages. Traces of monotheism seen across all civilizations, however corrupt, indicate the presence of past prophets among them and their *fitra*. Even apparently polytheistic ancient religions of Egypt trace their origin back to Atum, who bears an uncanny resemblance to Adam. Atum reflected on his existence with all the other souls in the primordial form of "nun" and the subsequent creation of all of humanity from himself. Memphis theology, in particular, speaks of all creation originating as a simple "word," similar to the Abrahamic conception. Moreover, from Atum first came Shu, the god of air or wind, which translates to the name of Eve in Arabic and Hebrew Hawwah. The similarities continue to one of their offspring Set—representing disorder and evil—murdering his brother Osiris, just as in the story of Cain and Abel. As God confirms, "We surely sent a messenger to every community, saying, 'Worship God and shun false gods.' But some of them were guided by God, while others were destined to stray. So travel throughout the land and see the fate of the deniers!" (*an-Naml* 16:36).

We can never be certain whom God guides or guided in the past. Seneca's writings, for instance, resemble various Prophetic teachings, even when he was advising his friend Lucius to weep but not wail (e.g., *Sunan Abi Dawud* 3127).[1014] Socrates and Plato's criticism of Homeric polytheism along with their counterarguments for monotheism also hint at divine guidance. Many of the charges of cultural plagiarism in world religions are instead reflective of the dilution of that divine light originating from the same God. Thus, even the oldest religions, like Hinduism, have monotheism in their roots. Their concept of an *avatar* as "the one sent down" is arguably the same as a messenger, as is the concept of the *antim avatar* a foretelling of the last Prophet. This last messenger in the Vedas was also called *narashansa*, which translates to "the praised human." God informs us that prior messengers foretold the coming of the last messenger Ahmad, whose name in Arabic also means "the praised one" (*as-Saf* 61:6). Thomas Cleary noted a similar prophecy of "the praised one" in his translation of *Dhammapada* (Chap XVII), and connected it to another hymn in the Torah. Some scholars believe the Kalki avatar (mentioned in the *Puranas*) coming in the *Kali Yuga* (the age of darkness) to be another reference to prophet Muhammad. Indeed, he described himself as the last messenger before the end of time (*Sahih al-Bukhari* 5301). The description of this period in *Mahabharata* has remarkable similarities to the Prophet's foretelling of the signs of the Hour (e.g., *Jami` at-Tirmidhi* 2205).

The Holy Spirit mentioned several passages prior, was described as the most magnificent among the angels, all of whom are made of light (*Sahih Muslim* 2996). Perhaps their creation from light gives them the ability to break our light-speed barrier and carry out their divinely imbued tasks. For those within the universe, $E=mc^2$ translates to an infinite mass required for an object to approach lightspeed, making acceleration that much more difficult. While these laws break down near a black hole within our universe, they become meaningless for creations of the outer realms. Accordingly, angels are exceptions to the light-speed limit, just like the spin particles we discovered. It may be ordinary for them to travel through event horizons, potential wormholes, the future, the past, and additional unknown realms. "God, the Lord of the Ways of Ascent, by which the angels and the Spirit ascend to Him" (*al-Ma'arij* 70:3-4).

In his popular book *Cosmos*, Carl Sagan artfully described the concept of multidimensionality and curved spacetime through the example of a flat nation of two-dimensional citizens.[1015] Although they may have complex shapes, to each other, they appear as lines, unaware and unable to look up and down. Then, he entertains a three-dimensional apple approaching from above, which can see through the actual shapes of the Flatland. When the apple speaks to a square below, the latter cannot see and only hears a voice that appears to come from within. If the apple descended to the square's level, it would suddenly appear as an enlarging line at the square's sight and then disappear. Only if the square was elevated to the privilege of a view from above would he finally see things from a higher dimension.

Sagan's example immediately resembles the entire prophetic legacy to those familiar with the Islamic tradition. The angels, being from a higher dimension, speaking to human prophets and messengers can be similarly explained, as exemplified through the first revelation encounter of prophet Muhammad upon the Mountain of Light. We can presume how the angels can make themselves be seen, while God's dimensionless existence makes us physically incapable of withstanding His magnificence. The Prophet's ascension on his Night Journey to the multiverse would similarly be achieved, defying the limits of imagination of the ordinary four-dimensional inhabitants of the earth. In the subsequent chapter of his book, Sagan interestingly included a pictorial reference to the Prophet's Night Journey without any connection or further explanation.[1016]

The Prophet was blessed with glimpses of the unseen world and described the heavens to be so tightly packed with angels as to not even have space of four-fingers width (*Sunan Ibn Majah* Book 37, Hadith 91). What we call dark matter may just be our perception of these angels following God's commands in performing their various duties, including holding the universe together. We can only wonder how the atmospheric whirls from their busy wings would manifest in the mortal world of molecules and winds, perhaps contributing to the background noise of the universe. Astronomer Rebecca Elson (1960-99 CE) wrote in *Searching for Dark Matter*:

> Whatever they turn out to be,
> Let there be swarms of them,
> Enough for immortality,
> Always a star where we can warm ourselves.
>
> Let there be enough to bring it back

> From its own edges,
> To bring us all so close we ignite
> The bright spark of resurrection.

On the other hand, *jinns* are made from a smokeless fire, which presents an intriguing puzzle from a scientific standpoint. Smoke is typically a byproduct of incomplete combustion, which suggests that this unique type of flame is the result of something else entirely. It could potentially stem from a complete combustion of pure fuel and an abundance of oxygen, or it could be made up of antiparticles, for example. The Arabic word *jinn* also adds to the mystery, as it translates to "hidden" or "unseen" in other parts of the Qur'an. Regardless of its composition, this fire is different from light, which makes *jinns* bound by the same spacetime light cone as the rest of us inhabiting this universe. The little we know about these partners of crime in the world of free will results in many misconceptions and likely all of the paranormal activities.

Ultimately, trying to reconcile these divine phenomena with scientific interpretations is akin to a delivery man speculating about the contents of the packages he carries. The only way we may be able to peek into the darkness of this blinding barrier is by transforming into something extra-universal to escape its physical boundaries. Hence, at death, we are freed from the limitations of our shells and revert to our souls, which are the extraterrestrial parts of us that originated on the back of Adam in heaven.

TO DUST WE RETURN

All that has been discussed here concerns our temporary life on earth, where God "created from water every living thing" (*al-Anbiya'* 21:30). Water's significance is tied to our every breath, which obviates the need for its mention but results in our forgetfulness. God reminds us that it is ultimately His rule over water that ensures our sustenance down to the small sips we take ungratefully (*al-Waqi'ah* 56:68). This dependence was recognized by the first single-celled organism to the multicellular philosophers like Thales of Miletus (620-540 BC), who deemed water as the first principle of life and material world.[1017] Even Homer's gods swore by it in *The Iliad* (xiv, 271).

The flow of water shapes the physical world we see and our history, running deeper than its apparent surface. As we continue to deplete Earth's natural resources, making it unlivable, any search for an alternative planet is focused on the availability of water. We are made of 65% water ourselves and would only last 3-4 days without it. Even the search for extraterrestrials usually consists of searching for water elsewhere that would sustain intelligent life as we know it. Therefore, it is no less than a miracle every time water *falls from the sky* when we cannot find another such planet in our vast universe. Only 0.001% of our freshwater is contained within the clouds, 0.036% in the lakes, rivers, and reservoirs, and the rest as ice sheets—all adding up to 3% of the earth's water. The remaining 97% is in the seas as virtually unusable salt water. God reminds us that both bodies of water are not alike, yet we still eat tender seafood and extract ornaments to wear from them (*Fatir* 35:12). Between them is a boundary preventing contamination where lethal saltwater meets the rivers of freshwater, defying expectations (*al-Rahman* 55:19-21). Similar "lakes" have been recently discovered deep within the ocean with an entirely different composition from their surroundings, supporting diverse life forms.

Water has been here for 4.3 billion years to sustain life, serving as the bloodstream of the planet. The transformation it brings to even the driest regions was recently captured by filmmaker Harun Mehmedinović. "And among His Signs, that you see the earth barren; but when We send down water to it, it is stirred to life and growth. Verily, He Who gives it life, can surely give life to the dead [on the Day of Resurrection]. Indeed He can do all things" (*Fussilat* 41:39). Some desert plant seeds remain dormant for thousands of years, waiting for a drop of rainfall to germinate. What nature does with a tiny seed, some water, and sunshine is unmatched by even our most advanced technology.

It is He who sends down water from the sky. With it We produce the shoots of each plant...From the date palm come clusters of low-hanging dates, and there are gardens of vines, olives, and pomegranates, alike yet different. Watch their fruits as they grow and ripen! In all this there are signs for those who would believe. (al-An'am 6:99)

Rain also dictates global migrations of large mammals down to small dragonflies that travel from India across an entire ocean to Africa. There they lay eggs in pools formed by the continent's first rainfall of the season. Nymphs hatching from those eggs feed on mosquito larvae in the same ponds, which is Africa's most effective measure against mosquito-borne diseases. In this global chain of events, if farmers in India spray too much pesticide killing dragonflies, it results in a deadly malaria outbreak in Africa later that season. It highlights one of the infinite ways the flow of water connects all living things on Earth, supporting over eight million documented species and their unique identities. "It is God who sends the winds, bearing good news of His coming grace, and when they have gathered up the heavy clouds, We drive them to a dead land where We cause rain to fall, bringing out all kinds of crops, just as We shall bring out the dead. Will you not reflect?" (*al-A'raf* 7:57).

Instead of being grateful for such blessings, this anthropic picture leads some to hunt for trophies. But God kept his rule over water for a clear purpose: "His throne [rule] was on water—so as to test which of you does best" (*Hud* 11:7). All of our quarrels and qualms since the dawn of humanity have revolved around this truism. Humans have always settled near fresh water, with ancient civilizations sprouting along the Nile, Tigris/Euphrates, Indus, and Yellow Rivers. Only recently have we been able to bring fresh water far from its source to accommodate large settlements in remote areas. That comes at the cost of ever-increasing dependence on fresh water, creating a wider economic disparity. While developed countries have readily made fresh water available, there remain places worldwide where the closest water sources are miles away. Indeed, water is a test for us as some animals remain *more equal than others*.[1018] The prosperous are afforded better access to water and the poor are left to their generosity for a meager sip.

This fight for water dominates world history and is more prevalent today than ever. More than two-thirds of the world's rivers no longer connect to the sea because of the artificial dams along their course. These growing numbers of dams reveal a new face of the hemispheric economic disparity that is literally pushing the entire planet off balance. "There is now so much water stored behind dams in the northern hemisphere, the weight of the water has tilted the axis of the planet, affecting the speed of its spin," narrates McEvers.[1019] This imbalance is a direct result of the location of most of the world's developed countries at the top, for even geographically, we have deviated from the middle. This is just a minor note on the melodrama enacted globally by water's abundance and privation. Once a Great Flood gave Noah and those aboard the Ark a fresh start. Another served as the Pharaoh's exquisite comeuppance after he claimed to be a god and chased the Israelites into the sea. On the other hand, water gushed out at Ishmael's heels and brought life to a barren Arabian desert. We are continually tested by floods and stormy conditions, as seen in China's Yellow and Yangtze River floods, which resulted in over two million deaths in 1887 and 1931. Even in recent years, record rains and flooding have devastated many regions globally.

The Prophet added: "I was raised to the Lote Tree and saw four rivers...Those coming out were the Nile and the Euphrates, and those which were going in were two rivers in paradise." (Sahih al-Bukhari 5610)

Other times we are tested with droughts that have also played a pivotal role in shaping our history. A series of megadroughts between 135,000 and 75,000 years ago led to the first migrations of early humans out of Africa.[1020] Archeological evidence of massive droughts some 4,500 years ago in the Middle East and parts of Europe was discovered in royal tombs of Egypt.[1021] Centuries thereafter, a similar drought played a key role in the migration of Israelites—known to Egyptians as Hyksos—from Canaan until their Exodus with Moses. Joseph's tragic circumstances once brought him from Canaan to Egypt as an enslaved child. His eventual rise to power as the treasury minister was through his divine gift of dream interpretation, allowing him to foresee seven years of drought and prepare accordingly (*Yusuf* 12:47-9). The drought caused neighboring regions to crumble and rely on Egyptian rations, perhaps leading to the rise of the Middle/New Kingdom of Egypt.

The full scale of the Egyptian Empire is often underappreciated, as it is unheard of in our times to see another similar empire lasting nearly three millennia. That domination of history was made possible by the Nile, whose tidal waves left ripples through the rise and fall of the various dynasties trying to leave a mark along its course. Owing to its fertile banks from the annual floods, Egypt could produce enough to meet the needs of its citizens and the surrounding dependent regions. Therefore, at the height of Pharaoh's aggression, he was punished by years of droughts for his aggression and oppression of the Israelites (*al-A'raf* 7:130).

Most crises in human history can be linked to water in one way or another. The Mayan empire in Mesoamerica is believed to have failed through a sharp decline in rainfall about 1200 years ago.[1022] "Say, 'Just think: if all your water were to sink deep into the earth, who could give you flowing water in its place?'" asks God (*al-Mulk* 67:30). Despite warnings from experts, we have failed to change our track towards global warming, which has already caused irreversible changes in the planetary water flow (i.e., the *rivers* that fly above the forest). Chomsky reports that "'in the middle latitudes of the Northern hemisphere, average temperatures are increasing at a rate that is equivalent to moving south about 10 meters (30 feet) each day,' a rate 'about 100 times faster than most climate change that we can observe in the geological record'—and perhaps 1,000 times faster, according to other technical studies."[1023]

The past droughts were relatively rare events with consequent historical milestone casualties. We now see that same theme more frequently in global politics where nearly all of our recent socio-political crises can be traced back to droughts. The 2015 droughts in the Amazon Rainforest resulted in a shortage of tap water in Sao Paulo, Brazil, causing massive uprising, rioting, and bubbling toxic phosphate foams in Rio Tietê. The number of Amazon forest fires increased by 72% that year, and the situation has only worsened since then. These numbers are not in our favor, nor are they isolated to just the Amazon. The 2011 drought in California lasted six years, leading to the 2018 wildfires, the worst in its history, and each subsequent year breaking the previous year's record. Australia, Turkey, and Greece experienced similar devastating wildfires in 2020 and 2021. Cape Town faced a drought in 2015 when its tap water ran dry, and some farmers in the region did not see much rainfall for seven years, resembling the drought of Joseph. These places are now gradually becoming unlivable due to the escalating climate calamities.[1024]

The increase in droughts worldwide reflects a shift in the global water flow, as the total amount of water on earth remains the same. Droughts in some regions translate to storms and catastrophic floods in others, overall indicating a planet off balance. The Prophet's warning about the end of time is striking in its resemblance to ours, saying: "The famine would not break out because of drought, but there would be famine despite heavy rainfall as nothing would grow from the earth" (*Sahih Muslim* 2904). It is as if we are being tested through them because of our aggression against each other and the divine.

Groundwater plays a vital role in the locations of the natural wells, which vary from far and few in deserts versus the extensive network of underground rivers in the Yucatan peninsula. Recent technological advancements have allowed us to tap deeper into underground reservoirs called aquifers, making it possible to even farm in the middle of deserts. The only problem is that the rate we are pumping out these aquifers is much higher than the thousands of years of cumulative rainfall replenishing them. In most places, as long as you own the land it is free to pump the aquifers that lie beneath, even when an entire geological region is dependent on them. In our capitalistic world, food production in a barren wasteland is exceedingly profitable with enough surplus to keep the media and the politicians happy, as well as the rest of us in the dark.

Have they not seen how many generations We destroyed before them which We had established upon the earth as We have not established you? And We sent [rain from] the sky upon them in showers and made rivers flow beneath them; then We destroyed them for their sins and brought forth after them a generation of others. (al-Ana'am 6:6)

Interestingly, some of the most prominent desert farms in the US are owned by Saudi Arabia. It should come as no surprise that while drilling for oil in the 1970s, they discovered aquifers that were just as lucrative. Arabia witnessed an explosion of desert farms, visible even from space, making them the world's sixth-largest wheat exporter in the '90s. Within two decades, they pumped 80% of their aquifers dry (remarkably, the Zamzam is still flowing). This loss of revenue prompted a search for similar aquifers worldwide, leading to the emergence of desert farms in places like Arizona. Consequently, 66% of Saudi's total water usage is now located outside of the country. "They do not cheat in weights and measures but they will be stricken with famine, severe calamity, and the oppression of their rulers," warned the Prophet. "They do not withhold the Zakah of their wealth, but rain will be withheld from the sky, and were it not for the animals, no rain would fall on them" (*Sunan Ibn Majah* 4019).

Today, 92% of our daily water usage is for agriculture, with many developed countries relying on aquifers for half of that water. The more we pump, the deeper we must dig to access them. The Ogallala Aquifer, one of the world's largest, has already been nearly depleted through industrial agriculture, turning the farmlands at its penumbra into ghost towns. Places like Happy, Texas, offer a glimpse of the misery that lies ahead. The Canning Basin aquifer in Australia is also depleting at a similar rate, contributing to recent droughts in the region, which in turn directly affects global agriculture and politics.

Our consumerism fuels an ever-increasing demand for cheaper products from poorer countries. We are witnessing a new level of global oppression resulting from what political economist Thorstein Veblen (1857-1929 CE) called "fabricating wants." Business leaders admit to directing people to "the superficial things" and "fashionable consumption," which helps atomize them to individualism without challenging authority.[1025] Poorer countries resort to unsustainable measures to meet the demand, leading to a virtual water shift with devastating consequences. An unfortunate example was the drying up of the rivers draining into the Aral Sea from diversion to irrigate cotton fields needed for cheap jeans worldwide. This sea was drained in just 30 years of capitalism, turning it into a barren desert. Similarly, the mighty Colorado River, which created the Grand Canyon, no longer connects to the ocean. Containing the river's water within the dams in our country directly deprives those dependent on its water south of the border. As their farms dry up, they are left with no option but to abandon their barren native lands and migrate upstream.

Adam Smith's *The Wealth of Nations* popularized the delusion of "unintended consequences of intended action" somehow benefiting society at large. It justified unbridled capitalism by making the pursuit of self-interest appear philanthropic, which facilitated the exploitation of the Industrial Revolution. The resulting extreme poverty of Britain was only alleviated by shifting those exploitative practices to the colonies. That model was further honed by the emerging industrial empires of the new millennium, who now regularly inject fresh capital into the Third World through loans and aid to prevent exsanguination. Thus, maintaining their buying power but always favoring the developed world. Even when the World Bank spent $12 million in Bangladesh to install deep tubewells, it was controlled by local strongmen, ultimately benefiting large agribusiness.[1026] While only a fraction of it trickles down to the subaltern, most end up in the pockets of local elites and rulers who use it to maintain the *status quo*.[1027]

That "aid" also comes with strings, adding to the Third World debt and misery, which is then passed onto the poor. Subsequent generations inheriting it drown in their grief against the powers that rule. Their uprisings are brutally suppressed, often with the help of the same developed powers who use the usual propagandistic formulae and language to justify it in the eyes of a distracted world. "Until recently, it was convenient to call those justice seekers 'communists.' Since the collapse of communism the new label is 'Islamic fundamentalists,'" explained Dr. Hathout.[1028] These practices are also employed in domestic uprisings against institutional oppression and injustice, as demonstrated through movements like the Civil Rights and Black Lives Matter. The political confusion among the masses is highlighted in the case study of Texas, where the majority favors taxing the wealthy and big corporations yet claims to be Republicans.[1029]

These economic and moral depressions permeate through a raging planet with sinking and cracking ground due to the drying aquifers in regions including the US, Mexico, Saudi Arabia, Thailand, and Japan. Similarly, the fast-melting Arctic permafrost is rapidly reshaping the northern landscape with giant sinkholes of ever-increasing size. The resultant expelled methane further adds to the greenhouse gasses as we desperately pray for the planet's obstipation. These sinking realities give new meaning to God's warnings, like: "Do those who devise evil plots feel secure that God will not cause the earth to swallow them? Or that the torment will not come upon them in ways they cannot comprehend?" (*al-Nahl* 16:45).

While the political unrest on the surface has become a cliche, the underlying causes have remained underground. Geographical open-air concentration camps like Gaza have been hit hard, as their depleting aquifers have resulted in saltwater seepage into wells that residents have depended on for centuries. Currently, over 97% of Gaza's wells are unfit for human consumption, resulting in severe chronic illnesses. Norwegian trauma surgeon Mads Gilbert's outcries were ignored in 2014 when he reported 57% of Gazan households to be food insecure and 80% relying on foreign aid due to the continued embargo. It prevents them from meeting their daily caloric requirements, used as a drawn-out ethnic cleansing. "Prevalence of anaemia in children <2yrs in Gaza is at 72.8 percent, while prevalence of wasting, stunting, underweight have been documented at 34.3 percent, 31.4 percent, 31.45 percent respectively," reported Gilbert before the active genocide.[1030] At this rate, Gaza will soon be uninhabitable, and whatever comes out of that desperate situation would be wholly justified.

The collective punishment of such injustice looms over our horizon, with experts like Dr. Giulio Boccaletti predicting that the demand for fresh water will outstrip supply by 40% globally in less than a decade. God warns, "and fear a trial which will not strike those who have wronged among you exclusively, and know that God is severe in penalty" (*al-Anfal* 8:24-25). Until simple basic necessities are restored, anyone with running tap water is not in a place to criticize their anger. Preventing some from their access to fundamental rights while the rest of the world is drowning in surplus is an unforgivable crime. Places like Gaza and the Salton Sea are merely glimpses into our near future. In hindsight, it is apparent that Chomsky's prescient warning in 2016 about "other dangers, like pandemics," was not a prophecy but an inevitable outcome of recent events.[1031] Despite being fully aware of these potential catastrophes, we have failed to take any meaningful action.

The American Empire is undoubtedly one of the world's greatest, whose overt religiosity is celebrated by evangelists like Rick Warren. This empire sees its nationalistic greed as an end in itself without using its power to promote global justice. History shows that every empire eventually falls, and we have done little to thwart this fate. We have neglected to share our success with our people and those we exploit worldwide. While producing a disproportionate amount of greenhouse gasses, we refuse to participate in global justice movements such as climate change, leaving poorer countries to bear the brunt of our actions without adequate resources to combat them effectively. This only shows how overt religiosity in a society does not guarantee justice but can even counterintuitively impede it.

Shedinger explains, "As long as people are flocking into the churches (and Americans *are* flocking to conservative evangelical churches), involvement in larger social justice movements, though not actively discouraged, is often secondary to the primary 'religious' purpose of these churches."[1032] That is not to reject religion altogether, as we are already suffering from the adverse effects of secularism. Instead, we should rethink whatever prevents us from acting in a noble manner, which essentially is the most authentic *selfish* act that benefits all. As we dawdle about, distracted by our devices and social media, these global events seem too distant to be relevant to our daily lives. Our consumerism and disregard for the vulnerable are gainfully utilized by the powerful, "and those who survive will be left to contemplate the outcome," warns Chomsky.[1033] Fittingly, God compares such existence with locusts, whose sole purpose is to consume, consummate, and create chaos (*al-Qamar* 54:7).

Apart from the moral implications, we are directly impacted by events in faraway lands through the global economy. As millions of Bangladeshis are on the brink of becoming climate change refugees, scientist Atiq Rahman aptly proposed that these migrants should have the right to move to the developed countries responsible for global warming, such as the US.[1034] The level of poverty in that region is unimaginable for those without first-hand experience. Moreover, in 1971, Bangladesh narrowly escaped a total massacre aided by President Nixon and Kissinger. Today it continues to struggle with Muslim Rohingya refugees fleeing from an ongoing genocide in Myanmar.[1035] With the looming climate crisis, millions of more Muslim refugees will be forced to push into neighboring India, which will inevitably spell savagery scaling the partition, given the current overtly racist BJP government's anti-Muslim sentiment.[1036]

Humanity exists as a whole. The Prophet explained, "The believers in their mutual kindness, compassion, and sympathy are just like one body. When one of the limbs suffers, the whole body responds to it with wakefulness and fever" (*Riyad as-Salihin* 224). Aristotle used the same metaphor to explain why the well-being of the entire body of people naturally comes before the family and the individual, as the latter is not self-sufficient without the support of a community. Therefore, all virtuous people must be concerned with the well-being of the entire global community. A failure to do so renders them down to the level of an apolitical and unjust beast.[1037]

At the turn of this millennium, NASA's GRACE satellites detected dangerously depleted aquifers in the Syriac region, whose governments ignored the warning due to other pressing matters, including unrelenting Western interference. Continued over-pumping for agriculture led to a drought in 2006, resulting in an 85% loss of Syria's livestock. This forced farmers to relocate to cities, exacerbating existing stress and pushing the country closer to its breaking point. The resultant food shortage and shattered economy directly led to uprisings and subsequent regime change. What devolved from that desperation is an ongoing humanitarian crisis that continues to spread throughout the neighboring countries. A landlocked Jordan now faces a similar disaster as it pumps 160% more than the replenishing rate of its aquifers to meet the demands of an ever-increasing refugee population. Lebanon, Libya, and Yemen have already collapsed under the aftershocks of these issues, spreading further into surrounding lands. Desperate measures only lead to desperate times.

Our treatment of the planet reflects a global secular scientific trend where everything is a soulless inanimate object meant to serve our capitalistic needs. This corrupted worldview fuels an unsustainable relationship where everyone suffers. Dr. al-Attas pointed out that God created the world perfectly, and it remained that way for nearly its entire existence until the secular development of the last few centuries. As both this world and ourselves have an end, we are the only ones who need to *develop* toward the final objective of the hereafter and the natural world.[1038] Until we unlearn our misconceptions and get back in touch with our roots, all paths to a different future will remain obscured. "I believe the only way out of our current predicament will come through a fundamental shift in the way we understand and relate to nature—not simply through sentiment, government programs, or green technology," writes Ogunnaike. "Many traditions—Shinto, Taoist, Native American, African, ancient Norse, Celtic, and Germanic, as well as some Hindu and Islamic traditions—provide more sustainable models of understanding and interacting with the natural world from which we must eventually learn."[1039]

Geographer Troy Sternberg paints a global picture starting with the Millennium drought in Australia, which affected its wheat supply to the northern hemisphere during their winter months. The next domino was the Chinese drought of 2010, resulting in food prices skyrocketing in places like Syria and Egypt, which were simultaneously affected by their own droughts. The same year, Russia—one of the largest exporters of wheat to the Middle East—also had one of its worst droughts, resulting in an 80% reduction in their exports.[1040] Hence, Russia is again ogling the eastern European wheat fields that had once motivated Hitler and Napoleon. Wheat prices worldwide rose 130% that year, providing an excellent opportunity for some wealthy countries to profit from inflation. Poorer countries like Egypt saw prices rise more than 300%, enough to bring hungry people out into the streets, causing food riots in Cairo.

The spark that ignited the Arab Spring and its aftermath had a ripple effect on neighboring regions, where the influx of refugees from destabilized countries began to impact local economies. In Lebanon, for instance, it is estimated that over 40% of the current population are refugees.[1041] The fear of mass migration played into the Brexit debates and anti-refugee sentiment led to the election of far-right governments worldwide. This knee-jerk reaction to economic distress is a common phenomenon, as people often seek scapegoats to displace their fears and anxieties. Today, Islam serves as that *otherized* receptacle, "into which can be tossed all the angst and apprehension people feel about the faltering economy, about the new and unfamiliar political order, about the shifting cultural, racial, and religious landscapes that have fundamentally altered the world," explains Aslan.[1042] This labeling of Islam as a catch-all for anything foreign or alien is not limited to Europe, as even domestic Christian patriarchy, misogyny, and racist white supremacy are often labeled in mainstream media as the "Texas Taliban" or the "American Sharia."

Oppressive totalitarian agencies have always used such fear tactics to assert control by exploiting people's insecurities. "The fearful seek strong leaders who appear to have conquered their own Fears to lead them out of its slavery," explained Dr. Hawkins.[1043] However, when we immediately look to vituperate others at times of distress instead of taking responsibility for our actions, we are only following the *sunnah* of the devil. Recall when God called out his defiance, "He said, 'My Lord, since You made me go astray, I swear that I shall beautify for them [evils] on the earth, and shall lead all of them astray'" (*al-Hijr* 15:39). This blame-game is driven by that original sin, which only displays one's arrogance, ingratitude, and unhappiness.

Without a realistic solution to these issues, no *wall* will be big enough to stop the effects of climate change from being felt in every home. We are already witnessing the economic despair brought partly by recent droughts and a global pandemic. While regional droughts like the ones in ancient Egypt were their divine tests that resulted in their downfall, our abuse of the entire planet is culminating in a global trial that threatens to wipe out our entire species. For humanity hath seen no fury like mother nature scorned.

In the face of global injustice and chaotic hateful rhetoric, even the faithful can fall into despair and cry like our pious predecessors: "When will God's help arrive?" Indeed, God promises that His help is near (*al-Baqarah* 2:214). None of it makes sense if we think of our worldly lives as an end. "Repent, for the kingdom of heaven is near," preached John the Baptist in the wilderness of Judea before meeting his unjust fate (*Matthew* 3:2). Regardless of when the world actually ends, it effectively ends for all individuals when they die. But what have we prepared for our Afterlife? There is no causation nor correlation between one's status in this world and the next. The Prophet reminded us that if God wants good for somebody, He tests him with trials (*Sahih al-Bukhari* 5645). Those who are too far gone are given respite because this world is all they are struggling for.

Nonetheless, God sustains us all with His infinite mercy, "And the bounty of your Lord can never be withheld" (*al-Isra'* 17:20). Most certainly, all trials come to pass, but what matters is the state they leave us in. Only the faithless lose hope in God's mercy (*Yusuf* 12:87). We should not question His infinite wisdom when faced with a calamity. Instead, we must continue to play our parts as exemplified by His prophets and messengers till the brink of oblivion. The Prophet commanded: "Even if the Resurrection were established upon one of you while he has in his hand a sapling, let him plant it" (*Musnad Aḥmad* 12902).

No soul can ever die without God's Will at the destined time. Those who desire worldly gain, We will let them have it, and those who desire heavenly reward, We will grant it to them. And We will reward those who are grateful. (al-'Imran 3:145)

Ultimately, our worldly end is related to our failure to live a temperate life and be a moderate nation. Our current state of moral bankruptcy sets us on a particularly predictable trajectory in Ibn Khaldun's cycle of civilization. At the same time, we appear to be hurtling relatively straight to our demise in Einstein's curved spacetime. We are the apocryphal frogs in ethical sedentation as our world approaches its boiling point. Perhaps our sum over history is inevitable, but our individual salvation and success still depend on our humility and struggle to make the world a better place for all. The choice is always ours.

Before leaving our solar system in 1990, Voyager-I turned its camera around one last time to take a few more pictures of our home. One of them became known as the iconic Pale Blue Dot, depicting our planet as an unpretentious, lonesome pixel suspended in an unimaginable void. Carl Sagan's comments were weighty in capturing the relative insignificance of the entire spectrum of human conditions within the backdrop of such cosmic enormity. Yet, all our individual experiences—including everything discussed in this book—only occupy a microscopic flicker of this spacetime. As dominant and indestructible as we may seem today, our entire legacy only represents 0.007% of our planet's history. Our current conflicts and grievances will also come to pass, just like those historical ones. The only surviving factors from it all are human characteristics and whether we can navigate the constantly evolving present virtuously.

The righteous path is a lonely one walked by all of our pious predecessors. The prophets were treated harshly, unlike the flatterers at the court, who were later condemned as false prophets. Our earthly lives are illusory in every sense and ultimately nothing but a temporal prison. True freedom awaits us in our eternal life in the Hereafter, where the answers to all of our questions, prayers, and strife will be realized. Thus, the ease promised to believers is seldom manifested terrestrially.

To opine over all matters is corrosive to the soul. Once we have gained a reasonable understanding of our present condition, the spectator should relieve himself of the burdens of opinions and events beyond his control. Referring back to the opening hadith, while actions are judged by their intentions, the utmost emphasis lies on the *act*. If all of these discussions fail to spring us into action and change ourselves for the better, then our inaction is what ultimately allows evil to prosper. May God grant forgiveness and reward His servants who struggle in His path with His boundless mercy and approval.

So, indeed with hardship comes ease. Indeed with [that] hardship comes [more] ease. (ash-Sharh 94:5-6)

NOTES

[1] Ibn Khaldun. *The Muqaddimah: An Introduction to History*. Translated by Franz Rosenthal, abridged by N. J. Dawood, Princeton Classics Edition, 2015, pp. 414

[2] Orwell, George. *1984*. Thorndike Press, 2017, pp. 17

[3] Rovelli, Carlo. *The Order of Time*. Riverhead Books, 2018, pp. 178

[4] Hawkins, David R. *Power vs. Force: The Hidden Determinants of Human Behavior*. Hay House Inc, 1995, pp. 82

[5] Berlinski, David. *The Devil's Delusion: Atheism and Its Scientific Pretensions*. Basic Books, 2009, pp. 39

[6] Al-Attas, Syed M N. *Islam and Secularism*. Art Printing Works, 1993, pp. xv

[7] "The tendency of our culture: On Arnold Toynbee's analysis of 'prole culture.'" *The New Criterion*. Vol. 19, no. 7, March 2001, pp. 1

[8] Smith, John M. "Mongol Manpower and Persian Population." *Journal of the Economic and Social History of the Orient*, vol. 18, no. 3, 1975, pp. 271–99

[9] *Prester John, the Mongols and the Ten Lost Tribes*. Edited by Charles F Beckingham and Bernard Hamilton, Aldershot, 1996

[10] Morgan, David. *The Mongols*. Wiley & Sons, 1987, pp. 74

[11] From 'Abdallah b Fadlallah Wassaf, *Tarjiyat al-amsar wa-tajziyat al-a'sar*, in Bertold Spuler's *History of the Mongols*. Translated by Helga Drummond and Stuart Drummond, Hippocrene Books, 1989, pp. 120-1

[12] Frankopan, Peter. *The Silk Roads*. First Vintage Books, 2017, pp. 165

[13] Locke, John. *An Essay Concerning Human Understanding*. Penguin Books, 1997, pp. 238

[14] NIDA. "What are MDMA's effects on the brain?" *NIH*. April 13, 2021

[15] Adamson, Peter. *Al-Kindi*. Oxford University Press, 2007, pp. 151

[16] Mauss, Iris B, et al. "Can seeking happiness make people unhappy? [corrected] Paradoxical effects of valuing happiness." *Emotion*, vol. 11, no. 4, 2011, pp. 807-15

[17] Grant, Adam. *Think Again: The Power of Knowing What You Don't Know*. Viking, 2021, pp. 237-8

[18] Lama, Dalai, and Howard Cutler. *The Art of Happiness: A Handbook for Living*. Riverhead books, 2009, pp. 23

[19] Watkins, Philip C. *Gratitude and the Good Life: Toward a Psychology of Appreciation*. Springer, 2014, pp. 3

[20] Watkins, Philip C. *Gratitude and the Good Life: Toward a Psychology of Appreciation*. Springer, 2014, pp. 8

[21] Howell, Ryan T, et al. "Health benefits: Metaanalytically determining the impact of well-being on objective health outcomes." *Health Psychology Review*, vol. 1, 2007, pp. 83–136

[22] Ibn Daqiq al-'Id. *A Treasury of Hadith: A Commentary on Nawawi's Forty Prophetic Traditions*. Translated by Mokrane Guezzou, Kube Publishing, 2014, pp. 137-138

[23] Lama, Dalai, and Howard Cutler. *The Art of Happiness: A Handbook for Living*. Riverhead books, 2009, pp. 141

[24] Locke, John. *An Essay Concerning Human Understanding*. Penguin Books, 1997, pp. 130

[25] Pluckrose, Helen and James Lindsay. *Cynical Theories: How Activist Scholarship Made Everything about Race, Gender, and Identity*. Pitchstone Publishing, 2020, pp. 227

[26] Fideler, David. *Breakfast With Seneca: A Stoic Guide to the Art of Living*. W. W. Norton & Co, 2022, pp. 53

[27] Aristotle. *Nicomachean Ethics*. Translated by W. D. Ross, Modern Library, 2001, Bk. III: Ch. 2

[28] Seneca. *On The Shortness of Life*. Translated by C. D. N. Costa, Penguin Books, 2005, 15.5-16.1

[29] Fideler, David. *Breakfast With Seneca: A Stoic Guide to the Art of Living.* W. W. Norton & Co, 2022, pp. 123

[30] Hawkins, David R. *Power vs. Force: The Hidden Determinants of Human Behavior.* Hay House Inc, 1995, pp. 18-9

[31] Keles, Betul, et al. "A systematic review: the influence of social media on depression, anxiety and psychological distress in adolescents." *International Journal of Adolescence and Youth*, vol. 25, Match 21, 2019, pp. 79-93

[32] Carr, Nicholas. *The Shallows: What the Internet is Doing to Our Brains.* Norton, 2010

[33] Seneca. *Letters from a Stoic.* Translated by Robin Campbell, Penguin, 1969, 115.9

[34] Sheldon, OJ, et al. "Emotionally unskilled, unaware, and uninterested in learning more: Reactions to feedback about deficits in emotional intelligence." *Journal of Applied Psychology*, vol. 99, 2014, pp. 125–137

[35] Seneca. *Letters from a Stoic.* Translated by Robin Campbell, Penguin, 1969, 78.2

[36] Aristotle. *Nicomachean Ethics.* Translated by W. D. Ross, Modern Library, 2001, Bk. III: Ch. 9

[37] Kreeft, Peter. *The Platonic Tradition.* St. Augustine's Press, 2018, pp. 108

[38] Fredrickson, Barbara L, et al. "A functional genomic perspective on human well-being." *Proceedings of the National Academy of Sciences of the United States of America*, vol. 110, 33, August 13, 2013, pp. 13684-9

[39] Einstein, Albert. "Religion and Science: On Prayer; Purpose in Nature; Meaning of Life; the Soul; A Personal God." *New York Times Magazine*, November 9, 1930, pp. 1-4

[40] Locke, John. *An Essay Concerning Human Understanding.* Penguin Books, 1997, pp. 7

[41] Al-Ghazali. *The Alchemy of Happiness.* Translated by Claud Field, Martino Fine Books, 2017

[42] Mill, John S. *Autobiography.* Penguin Classics, 1883/1990

[43] Seneca. *Letters from a Stoic.* Translated by Robin Campbell, Penguin, 1969, 78.13

[44] Rafi-ud-din, Mohammad. *The Manifesto of Islam: an exposition of Islam as the inevitable world ideology of the future.* Forgotten Books, 2012, pp. 6

[45] Seneca. *Letters from a Stoic.* Translated by Robin Campbell, Penguin, 1969, 69.1

[46] Eyal, Tal, et al. "Perspective mistaking: Accurately understanding the mind of another requires getting perspective, not taking perspective." *Journal of personality and social psychology*, vol. 114,4, April 2018, pp. 547-571

[47] Hastings, James, et al. *Encyclopædia of Religion and Ethics.* T. & T. Clark, 1923, pp. 616–618

[48] Al-Biruni. *On Hinduism (1030).* Oxford Islamic Studies Online, Accessed Dec 28, 2021

[49] Yuvraj, Krishan. *The Doctrine of Karma: Its Origin and Development in Brāhmaṇical, Buddhist, and Jaina Traditions.* Motilal Banarsidass Publishers, 1997, pp. 17–27

[50] Parenti, Michael. *God And His Demons.* Prometheus Books, 2010, pp. 202

[51] See for example: Parenti, Michael. *God And His Demons.* Prometheus Books, 2010, Ch. 12

[52] Thackston Jr, WM. *Signs of the Unseen: The Discourse of Jalaluddin Rumi.* Shambhala, 1999, pp. xx

[53] Lang, Jeffrey. *Struggling to Surrender.* Amana Publications, 1995, pp. 59

[54] Pope, Alexander. *An Essay on Man.* Epistle 1:161-4

[55] Aristotle. *Metaphysics.* Translated by W. D. Ross, Modern Library, 2001, Bk. III: Ch. 4

[56] Lang, Jeffrey. *Struggling to Surrender.* Amana Publications, 1995, pp. 59

[57] Aurelius, Marcus. *The Emperor's Handbook.* Translated by C. Scot Hicks and David V. Hicks. Scribner, 2002, Bk. IX:4

[58] Sun Tzu. *The Art of War.* Thomas Cleary's introduction, Shambhala Publications, 1988, pp. 4

[59] Thackston Jr, WM. *Signs of the Unseen: The Discourse of Jalaluddin Rumi.* Shambhala, 1999, pp. xix

[60] Messerly, John "W. H. Auden's, 'We must love one another or die.'" *reasonandmeaning.com*, May 2014

[61] Ansary, Tamim. *The Invention of Yesterday.* Public Affairs, 2019, pp. 355

[62] McAuliffe Jr, Dennis. *The Deaths of Sybil Bolton: An American History.* Times Books, 1994, pp. 116

[63] Zinn, Howard. *A People's History of the United States.* Harper Collins, 1999, pp. 138

[64] Chomsky, Noam. *Who Rules the World?* Metropolitan Books, 2016, pp. 34

[65] King Jr, Martin L. *Why We Can't Wait.* New American Library, 1964

[66] Ogilvy, James. "Greed." *Wicked Pleasures: Meditations on the Seven "Deadly" Sins*, edited by Robert C. Solomon, Rowman & Littlefield, 1999

[67] Ibn Taymiyyah. *Al-'Ubudiyyah.* Edited by Muhammad Zuhair Shawish, al-Maktab al-Islami, 2005, pp. 81

[68] Staw, Barry M and Jerry Ross. "Understanding Behavior in Escalation Situations." *Science*, vol. 246, no. 4927 November 1989, pp. 216–20

[69] Fildis, Ayse T. "The Troubles in Syria: Spawned by French Divide and Rule," *Middle East Policy*, vol. 18, no. 4, Winter 2011

[70] Briggs, Helen. "Neanderthals 'self-medicated' for pain." *BBC News*, March 8, 2017

[71] Frankopan, Peter. *The Silk Roads*. First Vintage Books, 2017, pp. 252-3

[72] Dunbar-Ortiz, Roxanne. *An Indigenous Peoples' History of The United States*. Beacon Press, 2014, pp. 139-40

[73] Eisenhardt, Kathleen M, et al. "How Management Teams Can Have a Good Fight." *Harvard Business Review*, July-Aug 1997

[74] Lama, Dalai, and Howard Cutler. *The Art of Happiness: A Handbook for Living*. Riverhead books, 2009, pp. 147

[75] Turkle, Sherry. *Alone Together: Why We Expect More from Technology and Less from Each Other*. Basic Books, 2011

[76] Russell, Bertrand. *An Outline of Philosophy*. Meridian Printing, 1960, pp. 30-31

[77] Feynman, Richard P. "There's Plenty of Room at the Bottom," *Caltech Engineering and Science*, vol. 23, no. 5, 1960, pp. 36

[78] Thant, U. "The Decade of Development." *Public Papers of the Secretaries-General of the United Nations*, edited by Andrew W. Cordier and Max Harrelson, vol. 6, 1976, pp. 118

[79] Immerwahr, Daniel. *How To Hide An Empire: A History of the Greater United States*. Farrar, Straus and Giroux, 2019, pp. 276

[80] Mejcher, Helmut. "Oil and British Policy towards Mesopotamia, 1914-1918." *Middle Eastern Studies*, vol. 8, no. 3, 1972, pp. 377–91

[81] War Cabinet minutes, August 13, 1918, CAB 23/42

[82] Buchan, James. *Days of God: The Revolution in Iran and its Consequences*. John Murray Publishers, 2012, pp. 27

[83] Goldberg, Suzanne. "Exxon Knew of Climate Change in 1981, but it Funded Deniers for 27 More Years," *Guardian*, July 8, 2015

[84] Plumer, Brad and Henry Fountain. "A Hotter Future Is Certain, Climate Panel Warns. But How Hot Is Up to Us." *The New York Times*. Aug 9, 2021; Spring, Jake, et al. "UN climate report urges world to adapt now, or suffer later." *Reuters*. Feb 28, 2022

[85] Chomsky, Noam. *Who Rules the World?* Metropolitan Books, 2016, pp. 160

[86] Bryson, Bill. *A Short History of Nearly Everything*. Broadway Books, 2003, pp. 280

[87] Chomsky, Noam. *Who Rules the World?* Metropolitan Books, 2016, pp. 231

[88] Holley, Peter. et al. "The Doomsday Clock Just Advanced, 'Thanks to Trump': It's Now Just 2 1/2 Minutes to 'Midnight,'" *Washington Post*, Jan 26, 2017

[89] Grant, Richard. "Do Trees Talk to Each Other?" *Smithsonian*, March 2018

[90] Norden, Natalia. et al. "Mast Fruiting Is a Frequent Strategy in Woody Species of Eastern South America."*PLoS One*, vol. 2, no, 10, Oct 24, 2007

[91] Gorman, James. "Baboon Study Shows Benefits for Nice Guys, Who Finish 2nd." *The New York Times*, July 14, 2011

[92] Hathout, Hassan. *Reading the Muslim Mind*. American Trust Publications, 1995, pp. 90

[93] MacIntyre, Alasdair. *AfterVirtue*. University of Notre Dame Press, 2007, pp. 69

[94] Russell, Bertrand. *An Outline of Philosophy*. Meridian Printing, 1960, pp. 30

[95] Said, Edward W. *Orientalism*. Vintage Books, 1979, pp. 251

[96] Deneen, Patrick J. *Why Liberalism Failed*. Yale University Press, 2018, pp. 143

[97] Homes, John. "Losing 25,000 to Hunger Every Day." *The UN Chronicle*.

[98] Orwell, George. *1984*. Thorndike Press, 2017, pp. 304

[99] Deneen, Patrick J. *Why Liberalism Failed*. Yale University Press, 2018, pp. 179

[100] MacIntyre, Alasdair. *AfterVirtue*. University of Notre Dame Press, 2007, pp. xv

[101] "Poverty Myths." https://4thworldmovement.org/

[102] Shelton, Scarlet. "Effects of Poverty on Society." *The Borgen Project*, Aug 3, 2016

[103] Anser, Muhammad K, et al. "Dynamic linkages between poverty, inequality, crime, and social expenditures in a panel of 16 countries: two-step GMM estimates." *Economic Structures*, vol. 9, 2020, pp. 43

[104] Brocht, Chauna, et al. "Any Way You Cut It: Income Inequality on the Rise Regardless of How It's Measured," Briefing Paper, *Economic Policy Institute*, September 1, 2000

[105] Seneca. *On Anger*. Translated by Aubrey Stewart. Book 2.31.7

[106] Fry, Richard and Rakesh Kochhar. "America's Wealth Gap Between MIddle-Income and Upper-Income Families Is Widest on Record," *Pew Research Center*, December 17, 2014

[107] White, Martha C. "Wall Street minted 56 new billionaires since the pandemic began - but many families are left behind. *NBC News*, December 30, 2020

[108] Baker, Dean. "Health Care Costs and the Budget." *Center for Economic and Policy Research*, February 27, 2019

[109] Editors, "The Secret Behind Big Bank Profits," *Bloomberg News*, February 21, 2013

[110] Chomsky, Noam. *Who Rules the World?* Metropolitan Books, 2016, pp. 53, 63

[111] Stockholm International Peace Research Institute, *SIPRI Military Expenditure Database*, April 2020

[112] Routley, Nick. "The Anatomy of the $2 Trillion COVID-19 Stimulus Bill." *Visual Capitalist*. March 30, 2020

[113] Parenti, Michael. *The Sword And The Dollar: Imperialism, Revolution, and the Arms Race*. St. Martin Press, 1989, pp. 8

[114] Marx, Karl. "Wages of Labour." *Economic and Philosophic Manuscripts of 1844*. Progress Publishers, 1959

[115] Parenti, Michael. *The Sword And The Dollar: Imperialism, Revolution, and the Arms Race*. St. Martin Press, 1989, pp. 13, 20

[116] Gay, Chris. "Why is America so opposed to universal health care?" *South China Morning Post*, May 19, 2017

[117] Smith, Emily E. "Meaning Is Healthier Than Happiness." *The Atlantic*, August 1, 2013

[118] Shedinger, Robert F. *Was Jesus A Muslim?* Fortress Press, 2009, pp. 54

[119] Seneca. *Of Consolation to Helvia*. Translated by Aubrey Stewart, 10.8-11

[120] Hathout, Hassan. *Reading the Muslim Mind*. American Trust Publications, 1995

[121] Aristotle. *Politics*. Translated by Benjamin Jowett, Modern Library, 2001, Bk. I: Ch. 10

[122] Bayyah, Shaykh A. "Religious Minorities in Muslim-Majority Lands: A Legal Framework and a Call to Action." *The Marrakesh Declaration*, 2018, pp. 14

[123] Bryson, Bill. *A Short History of Nearly Everything*. Broadway Books, 2003, pp. 158

[124] Chomsky, Noam. *Who Rules the World?* Metropolitan Books, 2016, pp. 64

[125] Orwell, George. *1984*. Thorndike Press, 2017, pp. 421

[126] Hawkins, David R. *Power vs. Force: The Hidden Determinants of Human Behavior*. Hay House Inc, 1995, pp. 154

[127] Aristotle. *Politics*. Translated by Benjamin Jowett, Modern Library, 2001, Bk. III: Ch. 7

[128] Aristotle. *Politics*. Translated by Benjamin Jowett, Modern Library, 2001, Bk. IV: Ch. 2

[129] Deneen, Patrick J. *Why Liberalism Failed*. Yale University Press, 2018, pp. 159

[130] Bayyah, Shaykh A. "Religious Minorities in Muslim-Majority Lands: A Legal Framework and a Call to Action." *The Marrakesh Declaration*, 2018, pp. 30

[131] Kramer, Caroline K, et al. "Are metabolically healthy overweight and obesity benign conditions?: A systematic review and meta-analysis." *Annals of Internal Medicine*, vol. 159, no. 11, December 2013, pp. 758-69

[132] Ibn Khaldun. *The Muqaddimah: An Introduction to History*. Translated by Franz Rosenthal, abridged by N. J. Dawood, Princeton Classics Edition, 2015, pp. 324

[133] Fagin, Dan and Marianne Lavelle. *Toxic Deception: How the Chemical Industry Manipulates Science, Bends the Law, and Endangers Your Health*, Birch Lane Press, 1996

[134] Wells, Jane. "Is 'organic' really organic? A deep dive into the dirt." *CNBC*, November 4, 2015

[135] Chomsky, Noam. *Manufacturing Consent: The Political Economy of the Mass Media*. Pantheon Books, 2002, pp. xlvi

[136] Thornton, Joseph. *Pandora's Poison: Chlorine, Health, and a New Environmental Strategy*. MIT Press, 2000,

pp. 100

[137] O'Dea, K. "Marked improvement in carbohydrate and lipid metabolism in diabetic Australian Aborigines after

temporary reversion to traditional lifestyles." *Diabetes*, vol. 33, no. 6, June 1984, pp. 596-603

[138] Pollan, Michael. *In Defense of Food*. Thorndike Press, 2008, pp. 68-9

[139] Sens, Josh. "Racing Like Rats / Stress: Are too many people using it as an excuse for bad behavior?" *SFGate*, September 16, 2001

[140] Luo, Jia et al. "Ingestion of Lactobacillus strain reduces anxiety and improves cognitive function in the hyperammonemia rat." *Science China. Life sciences*, vol. 57, no. 3 (2014), pp. 327-335; Mindus, Claire et al. "*Lactobacillus*-Based Probiotics Reduce the Adverse Effects of Stress in Rodents: A Meta-analysis." *Frontiers in behavioral neuroscience*, vol. 15 642757. 16 June 2021; Bravo, Javier A., et al. "Ingestion of Lactobacillus Strain Regulates Emotional Behavior and Central GABA Receptor Expression in a Mouse via the Vagus Nerve." *Proceedings of the National Academy of Sciences of the United States of America*, vol. 108, no. 38, 2011, pp. 16050–55

[141] Patangia, Dhrati V et al. "Impact of antibiotics on the human microbiome and consequences for host health." *MicrobiologyOpen*, vol. 11, no1, 2022: e1260

[142] Ramirez, Jaime et al. "Antibiotics as Major Disruptors of Gut Microbiota." *Frontiers in cellular and infection microbiology*, vol. 10 572912, Nov. 24, 2020

[143] Wansink, Brian, et al. "Internal and external cues of meal cessation: the French paradox redux?" *Obesity*, vol. 15, no. 12, December 2007, pp. 2920-4.

[144] Netz, Yael. "Is the Comparison between Exercise and Pharmacologic Treatment of Depression in the Clinical Practice Guideline of the American College of Physicians Evidence-Based?" *Frontiers in pharmacology*, vol. 8, no. 257, May 15, 2017

[145] Ibn Khaldun. *The Muqaddimah: An Introduction to History*. Translated by Franz Rosenthal, abridged by N. J. Dawood, Princeton Classics Edition, 2015, pp. 67

[146] Al-Ghazali. *The Alchemy of Happiness*. Translated by Claud Field, Martino Fine Books, 2017

[147] Immerwahr, Daniel. *How To Hide An Empire: A History of the Greater United States*. Farrar, Straus and Giroux, 2019, pp. 140

[148] Scherwitz, L. et al. "Self-involvement and coronary heart disease incidence in the multiple risk factor intervention trial." *Psychosomatic Medicine*, vol. 48, no. 3-4, Mar-Apr 1986, pp. 187-99

[149] Bryson, Bill. *A Short History of Nearly Everything*. Broadway Books, 2003, pp. 284

[150] Rosane, Olivia. "Humans and Big Ag Livestock Now Account for 96 Percent of Mammal Biomass." *EcoWatch*, May 23, 2018

[151] Bryson, Bill. *A Short History of Nearly Everything*. Broadway Books, 2003, pp. 472

[152] Tolstoy, Leo. *Hadji Murat*. Hesperus Classics, 2003, pp. 4

[153] Hawkins, David R. *Power vs. Force: The Hidden Determinants of Human Behavior*. Hay House Inc, 1995, pp. 291

[154] Bosick, Stacey, and Paula Fomby. "Family Instability in Childhood and Criminal Offending during the Transition into Adulthood." *The American behavioral scientist*, vol. 62, no. 11, 2018, pp. 1483-1504

[155] Aristotle. *Politics*. Translated by Benjamin Jowett, Modern Library, 2001, Bk. I: Ch. 3

[156] Stowasser, Barbara F. "The End is Near: Minor and Major Signs of the Hour in Islamic Texts and Contexts." *Georgetown University*.

[157] Bracken, HM. "Essence, Accident, and Race." *Hermathena*, Trinity College Dublin, no 116, 1973, pp. 81-96; Weikart, Richard. *From Darwin to Hitler: Evolutionary Ethics, Eugenics, and Racism in Germany*, Palgrave Mcillan, 2006

[158] Mill, John Stuart. "Considerations on Representative Government." *On Liberty and Other Essays*, edited by John Gray, Oxford University Press, 2008, pp. 232

[159] Orwell, George. "Politics and the English Language." Online article, pp. 10, http://www.public-library.uk/ebooks/72/30.pdf

[160] Epictetus. *Discourses, Fragments, and Encheiridion*. Translated by W. A. Oldfather, Loeb Classical Library, 1925-8, 4.1.113

[161] MacIntyre, Alasdair. *AfterVirtue*. University of Notre Dame Press, 2007, pp. 69-70

[162] Bryson, Bill. *A Short History of Nearly Everything*. Broadway Books, 2003, pp. 388

[163] Ibn Khaldun. *The Muqaddimah: An Introduction to History*. Translated by Franz Rosenthal, abridged by N. J. Dawood, Princeton Classics Edition, 2015, pp. 138

[164] Toynbee, Arnold J. *A Study of History*, vol. 3, *The Growths of Civilizations*, 2nd ed. Oxford University Press, 1935, pp. 322

[165] Cowan, James. Introduction. *Hayy Ibn Yaqzan*, by Ibn Tufail, Azafran Books, 2018, pp. 9

[166] Draper, John W. *History Of The Conflict Between Religion And Science*. Cambridge University Press

[167] Bryson, Bill. *A Short History of Nearly Everything*. Broadway Books, 2003, pp. 386

[168] Bryson, Bill. *A Short History of Nearly Everything*. Broadway Books, 2003, pp. 384

[169] Sagan, Carl. *Cosmos*. Random House, 1980, pp. 20

[170] Shanavas, TO. *Islamic Theory of Evolution: The Missing Link between Darwin and the Origin of Species*. Brainbowpress, 2005, pp. 70

[171] Russell, Bertrand. *An Outline of Philosophy*. Meridian Printing, 1960, pp. 260

[172] Al-Ghazali. *The Alchemy of Happiness*. Translated by Claud Field, Martino Fine Books, 2017

[173] Bryson, Bill. *A Short History of Nearly Everything*. Broadway Books, 2003, pp. 166

[174] Seife, Charles. *Zero: The Biography of a Dangerous Idea*. Penguin Books, 2000, pp. 101

[175] Feyerabend, Paul. *Farewell to Reason*. Verso, 1987, pp. 26-7

[176] Berlinski, David. *The Devil's Delusion: Atheism and Its Scientific Pretensions*. Basic Books, 2009, pp. 156-9

[177] Arntzen, Jan W. "The Midwife Toad Challenge After (Half) a Century." *Frontiers in Ecology and Evolution*, Feb 10, 2022

[178] Champagne, Frances A, et al. "Variations in maternal care in the rat as a mediating influence for the effects of environment on development." *Physiology & Behavior*, vol. 79, no. 3, August 2003, pp. 359-71

[179] Vågerö, Denny, et al. "Paternal grandfather's access to food predicts all-cause and cancer mortality in grandsons." *Nature Communications*, vol. 9, no.1, December 2018, pp. 5124

[180] Shanavas, TO. *Islamic Theory of Evolution: The Missing Link between Darwin and the Origin of Species*. Brainbowpress, 2005, pp. 96

[181] Bryson, Bill. *A Short History of Nearly Everything*. Broadway Books, 2003, pp. 348

[182] Bryson, Bill. *A Short History of Nearly Everything*. Broadway Books, 2003, pp. 441

[183] Bryson, Bill. *A Short History of Nearly Everything*. Broadway Books, 2003, pp. 343, 345

[184] Qadhi, Yasir. "The Stories of the Prophets: The Story of Adam Pt 3." *MuslimCentral.com* podcast August 18, 2021

[185] Shanavas, TO. *Islamic Theory of Evolution: The Missing Link between Darwin and the Origin of Species*. Brainbowpress, 2005, pp. 167

[186] Thackston Jr, WM. *Signs of the Unseen: The Discourse of Jalaluddin Rumi*. Shambhala, 1999, pp. xx

[187] Bryson, Bill. *A Short History of Nearly Everything*. Broadway Books, 2003, pp. 291

[188] Kuhn, Thomas S. *The Structure of Scientific Revolutions*. 4th ed, The University of Chicago Press, 2012, pp. 141

[189] Russell, Bertrand. *An Outline of Philosophy*. Meridian Printing, 1960, pp. 5

[190] MacIntyre, Alasdair. *AfterVirtue*. University of Notre Dame Press, 2007, pp. 234

[191] Bryson, Bill. *A Short History of Nearly Everything*. Broadway Books, 2003, pp. 293

[192] Berlinski, David. *The Devil's Delusion: Atheism and Its Scientific Pretensions*. Basic Books, 2009, pp. 111

[193] Kierkegaard, Soren. *Kierkegaard's Writings, VI, Volume 6: Fear and Trembling/Repetition*. Edited and translated by Edna H Hong and Howard V Hong, Princeton University Press, 1983, pp. 200

[194] Rovelli, Carlo. *The Order of Time*. Riverhead Books, 2018, pp. 16

[195] Gould, Stephen J. *Ever Since Darwin*. W W Norton & Company, 1992, pp. 60

[196] Husaini, Abdul Q. *The Pantheistic Monism of Ibn al-'Arabi*. Sh. Muhammad Ashraf, 2nd edition, 1979

[197] Hakim, KA. *The Metaphysics of Rumi: A critical and historical sketch*. Institute of Islamic Culture, 1977, pp. 37

[198] Shanavas, TO. *Islamic Theory of Evolution: The Missing Link between Darwin and the Origin of Species*. Brainbowpress, 2005, pp. 116-117

[199] Stokes, Philip. *Philosophy 100 Essential Thinkers*. Enchanted Lion Books, 2006, pp. 119

[200] Shanavas, TO. *Islamic Theory of Evolution: The Missing Link between Darwin and the Origin of Species*. Brainbowpress, 2005, pp. 121

[201] Darwin, Charles. *On the Origin of The Species*. Down, Bromley, Kent, 1859, pp. 32, 61, 63

[202] Braterman, Paul. "Islamic Foreshadowing of Evolution." *Muslim Heritage*, March 21, 2017

[203] Al-Biruni. *Athar-ul-Bakya (The Chronology of Ancient Nations)*. Translated by Eduard Sachau, W. H. Allen & Co., 1879

[204] Berlinski, David. *The Devil's Delusion: Atheism and Its Scientific Pretensions*. Basic Books, 2009, pp. 190-1

[205] Shohat, Ella. "Notes on the 'Post-Colonial.'" *Social Text*, Duke University Press, no. 31/32, pp. 99–113

[206] Southern, R.W. *Western Views of Islam in the Middle Ages*. Harvard University Press, 1978, pp. 91-2, 108-9

[207] Al-Qazzaz, Ayad, et al. *The Arabs in American Textbooks*. California State Board of Education, 1975

[208] Hourani, Albert. "Islam and the philosophers of history." *Middle Eastern Studies*, vol. 3:3, 1967, pp. 222

[209] Elsbach, Kimberly D, and C B Bhattacharya. "Defining Who You Are by What You're Not: Organizational Disidentification and the National Rifle Association." *Organization Science*, vol. 12, no. 4, August 2001, pp. 393–413

[210] Said, Edward W. *Orientalism*. Vintage Books, 1979, pp. 235-7

[211] Cust, R. N. "The International Congresses of Orientalists." *Hellas*, vol. 6, no. 4, 1897, pp. 349

[212] Said, Edward W. *Orientalism*. Vintage Books, 1979, pp. 153-6

[213] Feyerabend, Paul. *Farewell to Reason*. Verso, 1987, pp. 11

[214] Said, Edward W. *Orientalism*. Vintage Books, 1979, pp. 262

[215] Said, Edward W. *Orientalism*. Vintage Books, 1979, pp. 292-3

[216] Said, Edward W. *Orientalism*. Vintage Books, 1979, pp. 107

[217] Masalha, Nur. *Palestine: A Four Thousand Year History*. I. B. Tauris, 2022, pp. 63

[218] Thomas, Jake. "Russia Accused of 'Under Reporting' Civilian Casualties Just Like in Syria." *Newsweek*, March 23, 2022

[219] Wolf, Eric R. *Europe and the People without History*. University of California Press, 1982, pp. 5

[220] Chateaubriand, Francois-Rene. *Oeuvres*, 2: 1011, 979, 990, 1052

[221] Chateaubriand, Francois-Rene. *Oeuvres*, 2: 1069

[222] Said, Edward W. *Orientalism*. Vintage Books, 1979, pp. 171

[223] Roth, Norman. *Conversos, Inquisition, and the Expulsion of the Jews from Spain*. University of Wisconsin Press, 2002, pp. 229

[224] Roberts, Dorothy E. *Four Hundred Souls*. Edited by Ibram X Kendi and Keisha N Blain, One World, 2021, pp. 119

[225] MacIntyre, Alasdair. *A Short History of Ethics*. The Macmillan Company, 1966, pp. 183

[226] Eze, Emmanuel C. *Race and the Enlightenment: A Reader*. Wiley-Blackwell, 1997

[227] Roberts, Dorothy E. *Four Hundred Souls*. Edited by Ibram X Kendi and Keisha N Blain, One World, 2021, pp. 120

[228] Pluckrose, Helen and James Lindsay. *Cynical Theories: How Activist Scholarship Made Everything about Race, Gender, and Identity*. Pitchstone Publishing, 2020, pp. 112

[229] Keel, Terence. *Divine Variations: How Christian Thought Became Racial Science*. Stanford University Press, 2018

[230] Said, Edward W. *Orientalism*. Vintage Books, 1979, pp. 228

[231] Deneen, Patrick J. *Why Liberalism Failed*. Yale University Press, 2018, pp. 186

[232] Quoted in: Zinn, Howard. *A People's History of the United States*. Harper Collins, 1999, pp. 28

[233] Sowell, Thomas. *Black Rednecks and White Liberals*. Encounter Books, 2005, pp. 157-9

[234] Cherfils, Christian. *Bonaparte Et L'Islam: D'Apres Les Documents Francais Et Arabes (1914)*. Kessinger Publishing 2010

[235] Sowell, Thomas. *Black Rednecks and White Liberals*. Encounter Books, 2005, pp. 126-7

[236] Ansary, Tamim. *Destiny Disrupted: A History of the World Through Islamic Eyes*. Public Affairs, 2010

[237] Mumisa, Michael. *Islamic Law: Theory & Interpretation*. Amana Publications, 2002, pp. 45

[238] Ibn Ashur. *Treatise on Maqasid al-Shari'ah*. Translated by muhammad al-Tahir Ibn Ashur. The International Institute of Islamic Thought, 2006, ch. 18

[239] Phillips, Kevin P. *The Cousins' Wars: Religion, Politics, Civil Warfare, And The Triumph Of Anglo-America*. Basic Books, 1999, pp. 177-90

[240] Dunbar-Ortiz, Roxanne. *An Indigenous Peoples' History of The United States*. Beacon Press, 2014, pp. 51-2
[241] Dunbar-Ortiz, Roxanne. *An Indigenous Peoples' History of The United States*. Beacon Press, 2014, pp. 54
[242] Reynolds, David S. *John Brown, Abolitionist: The Man Who Killed Slavery, Sparked the Civil War, and Seeded Civil Rights*. Vintage, 2006, pp. 449
[243] Said, Edward W. *Orientalism*. Vintage Books, 1979, pp. 14
[244] Shanavas, TO. *Islamic Theory of Evolution: The Missing Link between Darwin and the Origin of Species*. Brainbowpress, 2005, pp. 80
[245] Graham, Mark. *How Islam Created The Modern World*. Amana Publications, 2006, pp. 47
[246] Frankopan, Peter. *The Silk Roads*. First Vintage Books, 2017, pp. 142
[247] Strogatz, Steven. *Infinite Powers: How Calculus Reveals the Secrets of the Universe*. Houghton Mifflin Harcourt, 2019, pp. 90-1
[248] Kwan, Alistair, et al. "Who Really Discovered Snell's Law?" *Physics World*, vol. 15, no. 4, April 2002
[249] Parenti, Michael. *God And His Demons*. Prometheus Books, 2010, pp. 182
[250] Awaad, Rania, and Sara Ali. "Obsessional Disorders in al-Balkhi's 9th century treatise: Sustenance of the Body and Soul." *Journal of affective disorders*, vol. 180, July 2015, pp. 185-9
[251] Brown, Peter. *The Rise of Western Christendom: Triumph and Divinity, 200-1000 AD*. Blackwell, 1996, pp. 194
[252] Greifenhagen, F Volker. "Why did Luther want the Qur'an to be published?" Table Talk given at Luther College at the University of Regina, March 7, 2017
[253] Berkey, Jonathan P. *The Transmission of Knowledge in Medieval Cairo: A Social History of Islamic Education*. Princeton University Press, 1992, pp. 296
[254] Curiel, Jonathan. "Muslim roots of the blues/The music of famous American blues singers reaches back through the South to the culture of West Africa." *SFGate*, Aug 15, 2004
[255] Graham, Mark. *How Islam Created The Modern World*. Amana Publications, 2006, pp. 79
[256] Al-Juwaynī, *The End of the Pursuit (Nihāyat al-maṭlab)*, quoted in *The Marrakesh declaration*, pp. 37
[257] Bayyah, Shaykh A. "Religious Minorities in Muslim-Majority Lands: A Legal Framework and a Call to Action." *The Marrakesh Declaration*, 2018, pp. 38
[258] Aslan, Reza. *No god but God: The Origins, Evolution, and Future of Islam*. Random House Trade, 2011, pp. 96
[259] Fletcher, Richard. *The Barbarian Conversion: From Paganism to Christianity*. University of California Press, 1999, pp. 24
[260] Murray, Alexander. *Reason and Society in the Middle Ages*. Oxford University Press, 1978, pp. 158-9
[261] Dickens, Mark. "Patriarch Timothy I and the Metropolitan of the Turks." *Journal of the Royal Asiatic Society*, vol. 20, no. 2, 2010, pp. 117–39
[262] Stillman, Norman A. *The Jews of Arab Lands: A History and Source Book*. Jewish Publication Society of America, 1979, pp. 25-6
[263] Dirks, Jerald F. *Muslims In American History: A Forgotten Legacy*. Amana Publications, 2006, pp. 29
[264] Diamond, Jared M. *Guns, Germs, and Steel: The Fates of Human Societies*. W. W. Norton & Company Ltd, 2017, pp. 75
[265] Dirks, Jerald F. *Muslims In American History: A Forgotten Legacy*. Amana Publications, 2006, pp. 47
[266] Haselby, Sam. "Muslims of early America." Edited by Brigid Hains for *Aeon*, May 20, 2019
[267] Marcus, Steven. *The Other Victorians: A Study of Sexuality and Pornography in Mid-Nineteenth Century England*. Bantam Books, 1967, pp. 200-19
[268] Said, Edward W. *Orientalism*. Vintage Books, 1979, pp. 188-90
[269] Chomsky, Noam. *Global Discontents*. Interviews with David Barsamian. Metropolitan Books, 2017, pp. 84
[270] Hammond, Robert. *The Philosophy Of Al Farabi And Its Influence On Medieval Thought*. Kessinger Publishing, 2010
[271] Chomsky, Noam. *Who Rules the World?* Metropolitan Books, 2016, pp. 9-10
[272] United Nations Inter-Agency Task Force, Africa Recovery Programme/Economic Commission for Africa, *South African Destabilization: The Economic Cost of Frontline Resistance to Apartheid*, 1989, pp. 13
[273] Parenti, Michael. *The Sword And The Dollar: Imperialism, Revolution, and the Arms Race*. St. Martin Press, 1989, pp. 11

[274] See for eg.: Letter from Theodor Herzl to Yusuf Diya Pasha al-Khalidi, March 19, 1899, reprinted in Khalidi, Walid, *From Haven to Conquest: Readings in Zionism and the Palestine Problem*. Institute for Palestinian Studies, 1971, pp. 91-3

[275] Khalidi, R. *The Hundred Year's War on Palestine: A History of Settler Colonialism, 1917-2017*. Metropolitan Books, 2020, pp. 160-1

[276] Said, Edward W. *Orientalism*. Vintage Books, 1979, Preface pp. xxvi

[277] Shavit, Ari. "The Big Freeze," *Ha'aretz*, 7 October 2004; Chomsky, Noam. *Who Rules the World?* Metropolitan Books, 2016, pp. 11, 169

[278] Chomsky, Noam. *Who Rules the World?* Metropolitan Books, 2016, pp. 78-9

[279] Chomsky, Noam. *Who Rules the World?* Metropolitan Books, 2016, pp. 11, 189

[280] Wilkins, Brett. "Israeli Man Trying to Take Over Palestinian Home Says 'If I Don't Steal It, Someone Else' Will." *Common Dreams*, May 4, 2021

[281] Immerwahr, Daniel. *How To Hide An Empire: A History of the Greater United States*. Farrar, Straus and Giroux, 2019, pp. 38

[282] Immerwahr, Daniel. *How To Hide An Empire: A History of the Greater United States*. Farrar, Straus and Giroux, 2019, pp. 43

[283] Zertal, Idith, and Akiva Eldar. *Lords of the Land: The War for Israel's Settlements in the Occupied Territories, 1967-2007*, Nation books, 2007, pp. 13

[284] Frantzman, Seth J. "New joint ventures hint at 'burgeoning relationship' between Israel and India." *Defense News*, Feb 18, 2020

[285] Chomsky, Noam. *Global Discontents*. Interviews with David Barsamian. Metropolitan Books, 2017, pp. 7

[286] Becker, Jo, and Scott Shane. "Secret 'Kill List' Proves a Test of Obama's Principles and Will." *New York Times*. May 29, 2012

[287] Brzezinski, Matthew. "The Unmanned Army." *The New York Times*, April 20, 2003

[288] Knickmeyer, Ellen. "Costs of the Afghanistan war, in lives and dollars." *AP News*, Aug 16, 2021

[289] Dunbar-Ortiz, Roxanne. *An Indigenous Peoples' History of The United States*. Beacon Press, 2014, pp. 58-9

[290] Kaplan, Robert D. *Imperial Grunts: On the Ground with the American Military, from Mongolia to the Philippines to Iraq and Beyond*. Vintage, 2006, pp. 3-5

[291] Dunbar-Ortiz, Roxanne. *An Indigenous Peoples' History of The United States*. Beacon Press, 2014, pp. 193-4

[292] Massey, Eli. "Shireen Al-Adeimi on the U.S.-Backed War in Yemen." *Current Affairs*, Jan 8, 2021

[293] Jentleson, Bruce W. *Friends Like These: Reagan, Bush, and Saddam, 1982-1990*. W. W. Norton Co, 1994, pp. 35

[294] Woods, Kevin M. *Mother of All Battles: Saddam Hussein's Strategic Plan for the Persian Gulf War*. Naval Institute Press, 2008, pp. 50

[295] Frankopan, Peter. *The Silk Roads*. First Vintage Books, 2017, pp. 466

[296] Bush, George HW. "Grant of Executive Clemency," *Federal Register* 57.251, Proclamation 6518, Dec 24, 1992, pp. 62145-6

[297] Frankopan, Peter. *The Silk Roads*. First Vintage Books, 2017, pp. 490

[298] Michael, Maggie, et al. "AP Investigation: US allies, al-Qaida battle rebels in Yemen." *AP News*, Aug 6, 2018

[299] Immerwahr, Daniel. *How To Hide An Empire: A History of the Greater United States*. Farrar, Straus and Giroux, 2019, pp. 385

[300] Daum, Werner. "Universalism and the West." *Harvard International Review*, vol. 23, issue 2, Summer 2001, pp. 19

[301] Chappell, Bill. "Sudan And Israel Agree To Normalize Relations In U.S.-Brokered Deal." *NPR*, October 23, 2020

[302] McKenna, Matthew. "On Memorial Day, We Should Remember Most U.S. Wars Were Started for Resource Theft, Imperial Hubris and Racist Animus." *CovertAction Magazine*, May 30, 2021

[303] Churchill, Winston S. *The World Crisis, 1911-1918*. Free Press, 2005, pp. 667-8

[304] HM Stationery Office, *Statistics of the Military efforts of the British Empire during the Great War, 1914-1920*. 1922, pp. 643

[305] Frankopan, Peter. *The Silk Roads*. First Vintage Books, 2017, pp. 306

[306] Heyden, Tom. "The 10 greatest controversies of Winston Churchill's career." *BBC News*, January 26, 2015

[307] Zinn, Howard. *A People's History of the United States*. Harper Collins, 1999, pp. 303

[308] Strachan, Hew. *Financing the First World War*. Oxford University Press, 2004, pp. 188

[309] Bayly, Christopher A, and Tim Harper. *Forgotten Armies: The Fall of British Asia, 1841-1945*. Penguin UK, 2004

[310] Chomsky, Noam. *Manufacturing Consent: The Political Economy of the Mass Media*. Pantheon Books, 2002, Ch. 1

[311] Zinn, Howard. *A People's History of the United States*. Harper Collins, 1999, pp. 356

[312] Franklin, Bruce. *Vietnam and Other American Fantasies (Culture, Politics, and the Cold War)*. University of Massachusetts Press, 2001

[313] Greene, Bryce. "NPR Devotes Almost Two Hours to Afghanistan Over Two Weeks—and 30 Seconds to US Starving Afghans." *Fair*, September 2, 2022

[314] Chomsky, Noam. *Manufacturing Consent: The Political Economy of the Mass Media*. Pantheon Books, 2002, pp. xxxvi

[315] Sorensen, Christian. "Who Are the Ultimate War Profiteers? U.S. Air Force Veteran Removes the Veil." *CovertAction Magazine*, February 10, 2021

[316] Hochschild, Arlie R. *Strangers in Their Own Land: Anger and Mourning on the American Right*. New Press, 2016

[317] Aikins, Matthieu. "Times Investigation: In U.S. Drone Strike, Evidence Suggests No ISIS Bomb." *The New York Times*, September 10, 2021

[318] Xiong, Jack. "The Fake News in 1990 That Propelled the US into the First Gulf War." *Citizen Truth*, May 7, 2018

[319] Miklaszewski, Jim. "US intel: No evidence of Viagra as weapon in Libya." *NBC News*, April 29, 2011

[320] Shalom, Stephen R. *Imperial Alibis: Rationalizing U.S. Intervention After the Cold War*. South End Press, 1999

[321] Shedinger, Robert F. *Was Jesus A Muslim?* Fortress Press, 2009, pp. 83, 84

[322] Al-Attas, Syed M N. *Islam and Secularism*. Art Printing Works, 1993, pp. 41-2

[323] Karamustafa, Ahmet. "Islam: A Civilizational Project in Progress." *Progressive Muslims: On Justice, Gender, and Pluralism*. Edited by Omid Safi, Oneworld, 2003, pp. 99

[324] Bayyah, Shaykh A. "Religious Minorities in Muslim-Majority Lands: A Legal Framework and a Call to Action." *The Marrakesh Declaration*, 2018, pp. 14

[325] Shedinger, Robert F. *Was Jesus A Muslim?* Fortress Press, 2009, pp. 167

[326] Haselby, Sam. "Muslims of early America." Edited by Brigid Hains for *Aeon*, May 20, 2019

[327] Dirks, Jerald F. *Muslims In American History: A Forgotten Legacy*. Amana Publications, 2006, pp. 70

[328] Williams, Jennifer. "A brief history of Islam in America." *Vox*, January 29, 2017

[329] Shedinger, Robert F. *Was Jesus A Muslim?* Fortress Press, 2009, pp. xi

[330] Yusuf, Hamza. "A Spiritual Witness *Imam al-Tahawi's Gift of Simplicity*," *Seasons*, Zaytuna Institute, vol 4, no.1 2007, pp. 47

[331] Said, Edward W. *Orientalism*. Vintage Books, 1979, Ch.1

[332] Cromer, Evelyn B (Earl of). *Modern Egypt*. Macmillan Co, 1908, pp. 146-67

[333] Bayyah, Shaykh A. "Religious Minorities in Muslim-Majority Lands: A Legal Framework and a Call to Action." *The Marrakesh Declaration*, 2018, pp. 15

[334] Yusuf, Hamza. "When No News Is Good News." Sacred Text Messages podcast, season 1, episode 3, July 15, 2021

[335] Muggeridge, Malcolm. "The Oddest Prophet – Søren Kierkegaard," *Plough.com*, November 24, 2015

[336] Stanton, Gegory. "The Ten Stages of Genocide," *Genocidewatch.net*, 2016

[337] Rahman, Fazlur. *Major Themes of the Qur'an*. Biblioteca Islamica, 1980, pp. 37

[338] Hay, Denys. *Europe: The Emergence of an Idea*. Edinburgh University Press, 1968

[339] Hathout, Hassan. *Reading the Muslim Mind*. American Trust Publications, 1995, pp. 16-7

[340] "The Iron Age: The Israelites in Palestine." *Britannica*

[341] "Hebrew: people." *Britannica*.

[342] Jeffries, J M N. *Palestine: The Reality*. Skyscraper Publications, 2017, pp. 6

[343] Lewis, David L. *God's Crucible: Islam and the Making of Europe, 570-1215*. W.W. Norton & Co, 2008, pp. 60-2

[344] Baer, Yitzhak. *A History of the Jews in Christian Spain*. Jewish Publication Society of America, 1961-66, pp. 16

[345] Frankopan, Peter. *The Silk Roads*. First Vintage Books, 2017, pp. 185

[346] Dirks, Jerald F. *The Abrahamic faiths: Judaism, Christianity, and Islam: similarities & contrasts*. Amana Publications, 2004, pp. 162

[347] Frankopan, Peter. *The Silk Roads*. First Vintage Books, 2017, pp. 83-4

[348] Aslan, Reza. *No god but God: The Origins, Evolution, and Future of Islam*. Random House Trade, 2011, pp. 96

[349] Lord Balfour, House of Lords Speeches, Hansard, vol. 50, June 21, 1922, pp. 1016-7

[350] *The Times*, Nov 7, 1917 referenced by Peter Frankopan, *The Silk Roads*. First Vintage Books, 2017

[351] Khalidi, R. *The Hundred Year's War on Palestine: A History of Settler Colonialism, 1917-2017*. Metropolitan Books, 2020, pp. 13

[352] Frankopan, Peter. *The Silk Roads*. First Vintage Books, 2017, pp. 377

[353] Barr, James. *A Line in the Sand: Britain, France and the Struggle that shaped the MIddle East*. Simon & Schuster UK, 2011, pp. 163

[354] Nutting, Anthony. *Balfour and Palestine, a Legacy of Deceit*. The Council for the Advancement of Arab-British Understanding, 1975

[355] House, Edward M. *The Intimate Papers of Colonel House*. Edited by Charles Seymour, Houghton Mifflin company, 1926, p. p48

[356] Lang, Jeffrey. *Struggling to Surrender*. Amana Publications, 1995, pp. 221

[357] Masalha, Nur. *Palestine: A Four Thousand Year History*. I. B. Tauris, 2022, pp. 308

[358] Khalidi, R. *The Hundred Year's War on Palestine: A History of Settler Colonialism, 1917-2017*. Metropolitan Books, 2020, pp. 34

[359] Lang, Jeffrey. *Struggling to Surrender*. Amana Publications, 1995, pp. 222

[360] Wright, Clifford A. *Facts and Fables: The Arab-Israeli Conflict*. Routledge, 1989, pp. 16-7

[361] Lang, Jeffrey. *Struggling to Surrender*. Amana Publications, 1995, pp. 223

[362] Masalha, Nur. *Palestine: A Four Thousand Year History*. I. B. Tauris, 2022, pp. 380-2

[363] Dayan, Moshe. Speech to Technion University students on March 19, 1969. A transcript of the speech appeared in Ha'aretz on April 4, 1969. Found on: https://imeu.org/article/what-leading-israelis-have-said-about-the-nakba, 15/05/2023.

[364] Baker, William W. *Theft of a Nation*. Defenders Publications, 1982, pp. 6

[365] Brenner, Michael. *The Renaissance of Jewish Culture in Weimar Germany*. Yale University Press, 1996, pp. 32

[366] Ingrams, Doreen. *Palestine Papers 1917-1922: Seeds of Conflict*. Cox & Syman, 1972, pp. 10

[367] Chomsky, Noam. *Who Rules the World?* Metropolitan Books, 2016, pp. 80

[368] Yoav Biran, Minister Plenipotentiary, Embassy of Israel, letter, *Manchester Guardian Weekly*, July 25, 1982; Gad Becker, *Yediot Ahronot*, April 13, 1983; Reuters, "Shamir Promises to Crush Rioters," *New York Times*, April 1, 1988

[369] Sengupta, Somini. "U.N. Will Weigh Asking Court to Investigate War Crimes in Syria," *New York Times*, May 22, 2014

[370] Chomsky, Noam. *Who Rules the World?* Metropolitan Books, 2016, pp. 118-9

[371] Raz, Avi. *The Bride and The Dowry: Israel, Jordan and the Palestinians in the Aftermath of the June 1967 War*. Yale University Press, 2012, pp. 244

[372] Dunbar-Ortiz, Roxanne. *An Indigenous Peoples' History of The United States*. Beacon Press, 2014, pp. 87-90

[373] Waage, Hilde H. "Postscript to Oslo: the Mystery of Norway's Missing Files." *Journal of Palestine Studies*, vol. 38, no. 1, 2008, pp. 54–65

[374] Lang, Jeffrey. *Struggling to Surrender*. Amana Publications, 1995, pp. 218

[375] Lewis, David L. *God's Crucible: Islam and the Making of Europe, 570-1215*. W.W. Norton & Co, 2008, pp. 172

[376] Lewis, David L. *God's Crucible: Islam and the Making of Europe, 570-1215*. W.W. Norton & Co, 2008, pp. 161

[377] Fouracre, Paul. *Age of Charles Martel*. Routledge, 2000, pp. 136-9

[378] Heer, Friedrich. *Charlemagne and His World.* Macmillian, 1975, pp. 14

[379] Heer, Friedrich. *Charlemagne and His World.* Macmillian, 1975, pp. 23-4

[380] Heer, Friedrich. *Charlemagne and His World.* Macmillian, 1975, pp. 99

[381] Becher, Matthias. *Charlemagne.* Yale University Press, 2005, pp. 60

[382] Al-Masudi. *The Meadows of Gold.* Translated by Paul Lunde and Caroline Stone, Routledge, 1989, vol 1

[383] Lewis, David L. *God's Crucible: Islam and the Making of Europe, 570-1215.* W.W. Norton & Co, 2008, pp. 174

[384] Said, Edward W. *Orientalism.* Vintage Books, 1979, Afterword pp. 343

[385] Lewis, David L. *God's Crucible: Islam and the Making of Europe, 570-1215.* W.W. Norton & Co, 2008, pp. xxiii

[386] Parenti, Michael. *The Sword And The Dollar: Imperialism, Revolution, and the Arms Race.* St. Martin Press, 1989, pp. 41-2

[387] Bowman, Sam. "Are 70% of France's Prison Inmates Muslims?" *Adam Smith Institute*, Mar 29, 2017

[388] Lewis, David L. *God's Crucible: Islam and the Making of Europe, 570-1215.* W.W. Norton & Co, 2008, pp. 136

[389] Boas, Roger. "Arab Influences on European Love-Poetry." *Legacy of Muslim Spain.* Edited by Salma K Jayyusi, Brill, vol. 1, 1994, pp. 462-5

[390] Graham, Mark. *How Islam Created The Modern World.* Amana Publications, 2006, pp. 89

[391] Cowan, James. Introduction. *Hayy Ibn Yaqzan,* by Ibn Tufail, Azafran Books, 2018, pp. 1

[392] Lewis, David L. *God's Crucible: Islam and the Making of Europe, 570-1215.* W.W. Norton & Co, 2008, pp. 106

[393] Lewis, David L. *God's Crucible: Islam and the Making of Europe, 570-1215.* W.W. Norton & Co, 2008, pp. 203; Menocal, Maria R. *The Ornament of the World: How Muslims, Jews and Christians Created a Culture of Tolerance in Medieval Spain.* Back Bay Books, 2003, pp. 32

[394] Shedinger, Robert F. *Was Jesus A Muslim?* Fortress Press, 2009, pp. 81

[395] Oman, Charles. *The Dark Ages 476-918 A.D.* Independently published, 2017, pp. 144

[396] Tyerman, Christopher. *God's War: A New History of the Crusades.* Belknap Press, 2009, pp. 660

[397] Frankopan, Peter. *The Silk Roads.* First Vintage Books, 2017, pp. 83

[398] Gandhi, Mohandas. *Letters from One: Correspondence (and More) of Leo Tolstoy and Mohandas Gandhi; Including "Letter to a Hindu."* River Drafting Spirit Series, Book 3 (locs. 367-70), Kindle

[399] Ward-Perkins, Bryan. *The Fall of Rome and the End of Civilization.* Oxford University Press, 2005

[400] Wickham, Chris. *The Inheritance of Rome: Illuminating the Dark Ages 400-1000.* Penguin Books, 2010

[401] Ibn Fadlan. *Ibn Fadlan and the Land of Darkness.* Translated by Paul Lunde and Caroline Stone. Penguin Classics, 2012, pp. 204-7

[402] Lewis, David L. *God's Crucible: Islam and the Making of Europe, 570-1215.* W.W. Norton & Co, 2008, pp. 126

[403] Marcellinus, Ammianus. *The Roman History of Ammianus Marcellinus.* Translated by C. Yonge, G. Bell, 1894, pp. 283

[404] Bar Penkaye, John. *Ktaba d-res melle (Summary of World History).* Translated by Alphonse Mingana and Roger Pearse, 2010, book 15, online version from www.tertullian.org

[405] Dirks, Jerald F. *The Abrahamic faiths: Judaism, Christianity, and Islam: similarities & contrasts.* Amana Publications, 2004, pp. 157-8

[406] Cole, Juan. *Muhammad: Prophet of Peace Amid The Clash of Empires.* Bold Type Books, 2018, pp. 123

[407] Bayyah, Shaykh A. "Religious Minorities in Muslim-Majority Lands: A Legal Framework and a Call to Action." *The Marrakesh Declaration,* 2018, pp. 27

[408] Aslan, Reza. *No god but God: The Origins, Evolution, and Future of Islam.* Random House Trade, 2011, pp. 80

[409] Altabe, David F. *Spanish and Portuguese Jewry Before and After 1492.* Sepher Hermon Pr, 1983, pp. 45

[410] Frankopan, Peter. *The Silk Roads.* First Vintage Books, 2017, pp. 195

[411] Dirks, Jerald F. *The Abrahamic faiths: Judaism, Christianity, and Islam: similarities & contrasts.* Amana Publications, 2004, pp. 163

[412] Dirks, Jerald F. *Muslims In American History: A Forgotten Legacy.* Amana Publications, 2006, pp. 61

[413] Frankopan, Peter. *The Silk Roads.* First Vintage Books, 2017, pp. 201

[414] Subrahmanyam, Sanjay. *The Career and Legend of Vasco da Gama.* Cambridge University Press, 1998, pp. 205

[415] Frankopan, Peter. *The Silk Roads*. First Vintage Books, 2017, pp. 221
[416] Dirks, Jerald F. *Muslims In American History: A Forgotten Legacy*. Amana Publications, 2006, pp. 37
[417] Haselby, Sam. "Muslims of early America." Edited by Brigid Hains for *Aeon*, May 20, 2019
[418] Dirks, Jerald F. *Muslims In American History: A Forgotten Legacy*. Amana Publications, 2006, pp. 41
[419] Haselby, Sam. "Muslims of early America." Edited by Brigid Hains for *Aeon*, May 20, 2019
[420] Mikhail, Alan. "Op-Ed: Columbus' fear of Islam, rooted in Europe's Crusades, shaped his view of Native Americans." *Los Angeles Times*, October 11, 2021
[421] Lewis, David L. *God's Crucible: Islam and the Making of Europe, 570-1215*. W.W. Norton & Co, 2008, pp. 254-5
[422] Linebaugh, Peter. *The Magna Carta Manifesto: Liberties and Commons for All*. University of California Press, 2009, pp. 26-7
[423] Stone, I F. *In a Time of Torment*. Random House, 1967, pp. 432
[424] Cole, Juan. *Muhammad: Prophet of Peace Amid The Clash of Empires*. Bold Type Books, 2018, pp. 145
[425] Aboul-Enein, Youssef H, and Sherifa Zuhur. *Islamic Rulings on Warfare*. Strategic Studies Institute, US Army War College, Diane Publishing Co, 2004, pp. 22
[426] Cohn, Norman. *The Pursuit of the Millennium*. Quoted in Bamber Gascoigne, *The Christians*. Jonathan Cape, 1977, pp. 113
[427] Dirks, Jerald F. *The Abrahamic faiths: Judaism, Christianity, and Islam: similarities & contrasts*. Amana Publications, 2004, pp. 170
[428] Frassetto, Michael. *Christian Attitudes Toward the Jews in the Middle Ages: A Casebook*. Routledge Medieval Casebooks, 2006, pp. 61-82
[429] Cohn, Norman. *The Pursuit of the Millennium*. Quoted in Bamber Gascoigne, *The Christians*. Jonathan Cape, 1977, pp. 113
[430] Dirks, Jerald F. *The Abrahamic faiths: Judaism, Christianity, and Islam: similarities & contrasts*. Amana Publications, 2004, pp. 170
[431] Robert of Clari. *The Conquest of Constantinople*. Translated by Edgar H McNeal, Columbia University Press, 2005, pp. 71
[432] Dirks, Jerald F. *The Abrahamic faiths: Judaism, Christianity, and Islam: similarities & contrasts*. Amana Publications, 2004, pp. 159
[433] Graham, Mark. *How Islam Created The Modern World*. Amana Publications, 2006, pp. 136-7
[434] Parenti, Michael. *God And His Demons*. Prometheus Books, 2010, pp. 137
[435] Zinn, Howard. *A People's History of the United States*. Harper Collins, 1999, pp. 1-4
[436] Zinn, Howard. *A People's History of the United States*. Harper Collins, 1999, pp. 6
[437] Blackburn, Robin. *The Making of New World Slavery: From the Baroque to the Modern, 1492-1800*. Verso, 1998, pp. 36-8
[438] Dunbar-Ortiz, Roxanne. *An Indigenous Peoples' History of The United States*. Beacon Press, 2014, pp. 199
[439] Hochschild, Adam. *King Leopold's Ghost: A Story of Greed, Terror, and Heroism in Colonial Africa*. Houghton Mifflin, 1999
[440] Parenti, Michael. *The Sword And The Dollar: Imperialism, Revolution, and the Arms Race*. St. Martin Press, 1989, ch. 2
[441] Jennings, Francis. *The Invasion of America: Indians, Colonialism, and the Cant of Conquest*. Omohundro Institute and University of North Carolina Press, 2009, pp. 168
[442] Tinker, George E. *Missionary Conquest: The Gospel and Native American Cultural Genocide*. Fortress Press, 1993, pp. 42
[443] Aslan, Reza. *No god but God: The Origins, Evolution, and Future of Islam*. Random House Trade, 2011, pp. 263
[444] DeGolyer, Everette L. "Preliminary Report of the Technical Oil Mission to the Middle East," *Bulletin of the American Association of Petroleum Geologists*, vol. 28, 1944, pp. 919-23
[445] Halifax to Foreign Office, February 20, 1944, FO 371/42688
[446] Leffler, Melvyn P. *A Preponderance of Power: National Security, the Truman Administration, and the Cold War*. Stanford University Press, 1993, pp. 144
[447] Malcolm X, and Alex Haley. *The Autobiography of Malcolm X*. Ballantine Books, 1964, pp. 176-7
[448] *Lord Curzon in India: Being a Selection from His Speeches as Viceroy & Governor General of India, 1898-1905*. McMillan, 1906, pp. 589-90

[449] Ansary, Tamim. *The Invention of Yesterday*. Public Affairs, 2019, pp. 266

[450] Aslan, Reza. *No god but God: The Origins, Evolution, and Future of Islam*. Random House Trade, 2011, pp. 228

[451] Malcolm X, and Alex Haley. *The Autobiography of Malcolm X*. Ballantine Books, 1964, pp. 176-178.

[452] Aslan, Reza. *No god but God: The Origins, Evolution, and Future of Islam*. Random House Trade, 2011, pp. 237

[453] Ogunnaike, Oludamini. "Of Cannons and Canons: The Promise and Perils of Postcolonial Education." *Renovatio*, December 11, 2018

[454] Clymer, Kenton J. "Review of *Not so Benevolent Assimilation: The Philippine-American War*, by Stuart Creighton Miller." *Reviews in American History*, vol. 11, no. 4, 1983, pp. 547–52

[455] Lee, Ian. "How Jewish American pedophiles hide from justice in Israel." *CBS News*, February 19, 2020; Wight, Emily. "Stripped, beaten and blindfolded: new research reveals ongoing violence and abuse of palestinian children detained by Israeli military." *Save the Children*, July 10, 2023

[456] Smith, Maureen. "Forever Changed: Boarding School Narratives of American Indian Identity in the U.S. and Canada." *Indigenous Nations Journal*, vol. 2, no. 2, Fall 2001, pp. 57-82; Cook-Lynn, Elizabeth. *Why I Can't Read Wallace Stegner and Other Essays: A Tribal Voice*. University of Wisconsin Press, 1996, pp. 88

[457] Said, Edward W. *Orientalism*. Vintage Books, 1979, pp. 324

[458] Ibn Khaldun. *The Muqaddimah: An Introduction to History*. Translated by Franz Rosenthal, abridged by N. J. Dawood, Princeton Classics Edition, 2015, pp. 196

[459] Hickel, Jason. "How Britain stole $45 trillion from India and lied about it." *Al-Jazeera*, December 19, 2018

[460] McLane, John R. *Land and Local Kingship in Eighteenth-Century Bengal*. Cambridge University Press, 1993, pp. 194-207

[461] Lawson, Philip. *The East India Company: A History*. Routledge, 1993

[462] Parenti, Michael. *The Sword And The Dollar: Imperialism, Revolution, and the Arms Race*. St. Martin Press, 1989, pp. p27

[463] Reid, Helen. "Zambia's Chinese debt nearly twice official estimate, study finds." *Reuters*, September 28, 2021

[464] Kumar, Deepa. "Afghan Women Betrayed." *Spectre*, September 4, 2021

[465] See for example: Feingold, Henry L. *The Politics of Rescue: The Roosevelt Administration and the Holocaust, 1938-1945*. Rutgers University Press, 1970

[466] Gopal, Anand. "The Other Afghan Women," *The New Yorker*, September 6, 2021

[467] Chomsky, Noam. *Who Rules the World?* Metropolitan Books, 2016, pp. 73

[468] Parenti, Michael. *The Sword And The Dollar: Imperialism, Revolution, and the Arms Race*. St. Martin Press, 1989, pp. 87

[469] Haselby, Sam. "Muslims of early America." Edited by Brigid Hains for *Aeon*, May 20, 2019

[470] Sowell, Thomas. *Black Rednecks and White Liberals*. Encounter Books, 2005

[471] Lowery, Wesley. *Four Hundred Souls*. Edited by Ibram X Kendi and Keisha N Blain, One World, 2021, pp. 112

[472] Johnson, Samuel. *Taxation No Tyranny; An Answer to the Revolutions and Address of the American Congress*. 1775

[473] Rovelli, Carlo. *The Order of Time*. Riverhead Books, 2018, pp. 11

[474] Jefferson, Thomas. *Notes on the State of Virginia*. Edited by David Waldstreicher, Palgrave, 2002, pp. 176-7

[475] Deneen, Patrick J. *Why Liberalism Failed*. Yale University Press, 2018, pp. 161-3

[476] Jan, Tracy. "Report: No progress for African Americans on homeownership, unemployment and incarceration in 50 years." *The Washington Post*, February, 1018

[477] McDermott, Stacy P. "Emancipator didn't advocate racial equality. But was he a racist?" *NPR Illinois*, February 2004

[478] Sagan, Carl. *Cosmos*. Random House, 1980, pp. 187

[479] Ansary, Tamim. *The Invention of Yesterday*. Public Affairs, 2019, pp. 125

[480] Haselby, Sam. "Muslims of early America." Edited by Brigid Hains for *Aeon*, May 20, 2019

[481] Zinn, Howard. *A People's History of the United States*. Harper Collins, 1999, pp. 180

[482] Douglass, Frederick. "What to the Slave Is the Fourth of July?" *Teaching American History*, 1852

[483] Malcolm X, and Alex Haley. *The Autobiography of Malcolm X*. Ballantine Books, 1964, pp. 2

[484] Wilkerson, Isabel. *Four Hundred Souls*. Edited by Ibram X Kendi and Keisha N Blain, One World, 2021, pp. 278

[485] Ibn Khaldun. *The Muqaddimah: An Introduction to History*. Translated by Franz Rosenthal, abridged by N. J. Dawood, Princeton Classics Edition, 2015, pp. 241

[486] Miles, Tiya. *Four Hundred Souls*. Edited by Ibram X Kendi and Keisha N Blain, One World, 2021, pp. 129

[487] Feigenbaum, Anna. "How Tear Gas Became the White Supremacist's Favorite Poison." *Mother Jones*, June 8, 2020

[488] Romo, Vanessa. "Kyle Rittenhouse Released On $2 Million Bail, Awaiting Trial in Kenosha, Wis., Deaths." *NPR*, November 20, 2020

[489] Malcolm X, and Alex Haley. *The Autobiography of Malcolm X*. Ballantine Books, 1964, pp. 378

[490] Dunbar-Ortiz, Roxanne. *An Indigenous Peoples' History of The United States*. Beacon Press, 2014, pp. 2-14

[491] Van Alstyne, Richard W. *The Rising American Empire*. Norton, 1960

[492] Wright, Kai. *Four Hundred Souls*. Edited by Ibram X Kendi and Keisha N Blain, One World, 2021, pp. 79

[493] Harris, Leslie M. *In the Shadow of Slavery: African Americans in New York City, 1626-1863*. University of Chicago Press, 2004, pp. 17

[494] Akenson, Donald H. *God's Peoples: Covenant and Land in South Africa, Israel, and Ulster*. McGill-Queen's University Press, 1991, pp. 151-82, 227-62, 311-48

[495] Shedinger, Robert F. *Was Jesus A Muslim?* Fortress Press, 2009, pp. 85

[496] Smyth, Patrick. *The Present State of the Catholic Missions Conducted by the Ex-Jesuits in North America*. P. Byrne, 1788

[497] Brissot De Warville, JP. *New Travels in the United States of America in 1788*. Harvard University Press, 1964, pp. 346

[498] Zinn, Howard. *A People's History of the United States*. Harper Collins, 1999, pp. 29-30

[499] Ibn Khaldun. *The Muqaddimah: An Introduction to History*. Translated by Franz Rosenthal, abridged by N. J. Dawood, Princeton Classics Edition, 2015, pp. 59-60

[500] Tisby, Jemar. *Four Hundred Souls*. Edited by Ibram X Kendi and Keisha N Blain, One World, 2021, pp. 45

[501] Shedinger, Robert F. *Was Jesus A Muslim?* Fortress Press, 2009, pp. 55

[502] McVeigh, Rory, et al. "Political Polarization as a Social Movement Outcome: 1960s Klan Activism and its Enduring Impact on Political Realignment in Southern Counties, 1960-2000," *American Sociological Review*, vol. 79, no. 6, 2014, pp. 1144-71

[503] Immerwahr, Daniel. *How To Hide An Empire: A History of the Greater United States*. Farrar, Straus and Giroux, 2019, pp. 116-17

[504] Khalidi, R. *The Hundred Year's War on Palestine: A History of Settler Colonialism, 1917-2017*. Metropolitan Books, 2020, pp. 27-8

[505] Zinn, Howard. *A People's History of the United States*. Harper Collins, 1999, pp. 130

[506] Accusation of Dreyfusards as quoted in Geoffrey Hawthorn, *Enlightenment and Despair: A History of Social Theory*, Cambridge University Press, 1976, pp. 117

[507] Whitman, James Q. "Why the Nazis Loved America." *Time*. March 2017

[508] Kershaw, Ian. *Hitler: 1936-1945 Nemesis*. W. W. Norton & Company, 2001, pp. 401

[509] Dunbar-Ortiz, Roxanne. *An Indigenous Peoples' History of The United States*. Beacon Press, 2014, pp. 142-3

[510] Malcolm X, and Alex Haley. *The Autobiography of Malcolm X*. Ballantine Books, 1964, pp. 333, 340-41

[511] Grant, Adam. *Think Again: The Power of Knowing What You Don't Know*. Viking, 2021, pp. 124

[512] See for example: Mascall, E L. *The Secularization of Christianity*. Holt, Rinehart and Winston, 1967

[513] Chrysostom, Dio. *Discourses*. Translated by H. Lamar Crosby, Loeb Classical Library, 1946, vol. 4, pp. 363; Derrett, J, and M Derrett. "Homer in India: The Birth of the Buddha." *Journal of the Royal Asiatic Society*, vol. 2, no. 1, Cambridge University Press, 1992, pp. 47–57

[514] Frankopan, Peter. *The Silk Roads*. First Vintage Books, 2017, pp. 9,86

[515] Shedinger, Robert F. *Was Jesus A Muslim?* Fortress Press, 2009, pp. 16

[516] Aslan, Reza. *Zealot: The Life and Times of Jesus of Nazareth*. Random House, 2013, pp. 37

[517] Aslan, Reza. *Zealot: The Life and Times of Jesus of Nazareth*. Random House, 2013, pp. p31

[518] Adler, Yonatan. "Was Jesus a "Jew"?" *Yale University Press*. February 2024

[519] Aslan, Reza. *Zealot: The Life and Times of Jesus of Nazareth*. Random House, 2013, pp. 144, 150, 152

[520] Aslan, Reza. *Zealot: The Life and Times of Jesus of Nazareth*. Random House, 2013, pp. 187
[521] Aslan, Reza. *Zealot: The Life and Times of Jesus of Nazareth*. Random House, 2013, pp. 170-171
[522] MacIntyre, Alasdair. *AfterVirtue*. University of Notre Dame Press, 2007, pp. 166
[523] Norwich, John J. *Byzantium: The Early Centuries*. Knopf, 2001, pp. 148-56
[524] Al-Attas, Syed M N. *Islam and Secularism*. Art Printing Works, 1993, pp. 3-11
[525] Aslan, Reza. *Zealot: The Life and Times of Jesus of Nazareth*. Random House, 2013, pp. 149
[526] Aslan, Reza. *Zealot: The Life and Times of Jesus of Nazareth*. Random House, 2013, pp. 215
[527] Aslan, Reza. *Zealot: The Life and Times of Jesus of Nazareth*. Random House, 2013, pp. 144, 150, 152
[528] Lang, Jeffrey. *Struggling to Surrender*. Amana Publications, 1995, pp. 207
[529] Frankopan, Peter. *The Silk Roads*. First Vintage Books, 2017, pp. 79-80
[530] Dirks, Jerald F. *The Abrahamic faiths: Judaism, Christianity, and Islam: similarities & contrasts*. Amana Publications, 2004, pp. 118
[531] Shedinger, Robert F. *Was Jesus A Muslim?* Fortress Press, 2009, pp. 135
[532] Aslan, Reza. *Zealot: The Life and Times of Jesus of Nazareth*. Random House, 2013, pp. 70
[533] See for example: Parenti, Michael. *God And His Demons*. Prometheus Books, 2010
[534] Parenti, Michael. *God And His Demons*. Prometheus Books, 2010, pp. 57
[535] Lang, Jeffrey. *Struggling to Surrender*. Amana Publications, 1995, pp. 74-5
[536] Einstein, Albert. "Religion and Science: On Prayer; Purpose in Nature; Meaning of Life; the Soul; A Personal God." *New York Times Magazine*, November 9, 1930, pp. 1-4
[537] Aslan, Reza. *No god but God: The Origins, Evolution, and Future of Islam*. Random House Trade, 2011, pp. 182
[538] Dirks, Jerald F. *The Abrahamic faiths: Judaism, Christianity, and Islam: similarities & contrasts*. Amana Publications, 2004, pp. 100
[539] Frankopan, Peter. *The Silk Roads*. First Vintage Books, 2017, pp. 79
[540] Dirks, Jerald F. *The Abrahamic faiths: Judaism, Christianity, and Islam: similarities & contrasts*. Amana Publications, 2004, pp. 135
[541] Al-Mubarakpuri, Safiur-Rahman. *The Sealed Nectar*. Darussalam, 2015, pp. 71
[542] Chomsky, Noam. *Global Discontents*. Interviews with David Barsamian. Metropolitan Books, 2017, pp. 89
[543] Shedinger, Robert F. *Was Jesus A Muslim?* Fortress Press, 2009, pp. 11-12
[544] Dirks, Jerald F. *The Abrahamic faiths: Judaism, Christianity, and Islam: similarities & contrasts*. Amana Publications, 2004, pp. 131
[545] Al-Muqaddasi. *The Best Divisions for Knowledge of the Regions: Ahsan al-Taqasim fi Marifat al-Aqalim*. Translated by Basil Anthony Collins, 1994 Garnet Publishing, 2000, pp. 11
[546] Aslan, Reza. *No god but God: The Origins, Evolution, and Future of Islam*. Random House Trade, 2011, pp. 9
[547] Rodinson, Maxime. *Muhammad*. The New Press, 2002, pp. 66
[548] Euripides. *The Bacchae*. Line 16
[549] Dirks, Jerald F. *The Abrahamic faiths: Judaism, Christianity, and Islam: similarities & contrasts*. Amana Publications, 2004, pp. 133
[550] Diamond, Jared M. *Guns, Germs, and Steel: The Fates of Human Societies*. W. W. Norton & Company Ltd, 2017, pp. 440
[551] Aurelius, Marcus. *The Emperor's Handbook*. Translated by C. Scot Hicks and David V. Hicks. Scribner, 2002, Bk. XI:4
[552] Ibn Khaldun. *The Muqaddimah: An Introduction to History*. Translated by Franz Rosenthal, abridged by N. J. Dawood, Princeton Classics Edition, 2015, pp. 67
[553] Suedfeld, Peter, et al. "Changes in the hierarchy of value references associated with flying in space." *Journal of Personality*, vol. 78, no. 5, October 2010, pp. 1411-35
[554] "Edgar Mitchell's Strange Voyage." *People*, April 8, 1974
[555] Aslan, Reza. *No god but God: The Origins, Evolution, and Future of Islam*. Random House Trade, 2011, pp. 262
[556] Chomsky, Noam. *Global Discontents*. Interviews with David Barsamian. Metropolitan Books, 2017, pp. 73

[557] Hawkins, David R. *Power vs. Force: The Hidden Determinants of Human Behavior.* Hay House Inc, 1995, pp. 82-3

[558] For a more academic discussion on the topic see: MacIntyre, Alasdair. *AfterVirtue.* University of Notre Dame Press, 2007, ch. 17

[559] Graham, Mark. *How Islam Created The Modern World.* Amana Publications, 2006, pp. 20

[560] Moon, David. *The Abolition of Serfdom in Russia, 1862-1907.* Routledge, 2002, pp. 54

[561] Frankopan, Peter. *The Silk Roads.* First Vintage Books, 2017, pp. 382

[562] Malcolm X, and Alex Haley. *The Autobiography of Malcolm X.* Ballantine Books, 1964, pp. 277-78

[563] Berlinski, David. *The Devil's Delusion: Atheism and Its Scientific Pretensions.* Basic Books, 2009, pp. 28

[564] Orwell, George. *1984.* Thorndike Press, 2017

[565] Orwell, George. "Politics and the English Language." Online article, pp. 5, http://www.public-library.uk/ebooks/72/30.pdf

[566] Aristotle. *Politics.* Translated by Benjamin Jowett, Modern Library, 2001, Bk. II: Ch. 9

[567] Zinn, Howard. *A People's History of the United States.* Harper Collins, 1999, pp. 83-4

[568] Hernandez, Joe. "Yeshiva University cancels all clubs after it was ordered to allow an LGBTQ group." *NPR*, September 17, 2002

[569] Zinn, Howard. *A People's History of the United States.* Harper Collins, 1999, pp. 83

[570] Lewis, Clive Staples. *The Abolition of Man.* Harper One, 1944, pp. 43

[571] Aristotle. *Politics.* Translated by Benjamin Jowett, Modern Library, 2001, Bk. I: Ch. 2

[572] Rafi-ud-din, Mohammad. *The Manifesto of Islam: an exposition of Islam as the inevitable world ideology of the future.* Forgotten Books, 2012, pp. 117

[573] Hathout, Hassan. *Reading the Muslim Mind.* American Trust Publications, 1995, pp. 91-4

[574] Curtis, Mark. *Secret Affairs: Britain's Collusion with Radical Islam.* Serpent's Tail, 2010

[575] Chomsky, Noam. *Who Rules the World?* Metropolitan Books, 2016, pp. 46

[576] Koven, Ronald. "Moslem Faction Opposes Monarchy." *The Washington Post*, November 12, 1978

[577] Immerwahr, Daniel. *How To Hide An Empire: A History of the Greater United States.* Farrar, Straus and Giroux, 2019, pp. 401

[578] See for example: http://www.electproject.org/national-1789-present

[579] Deneen, Patrick J. *Why Liberalism Failed.* Yale University Press, 2018, pp. 162-5

[580] See for example: Zinn, Howard. *A People's History of the United States.* Harper Collins, 1999, ch. 11

[581] Parenti, Michael. *The Sword And The Dollar: Imperialism, Revolution, and the Arms Race.* St. Martin Press, 1989, pp. 95-6

[582] McMahon, Jeff. *Reagan and the World.* Monthly Review Press, 1985, pp. 13

[583] Ferguson, Thomas. *Golden Rule:The Investment Theory of Party Competition and the Logic of Money-Driven Political Systems.* University of Chicago Press, 1995

[584] Liptak, Adam. "Supreme Court Invalidates Key Part of Voting Rights Act," *The New York Times*, June 25, 2013

[585] "Peabody Energy Shares Rocket After Trump Wins Presidency." *Market Insider CNBC*, November 9, 2016

[586] Immerwahr, Daniel. *How To Hide An Empire: A History of the Greater United States.* Farrar, Straus and Giroux, 2019, pp. 195

[587] Chomsky, Noam. *Who Rules the World?* Metropolitan Books, 2016, pp. 219-20

[588] Butler, S. "America's Armed Forces: 2. 'In Time of Peace': The Army." *Common Sense*, vol. 4, no. 11, November, 1935, pp. 8-12

[589] Immerwahr, Daniel. *How To Hide An Empire: A History of the Greater United States.* Farrar, Straus and Giroux, 2019, pp. 150

[590] Cole, Leonard A. *Clouds of Secrecy: The Army's Germ Warfare Tests Over Populated Areas.* Rowman & Littlefield Publishers, 1989

[591] Smith, Susan L. "Mustard Gas and American Race-Based Human Experimentation in World War II." *Journal of Law, Medicine and Ethics*, vol 36, Fall 2008, pp. 517-21

[592] Clark, Truman R. *Puerto Rico and the United States, 1917-1933.* University of Pittsburgh Press, 1975, pp. 152-3

[593] Zinn, Howard. *A People's History of the United States.* Harper Collins, 1999, pp. 469-72

[594] Parenti, Michael. *The Sword And The Dollar: Imperialism, Revolution, and the Arms Race*. St. Martin Press, 1989, pp. 173

[595] Chomsky, Noam. *Manufacturing Consent: The Political Economy of the Mass Media*. Pantheon Books, 2002, pp. xxx

[596] Chomsky, Noam. *Who Rules the World?* Metropolitan Books, 2016, pp. 68

[597] Dunbar-Ortiz, Roxanne. *An Indigenous Peoples' History of The United States*. Beacon Press, 2014, pp. 192

[598] Quoted in William A Buckingham, Jr. *Operation Ranch Hand: The Air Force and Herbicides in Southeast Asia, 1961-1971*. U.S. Air Force, 1982, pp. 82

[599] McCoy, Alfred. "Foreword: Reflections on History's Largest Air War," in *Voices from the Plain of Jars*. Edited by Fred Branfman, University of Wisconsin Press, 2013, pp. xii

[600] Branfman, Fred. *Voices from the Plain of Jars: Life under an Air War*. University of Wisconsin Press, 2013, pp. 36

[601] Orwell, George. "Marrakech," *A Collection of Essays*. Doubleday Anchor Books, 1954, pp. 187

[602] Chomsky, Noam. *Who Rules the World?* Metropolitan Books, 2016, pp. 74

[603] Said, Edward W. *Orientalism*. Vintage Books, 1979, pp. 108

[604] Frankopan, Peter. *The Silk Roads*. First Vintage Books, 2017, pp. 253

[605] See for example: Bell, Gertrude. *The Desert and the Sown*. William Heinemann, 1907, pp. 244

[606] Vine, David. *Island of Shame: The Secret History of the U.S. Military Base on Diego Garcia*. Princeton University Press, 2011, pp. 2

[607] Vine, David. *Island of Shame: The Secret History of the U.S. Military Base on Diego Garcia*. Princeton University Press, 2011, pp. 15

[608] Immerwahr, Daniel. *How To Hide An Empire: A History of the Greater United States*. Farrar, Straus and Giroux, 2019, pp. 354

[609] Jacobsen, Annie. *Nuclear War: a scenario*. Dutton, 2024, pp. 80

[610] Jacobsen, Annie. *Nuclear War: a scenario*. Dutton, 2024, pp. 18

[611] Jacobsen, Annie. *Nuclear War: a scenario*. Dutton, 2024, pp. 27

[612] Sagan, Carl. *Cosmos*. Random House, 1980, pp. 328-9

[613] Quoted in: Zinn, Howard. *A People's History of the United States*. Harper Collins, 1999, pp. 18

[614] Shedinger, Robert F. *Was Jesus A Muslim?* Fortress Press, 2009, pp. 165

[615] Chomsky, Noam. *Who Rules the World?* Metropolitan Books, 2016, pp. 149-50

[616] Chomsky, Noam. *Who Rules the World?* Metropolitan Books, 2016, pp. 158

[617] Parenti, Michael. *The Sword And The Dollar: Imperialism, Revolution, and the Arms Race*. St. Martin Press, 1989, ch. 13

[618] Zinn, Howard. *A People's History of the United States*. Harper Collins, 1999, pp. 584

[619] Hiatt, Fred, and Joanne Omang. "CIA Helped To Mine Ports In Nicaragua." *The Washington Post*, April 7, 1984

[620] Zinn, Howard. *A People's History of the United States*. Harper Collins, 1999, pp. 424-5

[621] Bowman, Robert. "Truth is, we're terrorized because we're hated." *National Catholic Reporter*, October 2, 1998

[622] Zane, Damian. "The Kenyan school that was once a British detention camp." *BBC News*, August 27, 2019

[623] Paquette, Danielle. "A family's 76-year quest for truth — and justice." *The Washington Post*. September 9, 2020

[624] Aslan, Reza. *No god but God: The Origins, Evolution, and Future of Islam*. Random House Trade, 2011, pp. 252

[625] Tharoor, Ishaan. "The Taliban indoctrinates kids with jihadist textbooks paid for by the U.S." *The Washington Post*, December 8, 2014

[626] Gopal, Anand. *No Good Men Among The Living*. Metropolitan Books, 2014, pp. 56-7

[627] Aslan, Reza. *No god but God: The Origins, Evolution, and Future of Islam*. Random House Trade, 2011, pp. 252

[628] "Osama bin Laden: Taliban Spokesman Seeks New Proposal for Resolving bin Laden Problem," U.S. Department of State cable, *National Security Archive*, November 28, 1998

[629] Gopal, Anand. *No Good Men Among The Living*. Metropolitan Books, 2014, pp. 67

[630] Veblen, Thorstein. *The Theory of the Business Enterprise*. Charles Scribner's Sons, 1932, pp. 217

[631] Finnegan, Michael. "Cheney Gets $33.7-Million Retirement Deal, Firm Says," *Los Angeles Times*. August 17, 2000

[632] Young, Angelo. "Former Halliburton Subsidiary Received $39.5 Billion In Iraq-Related Contracts Over The Past Decade," *Business Insider*, March 19, 2013

[633] Gopal, Anand. *No Good Men Among The Living*. Metropolitan Books, 2014, pp. 273

[634] Hakimi, Mohammad H. "Afghanistan: The Ghost Teachers of Ghor," *Institute for War and Peace Reporting*, March 29, 2012

[635] Mojumdar, Aunohita. "An Inflated Claim of Health Success in Afghanistan Exposed," *Christian Science Monitor*, December 5, 2010

[636] Gopal, Anand. *No Good Men Among The Living*. Metropolitan Books, 2014, pp. 274

[637] Kimball, Jill. "Costs of the 20-year war on terror: $8 trillion and 900,000 deaths." *Brown University*, September 1, 2021

[638] Wilber, Donald N. *Clandestine Services History: Overthrow of Premier Mossadeq of Iran: November 1952- August 1953*. National Security Archive, 1969, pp. 7

[639] Frankopan, Peter. *The Silk Roads*. First Vintage Books, 2017, pp. 406

[640] See detailed examples in: Parenti, Michael. *The Sword And The Dollar: Imperialism, Revolution, and the Arms Race*. St. Martin Press, 1989

[641] Parsi, Trita. *The Treacherous Alliances: The Secret Dealings of Iran, Israel and the United States*. Yale University Press, 2008, pp. 107

[642] Dorman, William A, and Mansour Farhang. *The U.S. Press and Iran: Foreign Policy and the Journalism of Deference*. University of California Press, 1988

[643] Said, Edward W. *Orientalism*. Vintage Books, 1979, pp. 245-51

[644] From an October 27, 1964 speech delivered in Qum, published in: Imam Khomeini. *Islam and revolution: Writings and Declarations of Imam Khomeini*. Translated by Hamid Algar, Mizan Press, 1981, pp. 28

[645] Aslan, Reza. *No god but God: The Origins, Evolution, and Future of Islam*. Random House Trade, 2011, pp. XIII, 262

[646] Chomsky, Noam. *Who Rules the World?* Metropolitan Books, 2016, pp. 44

[647] Frankopan, Peter. *The Silk Roads*. First Vintage Books, 2017, pp. 335

[648] Hardinge to Gertrude Bell, March 27, 1917, Harding MSS 30

[649] Lawrence, T.E. *The Seven Pillars of Wisdom: A Triumph*. Doubleday, Doran & Co, 1926 (1935 reprint edition), pp. 28

[650] Parenti, Michael. *The Sword And The Dollar: Imperialism, Revolution, and the Arms Race*. St. Martin Press, 1989, ch. 6

[651] Immerwahr, Daniel. *How To Hide An Empire: A History of the Greater United States*. Farrar, Straus and Giroux, 2019, pp. 51

[652] "Talking Points for Ambassador Rumsfeld's Meeting with Tariq Aziz and Saddam Hussein," December 4, 1983, cited by Bryan R Gibson, *Covert Relationship: American Foreign Policy, Intelligence, and the Iran-Iraq War, 1980-1988*. Praeger, 2010, pp. 111, 113-18

[653] Savage, Charlie. "Bush Declares Exceptions to Sanctions of two Bills He Signed into Law." *The New York Times*, October 15, 2008

[654] Rosenthal, Andrew. "In a Speech, President Returns to Religious Themes." *The New York Times*, January 28, 1992; Rubin, Joshua. "God Speaks Through Bush, Again." *The Philadelphia Inquirer*, October 7, 2005

[655] Mason, John G. "Leo Strauss and the Noble Lie: the Neo-Cons at War," *Logos*, William Paterson University, January 2006

[656] "Were 1998 Memos a Blueprint for War?" *ABC News*, January 6, 2006

[657] Hartung, William. "We're #1: The U.S. Government is the World's Largest Arms Dealer." *Forbes*, Mar 18, 2022

[658] Mahajan, Rahul. "'We Think the Price Is Worth It': Media uncurious about Iraq policy's effects--there or here," *fair.org*, November 1, 2001

[659] Ezgi Basaran interview with Graham Fuller, "Former CIA Officer Says US Helped Create IS," *Al-Monitor*, September 2, 2014

[660] Mooney, James. *Historical Sketch of the Cherokee*. Routledge, 2005, pp. 124

[661] Zinn, Howard. *A People's History of the United States*. Harper Collins, 1999, pp. 297

[662] Immerwahr, Daniel. *How To Hide An Empire: A History of the Greater United States*. Farrar, Straus and Giroux, 2019, pp. 72

[663] Immerwahr, Daniel. *How To Hide An Empire: A History of the Greater United States*. Farrar, Straus and Giroux, 2019, pp. 100

[664] Immerman, Richard H. *Empire for Liberty: A History of American Imperialism from Benjamin Franklin to Paul Wolfowitz*. Princeton University Press, 2012

[665] Kristof, Nicholas D. "U.S. Apologizes to Japan for Rape of 12-Year-Old in Okinawa." *The New York Times*, November 2, 1995

[666] Hasan, Mehdi. "Everyone Is Denouncing the Syrian Rebels Now Slaughtering Kurds. But Didn't the U.S. Once Support Some of Them?" *The Intercept*, October 26, 2019

[667] Schorr, Daniel. "Telling It Like It Is: Kissinger and the Kurds." *Christian Science Monitor*, October 18, 1996

[668] United Press International, "Vincennes Too Aggressive in Downing Jet, Officer Writes," *Los Angeles Times*, September 2, 1989.

[669] Evans, David. "Vincennes Medals Cheapen Awards for Heroism." *Daily Press*, April 15, 1990

[670] Van Creveld, Martin. "Sharon on the Warpath: Is Israel Planning to Attack Iran?" *The New York Times*, August 21, 2004

[671] Frank, Joshua. "The Looming Threat of Israel's Nuclear Option." *The Nation*, November 24, 2023

[672] Immerwahr, Daniel. *How To Hide An Empire: A History of the Greater United States*. Farrar, Straus and Giroux, 2019, pp. 114

[673] Fein, Bruce. "Embracing dictators is nothing new," *The Washington Post*, May 4, 2017

[674] Parenti, Michael. *The Sword And The Dollar: Imperialism, Revolution, and the Arms Race*. St. Martin Press, 1989, ch. 4

[675] Chomsky, Noam. *Who Rules the World?* Metropolitan Books, 2016, pp. 19

[676] Zinn, Howard. *A People's History of the United States*. Harper Collins, 1999, pp. 545

[677] Nevins, Joseph. "How US Policy in Honduras Set the Stage for Today's Mass Migration," *Conversation*, November 1, 2016

[678] Zinn, Howard. *A People's History of the United States*. Harper Collins, 1999, pp. 607

[679] Gilens, Martin. "Inequality and Democratic Responsiveness: Who Gets What They Want from Government?" *Princeton University*, August 2004

[680] Dostoevsky, Fyodor. *Notes From Underground*. Translated by Mirra Ginsburg, Bantam Classics, 1974, pp. 22-3

[681] Davies, Nicolas JS. "35 countries where the U.S. has supported fascists, drug lords and terrorists." *Salon*, March 8, 2014

[682] Wilford, Hugh. *America's Great Game: The CIA's Secret Arabists and the Shaping of the Modern Middle East*, Basic Books, 2017, pp. 73; Herman, Edward S. *The Real Terror Network*. South End Press, 1982

[683] Beit-Hallahmi, Benjamin. "Israel's Global Ambitions," *The New York Times*, January 6, 1983

[684] Kaplan, Robert D. *Imperial Grunts: On the Ground with the American Military, from Mongolia to the Philippines to Iraq and Beyond*. Vintage, 2006, pp. 7-8

[685] 2010 Arab Public Opinion Survey, Zogby International/Brookings Institution, 2010

[686] WIN/Gallup, "Optimism is Back in the World," December 30, 2013

[687] Jarvis, Robert. "Weapons Without Purpose? Nuclear Strategy in the Post-Cold War Era," review of *The Price of Dominance: The New Weapons of Mass Destruction and Their Challenge to American Leadership*, by Jan Lodal, *Foreign Affairs*, vol. 80, no.4, July/August 2001, pp. 143-8

[688] Immerwahr, Daniel. *How To Hide An Empire: A History of the Greater United States*. Farrar, Straus and Giroux, 2019, pp. 14

[689] Seneca. *Letters from a Stoic*. Translated by Robin Campbell, Penguin, 1969, 117.33

[690] MacIntyre, Alasdair. *AfterVirtue*. University of Notre Dame Press, 2007, pp. 233-4

[691] Seneca. *Letters from a Stoic*. Translated by Robin Campbell, Penguin, 1969, 122.7

[692] Sun Tzu. *The Art of War*. Thomas Cleary's introduction, Shambhala Publications, 1988, pp. 5

[693] Auerbach, Erich. "Philology and *Weltliteratur*." Translated by M. and Edward W Said, *Centennial Review*, vol. 13, no. 1, Winter 1969, pp. 17

[694] Rumi, *Divan*, II, ghazal 918, line 9669

[695] Al-Ghazali. *The Alchemy of Happiness*. Translated by Claud Field, Martino Fine Books, 2017

[696] Locke, John. *An Essay Concerning Human Understanding*. Penguin Books, 1997, pp. 258

[697] Epictetus. *Discourses, Fragments, and Encheiridion*. Translated by W A Oldfather, 2 vols, Loeb Classical Library, 1925-8, 4.1.52

[698] Al-Attas, Syed M N. *Islam and Secularism*. Art Printing Works, 1993, pp. 20-1

[699] Gibbons, Ann. "Why 536 was 'the worst year to be alive': Glacier cores reveal Icelandic volcano that plunged Europe into darkness." *Science*, November 15, 2018

[700] Stokes, Philip. *Philosophy 100 Essential Thinkers*. Enchanted Lion Books, 2006, pp. 61

[701] Parenti, Michael. *God And His Demons*. Prometheus Books, 2010, Ch. 8

[702] Goodstein, Laurie, et al. "Embezzlement Is Found in Many Catholic Dioceses." *The New York Times*, January 5, 2007

[703] Stokes, Philip. *Philosophy 100 Essential Thinkers*. Enchanted Lion Books, 2006, pp. 145, 85

[704] MacIntyre, Alasdair. *A Short History of Ethics*. The Macmillan Company, 1966, pp. 158

[705] Zinn, Howard. *A People's History of the United States*. Harper Collins, 1999, pp. 74-9

[706] Shy, John. *A People Numerous and Armed*. Oxford University Press, 1976, pp. 146

[707] Zinn, Howard. *A People's History of the United States*. Harper Collins, 1999, pp. 80

[708] GQ quoted in: Drinnon, Richard. *Facing West: The Metaphysics of Indian-Hating and Empire-Building*. OUP, 1997 pp. 331

[709] Dunbar-Ortiz, Roxanne. *An Indigenous Peoples' History of The United States*. Beacon Press, 2014, pp. 3, 77

[710] Zinn, Howard. *A People's History of the United States*. Harper Collins, 1999, pp. 47

[711] Paine, Thomas. "Of Monarchy And Hereditary Succession." *Common Sense*, 1776

[712] Dunbar-Ortiz, Roxanne. *An Indigenous Peoples' History of The United States*. Beacon Press, 2014, pp. 127

[713] Zinn, Howard. *A People's History of the United States*. Harper Collins, 1999, pp. 149-51

[714] Jay, William. *The Life of John Jay*. J & J Harper, 1833, vol. 1, ch. 3

[715] Chomsky, Noam. *Global Discontents*. Interviews with David Barsamian. Metropolitan Books, 2017, pp. 15

[716] Owens, Deirdre C. *Four Hundred Souls*. Edited by Ibram X Kendi and Keisha N Blain, One World, 2021, pp. 162

[717] *The Statutes at Large: Being a Collection of All the Laws of Virginia, from the First Session of the Legislature in the Year 1619*. Edited by William W Hening, Samuel Pleasante, 1823, pp. 146

[718] Immerwahr, Daniel. *How To Hide An Empire: A History of the Greater United States*. Farrar, Straus and Giroux, 2019, pp. 31

[719] Zinn, Howard. *A People's History of the United States*. Harper Collins, 1999, pp. 636

[720] Russell, Bertrand. *An Outline of Philosophy*. Meridian Printing, 1960, pp. 237

[721] Russell, Bertrand. *An Outline of Philosophy*. Meridian Printing, 1960, pp. 243

[722] Adler, Mortimer J. *How to Read a Book*. Simon And Schuster, 1940, pp. 365

[723] Grant, Adam. *Think Again: The Power of Knowing What You Don't Know*. Viking, 2021, pp. 147

[724] Russell, Bertrand. *An Outline of Philosophy*. Meridian Printing, 1960, pp. 242

[725] Russell, Bertrand. *An Outline of Philosophy*. Meridian Printing, 1960, pp. 243

[726] Aslan, Reza. *No god but God: The Origins, Evolution, and Future of Islam*. Random House Trade, 2011, pp. 252

[727] Al-Qushayri. *Al-Risalat al-Qushayriyyah*. Edited by 'Abd al-Halim Mahmud and Mahmud bin al-Sharif, Dar al-Ma'arif, 2:369

[728] Seneca. *Letters from a Stoic*. Translated by Robin Campbell, Penguin, 1969, 106.12

[729] Aristotle. *Nicomachean Ethics*. Translated by W. D. Ross, Modern Library, 2001, Bk. III: Ch. 2.3

[730] Al-Attas, Syed M N. *Islam and Secularism*. Art Printing Works, 1993, pp. 116-25

[731] Lick, David J, et al. "Superior pattern detectors efficiently learn, activate, apply, and update social stereotypes." *Journal of experimental psychology*, vol. 147, no. 2, February 2018, pp. 209-227

[732] Kahan, Dan M, et al. "Motivated Numeracy and Enlightened Self-Government." *Behavioural Public Policy*, Yale Law School, Public Law Working Paper, vol. 1, no. 307, September 2013, pp. 54-86

[733] Sun Tzu. *The Art of War*. Translated by Thomas Cleary, Shambhala Publications, 1988, pp. 112

[734] Abd al-Fattah Abu Ghuddah. *Prophet Muhammad: The Teacher*. Awakening Publications, 2017

[735] Zinn, Howard. *A People's History of the United States*. Harper Collins, 1999, pp. 365-6

[736] Al-Sulami. *Uyub al-nafs wa adwiyatuha (Infamies of the Soul & Their Treatments)*. Translated by Musa Furber. Islamosaic, 2018, pp. 17

[737] Adler, Mortimer J, and Charles Van Doren. *How To Read A Book: The Classic Guide To Intelligent Reading*. Touchstone, 1972, pp. 163

[738] Seife, Charles. *Zero: The Biography of a Dangerous Idea*. Penguin Books, 2000, pp. 4

[739] Dostoevsky, Fyodor. *Notes From Underground*. Translated by Mirra Ginsburg, Bantam Classics, 1974, pp. 22

[740] Pluckrose, Helen and James Lindsay. *Cynical Theories: How Activist Scholarship Made Everything about Race, Gender, and Identity*. Pitchstone Publishing, 2020, pp. 39

[741] Magdoff, Harry. "Globalization–To What End?" *Socialist Register 1992: New World Order?* Edited by Ralph Milliband and Leo Panitch. Monthly Review Press, 1992, pp. 44-75

[742] Diamond, Jared M. *Guns, Germs, and Steel: The Fates of Human Societies*. W. W. Norton & Company Ltd, 2017, pp. 183

[743] Du Bois, W E B. *Black Reconstruction in America, 1860-1880*. Free Press, 1998, pp. 714

[744] Wali, Omid. "Sayed Jamaluddin Afghan as a Social Reformer in Islamic World." Andhra University, 2020, pp. 11

[745] Shah, Zulfiqar A. *Islam and The English Enlightenment*. Claritas books, 2022

[746] Al-Attas, Syed M N. *Islam and Secularism*. Art Printing Works, 1993, pp. 119

[747] Haleem, Abdul. *The Qur'an*. Oxford University Press, 2004, introduction, pp. xxii-xxiii

[748] Byrd, Jodi. *The Transit of Empire: Indigenous Critiques of Colonialism*. University of Minnesota Press, 2011, pp. xii-iv

[749] Grant, Adam. *Think Again: The Power of Knowing What You Don't Know*. Viking, 2021, pp. 182

[750] MacIntyre, Alasdair. *AfterVirtue*. University of Notre Dame Press, 2007

[751] Chomsky, Noam. *The Responsibility of Intellectuals*. The New Press, 2017

[752] Said, Edward W. *Orientalism*. Vintage Books, 1979, pp. 11

[753] Grant, Adam. *Think Again: The Power of Knowing What You Don't Know*. Viking, 2021, pp. 31

[754] Petersen, Alexander M, et al. "Discrepancy in scientific authority and media visibility of climate change scientists and contrarians." *Nature Communications*, vol. 10, article 3502, August 2019

[755] Dirks, Jerald F. *The Abrahamic faiths: Judaism, Christianity, and Islam: similarities & contrasts*. Amana Publications, 2004, pp. 21

[756] Graham, Mark. *How Islam Created The Modern World*. Amana Publications, 2006, pp. 171

[757] Ahmed, Akbar. "OP-ED: Goethe's tribute to Islam." *Daily Times*, May 12, 2017

[758] Levine, Mark, et al. "Identity and Emergency Intervention: How Social Group Membership and Inclusiveness of Group Boundaries Shape Helping Behavior." *Personality and Social Psychology Bulletin*, vol. 31, no. 4, April 2005, pp. 443–453

[759] Jussim, Lee, et al. "Stereotype (In)Accuracy in Perceptions of Groups and Individuals." *Current Directions in Psychological Science*, vol. 24, no. 6, December 2015, pp. 490–497

[760] Kelman, Herbert C. "Group processes in the resolution of international conflicts: Experiences from the Israeli-Palestinian case." *American Psychologist*, vol. 52, 1997, pp. 212-20

[761] Grant, Adam. *Think Again: The Power of Knowing What You Don't Know*. Viking, 2021, pp. 135

[762] Grant, Adam. *Think Again: The Power of Knowing What You Don't Know*. Viking, 2021, pp. 141

[763] Maio, Gregory, and James M Olson. "Values As Truisms: Evidence and Implications." *Journal of Personality and Social Psychology*, vol. 74, February 1998, pp. 294-311

[764] Said, Edward W. *Orientalism*. Vintage Books, 1979, Preface pp. xx

[765] Cleary, Thomas. *The Essential Koran: The Heart of Islam*. Introduction, HarperCollins, 1994, pp. viii

[766] Elmasry, Shadee M. "Yemen's Good Fortune: Imam 'Abd Allah b 'Alawi al-Haddad." *Seasons*, Zaytuna Institute, vol 4, no.1, 2007, pp. 88

[767] Chomsky, Noam. *Global Discontents*. Interviews with David Barsamian. Metropolitan Books, 2017, pp. 85

[768] Al-Mubarakpuri, Safiur-Rahman. *The Sealed Nectar*. Darussalam, 2015, pp. 128

[769] Cicero. *Pro Plancio*. Translated by C D Yonge, George Bell & Sons, 1891, pp. 80

THE OPINIONATED SPECTATOR

[770] Bergman, Peter. "The Next Time You Want to Complain at Work, Do This Instead." *Harvard Business Review*. May 17, 2018

[771] Kierkegaard, Soren. *Concluding Unscientific Postscript to Philosophical Fragments: Kierkegaard's Writings 12*. Edited and translated by Howard V Hong and Edna H Hong, Princeton University Press, vol. 1, 1992, pp. 178

[772] Fideler, David. *Breakfast With Seneca: A Stoic Guide to the Art of Living*. W. W. Norton & Co, 2022, pp. 106

[773] Seneca. *Of Consolation: To Marcia*. Translated by Aubrey Stewart, 10.1-3

[774] Kierkegaard, Soren. *Eighteen Upbuilding Discourses: Kierkegaard's Writings 5*. Edited and translated by Howard V Hong and Edna H Hong, Princeton University Press, 1990, pp. 18-9

[775] Einstein, Albert. "Religion and Science: On Prayer; Purpose in Nature; Meaning of Life; the Soul; A Personal God." *New York Times Magazine*, November 9, 1930, pp. 1-4

[776] Al-Attas, Syed M N. *Islam and Secularism*. Art Printing Works, 1993, pp. 51-4

[777] Kuhn, Thomas S. *The Structure of Scientific Revolutions*. 4th ed, The University of Chicago Press, 2012, pp. 170-1

[778] Kreeft, Peter. *The Platonic Tradition*. St. Augustine's Press, 2018, pp. 79

[779] Lewis, Clive Staples. *The Abolition of Man*. Harper One, 1944, pp. 81

[780] Kuhn, Thomas S. *The Structure of Scientific Revolutions*. 4th ed, The University of Chicago Press, 2012, pp. 23-7, 34

[781] Meyer, Stephen C. *Return of the God Hypothesis*. HarperCollins, 2021, pp. 270

[782] Feyerabend, Paul. *Farewell to Reason*. Verso, 1987, pp. 13

[783] Dirks, Jerald F. *Abraham: The Friend of God*. Amana Publications, 2002, pp. 149

[784] Ayub, Ayub. "Matn criticism and its role in the evaluation of hadith authenticity." *International Journal of Islamic Studies and Humanities*, vol, no.1, April 2018, pp. 69-75

[785] Berlinski, David. *The Devil's Delusion: Atheism and Its Scientific Pretensions*. Basic Books, 2009, pp. 50

[786] Kuhn, Thomas S. *The Structure of Scientific Revolutions*. 4th ed, The University of Chicago Press, 2012, pp. 156-7

[787] Stokes, Philip. *Philosophy 100 Essential Thinkers*. Enchanted Lion Books, 2006, pp. 205

[788] Kuhn, Thomas S. *The Structure of Scientific Revolutions*. 4th ed, The University of Chicago Press, 2012, pp. 3

[789] Frankopan, Peter. *The Silk Roads*. First Vintage Books, 2017, pp. 95-6

[790] Shedinger, Robert F. *Was Jesus A Muslim?* Fortress Press, 2009, pp. 82

[791] Stokes, Philip. *Philosophy 100 Essential Thinkers*. Enchanted Lion Books, 2006, pp. 93

[792] Said, Edward W. *Orientalism*. Vintage Books, 1979, pp. 114-6

[793] Cleary, Thomas. *The Essential Koran: The Heart of Islam*. Introduction, HarperCollins, 1994, pp. vii

[794] Russell, Bertrand. *An Outline of Philosophy*. Meridian Printing, 1960, pp. 47

[795] Heckscher, Christopher M. "A Nearctic-Neotropical Migratory Songbird's Nesting Phenology and Clutch Size are Predictors of Accumulated Cyclone Energy." *Scientific Reports*, issue 8, July 2, 2018

[796] Geological Society of America. "Raising giant insects to unravel ancient oxygen." *ScienceDaily*, Oct 30, 2010.

[797] Staedter, Tracy. "Big Mammals Evolved Thanks to More Oxygen." *Scientific American*, Oct 3, 2005

[798] Russell, Bertrand. *An Outline of Philosophy*. Meridian Printing, 1960, pp. 127

[799] Hawkins, David R. *Power vs. Force: The Hidden Determinants of Human Behavior*. Hay House Inc, 1995, pp. 28

[800] Diamond, Jared M. *Guns, Germs, and Steel: The Fates of Human Societies*. W. W. Norton & Company Ltd, 2017, pp. 91

[801] Bryson, Bill. *A Short History of Nearly Everything*. Broadway Books, 2003, pp. 441, 442

[802] Russell, Bertrand. *An Outline of Philosophy*. Meridian Printing, 1960, pp. 169

[803] Hawkins, David R. *Power vs. Force: The Hidden Determinants of Human Behavior*. Hay House Inc, 1995, pp. 26

[804] Burckhardt, Titus. *An Introduction to Sufi Doctrine*. Translated by D M Matheson, Thorsons Publishing, 1976, pp. 41

[805] "Popol Vuh: The Mayan Book of the Dawn of Life." Translated by Dennis Tedlock, 1996, *Annenberg Learner.org*

[806] Al-Ghazali. *Path to Sufism: his deliverance from error al-Munqidh min al-Dalal*. Translated by R J Mccarthy, Fons Vitae, 2006, pp. 77

[807] Locke, John. *An Essay Concerning Human Understanding*. Penguin Books, 1997, pp. 576

[808] Rodinson, Maxime. *Islam and Capitalism*. University of Texas Press, 1979, pp. 79-80

[809] Cleary, Thomas. *The Essential Koran: The Heart of Islam*. Introduction, HarperCollins, 1994, pp. vii

[810] Carlyle, Thomas. *On Heroes, Hero-Worship, and the Heroic in History*. Longmans, Green & Co, 1841 reprint ed, 1906, pp. 63

[811] Russell, Bertrand. *An Outline of Philosophy*. Meridian Printing, 1960, pp. 272

[812] Aslan, Reza. *No god but God: The Origins, Evolution, and Future of Islam*. Random House Trade, 2011, pp. 269

[813] For more detailed discussion, see: Al-Attas, Syed M N. *Islam and Secularism*. Art Printing Works, 1993, pp. 47

[814] Shedinger, Robert F. *Was Jesus A Muslim?* Fortress Press, 2009, pp. 37

[815] Bloom, Harold. *The Western Canon*, Harcourt Brace, 1994, pp. 29

[816] Berlinski, David. *The Devil's Delusion: Atheism and Its Scientific Pretensions*. Basic Books, 2009, pp. 20,26

[817] Kierkegaard, Soren. *Works of Love: Some Christian Reflections in the Form of Discourses*. Translated by Howard and Edna Hong, Harper, 1962, pp. 95

[818] Adamson, Peter. *Al-Kindi*. Oxford University Press, 2007, pp. 135-43

[819] Adamson, Peter. *Al-Kindi*. Oxford University Press, 2007, pp. 127-35

[820] Schmoeger, Michaela, et al. "Maternal bonding behavior, adult intimate relationship, and quality of life." "Mütterliches Bonding, partnerschaftliche Beziehungen im Erwachsenenalter und Lebensqualität." *Neuropsychiatrie: Klinik, Diagnostik, Therapie und Rehabilitation: Organ der Gesellschaft Osterreichischer Nervenarzte und Psychiater*, vol. 32, no. 1, January, 2018, pp. 26-32

[821] Stokes, Philip. *Philosophy 100 Essential Thinkers*. Enchanted Lion Books, 2006, pp. 77

[822] Gohlman, William E. *The Life of Ibn Sina: A Critical Edition and Annotated Translation*. SUNY Press, 1974, pp. 35

[823] Kreeft, Peter. *The Platonic Tradition*. St. Augustine's Press, 2018, pp. 44

[824] Russell, Bertrand. *An Outline of Philosophy*. Meridian Printing, 1960, pp. 3

[825] Russell, Bertrand. *An Outline of Philosophy*. Meridian Printing, 1960, pp. 309

[826] Morris, Richard. *The Nature of Reality*. McGraw-Hill, 1986, pp. 15

[827] Hawkins, David R. *Power vs. Force: The Hidden Determinants of Human Behavior*. Hay House Inc, 1995, pp. 249-50

[828] Russell, Bertrand. *An Outline of Philosophy*. Meridian Printing, 1960, pp. 2

[829] Meyer, Stephen C. *Return of the God Hypothesis*. HarperCollins, 2021, pp. 185-8

[830] Kierkegaard, Soren. *Philosophical Fragments (with Johannes Climacus): Kierkegaard's Writings 7*. Edited and translated by Howard V Hong and Edna H Hong, Princeton University Press, 1998, pp. 39-44

[831] Yusuf, Hamza. "A Spiritual Witness *Imam al-Tahawi's Gift of Simplicity*," *Seasons*, Zaytuna Institute, vol. 4, no.1 2007, pp. 45

[832] Naved Islam: https://navedislam.com/stories/imam-abu-hanifa-debate-atheist/

[833] MacIntyre, Alasdair. *AfterVirtue*. University of Notre Dame Press, 2007, pp. 54-5

[834] 'Abdullah Ibn 'Alawi al-Haddad. *Kitab al-hikam*. Translated by Mostafa al-Badawi, Ihya Publishing, 2017

[835] Stokes, Philip. *Philosophy 100 Essential Thinkers*. Enchanted Lion Books, 2006, pp. 45

[836] MacIntyre, Alasdair. *AfterVirtue*. University of Notre Dame Press, 2007, pp. 2

[837] Ibn Khaldun. *The Muqaddimah: An Introduction to History*. Translated by Franz Rosenthal, abridged by N. J. Dawood, Princeton Classics Edition, 2015, pp. 240-1

[838] Lewis, Clive Staples. *The Abolition of Man*. Harper One, 1944, pp. 65-6

[839] Ibn Khaldun. *The Muqaddimah: An Introduction to History*. Translated by Franz Rosenthal, abridged by N. J. Dawood, Princeton Classics Edition, 2015, pp. 97

[840] Stokes, Philip. *Philosophy 100 Essential Thinkers*. Enchanted Lion Books, 2006, pp. 129

[841] Quoted by: Berlinski, David. *The Devil's Delusion: Atheism and Its Scientific Pretensions*. Basic Books, 2009, pp. 14

[842] Einstein, Albert. "Religion and Science: On Prayer; Purpose in Nature; Meaning of Life; the Soul; A Personal God." *New York Times Magazine*, November 9, 1930, pp. 1-4

[843] Ibn Khaldun. *The Muqaddimah: An Introduction to History*. Translated by Franz Rosenthal, abridged by N. J. Dawood, Princeton Classics Edition, 2015, pp. 96-7

[844] Ibn Ashur. *Treatise on Maqasid al-Shari'ah*. Translated by Muhammad al-Tahir Ibn Ashur. The International Institute of Islamic Thought, 2006, ch. 27

[845] Dawkins, Richard. Speaking during the Intelligence Squared Debate, "Atheism Is the New Fundamentalism," November 2019

[846] Nietzsche, Friedrich W. *Ecce Homo: Nietzsche's Autobiography*. Translated by Anthony M Ludovici, Mcmillan, 1911, pp. 7

[847] MacIntyre, Alasdair. *AfterVirtue*. University of Notre Dame Press, 2007, pp. 107

[848] Lang, Jeffrey. *Struggling to Surrender*. Amana Publications, 1995, pp. 4

[849] Also argued by Locke, John. *An Essay Concerning Human Understanding*. Penguin Books, 1997, pp. 58

[850] Russell, Bertrand. *An Outline of Philosophy*. Meridian Printing, 1960, pp. 1

[851] Aristotle. *Nicomachean Ethics*. Translated by W. D. Ross, Modern Library, 2001, Bk. VI: Ch. 6

[852] Alborn, Mitch. *Tuesdays with Morrie: An Old Man, a Young Man, and Life's Greatest Lesson*. Broadway Books, 1997, pp. 196

[853] Thackston Jr, WM. *Signs of the Unseen: The Discourse of Jalaluddin Rumi*. Shambhala, 1999, pp. 114

[854] Bryson, Bill. *A Short History of Nearly Everything*. Broadway Books, 2003, pp. 380

[855] Meyer, Stephen C. *Return of the God Hypothesis*. HarperCollins, 2021, pp. 194

[856] Al-Ghazali. *Path to Sufism: his deliverance from error al-Munqidh min al-Dalal*. Translated by R J Mccarthy, Fons Vitae, 2006, pp. 60-61, 64

[857] Bryson, Bill. *A Short History of Nearly Everything*. Broadway Books, 2003, pp. 288

[858] Parenti, Michael. *God And His Demons*. Prometheus Books, 2010, pp. 83-85

[859] Pope, Alexander. *An Essay on Man*. Epistle 1:115-18

[860] Ibn Khaldun. *The Muqaddimah: An Introduction to History*. Translated by Franz Rosenthal, abridged by N. J. Dawood, Princeton Classics Edition, 2015

[861] Rovelli, Carlo. *The Order of Time*. Riverhead Books, 2018, pp. 101

[862] Stokes, Philip. *Philosophy 100 Essential Thinkers*. Enchanted Lion Books, 2006, pp. 63

[863] Deneen, Patrick J. *Why Liberalism Failed*. Yale University Press, 2018, pp. 137-8

[864] Prashad, Vijay. *The Darker Nations: A People's History of the Third World*. The New Press, 2007, pp. xvii

[865] Shakir, Zaid. "From Socialism to Nihilism: The Decline of Radical Modern Muslim Thought," *Seasons*, Zaytuna Institute, vol 4, no.1, 2007, pp. 18-19

[866] Locke, John. *An Essay Concerning Human Understanding*. Penguin Books, 1997, pp. 62

[867] Plato. *Great Dialogues of Plato: Meno*. Translated by W. H. D. Rouse, Signet Classics, 1999, pp. 48

[868] Ibn Qayyim al-Jawziyya. *Shifā' al-'alīl fī masā'il al-qaḍā' wa-al-qadar wa-al-ḥikma wa-al-ta'līl*. Edited by al-Sayyid Muḥammad al-Sayyid and Sa'īd Maḥmūd, Dār al-Ḥadīth, 1994, pp. 639; for al-Barr's views see Adang, Camilla. "Islam as the inborn religion of mankind: the concept of fiṭra in the works of Ibn Ḥazm." *Al-Qanṭara*, vol. 21, no. 2, February 2019, pp. 391

[869] Lang, Jeffrey. *Struggling to Surrender*. Amana Publications, 1995, pp. 67

[870] Ibn Qayyim al-Jawziyya. *Shifā' al-'alīl fī masā'il al-qaḍā' wa-al-qadar wa-al-ḥikma wa-al-ta'līl*. Edited by al-Sayyid Muḥammad al-Sayyid and Sa'īd Maḥmūd, Dār al-Ḥadīth, 1994, pp. 618

[871] Russell, Bertrand. *An Outline of Philosophy*. Meridian Printing, 1960, pp. 7

[872] Ibn Qayyim al-Jawziyya. *Shifā' al-'alīl fī masā'il al-qaḍā' wa-al-qadar wa-al-ḥikma wa-al-ta'līl*. Edited by al-Sayyid Muḥammad al-Sayyid and Sa'īd Maḥmūd, Dār al-Ḥadīth, 1994, pp. 609

[873] Al-Ghazali. *Path to Sufism: his deliverance from error al-Munqidh min al-Dalal*. Translated by R J Mccarthy, Fons Vitae, 2006, pp. 27

[874] Russell, Bertrand. *An Outline of Philosophy*. Meridian Printing, 1960, pp. 84

[875] Stokes, Philip. *Philosophy 100 Essential Thinkers*. Enchanted Lion Books, 2006, pp. 105

[876] Cowan, James. Introduction. *Hayy Ibn Yaqzan*, by Ibn Tufail, Azafran Books, 2018, pp. 14

[877] Russell, Bertrand. *An Outline of Philosophy*. Meridian Printing, 1960, pp. 285

[878] Deneen, Patrick J. *Why Liberalism Failed*. Yale University Press, 2018, pp. 17-8

[879] Russell, Bertrand. *An Outline of Philosophy*. Meridian Printing, 1960, pp. 251

[880] Stokes, Philip. *Philosophy 100 Essential Thinkers*. Enchanted Lion Books, 2006, pp. 153
[881] Frankopan, Peter. *The Silk Roads*. First Vintage Books, 2017, pp. 41
[882] See Ehrman, Bart D. *Misquoting Jesus: The Story behind Who Changed the Bible and Why*. HarperCollins, 2005
[883] Aslan, Reza. *No god but God: The Origins, Evolution, and Future of Islam*. Random House Trade, 2011, pp. 11
[884] Hawkins, David R. *Power vs. Force: The Hidden Determinants of Human Behavior*. Hay House Inc, 1995, pp. 273
[885] Shedinger, Robert F. *Was Jesus A Muslim?* Fortress Press, 2009, pp. 59
[886] Dirks, Jerald F. *The Abrahamic faiths: Judaism, Christianity, and Islam: similarities & contrasts*. Amana Publications, 2004, pp. 9-10
[887] May, Herbert G, and Bruce M Metzger. *The New Oxford Annotated Bible with the Apocrypha*. Oxford University Press, 1977, pp. 1169
[888] Pregill, Michael E. "The Hebrew Bible and the Quran: The Problem of the Jewish 'Influence' on Islam." *Religion Compass*, 1 (2007): 10.1111/j.1749-8171.2007.00044.x
[889] Moshfegh, David. *Ignaz Goldziher and the Rise of Islamwissenschaft as a "Science of Religion."* University of California at Berkeley, 2012, pp. 333
[890] Haleem, Abdul. *The Qur'an*. Oxford University Press, 2004. Introduction, pp. xv-xvi
[891] Gibb, H A R. *Mohammedanism*. Oxford University Press, 1962, pp. 50
[892] Gibb, H A R. *Modern Trends in Islam*. University of Chicago Press, 1947, pp. 7
[893] Said, Edward W. *Orientalism*. Vintage Books, 1979, pp. 138
[894] Al-Ghazali. *Path to Sufism: his deliverance from error al-Munqidh min al-Dalal*. Translated by R J Mccarthy, Fons Vitae, 2006, pp. 31-32
[895] Hawking, Stephen. *A Brief History of Time*. Bantam Books, 1988, pp. 139
[896] Aristotle. *Nicomachean Ethics*. Translated by W. D. Ross, Modern Library, 2001, Bk. VI: Ch. 9
[897] Grant, Adam. *Think Again: The Power of Knowing What You Don't Know*. Viking, 2021, pp. 4
[898] Graham, Mark. *How Islam Created The Modern World*. Amana Publications, 2006, pp. 74
[899] Bayyah, Shaykh A. "Religious Minorities in Muslim-Majority Lands: A Legal Framework and a Call to Action." *The Marrakesh Declaration*, 2018, pp. 14
[900] Sagan, Carl. *Cosmos*. Random House, 1980, pp. 59
[901] Hawking, Stephen W. *The Theory of Everything*. New MIllennium Press, 2002, pp. 23
[902] Sagan, Carl. *Cosmos*. Random House, 1980, pp. 188
[903] Krumrei-Mancuso, Elizabeth J, et al. "Links between intellectual humility and acquiring knowledge." *The Journal of Positive Psychology*, vol. 15, no. 2, February 2019, pp. 155-170
[904] Kelly, George A. *The Psychology of Personal Constructs, vol 1, A Theory of Personality*. W W Norton, 1995
[905] Al-Attas, Syed M N. *Islam and Secularism*. Art Printing Works, 1993, pp. 44
[906] Rovelli, Carlo. *The Order of Time*. Riverhead Books, 2018, pp. 118-119
[907] Strogatz, Steven. *Infinite Powers: How Calculus Reveals the Secrets of the Universe*. Houghton Mifflin Harcourt, 2019, pp. xvii
[908] Russell, Bertrand. *An Outline of Philosophy*. Meridian Printing, 1960, pp. 121
[909] Strogatz, Steven. *Infinite Powers: How Calculus Reveals the Secrets of the Universe*. Houghton Mifflin Harcourt, 2019, Appendix
[910] Aristotle. *Metaphysics*. Translated by W. D. Ross, Modern Library, 2001, Bk. III: Ch. 4
[911] Al-Ghazali. *The Alchemy of Happiness*. Translated by Claud Field, Martino Fine Books, 2017
[912] Bruner, Jérôme S, and Leo Postman. "On the perception of incongruity; A paradigm." *Journal of personality*, vol. 18, no. 2, 1949, pp. 206-23
[913] Stratton, George M. "Vision without Inversion of the Retinal Image," *Psychological Review*, vol. 4, 1897, pp. 341-60, 463-81
[914] Thackston Jr, WM. *Signs of the Unseen: The Discourse of Jalaluddin Rumi*. Shambhala, 1999, pp. 9
[915] Thackston Jr, WM. *Signs of the Unseen: The Discourse of Jalaluddin Rumi*. Shambhala, 1999, pp. 18
[916] Thackston Jr, WM. *Signs of the Unseen: The Discourse of Jalaluddin Rumi*. Shambhala, 1999, pp. pxxiv

[917] Al-Ghazali. *Path to Sufism: his deliverance from error al-Munqidh min al-Dalal*. Translated by R J Mccarthy, Fons Vitae, 2006, pp. 65-66

[918] Kuhn, Thomas S. *The Structure of Scientific Revolutions*. 4th ed, The University of Chicago Press, 2012, pp. 132

[919] Kuhn, Thomas S. *The Structure of Scientific Revolutions*. 4th ed, The University of Chicago Press, 2012, pp. 138

[920] Adler, Mortimer J, and Charles Van Doren. *How To Read A Book: The Classic Guide To Intelligent Reading*. Touchstone, 1972, pp. 4

[921] Boissoneault, Lorraine. "The True Story of Brainwashing and How It Shaped America." *Smithsonian*, May 22, 2017

[922] Hoyt, Alia. "Ghost Tape No. 10: The Haunted Mixtape of the Vietnam War." howstuffworks.com

[923] Sun Tzu. *The Art of War*. Thomas Cleary's introduction, Shambhala Publications, 1988, pp. 5

[924] Ogunnaike, Oludamini. "Of Cannons and Canons: The Promise and Perils of Postcolonial Education." *Renovatio*, December 11, 2018

[925] Cole, Juan. *Muhammad: Prophet of Peace Amid The Clash of Empires*. Bold Type Books, 2018, pp. 104

[926] Aslan, Reza. *No god but God: The Origins, Evolution, and Future of Islam*. Random House Trade, 2011, pp. 168

[927] Aristotle. *Nicomachean Ethics*. Translated by W. D. Ross, Modern Library, 2001, Bk. IX: Ch. 8

[928] Bayyah, Shaykh A. "Religious Minorities in Muslim-Majority Lands: A Legal Framework and a Call to Action." *The Marrakesh Declaration*, 2018, pp. 23

[929] "The Wahhabi Movement." *Britannica*. https://www.britannica.com/place/Saudi-Arabia/The-Wahhabi-movement

[930] "A Chronology: The House of Saud." *PBS Frontline*, https://www.pbs.org/wgbh/pages/frontline/shows/saud/cron/

[931] Eden, Jeff. "Did Ibn Saud's militants cause 400,000 casualties? Myths and evidence about the Wahhabi conquests, 1902–1925." *British Journal of Middle Eastern Studies*, vol. 46, no. 4, February 2018, pp. 519-34

[932] Aslan, Reza. *No god but God: The Origins, Evolution, and Future of Islam*. Random House Trade, 2011, pp. 251

[933] al-Mas'udi, cited by Gutas, Dimitri. *Greek Thoughts, Arabic Culture*. Routledge, 1998, pp. 89

[934] Mumisa, Michael. *Islamic Law: Theory & Interpretation*. Amana Publications, 2002, pp. 147

[935] Frankopan, Peter. *The Silk Roads*. First Vintage Books, 2017, pp. p96

[936] Mumisa, Michael. *Islamic Law: Theory & Interpretation*. Amana Publications, 2002, ch. 3

[937] Aslan, Reza. *No god but God: The Origins, Evolution, and Future of Islam*. Random House Trade, 2011, pp. 244

[938] Aslan, Reza. *No god but God: The Origins, Evolution, and Future of Islam*. Random House Trade, 2011, pp. 244

[939] Shakir, Zaid. "From Socialism to Nihilism: The Decline of Radical Modern Muslim Thought," *Seasons*, Zaytuna Institute, vol 4, no.1, 2007, pp. 17

[940] "Where did the names of the days of the week come from?" *The Old Farmer's Almanac*, https://www.almanac.com/fact/where-did-the-names-of-the-days#

[941] Clot, Andre. *Harun al-Rashid and the World of a Thousand and One Night*. Translated by John Howe, New Amsterdam Books. 1989, pp. 97

[942] Rovelli, Carlo. *The Order of Time*. Riverhead Books, 2018, pp. 3

[943] Rovelli, Carlo. *The Order of Time*. Riverhead Books, 2018, pp. 68

[944] Hawking, Stephen W. *The Theory of Everything*. New MIllennium Press, 2002, pp. 9

[945] Hawking, Stephen W. *The Theory of Everything*. New MIllennium Press, 2002, pp. 126

[946] Brown, Malcolm W. "Clues to Universe Origin Expected." *The New York Times*, March 12, 1978

[947] Bryson, Bill. *A Short History of Nearly Everything*. Broadway Books, 2003, pp. 15

[948] Aristotle. *Nicomachean Ethics*. Translated by W. D. Ross, Modern Library, 2001, Bk. VI: Ch. 7

[949] Hawkins, David R. *Power vs. Force: The Hidden Determinants of Human Behavior*. Hay House Inc, 1995, pp. 54

[950] Graham, Mark. *How Islam Created The Modern World*. Amana Publications, 2006, pp. 44

[951] Griffel, Frank. "Al-Ghazali." *Stanford Encyclopedia of Philosophy*, August 2007

[952] Holtzman, Livnat. "Human Choice, Divine Guidance and the Fitra Tradition- The Use of Hadith in Theological Treatises by Ibn Taymiyya and Ibn Qayyim al-Jawziyya." *Ibn Taymiyya and His Times*. Edited by Yossef Rapoport and Shahab Ahmed, Oxford University Press, 2010, pp. 169

[953] Ibn Qayyim al-Jawziyya. *Shifā' al-'alīl fī masā'il al-qaḍā' wa-al-qadar wa-al-ḥikma wa-al-ta'līl*. Edited by al-Sayyid Muḥammad al-Sayyid and Sa'īd Maḥmūd, Dār al-Ḥadīth, 1994, pp. 625

[954] Locke, John. *An Essay Concerning Human Understanding*. Penguin Books, 1997, pp. 175

[955] Lang, Jeffrey. *Struggling to Surrender*. Amana Publications, 1995, pp. 51

[956] Abū al-Ḥasan al-Ash'arī. *Kitāb maqālāt al-islāmiyyīn wa-ikhtilāf al-muṣallīn*. Edited by H. Ritter, 2nd edition. Franz Steiner, 1963, pp. 259

[957] Ibn Qayyim al-Jawziyya.*Shifā' al-'alīl fī masā'il al-qaḍā' wa-al-qadar wa-al-ḥikma wa-al-ta'līl*. Edited by al-Sayyid Muḥammad al-Sayyid and Sa'īd Maḥmūd, Dār al-Ḥadīth, 1994, pp. 629

[958] Hawking, Stephen W. *The Theory of Everything*. New MIllennium Press, 2002, pp. 29

[959] Schroeder, Gerald L. *The science of God: The Convergence of Scientific and Biblical Wisdom*. Free press, 2009 pp. 164

[960] Meyer, Stephen C. *Return of the God Hypothesis*. HarperCollins, 2021, pp. 54-5

[961] Russell, Bertrand. *An Outline of Philosophy*. Meridian Printing, 1960, pp. 83

[962] Seife, Charles. *Zero: The Biography of a Dangerous Idea*. Penguin Books, 2000, pp. 123

[963] Sagan, Carl. *Cosmos*. Random House, 1980, pp. 68

[964] Bryson, Bill. *A Short History of Nearly Everything*. Broadway Books, 2003, pp. 145

[965] Rovelli, Carlo. *The Order of Time*. Riverhead Books, 2018, pp. 16

[966] Asad, Muhammad. *The Message of the Qur'an*. The Book Foundation, 2005, pp. 513

[967] Hakim, Khalifa A. *The Metaphysics of Rumi: A critical and historical sketch*. Institute of Islamic Culture, 1977, pp. 18

[968] Flatow, Ira. "Resetting the Theory of Time." *Science* NPR, May 2013

[969] Strogatz, Steven. *Infinite Powers: How Calculus Reveals the Secrets of the Universe*. Houghton Mifflin Harcourt, 2019, pp. 280

[970] Ibn Khaldun. *The Muqaddimah: An Introduction to History*. Translated by Franz Rosenthal, abridged by N. J. Dawood, Princeton Classics Edition, 2015, pp. 78

[971] Rovelli, Carlo. *The Order of Time*. Riverhead Books, 2018, pp. 9

[972] Hawking, Stephen W. *The Theory of Everything*. New MIllennium Press, 2002, pp. 54-55

[973] Munroe, Randall. "Is Earth Getting Bigger Over Time?" *The New York Times*, December 10, 2019

[974] Rovelli, Carlo. *The Order of Time*. Riverhead Books, 2018, pp. 38

[975] Hafele, JC, and Richard E Keating. "Around-the-World Atomic Clocks: Observed Relativistic Time Gains." *Science*, vol. 177, issue 4044, 1972, pp. 166-8

[976] Rovelli, Carlo. *The Order of Time*. Riverhead Books, 2018, pp. 43-4

[977] Sagan, Carl. *Cosmos*. Random House, 1980, pp. 231

[978] Rovelli, Carlo. *The Order of Time*. Riverhead Books, 2018, pp. 24, 27

[979] Hawking, Stephen W. *The Theory of Everything*. New MIllennium Press, 2002, pp. 77-78

[980] Rovelli, Carlo. *The Order of Time*. Riverhead Books, 2018, pp. 32

[981] Dunbar-Ortiz, Roxanne. *An Indigenous Peoples' History of The United States*. Beacon Press, 2014, pp. 96

[982] Al-Ghazali. *The Alchemy of Happiness*. Translated by Claud Field, Martino Fine Books, 2017, pp. 35

[983] Hawking, Stephen W. *The Theory of Everything*. New MIllennium Press, 2002, pp. 166

[984] Strogatz, Steven. *Infinite Powers: How Calculus Reveals the Secrets of the Universe*. Houghton Mifflin Harcourt, 2019, pp. 168

[985] Russell, Bertrand. *An Outline of Philosophy*. Meridian Printing, 1960, pp. 163

[986] Meyer, Stephen C. *Return of the God Hypothesis*. HarperCollins, 2021, pp. 42-3

[987] Rovelli, Carlo. *The Order of Time*. Riverhead Books, 2018, pp. 12-13

[988] Lama, Dalai, and Howard Cutler. *The Art of Happiness: A Handbook for Living*. Riverhead books, 2009, pp.

[989] Al-Ghazali. *The Alchemy of Happiness*. Translated by Claud Field, Martino Fine Books, 2017

[990] Russell, Bertrand. *An Outline of Philosophy*. Meridian Printing, 1960, pp. 118

[991] Stokes, Philip. *Philosophy 100 Essential Thinkers*. Enchanted Lion Books, 2006, pp. 125

[992] Rovelli, Carlo. *The Order of Time*. Riverhead Books, 2018, pp. 85

[993] Maimonides, Moses. *The Guide for the Perplexed*. Translated by M. Friedlander, Dover Publications, 2000, I.73.106a

[994] Ijzerman, Hans R. "Warming to Each Other." *Psychology Today*, March 2, 2021

[995] Lama, Dalai, and Howard Cutler. *The Art of Happiness: A Handbook for Living*. Riverhead books, 2009, pp. 58

[996] Hawking, Stephen W. *The Theory of Everything*. New MIllennium Press, 2002, pp. 57

[997] Thackston Jr, WM. *Signs of the Unseen: The Discourse of Jalaluddin Rumi*. Shambhala, 1999, pp. xviii-xix

[998] Aslan, Reza. *No god but God: The Origins, Evolution, and Future of Islam*. Random House Trade, 2011, pp. 153

[999] Adamson, Peter. *Al-Kindi*. Oxford University Press, 2007, pp. 52

[1000] Strogatz, Steven. *Infinite Powers: How Calculus Reveals the Secrets of the Universe*. Houghton Mifflin Harcourt, 2019, pp. 16

[1001] Seife, Charles. *Zero: The Biography of a Dangerous Idea*. Penguin Books, 2000, Appendix A

[1002] Seife, Charles. *Zero: The Biography of a Dangerous Idea*. Penguin Books, 2000, pp. 106, 113

[1003] Seife, Charles. *Zero: The Biography of a Dangerous Idea*. Penguin Books, 2000, pp. 61

[1004] Seife, Charles. *Zero: The Biography of a Dangerous Idea*. Penguin Books, 2000, pp. 215

[1005] Hawking, Stephen W. *The Theory of Everything*. New MIllennium Press, 2002, pp. 162-163

[1006] Seife, Charles. *Zero: The Biography of a Dangerous Idea*. Penguin Books, 2000, pp. 215

[1007] Berlinski, David. *The Devil's Delusion: Atheism and Its Scientific Pretensions*. Basic Books, 2009, pp. 107

[1008] Thackston Jr, WM. *Signs of the Unseen: The Discourse of Jalaluddin Rumi*. Shambhala, 1999, pp. xvi-xviii

[1009] Chanda, Avik. "Dara Shikoh and the Upanishads." *Live History India*, November 15, 2019

[1010] *The Hymns of the Rig Veda*. Translated by Ralph T H Griffith, WWNorton.com, 1896, ch. 5, 10, 129

[1011] Boyce, Mary. *Zoroastrians: Their Religious Beliefs and Practices*. Routledge, 2001, pp. 18-20

[1012] Aslan, Reza. *No god but God: The Origins, Evolution, and Future of Islam*. Random House Trade, 2011, pp. 11

[1013] Yusuf, Hamza. "Buddha in the Qur'an?" *Common Ground Between Islam and Buddhism*. Fons Vitae, 2010, pp. 119-22

[1014] Seneca. *Letters from a Stoic*. Translated by Robin Campbell, Penguin, 1969, 63.1

[1015] Sagan, Carl. *Cosmos*. Random House, 1980, pp. 262-5

[1016] Sagan, Carl. *Cosmos*. Random House, 1980, pp. 281

[1017] Aristotle. *Metaphysics*. Translated by W. D. Ross, Modern Library, 2001, Bk. I: Ch. 3

[1018] Orwell, George. *Animal Farm*. PLUME Penguin Group, 1983.

[1019] McEvers, Kelly. *The Molecule That Made Us*. PBS documentary, 2020

[1020] Scholtz, Christopher A, et al. "East African megadroughts between 135 and 75 years ago and bearing on early-modern human origins." *PNAS*, vol. 104, no. 42, October 16, 2007, pp. 16416-21

[1021] Barta, Miroslav, and Ales Bezdek. "Beetles and the decline of the Old Kingdom: Climate change in ancient Egypt." *Chronology and Archaeology in Ancient Egypt (The Third Millennium B.C.)*. Czech Institute of Egyptology, pp. 214-22

[1022] Evans, Nicholas P, et al. "Quantification of drought during the collapse of the classic Maya civilization." *Science*, vol. 361, issue 6401, August 2018, pp. 498-501

[1023] Chomsky, Noam. *Who Rules the World?* Metropolitan Books, 2016, pp. 4

[1024] Khalil, Shaimaa, and Tiffanie Turnbull. "Australia election: How climate is making Australia more unliveable." *BBC News*, May 19, 2022

[1025] Chomsky, Noam. *Who Rules the World?* Metropolitan Books, 2016, pp. 88

[1026] Lenoux, P. "The World Bank." *How the World Works*. Ed. Gary L Olson, Scott Foresman/Addison-Wesley, 1984, pp. 28

[1027] Hathout, Hassan. *Reading the Muslim Mind*. American Trust Publications, 1995, pp. 85

[1028] Hathout, Hassan. *Reading the Muslim Mind*. American Trust Publications, 1995, pp. 93

[1029] Chomsky, Noam. *Global Discontents*. Interviews with David Barsamian. Metropolitan Books, 2017, pp. 7

[1030] Gilbert, Mads. "Brief Report to UNRWA: The Gaza Health Sector as of June 2014." University Hospital of North Norway, July 3, 2014

[1031] Chomsky, Noam. *Who Rules the World?* Metropolitan Books, 2016, pp. 128-9

[1032] Shedinger, Robert F. *Was Jesus A Muslim?* Fortress Press, 2009, pp. 141

[1033] Chomsky, Noam. *Who Rules the World?* Metropolitan Books, 2016, pp. 56

[1034] Harris, Gardiner. "Borrowed Time on Disappearing Land." *The New York Times*, March 28, 2014

[1035] Human Rights. "Genocide threat for Myanmar's Rohingya greater than ever, investigators warn Human Rights Council," *UN News*, September 16, 2019

[1036] Waikar, Prashant. "Reading Islamophobia in Hindutva: An Analysis of Narendra Modi's Political Discourse." *Islamophobia Studies Journal*, vol. 4, no. 2, Pluto Journals, 2018, pp. 161–80

[1037] Aristotle. *Politics*. Translated by Benjamin Jowett, Modern Library, 2001, Bk. I: Ch. 2

[1038] Al-Attas, Syed M N. *Islam and Secularism*. Art Printing Works, 1993, pp. 42

[1039] Ogunnaike, Oludamini. "Of Cannons and Canons: The Promise and Perils of Postcolonial Education." *Renovatio*, December 11, 2018

[1040] World Bank. *World Price Watch*. Washington DC, 2012

[1041] United Nations High Commissioner for Refugees. *Global Trends: Forced Displacement in 2015*: http://www.unhcr.org/576408cd7.pdf

[1042] Aslan, Reza. *No god but God: The Origins, Evolution, and Future of Islam*. Random House Trade, 2011, pp. XIV

[1043] Hawkins, David R. *Power vs. Force: The Hidden Determinants of Human Behavior*. Hay House Inc, 1995, pp. 80

Made in the USA
Monee, IL
26 June 2025

19828838R00225